Porsche 911 Owners Workshop Manual

by J H Haynes
Member of the Guild of Motoring Writers
and Peter Ward

Models covered:

Porsche 911, 911L, 911E, 911S, 911T and Carrera

2.0 Litre (1991 cc/121.5 cu in)
2.2 Litre (2195 cc/134 cu in)
2.4 Litre (2341 cc/142.8 cu in)
2.7 Litre (2687 cc/163.97 cu in)

Covers Cape and Targa versions of above

Does not cover 3 Litre or Turbo models

ISBN 0 85696 264 3

HAYNES PUBLISHING GROUP
SPARKFORD YEOVIL SOMERSET ENGLAND
distributed in the USA by
HAYNES PUBLICATIONS INC
861 LAWRENCE DRIVE
NEWBURY PARK
CALIFORNIA 91320
USA

Acknowledgements

Thanks are due to Porsche Cars Great Britain Limited for the supply of technical information and certain illustrations. AFN Limited of Isleworth, Middlesex supplied us with spare parts for our project cars. Castrol Limited provided lubrication data.

Car Mechanics magazine kindly supplied many of the photographs used in the bodywork repair Section of Chapter 10.

Special thanks are due to Squadron Leader H. Mayes, who kindly loaned his 1969 911 Targa as one of our project cars.

Lastly thanks are due to all of the people at Sparkford who helped in the production of this manual. Particularly, Brian Horsfall and Martin Penny who carried out the mechanical work; Stanley Randolph who planned the layout of each page and Rod Grainger the editor.

About this manual

Its aims

The aim of this book is to help you get the best value from your car. It can do so in two ways. First it can help you decide what work must be done, even should you choose to get it done by a garage, the routine maintenance and the diagnosis and course of action when random faults occur. However it it hoped that you will also use the second and fuller purpose by tackling the work yourself. This is not only satisfying, but on the simpler jobs it may even be quicker than booking the car into a garage and going there twice, to leave and collect it. Perhaps most important, much money can be saved by avoiding the costs a garage must charge to cover labour and overheads. To avoid labour costs a garage will often give a cheaper repair by fitting a reconditioned assembly. The home mechanic can be helped by this book to diagnose the fault and make a repair using only a minor spare part.

The book has drawings and descriptions to show the function of the various components so that their layout can be understood. Then the tasks are described and photographed in a step-by-step sequence so that even a novice can cope with complicated work.

The jobs are described assuming only normal tools are available, and not special tools unless absolutely necessary. However a reasonable outfit of tools will be a worthwhile investment. Many special workshop tools produced by the makers merely speed the work, and in these cases guidance is given as to how to do the job without them. On a very few occasions a special tool is essential to prevent damage to components; then its use is described. Though it might be possible to borrow the tool, such work may have to be entrusted to the official agent.

Using the manual

The manual is divided into ten Chapters. Each Chapter is divided into numbered Sections which are headed in **bold** type between horizontal lines. Each Section consists of serially numbered paragraphs.

There are two types of illustration: (1) Figures which are numbered according to Chapter and sequence of occurrence in that Chapter. (2) Photographs which have a reference number in their caption. All photographs apply to the Chapter in which they occur so that the reference figure pinpoints the pertinent Section and paragraph number.

Procedures, once described in the text, are not normally repeated. If it is necessary to refer to another Chapter the reference will be given. Cross-references given without use of the word 'Chapter' apply to Sections and/or paragraphs in the same Chapter, eg, 'see Section 8' means also 'in this Chapter'.

When the left or right side of the car is mentioned it is as if one is seated in the driver's seat looking forward.

Whilst every care is taken to ensure that the information in this manual is correct no liability can be accepted by the authors or publishers for loss, damage or injury caused by any errors in, or omissions from, the information given.

Contents

Use of English

As this book has been written in England, it uses the appropriate English component names, phrases, and spelling. Some of these differ from those used in America. Normally, these cause no difficulty, but to make sure, a glossary is printed below. In ordering spare parts remember the parts list will probably use these words:

Glossary

English	American	English	American
Aerial	Antenna	Layshaft (of gearbox)	Counter shaft
Accelerator	Gas pedal	Leading shoe (of brake)	Primary shoe
Alternator	Generator (AC)	Locks	Latches
Anti-roll bar	Stabiliser or sway bar	Motorway	Freeway, turnpike etc.
Battery	Energizer	Number plate	Licence plate
Bodywork	Sheet metal	Paraffin	Kerosene
Bonnet (engine cover)	Hood	Petrol	Gasoline
Boot lid	Trunk lid	Petrol tank	Gas tank
Boot (luggage compartment)	Trunk	'Pinking'	'Pinging'
Bottom gear	1st gear	Propeller shaft	Driveshaft
Bulkhead	Firewall	Quarter light	Quarter window
Camfollower or tappet	Valve lifter or tappet	Retread	Recap
Carburettor	Carburetor	Reverse	Back-up
Catch	Latch	Rocker cover	Valve cover
Choke/venturi	Barrel	Roof rack	Car-top carrier
Circlip	Snap ring	Saloon	Sedan
Clearance	Lash	Seized	Frozen
Crownwheel	Ring gear (of differential)	Side indicator lights	Side marker lights
Disc (brake)	Rotor/disk	Side light	Parking light
Drop arm	Pitman arm	Silencer	Muffler
Drop head coupe	Convertible	Spanner	Wrench
Dynamo	Generator (DC)	Sill panel (beneath doors)	Rocker panel
Earth (electrical)	Ground	Split cotter (for valve spring cap)	Lock (for valve spring retainer)
Engineer's blue	Prussion blue	Split pin	Cotter pin
Estate car	Station wagon	Steering arm	Spindle arm
Exhaust manifold	Header	Sump	Oil pan
Fast back (Coupe)	Hard top	Tab washer	Tang; lock
Fault finding/diagnosis	Trouble shooting	Tailgate	Liftgate
Float chamber	Float bowl	Tappet	Valve lifter
Free-play	Lash	Thrust bearing	Throw-out bearing
Freewheel	Coast	Top gear	High
Gudgeon pin	Piston pin or wrist pin	Trackrod (of steering)	Tie-rod (or connecting rod)
Gearchange	Shift	Trailing shoe (of brake)	Secondary shoe
Gearbox	Transmission	Transmission	Whole drive line
Halfshaft	Axle-shaft	Tyre	Tire
Handbrake	Parking brake	Van	Panel wagon/van
Hood	Soft top	Vice	Vise
Hot spot	Heat riser	Wheel nut	Lug nut
Indicator	Turn signal	Windscreen	Windshield
Interior light	Dome lamp	Wing/mudguard	Fender

Miscellaneous points

An "Oil seal" is fitted to components lubricated by grease!

A "Damper" is a "Shock absorber", it damps out bouncing, and absorbs shocks of bump impact. Both names are correct, and both are used haphazardly.

Note that British drum brakes are different from the Bendix type that is common in America, so different descriptive names result. The shoe end furthest from the hydraulic wheel cylinder is on a pivot; interconnection between the shoes as on Bendix brakes is most uncommon. Therefore the phrase "Primary" or "Secondary" shoe does not apply. A shoe is said to be Leading or Trailing. A "Leading" shoe is one on which a point on the drum, as it rotates forward, reaches the shoe at the end worked by the hydraulic cylinder before the anchor end. The opposite is a trailing shoe, and this one has no self servo from the wrapping effect of the rotating drum.

Introduction to the Porsche 911

The Porsche 911 is a car in a class of its own in the world of the sporting motorist.

Originally produced as a Coupé of 2 litre engine capacity, it was a natural successor to the Type 356, which itself started life as a Porsche designed body assembled mainly around standard Volkswagen components with a modified VW Beetle type engine.

Although not differing greatly in body style, the 911 model, introduced in September 1964, was a very different car mechanically. A new rear-mounted, flat-six, dry-sump engine was introduced, with carburetion by a triple choke Solex carburettor for each cylinder bank. Power was transmitted through a conventional diaphragm spring clutch to a 5-speed transaxle which drove the rear wheels through twin drive-shafts. The result was an outstanding 130 mph plus sports coupé.

Subsequent development brought about both de-rated and up-rated versions, replacement of the Solex carburettors by Webers, the intro-duction of the Bosch plunger pump fuel injection system, and later the intake-airflow-controlled K-jetronic injection system. Concurrently there were minor transmission modifications, and in August 1971 a new transmission was introduced for the 1972 models. Meanwhile, the semi-automatic Sportomatic transmission had been introduced, which also underwent considerable modification for 1972.

The original rack and pinion steering, and MacPherson strut and torsion bar front suspension has undergone minor changes, but there was one major change with the introduction of optional self-levelling front suspension units. The rear suspension is a semi-trailing link layout with transverse torsion bars which, too, has undergone several changes.

The braking system, originally a single hydraulic circuit, was modified to a dual system in August 1967. This utilizes disc brakes on all four wheels, with the handbrake operating twin shoes in drums incorporated in the rear hubs.

Apart from the introduction of a removeable top Targa version, body styling has altered little, most changes having been incorporated in the interests of improved roadholding, handling and aerodynamics. This has particularly been the case with the Carrera models (although an increase in the wheelbase for 1969 models, without moving the engine position, effectively reduced the overhang weight and greatly improved these characteristics).

This has been but a brief introduction to a truly outstanding car, the history of which is far better related in the numerous books available covering the history of Porsche and the development of the 911 model.

Porsche 911T 'Targa'

Porsche 911E. (Inset Porsche Carrera RS)

Buying spare parts and vehicle identification numbers

Buying spare parts

Spare parts are available from many sources, for example: Porsche garages, other garages and accessory shops, and motor factors. Our advice regarding spare part sources is as follows:

Officially appointed Porsche garages - This is the best source of parts which are peculiar to your car and are otherwise not generally available (eg. complete cylinder heads, internal transmission components, badges, interior trim, etc). It is also the only place at which you should buy parts if your car is still under warranty - non-Porsche components may invalidate the warranty. To be sure of obtaining the correct parts it will always be necessary to give the storeman your car's chassis and engine numbers, and if possible, to take the 'old' part along for positive identification. Remember that many parts are available on a factory exchange scheme - any parts returned should always be clean! It obviously makes good sense to go straight to the specialists on your car for this type of part for they are best equipped to supply you.

Other garages and accessory shops - These are often very good places to buy materials and components needed for the maintenance of your car (eg, oil filters, spark plugs, bulbs, fan belts, oils and greases, touch-up paint, filler paste, etc). They also sell general accessories, usually have convenient opening hours, charge lower prices and can often be found not far from home.

Motor factors - Good factors may stock some of the more important components which wear out relatively quickly (eg, clutch components, pistons, valves, exhaust systems, brake cylinders/pipes/hoses/seals/pads etc). Remember, though, that the Porsche 911 is not exactly a run-of-the-mill car so you may find that you will have to resort to the Porsche garage after all. Motor factors will often provide new or reconditioned components on a part exchange basis - this can save a considerable amount of money.

Vehicle identification numbers

Although many individual parts, and in some cases sub-assemblies, fit a number of different models it is dangerous to assume that just because they look the same, they are the same. Differences are not always easy to detect except by serial numbers. Make sure, therefore, that the appropriate identity number for the model or sub-assembly is known and quoted when a spare part is ordered.

The *chassis serial number* is located on the luggage compartment floor on the right-hand side. On early models the *nomenclature plate* is alongside, but on later models it appears at the side of the luggage compartment lid catch on the transverse panel. Most models have a *paint code number* on one of the door pillars. The *engine number* appears on the right-hand support member for the fan housing, either on the rear or right-hand face (photos).

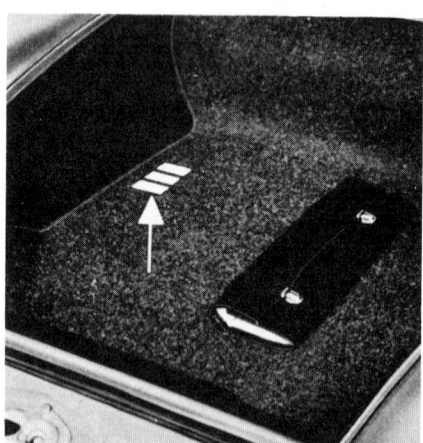

Fig. 1. Chassis number

Fig. 2. Engine number

Nomenclature plate (typical)

Paint code number

Routine Maintenance

Maintenance is essential for safety and desirable for the purpose of obtaining the best in terms of performance and economy, from your car.

Over the years, the need for periodic lubrication - oiling, greasing, and so on - has been drastically reduced if not totally eliminated. This has unfortunately tended to lead some owners to think that because no such action is required, components either no longer exist, or will last forever. This is a serious delusion since the largest initial element of maintenance is visual examination.

The routine maintenance summary is based upon the manufacturer's recommendation, but is supplemented by certain checks which the author feels will add up to improved reliability and an increase of component life. Those items listed which may not be applicable to your car should be ignored.

Every 250 miles (400 km) or weekly, whichever comes first

Steering/suspension
Check the tyre pressures.
Examine tyres for wear and damage.
Check steering for smooth and accurate response.

Brakes
Check reservoir fluid level. Check the system for leaks if there is a noticeable drop in level since last check (photo).
Check braking efficiency during an emergency stop.
Ensure handbrake will hold car on a steep gradient.

Lights, wipers, horns, instruments
Check operation of all exterior lights.
Check operation of all warning lights and systems.
Check operation of all instruments and gauges.
Check the windscreen washers and wipers, and top-up the fluid level, if necessary, using a water/antifreeze mixture (photo).
Check operation of headlamp washers.
Check operation of horn(s).

Engine
Check engine oil reservoir level and top-up if necessary (engine idling, car on level ground and oil at approximately 80ºC/176ºF) (photo).

Electrical
Check battery electrolyte level and top-up with distilled or de-ionized water to just cover separators.

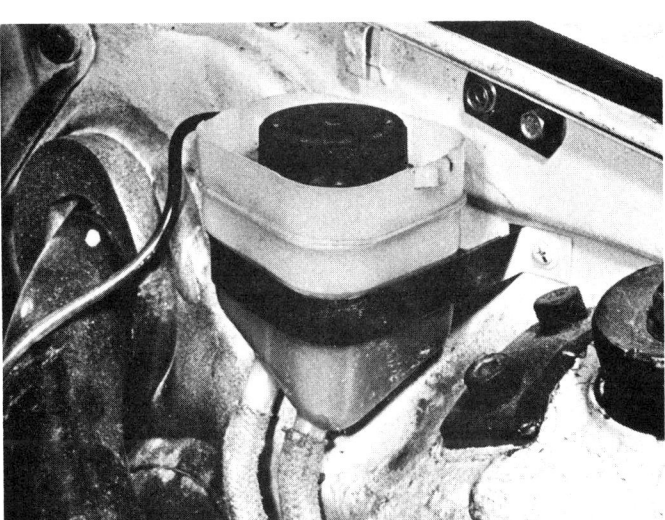

Brake fluid reservoir

Windscreen washer reservoir cap (typical)

Every 6000 miles (10000 km) or 6 months, whichever comes first

Suspension/steering

Check for free-play in ball joints and linkages.
Check rubber boots, bellows and bushes for deterioration.

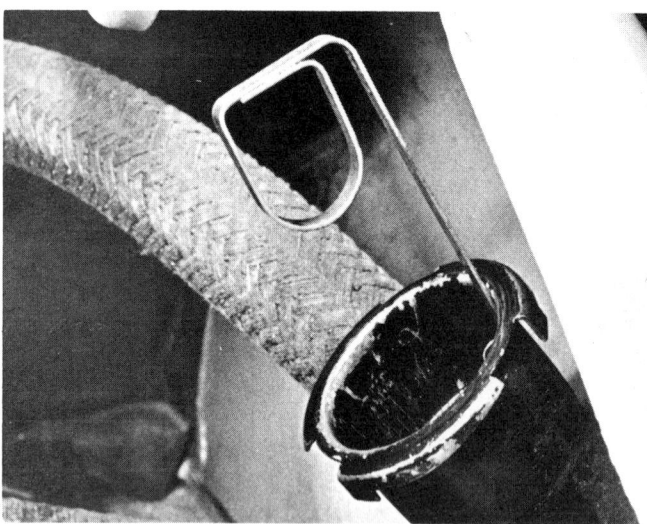

Engine oil level dipstick in filler tube in engine compartment
(also see Fig. 4 which shows one of the alternative filler tubes)

Brakes

Check brake pad wear.
Check free-play in master cylinder pushrod.
Inspect all brake lines for damage and corrosion.
Ensure vented disc vents are unobstructed.

Engine

Check valve clearances; renew valve cover gasket.
Renew engine oil and clean magnetic drain plug.
Renew engine oil filter.
Check for engine oil leaks.
Check tension of alternator drivebelt.
Check spark plug gap (except CDS).
Replace contact breaker points (except CDS).
Lubricate distributor. One drop of engine oil at each linkage/pivot point; trace of petroleum jelly on cam profile.
Check points gap/dwell angle and ignition timing.
Check all engine controls and lubricate pivots/linkages with engine oil.
Check idle speed.
Check condition of fuel system hoses.
Check exhaust system/heat exchanger for security and corrosion.

Transmission

Check clutch play and pedal adjustment.
Check transmission oil level.
Check for transmission oil leaks.
Check for free-play in driveshaft joints.

Bodywork

Lubricate all door locks and hinges (photo).
Check operation of heating system.

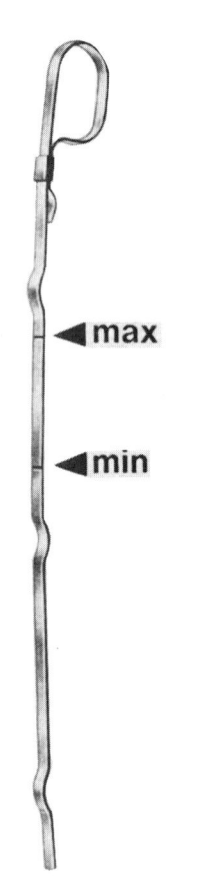

Fig. 3. Typical dipstick markings

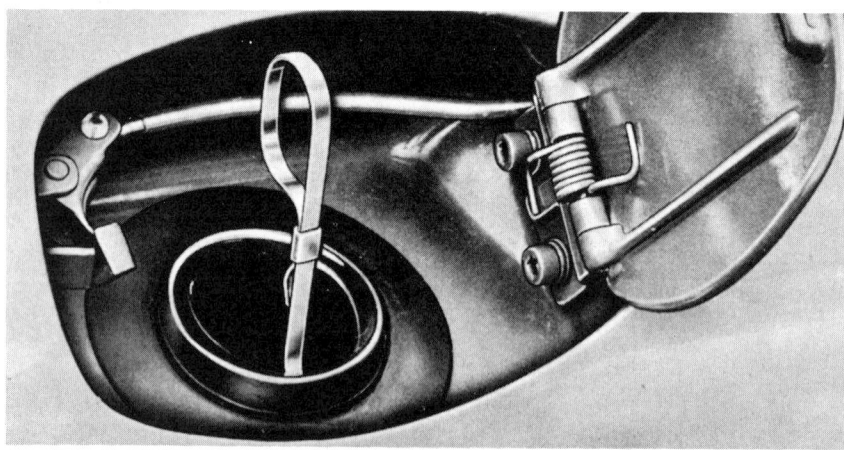

Fig. 4. Engine oil filler in rear wing (fender), applicable to some models

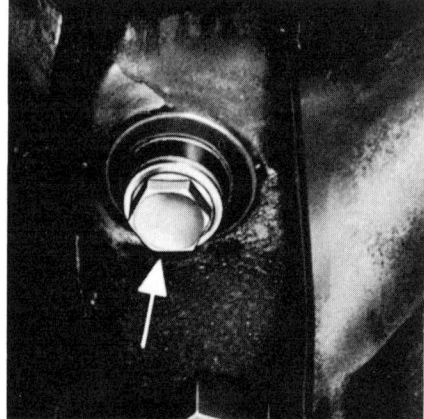

Fig. 5a. Engine and reservoir drain plugs.
On early models these have hexagon socket heads.

Every 12000 miles (20000 km) or 12 months, whichever comes first

Engine
Clean fuel pump strainer or replace cartridge.
Renew spark plugs.
Renew air filter cartridge, or clean wet filter and re-lubricate.
Clean crankcase breather vent cartridge and check condition of hoses and tightness of connections.

Transmission
Renew transmission oil and clean magnetic drain plugs.

Bodywork
Check condition of all rubber seals on doors etc.
Ensure door drain holes are unobstructed.

Fig. 6. Oil filter

The actual position varies according to the model, but it is always on the engine compartment sidewall at the right-hand side.

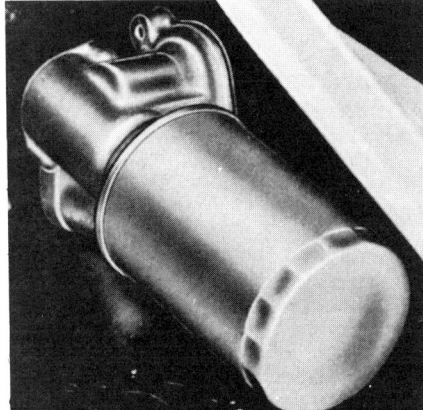

Every 24000 miles (40000 km) or 2 years, whichever comes first

Brakes
Renew oil supply line connecting socket and filter on mechanical injection pump.
Renew all fluid in brake hydraulic system.

Every 30000 miles (48000 km)

Engine
Check condition and tension of air pump drivebelt.
Clean or renew EGR valve.

Door hinge lubrication

Fig. 7. Transmission drain and filler plugs (typical).

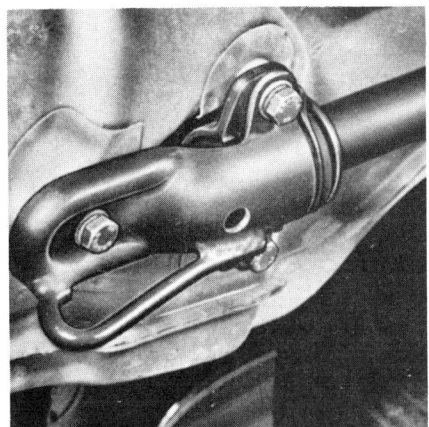

Fig. 8. Front towing eye on wishbone pivot end.

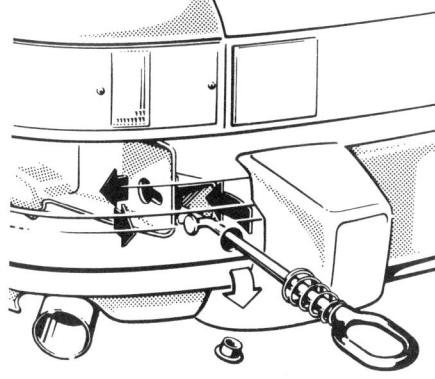

Fig. 9. Rear towing eye used on later models.

Jacking and towing

Jacking points
There is a jacking point on each side of the car which is for use with the jack supplied with the car. It raises the car to provide access to the front and rear at that side.
On cars with hydropneumatic suspension struts it will be noted that the body height drops after any jacking procedure. Normal level will be attained after driving a short distance.
The jack supplied with the car is not recommended for use when working under the car. Either use a workshop trolley jack or axle stands beneath the bodyframe sidemembers. Place wooden blocks on the jack or axle stand head to prevent damage. Never jack-up on the engine/transmission, driveshafts or steering gear components. Provided that care is taken, it is permissible to jack-up on the front suspension wishbones or rear suspension control arms.

Towing
A towing hook is provided at the front of the car. This is either on the forward end of one of the wishbone pivots or at the forward end of the fuel tank.
At the rear, later models have a towing hook provided with the car tool kit. To use it, remove the plastic plug in the rear bumper, insert the hook so that the cranked end slots into the side rail, and pull the hook rearwards to engage it.
Never be tempted to attach towropes to bumpers, steering gear components or the driveshafts.

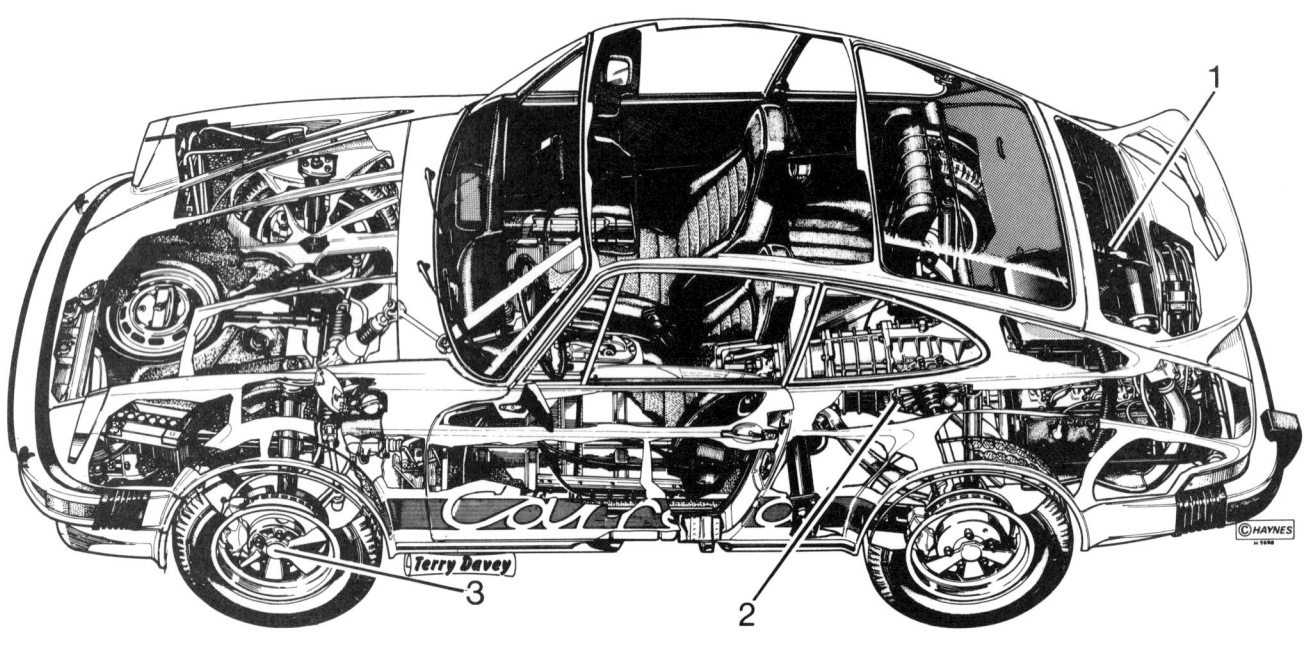

Recommended lubricants

Note: The following lubricants are recommended for use in temperate climates only. Different operating conditions require different lubricants. Consult the handbook supplied with the car.

Component	Castrol product
1 Engine (including Sportomatic torque converter)	**CRI 30**
2 Transmission and differential (Refer to Chapter 6 Specifications for limited slip differential)	**Hypoy or Hypoy B**
3 Wheel bearings and chassis/suspension lubrication	**Castrol LM Grease (MS3 where molybdenum disulphide grease is specified)**
Brake fluid	**Castrol Girling Universal Brake and Clutch Fluid**

In addition, engine oil or **Castrol Everyman Oil** *can be used for hinges, pivots, linkages etc.*

Chapter 1 Engine

Contents

Specifications

Due to the multiplicity of performance figures quoted over the years of production of the various engine types, these are not included in this manual but reference should be made to specialist publications or the manufacturer's literature or owner's handbook. Similarly, as this manual does not set out to be a parts list, manufacturing dimensions and tolerances are also kept to a minimum in order to give the maximum clarity to measurements and clearances connected with repair and maintenance - the manual's primary purpose.

The following guide will be helpful however, in identifying the particular engine, details of which are separated into capacities (displacement).

Until 1969 the engine was designated 2000 for external (public) reference but known as 901 (with suffix) for purposes of service, spares etc., within the Porsche organisation. The engine capacity was 1991 cc.

From 1970 the engine is designated 911 (with suffix E, S or T). Until July 1971, the engine capacity was 2195 cc; from August 1971 to July 1973 the engine capacity was 2341 cc (Carrera model 2687 cc). From August 1973, the engine capacity was increased to 2687 cc.

Other factors in engine identification may be useful particularly when purchasing a used vehicle:

E models - fuel injection
S models - carburettors (early) fuel injection (after late 1968)
T models - carburettors
January 1968   -   Fuel injection system of Bosch manufacture
August 1968   -   Magnesium crankcase introduced
August 1971   -   Nikasil type cylinder barrels fitted
August 1973   -   Alusil type cylinder barrels fitted

Engine general

Type	Air-cooled, four stroke, six cylinder horizontally opposed, overhead camshaft. Rear mounted in conjunction with transmission
No. of cylinders	6 (two banks of three opposing)

	1991 cc	2195 cc	2341 cc	2687 cc
Engine capacity				
Bore	3.15 in (80 mm)	3.31 in (84 mm)	3.31 in (84 mm)	3.54 in (90 mm)
Stroke	2.60 in (66 mm)	2.60 in (66 mm)	2.77 in (70.4 mm)	2.77 in (70.4 mm)
Displacement	121.5 cu in (1991 cc)	134 cu in (2195 cc)	142.9 cu in (2341 cc)	163.9 cu in (2687 cc)
Compression ratio	(2000) 9.0:1 (2000S) 9.8:1 (2000T) 8.6:1 (911E) 9.1:1 (911S) 9.9:1	(911T) 8.6:1 (911E) 9.1:1 (911S) 9.8:1	(911TV) 7.5 :1 (911T - N. America) 7.5:1 (911E) 8.0:1 (911S) 8.5:1	8.5:1
Firing order	1-6-2-4-3-5	1-6-2-4-3-5	1-6-2-4-3-5	1-6-2-4-3-5

Crankshaft

Main bearing running clearance:				
1 to 7	0.0003 to 0.0028 in (0.010 to 0.072 mm)	0.0003 to 0.0028 in (0.010 to 0.072 mm)	0.0003 to 0.0028 in (0.010 to 0.072 mm)	0.0003 to 0.0028 in (0.010 to 0.072 mm)
No. 8	0.002 to 0.004 in (0.048 to 0.104 mm)	0.002 to 0.004 in (0.048 to 0.104 mm)	0.002 to 0.004 in (0.048 to 0.104 mm)	0.002 to 0.004 in (0.048 to 0.104 mm)
Big-end bearing running clearance	0.0011 to 0.0034 in (0.030 to 0.088 mm)	0.0011 to 0.0034 in (0.030 to 0.088 mm)	0.0011 to 0.0034 in (0.030 to 0.088 mm)	0.0011 to 0.0034 in (0.030 to 0.088 mm)
Gudgeon pin clearance in connecting rod	0.0007 to 0.0015 in (0.020 to 0.039 mm)	0.0007 to 0.0015 in (0.020 to 0.039 mm)	0.0007 to 0.0015 in (0.020 to 0.039 mm)	0.0007 to 0.0015 in (0.020 to 0.039 mm)

Pistons
For dimensions see Section 19.

Piston rings

Number	2 compression, 1 oil control	2 compression, 1 oil control	2 compression, 1 oil control	'LS' piston ring gaps R (Top) 0.2 to 0.4 mm N (Second) 0.15 to 0.35 mm Oil control 0.4 to 1.4 mm
End gap	0.006 to 0.039 in (0.15 to 1.0 mm)	0.006 yo 0.039 in (0.15 to 1.0 mm)	0.006 to 0.039 in (0.15 to 1.0 mm)	
Groove clearance:				
Top	0.0029 to 0.0042 in (0.075 to 0.107 mm)	0.0029 to 0.0042 in (0.075 to 0.107 mm)	0.0029 to 0.0042 in (0.075 to 0.107 mm)	
Second	0.0023 to 0.0078 in (0.060 to 0.20 mm)	0.0023 to 0.0078 in (0.060 to 0.20 mm)	0.0023 to 0.0078 in (0.060 to 0.20 mm)	
Oil control	0.0009 to 0.0020 in (0.025 to 0.052 mm)	0.0009 to 0.0020 in (0.025 to 0.052 mm)	0.0009 to 0.0020 in (0.025 to 0.052 mm)	

Valves

Valve timing:	(To engine no. 911000)	(911E)	(911T)	(911T) N. America
Inlet opens	29° BTDC	20° BTDC	15° BTDC	0° BTDC
Inlet closes	39° ABDC	34° ABDC	29° ATDC	32° ABDC
Exhaust opens	39° BBDC	40° BBDC	41° BTDC	30° BBDC
Exhaust closes	19° ATDC	6° ATDC	5° BTDC	10° BTDC
	(From engine no. 911001)	(911S)	(911E)	(911)
Inlet opens	20° BTDC	38° BTDC	18° BTDC	1° ATDC
Inlet closes	34° ABDC	50° ABDC	36° ATDC	35° ABDC
Exhaust opens	40° BBDC	40° BBDC	38° BTDC	29° BBDC
Exhaust closes	6° ATDC	20° ATDC	8° ATDC	7° BTDC
	(2000S)	(911T)	(911S)	(911S)
Inlet opens	38° BTDC	15° BTDC	38° BTDC	6° ATDC
Inlet closes	50° ABDC	29° ABDC	50° ATDC	50° ABDC
Exhaust opens	50° BBDC	41° BBDC	40° BTDC	24° BBDC
Exhaust closes	20° ATDC	5° BTDC	20° ATDC	2° BTDC
	(2000T)		(911TV)	(Carrera)
Inlet opens	15° BTDC		15° BTDC	38° BTDC
Inlet closes	29° ATDC		29° ATDC	50° ABDC
Exhaust opens	41° BTDC		41° BTDC	40° BBDC
Exhaust closes	5° BTDC		5° BTDC	20° ATDC
	(911S)			
Inlet opens	38° BTDC			
Inlet closes	50° ABDC			
Exhaust opens	40° BBDC			
Exhaust closes	20° ATDC			

	1991 cc	2195 cc	2341 cc	2687 cc
Engine capacity	1991 cc	2195 cc	2341 cc	2687 cc
Valve clearances (cold):				
Inlet and exhaust	0.004 in (0.10 mm)	0.004 in (0.10 mm)	0.004 in (0.10 mm)	0.004 in (0.10 mm)
Valve stem-to-guide clearance:				
Inlet	0.0011 to 0.0059 in (0.030 to 0.15 mm)	0.0011 to 0.0059 in (0.030 to 0.15 mm)	0.0011 to 0.0059 in (0.030 to 0.15 mm)	0.0011 to 0.0059 in (0.030 to 0.15 mm)
Exhaust	0.0019 to 0.0078 in (0.050 to 0.20 mm)	0.0019 to 0.0078 in (0.050 to 0.20 mm)	0.0019 to 0.0078 in (0.050 to 0.20 mm)	0.0019 to 0.0078 in (0.050 to 0.20 mm)

Camshaft

Bearing running clearance ...	0.0009 to 0.0039 in (0.025 to 0.10 mm)	0.0009 to 0.0039 in (0.025 to 0.10 mm)	0.0009 to 0.0039 in (0.025 to 0.10 mm)	0.0009 to 0.0039 in (0.025 to 0.10 mm)
Endfloat	0.0059 to 0.0157 in (0.150 to 0.40 mm)	0.0059 to 0.0157 in (0.150 to 0.40 mm)	0.0059 to 0.0157 in (0.150 to 0.40 mm)	0.0059 to 0.0157 in (0.150 to 0.40 mm)

Rocker arms and shafts

Running clearance of arm to shaft	0.006 to 0.0031 in (0.016 to 0.080 mm)	0.006 to 0.0031 in (0.016 to 0.080 mm)	0.006 to 0.0031 in (0.016 to 0.080 mm)	0.006 to 0.0031 in (0.016 to 0.080 mm)
Rocker arm endfloat ...	0.0039 to 0.0196 in (0.100 to 0.50 mm)	0.0039 to 0.0196 in (0.100 to 0.50 mm)	0.0039 to 0.0196 in (0.100 to 0.50 mm)	0.0039 to 0.0196 in (0.100 to 0.50 mm)

Intermediate shaft

Bearing running clearance ...	0.0007 to 0.0039 in (0.020 to 0.10 mm)	0.0007 to 0.0039 in (0.020 to 0.10 mm)	0.0007 to 0.0039 in (0.020 to 0.10 mm)	0.0007 to 0.0039 in (0.020 to 0.10 mm)
Shaft endfloat	0.0031 to 0.0059 in (0.080 to 0.150 mm)	0.0031 to 0.0059 in (0.080 to 0.150 mm)	0.0031 to 0.0059 in (0.080 to 0.150 mm)	0.0031 to 0.0059 in (0.080 to 0.150 mm)

Lubrication

System type	Force feed, dry sump, separate oil tank and oil cooler	Force feed, dry sump, separate oil tank and oil cooler	Force feed, dry sump, separate oil tank and oil cooler	Force feed, dry sump, separate oil tank and oil cooler
Capacity	16 Imp. pints (9 litres/ 9.5 US qts)	16 Imp. pints (9 litres/ 9.5 US qts)	16 Imp. pints (9 litres/ 9.5 US qts)	23 Imp.pints (13 litres/ 13.7 US qts)

Torque wrench settings

	lb f ft	kg fm
Crankcase section bolts	25	3.5
Crankcase nuts (M8)	18	2.5
Flywheel securing bolts	106	14.6
Crankshaft pulley bolt	56	7.7
Connecting rod bolts	36	5.0
Cylinder head nuts	21	2.9
Camshaft sprocket nuts	71	9.8
Rocker arm shaft nuts	13	1.8
Pulley to alternator nut	28	3.9
Spark plugs	18	2.5
Blower housing clamp bolts	6	0.8

1 General description

1 The basic design of the engine is similar in all models and is of air-cooled, six-cylinder, horizontally opposed type with an overhead camshaft installed on each of the cylinder banks. The engine is mounted at the rear of the car.

2 Since its introduction in 1964, the engine has undergone many modifications, the most important being the increase in cylinder displacement and the changes in cylinder materials.

3 The crankshaft is supported in eight main bearings while each chain driven camshaft runs in four bearings.

4 Lubrication is by dry sump system. The dual oil pumps are located in the crankcase, one pump scavenging oil from the crankcase and the other one drawing oil from a remote tank and pressurising it for distribution to the engine working surfaces and bearings.

5 The crankshaft is geared to a short intermediate shaft which in turn drives the two camshafts by means of duplex chains.

6 This intermediate shaft also drives the dual oil pumps through a connecting shaft.

7 According to model and gear production, the engine may be fitted with carburettors or a fuel injection system. Reference should be made to Chapter 3 for details.

8 Perhaps one of the most interesting and unconventional features of the engine is the method of heating the car interior. This is designed around a heat exchanger attached to the exhaust system and provided with the necessary controls to regulate the airflow and temperature. A description is included in Section 47, of this Chapter.

9 Cooling of the engine is critical and is provided by a blower and the necessary ducts and covers.

10 Reference should be made to 'Specifications' at the beginning of this Chapter for detailed differences between the various engine versions, tabulated according to capacity.

11 It is emphasised that the engine is a rather specialised and complex unit and a working mechanical knowledge plus a fairly extensive tool kit (Metric) will greatly facilitate major overhaul operations on this car.

2 Operations possible with the engine still in the car

1 Many of the smaller ancillary components (engine oil filter, air cleaner, carburettors, distributor etc) may be removed and refitted with the engine still in position in the car.

2 However, the removal and refitting of components of the engine proper is limited to the following items:

3 The oil cooler.

4 The oil temperature thermostat (after first removing the air cleaner).

5 The oil pump for Sportomatic transmission. This is not the engine

oil pump.

6   The blower unit and alternator. This can be removed from the upper air cooling channel but the latter can only be removed after the engine has been lifted out of the car.

7   The blower fan drivebelt.

8   The chain tensioner (after having first removed the exhaust silencer and engine rear shroud).

9   The crankshaft oil seal which is located behind the pulley. The pulley will of course first have to be removed.

10   The rocker shafts and arms (after having removed the rocker covers).

11   When removing the oil cooler from 1973 onward cars with the engine still in position, the task is simplified compared with earlier cars, as they are fitted with a two-piece air shroud.

3   Engine - method of removal

1   The engine can only be removed together with the transmission as a combined assembly.

2   The car should be raised at the rear and supported on axlestands placed under the bodyframe. Make sure that it is sufficiently high to provide clearance for the engine/transmission between the underside of the body and the ground.

3   A trolley jack should be used to support the power unit so that it can be lowered and withdrawn rearwards with the minimum of man-handling.

4   Engine/transmission - removal

1   Open the engine compartment lid to its fullest extent.

2   Disconnect the lead from the battery negative terminal.

3   Remove the air cleaner and hot air duct (photo).

4   Disconnect the oil tank vent hose.

5   *On carburettor engines;* disconnect the leads from the electric pump. Plug the hoses. There is no need to disconnect the hoses from the carburettors or the secondary mechanical fuel pump unless they are going to get in the way of the lifting equipment (photo).

6   *On fuel injection engines;* disconnect the hoses from the fuel filter, the fuel distributor, the control pressure regulator. Plug all the hoses and make sure you identify them for correct reconnection (see Chapter 2).

7   Mark and then disconnect the leads from the alternator.

8   Disconnect the high tension (HT) and the low tension (LT) cables from the ignition coil (photo).

9   Disconnect the throttle linkage.

10   Disconnect the oil breather hose from the oil filler (photo).

11   Disconnect the lead from the oil pressure switch.

12   Drain the engine oil into a suitable container.

13   Disconnect the oil hoses from the oil tank and the oil lines from the oil cooler, see Section 51 and 52.

14   Disconnect the lead from the starter motor.

15   Disconnect the hot air ducts which run between the heat exchanger and the air grille, also disconnect the heater cables from the rotary valves of the heater body under the car.

16   Disconnect the clutch from the clutch release lever (photo).

17   Disconnect the earth strap which runs between the engine and the bodyframe (photo).

18   Disconnect the leads from the reversing lamp switch, the speedometer cable and the vacuum hose from its reservoir.

19   Remove the screws which secure the centre tunnel in the rear passenger compartment and withdraw the cover.

20   Pull the rubber bellows which are now exposed, towards the front of the car and then cut the lockwire and unscrew the lock bolt.

Fig. 1.1. Two-piece air shroud used on engine oil cooler (1973 on (Sec. 2)

4.3 Air cleaner

4.5 Disconnecting lead from electric fuel pump

4.8 Location of ignition coil

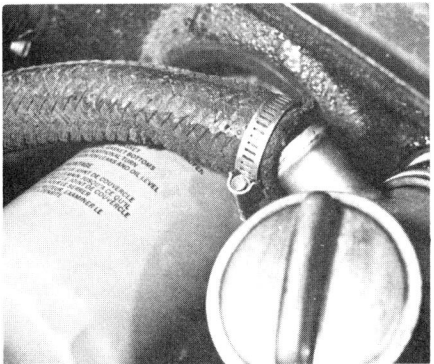

4.10 Oil breather hose connection to filler pipe

4.16 Clutch cable connection

4.17 Earth strap connection

21 Separate the gearshift rod sections.

22 Now raise the rear of the car and support it securely on axlestands placed under the bodyframe.

23 *On cars fitted with Sportomatic transmission,* disconnect the oil lines from the transmission oil supply pump.

On cars with emission control equipment, disconnect the hoses from the air pump and disconnect the air pump filter.

24 Place a 'trolley' jack under the engine/transmission and take its weight. The point on contact of the jack should be about two thirds along the length of the engine bottom cover, measured from the pulley end.

25 Disconnect the axleshafts from the transmission drive flanges by extracting the socket-headed screws. A few taps with a plastic-faced hammer may be required to separate the shaft from the flange once the

screws have been removed.

26 Disconnect the engine mountings and the mounting which supports the transmission.

27 Lower the jack carefully and remove the engine/transmission from below and to the rear of the car (photo).

5 Engine/transmission - separation (no : Sportomatic)

1 With the engine/transmission removed, the transmission must now be separated from the engine.

2 *On cars built up until 1970,* remove the starter motor and unscrew and remove the bolts which secure the engine to the transmission (photo).

3 Support the weight of the transmission and withdraw it from the engine in a straight-line. Ensure that the weight of the transmission does not hang upon the primary shaft while it is still engaged with the clutch mechanism (photo).

4 *On cars built after 1970,* unbolt and remove the starter motor and then turn the flywheel until the first of the three rivet heads comes into view through the starter motor aperture.

5 Obtain or make up sleeves or distance collars similar to those shown in Fig. 1.3 and then screw a socket-headed screw (M6 x 12) through the first spacer sleeve into the threaded bore of the rivet. Tighten the screw with an Allen key which will relieve the tension of the clutch release bearing.

6 Repeat these operations on the remaining two rivets after having turned the flywheel to bring them into view one by one.

7 On some 1970/71 models, it is possible to relieve the tension of the clutch release bearing by unscrewing the adjusting screw on the clutch release fork.

8 With the release bearing tension relieved, insert a screwdriver into the aperture in the transmission casing and prise the release bearing so that it turns through 90° (Fig. 1.4). The clutch release lever end fork can now be withdrawn past the release bearing.

9 Unbolt and remove the transmission from the engine, as described in paragraph 3.

Fig. 1.2. Oil supply pump fitted to engine exterior on cars with Sportomatic transmission (Sec. 4)

4.27 Removing the engine/transmission

5.2 Removing the starter motor

5.3 Separating transmission from engine

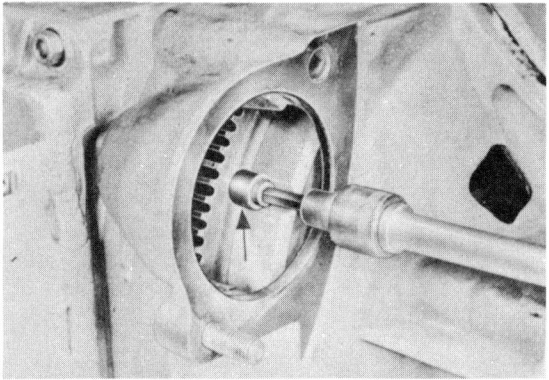

Fig. 1.3. Flywheel rivet and spacer (1970 onwards) (Sec. 5)

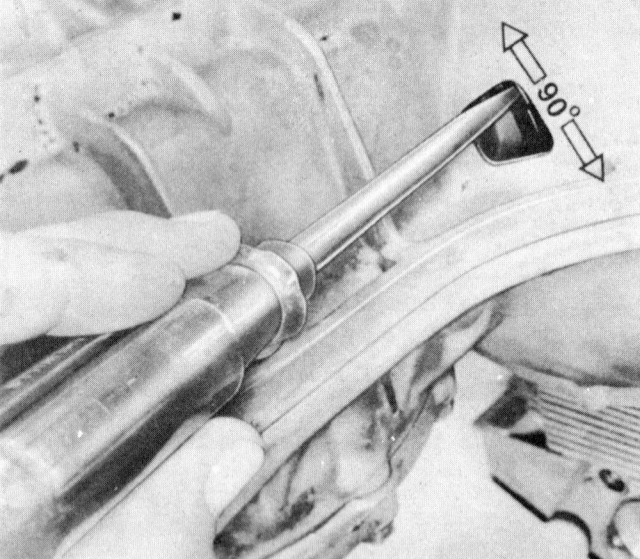

Fig. 1.4. Turning clutch release bearing through 90° (1970 onwards)
(Sec. 5)

6 Engine/transmission - separation (Sportomatic)

1 Unscrew and remove the nuts which secure the torque converter
housing to the gearbox.
2 Disconnect the intermediate lever from the actuating lever by
extracting the cotter pin. Remove the actuating lever.
3 Slide the torque connector housing away from the gearbox and at
the same time, disengage the clutch release fork from the release
bearing.

7 Engine ancillaries - removal

1 Before dismantling proper can begin, the engine must be stripped
of all external ancillary components.
2 Remove the throttle control rods and linkage and *on carburettor
type engines,* remove the carburettors complete with manifolds.
3 *On fuel injection type engines,* removed the injection pump or
fuel distributor (according to type) and disconnect the lines from the
fuel injectors. Refer to Chapter 2, for full details of these operations.
4 *On cars equipped with emission control systems,* disconnect and
remove the components of the system including the air pump and
regulating valve; see Chapter 2 for full details.
5 Remove the distributor cap complete with high tension leads.
6 Remove all the air cooling ducts and shrouds from the engine by

removing the securing screws.
7 Detach the air ducts which connect the air blower outlets and
heat exchanger inlets. Remove them together with the cover shrouds
(see Section 47) (photo).
8 Disconnect the leaf spring type engine rear mounting.
9 *On carburettor engines,* remove the fuel pump and hoses.
10 Unscrew the exhaust flange nuts and withdraw the exhaust assembly
(photo).
11 Remove the engine mounting and bracket from the engine (photo).
12 Remove the blower pulley nut and extract the drivebelt. Lock the
pulley for this operation by using a rod and 'C' spanner or similar
tool. Some car tool kits include one (photo).
13 Loosen both screws of the strap which secures the alternator to the
blower housing (photos).
14 Pull the blower housing to the rear and disconnect the leads from
the alternator. Remove the alternator and blower as an assembly.
Remove the strap (photo).
15 Unbolt and remove the heat exchanger (photo).
16 On all cars except those equipped with Sportomatic, mark the position
of the clutch pressure plate cover in relation to the flywheel and then
unscrew the cover screws a turn at a time each in diagonally opposite
sequence and then remove the pressure plate and driven plate from
the flywheel.
17 Unbolt and remove the rocker shaft covers.
18 With the engine stripped of ancillaries, clean the external surfaces
of the unit with paraffin and a stiff brush or a water soluble solvent.
19 Gather together tools and rag and dismantling proper may commence,
as described in the following Section.

8 Timing chains and sprockets - removal

1 Disconnect the oil hoses which connect the crankcase with the
chain covers (photo).
2 Unscrew the securing nuts and remove the chain covers.
3 Unscrew the nuts which secure the chain tensioner and then
withdraw the tensioners together with pivot levers and idler pulleys.
4 Remove the camshaft sprocket retaining nuts and extract the
sprocket dowel pin. The pin can be extracted by screwing a bolt into it
(photo).
5 Remove the chain guide slippers from the chain housing. The
slippers are retained by spring clips and these should be raised from
their grooves using a thin screwdriver.
6 Withdraw the chain sprockets. At this stage do not move the
positions of either the crankshaft or the camshafts as the valves may
dig into the piston crowns with consequent damage to both components.
Extract the hub and the thrust washers.
7 Extract the Woodruff keys from the camshafts.
8 Remove the three bolts from the sealing flange and withdraw the
flange, seal and gasket.
9 Unbolt the chain covers from the crankcase.
10 Withdraw the chain covers sideways over the lengths of the chain.
11 Within the crankcase aperture; additional chain guide slippers will
now be visible and these can be removed if the spring retainers are
lifted and the pivot bolts unscrewed (photo). (Fig. 1.5).

9 Cylinder head - removal and dismantling

1 Remove the oil cooler, as described in Section 13.
2 Each bank of three cylinder heads can be removed together with the
camshaft housing. Alternatively, by removing the camshaft housing
first, any one of the cylinder heads may be removed individually.
3 *To remove a single cylinder head,* release the rocker shafts using a
5 mm Allen key. The rocker shafts can only be pushed out if pressure
from the rocker arms is relieved, therefore the camshaft will have to be
turned to alter the position of the cam lobes as the rocker shaft is
pushed out. Take great care however that, now the engine valve
timing chains have been disconnected, the valve heads do not dig
into the piston crowns as the camshaft is turned.
4 Remove the camshaft housing securing nuts and their spring washers
and withdraw the camshaft housing.
5 Unscrew the retaining nuts from the cylinder head which is to be
removed and withdraw the head from the barrel.
6 *To remove the bank of three cylinder heads,* release all the cylinder
head nuts evenly and then remove the nuts.

7.7 An air duct

7.10 Exhaust silencer

7.11 Engine mounting and bracket

7.12 Releasing blower pulley nut

7.13a Blower housing strap bolts

7.13b Blower housing strap lower bolt

7.14a Alternator leads

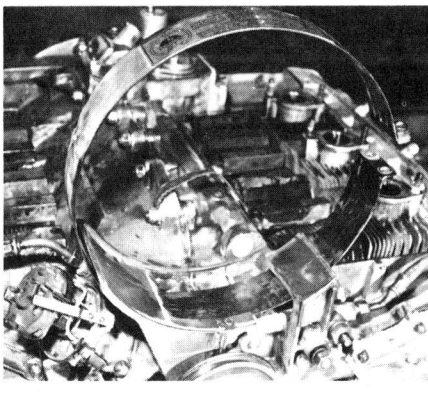

7.14b Blower housing strap (blower and alternator removal)

7.15 Removing a heat exchange

8.1 Crankcase to chain cover oil line

8.4 Camshaft sprocket showing dowel pin

8.11 A crankcase chain guide slipper

7   Withdraw the bank of three cylinder heads complete with the camshaft housing.

8   Remove the joint gaskets.

9   Dismantle the rocker shafts, as described in paragraph 3, and the camshaft housing. Mark all components for exact refitting, particularly the position of each cylinder head in relation to its barrel.

10 The valves can be removed from the cylinder head using a valve spring compressor. With the spring compressed, extract the split collets and then release the compressor.

11 Extract the retainer, the valve spring, lower washers and the oil seal.

10 Pistons, flywheel and crankshaft - removal

1   With all three cylinder heads removed from both sides of the engine, mark the location of the six cylinder barrels, remove the air deflector plates and then unbolt the cylinder barrels and withdraw them carefully off their pistons. Mark each piston in respect of its position and also which way round it is fitted to the connecting rod.

2   Extract the gudgeon pin circlips.

3   The gudgeon pins are an interference fit in the pistons and the pistons will have to be heated before the pins can be pushed out. If the pistons are to be used again, try wrapping cloths round the piston and soaking them in boiling water, alternatively, turn the engine so that the pistons can be immersed in boiling water. If the pistons are to

be discarded, then the careful use of a blow torch will be the quickest means of heating them.

4   Remove the crankcase breather attachment.

5   Unscrew and remove the thermostat and the oil pressure switch.

6   Remove all the (M8) nuts which hold the two halves of the crankcase together.

7   Unscrew the flywheel mounting bolts. To prevent the flywheel turning while the bolts are unscrewed, *on early cars,* lock the starter ring gear using a large screwdriver.

On later cars, the ring gear is attached to the clutch pressure plate and the flywheel will have to be locked by bolting a small plate between a flywheel bolt hole and a casing bolt hole.

8   On cars equipped with Sportomatic transmission, the driveplate which is bolted to the end of the crankshaft should be used to prevent the crankshaft turning. With this type of transmission, there is no flywheel attached directly to the crankshaft.

9   Unscrew and remove the two domed nuts which are visible within the oil cooler flange.

10 Remove the tie bolts which are accessible within the left-hand timing chain housing of the crankcase.

11 Pull both halves of the crankcase apart. Retain the bearing shells in their original positions if they are not to be renewed. No 1 main bearing is at the flywheel end of the crankshaft.

12 Remove the crankshaft complete with connecting rods which are still attached to it.

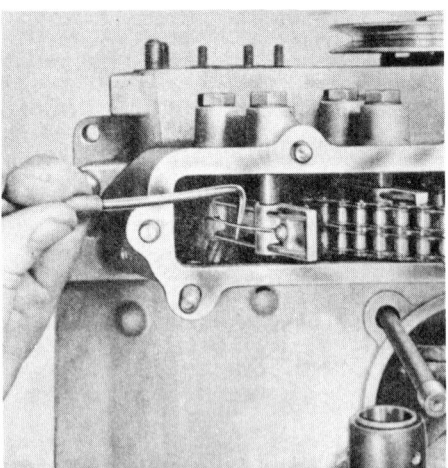

Fig. 1.5. Removing a chain guide slipper from crankcase (Sec. 8)

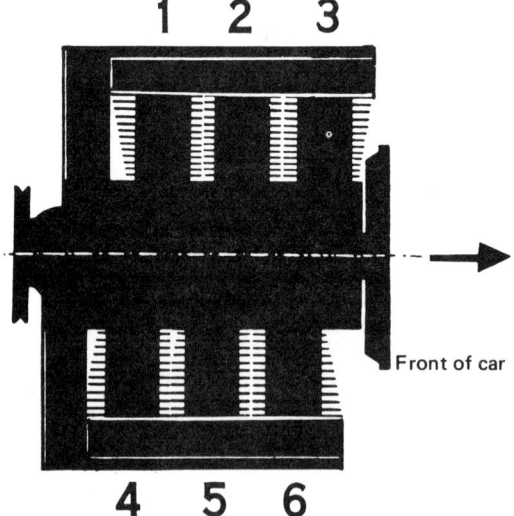

Fig. 1.6. Cylinder layout (firing order 1-6 - 2-4 - 3-5) (Sec. 10)

Fig. 1.7. Driveplate (Sportomatic transmission) (Sec. 10)

Fig. 1.8. Main bearing No 1 domed nuts accessible within oil cooler mounting flange (right-hand crankcase section) (Sec. 10)

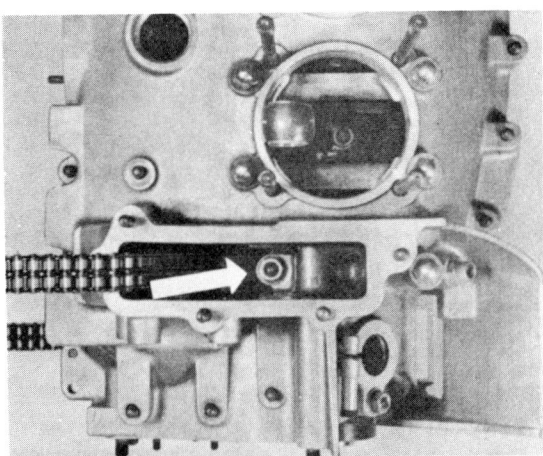

Fig. 1.9. Tie-bolt of main bearing No 7 accessible through left-hand chain housing (Sec. 10)

13 Remove the big-end bolts and withdraw the rods and caps. Mark the rods and caps in relation to their position on the crankshaft, also which way round they are fitted. If the bearing shells are to be used again, keep them identified (using masking tape or a spirit pen) not only in respect of position but also regarding cap or rod.

11 Oil pump, intermediate and connecting shafts - removal

1 These three components can be removed together, after unscrewing the oil pump retaining nuts.
2 The individual parts can be separated after removal.

12 Lubrication system and components - description

1 The lubrication system is of dry-sump type and the circuit contains two oil pumps housed in the crankcase.
2 One pump draws oil (free from air bubbles) from a separate oil tank and distributes it to the bearings.
3 The second pump extracts oil (which has already circulated) from the crankcase. This oil passes through a coarse strainer and then through a cartridge type filter before being returned to the oil tank.
4 An oil cooler is fitted but a thermostat monitors the oil temperature and a valve regulates the oil flow so that at 176°F (80°C) and below the oil does not pass through the cooler.
5 A pressure relief valve and a safety valve are built into the oil circuit.
6 Each main bearing is supplied with oil from a separate drilling while main bearings 1 and 8 are so designed that oil under pressure passes into the centre of the crankshaft to lubricate the connecting rod big-end bearings.
7 An oil passage leads to the front bearing of the intermediate shaft and a connection is provided to the rear bearing through the centre of the shaft itself.
8 Oil is supplied to the camshaft by means of an oil line connected centrally.
9 The rocker shafts and valve stems are splash lubricated.
10 A number of modifications and changes have been carried out over the years of production and the following summary gives details:

Supplementary oil cooler (911S models)
11 As from 1969, a supplementary oil cooler is located under the

right-hand front wing. Cars built after 1973 have a modified tubular type oil cooler.

Modified oil tank location
12 As from 1972, the oil tank is located under the right-hand rear wheel arch just ahead of the axle driveshaft.
13 The oil filler is accessible from outside the car after raising a small hinged lid.
14 The oil filter assembly is located on the right-hand rear wing valance.

Modified lubrication of camshaft and rocker arms
15 As from engine no. 903 070, oil is supplied to the camshaft lobes by means of aluminium tubes which are precisely perforated. Additional holes in the tubes permit oil to splash against the inlet valve cover so that it will then drip down onto the rocker arms and valve stems.

Piston oil cooling jets
16 As from the end of 1970 oil spray jets are installed in all engines in order to reduce the piston crown operating temperature by spraying oil onto the underside of the piston (Fig. 1.11).
17 The jets are installed during production and cannot be removed.

13 Lubrication system components - removal and refitting

1 At time of major engine overhaul it is recommended that the following components are removed and examined for wear:

Crankcase oil strainer
2 Unscrew and remove the nuts from the oil strainer cover plate.
3 Remove the cover plate, the strainer and gaskets (photo) (Fig. 1.12).
4 Remove the plug from the cover plate and wipe away any fillings adhering to its magnetised inner surface.
5 Clean the strainer and if its mesh is broken, renew it.
6 Refit the strainer so that it fits snugly round the oil pick-up tube. Use a new gasket on each side of the strainer.
7 Refit the other components by reversing the removal operations.

Oil pressure release and safety valves
8 Withdraw the plugs from the crankcase (Figs. 1.13 and 1.14).
9 Extract the springs and pistons (both springs are identical).
10 Check the pistons for scoring; if evident, renew them.
11 Check the spring free-lengths. They should be 2.75 in (70 mm). If they are below this figure, renew them.
12 On engines up to no. 901282, an aluminium sealing ring is used for the pressure release valve and this must be renewed where necessary by one of similar type. On engines no. 901283 onwards, both valve sealing rings are identical.

Oil cooler
13 With the upper, front and right-hand cover plates removed from the engine, unscrew and remove both nuts from the top of the oil cooler (photo) (Fig. 1.15).
14 Unscrew the lower retaining nuts from the oil cooler and lift the unit away. (Fig. 1.16). If you detach the inlet pipe from the cooler, hold the union nut tightly otherwise the joint may tear away.
15 When installing the oil cooler, make sure that the sealing rings are in good condition: if otherwise, renew them.

Oil filter
16 The oil filter cartridge is removed by unscrewing it in an anticlock-wise direction. A small strap or chain type wrench may be needed to do this. If all else fails drive a sharp-pointed tool right through the cartridge at about halfway down its length and use the tool as a lever.
17 When fitting the new filter, apply grease to its sealing washer and screw it on using hand-pressure only (photo).

Oil temperature thermostat
18 The thermostat is held in position in the crankcase by a flange.
19 Disconnect the lead from the oil pressure switch.
20 Disconnect the crankcase breather hose.
21 Unscrew and remove the oil pressure switch (photo).
22 Unscrew and remove the thermostat and withdraw the thermostat (photo).

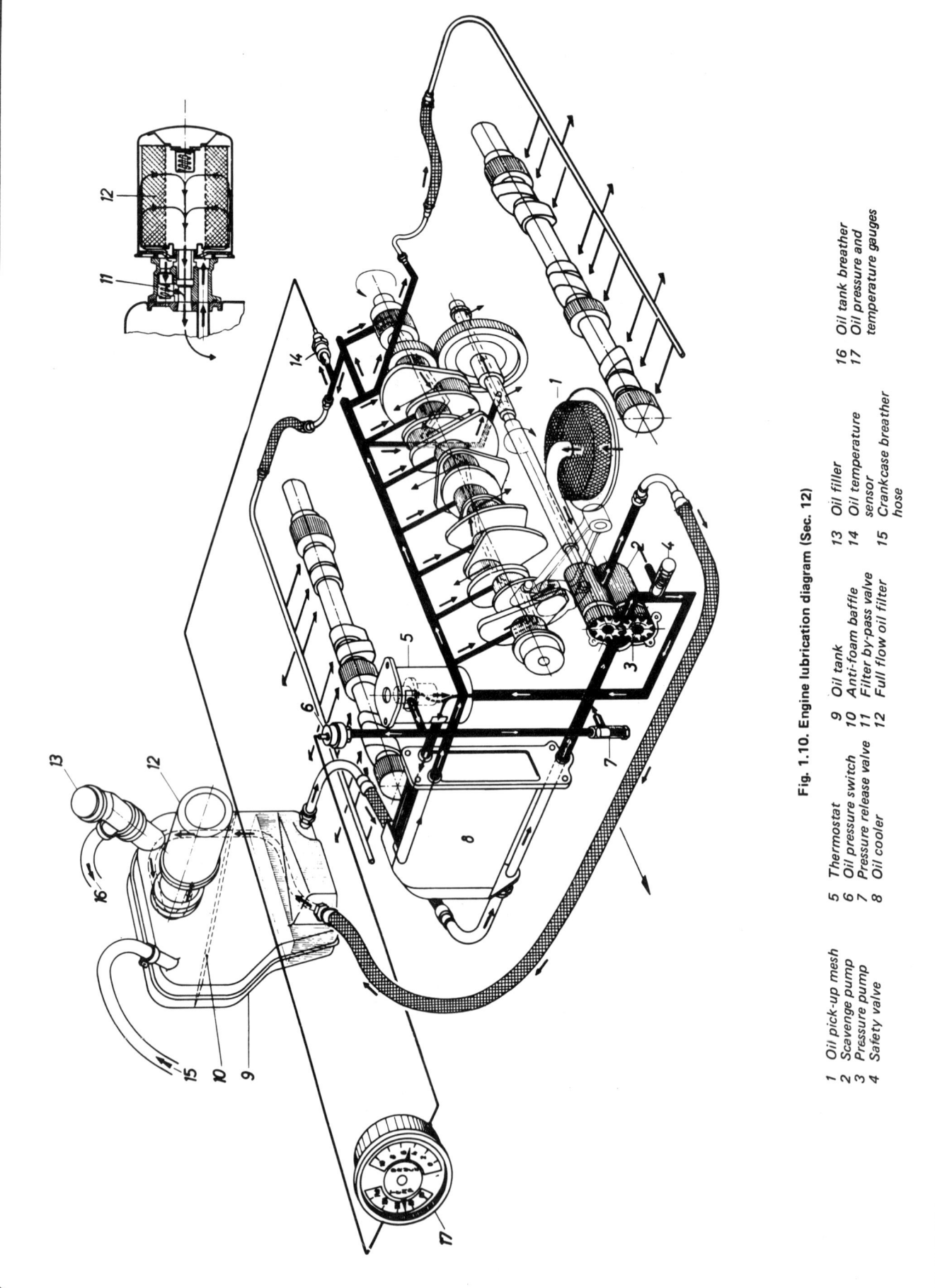

Fig. 1.10. Engine lubrication diagram (Sec. 12)

1 Oil pick-up mesh
2 Scavenge pump
3 Pressure pump
4 Safety valve

5 Thermostat
6 Oil pressure switch
7 Pressure release valve
8 Oil cooler

9 Oil tank
10 Anti-foam baffle
11 Filter by-pass valve
12 Full flow oil filter

13 Oil filler
14 Oil temperature
    sensor
15 Crankcase breather
    hose

16 Oil tank breather
17 Oil pressure and
    temperature gauges

Fig. 1.11. Location of piston oil cooling spray jets (1970 on) (Sec. 12)

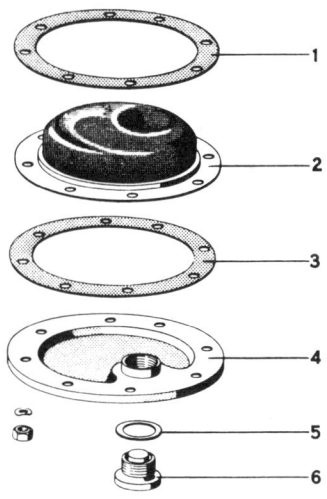

Fig. 1.12. Crankcase oil strainer (Sec. 13)

1	Gasket	4	Cover plate
2	Strainer	5	Sealing washer
3	Gasket	6	Magnetic drain plug

Fig. 1.13. Location of:

a   Safety valve

b   Oil pressure release valves (Sec. 13)

13.3 Crankcase oil strainer cover removed

Fig. 1.14. Exploded view of oil pressure valve (Sec. 13)

13.13 Removing an oil cooler cover plate

Fig. 1.16. Oil cooler lower securing nuts (Sec. 13)

Fig. 1.15 Oil cooler upper securing nuts (Sec. 13)

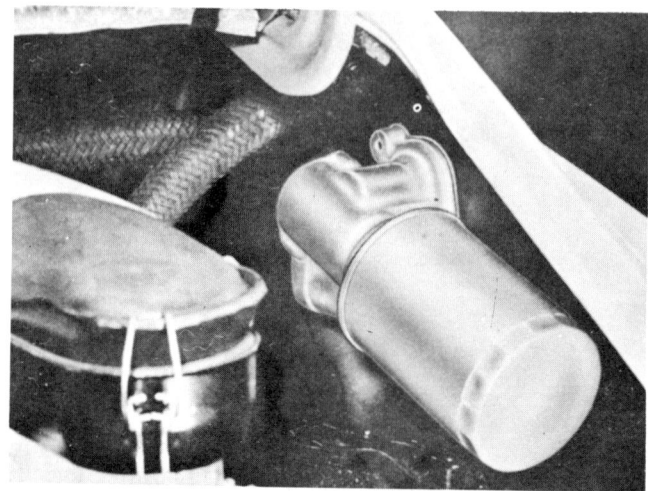

Fig. 1.17. Oil filter and mounting (Sec. 13)

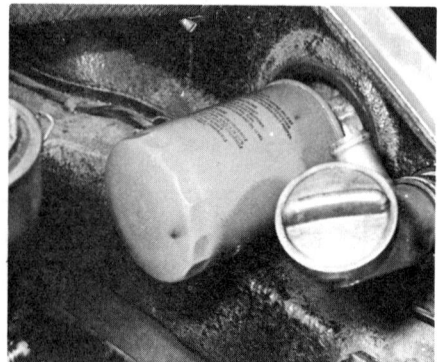

13.17 Oil filter cartridge and filler pipe

13.21 Oil pressure switch

13.22 Removing the oil temperature thermostat

23 Renew the 'O' ring seals before fitting. The mounting studs are offset so that the thermostat can only be installed one way round.

Oil pump (engine lubrication)
24 Removal and refitting of the pump and its intermediate and connecting drive shafts are described in Section 11.
25 It is not recommended that the oil pump is overhauled or repaired but if it is worn, it should be removed.

Oil pump (Sportomatic transmission)
26 This oil pump is accessible after removing the left rear road wheel and heat exchanger, without the need to remove the engine.
27 Disconnect the oil lines from the pump, unbolt and remove the pump.
28 To overhaul the pump, remove the cover from the pump body.

29 Drive the dowel pin from the rotor shaft and withdraw the inner and outer rotors.
30 Remove the nuts from the pressure relief valve cover and withdraw the cover, spring and plunger.
31 Check all parts for wear. The inner and outer rotors and shaft are supplied together as a matched assembly.
32 When reassembling the pump, make sure that the cover aligning dowel projects 0.16 im (4 mm) above the mating face of the housing. The outer rotor must have its levelled edge inserted first.
33 Apply oil liberally to the rotors and make that the 'O' ring is fitted in the pressure relief valve cover.
34 Make sure that the tension pins in the camshaft drive flange project 0.32 in (8 mm) above the flange face and install the pins so that their slots are aligned as shown in Fig. 1.20.

Fig. 1.18. Removing Sportomatic transmission oil pump cover (Sec. 13)

Fig. 1.19. Removing pressure relief valve cover (Sportomatic transmission oil pump) (Sec. 13)

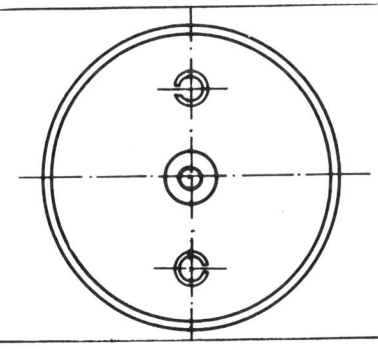

Fig. 1.20. Setting up tension pins in camshaft drive flange for Sportomatic transmission oil pump (Sec. 13)

14 Crankcase ventilation system

1   The system includes a vent hose from the crankcase and one from the oil tank. These are connected to the air cleaner so that oil fumes are drawn into the engine and burned during the normal combustion cycle.

2   A flame trap is incorporated at the air cleaner end of the hose as a safety feature to combat backfire.

3   Periodically inspect the condition and the security of the hoses. At intervals of 6000 miles (9600 km) detach the flame trap, wash it clean in paraffin and let in drain or blow it dry with air from a tyre pump before refitting it (photo).

15 Examination and renovation - general

With the engine stripped down and all parts thoroughly cleaned, it is now time to examine everything for wear. The items should be checked and where necessary renewed or renovated, as described in the following Sections.

16 Crankcase - examination and renovation

1   Carefully clean the mating surfaces until free from old gasket and jointing compound.

2   Clean out all oilways using a round wire brush, flush out all the oil passages with petrol and blow dry with air from a tyre pump. Clean the filter mesh (photo).

3   Check the two crankcase halves for cracks, stripped threads in the stud or bolt holes and general damage. It is possible to have the threads repaired by installing thread inserts and specialists can repair cracks in the engine castings where this is required.

4   The groove which is cut round main bearing no. 7 tie-bolt on the left-hand side of the crankcase is a pressure relief groove and it must be left absolutely clear of jointing compound and dirt.

17 Crankshaft, bearings and connecting rods - examination and renovation

1   The places to check for wear on the crankshaft are the main bearing journals and big-end crank pins.

2   A micrometer will be required to check for out-of-roundness or taper; measurements should be taken at several different points round, and along, each bearing journal or crankpin.

3   Examine the bearing surfaces for scoring.

4   Where out-of-roundness or taper is found to exceed 0.0004 in (0.01 mm) on any journal or crankpin then the crankshaft will have to be reground. Similarly, if general wear in a crankpin or journal is found to exceed 0.010 in (0.25 mm) then the crankshaft will have to be reground and undersize bearings fitted. This job is obviously one for your dealer or specialist engineering company and they will regrind to the correct size and supply the new bearing to provide the correct running clearance.

5   If the teeth of the distributor or intermediate shaft drive gears are

14.3 Detaching the flame trap

16.2 Crankcase filter mesh

17.5 Distributor drive gear and intermediate drive gear on crankshaft

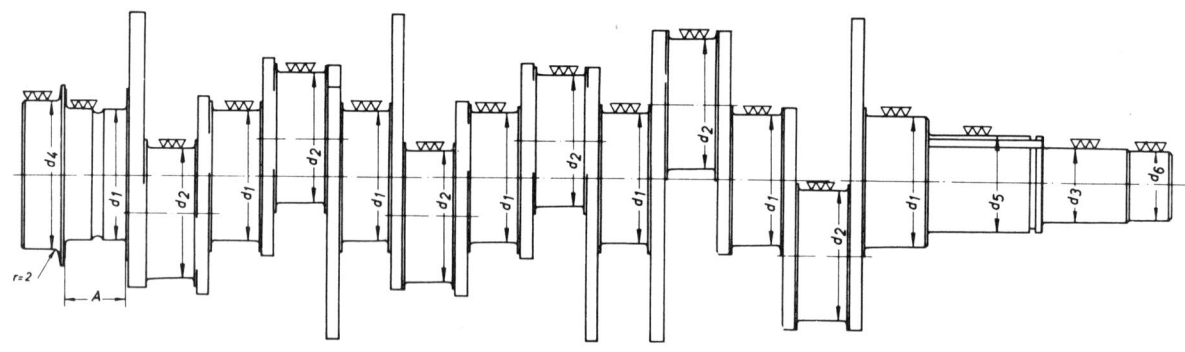

Fig. 1.21. Crankshaft regrinding details (Sec. 17)

Degree of wear	Crankcase bore diameter (bearings 1 - 8)		All main bearings d 1 and connecting rod bearings d2 on crankshaft (up to 1972)	Connecting rod bearings d 2 1972 onwards	Main bearing diameter d 3 on crankshaft bearing 8	Shoulder diameter	Timing gear seat diameter d 5	Bearing surface diameter d 6	Guide bearing Width A
Std.			56,990 - 56,971 (2,2437 - 2.2429")	51,990 - 51,971 (2,0468 - 2.0461")	30.993 - 30.980 (1.2202 - 1,2197")				
0.25	Normal 62,000 - 62,019 (2.4409" - 2.4117")	Oversize 62.269 - 62.250 (2.4515" - 2.4508")	56.740 - 56.721 (2,2338 - 2.2331")	51.740 - 51.721 (2.0382 - 2.0363")	30.743 - 30.730 1.2104 - 1.2098"	65,000 - (2.5591")	42.013 - (1.6540")	29.993 -2 (1.1808")	28.000 - (1.1024")
0.50			56.490 - 56.471 (2.2240 - 2.2232")	51.490 - 51.471 (2.0272 - 2.0264")	30.493 - 30.480 1.2005 - 1.999"	64.981 (2.5583")	42.002 (1.6536")	29.960 (1.1795")	28.052 (1.1044")
0.75			56.240 - 56.221 (2.2141 - 2.2134")	51.240 - 51.221 (2.0173 - 2.0166")	30.243 - 30.230 (1.1906 - 1.1901")				

worn or damaged, they should be drawn off together using a two-legged puller but having first extracted the circlip from the front face of the distributor gear (photo).

6   When installing the intermediate shaft gear to the crankshaft, heat it to 302°F (150°C) in an oil bath before driving it on. Make sure that the shoulder on the gear is towards the flywheel.

7   From the point of view of interest, the standard and undersize tolerances for the crankshaft are given in Fig. 1.21.

8   Whenever the crankshaft is reground, the oilway plugs should be removed and the oilways thoroughly cleaned out. Fit new plugs and stake them securely.

9   If a connecting rod is twisted or must be renewed for any other reason, make sure that its weight does not vary from that of any other rod by more than 0.12 oz (3 g).

10   The small end bush in the connecting rod can be renewed if worn by pressing the old one out and the new one in. No reaming is required and the gudgeon pin should be a push fit using light finger-pressure.

18 Intermediate shaft - examination and renovation

1   The gearwheel on the intermediate shaft is machined while it is in position on the shaft and if either component is worn then the shaft/gear must be renewed as an assembly.

2   It is recommended that at time of major overhaul, the aluminium plugs are removed from the end face of the shaft and residue cleaned from the oil ways. To remove the plugs, drill and tap a thread in them and extract them by screwing in a bolt through a distance piece of greater diameter than the plug.

3   Renew the plugs on completion.

4   All later pressure die-cast crankcases are fitted with a lapped bearing insert to support the rear journal of the intermediate shaft. This insert controls the shaft endfloat by means of its thrust flanges.

19 Cylinders, pistons and piston rings - examination and renovation

1   Over the years of production, the material used for the cylinder barrels has been changed. Originally, the liner was of cast-iron with

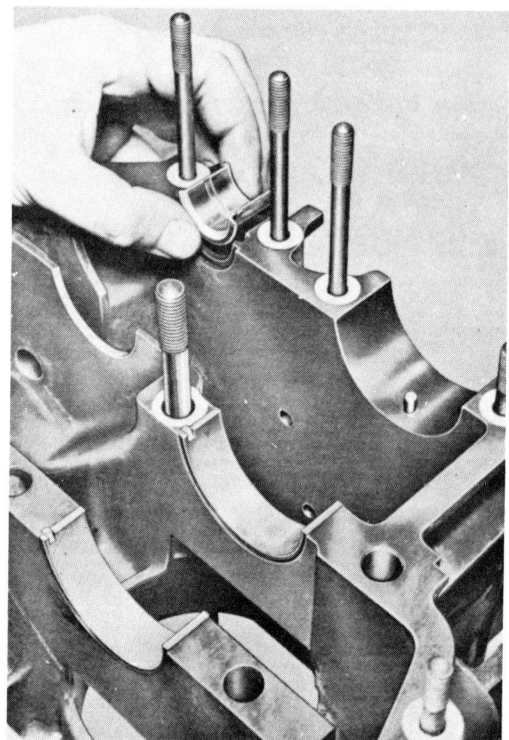

Fig. 1.22. Fitting an intermediate shaft rear bearing (Sec. 18)

aluminium casing and fins. Later cars have an aluminium cylinder with specially treated bores. The latest types have bores which have been silicon impregnated.

2 Cylinder barrels which have a cast-iron core can be rebored and oversize pistons installed but the latest types are renewed when they become worn unless a specialist company can be located to undertake the special treatment required for housing and silicon impregnation.

3 The necessity for reboring or renewal of cylinder barrels will normally be self evident from the engine's emission of blue smoke and high level of oil consumption but where the use of an internal micrometer can be obtained, the actual wear of the cylinder bore and the running clearance between piston and cylinder can be calculated.

4 Always measure a cylinder bore about 1.2 in (30 mm) above the bottom edge of the bore. The clearance between piston and cylinder must not exceed 0.0039 in (0.1 mm).

5 Normally your Porsche dealer will supply the correct oversize pistons compatible with the rebored or new cylinder barrels but the piston markings should be understood. All cylinder barrels in any one bank

should have the same marking. The mark is a figure enclosed in a triangle and represents the installed height of the cylinder barrel measured between the joint of the crankcase and the joint with the cylinder head.

Cylinder barrel mark		Installed height of cylinder barrel
△5	up to 1972	3.236 to 3.237 in (82.000 to 82.225 mm)
	1972 on	85.400 to 85.425 mm
△6	up to 1972	3.237 to 3.238 in (82.225 to 82.250 mm)
	1972 on	85.425 to 85.450 mm

6 Similarly the pistons should be selected so that their triangular mark matches the one on their respective cylinder barrels, also the grade mark on the piston is in accordance with the following table having already measured and recorded the individual cylinder bore diameter or selected new barrels with appropriate size markings:

Engines built up to 1968

Piston or cylinder marking	Piston diameter	Cylinder bore (internal diameter)	Gives piston to cylinder clearance of
Standard			
−1	3.1466 to 3.1470 in (79.925 to 79.935 mm)	3.1492 to 3.1496 in (79.990 to 80.000 mm)	
0	3.1470 to 3.1474 in (79.945 to 79.955 mm)	3.1496 to 3.1500 in (80.000 to 80.010 mm)	
+1	3.1474 to 3.1478 in (79.945 to 79.955 mm)	3.1500 to 3.1504 in (80.010 to 80.020 mm)	
Oversize			0.0022 to 0.0029 in (0.055 to 0.075 mm)
−1KD1	3.1663 to 3.1667 in (80.425 to 80.435 mm)	3.1689 to 3.1692 in (80.490 to 80.500 mm)	
0KD1	3.1667 to 3.1671 in (80.435 to 80.445 mm)	3.1692 to 3.1696 in (80.500 to 80.510 mm)	
+1KD1	3.1671 to 3.1675 in (80.445 to 80.455 mm)	3.1696 to 3.1700 in (80.510 to 80.520 mm)	

Engines built 1968 onwards

Piston or cylinder marking	Piston diameter	Cylinder bore	Gives piston to cylinder clearance of
Type 911S			
Standard			
0	79.950	80.00 to 80.01	
1	79.960	80.01 to 80.02	
2	79.970	80.02 to 80.03	0.045 to 0.065
Oversize			
0KD1	80.450	80.50 to 80.51	
1KD1	80.460	80.51 to 80.52	
2KD1	80.470	80.52 to 80.53	
Type 911L			
Standard			
0	79.960	80.00 to 80.01	
1	79.970	80.01 to 80.02	0.035 to 0.055
2	79.980	80.02 to 80.03	
Oversize - as for type 911S			
Type 911T			
Mahle Standard and Oversize - as Type 911L			0.025 to 0.045
Schmidt Standard and Oversize - as Type 911L (tolerance ± 0.006 to 0.007)			0.035 to 0.055

Engines built 1972 onwards

Piston or cylinder marking	Piston diameter	Cylinder bore	Gives piston to cylinder clearance of
Type 911S			
Standard			
0	83.950	84.000 to 84.010	
1	83.960	84.010 to 84.020	
2	83.970	84.020 to 84.030	
1st oversize			
0KD1	84.200	84.250 to 84.260	
1KD1	84.210	84.260 to 84.270	0.045 to 0.065
2KD1	84.220	84.270 to 84.280	
2nd oversize			
0KD2	84.450	84.500 to 84.510	
1KD2	84.460	84.510 to 84.520	
2KD2	84.470	84.520 to 84.530	
Type 911E			
Standard			
0	83.970	84.000 to 84.010	
1	83.980	84.010 to 84.020	
2	83.990	84.020 to 84.030	
1st oversize			
0KD1	84.220	84.250 to 84.260	
1KD1	84.230	84.260 to 84.270	0.025 to 0.045
2KD1	84.240	84.270 to 84.280	
2nd oversize			
0KD2	84.470	84.500 to 84.510	
1KD2	84.480	84.510 to 84.520	
2KD2	84.490	84.520 to 84.530	
Type 911T			
Standard			
(Mahle pistons)			
0	83.970	84.000 to 84.010	
1	83.980	84.010 to 84.020	
2	83.990	84.020 to 84.030	
1st oversize			
0KD1	84.220	84.250 to 84.260	
1KD1	84.230	84.260 to 84.270	0.025 to 0.045
2KD1	84.240	84.270 to 84.280	
2nd oversize			
0KD2	84.470	84.500 to 84.510	
1KD2	84.480	84.510 to 84.520	
2KD2	84.490	84.520 to 84.530	

Piston or cylinder marking	Piston diameter	Cylinder bore	Gives piston to cylinder clearance of
Standard (Schmidt pistons)			
0	83.970	84.000 to 84.010	
1	83.980	84.010 to 84.020	
2	83.990	84.020 to 84.030	
1st oversize			
0 KD 1	84.220	84.250 to 84.260	
1 KD 1	84.230	84.260 to 84.270	0.023 to 0.048
2 KD 1	84.240	84.270 to 84.280	
2nd oversize			
0 KD 2	84.470	84.500 to 84.510	
1 KD 2	84.480	84.510 to 84.520	
2 KD 2	84.490	84.520 to 84.530	

1973 onwards (Carrera 2687 cc)

Standard			
0	89.950	90.000 to 90.010	0.025
1	89.960	90.010 to 90.020	to
2	89.970	90.020 to 90.030	0.045

Oversizes not available in pistons or cylinder barrels.

1974 onwards

911 and 911S
Standard			
0	89.970	90.000 to 90.010	0.025
1	89.980	90.010 to 90.020	to
2	89.990	90.020 to 90.030	0.045

911 (LS version)
Standard			
0	89.952 to 89.967	90.000 to 90.010	0.035
1	89.962 to 89.977	90.010 to 90.020	to
2	89.972 to 89.987	90.020 to 90.030	0.060

911S (LS version Mahle pistons)
Standard			
0	89.960 to 89.972	90.000 to 90.012	0.028
1	89.972 to 89.984	90.012 to 90.024	to
2	89.984 to 89.996	90.024 to 90.036	0.052

7 It should be noted that the design of the piston crown and skirt differs between the various engine types, also with regard to the location of the piston oil control ring.

8 Piston rings should be removed and installed by sliding two or three old feeler blades behind the ring and spacing them at equidistant points. Remove or fit the piston ring using a twisting action. The feeler blades will act as slides and also prevent the upper rings from dropping into the lower piston grooves as they pass over them. Always remove and fit a ring from the top of the piston.

9 When fitting new piston rings, insert the compression rings into the cylinder bore. Place each ring in turn into the lower part of the bore and set it squarely with a piston. Measure the piston ring end

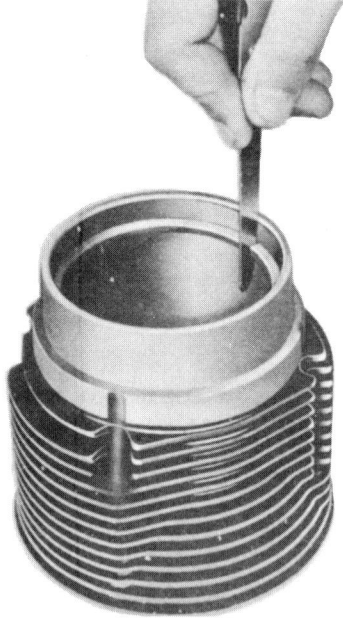

Fig. 1.23. Measuring a piston ring end gap (Sec. 19)

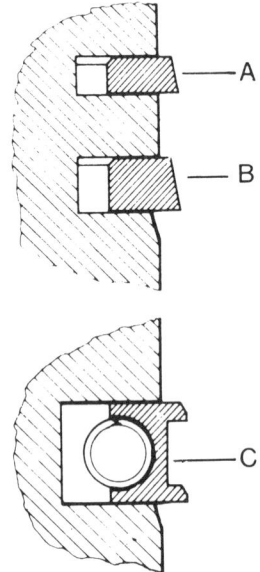

Fig. 1.24. Piston ring fitting diagram (Sec. 19)

A   *Top compression*   B   *Second compression*   C   *Oil control*

gap using a feeler blade. The gap should be as specified in 'Specifications' at the beginning of this Chapter otherwise the end faces may be rubbed down with a fine flat file or carborundum strip but keep the end faces square.

10 Now check the piston ring to groove clearance by fitting each compression ring into its respective groove and measuring the gap again using feeler blades. If the ring is slightly tight in its groove it can be rubbed down on a sheet of fine abrasive cloth held on a piece of plate glass. If the ring is very tight then the piston groove should be machined out to correct what must be a manufacturing fault.

11 Assemble the piston rings to the pistons so that the word 'TOP' is uppermost on all rings. This will ensure that the chamfers are correctly positioned. Stagger the ring and gaps at equidistant points of a circle to prevent gas blow-by.

20 Flywheel - examination and renovation

1 Examine the starter ring gear. If the teeth are worn or chipped, then

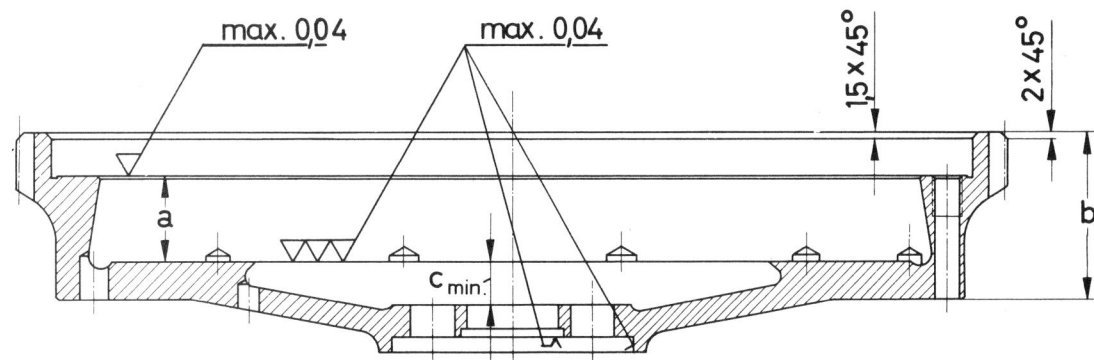

Fig. 1.25. Flywheel machining details (up to engine No P.901638) (Sec.20)

Measurement point	Dimensions when new		Re-machining stages				Tolerances
	mm	1	2	3	4		
a	22.5 mm (.886")	22.5 (.886")	—	—	—		+ 0.2 (.0078")
			38.2	37.8	37.4		
b	44.6 mm (1. (1.7559")	44.2 (1.7401")	(1.5039)	(1.4881)	(1.4724)		± 0.2 (.0078)
c		Minimum thickness 11.000 mm (.4330")					

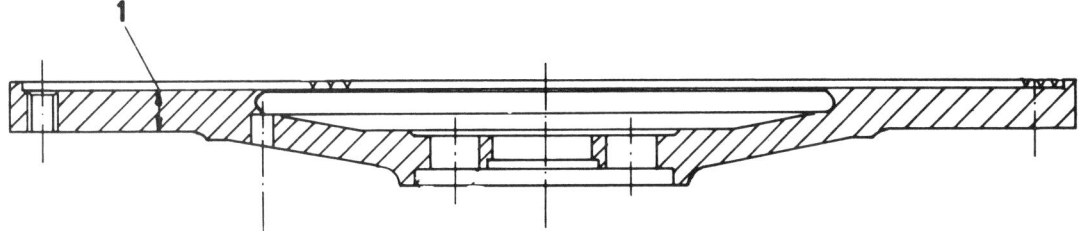

Fig. 1.26. Flywheel machining diagram (engine No. P.901639 on) (Sec. 20)

1 *Minimum thickness after refinishing 0.335 in (8.5 mm)*

the flywheel will have to be renewed.
2 If the starter ring gear is in good condition but the clutch driven plate contact surface is scored or shows a number of small cracks then it should be machined.
3 Machining of a flywheel is critical and on early cars the machining must be carried out in accordance with the diagram Fig. 1.25.
4 On later flywheels, the flywheel thickness (1) (Fig. 1.26) must not be reduced below 0.335 in (8.5 mm).
5 Take the opportunity while the flywheel is off to examine the central pilot bearing or bush for wear. If it needs renewal, extract it together with its retainer and install a new one (photo).

21 Camshafts and camshaft housings - examination and renovation

1 Examine the surfaces of the cam lobes at the bearing journals for scoring or wear. If these conditions are evident, renew the camshaft.
2 Check that the camshaft oil passages are clear by applying compressed air.
3 Examine the camshaft housings for cracks and carefully clean the mating surfaces of the housings free from old jointing compound.
4 On cars equipped with a Bosch fuel injection system, the left-hand camshaft drives the fuel injection pump through pulleys and a belt. If worn, the bearing retainer can be removed from the cover and the bearing drawn off the end of the camshaft. Renew the oil seal at the same time. (Fig. 1.27)

20.5 Flywheel central pilot bearing

Fig. 1.27. Camshaft bearing and retainer for Bosch fuel injection pump drive (Sec. 21)

22 Rocker shafts and arms - examination and renovation

1   Examine the shafts for scoring and the shaftends for distortion. The method of securing the shafts by expanding their ends with cones, ensures an oil seal which should be leakproof.
2   Check the rocker arm bushes for wear and also the condition of the cam lobe bearing surface. Any wear or scoring should be rectified by renewal of the arm.

23 Valves and valve seats - examination and renovation

1   Examine the heads of the valves for pitting and burning, especially the heads of the exhaust valves. The valve seatings should be examined at the same time. If the pitting on valve and seat is very slight the marks can be removed by grinding the seats and valves together with coarse, and then fine, valve grinding paste.
2   Where bad pitting has occurred to the valve seats then they will have to be recut. This is a tricky operation due to the small amount of metal which is permissible to remove and it is best to give the work to your Porsche dealer.
3   The valve seat should be cut in three stages: 45° followed by a 75° cutter to slightly level the lower edge of the seat and finally a 35° cutter to level the upper edge of the seat until the specified seat width is obtained.
4   If the valve seat is too badly burned away for recutting to be carried out then the cylinder head should be exchanged for a factory reconditioned one.
5   Valve grinding is carried out as follows:
    Smear a trace of coars carborundum paste on the seat face and apply a suction grinder tool to the valve head. With a semi rotary motion, grind the valve head to its seat, lifting the valve occasionally to redistribute the grinding paste. When a dull matt even surface finish is produced on both the valve seat and the valve, wipe off the paste, lifting and turning the valve to redistribute the paste as before. A light spring placed under the valve head will greatly ease this operation. When a smooth unbroken ring of light grey matt finish is produced, on both valve and valve seat faces, the grinding operation is complete (photo).
6   Scrape away all carbon from the valve head and the valve stem. Carefully clean away every trace of grinding compound, taking great care to leave none in the ports or in the valve guides. Clean the valves and valve seats with a paraffin soaked rag then with a clean rag, and finally if an air line is available, blow the valves, valve guides and valve ports clean.

24 Valve guides and springs - examination and renovation

1   Worn valve guides can be detected if the play between the valve stem and guide exceeds the following clearance:

Inlet   0.0011 to 0.0059 in (0.030 to 0.15 mm)
Exhaust   0.0019 to 0.0078 in (0.050 to 0.20 mm)

2   Obviously these tolerances are very difficult to measure but a good indication of wear will be obtained if a new valve is inserted in the guide and the valve is moved in a sideways direction. Any more than an

23.5 Grinding a valve into a cylinder head

imperceptible rocking movement will mean that the guide or stem or both, are worn.
3   If new guides are necessary the old guides have to be drilled out, and the new ones pressed in and reamed; this work is not within the scope of the home mechanic. In fact, if the valve guides are worn severely it will probably be more economical to exchange the cylinder head for a factory reconditioned one rather than renew the guides alone.
4   Compare the free-length of the valve springs with the free-length of a new spring. If the springs have been permanently compressed much below the new spring length, renew them. Where valve springs have been in use for 30000 miles (48000 km) or more, it is recommended that they are renewed.

25 Cylinder head - decarbonising and examination

1   With the cylinder head removed, use a blunt scraper to remove all trace of carbon and deposits from the combustion spaces and ports. Remember that the cylinder head is aluminium alloy and can be damaged easily during the decarbonising operations. Scrape the cylinder head free from scale or old pieces of gasket or jointing compound. Clean the cylinder head by washing it in paraffin and take particular care to pull a piece of rag through the ports and cylinder head bolt holes. Any dirt remaining in these recesses may well drop onto the gasket or cylinder block mating surfaces as the cylinder head is lowered into position and could lead to an air leak after reassembly is complete.
2   With the cylinder head clean, test for distortion. Carry out this test using a straight edge and feeler gauges or a piece of plate glass. If the surface shows any warping in excess of 0.0059 in (0.15 mm) then the cylinder head will have to be renewed.

26 Chain tensioner (early type) - examination and renovation

1   The timing chain is left under constant tension by a mechanical tensioner which incorporates a hydraulic vibration damper.
2   If the tensioner has become faulty and is causing slackness in the chain (even temporarily) then it must be dismantled.
3   Extract the small circlip, but cover the tensioner with a cloth as the piston is under tension from its spring.
4   Extract the piston and remove the cage which contains the ball valve and the spring and guide. The ball valve seat is pressed into the piston.
5   Clean all components and remove any fillings or swarf which could be the cause of any malfunction.
6   Renew any worn or corroded items.
7   Reassemble by reversing the dismantling procedure then carefully secure the tensioner in the jaws of a vice.
8   Fill the tensioner oil cup with engine oil then depress the ball valve

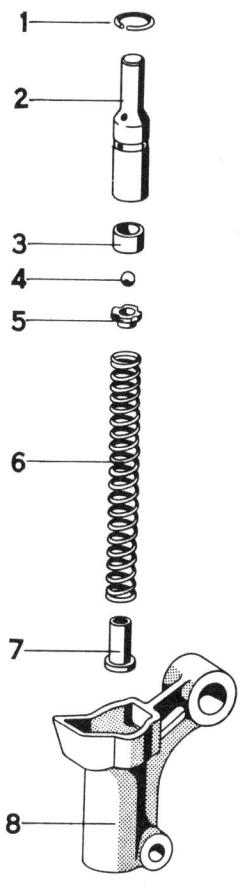

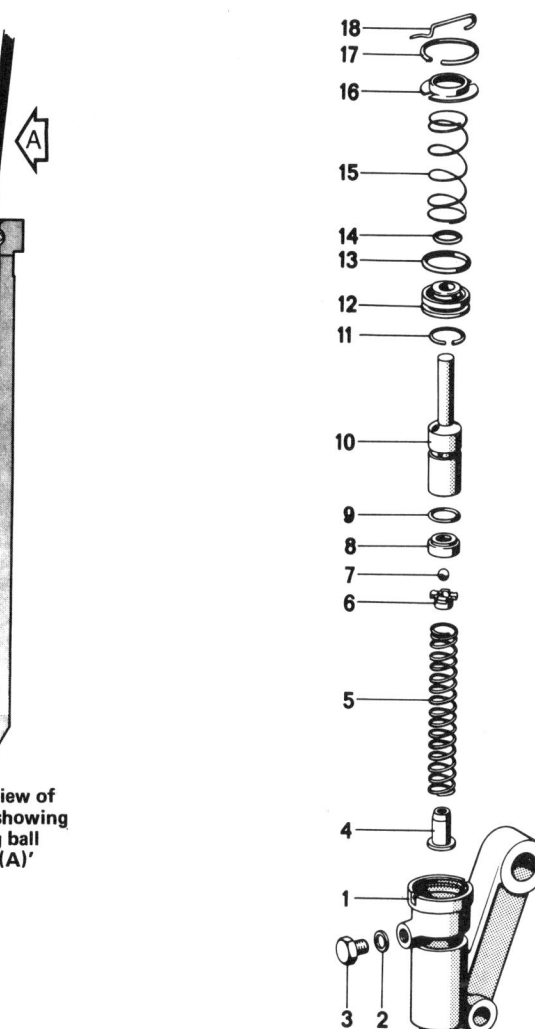

Fig. 1.29. Sectional view of early type tensioner showing method of depressing ball using a piece of wire (A)' (Sec. 26)

Fig. 1.28. Exploded view of early type chain tensioner (Sec. 26)

1 Circlip
2 Piston
3 Ball valve seat
4 Ball
5 Ball valve cage
6 Spring
7 Spring guide
8 Body

by inserting a cranked piece of wire as shown in Fig. 1.29. At the same time, move the piston up and down until air bubbles cease to emerge from the oil. Top-up the oil cup and remove the wire.

27 Chain tensioner (later type) - examination and renovation

1 A chain tensioner of modified design is fitted to engines commencing with the following numbers:

911T	6190834,	6193106,	6195622,	6198071
911E	6291723,	6391688		
911S	6298507			

2 On cars built after June 1970, the chain tensioner incorporates an intermediate piece with an 'O' ring.
3 Secure the chain tensioner in the jaws of a vice but do not overtighten the vice screw.
4 Extract the circlip, remove the spring retainer and the spring.
5 Withdraw the oil retainer piston with a pair of pliers but take care not to damage the soft aluminium of the piston.
6 Extract the plunger circlip. Depress the plunger while doing this as it is under tension.
7 Pull out the intermediate piece and 'O' ring (if fitted) and then extract the ball retainer and ball.
8 Examine all components for wear and renew as necessary. Discard the original 'O' rings and fit new ones. If the tensioner was not fitted with an intermediate piece and 'O' ring install these components when

Fig. 1.30. Exploded view of later type chain tensioner (Sec. 27)

1 Body
2 Copper seating washer
3 Bleed screw
4 Spring guide
5 Spring
6 Ball retainer
7 Ball
8 Intermediate piece
9 'O' ring
10 Plunger
11 Circlip
12 Oil retaining piston
13 'O' ring
14 'O' ring
15 Spring
16 Spring retainer
17 Circlip
18 Clamp (supplied with new tensioners only)

reassembling.
9 Fill the chain tensioner with engine oil and bleed it of air as described for earlier units in the preceding Section.
10 Insert the plunger spring and guide into the plunger and then insert the plunger assembly into the tensioner housing. Secure the plunger with the circlip.
11 Secure the tensioner in the vice at an angle as shown in Fig. 1.31 and fill the upper part of the tensioner housing with engine oil.
12 Install the new 'O' rings, and then press the oil retainer piston onto the plunger shaft. Open the bleed screw and depress the piston until it is well down the housing then close the bleed screw.
13 Install the spring, the spring retainer and the circlip.

28 Crankshaft oil seals renewal

1 The crankshaft oil seals will normally be renewed at the time of engine reassembly but if the crankcase is not to be separated into half

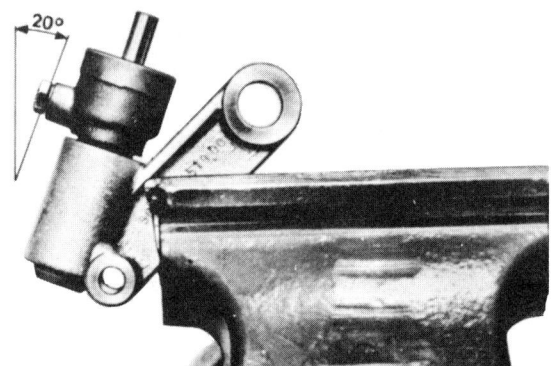

Fig. 1.31. Later type chain tensioner secured in vice ready for filling with oil (Sec. 27)

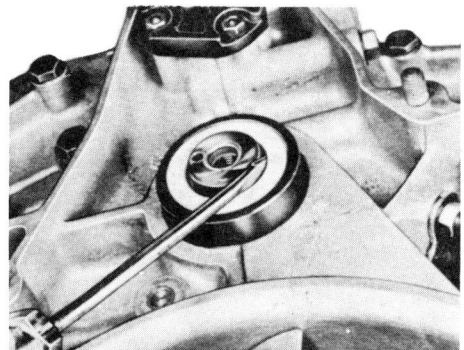

Fig. 1.32. Removing crankshaft oil seal (pulley end) (Sec. 28)

sections, the oil seals can still be renewed using the following methods.

2   To renew the seal at the pulley end (adjacent to main bearing No.8), prise it out with a screwdriver inserted under the rubber covered edge of the metal housing of the seal.

3   Pull the new seal into position using the tapped hole in the end of the crankshaft into which the bolt can be screwed and apply pressure through a suitably sized distance piece.

4   The oil seal at the flywheel end of the crankshaft (adjacent to main bearing no. 1) can also be prised out with a screwdriver and the new one tapped into position using a suitable piece of tubing.

5   Always apply grease to the seal lips before installation.

29 Engine - preparation for reassembly

1   To ensure maximum life with reliability from a rebuilt engine, not only must everything be correctly assembled but all components must be spotlessly clean and the correct spring or plain washers used where originally located. Always lubricate bearing and working surfaces with clean engine oil during reassembly of engine parts.

2   Before reassembly commences, renew any bolts or studs the threads of which are damaged or corroded.

3   As well as your normal tool kit, gather together clean rags, oil can, a torque wrench and a complete (overhaul) set of gaskets and oil seals.

30 Engine reassembly - crankcase components

1   Install the main bearing shells in the two crankcase half sections. Check that the oil holes in the shells align with the passages in the bearing seats (photos).

2   Note that no 8 shell in the crankcase sections incorporates thrust flanges to control crankshaft endfloat (photo).

3   Fit the oil sealing ring into the groove in the oil suction passage in the right-hand crankcase section (photo).

4   Lower the oil pump, connecting and intermediate shaft assembly

complete with chains into the right-hand crankcase section.

5   Note that the intermediate shaft rear bearing is of shell type on later engines. The thrust flanges of the shell control shaft endfloat (photo).

6   Make sure that the oil sealing ring has not become displaced and then tighten the oil pump securing nuts and bend up the lock tabs.

7   Reassemble the connecting rods to the crankshaft. To do this, install the big-end bearing shells and fit the connecting rod and cap with numbers adjacent. The caps and rods which were not punched before removal should be installed to their original crankpin and positioned the same way round on the shaft as they were originally. Due to the fact that the connecting rod bolts stretch when tightened, it is strongly recommended that new bolts are used for reassembly (photos).

8   Tighten the big-end bolts to the specified torque (photo).

9   To no. 8 crankshaft main bearing insert, fit a new 'O' ring and an inner oil seal (photo).

10 Mark the position of the dowel locating hole in the bearing insert on its end face and then slide the insert onto the crankshaft (photo).

11 Fit the crankshaft oil seal at the flywheel end (photo).

12 Support the connecting rods of cylinders 1, 2 and 3 in the vertical position. This can be done by carefully inserting a rod or tube through the connecting rod small end bushes (photo).

13 Apply oil to all the main bearing surfaces and lower the crankshaft assembly into the right-hand half of the crankcase. Make sure that the crankcase is supported high enough to allow the connecting rods of cylinders 4, 5 and 6, which are hanging straight down, to move far enough to ensure full seating of the crankshaft in its bearing. **Make quite sure that the dowel hole in no. 8 bearing insert engages with the dowel pin in the crankcase.** It is possible for this pin to engage in the oil passage and block the oil supply to the bearing.

14 Install the sealing rings to the oil pump body (photo).

15 Install the oil passage sealing ring which locates between the two halves of the crankcase.

16 Smear jointing compound on the mating faces of the crankcase halves and lower the left-hand crankcase section onto the right-hand

30.1a Main bearing shells fitted into right-hand crankcase section

30.1b Main bearing shells fitted into left-hand crankcase section

30.2 No. 8 main bearing shell showing thrust flanges

30.3 Sealing ring in right-hand crankcase section

30.5 Intermediate shaft rear bearing shell (later engines)

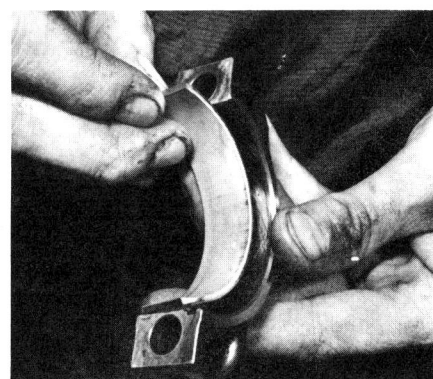

30.7a Fitting a big-end bearing shell

30.7b Fitting a connecting rod and cap to the crankshaft

30.7c Connecting rod and cap numbers

30.8 Tightening a big-end bolt

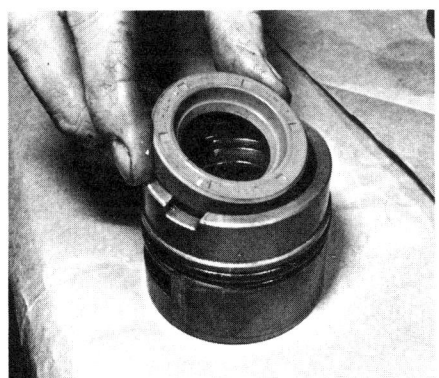

30.9 Fitting an oil seal to No 8 main bearing insert. NOTE: oil sealing 'O' ring already installed in groove

30.10 Fitting No 8 main bearing insert to crankshaft

30.11 Installing crankshaft oil seal (flywheel end)

30.12 Supporting connecting rods in vertical position and lowering crankshaft into crankcase

30.14 Sealing rings on oil pump

30.16 Joining crankcase halves

half. Keep the connecting rods for nos. 1, 2 and 3 cylinders in the vertical position during this operation. The help of an assistant will be useful (photo).

17 Pre-assemble the main bearing tie-bolts. First fit a washer to the bolt so that the smoother surface of the washer is towards the crankcase. Fit the 'O' ring (photo).

18 Insert the tie-bolts through the right-hand half of the crankcase. Fit the 'O' ring, the washer (again smoother side to crankcase) and fit the domed nut finger-tight (photo).

19 Installation of the 'O' rings, washers and domed nuts to the two studs within the oil cooler mounting flange is carried out in a similar manner to that described for the bolts (photo).

20 Note the stud within the chain housing of the left-hand crankcase half. A standard washer and nut is used on this stud (photo).

21 Tighten the tie-bolt and stud nuts to the specified torque wrench setting (photo).

22 Fit the plain and spring washers and nuts (or self-locking nuts) to the crankcase flange studs and tighten to the specified torque wrench setting (photo).

23 Fit the crankshaft pulley and securing bolt with washer.

31 Engine reassembly - flywheel, pistons and cylinder barrels

1 Install the flywheel to its mounting flange on the end of the crankshaft. The bolt holes are not symmetrical so the flywheel can only be fitted one way and so cannot upset the balance of the flywheel/crankshaft assembly (photo).

2 Insert the sock-headed screws and tighten them progressively and evenly to the specified torque wrench setting (photo).

3 Heat the first piston (complete with rings - see Section 19) by placing it in boiling water and then offer it to the connecting rod so that its location number, and the mark made to indicate which way round it was fitted originally, are correct. If new pistons are fitted the problem of which way round to fit them may be solved by making sure that the larger valve recess in the crown is towards the inlet valve (if the crown incorporates valve recesses).

4 Install the gudgeon pin and fit new circlips so that the open end of the clip faces the crankshaft or the piston crown (photos).

5 Check that the piston ring end-gaps are staggered, as described in Section 19, and oil them liberally.

6 Fit a piston ring compressor (photo).

7 Install a new gasket at the cylinder barrel mating surface of the crankcase.

8 Oil the bore of the first cylinder barrel to be fitted (check its location - marked before removal) and push the cylinder barrel squarely onto the piston so that it displaces the compressor and leaves the piston rings inside the barrel. Remove the compressor and push the cylinder into contact with its gasket (photos).

9 Temporarily retain the cylinder barrel in position by screwing on two nuts with distance pieces to two diagonally opposite cylinder head studs.

10 Repeat the foregoing operations on the remaining cylinders.

11 Install the air deflector plates and their clamps (photos).

32 Cylinder head - reassembly of valves

1 Oil the valve stem and insert it into its original seat or the seat into which it has been lapped (photo).

2 Fit the washers which determine the outer spring installed length (see paragraph 6) (photo).

3 Fit the spring seat and valve stem oil seal (photo).

4 Fit the valve springs (close coils of outer spring to cylinder head) and the spring retainer (photo).

5 Using a suitable compressor, compress the valve springs and insert the split cotters. These can be held in place with a dab of grease while the compresser is released (photo).

6 Tap the end of the valve stem with a hammer and hardwood block to settle the components and then measure the length of the outer valve spring (Fig. 1.33). The installed length should be as listed in the following table according to engine type. Where the measurement differs from that specified, dismantle the valve and extract or add spacer washers below the spring lower seat.

30.17 A main bearing tie-bolt

30.18 Tie-bolts showing 'O' rings, plain washer and domed nut

30.19 Domed nuts fitted to studs within oil cooler mounting flange

30.20 Chain housing internal stud with nut fitted   30.21 Tightening a tie-bolt domed nut

30.22 Crankcase flange nuts

31.1 Installing flywheel

31.2 Tightening flywheel bolts

31.4a Installing a piston

31.4b Piston rings and gudgeon pin circlip

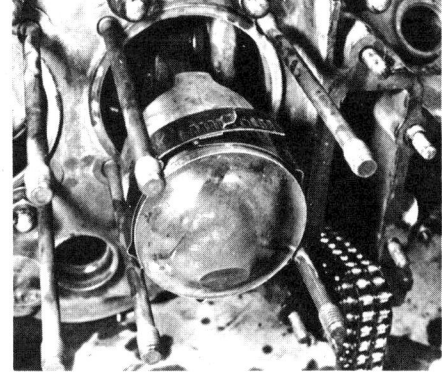
31.6 Piston ring compressor fitted

31.8a Installing a cylinder barrel

31.8b Cylinder barrel installed

31.11a Air deflector plates installed

31.11b Air deflector plate clamp bar

32.1 Installing a valve

32.2 Fitting valve spring length setting washers

32.3 Fitting valve stem oil seal

32.4 Fitting valve springs and retainer

32.5 Compressing valve springs

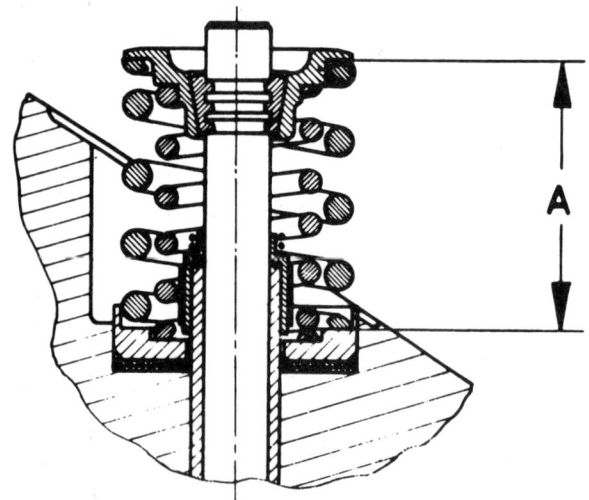

Fig. 1.33. Measuring points of installed valve spring (outer only): for A see table (Sec. 32)

7   Repeat the reassembly operations on the remaining valves and cylinder heads.

Installed length of outer valve spring

Valve	Engine	Length (inches)	Length (millimetres)
Inlet	2000 (1991 cc)	1.416 to 1.418	35.7 to 36.3
Exhaust		1.416 to 1.418	35.7 to 36.3
Inlet	2000T (1991 cc)	1.594 to 1.614	40.5 to 41.0
Exhaust		1.594 to 1.614	40.5 to 41.0
Inlet	No.911001 on (1991 cc)	1.366 to 1.390	34.7 to 35.3
Exhaust		1.366 to 1.390	34.7 to 35.3
Inlet	911T (2195 cc)	1.416 to 1.418	35.7 to 36.3
Exhaust		1.416 to 1.418	35.7 to 36.3
Inlet	911E (2195 cc)	1.416 to 1.418	35.7 to 36.3
Exhaust		1.37 to 1.39	34.7 to 35.3
Inlet	911S (2195 cc)	1.39 to 1.40	35.2 to 35.8
Exhaust		1.35 to 1.37	34.2 to 34.8
Inlet	911S, 911T 911TV (2341 cc)	1.37 to 1.39	34.7 to 35.3
Exhaust		1.37 to 1.39	34.7 to 35.3
Inlet	911G (2341 cc)	1.32 to 1.35	33.7 to 34.3
Exhaust		1.32 to 1.35	33.7 to 34.3
Inlet	911 (2687 cc)	1.37 to 1.39	34.7 to 35.3
Exhaust		1.39 to 1.40	35.2 to 35.8
Inlet	911S (2687 cc)	1.37 to 1.39	34.7 to 35.3
Exhaust		1.39 to 1.40	35.2 to 35.8
Inlet	Carrera (2687 cc)	1.39 to 1.40	35.2 to 35.8
Exhaust		1.35 to 1.37	34.2 to 34.8

33 Cylinder heads - refitting as bank of three with camshaft

1   The operations described in this Section and the next are alternatives, largely dependent upon which method was used to remove them.
2   Make sure that the rocker components are removed.
3   Locate new cylinder head gaskets so that the perforations are towards the cylinders.
4   Insert the oil pipes complete with 'O' rings into the crankcase.
5   Lower the cylinder head assembly (three) complete with camshaft housing into position on the cylinder barrels. Check that the oil pipe seals are not displaced.
6   Install the washers and screw on the cylinder head socket nuts finger-tight.

Fig. 1.34. Installing cylinder heads as bank of three (Sec. 33)

7 Insert the camshaft carefully into its bearings.
8 Tighten the cylinder head nuts progressively and in diagonally opposite sequence to the specified torque wrench setting.
9 Refitting the timing and rocker gear is as described in Section 37.

34 Cylinder head - refitting individually

1 Fit a new cylinder head gasket so that the perforations are towards the cylinder barrel.
2 Lower the cylinder head carefully into position (photo).
3 Fit the washers and screw on the cylinder head socket nuts finger-tight. Fit the remaining two cylinder heads (photos).
4 Smear the mating surfaces of the camshaft housing with jointing compound.
5 Fit new 'O' rings to the camshaft housing oil return pipes and install the pipes (photos).

6 Lower the camshaft housing into position and screw on the retaining nuts with their spring washers finger-tight (photo).
7 Tighten the cylinder head socket nuts progressively and evenly to the specified torque wrench setting (photo).
8 Tighten the camshaft housing retaining nuts progressively and evenly to the specified torque.

35 Engine reassembly - oil breather, oil pressure valves and oil cooler

1 Fit the oil breather outlet housing using a new gasket (photo).
2 Install the thermostat making sure that a new 'O' ring is fitted to its groove. The holes in the thermostat flange are offset and it can therefore only be fitted one way.
3 Install the pressure relief and safety valves.
4 Install the oil cooler but first make sure that the cooler to crankcase sealing rings are in position (photo).

34.2 Installing a cylinder head

34.3a Installing washer under cylinder head nut

34.3b Installing a cylinder head nut

34.5a Fitting an 'O' ring to a camshaft housing oil return pipe

34.5b Camshaft housing oil pipes installed

34.6 Camshaft housing installed

34.7 Tightening a cylinder head nut

35.1 Oil breather outlet housing

35.4 Oil cooler to crankcase sealing rings

36 Checking intermediate shaft endfloat

1   At this stage, check the endfloat of the intermediate shaft. To do this, use either a depth gauge or feeler blades and a straight edge to determine the projection of the intermediate shaft beyond the crankcase.

2   By simple calculation, work out the thickness of shims plus one paper gasket which will be required to be fitted between the end cover and crankcase to give the intermediate shaft an endfloat of between 0.003 and 0.005 in (0.08 and 0.12 mm).

3   Check the endfloat when the required shim pack thickness is known by prising the intermediate shaft backwards and forwards and reading off the movement on a dial gauge. Compare this reading with the shim pack thickness and add or remove shims as necessary.

4   Remove the shims and retain safely pending final assembly after the camshaft sprocket alignment has been checked; see Section 37.

37 Engine reassembly - camshafts and rocker shafts

1   Refit the chain guide slippers into the crankcase.

2   Locate new gaskets on the chain housing flanges of the crankcase (photo).

3   Draw the chains through the apertures in the chain housings and fit the chain housings to the crankcase (photo)

4   Oil the camshaft bearings and insert the camshaft carefully. Note the different design of the cam holes between the left-hand and right-hand camshafts (photo).

5   Turn the camshaft and observe that it turns freely. If it binds, loosen the camshaft housing nuts and try tightening them in a different sequence from that originally used.

6   Install the rocker arms and shafts. The shafts are of expanding type which seal in the camshaft housing by the tightening of a bolt and two cones (photo).

7   Install the rocker shaft, passing it through its rocker arm. Use a feeler blade inserted between the camshaft housing web and the rocker arm. Keep the blade depressed while the shaft is pushed in. When the feeler blade is felt to engage in the groove in the rocker shaft, withdraw the blade and continue to push the shaft for another 1/16 in (1.5 mm). Insert the cones.

8   Without moving the shaft, insert and tighten the bolt, which has a socket head, to the specified torque (photo).

9   Repeat the operations and install all the rocker shafts and arms.

10 Release the rocker arm adjusters to their maximum extent.

11 As the assembly of the rocker shafts proceeds, turn the camshaft as necessary to be able to alter the position of some of the lobes to facilitate fitting of the rocker arm.

12 It is very important that while the camshaft chains are disconnected the camshaft is not turned to a position which would cause the valves to dig into the pistons. If necessary, rotate the crankshaft to avoid this happening.

13 Press a new seal onto and up against the camshaft front bearing face.

14 Fit the aluminium sealing ring and a new 'O' ring to the camshaft endplate (photo).

15 Insert the screws and secure the endplate (photo).

16 Fit the thrust washer and spacers (photo).

17 Fit the Woodruff key.

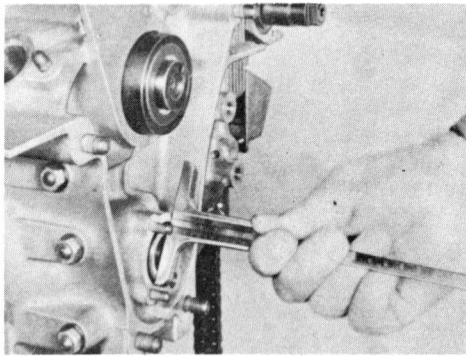

Fig. 1.35. Using a depth gauge to determine projection of the intermediate shaft (Sec. 36)

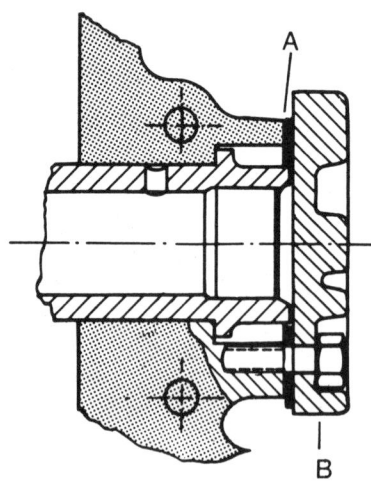

Fig. 1.36. Location of intermediate shaft shim pack (Sec. 36) .

A   Shim pack   B   Cover plate

37.2 Installing chain housing gasket on crankcase

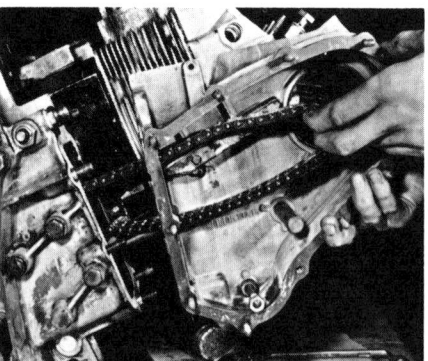

37.3 Installing chain housing

37.4 Installing a camshaft

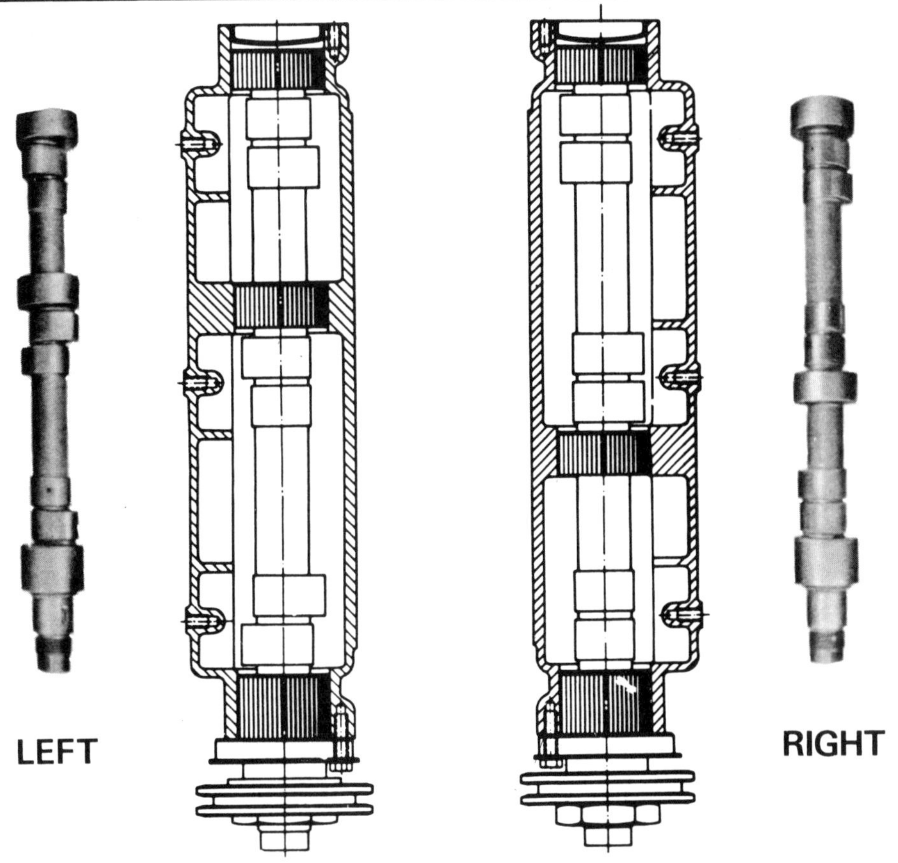

LEFT RIGHT

Fig. 1.37. Differences between left-hand and right-hand camshafts (Sec. 37)

37.6 Rocker arm and shaft components

37.8 Tightening a rocker shaft clamp bolt

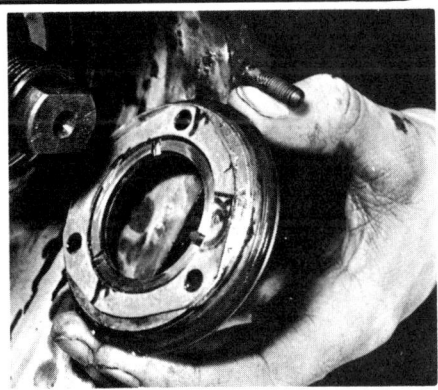

37.14 Crankshaft endplate

37.15 Camshaft endplate fitted

37.16 Installing camshaft thrust washers and spacers

37.18 Installing a camshaft sprocket flange

18 Fit the sprocket flange (photo).
19 Fit the sprockets to the camshaft flanges. The sprockets are inter-changeable but are offset. Make sure that the sprocket for cylinders 1, 2 and 3 is mounted so that the deeper recess is visible. The sprocket for cylinders 4, 5 and 6 should be mounted so that its shallower recess is visible when installed (photo).
20 Engage the chains with the teeth of the camshaft sprockets but do not screw on the sprocket nuts at this stage.
21 The alignment of the camshaft sprockets must now be checked with the front faces of the drive sprockets on the intermediate shaft. To do this, a straight edge and a depth gauge will be required. Insert the depth gauge into the hole at the base of the intermediate shaft and read off the distance between the rear edge of the straight-edge at the front face of the drive sprocket.
22 Now measure the distance between the rear edge of the straight edge at the front face of the camshaft sprocket for cylinders 4, 5 and 6. While taking these measurements, keep the intermediate shaft and camshaft pushed towards the flywheel.

23 If the alignment of the two sprockets is out by more than 0.01 in (0.25 mm) then the number of spacers used between the camshaft sprocket flange and the thrust plate must be adjusted.
24 Now check the alignment between the camshaft sprocket of cylinders 1, 2 and 3 and its drive sprocket. Measure the distance between the rear edge of the straight edge and the front face of the camshaft sprocket as previously described but as the rear drive sprocket is inaccessible, take the measurement of the front sprocket and add to this a fixed dimension of 2.157 in (54.8 mm) which is the installed distance between the two drive sprockets.
25 Correct any deviation in alignment as described in paragraph 16.
26 The cover plate on the intermediate shaft may now be installed (photo).

38 Engine reassembly - heat exchangers

1 Due to the design of the early camshaft chain tensioners, oil will be

37.19 Fitting a camshaft sprocket

Fig. 1.38. Checking alignment of camshaft sprockets with drive sprockets on the intermediate shaft (Sec. 37)

37.26 Fitting intermediate shaft cover plate

39.1 Installing a chain guide slipper into chain housing

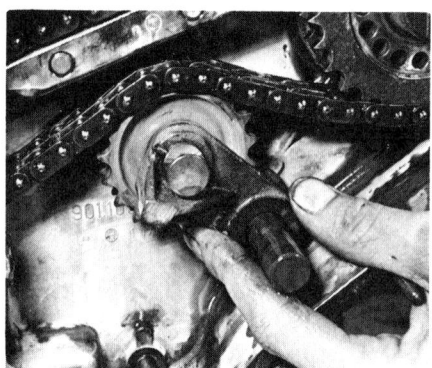
39.2 Installing a chain tensioner pivot lever and sprocket

39.4a Right-hand tensioner and chain installed

39.4b Left-hand tensioner and chain installed

40.1 Crankshaft TDC mark

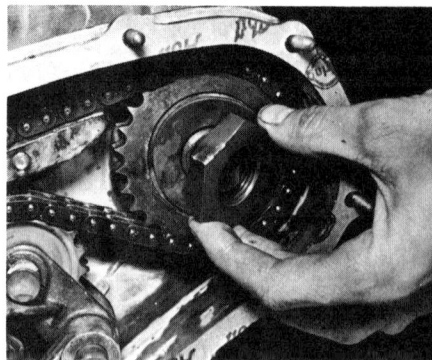
40.4 Fitting a camshaft sprocket nut (left-hand side)

lost if the engine is inverted. It is therefore recommended that the heat exchangers are installed at this stage on earlier engines. See also Section 47.

39 Engine reassembly - camshaft chains and tensioners

1 Lift the retaining spring clips and slide the chain guide slippers into position in the chain housings (photo).
2 Install the chain tensioner pivot lever with sprocket. The bearing studs are drilled to provide lubrication for the sprocket. Check that the holes face upwards (photo).
3 Install the chain tensioner. If the original tensioner is being installed, compress the assembly in a vice fitted with jaw protectors. Tighten the vice gently so that the 'O' rings are not damaged and until the plunger is depressed. Fit a clip similar to the one shown in Fig. 1.30 to hold the plunger depressed. If a new tensioner is being fitted, this is supplied with a temporary hold down clip already installed.
4 The right-hand tensioner may be fully installed and the temporary clip removed. The left-hand tensioner should only be installed by giving its retaining nut a couple of turns, otherwise the camshaft sprocket nut cannot be fitted at a later stage because of lack of clearance (photos).
5 At this stage, the valve timing must be adjusted as described in the next Section.

40 Valve timing

1 Turn the crankshaft until the 'Z1' mark on the pulley is in alignment with the crankcase joint (No. 1 at TDC) (photo).
2 Now turn both the camshafts (by means of the flats on the ends of the shaft) until the punch marks which are stamped on the faces of the camshafts are at their uppermost position. There is a possibility that as the camshafts are rotated, some valves may touch the piston crowns. If this happens, stop at once and reverse the direction of rotation slightly and adjust the position of the opposing camshaft until the valves are retracted.
3 When the crankshaft pulley and the camshaft sprocket marks are correctly positioned, find the hole in each camshaft sprocket which is in perfect alignment with the hole in the flange at its rear. Insert the dowel pins.
4 Fit the spring washers and screw on the camshaft sprocket retaining nuts and tighten to specified torque. The right hand nut is eccentric to drive the fuel pump plunger (carburettor only) (photo).
5 Fully tighten the left-hand chain tensioner securing nut.
6 Adjust the clearance of the inlet valve on No. 1 cylinder to 0.004 in (0.10 mm), as described in Section 41.
7 A dial gauge will now be required. Mount it on the camshaft housing so that its pointer (preloaded) rests against the valve spring retaining

cap of No. 1 inlet valve.
8 Compress the plunger of the chain tensioner fitted on the side of cylinder bank 1, 2 and 3. Use a screwdriver to do this and then wedge it with a piece of metal to prevent the chain sprocket of the tensioner from dropping.
9 Using a spanner on the crankshaft pulley bolt, rotate the crankshaft through 360° (one complete turn, and check that the 'Z1' mark is again in alignment with the crankcase joint.
10 The inlet valve of No. 1 cylinder will now be open and the dial gauge will have measured the distance through which the valve has moved.
11 Note the reading on the dial gauge which should be as shown in the following table according to engine models:

Engine	Dial gauge reading	
Type 2000 (901/01 901/05) up to engine no. 909927	Ideal Permissible	0.169 in (4.3 mm) 0.165 to 0.181 in (4.2 to 4.6 mm)
Type 2000 (901/06 901/07, 901/14 901/17)	Ideal Permissible	0.124 in (3.15 mm) 0.118 to 0.130 in (3.0 to 3.3 mm)
Type 2000S (901/02 901/08)	Ideal Permissible	0.205 in (5.2 mm) 0.197 to 0.213 in (5.0 to 5.4 mm)
Type 2000T (901/03 901/13)	Ideal Permissible	0.098 in (2.5 mm) 0.091 to 0.106 in (2.3 to 2.7 mm)

12 If the readings differ from those shown, remove the camshaft sprocket nut and washer, withdraw the dowel pin and turn the camshaft until the correct reading is obtained on the dial gauge. Insert the dowel pin into a different hole in the sprocket which has now taken up perfect alignment with one in the rear sprocket flange. Refit the nut and washer.
13 Now rotate the crankshaft two complete turns until the 'Z1' pulley mark is again in alignment with the crankcase joint and check the dial gauge reading again. If it is not within the specified range, carry out slight readjustment to the camshaft sprocket setting as previously described.
14 Repeat the foregoing checks and adjustments on cylinder No. 4 and the opposing camshaft sprocket.
15 Make sure that the wedges used on the chain tensioners have been removed at the end of operations.

41 Valve clearances - adjustment

1 The valve clearances should be adjusted COLD.
2 Turn the crankshaft by means of the pulley bolt until the 'Z1' mark on the pulley is opposite the crankcase joint. This represents No. 1 piston at TDC with both valves on that cylinder closed.
3 With the rocker cover removed, insert a feeler gauge of 0.004 in (0.10 mm) thickness between the end of the valve stem and the socket on the end of the rocker arm adjuster screw.
4 Adjust the clearance, if necessary, by releasing the locknut with a ring spanner and turning the adjuster screw. The feeler blade should be a stiff sliding fit. Tighten the locknut on completion without disturbing the adjuster screw (photo).
5 Repeat the operations on the other valve of the same cylinder. Inlet and exhaust valves have the same clearance.
6 To save unnecessary turning of the crankshaft, it is recommended that the valve clearances are adjusted in firing order sequence (1-6-2-4-3-5). The piston TDC positions are marked on the edge of the pulley wheel but if preferred, the crankshaft can be rotated and the valves of the particular cylinder observed to see when they are fully closed.
7 Adjustment of the valve clearances will be made easier if the spark plugs are first removed to release compression while the crankshaft pulley is being turned.

41.4 Adjusting a valve clearance

42 Engine reassembly - completion

1 Install the distributor, as described in Chapter 3. Make sure that a new sealing 'O' ring is fitted (photo).
2 Install new gaskets and fit the chain housing covers (photo).
3 It is recommended that before fitting the covers, the camshaft seals are inspected and renewed, if necessary. They can be removed and refitted using a small punch or cold chisel.
4 Install the oil supply pipes which lead from the main oil gallery to the chain housing cover.
5 Refit the mechanically-operated twin fuel pump unit to the right-hand chain cover. Make sure that at least two gaskets and the plastic insulating washer are installed between the pump mounting flange and the chain cover. The distance measured between the nearest point of the camshaft eccentric nut and the face of the pump mounting flange should be 2.02 in (51.4 mm). Add more gaskets, if necessary.

43 Engine ancillaries - refitting

1 The operations are largely a reversal of removal, as described in Section 7, but observe the following points.
2 Use new gaskets for the rocker covers and cover sprockets (photo).
3 Align the blower/alternator correctly in the mounting clamp, tighten bolts before fitting the upper air channel. Note the routing of the alternator leads through the grommet in the upper air channel (photo).

4 Fit and adjust the blower drivebelt to give a deflection of about ½ in (12.7 mm) at its centre. Adjust by adding or removing shims from between the pulley flanges (photo).

44 Engine - reconnecting to transmission

1 This is a reversal of operations described in Section 5 or 6 according to type of transmission.
2 On cars fitted with manually-operated tensioners, remember to centralise the clutch driven plate, as described in Chapter 4. On cars built after 1970, remember to remove the temporary screws and spacers from the clutch pressure plate.

45 Engine/transmission - installation

1 This is a reversal of the removal procedure described in Section 4 but watch the following points.
2 Tighten the engine mounting bolts to the specified torque wrench setting.
3 Make sure that the axle shaft flange mating surfaces are quite free from grease and then insert and tighten the connecting bolts to the specified torque wrench setting.
4 If the heat exchanger ducts tend to jam during installation of the engine/transmission, push the ducts a little way onto the heat exchanger outlets.
5 Refill the engine with oil and check the level in the transmission, topping-up if necessary.

42.1 Installing the distributor

42.2 Installing a chain housing cover

43.2 Rocker cover and shroud gaskets

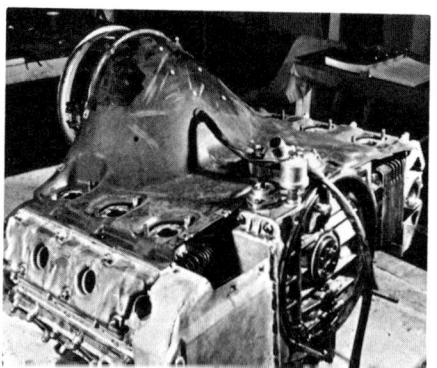

43.3 Upper air channel installed

43.4 Fitting blower drivebelt and pulley front flange

46 Start-up after major overhaul

1   Set the engine idling speed at a higher level than normal to offset the stiffness of new parts.
2   Start the engine and immediately check for oil leaks.
3   Run the engine until normal operating temperature is reached and then check the adjustment of carburettors, fuel injection system and ignition as described in the relevant Chapters.
4   If new internal components have been fitted, restrict the engine speed for the first few hundred miles.
5   After the first 500 miles (800 km) check the tightness of all nuts and bolts in accordance with specified torque wrench figures and change the engine oil.

47 Engine cooling and heater system

1   To prevent confusion and to ensure satisfactory operation of the system the identification of components is given in detail in this Section, while adjustment of the controls is described in the next Section.
2   The upper air channel which is constructed from glass-fibre reinforced plastic, conducts air from the belt-driven blower unit around the fins of the cylinder barrels and to other areas which require cooling.
3   Ducts from the upper air channel also connect with the heat exchangers which in turn supply the car interior with heated air.
4   In order to maintain the specified volume and flow of air, it is important that the upper air channel and the front, rear and side cover plates all fit together securely to minimise air loss.

5   The air deflector plates which are fitted between the cylinder barrels must always be correctly installed and have their spring retainers; secure them tightly to prevent rattle.
6   The blower can be removed and refitted with the engine still in the car but the upper air channel and cover plates are only detachable after the engine has been removed.
7   A heat exchanger is fitted to each bank of cylinder barrels. Airflow which is generated by the blower unit passes into the heat exchanger where it absorbs heat from the exhaust manifold contained within the heat exchanger. The exhaust gases are ejected in the normal way through a silencer while the heated air is directed to the car interior, or for screen demisting or for carburettor warming (Fig. 1.42).
8   The necessary controls are fitted to vary the direction, flow and temperature of the arrangement.
9   Removal and refitting of a heat exchanger can be carried out after disconnecting the hoses from it and unscrewing the retaining bolts. A cranked spanner will ease the job of removing and refitting the lower flange nuts (Fig. 1.43 and 1.44).

48 Heater control (early cars) - removal, refitting and adjustment

1   Disconnect the end of the control cable from the lever on the heat control box (Fig. 1.45).
2   Remove the cover from the gearshift rod tunnel.
3   Remove the heater control lever mounting screws and pull the knob from the lever.
4   Remove the mounting plate and ease the control lever/cable assembly from the car (Fig. 1.46).
5   Refitting is a reversal of removal, if the movement of the lever is too stiff or too slack adjust the self-locking nut on the pivot bolt.

Fig. 1.39. Engine upper air cooling channel (Sec. 47)

Fig. 1.40. An engine cooling system side cover plate (Sec. 47)

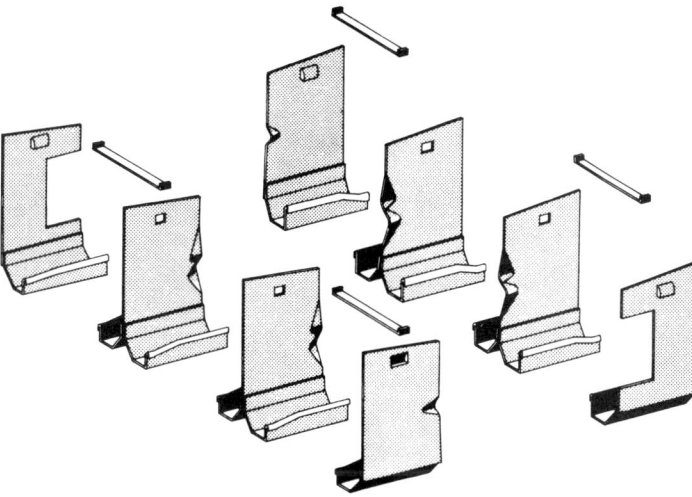

Fig. 1.41. Cylinder barrel air deflector plates (Sec. 47)

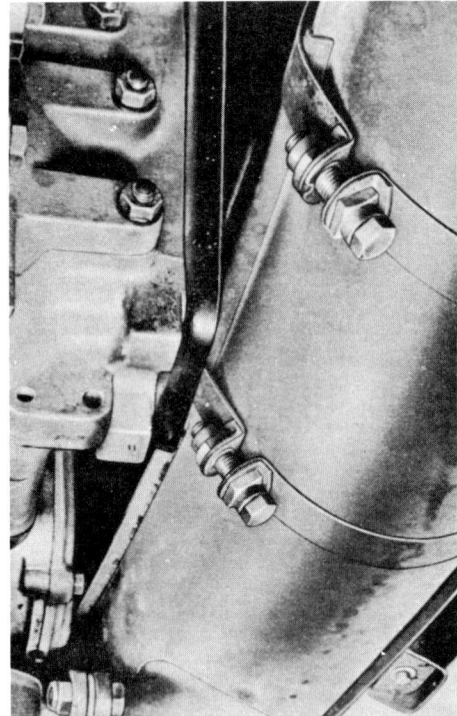

Fig. 1.42. Exhaust silencer and connections (Sec. 47)

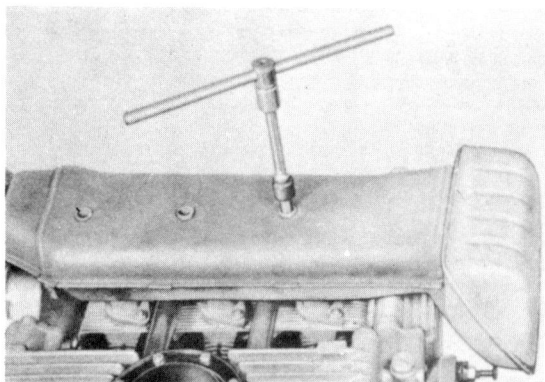

Fig. 1.43. Heat exchanger upper securing bolts (Sec. 47)

Fig. 1.44. Heat exchanger lower securing bolts (Sec. 47)

Fig. 1.45. Heater control cable connection (early cars) (Sec. 48)

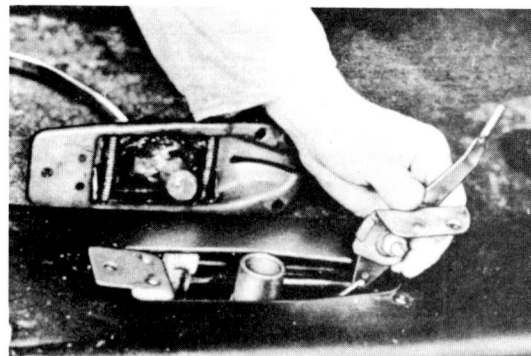

Fig. 1.46. Removing heater control cable/lever assembly (early cars) (Sec 48)

Fig. 1.47. Removing handbrake mounting plate bolt (1968 to 1974) (Sec. 49)

Fig. 1.48. Handbrake cable equaliser to lever connection (1968 to 1974) (Sec. 49)

49 Heater and hand throttle controls (1968 to 1974) - removal, refitting and adjustment

1   These levers are mounted adjacent to the handbrake lever.
2   Remove the gearshift rod tunnel cover and the dust excluding boot.
3   Remove the knob from the heater control lever by pulling it off.
4   Unscrew and remove the bolts which secure the handbrake mounting plate.
5   Remove the self-locking nut from the pivot bolt which runs through all three levers. Withdraw the cup spring, pressure disc, friction disc and heater control lever.
6   Raise the handbrake mounting plate slightly and unclip and disconnect the cable equaliser.
7   Pull out the lead for the handbrake warning lamp and remove the handbrake lever mounting plate.
8   Remove the snap-ring which secures the hand throttle link and withdraw the washer and link.
9   Remove the self-locking nut which secures the hand throttle and extract the cup spring, pressure disc, and friction discs. Withdraw the pivot pin.
10 The heater control cable can be removed after disconnecting it from the heater control box.
11 Refitting is a reversal of removal but observe the following points.
12 Grease the pivot pin sparingly. Do not let any grease come into contact with the friction discs.
13 Make sure that the cable dust excluding grommets are correctly fitted in the guide tubes of the heat control box cable clamps. Check operation of control flap.
14 The hand throttle control should set the engine speed at 4000 rev/min when fully open. Any adjustment required can be made by resetting the position of the collar on the throttle control rod visible through a hole in the centre tunnel.

50 Heater and hand throttle controls (1974 on) - removal, refitting and adjustment

1   The dismantling operations are very similar to those described in the preceding Section except that the heater and throttle lever knobs should be removed by knocking them off with a hammer and a small hardwood block. There are two heater levers plus the hand throttle lever.
2   When refitting, make sure that the longer of the two heater cables is connected to the left-hand lever.
3   To set the heater control levers, move both levers fully forward and then connect the cables to the clamps on the rotary valve plates of the heater control boxes.
4   Adjustment of the hand throttle is carried out as described in Section 49, except that when the lever is fully open, the engine speed should be between 3500 and 3800 rev/min.

51 Oil tanks - removal and refitting

1   The design and installation of oil tanks and coolers varies according to date of production.

Oil tanks
2   *On early models*, remove the right-hand rear road wheel, disconnect the oil hose clamps and detach the oil hose nearest the bottom of the tank and let the oil drain. Release the tank mounting strap and pull the tank far enough away to be able to disconnect the oil lines, breather hose and level sender leads.
3   *On cars built between 1973 and 1974*, remove the right-hand rear road wheel. Drain the oil from the tank, detach the oil hoses and pressure relief valve (Fig. 1.52) also the leads from the oil lever sender unit. Detach the tubular support from the outer end of the bumper and turn the support to one side. Unscrew the oil filter and disconnect the oil breather hoses from the tank. Remove the oil tank securing nuts (these are accessible from within the engine compartment). Remove the oil tank and the oil filter base.
4   *On cars built after 1974*, remove the right-hand rear road wheel, drain the oil and detach the oil hoses from the tank (Fig. 1.53). Remove the bolt from the lower section of the wing. Remove the screws from

Fig. 1.49. Heater control cable connection (1968 to 1974) (Sec 49)

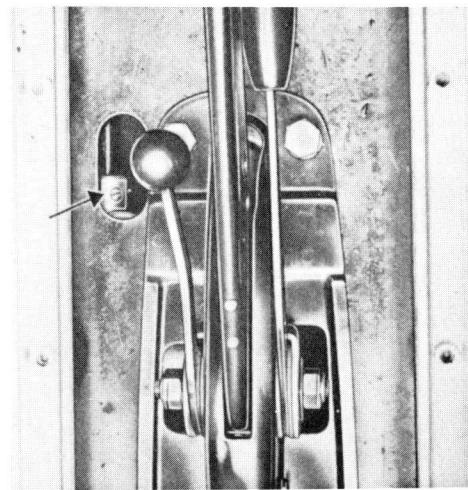

Fig. 1.50. Hand throttle cable adjuster (1968 to 1974) (Sec. 49)

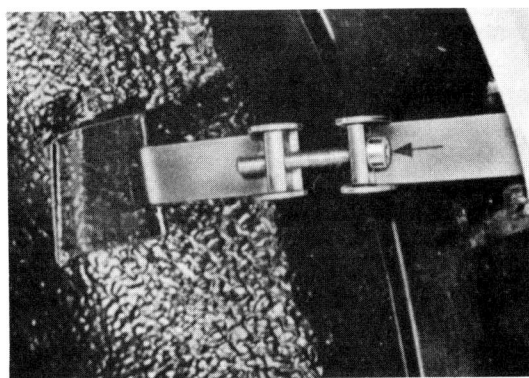

Fig. 1.51. Oil tank securing strap (early models) (Sec. 51)

the support tube of the bumper and turn it on its side. Diconnect the leads from the oil level sender unit and detach the breather hoses and remove the cover from the tank. Unscrew the oil filter, bend down the tab of the lockplate, remove the nut and pull out the support tube from the bottom. (Fig. 1.54) Remove the oil tank retaining nuts and lift the tank away (Fig. 1.55).
5   Refitting in all cases is a reversal of removal but on later models stick the gasket to the oil tank in its correct position before offering the tank into place.
6   Make sure that the 'O' ring is correctly seated in the oil filter base.

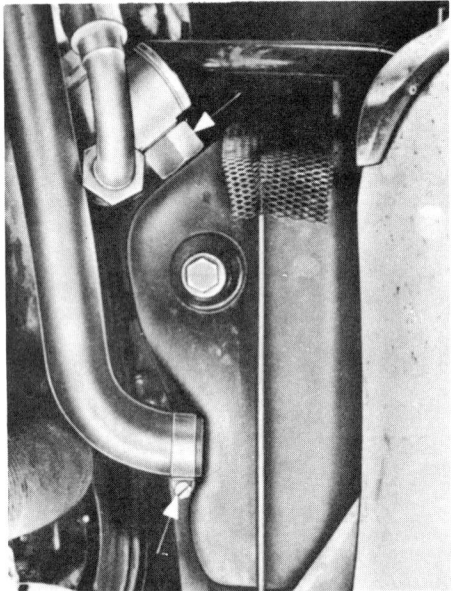

Fig. 1.52. Oil tank (1973 and 1974). Pressure relief valve and oil hose clip arrowed (Sec. 51)

Fig. 1.53. Oil tank (after 1974). Hose connections arrowed (Sec. 51)

Fig. 1.54. Oil tank support nut (arrowed) 1974 onwards (Sec. 51)

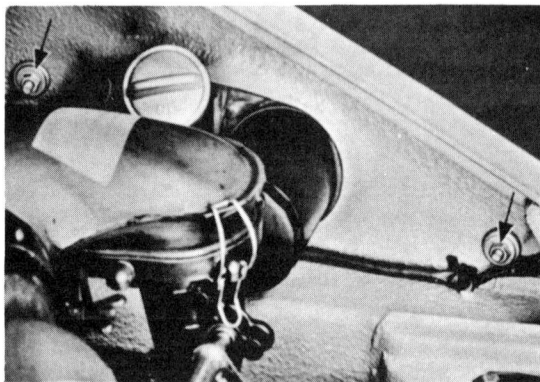

Fig. 1.55. Oil tank retaining nuts (1974 onwards) arrowed (Sec. 51)

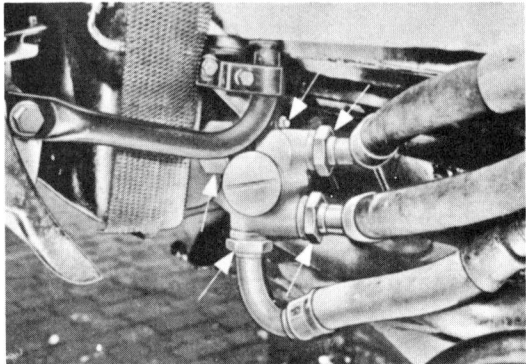

Fig. 1.56. Pressure relief valve adjacent to oil tank (Sec. 53)

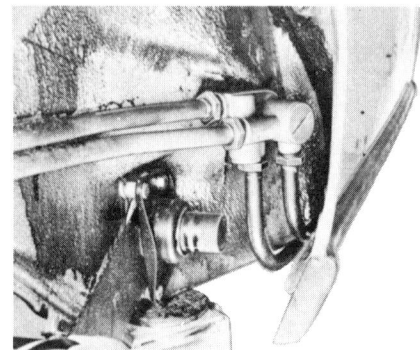

Fig. 1.57. Pressure relief valve adjacent to oil cooler (Sec. 53)

52 Supplementary oil cooler - removal and refitting

1   The design of the supplementary oil cooler varies according to date of production of the car but it is in all cases mounted beneath the right-hand front wing.

2   Remove the road wheel and brush away all dirt from the oil cooler pipe connections.

3   Disconnect the hoses taking care not to twist or strain them. Hold the union body with a second open-ended spanner.

4   Always observe strict cleanliness during the operations and cover any openings in the oil lines or cooler immediately to prevent dirt from entering.

5   On some cars, the right-hand headlamp assembly and the horn may have to be removed in order to gain access to one of the oil cooler mounting bolts.

6   Remove the grille (where fitted) and unbolt and remove the cooler unit.

7   Refitting is a reversal of removal.

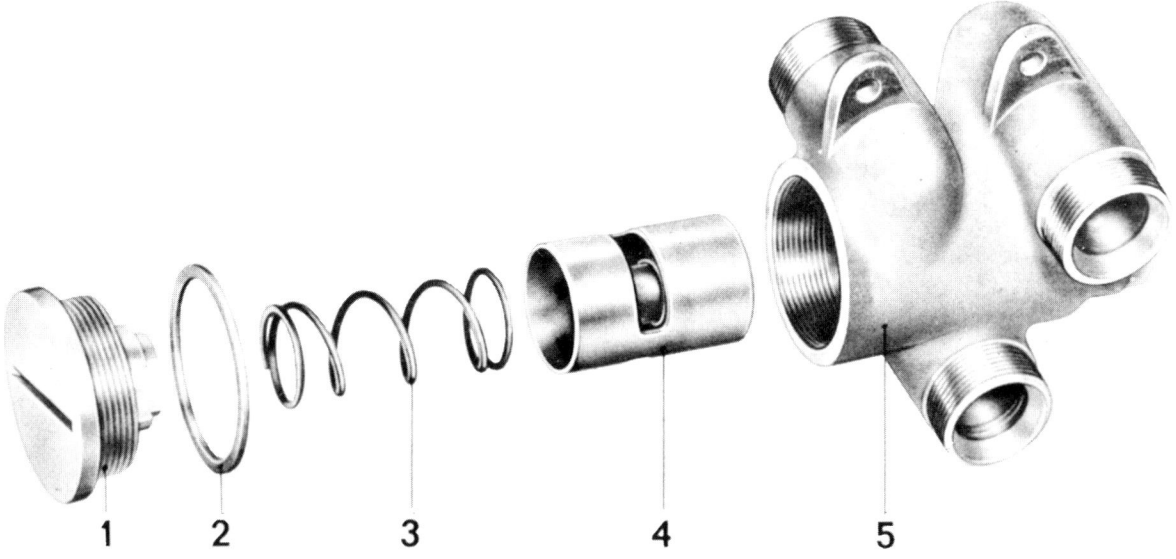

Fig. 1.58. Exploded view of pressure relief valve (adjacent to oil tank) (Sec. 53)

1 Plug	2 Sealing ring	3 Spring	4 Plunger	5 Valve body

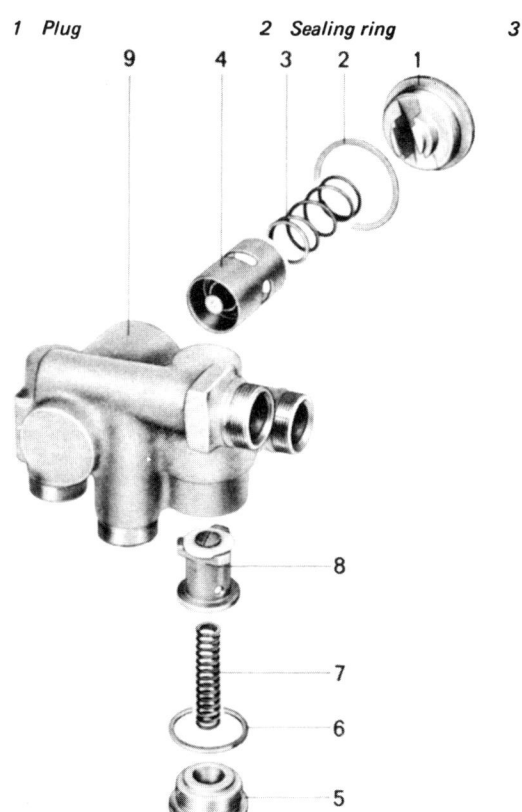

Fig. 1.59. Exploded view of pressure relief valve (adjacent to oil cooler) (Sec. 53)

1 Plug	4 Plunger	7 Spring
2 Gasket	5 Plug	8 Plunger
3 Spring	6 Gasket	9 Body

---

53 External oil pressure relief valves

1 Depending upon the particular model, a pressure relief valve may be encountered in the oil tank or adjacent to the oil cooler.

2 Removal is simply carried out after disconnecting the oil lines from the valve.

3 Wear is unlikely but should a fault develop in a pressure relief valve, it is recommended that a new valve assembly is fitted.

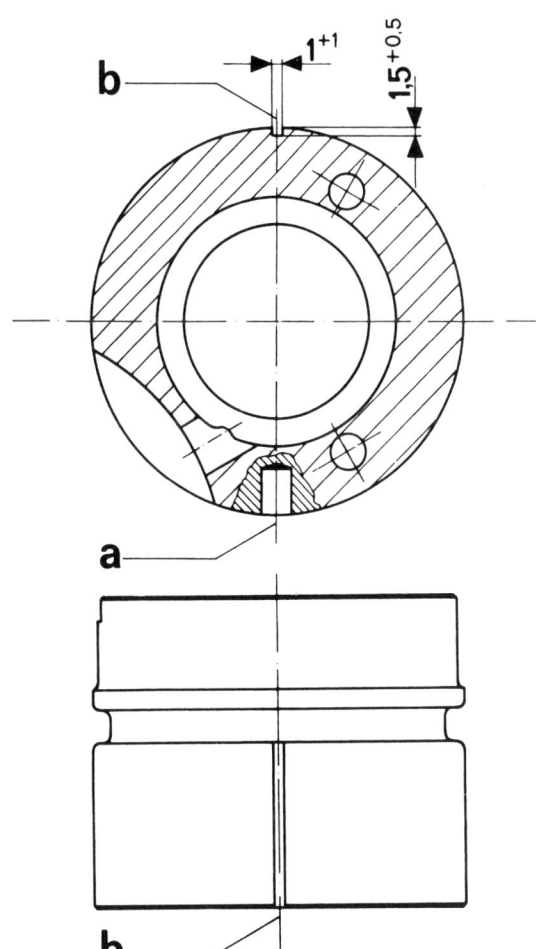

Fig. 1.60. Main bearing No 8 insert modification diagram (Sec. 54)

a) Dowel pin bore   b) Oil pressure relief groove
(Dimensions in millimetres)

54 Main bearing insert - modification

1   On cars built up until 1970, the insert used at main bearing No. 8

did not incorporate an oil pressure relief groove.
2   With such cars, it is worthwhile cutting a groove as shown in Fig.
1.60 to improve the oil sealing qualities of the component.
3   Use a fine hacksaw blade to cut the groove.

55 Fault diagnosis - engine

Symptom	Reason/s
Engine will not turn over when starter switch is operated	Flat battery. Bad battery connections. Bad connections at solenoid switch and/or starter motor. Defective starter motor.
Engine turns over normally but fails to start	No spark at plugs. No fuel reaching engine. Too much fuel reaching the engine (flooding),
Engine starts but runs unevenly and misfires	Ignition and/or fuel system faults. Incorrect valve clearances. Burnt out valves. Worn out piston rings.
Lack of power	Ignition and/or fuel system faults. Incorrect valve clearances. Burnt out valves. Worn out piston rings.
Excessive oil consumption	Oil leaks from crankshaft, rear oil seal, timing cover gasket, rocker cover gasket, oil filter gasket, tank or cooler lines. Worn piston rings or cylinder bores resulting in oil being burnt by engine. Worn valve guides and/or defective valve stem seals.
Excessive mechanical noise from engine	Wrong valve to rocker clearances. Worn crankshaft bearings. Worn cylinders (piston slap). Slack or worn timing chain and sprockets.

Note: When investigating starting and uneven running faults do not be tempted into snap diagnosis. Start from the beginning of the check procedure and follow it through. It will take less time in the long run. Poor performance from an engine in terms of power and economy is not normally diagnosed quickly. In any event the ignition and fuel systems must be checked first before assuming any further investigation needs to be made.

Chapter 2 Fuel and exhaust systems

Contents

Specifications

System type ... ...   Front mounted fuel tank, mechanical or electric fuel pumps, carburettors or fuel injection system.

Fuel tank

Up to 1971	13.6 Imp. gals. (16.3 US gals/62 litres)
1971 to 1974	18.7 Imp. gals. (22.4 US gals/85 litres)
1974 onwards	17.6 Imp. gals. (21.1 US gals/80 litres)

Fuel pump application

Solex carburettors	Twin mechanical and Bendix electric
Weber carburettors	Hardi electric
Zenith carburettors	Hardi electric
Fuel injection	Roller type electric

Carburettor application

Year	Engine	Capacity (cc)	Carburettors or injection system
	911 (except N.America)	1991	Solex 40 PI (Two triple throat)
1965 to 1967	911L	1991	Weber 40 IDA 3C and 3CI
	911S	1991	Weber 40 IDA 3C and 3CI
	911T	1991	Weber 40 IDA 3C and 3CI
	911 (N.America)	1991	Weber 40 IDAP 3C and 3CI
1968 (early)	911S	1991	Weber 40 IDA 3C and 3CI
	911T	1991	Weber 40 IDT 3C and 3CI*
1968 (later)	911S	1991	Bosch fuel injection system

Year	Engine	Capacity (cc)	Carburettors or injection system
1969	911T	2195	Zenith 40 TIN **
to	911S	2195	Bosch fuel injection system
1971	911E	2195	Bosch fuel injection system
1972	911E, S and T (except N.America)	2341	Bosch fuel injection system
to			
1973	N.America	2341	K-jetronic fuel injection system
1974	911	2687	K-jetronic fuel injection system
to	911S	2687	K-jetronic fuel injection system
1975	Carrera	2687	K-jetronic fuel injection system

* With Sportomatic transmission Weber 40 IDS 3C
** Some 1969 to 1971 models may be fitted with Weber 40 IDTP 3C/3CI or 40 IDTP 13C/3CI

Carburettor Specifications (Solex and Zenith

	Solex 40 PI	Zenith 40 TIN
Venturi	30	28.5
Main jet	125	120
Fuel jet	—	50
Air correction jet	180	190
Air correction jet (submersion)	—	100
Idle metering jet	55	47.5
Idle air bleed	1.0	160
Accelerator pump nozzle	0.8 mm	—
Pump jet	0.5 mm	—
Emulsion tube	8	4.3 mm
Float needle valve	2.0	1.5
Slow-running speed	850 to 950 rev/min	850 to 950 rev/min
CO level from exhaust	—	3 to 4%

Carburettor specifications (Weber)

	40IDA3C	40IDAP3c	40IDT3C	40IDA(S)	40IDS	401DS3C	40IDTP3C	40IDTP13C
Venturi	30	30	27	32	32	32	27	27
Pre-atomiser	4.5	4.5	4.5	4.5	4.5	4.5	4.5	4.5
Main jet	125	125	110	135	125	130	110	105
Air correction jet	180	180	185	170	185	180	185	170
Emulsion tube	F26	F26	F2	F26	F3	F3	F1	F1
Idle metering jet	55	52	50	55	55	55	45	55
Pump jet	50	50	50	50	50	50	50	50
Idle air bleed	110	110	110	110	110	110	145	145
Float needle valve	1.75	1.75	1.75	1.75	1.75	1.75	1.75	1.75
Float chamber vent	6	6	—	4.5	4.5	—	—	—
Enrichment jet	—	70	—	—	—	—	—	—
Mixture outlet	—	5.0 mm	5.0 mm	—	—	5.0 mm	5.0 mm	5.0 mm
Idle mixture outlet	—	1.0 mm	1.0 mm	—	—	1.0 mm	1.0 mm	1.0 mm
Bypass orifices {	—	—	1.0 mm	—	—	0.80 mm	0.70 mm	0.70 mm
	—	—	1.1 mm	—	—	1.1 mm	1.30 mm	1.30 mm
	—	—	1.35 mm	—	—	1.35 mm	1.20 mm	1.20 mm
Slow-running speed	850 to 950 rev/min	850 to 950 rev/min	850 to 950 rev/min	850 to 950 rev/min	850 to 950 rev/min	850 to 950 rev/min	850 to 950 rev/min	850 to 950 rev/min

Torque wrench settings
Fuel injection system

	lb f ft	kg f m
Injection pump pulley	18	2.5
Injection valve nozzle	22	3
Injection pump fuel inlet connector	29	4
Injection fuel lines to injection valves	8	1.1

1 General description

1   The fuel system comprises a front mounted fuel tank, mechanical or electric fuel pump and either carburettors or a fuel injection system dependent upon car model and date of production.
2   The carburettors may be of Solex, Weber or Solex-Zenith manufacture: reference should be made to Specifications for application and data.
3   With Solex installations, a camshaft driven, dual, mechanically operated, fuel pump arrangement is fitted plus an electrically operated Bendix pump.
4   With Weber installations, a Hardi type electric fuel pump is fitted.
5   A roller type electric fuel pump is fitted in conjunction with fuel injection systems.
6   On cars destined for operation in North America and certain other territories, a fuel evaporative control system and an exhaust emission control system are fitted.

2 Air cleaner - element renewal and air intake removal and refitting

1   Two types of air cleaner may be encountered. *To remove the circular type element.* loosen wing nuts and turn the air cleaner slightly to the left and remove it. Extract the filter element (photo).
2   *On the rectangular type cleaner,* disconnect both rubber fastening straps and remove the cover. Extract the element
3   Wipe out the interior of the air cleaner and install the new element. Refit the housing or cover.
4   The air intakes can be removed after releasing the toggle clips (photo).

2.1 Circular type air filter element

Fig. 2.1. Renewing rectangular type air cleaner element (Sec. 2)

2.4 Air intake toggle clips (carburettors)

3 Induction pre-heater (1972 models onwards)

1   On all fuel injection models commencing with 1972 models, an induction pre-heating system is installed.
2   The device ensures that the intake air is maintained at a pre-determined level by means of a thermostat and flap valves to improve performance and to reduce exhaust emission.
3   Air is drawn from the left-hand heat exchanger and from a fresh air source and mixed in precise quantities.
4   The intake air temperature is maintained at 112°F (45°C) as soon as possible after the engine has started up.
5   The hot air flap must be open when the engine is cold. This can be checked by inserting the fingers into the hole in the regulator housing, the flap will have closed the bypass duct and it is retained in position by spring tension.
6   Warm up the engine and observe that the flap closes. The hot air flap is controlled by a thermostat and if this fails then the complete regulator housing will have to be renewed.

Fresh air flap
7   This flap must be adjusted while the throttle valve linkage is in the idle position.
8   Adjust the position of the fresh air flap rollers so that the rollers touch the control lever but have no free play, neither are they under tension.
9   When correctly adjusted, the fresh air flap should begin to open when the throttle valves are at 20° open.

4 Mechanical fuel pump - routine cleaning

1   At the intervals specified in 'Routine Maintenance' unscrew the bolt and remove the cover from the fuel pump.
2   Extract the filter screen and wash any dirt from it using clean petrol.
3   Clean out the pump housing and then refit the filter screen and cover making sure that the cover gasket is in good condition.
4   Repeat the operations on the other pump and then start the engine and check for leaks.

5 Mechanical fuel pumps - testing, removal and overhaul

1   The twin mechanical fuel pump unit is designed to operate on a recirculating principle of drawing fuel from a common float chamber and delivering it to the individual Solex carburettors.
2   The pumps are actuated by a pushrod in contact with the eccentric nut on the front of the right-hand camshaft.
3   Failure of the fuel supply at the carburettors may be due to a fault in the pump unit. To test, disconnect the LT lead from the negative terminal of the coil (to prevent the engine firing) and also disconnect one of the fuel inlet pipes from a carburettor.
4   Operate the starter when a well defined spurt of fuel should be ejected from the open end of the hose. If this does not happen and the tank is known to contain fuel, the pump should be removed and overhauled in the following way.
5   Disconnect the fuel lines from the pumps.
6   Unscrew and remove the securing bolts and withdraw the dual pump assembly.
7   Remove the pump cover and extract the filter screen.
8   Scribe a line across the edges of the upper and lower pump body flanges and remove the securing screws. Separate the upper and

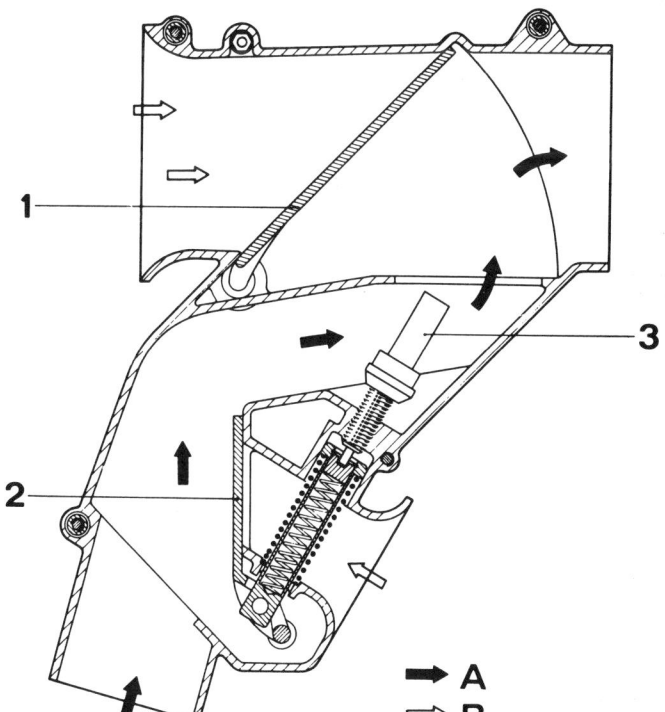

1

3

2

➡ A
⇨ B

Fig. 2.2. Induction pre-heater (1972 on) (Sec. 3)

1 *Fresh air flap*	2 *Warm air flap*	A *Warm air*
	3 *Thermostat*	B *Fresh air*

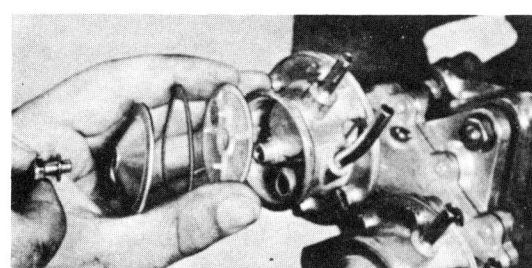

Fig. 2.3. Removing a filter screen from a mechanical fuel pump (Sec. 4)

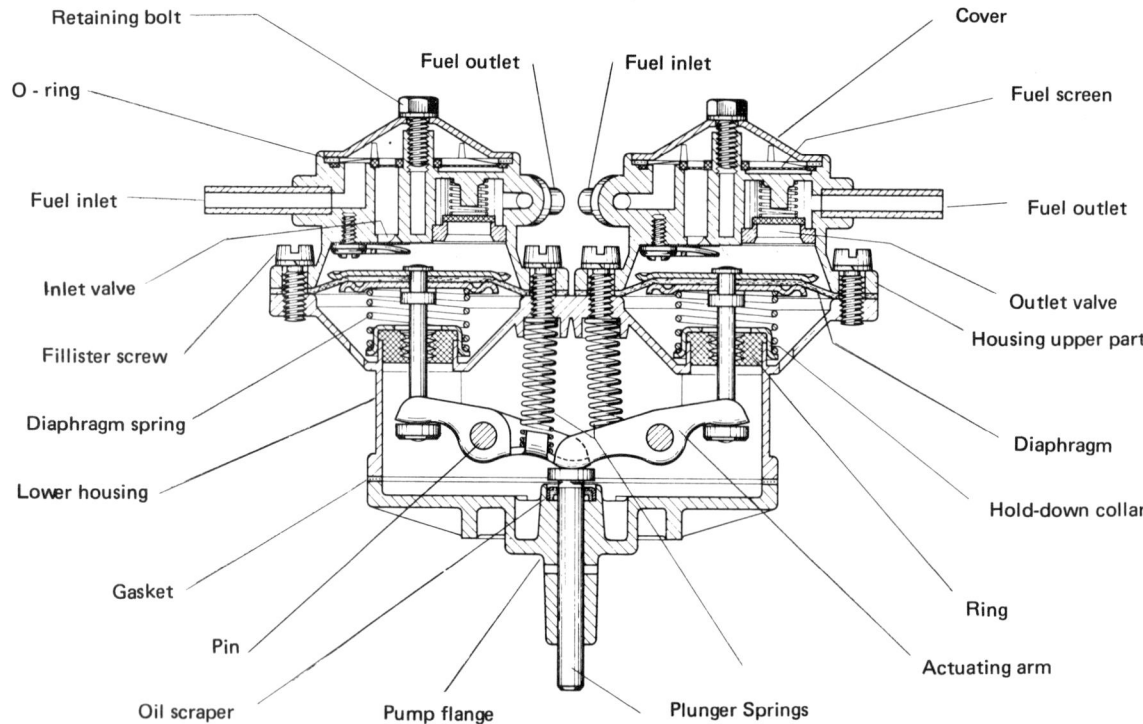

Fig. 2.4. Sectional view of twin mechanical fuel pump (Sec. 5)

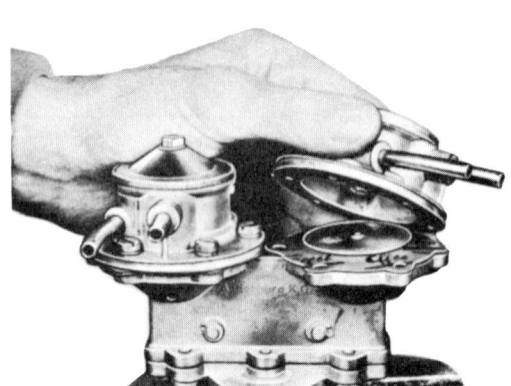

Fig. 2.5. Removing upper body from mechanical fuel pump (Sec. 5)

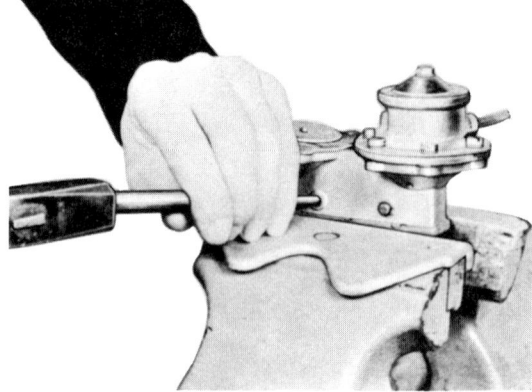

Fig. 2.6. Removing pivot pin from mechanical fuel pump (Sec. 5)

lower bodies (Fig. 2.5).

9   Disconnect the pump mounting flange from the lower bodies after extracting the securing screws.

10 Extract the circlip from the rocker shaft pivot and drive the pin out.

11 Withdraw the diaphragm and spring assembly.

12 The inlet valve can be removed if necessary, after withdrawing the screw, valve limiter and spring. The outlet valve is not removable.

13 Wash all components in clean petrol and renew any that are worn.

14 Reassembly is a reversal of dismantling but make sure that the diaphragm is not twisted and ensure that the upper body is correctly aligned with the lower body by having the flange edge marks opposite to each other.

15 Repeat the foregoing operations on the second pump.

16 Refit the fuel pump assembly making sure that at least two gaskets and the plastic insulating washer are installed between the pump mounting flange and the camshaft chain cover. The distance measured between the nearest point of the camshaft sprocket eccentric nut and the face of the pump mounting flange should be 2.02 in (51.4 mm). Add more gaskets, if necessary, to achieve this measurement.

6   Electric fuel pump (Bendix type) - cleaning

1   The Bendix electric fuel pump is installed together with the mechanical fuel pumps on engines equipped with Solex carburettors. As certain sections of the pump are filled with gas and sealed to prevent corrosion, it is recommended that servicing operations are limited to the following.

2   Unscrew the pump bottom cover. This is of bayonet fitting type and should be turned in an anticlockwise direction.

3   Extract the filter and clean it; also clean out the bottom cover.

4   Refitting is a reversal of removal but make sure that the gasket is in good condition and then start the engine and check for leaks.

7   Electric fuel pump (Hardi type) - cleaning

1   This type of pump is installed where Weber carburettors are fitted.

2   Unscrew and remove the plug from the valve housing of the pump. Clean the filter and refit the components.

8 Electric fuel pump (Hardi type) - removal, overhaul and refitting

1 Disconnect the fuel lines from the pump.
2 Unscrew and remove the pump mounting bolts and disconnect the earth strap.
3 Disconnect the lead from the positive (+) terminal of the pump.
4 Remove the six screws which secure the pump body to the valve housing and withdraw the body.
5 The diaphragm can now be removed by turning it in an anticlockwise direction. Withdraw the diaphragm complete with armature and spring.
6 To remove the breaker points, unclip the plastic cap and extract the adjusting screw from the upper part of the breaker assembly, also the condenser and breaker mounting screws. Withdraw the condenser and the upper part of the breaker assembly.
7 Extract the pivot pin from the lower part of the breaker assembly and withdraw the lower part.
8 Renew any worn or damaged components.
9 To install the diaphragm, place the spring on the pressure rod so that the smaller coil is against the armature.
10 Insert the diaphragm with the spring into the pump housing. Screw the pressure rod so far into the lower part of the rocker assembly that the contacts will not open when the diaphragm is pushed upwards.
11 Now turn the diaphragm and pressure rod in an anticlockwise direction until the points just begin to open when the diaphragm is pushed upwards.
12 To ensure that the breaker operates correctly, turn the diaphragm and pressure rod through 300° (5 screw holes) in an anticlockwise direction from the stage reached in paragraph 11.
13 Apply a little oil to the breaker pivots: make sure that the contacts are not contaminated with the oil.
14 Adjust the breaker gap by pushing the diaphragm upwards so that the points are open and then adjust the gap to 0.05 in (1.2 mm) by turning the adjuster screw. Make sure that the adjuster screw is engaged with the contact spring.
15 Fit the plastic cap and gaskets.
16 Install the valve housing and screws.

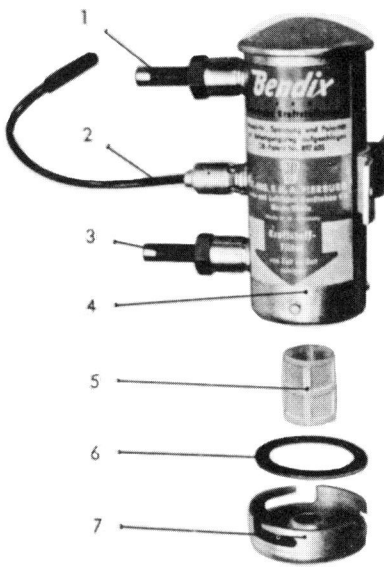

Fig. 2.7. Bendix type electric fuel pump (Sec. 6)

1	Fuel outlet	5	Filter
2	Lead	6	Gasket
3	Fuel inlet	7	Cover with
4	Body		magnet

9 Electric fuel pump (roller-cell type) - removal and refitting

1 This type of pump is fitted in conjunction with fuel injection systems. It is mounted on a bracket on the support member under the fuel tank.
2 The current draw and fuel delivery volume varies between the models. In the event of lack of fuel being attributed to the fuel pump, disconnect the electrical leads from it and uncouple and plug the fuel lines.
3 No provision is made for overhaul and the faulty pump should be replaced by a new one.

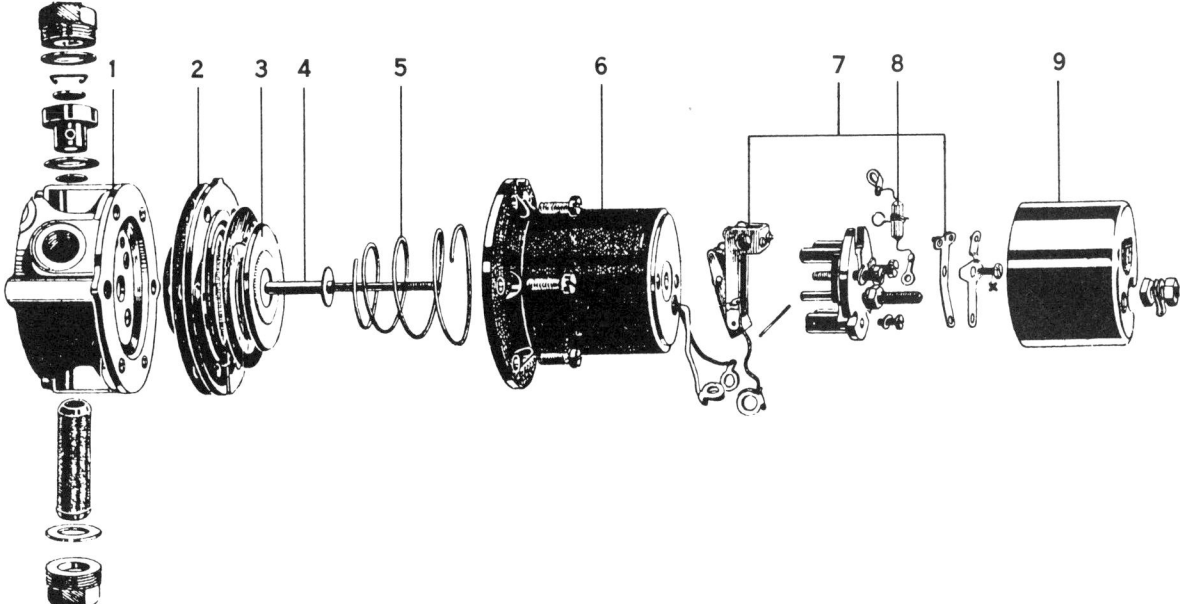

Fig. 2.8. Hardi type electric fuel pump (Secs. 7 and 8)

1	Valve housing	4	Rod	7	Breaker points
2	Diaphragm	5	Spring	8	Condenser
3	Armature	6	Body	9	Cap

10 Fuel tank (up to 1971) - removal and installation

1   Remove the drain plug and drain the fuel into a suitable container.
2   Disconnect both fuel lines from the tank.
3   Open the luggage compartment at the front of the car and remove the padding and the spare wheel.
4   Disconnect the vent pipe from the tank.
5   Disconnect the leads from the fuel level sender unit.
6   Remove the tank securing screws (socket heads).
7   Remove the clips on the flexible section of the filler pipe and disconnect the pipe from the tank.
8   Remove the fuel tank upwards from the luggage compartment. **Never attempt to solder or weld a leak in a fuel tank - leave the repair to specialists.**
9   Installation is a reversal of removal but make sure that the mounting flange gasket is in good condition otherwise water will leak into the luggage compartment.

11 Fuel tank (1971 to 73) - removal and installation

1   Remove the stoneguard from the front of the car.
2   Disconnect the fuel lines from the tank and drain the fuel into a suitable container.
3   Unscrew and remove the tank support bracket bolt.
4   Disconnect the vent hose from the tank.
5   Disconnect the electrical plug from the fuel tank sender unit (photo).
6   Remove both tank support brackets.
7   Slacken the hose clip on the flexible section of the filler hose,

disconnect the filler pipe and withdraw the tank upwards from the luggage compartment.
8   Never attempt to weld or solder a fuel tank. A leak may be temporarily repaired with fibreglass or a proprietary product but permanent repairs should be left to specialists or a new tank installed.
9   Installation is a reversal of removal.
10 On cars equipped with K-jetronic fuel injection systems, the fuel tank drain plug is fitted with a filter. This should be removed periodically when the fuel level is very low and the filter thoroughly cleaned. Use a new rubber seal when refitting.

12 Fuel tank (1974 onwards) - removal and installation

1   Raise the front of the car and remove the undershield.
2   Unscrew the drain plug and let the fuel drain into a suitable container.
3   Disconnect the fuel lines from the tank.
4   Disconnect the vent hose from the tank.
5   Remove the cover from the fuel level sender unit and pull off the wiring connector plug.
6   Remove the tank support brackets. The battery may have to be pushed slightly to one side to give access to these brackets.
7   Remove the clip which secures the flexible section of the filler pipe to the tank.
8   Disconnect the flexible filler hose from the tank and then remove the tank from the car upwards through the luggage compartment.
9   Installation is a reversal of removal but stick a new tank flange sealing gasket in position before lowering the tank into the luggage compartment.

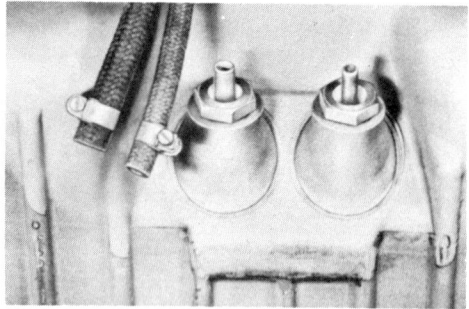

Fig. 2.9. Fuel tank connections (1971 to 1973) (Sec. 11)

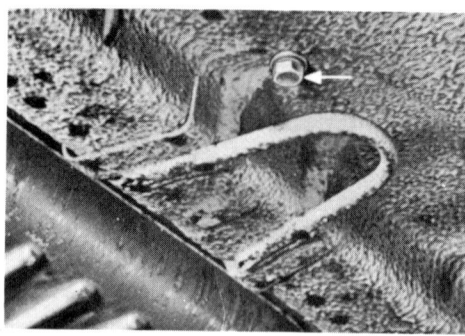

Fig. 2.10. Fuel tank support bracket bolt (1971 to 1973) (Sec. 11)

11.5 Fuel tank sender unit and connector plug

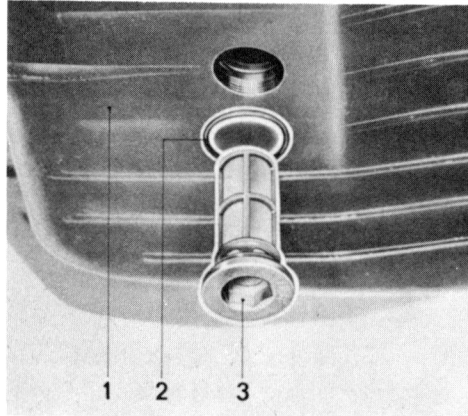

Fig. 2.11. Fuel tank filter 1973 K-jetronic only) (Sec. 11)

1   Tank   2   Gasket   3   Plug/filter assembly

13 Solex 40 PI carburettors - description

1 A triple bank of these carburettors is used on earlier models. One bank is fitted to each opposing cylinder intake.
2 A common float chamber is used for all three carburettors which is supplied by an electrically operated (primary) pump.
3 The fuel in the float chamber is then delivered to the carburettors by a mechanically operated (secondary) pump which works on a recirculatory principle returning excess fuel to an overflow reservoir.
4 The jets are located together in a cluster which is easily removable.
5 A diaphragm type accelerator pump is fitted, also the pump circuit incorporates valves to provide extra fuel at high engine load and revolutions.

14 Solex 40 PI carburettors - slow running adjustment

1 Bring the engine to normal operating temperature and remove the air cleaner assembly.
2 Disconnect the short connecting link from the throttle shaft.
3 Set the engine throttle speed to between 1200 and 1400 rev/min. by turning the throttle stop screws on the shaft.

4 A carburettor balancing device (flowmeter) will now be required to ensure that all three carburettors are synchronised.
5 Synchronisation is carried out first by making sure that the throttle valve link rods are set to provide the same movement of the valve plates when the shaft is rotated. Knurled nuts are provided on the link rods for adjustment purposes.
6 Now adjust the volume control screws until the engine runs as smoothly as possible.
7 When the balancing device indicates that the units are properly synchronised, reduce the throttle speed screw to give an idling speed of between 800 and 1000 rev/min. Re-adjust the volume control screws, if necessary.

15 Solex 40 PI carburettors - removal and installation

1 Remove the air cleaner and hot air duct.
2 Disconnect the throttle linkage.
3 Withdraw the float chamber vent hose.
4 Unscrew the retaining nuts and remove the air horns and baseplate. (Fig. 2.15).
5 Unscrew the carburettor flange mounting nuts and lift the carburettors individually from the engine. (Fig. 2.16)

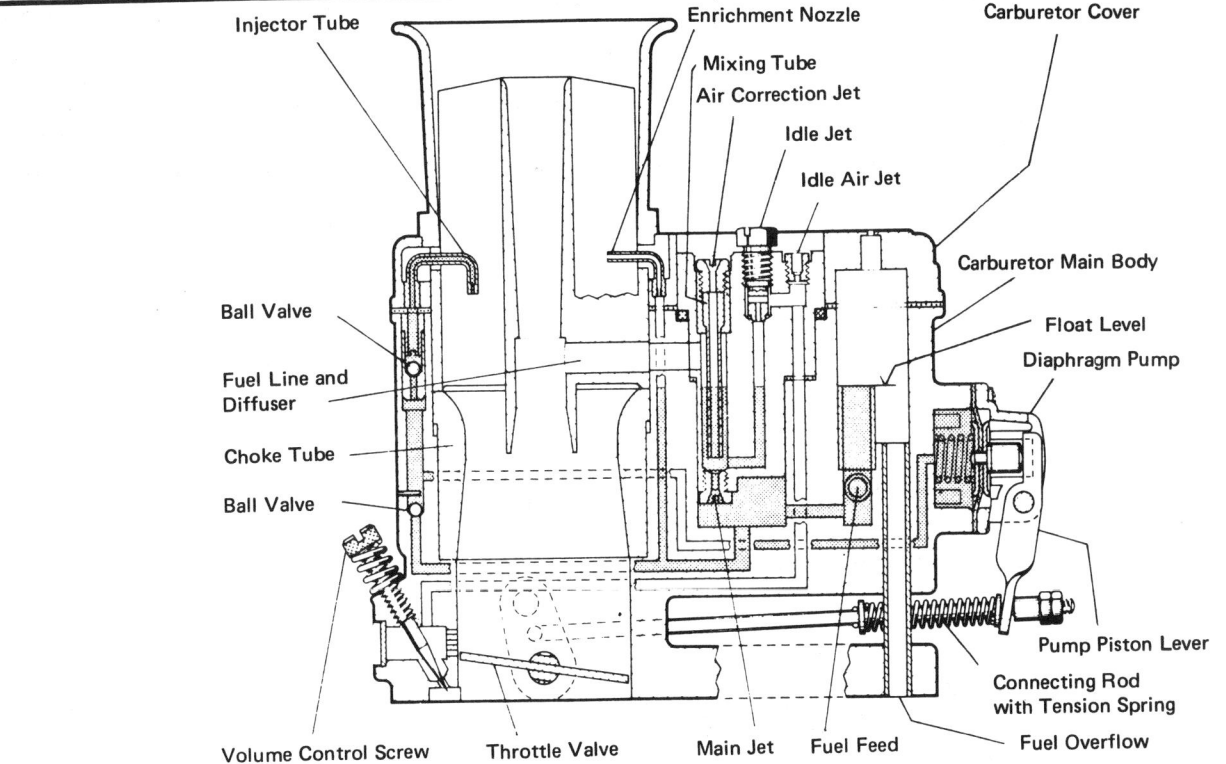

Fig. 2.12. Solex 40 PI carburettor showing jet locations (Sec. 13)

Fig. 2.13. Throttle link and throttle speed screw (A) Solex 40 PI carburettor (Sec. 14)

Fig. 2.14. Adjusting volume control screw (Solex 40 PI carburettor) (Sec. 14)

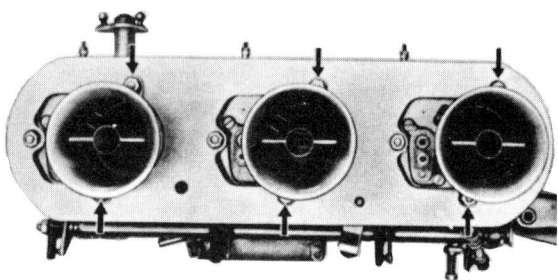

Fig. 2.15. Air horns and baseplate (Solex 40 PI carburettor) (Sec. 15)

Fig. 2.16. Removing a Solex 40 PI carburettor (Sec. 15)

Fig. 2.17. Cover securing screws (Solex 40 PI carburettor) (Sec. 16)

Fig. 2.18. Removing the jet carrier (Solex 40 PI carburettor) (Sec. 16)

Fig. 2.19. Pre-atomiser retaining pin and locknut (Solex 40 PI carburettor) (Sec. 16)

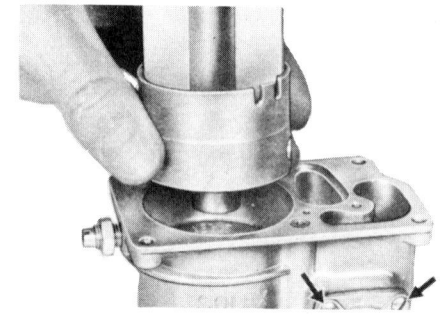

Fig. 2.20. Removing venturi (Solex 40 PI carburettor) (Sec. 16)

Fig. 2.21. Accelerator pump rod nuts (Solex 40 PI carburettor) (Sec. 16)

Fig. 2.22. Accelerator pump cover screws (Solex 40 PI carburettor) (Sec. 16)

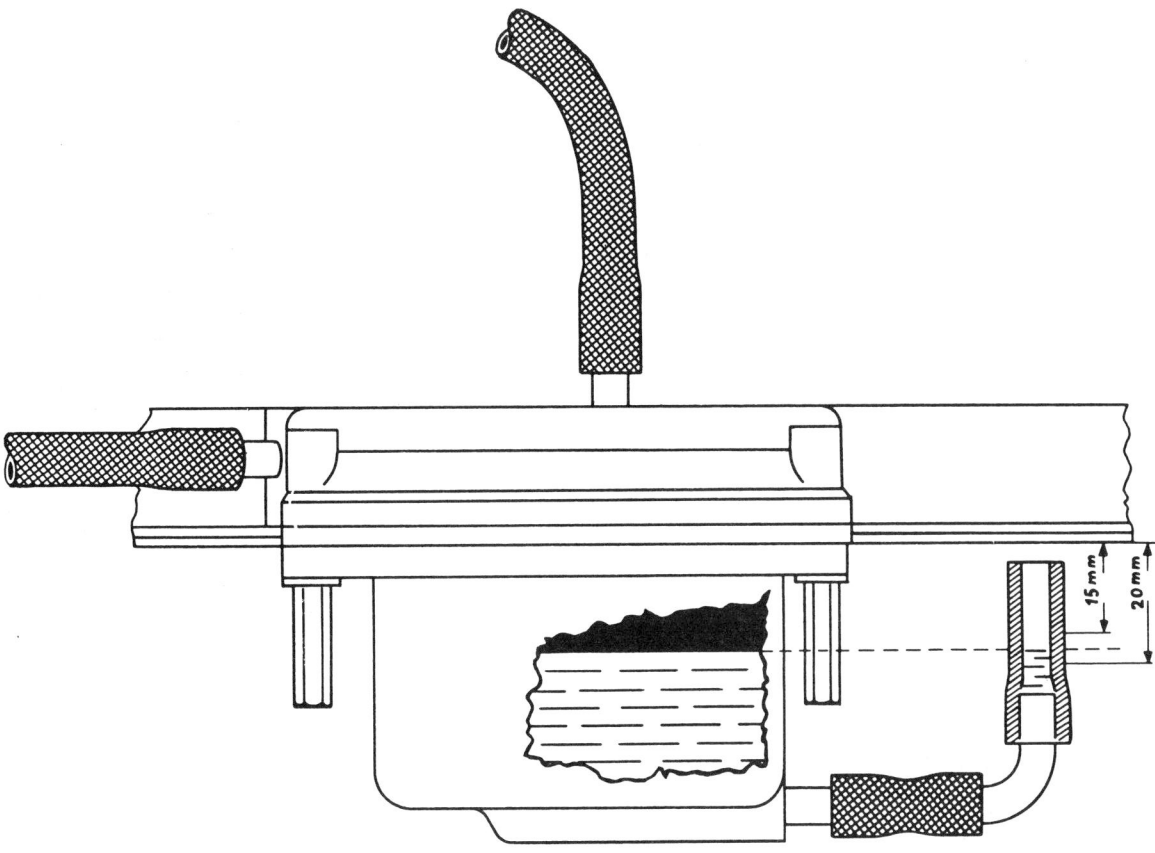

Fig. 2.23. Checking fuel level on Solex 40 PI carburettor (Sec. 16)

6   Installation is a reversal of removal but always use new flange gaskets.

16 Solex 40 PI carburettors   overhaul and adjustment

1   With the carburettor removed, remove the cover securing screws and pull off the cover.
2   Release the retaining nuts and remove the jet carrier.
3   The individual jets can now be unscrewed and cleaned with air from a tyre pump. Never clean jets with wire or their calibration will be ruined.
4   The operations so far described will normally be sufficient to clean any obstruction. If wear or damage has occurred to the carburettor then continue to dismantle in the following way.
5   Unscrew the idle mixture screw and spring.
6   Withdraw the pre-atomiser.
7   Remove the venturi upwards.
8   Release the accelerator pump rod nuts but not until their position on the rod has been carefully measured.
9   Remove the accelerator pump cover, diaphragm and spring.
10 Inspect all components for wear and renew as necessary. It is worthwhile checking the jet sizes with those listed in the Specifications in case a previous owner has changed any.
11 Reassembly is a reversal of dismantling but observe the following points.
12 Use a new 'O' ring seal under the jet carrier and tighten the securing screws carefully in diagonal sequence. A leak here can cause high fuel consumption.
13 Adjustment of the accelerator pump can only be carried out precisely if the amount of fuel ejected from the pump nozzle can be collected and measured. The fuel supply will have to be connected to the carburettor for this and for every two strokes of the pump rod the volume of fuel ejected should be as follows:

Summer   *0.40 to 0.50 cc*
Winter   *0.55 to 0.65 cc*

In practice, the accelerator pump stroke is adjusted by moving the nuts on the rod by not more than half a turn at a time from their original position and evaluating the acceleration quality.
14 The fuel level in the carburettor should not normally vary from its preset position. The level can be checked if a plastic tube is connected to the nozzle on the float chamber as shown in Fig. 2.23. The distance between the underside (milled face) of the intake duct and the fuel level shown in the plastic tube should be between 0.6 and 0.8 in (15 and 20 mm).

17 Weber carburettors - description

1   The carburettor arrangement is very similar to Solex units except that a mechanical fuel pump is no longer used, only the electrically operated pump being employed (photo).
2   Each bank of three carburettors incorporates two float chambers and one accelerator pump.

18 Weber carburettors - slow-running adjustment

1   This adjustment is carried out in a similar way and using a similar device to that described for Solex carburettors in Section 14.
2   Synchronisation of air flow should be made firstly by setting the throttle stop screws and then using the air adjustment screws. (Fig. 2.24)
3   Finally adjust the individual mixture control screws.

19 Weber carburettors - removal and installation

1   Disconnect the pre-heater hose from the air cleaner.
2   Withdraw the air cleaner element.
3   Disconnect the breather hose from the engine oil filler neck.
4   Disconnect the condensation hose from the base of the air cleaner housing.

5   Remove the air cleaner.
6   Disconnect the fuel hoses from the carburettors.
7   Disconnect the throttle linkage.
8   Unscrew and remove the nuts from the carburettor mounting flanges and withdraw the carburettors as an assembly. Take care that the spring washers from the flange studs do not drop into the intake ducts.
9   Installation is a reversal of removal but always use new flange gaskets.

20 Weber carburettors - overhaul and adjustment

1   With the carburettors removed as previously described, remove the upper body.
2   The main jet, air correction jet, emulsion tube, idle metering jet and idle air bleed can all be removed and cleaned using air from a tyre pump.

17.1 Weber carburettors on one cylinder bank

20.4 Carburettor banjo unions and filter bolts

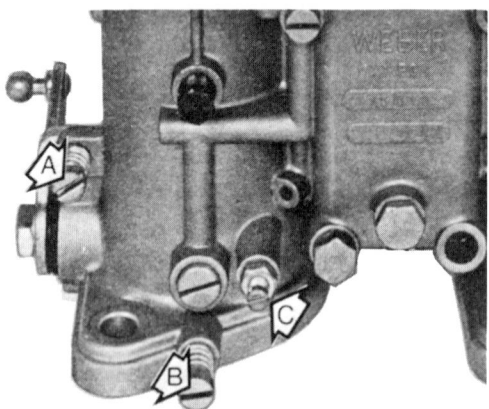

Fig. 2.24. Adjustment screws (Weber carburettor) (Sec. 18)

A   Throttle speed   B   Mixture   C   Air adjustment

Fig. 2.26. Plug removed to expose fuel inlet needle valve (Weber carburettors) (Sec. 20)

Fig. 2.25. Removing upper body (Weber carburettors) (Sec 20)

Fig. 2.27. Removing pre-atomiser (Weber carburettors) (Sec. 20)

Never probe the jets with wire or their calibration will be upset.

3   The operations so far described will normally be sufficient to clear any obstruction. If wear or damage has occurred to the carburettors then continue to dismantle in the following way.

4   Unscrew and remove the filter bolts and banjo unions from the upper body (photo).

5   Unscrew the plug and fuel inlet needle valve.

6   Remove the accelerator pump non-return valve and pump nozzle.

7   Withdraw the pre-atomiser. If it is stuck, release it with a few light taps.

8   Withdraw the venturis.

9   Unscrew the float pivot pin and withdraw the float.

10   Remove the accelerator pump cover and extract the diaphragm, springs and valve.

11   Clean all components and renew any that are worn.

12   Reassembly is a reversal of dismantling but check the setting of the float. The top edge of the float from the top edge of the carburettor body flange (without gasket fitted) should be 0.492 to 0.512 in (12.5 to 13 mm). Adjustment of the fuel level can be made by altering the thickness of gaskets under the fuel inlet needle valve or by bending the float arm tab gently.

Fig. 2.28. Withdrawing venturi (Weber carburettor) (Sec. 20)

Fig. 2.29. Removing float pivot pin (Weber carburettors) (Sec. 20)

Fig. 2.30. Accelerator pump cover (Weber carburettors) (Sec. 20)

21 Zenith 40 TIN carburettor - description

1   Two carburettor assemblies are installed, one assembly being fitted to each bank of cylinders.

2   Each carburettor assembly incorporates three venturis, two float chambers and an individually adjustable accelerator pump connected to each venturi.

3   An auxiliary enrichment system helps reduce exhaust emissions to a minimum

22 Zenith 40 TIN carburettor - slow-running adjustment

1   Ensure that the ignition system is correctly set, with regard to timing and dwell angle.

2   Bring the engine to normal operating temperature and check that the throttle hand control lever is fully depressed (OFF). Switch off the engine.

3   Remove the air cleaner and disconnect the throttle linkage from the cross shaft.

4   Turn the mixture control screws, (b) (Fig. 2.31) fully in and then unscrew them 2½ turns each.

5   Screw the air bypass screw (c) fully in.

6   Start the engine and using a balancer (airflow meter) synchronise cylinders 1 and 4 by turning their throttle stop screws. The engine should be running at about 1000 rev/min. during the synchronising operation.

7   Now synchronise cylinders 1 and 3 and 4 and 6 by turning the air bypass control screws. Open the air bypass screws as little as possible during the adjusting procedure and the screw which is in the venturi which had the highest airflow rate during the adjustment described in paragraph 6, should remain closed.

8   Adjust all the idle mixture control screws until the smoothest idling speed is obtained. Screwing in weakens the mixture, unscrewing enrichens the mixture.

9   If the idling speed has altered, readjust the throttle speed screws so that the engine is running at between 850 and 950 rev/min. Check the balance airflow) between the left-hand and right-hand carburettor installations.

10   The exhaust emission level should now be checked. CO value should not exceed 3 to 4%. Readjust the idle mixture control screws, if necessary.

11   Reconnect the throttle linkage making sure that the balljoints engage without preloading the throttle cross shaft.

Fig. 2.31. Adjustment screws (Zenith 40 TIN carburettor) (Sec. 22)

a) Throttle stop   *b) Idle mixture*   *c) Air by-pass*

23 Zenith 40 TIN carburettor - adjusting auxiliary enrichment device

1 Before carrying out this adjustment, make sure that the ignition and emission settings are correct, also the slow-running speed.

2 Run the engine to normal operating temperature and switch off.

3 Set the two enrichment device screws initially by screwing them right in and then unscrewing them two complete turns.

4 Turn the adjusting screw on the microswitch until the points close (audible by a 'click') then continue turning the screw in the same direction by another half turn.

5 Disconnect the grey/red lead from the enrichment device solenoid and then connect a jump lead from the battery positive (+) terminal or the top fuse on the fuse box to the free terminal on the solenoid.

6 Start the engine. The slow-running speed will increase slightly due to the fact that the solenoid has been activated.

7 Turn the flow adjusting screw on both the left-hand and right-hand carburettor assemblies until the engine idles at between 1150 and 1250 rev/min.

8 Using a flowmeter, check the balance between the venturis on cylinders 2 and 5. Synchronise by adjusting the flow-rate screws. If the idling speed changes, the flow rate screws should be screwed in to lower the speed or out to increase it.

9 Now the enrichment device mixture control screw clockwise on both carburettor assemblies (left-and right-hand) until any increase in slow-running reaches the point where it just begins to drop. Now unscrew the screws until the highest slow-running speed is achieved. Carry out this last operation separately on both carburettors.

10 A CO meter will now be required to analyse the exhaust gas. The CO level should be 3% at the increased idling speed of 1150 to 1250 rev/min. Any deviation from the specified CO level can be rectified by turning the flow rate screws equally (out richer, in weaker).

11 Now check that the engine slow-running speed of between 1150 and 1250 rev/min. is resumed after the accelerator is quickly depressed. If the slow-running speed stays at about 1800 rev/min instead of falling, reduce the engine speed by turning in both the flow rate adjusting screws.

12 Disconnect the jump lead and re-make the original connections.

24 Zenith 40 TIN carburettor auxiliary enrichment micro-switch and solenoid - testing

1 Disconnect both leads from the micro-switch.

2 Connect a jump lead between the battery positive (+) terminal (or top fuse in the fusebox) and one of the terminals on the micro-switch.

3 Connect the other terminal on the micro-switch to a test lamp and earth. Depress the micro-switch when the test lamp should illuminate and go out when the switch is released. Any deviation from this will indicate the need for renewal of the switch.

4 If the preceding test has proved satisfactory, re-make the original connections and then disconnect the lead from the left-hand terminal of the micro-switch and connect the lead to earth, routing it through a test lamp.

5 Start the engine and depress the accelerator. The test lamp should come on at about 1350 rev/min.

6 Release the throttle and the lamp should go out at about 1300 rev/min. Renew the micro-switch if its operation does not conform to specification.

7 If the test is satisfactory, re-make the original connections and then disconnect the right-hand lead from the micro-switch.

8 Connect a jump lead as previously described and touch the end of the lead to the terminal. This should cause the solenoid to make a 'clicking' sound. If it does re-make the original connections; if it does not, renew the solenoid.

25 Zenith 40 TIN carburettor - accelerator pump adjustment

1 Turn the self-locking adjusting screws (a) (Fig. 2.34) until the three actuating fingers (b) on the cross-shaft are located vertically.

2 Release the adjuster screws on the fingers and then screw the adjuster screws in until they just make contact with the pump plungers. Tighten the locknuts. When carrying out this adjustment, have the engine cold and commence with the pump for cylinders 1 and 4.

3 Repeat the foregoing operations on the other accelerator pump

Fig. 2.32. Auxiliary enrichment device (Zenith 40 TIN carburettor) (Sec. 23)

1   Flow rate adjusting screw
2   Auxiliary mixture control screw

Fig. 2.33. Jump lead connected to engine compartment fuse for testing enrichment device solenoid (Zenith 40 TIN) (Sec. 23)

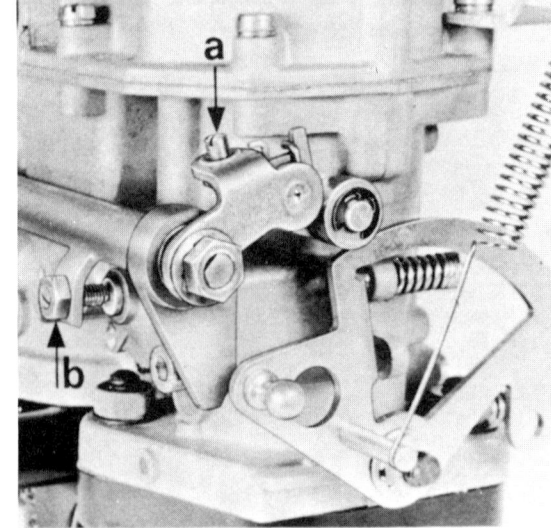

Fig. 2.34. Accelerator pump adjuster screws (Zenith 40 TIN carburettor) (Sec. 25)

a)   Shaft lever self-locking screw
b)   Pump shaft finger and adjuster screw and locknut

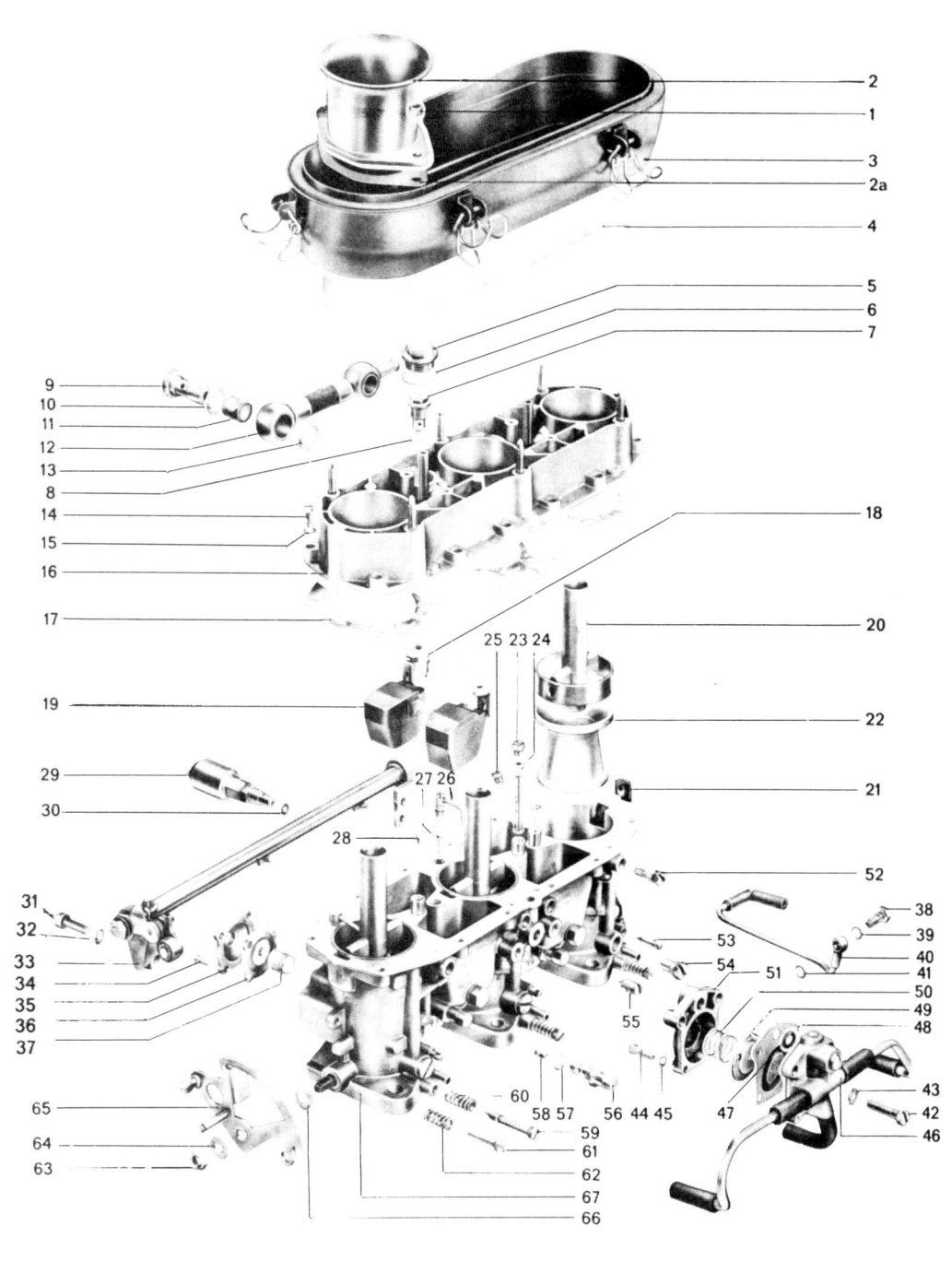

Fig. 2.35. Exploded view of Zenith 40 TIN carburettor

1 Nut
2 Stack
2a Gasket
3 Pan
4 Gasket
5 Plug
6 Seal
7 Fuel inlet needle valve
8 Gasket
9 Hollow bolt
10 Gasket
11 Filter
12 Banjo connector
13 Gasket
14 Screw
15 Lockwasher
16 Upper body
17 Gasket
18 Screw
19 Float assembly
20 Pre-atomiser
21 Clip
22 Venturi
23 Air correction jet
24 Emulsion tube
25 Pump inlet valve
26 Injection tube
27 Plug
28 Enrichment valve fuel jet
29 Enrichment solenoid
30 Gasket
31 Screw
32 Lockwasher
33 Pump shaft
34 Screw
35 Pump cover
36 Diaphragm
37 Pump spring
38 Hollow bolt
39 Gasket
40 Fuel line
41 Gasket
42 Screw
43 Lockwasher
44 Screw
45 Lockwasher
46 Enrichment valve cover
47 'O' ring
48 Diaphragm
49 Diaphragm plunger
50 Spring
51 Enrichment valve base
52 Idle jet
53 Air by-pass control screw
54 Plug
55 Auxiliary mixture control screw
56 Jet carrier
57 Gasket
58 Main jet
59 Idle mixture control screw
60 Spring
61 Idle speed adjusting screw
62 Spring
63 Nut
64 Lockplate
65 Cam
66 Spring washer
67 Body

screws.

4   Ideally, accelerator pump discharge should now be measured in a measuring tube. Correct volume of fuel discharged per stroke should be between 0.4 and 0.6 cc. If the amount of fuel discharged by the pump is too high, turn the adjuster screws on the fingers further in.

5   Fuel should flow from the accelerator pump nozzle as-soon as the throttle is touched. If this does not happen, the pump inlet valve may be faulty.

26 Zenith 40 TIN carburettor - float level adjustment

1   Before the fuel level in the float chamber can be measured, a measuring device will be needed (P226b fuel level gauge). One can be made up from plastic tubing and marked with two lines 17 and 18 mm measured from top face of the carburettor flange.

2   Remove the threaded plug from the float chamber and fit the measuring device.

3   Start the engine and let it run at idling speed when the fuel level should be seen to be within the two marks on the gauge.

4   If the level is incorrect, alter the thickness of the washer under the fuel inlet needle valve. This will mean removing the air cleaner, the upper bodies and the pan with clips.

27 Zenith 40 TIN carburettor - removal and installation

1   Remove the upper part of the air cleaner complete with connecting hoses.

2   Disconnect the fuel line from the carburettor.

3   Disconnect the throttle linkage.

4   Remove the carburettor securing nuts and washers.

5   Disconnect the lead from the solenoid valve.

6   Disconnect the vacuum pipe.

7   Remove the triple carburettor assembly from the intake.

8   Installation is a reversal of removal but always use new flange gaskets.

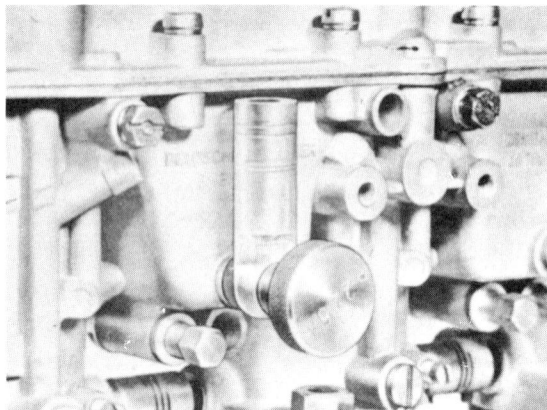

Fig. 2.36. Fuel level gauge attached to Zenith 40 TIN carburettor (Sec. 26)

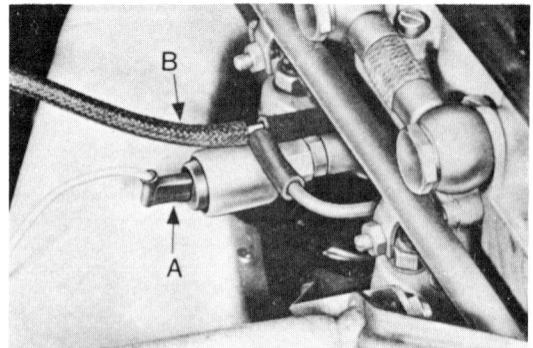

Fig. 2.37. Zenith 40 TIN carburettor solenoid valve lead (A) and vacuum pipe (B) (Sec. 27)

28 Zenith 40 TIN carburettor - overhaul

1   With the carburettors removed from the engine, commence dismantling by removing the stack (2) and the pan (3). (Fig. 2.35)

2   Remove the upper body.

3   At this stage, the jets, float, filter bolts and other items are all accessible. Do not dismantle unnecessarily.

4   Clean out the float chamber and clean the jets using air from a tyre pump only. Never probe them with wire or their calibration will be ruined.

5   If further dismantling is essential, the pre-atomiser and venturis can be withdrawn and also the accelerator pump and enrichment valve taken to pieces.

6   Clean all components in fuel only and always renew gaskets and seals when reassembling.

7   Whenever the carburettor unit has been overhauled, make sure that the checks and adjustments described earlier for this type of carburettor are carried out.

29 Bosch fuel injection system - description

1   This system is based upon a six plunger injection pump which is driven by a toothed belt running off the left-hand camshaft.

2   The fuel is drawn from the tank and delivered to the injection pump by an electrically-operated fuel pump. All fuel passes through a filter.

3   The injection plungers which are actuated by cams, force the fuel through lines to the injector nozzles located in the intake manifold.

4   Provided all adjustments have been correctly carried out, this system will give increased power without increasing fuel consumption, better acceleration and good cold starting.

5   Due to the need for special equipment, the servicing operations which the home mechanic can carry out should be limited to those described in the following Sections.

30 Bosch fuel injection system - slow-running adjustment

1   Before carrying out this work, make sure that the valve clearances are correct, also the ignition settings. Run the engine to normal operating temperature.

2   Start the engine and, if necessary, adjust the air screws on the throttle valve housings until the idling speed is within that specified (photo).

3   The airflow must now be checked between the individual cylinders. Use a suitable flowmeter and carry out minor adjustments to the air screws until the cylinders are synchronised (Fig. 2.40).

30.2 Throttle valve housing air screw (Bosch fuel injection)

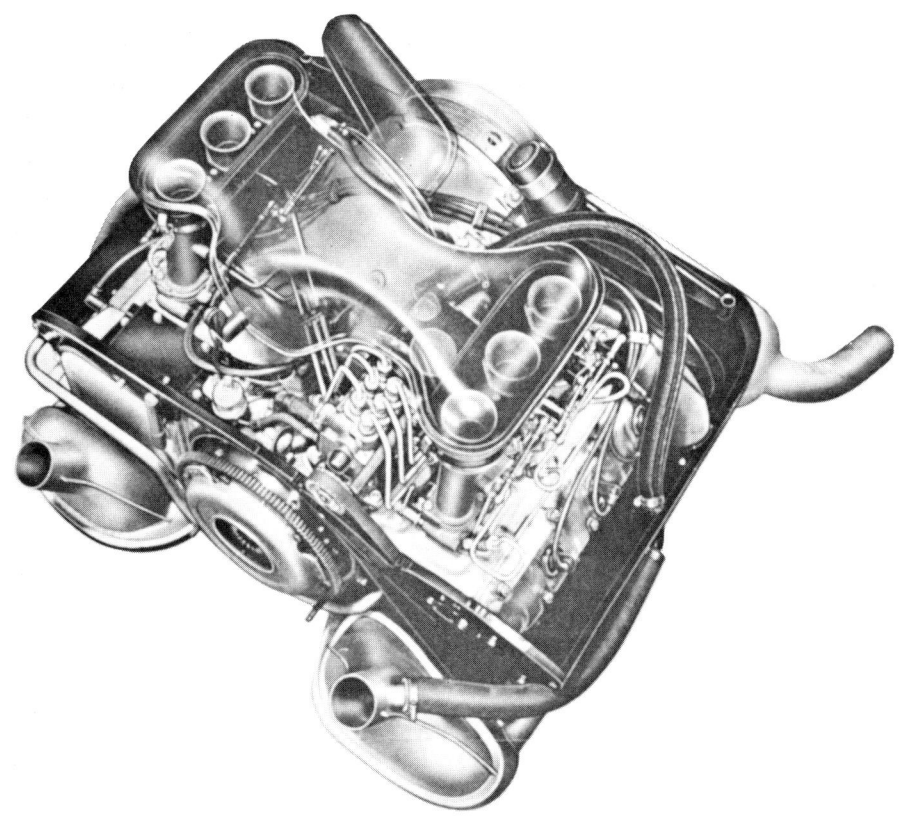

Fig. 2 38. Engine fitted with Bosch fuel injection system (Sec 29)

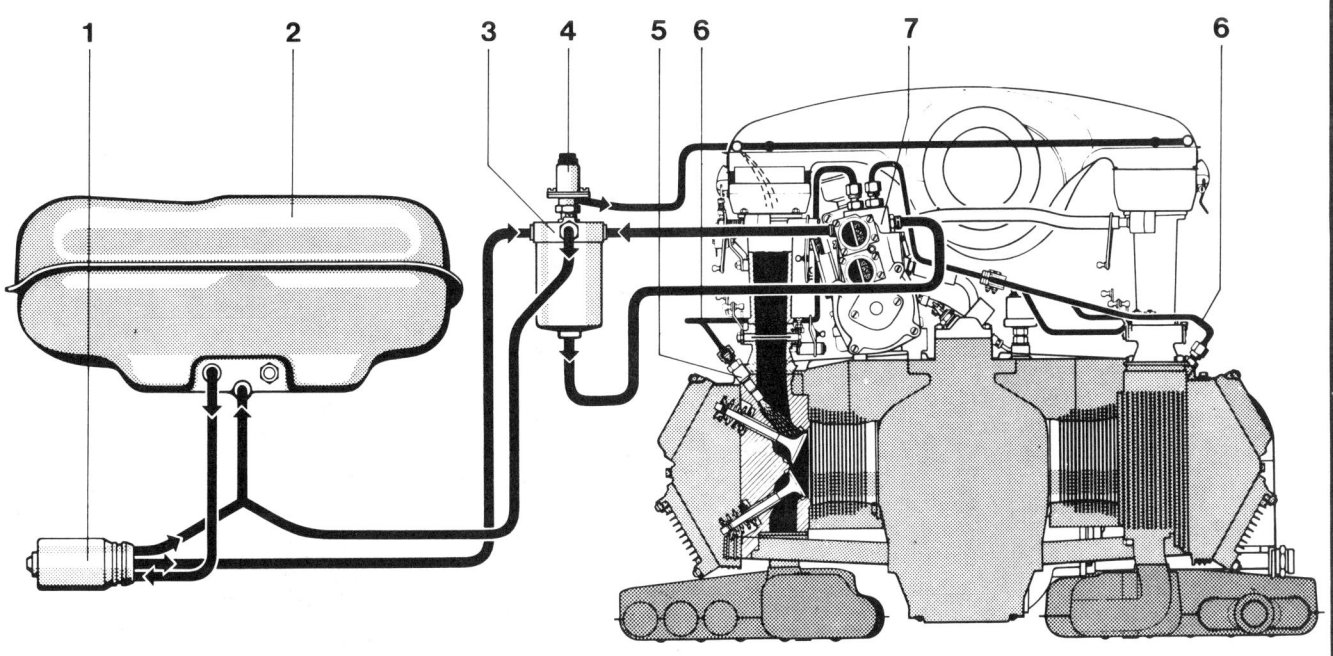

Fig. 2.39. Bosch fuel injection system (Sec. 29)

1	Electric fuel pump	3	Fuel filter	5	Injector	7	Injection pump
2	Fuel tank	4	Start enrichment solenoid	6	Injection line		

4   A CO meter (exhaust gas analyser) is required before any adjustment is made to the injection pump.

5   With the meter connected, check the CO content with the engine idling. If it is not within the range specified, push the flexible idle speed adjusting screw on the injection pump down until it locks.

6   To weaken the mixture, turn the adjusting screw anticlockwise and to enrich the mixture turn it clockwise. Do not turn the screw more than one notch at a time with a maximum of three notches in either direction.

7   When the CO level is correct, adjust the slow-running speed with the air screws and synchronise the intake pipes with the flowmeter.

31 Bosch fuel injection - delivery stroke adjustment

1   Turn the crankshaft pulley bolt until no. 1 piston is at TDC on the compression stroke. Now turn the crankshaft one complete revolution (360°).

2   Continue turning the crankshaft until the 'FE' mark on the crankshaft pulley is opposite the notch on the blower housing.

Fig. 2.40. Checking individual cylinder airflow (Bosch fuel injection) (Sec. 30)

Fig. 2.41. Bosch fuel injection pump alignment marks (Sec. 31)

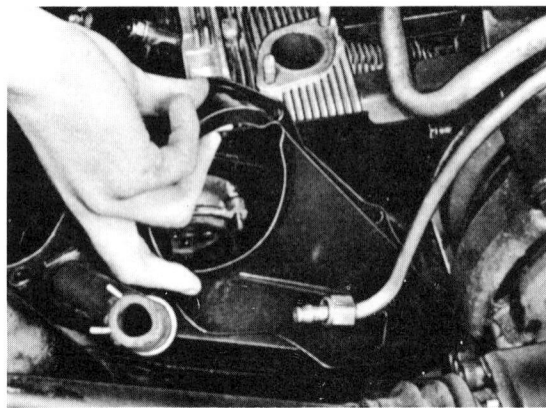

Fig. 2.42. Removing left-hand front engine cover (Sec. 32)

Fig. 2.43. Removing Bosch fuel pump drivebelt from camshaft sprocket) (Sec. 32)

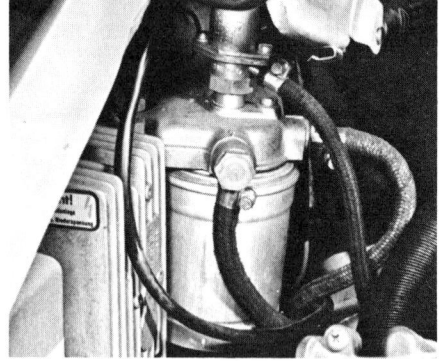

33.2 Fuel line filter (Bosch fuel injection)

34.7a Fuel injection valve connection

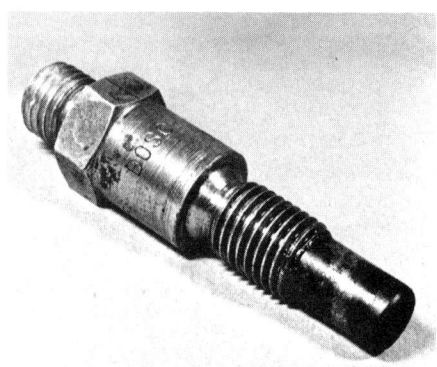

34.7b Bosch type fuel injection valve

3 Using a small mirror, check that the marks on the pump driven hub and the pump bearing cover are in alignment.
4 If the marks are out of alignment, the toothed belt will have to be removed as described in Section 32 and the camshaft drive sprocket slightly re-positioned. This can be done after releasing the three socket headed bolts which secure the camshaft sprocket.

32 Bosch fuel injection - pump drivebelt renewal

1 Set the crankshaft pulley 'FE' mark, as described in paragraphs 1 and 2 of the preceding Section.
2 Remove the left-hand heat exchanger.
3 Remove the left-hand engine front cover.
4 Release the injection pump mounting bolts and move the pump as far to the left as the elongated bolt holes will permit.
5 Slip the toothed belt from the camshaft drive sprocket and then detach it from the pump sprocket.
6 Install the new belt and then push the injection pump sideways until the belt tension is approximately ¼ in. (6.4 mm) at the centre of its run. Tighten the pump bolts.
7 Fit the cover plate and heat exchanger using a new gasket.
8 *On cars equipped with Sportomatic transmission,* before the injection pump belt can be removed, the transmission oil pressure pump must be removed and the connecting hoses detached from the pump.

33 Bosch fuel injection - fuel line filter renewal

1 The fuel filter assembly is located within the engine compartment.
2 To renew the disposable type filter element, disconnect the hose from the base of the filter and drain the fuel into a suitable container (photo).
3 Unscrew the filter body but before discarding it, unscrew the hose connecting union from it.
4 Screw the hose connector into the new filter using a new gasket.
5 Screw the new filter into position and connect the hose to it.

34 Bosch fuel injection pump - removal and refitting

1 Disconnect the lead from the battery negative terminal.
2 Remove the air filter assembly.
3 Align the 'FE' mark on the crankshaft pulley with the mark on the blower housing, as described in paragraphs 1 and 2, of Section 30.
4 Disconnect the leads from the micro-switch.
5 Disconnect the leads from the enrichment and shut-off solenoids (grey lead - enrichment, grey/red lead - shut off).
6 Loosen the warm air supply hose to the thermostat.
7 Disconnect the injector lines from the injection pump. The injection valves can be disconnected and removed if necessary by unscrewing them (photos).
8 Disconnect the fuel inlet line on the right-hand side of the injection pump.
9 Disconnect the fuel return line from the left-hand side of the injection pump.
10 Disconnect the oil inlet and return lines from the pump.
11 Disconnect the linkage between the guide shaft and the governor.
12 Release the injection pump mounting bolts and then push the toothed belt from the pump sprocket. Retain the belt with an elastic band to prevent it coming off the camshaft sprocket.
13 Remove the injection pump from its mounting taking care not to lift it by its barometric cell.
14 If a new pump is being installed, fill it with approximately 10 fl oz (300 cc) of engine oil injected through the oil return pipe connection (top hole).
15 Set the mark on the pump sprocket in alignment with the one on the pump bearing cover. Check that the crankshaft pulley alignment has not been disturbed and then install the pump leaving the mounting nuts finger-tight.
16 Engage the toothed belt with the pump sprocket. If the teeth on the sprocket do not mesh with those of the belt, the pump will have to be removed and the position of the sprocket slightly adjusted after loosening the socket headed bolts with an Allen key.
17 With the mounting nuts just tight enough to permit the pump to be

moved sideways stiffly, adjust the tension of the belt as described in Section 32, paragraph 6.

35 Bosch fuel injection - testing of control unit components

Enrichment solenoid
1 *On cars built up until 1970* an enrichment solenoid was incorporated in the fuel injection system. To test the solenoid, remove the rubber cap from the drive end of the injection pump and insert a bolt (M5 x 30) into the plunger control rack. Pull the control rack in the normal direction of travel and then release it. If it does not snap back to its normal position, then the injection pump should be renewed complete.
2 Disconnect the leads from the enrichment solenoid and connect a jump lead to fuse box terminal '15'. Observe the bolt which was fitted to the plunger control rack and touch the solenoid with the jump lead. The control rack should move in the driving direction. Failure to move will necessitate renewal of the solenoid. When installing a new solenoid, make sure that the length of the plunger is set to the same length as the original.

Fig. 2.44. Bosch fuel pump sprocket screw (Sec. 34)

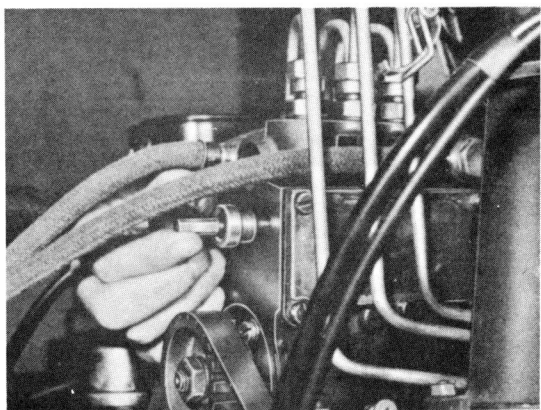

Fig. 2.45. Checking enrichment solenoid (Bosch fuel injection) (Sec. 35)

Fig. 2.46. Plunger setting diagram (Bosch fuel injection) (Sec. 35)

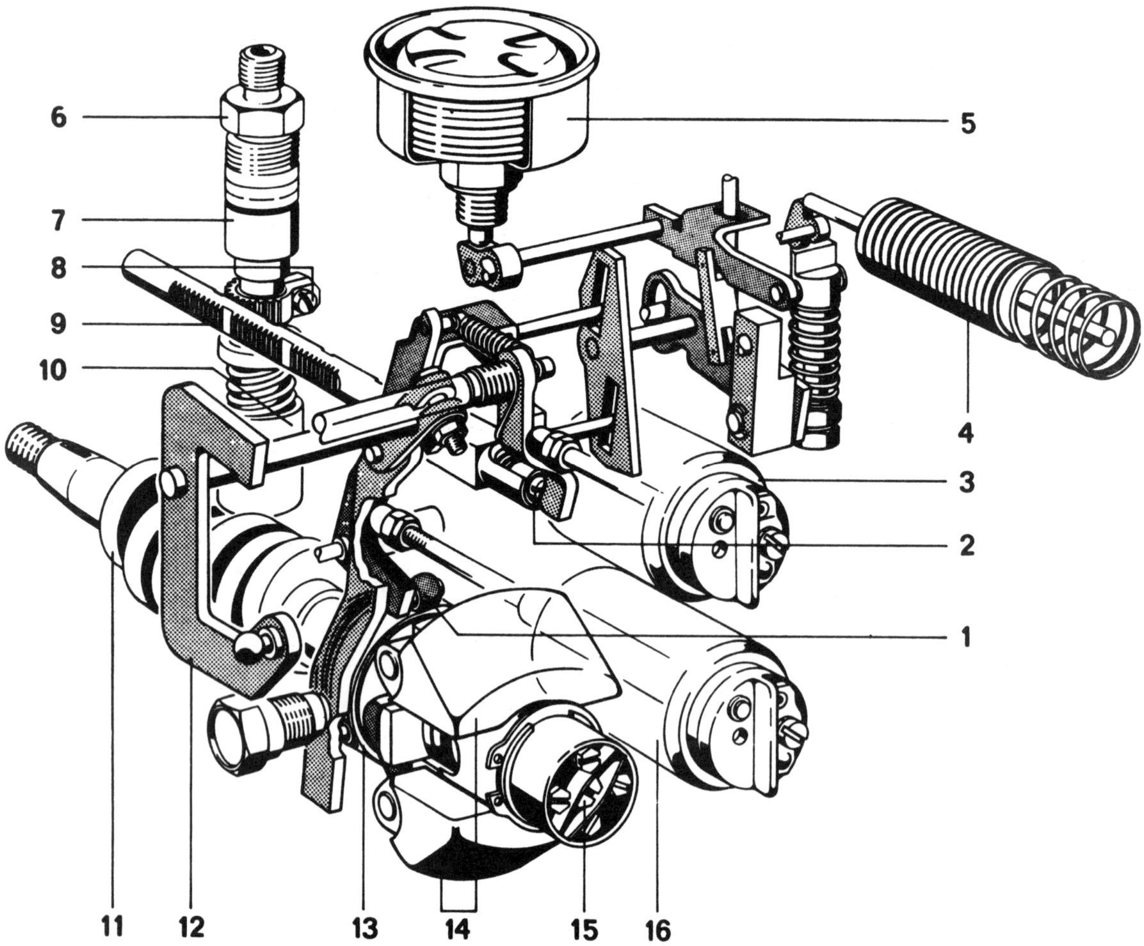

Fig. 2.47. Control unit components (Bosch fuel injection system) (Sec. 25)

1 Cam roller	5 Barometric cell	9 Control rack	13 Cam
2 Control rack head	6 Non-return valve	10 Roller tappet	14 Centrifugal governor
3 Enrichment solenoid	7 Plunger unit	11 Camshaft	15 Idle adjusting screw
4 Thermostat	8 Toothed segment	12 Governor control lever	16 Shut off solenoid

3   *On cars built after 1970,* as no enrichment solenoid is fitted, checking the movement of the control rack must be done by pushing the rack against its normal driving direction with a blunt tool. When the rack is released, it should snap back to its starting position. If it does not, or sticks, then the injection pump should be renewed.

Time limit relay (up to 1970)
4   To check this, connect a test lamp to the terminal on the enrichment solenoid and earth the other end of the test lamp lead.
5   Start the engine and observe if the lamp stays on for two seconds. If it does not, renew the relay.

Thermo-limit switch
6   This test can only be carried out in temperatures between −25°C and 2°C (−14° and 35°F).
7   Connect the test lamp to the terminal on the enrichment solenoid, start the engine and check that the test lamp stays on for more than two seconds. If it does not, renew the switch.

Shut-off solenoid
8   To test this solenoid, remove the rubber cap from the injection pump and insert a M5 x 30 bolt into the control rod.
9   Start the engine and run it at between 3000 and 4000 rev/min. Decelerate and observe the movement of the control rod. It should move towards the rear.
10 If the control rod does not move as specified, check the speed switch (paragraph 11) and the micro-switch adjustment (paragraph 14). If these switches are proved to be satisfactory, then the shut-off solenoid is faulty but renewal can only be carried out by your Porsche dealer.

Fig. 2.48. Testing speed switch (Bosch fuel injection) (Sec. 35)

Speed switch
11 Connect a test lamp between terminal '30b' of the switch and earth.
12 Start the engine and accelerate, when the test lamp should come on at about 1500 rev/min.
13 Now decelerate and the test lamp should go out at about 1300 rev/min. If the switch does not perform as stated, renew it.

Micro-switch

14 Connect a hot wire to the micro-switch lead connector.
15 Connect a test lamp from the micro-switch terminal to earth.
16 Turn on the ignition and actuate the micro-switch when the test lamp should go on. When the switch button is released, the lamp should go out.
17 The purpose of the micro-switch is to interrupt the fuel supply under over-running conditions. If adjustment is needed, release the locknut and adjuster screw.
18 With the engine idling, screw the adjuster screw down until the switch can just be heard to 'click'. Turn the screw a further ½ to ¾ turn and tighten the locknut.

36 K-Jetronic fuel injection system - description

1 This system which was first installed on cars destined for North America in January 1973 operates on the principle of measuring intake air flow in order that a precise quantity of fuel can be injected in relation to the volume of air being drawn into the engine.
2 Fuel is drawn from the fuel tank by an electrically operated pump, passed through an accumulator and a filter to the mixture control unit.
3 A pressure regulator maintains a constant pressure in the system.
4 From the mixture control unit, fuel lines carry the fuel to the injection nozzles and to a start (enrichment) valve.
5 System pressure is varied by two pressure regulators, one controlled by engine and outside temperatures and the other according to accelerator pedal movement.
6 The system varies slightly according to date of production.
7 Due to the complexity of the system and to the need for special tools and equipment, it is recommended that operations are limited to those described in the following Sections.

37 K-Jetronic fuel injection - slow-running adjustment

1 The procedure is very similar to that described for the Bosch system in Section 30 but synchronise the air intake pipes while the engine is idling at between 1600 and 2000 rev/min.
2 Where the fuel injection pump requires adjustment, the adjusting screw is accessible after removing the plastic cap from the air cooling upper shroud. (Fig. 2.51) Then insert a tool to depress the screw until the screw can be felt to engage in the slot in the centrifugal governor. Do not run the engine while the injection pump adjuster screw is being moved but swtich it off and re-start after having altered the position of the screw. On cars with an air pump (emission control), always disconnect the pressure hose at pump and plug it before checking CO level. (Fig. 2.52).

38 K-Jetronic fuel injection - adjustment and testing of components

Micro-switch

1 Disconnect the leads from the micro-switch.
2 Connect a buzzer between the contacts of the micro-switch.
3 Open the throttle and insert a feeler blade (0.80 in - 2 mm) between the idle stop screw and the throttle valve lever.
4 Now turn the micro-switch adjuster screw beyond the point where the buzzer goes off. (Fig. 2.53)
5 Unscrew the adjuster screw until the buzzer just actuates.
6 Remove the temporary feeler blade and check that the micro-switch arm has a free-movement of at least 0.02 in. (0.5 mm).
7 Check that the micro-switch is on when the hand throttle is fully open. If not, check the adjustment of the hand throttle (see Chapter 1).

Fig. 2.49. Engine fitted with K-jetronic fuel injection system (Sec. 36)

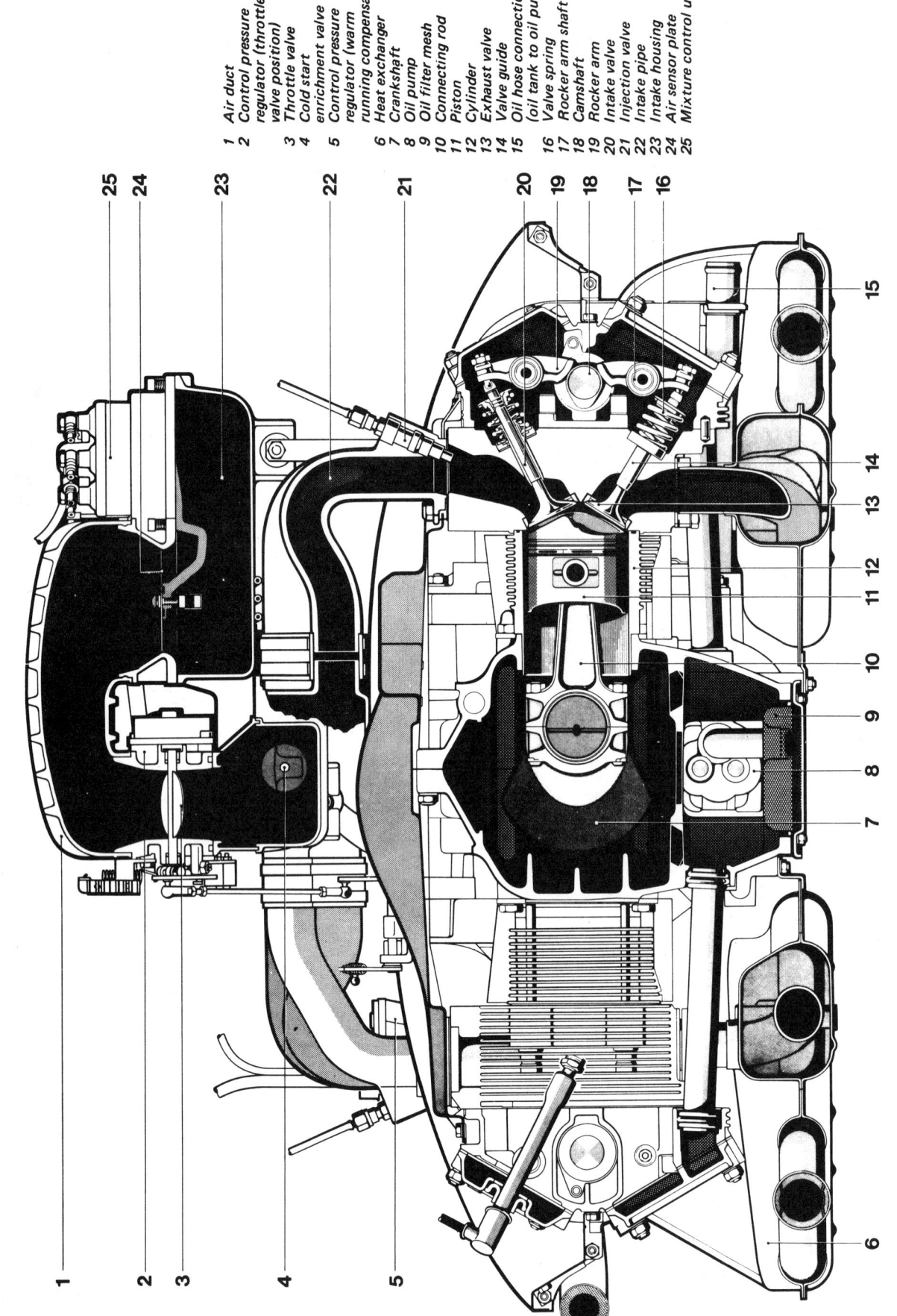

1 Air duct
2 Control pressure regulator (throttle valve position)
3 Throttle valve
4 Cold start enrichment valve
5 Control pressure regulator (warm running compensator)
6 Heat exchanger
7 Crankshaft
8 Oil pump
9 Oil filter mesh
10 Connecting rod
11 Piston
12 Cylinder
13 Exhaust valve
14 Valve guide
15 Oil hose connection (oil tank to oil pump)
16 Valve spring
17 Rocker arm shaft
18 Camshaft
19 Rocker arm
20 Intake valve
21 Injection valve
22 Intake pipe
23 Intake housing
24 Air sensor plate
25 Mixture control unit

Fig. 2.50. Cut-away view of K-jetronic fuel injection engine (1974 shown, slight difference on earlier versions)

Fig. 2.51. Centrifugal governor adjuster screw (K-jetronic fuel injection pump) (Sec. 37)

Fig. 2.52. Pressure hose connection to emission control air pump (Sec. 37)

Fig. 2.54. Auxiliary air device and connecting hose (K-jetronic fuel injection) (Sec. 38)

Auxiliary air device
11 Check and note the engine idling speed (rev/min).
12 Switch off the engine, remove the air cleaner and element with duct.
13 Disconnect the hose which leads to the auxiliary air device above the throttle valve at the throttle valve housing. Seal the connector and the hose.
14 Refit the duct, start the engine and note the idling speed. If the speed differs from that previously recorded, then the auxiliary air valve is probably leaking. This will be confirmed if it is found impossible to adjust the idling speed.
15 Renew the auxiliary air device

---

39 K-Jetronic fuel injection - removal and refitting of components

Regulator housing
1   Detach the air hose which runs between the left-hand heat exchanger and the regulator housing.
2   Remove the hose which runs between the regulator housing and the air cleaner intake.
3   Remove the three retaining bolts from the velocity stack and remove the regulator housing.
4   Refitting is a reversal of removal.

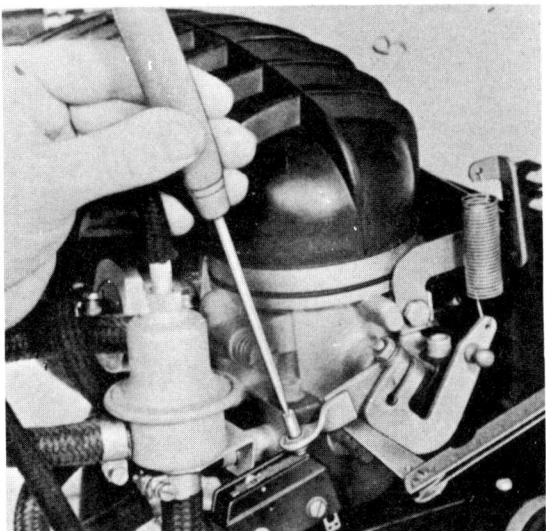

Fig. 2.53. Checking micro-switch adjustment (K-jetronic fuel injection pump) (Sec. 38)

Start valve
8   Remove the start (enrichment) valve as described in Section 39, leaving the fuel line attached to it.
9   Hold the start valve in a suitable container and connect it to the upper fuse in the engine fusebox, also to earth. Switch on the ignition momentarily. The valve should spray an even conical pattern of fuel.
10 Remove the temporary jumper leads and switch on the ignition. Wait ten seconds, wipe the nozzle of the valve dry and check that no fuel seeps out.

Mixture control unit
5   Disconnect all fuel lines from the mixture control unit.
6   Disconnect the fuel supply line from the fuel filter.
7   Unscrew and remove the socket-headed bolts and withdraw the mixture control unit and gasket.
8   When refitting the unit, fully tighten the bolts and then unscrew them one complete turn each.
9   Bleed the fuel system, as described in Section 40.

Throttle valve housing and control pressure regulator

10 Disconnect the fuel line which runs between the mixture control unit and the control pressure regulator (for the throttle valve position) (see Fig. 2.55)

11 Unscrew the four socket-headed screws and withdraw the throttle valve housing with control pressure regulator.

12 Before releasing the regulator from the throttle valve housing by withdrawing the two screws, mark the position of the regulator on the throttle valve housing.

13 If new components are installed, the control pressure regulator and the throttle valve position will have to be set by your Porsche dealer as special equipment is required. The regulator can be adjusted within the limits of its elongated bolt holes, lower pressure being obtained when it is moved in the forward direction of travel of the car.

Control pressure regulator (warm running compensator)

14 Disconnect the battery earth leads.

15 Disconnect the electrical leads from the regulator.

16 Disconnect the fuel hose from the regulator.

17 Remove the socket-headed securing bolts.

18 Disconnect the fuel line which runs between the mixture control unit and the regulator.

19 Refitting is a reversal of removal but bleed the fuel line system on completion.

Start (enrichment) valve

20 Disconnect the battery earth leads.

21 Remove the auxiliary air device from the throttle valve housing (see Fig. 2.54).

Fig. 2.55. Mixture control unit (K-jetronic fuel injection): control pressure regulator (throttle position) fuel line - arrowed (Sec. 39)

Fig. 2.56. Throttle valve housing screws (arrowed) on K-jetronic fuel injection (Sec. 39)

Fig. 2.57. Control pressure regulator (throttle position) securing screws - K-jetronic fuel injection (Sec. 39)

Fig. 2.58. Control pressure regulator (warm running compensator) attachments and connections - K-jetronic fuel injection (Sec. 39)

Fig. 2.59. Start valve and connection (K-jetronic fuel injection) (Sec. 39)

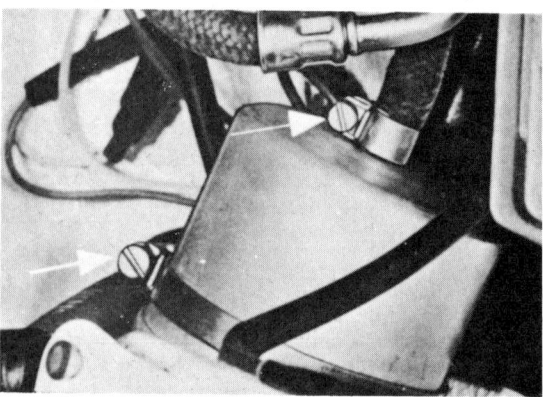

Fig. 2.60. Fuel filter (K-jetronic fuel injection) (Sec. 39)

22 Pull out the electrical connector plug from the start valve.
23 Remove the socket-headed securing bolts.
24 Disconnect the fuel line from the valve.
25 Refitting is a reversal of removal but make sure that the 'O' ring is properly positioned and that the connector plug is uppermost.
26 Bleed the fuel line system on completion (Section 40).

Fuel filter
27 Disconnect the battery earth leads.
28 Unscrew the fuel line coupling nut.
29 Disconnect the fuel hose from the filter and then disconnect the filter clamp.
30 Fit the new filter and bleed the fuel system on completion (Section 40).

Fuel pressure accumulator
31 Disconnect the fuel lines and plug them.
32 Remove the securing clamp.
33 Fit the fuel pressure accumulator by reversing the removal procedure. Bleed the fuel system on completion (Section 40).

Injection valve
34 Disconnect the fuel line from the injection valve by unscrewing the union nut.
35 The valve will need a sharp jerk to remove it and the best way to do this is to use an old union coupling nut to which is attached a length of cable.
36 Prise out the rubber bush from the support sleeve.
37 When refitting, make sure that the rubber bush is fully seated

below the bulge in the support sleeve.
38 Bleed the fuel system on completion (Section 40).

Vacuum controlled warm up regulator
39 Disconnect the battery and the warm intake air connection.
40 Release the fuel system pressure by slackening the warm up regulator pressure line connection at the mixture control unit.
41 Remove the air pump air filter.
42 Remove the left-hand and right-hand heater hoses.
43 Loosen the clamp at the heater blower and swing the heater blower upwards.
44 Disconnect all the hoses and fuel lines from the regulator and then unbolt the regulator and remove it.
45 Refitting is a reversal of removal but make sure that the base of the regulator and the mounting plate are absolutely clean.

---

40 K-Jetronic fuel system - bleeding

1 The fuel line system must be bled whenever any component has been disconnected and subsequently refitted.
2 Remove the air intake assembly with filter element.
3 **Switch on the ignition.**
4 Press the diaphragm lever of the airflow sensor upwards to its

Fig. 2 61. Fuel pressure accumulator (K-jetronic fuel injection) (Sec. 39)

Fig. 2.62. Removing an injector (K-jetronic fuel injection) (Sec. 39)

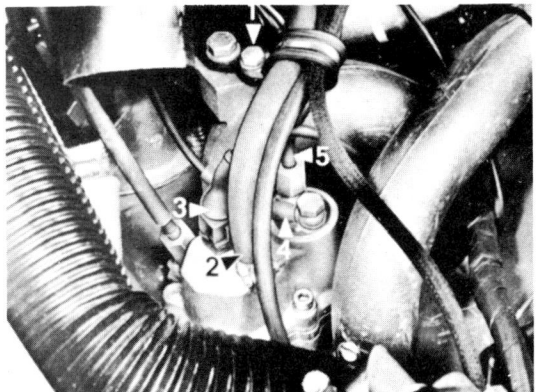

Fig. 2.63. Vacuum controlled warm-up regulator (K-Jetronic fuel injection (Sec. 39)

1 Securing clamp	3 Connector plug	5 Fuel feed line
2 Vacuum hose	4 Fuel return line	

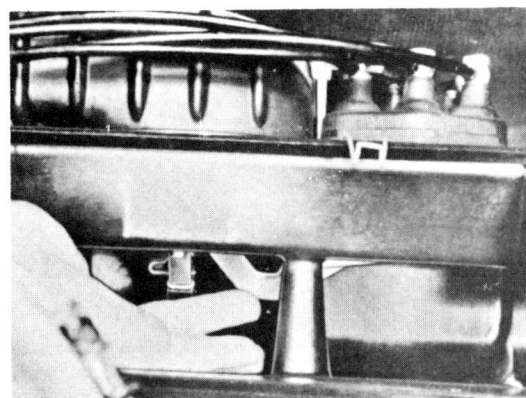

Fig. 2.64. Depressing airflow sensor lever to bleed K-Jetronic fuel lines (Sec. 40)

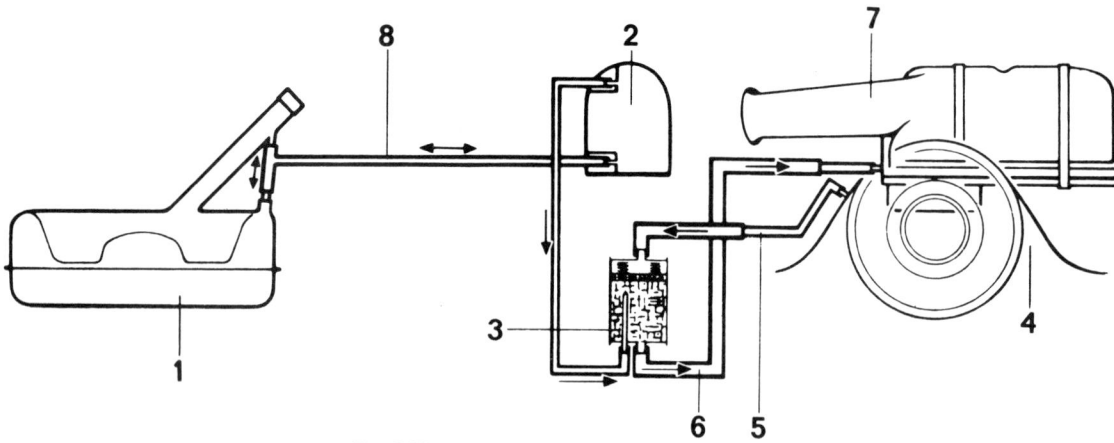

Fig. 2.65. Diagram of fuel evaporative control system (Sec 41)

1 *Fuel tank*
2 *Expansion chamber*
3 *Charcoal filter*
4 *Cooling fan upper shroud*

5 *Hose from cooling fan to charcoal filter*
6 *Hose from charcoal filter to engine air cleaner*

7 *Air cleaner*
8 *Fuel tank to expansion chamber return hose*

stop and hold it up for a maximum of 5 seconds or until the injection valves can be heard to spray fuel.

5   Release the lever, switch off the ignition and refit the air intake assembly.

41 Fuel evaporative control system

1   This system, which is fitted to all cars destined for operation in North America, stores the vapour from the fuel tank in a charcoal canister mounted within the luggage boot.

2   When the engine is running, the vapour is drawn into the engine air intake and having mixed with air, it is burned during the normal combustion processes.

3   Maintenance consists of keeping the connecting hose unions tight. The carbon filter (charcoal canister) only requires renewing after very high mileages (50,000 miles - 80,000 km).

42 Emission control system - description

1   On later cars, particularly those destined for operation in North America, an exhaust emission control system is fitted, its purpose being to reduce the emission of noxious fumes from the exhaust system (Figs. 2.67 and 2.68).

2   One of two systems may be fitted according to model. Either an *exhaust gas recirculation system* which recycles the exhaust gases by returning them to the combustion chambers where they reduce the combustion temperature and so minimise the volume of pollutant gases ejected, or an *air injection system*. The latter is a method of injecting clean air to the exhaust parts in order to dilute the combustion gases before they are emitted from the exhaust pipe. The air supply is taken from a separate air filter, compressed by an air pump which is driven by a bolt from a pulley attached to the engine cooling blower fan hub.

3   Some models are equipped with a throttle valve compensator to hold the throttle slightly open during periods of deceleration (a period when emission of unburned fuel vapour is at its greatest concentration).

43 Air pump drivebelt - tensioning

1   Release the adjuster link bolt and prise the air pump away from

Fig. 2.66. Adjusting air pump drive belt tension (Sec. 43)

the engine until there is a total deflection of about 5/8 in (15 mm) at the centre of the belt. Retighten the link bolt.

44 Air injection system - inspection and testing

1   Check the drivebelt tension, the pump air filter (renew if clogged) and the security of the connecting hoses.

2   Disconnect the air injection hose from the air pump. Plug the open end of the hose (See Fig. 2.52).

3   With the engine at normal operating temperature, check the CO level with a suitable meter. This should be between 1.5 and 2% at an idling speed of between 850 and 950 rev/min.

4   Now reconnect the hose to the air pump and with the engine still idling, the CO level should drop below 1%. If the level is above that specified, there is a leak or fault in the system.

45 Exhaust gas recirculation (EGR) system - inspection

1   Set a cold engine to run at a slightly higher idling speed than normal and then start the engine.

2   The outlet pipe between the EGR filter and the EGR valve will now heat up. (Fig. 2.69)

3   Increase the engine speed to about 4,000 rev/min. The outlet pipe from the EGR valve to the intake housing should now be hot as well. If it is not, one of the following faults may be the cause:

Defective EGR valve
Choked EGR lines
Choked vacuum bores in throttle valve housing
Leaking or choked vacuum hoses
Filter between silencer and EGR valve choked

1 EGR filter
2 Nut
3 Bolt
4 Screw
5 Clamp
6 Silencer
7 Gasket
8 Nut
9 Bolt
10 Heat exchanger
11 Gasket
12 Nut
13 Washer
14 Reactor
15 Seal
16 Nut
17 Bolt
18 Heat exchanger
19 Gasket
20 Nut
21 Washer
22 Reactor
23 Seal
24 Nut
25 Washer
26 Bolt
27 Vacuum hoses
28 Vacuum hoses
29 EGR connecting pipe
30 Nut
31 Washer
32 Bolts
33 Bolts
34 EGR valve
35 Gasket
36 EGR connecting pipe

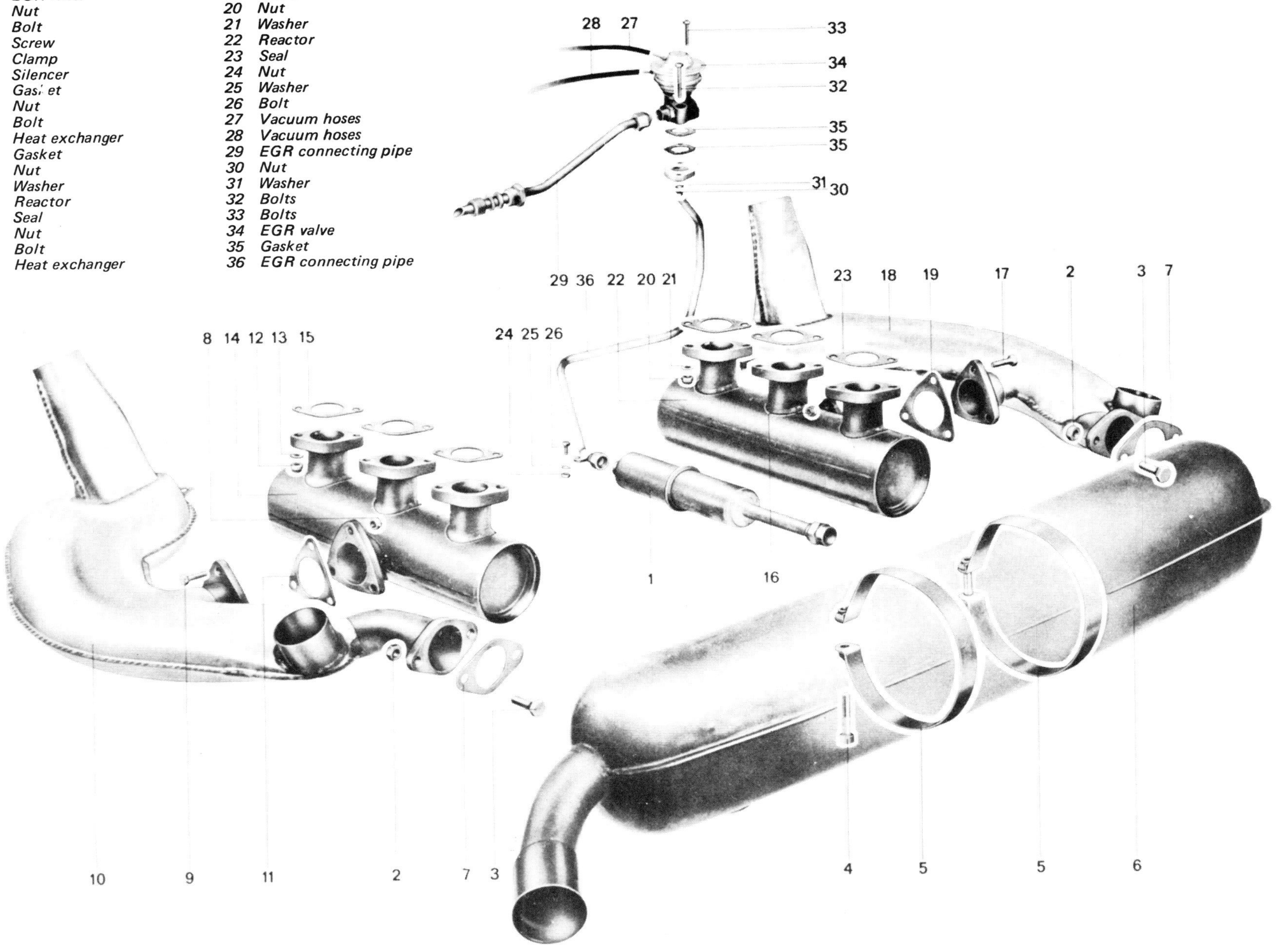

Fig. 2.67. Exhaust system and exhaust gas recirculation (EGR) components (Secs 42 and 50) (See also Fig. 2.74.)

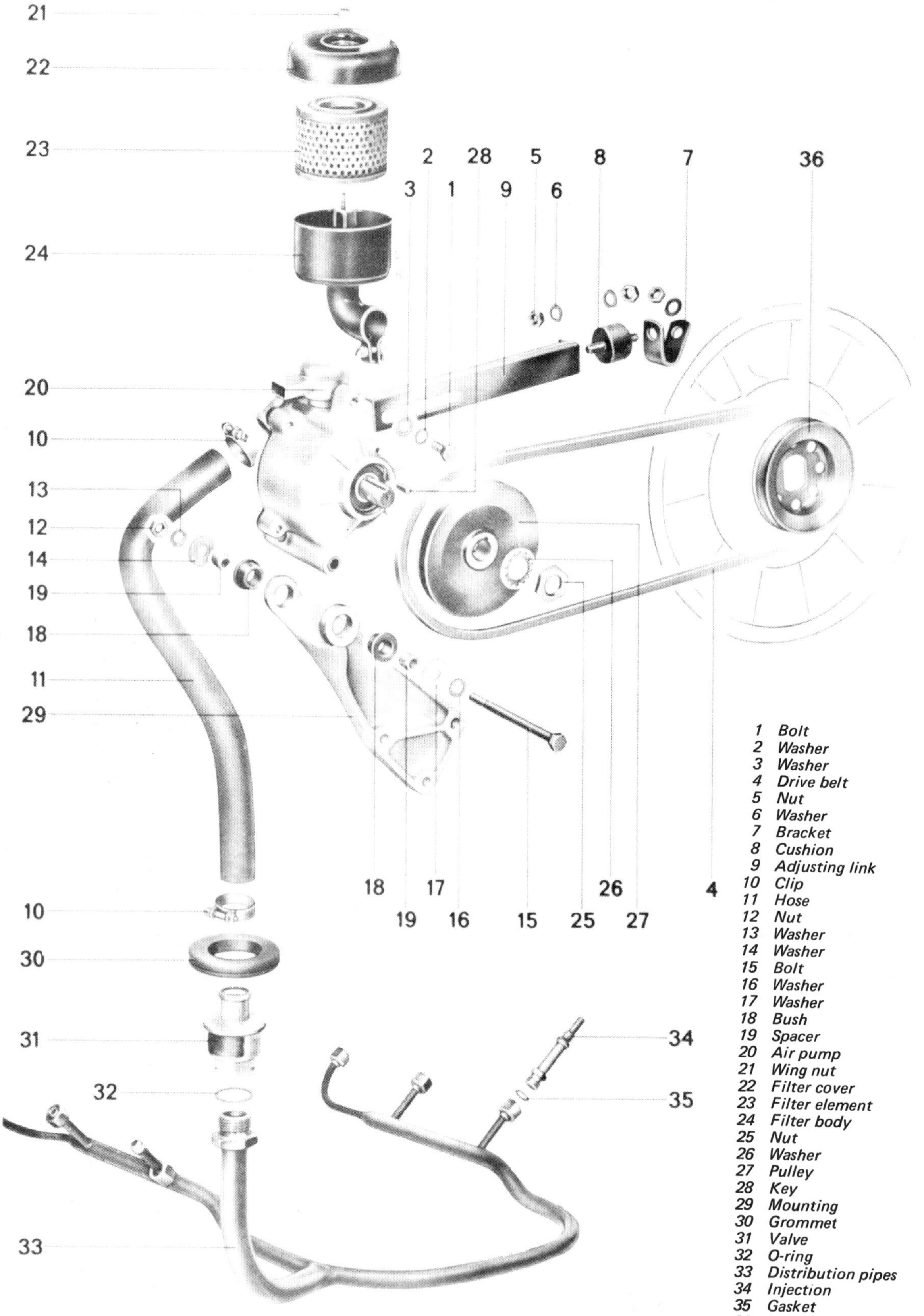

21
22
23
24
20
10
13
12
14
19
18
11
29
10
30
31
32
33

3 2 28 5 8 7 36
   1 9 6

18 17   26   4
  19 16 15 25 27

34
35

1   Bolt
2   Washer
3   Washer
4   Drive belt
5   Nut
6   Washer
7   Bracket
8   Cushion
9   Adjusting link
10 Clip
11 Hose
12 Nut
13 Washer
14 Washer
15 Bolt
16 Washer
17 Washer
18 Bush
19 Spacer
20 Air pump
21 Wing nut
22 Filter cover
23 Filter element
24 Filter body
25 Nut
26 Washer
27 Pulley
28 Key
29 Mounting
30 Grommet
31 Valve
32 O-ring
33 Distribution pipes
34 Injection
35 Gasket
36 Pulley

Fig. 2.68. Air injection system components (Sec. 42)

46 EGR valve - removal and installation

1   The EGR valve should be renewed at 30,000 mile (48,000 km) intervals.
2   Disconnect the vacuum hoses from the valve, marking them carefully for exact replacement.
3   Disconnect the outlet pipes from the valve.
4   Unscrew the mounting bolts and lift the valve away.
5   Installation is a reversal of removal, use new gaskets.

47 Throttle compensator - adjustment

1   To adjust this device on earlier engines, disconnect the lead from the insulated terminal on the compensator.
2   Connect battery power to this terminal so that the solenoid valve is actuated.
3   Start the engine and open the throttle to give an engine speed of between 3,000 and 4,000 rev/min. Let the throttle close slowly when the engine speed should reduce to between 1,250 and 1,300 rev/min. If the speed does not reduce to the level indicated, adjust the compensator link rod and repeat the operation.
4   Re-make the original connections, raise the engine speed to between 3,000 and 4,000 rev/min, release the throttle and check that the idle speed is now reduced to between 850 and 950 rev/min.

48 Throttle hand control

1   Adjustment of this device is described in Chapter 1, Sections 49 and 50.

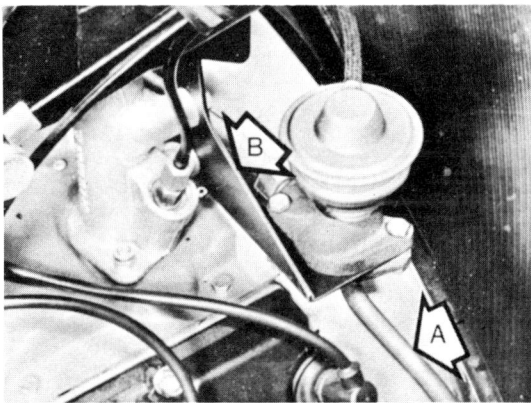

Fig. 2.69. EGR valve outlet pipe (filter to valve):A
EGR valve outlet pipe (valve to intake housing): B
(Sec. 45)

Fig. 2.70. Throttle valve compensator (Sec. 47)

49 Accelerator pedal - adjustment and removal

1   The accelerator pedal cross-shaft runs in two bushes which are mounted in the support bracket for the clutch and brake pedals. (photo). (Figs. 2.72 and 2.73)
2   Adjustment of the accelerator pedal should be carried out so that when the pedal is fully depressed, there is a clearance between the throttle valve lever at its stop of at least 0.04 in (1 mm). Depression of the pedal is controlled by a stop bolt which is adjustable.
3   The accelerator pedal can be removed independently of the other two pedals but if the support bracket must be withdrawn or the other pedals removed, note that two of the studs are attached to the brake master cylinder. There is no need to remove the brake master cylinder or disconnect the hydraulic lines when removing the pedal support bracket.

50 Exhaust system and manifolds

1   The exhaust, manifold and heat exchanger assemblies vary in design between models.
2   With the rear location of the engine, the exhaust system is compact and less difficult to service than systems which run the complete length of the car.
3   As shown in Fig. 2.74, short sections are removable for renewal when corrosion or damage has occurred.
4   When installing, always use new flange gaskets and check the condition of the supports and mountings.

49.1 Control pedal assembly

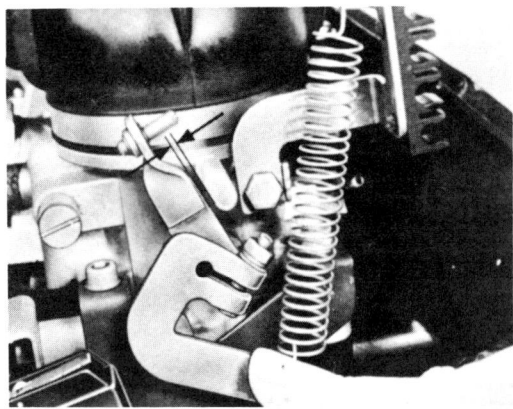

Fig. 2.71. Throttle valve clearance diagram (Sec. 49)

Fig, 2.72. Control pedal arrangement (up to 1974) (Sec. 49)

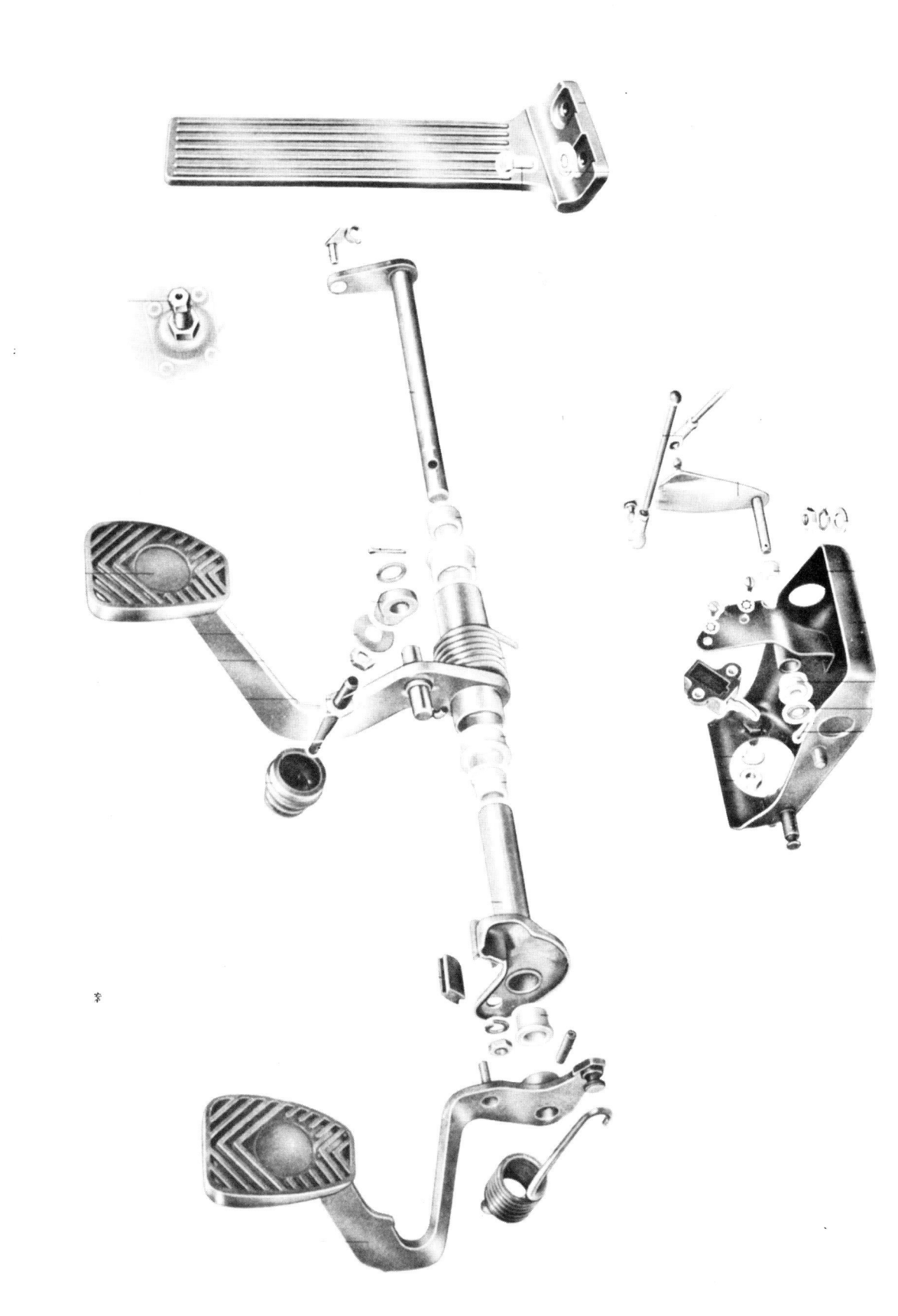

Fig. 2.73. Control pedal arrangement (1974 on) (Sec. 49)

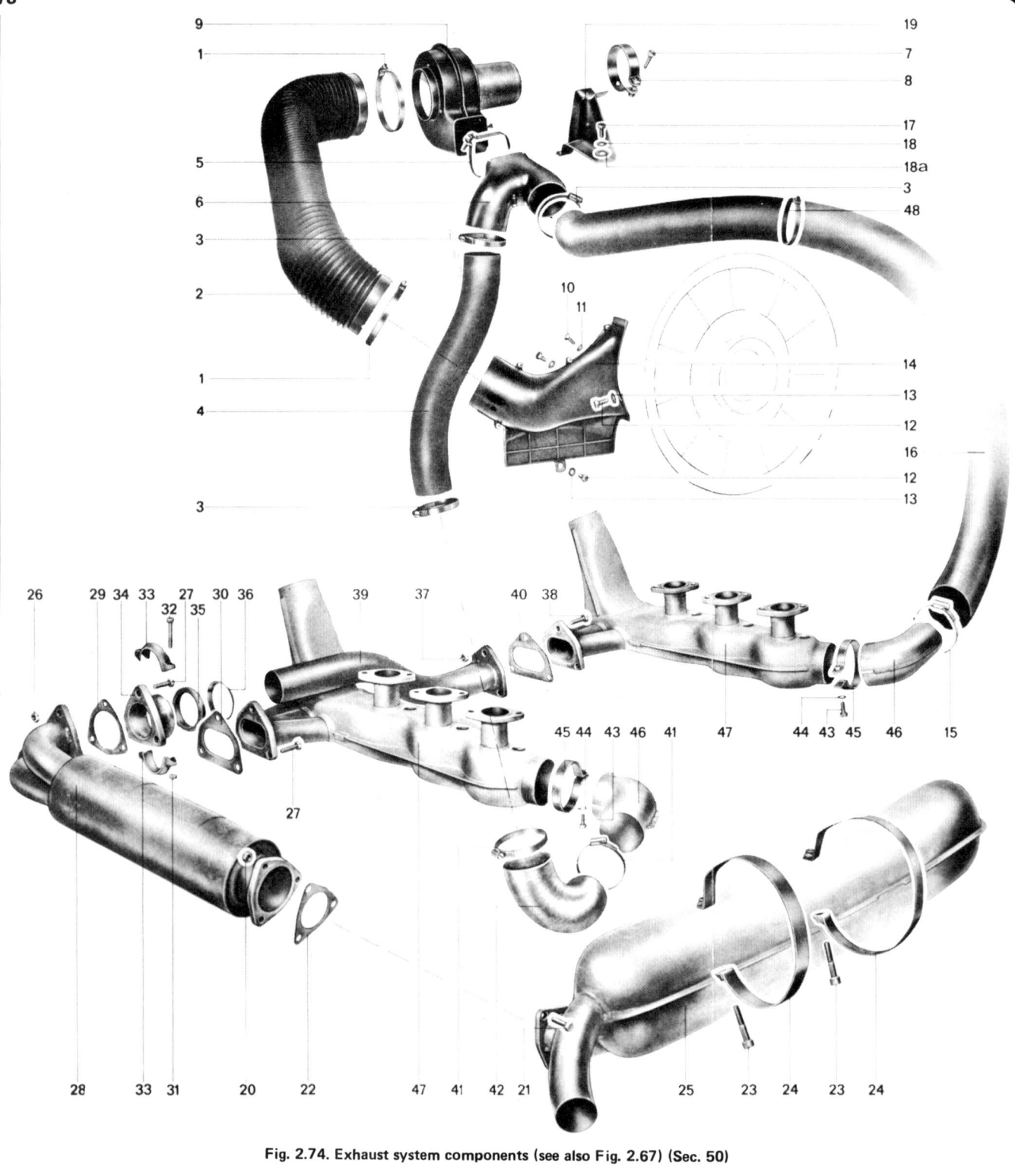

Fig. 2.74. Exhaust system components (see also Fig. 2.67) (Sec. 50)

1	Hose clip	13	Washer	24	Clamp	36	Collar
2	Hose	14	Heater air deflector	25	Silencer (secondary)	37	Nut
3	Hose clip	15	Hose clip	26	Nut	38	Bolt
4	Heater hose	16	Heater hose	27	Bolt	39	Adaptor pipe
5	Clamp	17	Bolt	28	Silencer (secondary)	40	Gasket
6	Adaptor	18	Lockwasher	29	Gaskets	41	Hose clip
7	Screw	18a	Washer	30	Gaskets	42	Flexible hose
8	Clip	19	Support bracket	31	Nut	43	Screw
9	Blower	20	Nut	32	Bolt	44	Washer
10	Self-tapping screw	21	Bolt	33	Clamp	45	Clamp
11	Washer	22	Gasket	34	Flange	46	Adaptor
12	Bolt	23	Screw	35	Seal	47	Heat exchanger

51 Fault diagnosis - fuel system

Symptom	Reason/s

Carburettors

Fuel consumption excessive	Air cleaner choked and dirty giving rich mixture.
	Fuel leaking from carburettors, fuel pumps, or fuel lines.
	Float chambers flooding.
	Generally worn carburettor.
	Distributor condenser faulty.
	Balance weights or vacuum advance mechanism in distributor faulty.
	Carburettors incorrectly adjusted, mixture too rich.
	Idling speed too high
	Contact breaker gap incorrect.
	Valve clearances incorrect.
	Incorrectly set spark plugs.
	Tyres under-inflated.
	Wrong spark plugs fitted.
	Brakes dragging.
	Emission control system faulty.
Insufficient fuel delivery or weak mixture due to air leaks	Partially clogged filters in pump and carburettors.
	Incorrectly seating valves in fuel pump.
	Fuel pump diaphragm leaking or damaged.
	Gasket in fuel pump damaged.
	Fuel pump valves sticking due to fuel gumming.
	Too little fuel in fuel tank (prevalent when climbing steep hills).
	Union joints on pipe connections loose
	Split in fuel pipe on suction side of fuel pump.
	Inlet manifold to block or inlet manifold to carburettor gaskets leaking.
	Fuel tank relief valve stuck closed.

Fuel injection system

Difficult starting from cold	Faulty enrichment solenoid.
	Defective starting relay.
	Faulty thermo-limit switch
	Time control switch defective
	Control rod stuck, not releasing rack.
Rough idling	Incorrectly adjusted idle air control.
	Incorrect ignition timing
	Defective injection pump thermostat.
	Defective injection valves.
	Cold start device not shutting off.
Engine will not start at all	Faulty fuel delivery pump.
	Starter relay defective.
	Defective thermo-time switch.
	Control rack stuck.
	Time limit relay switch defective.
Engine misfires	Choked fuel filter.
	Ignition incorrectly adjusted.
	Faulty injection valves.
	Injection pump out of adjustment.
Backfiring during overrun	Throttle valve housing not synchronised.
	Micro-switch incorrectly adjusted.
	Rev/min. transducer defective.

Chapter 3 Ignition system

Contents

Specifications

System type

Pre-1969 models	Conventional coil and distributor
1969 models onwards	Capacitive discharge system (CDS)

Distributor type ... ...   Bosch or Marelli according to model and year of manufacture

Firing order 1, 6, 2, 4, 3, 5

Cylinder numbering from rear of car ... ...   1, 2, 3, — left bank   4, 5, 6 — right bank

Dwell angle (conventional system) ... ... $40 \pm 3^{\circ}$

Distributor points gap (conventional system) ... ...   0.016 in (0.4 mm)

Dwell angle (CDS)

Bosch distributor	$38 \pm 3^{\circ}$
Marelli distributor (pre-1973)	$40 \pm 3^{\circ}$
Marelli distributor (1973 onwards)	$37 \pm 3^{\circ}$

Distributor points gap (CDS)

Bosch distributor	0.012 in (0.3 mm)
Marelli distributor (pre-1973)	0.016 in (0.4 mm)
Marelli distributor (1973 onwards)	0.014 in (0.35 mm)

Ignition timing (static/dynamic*)

911 911L (pre-1968 models)	TDC/30° BTDC at 6000 rpm
911T (pre-1968 models)	TDC/35° BTDC at 6000 rpm
911S and performance tuned version (pre-1968 models)	5° BTDC/30° BTDC at 6000 rpm
911S (1968 models)	5° BTDC/31° BTDC at 6000 rpm
911T, 911L (1968 models)	TDC/35° BTDC at 6000 rpm
911E, 911S (1969 models)	— /30° BTDC at 6000 rpm
911T (1969 models)	— /35° BTDC at 6000 rpm
911T (1970/71 models)	— /35° BTDC at 6000 rpm
911E, 911S (1970/71 models)	— /30° BTDC at 6000 rpm
911TV, 911T USA, 911E, 911S, (1972 models onwards)	— /5° ATDC at 900 ± 50 rpm/32 to 38° BTDC at 6000 rpm
Carrera 2.7	— /TDC at 900 ± 50 rpm

*Note: All ignition timing check at 6000 rpm are with the vacuum line disconnected (where applicable)

Ignition timing marks ... ...   On crankshaft pulley and blower housing

Spark plugs**/gaps

911 (pre-1969 models)	Bosch W250P21	0.014 in/0.35 mm
911T (pre-1967 models)	Bosch W250P21	0.014 in/0.35 mm
911S and performance tuned version (pre-1967 models)	Bosch W265P21	0.014 in/0.35 mm
911S (1967/68 models)	Bosch W265P21	0.014 in/0.35 mm
	Bosch WG265T2SP	0.016 in/0.40 mm
	Bern 260/14/3S	0.020 in/0.50 mm
911T (1967/68 models)	Bern 240/14/3	0.024 in/0.60 mm
	Bosch W230T30	0.024 in/0.60 mm

911L (1967 models)	...	...	...	...	...	...	...	Bosch W250P21	0.014 in/0.35 mm	
								Bosch WG265T2SP	0.016 in/0.40 mm	
								Bern 260/14/3S	0.020 in/0.50 mm	
								Champion N6Y	0.022 in/0.55 mm	
911T (1969 models)	...	...	...	...	...	...	...	Bosch W230T30	0.024 in/0.60 mm	
								Bern 240/14/3	0.024 in/0.60 mm	
911E, 911S (1969 models)	...	...	...	...	...	...	...	Bosch W265P21	0.014 in/0.35 mm	
								Bosch W265T2SP	0.014 in/0.35 mm	
911T (1970/71 models)	...	...	...	...	...	...	...	Bern 240/14/3	0.024 in/0.60 mm	
								Bern 250/14/3P	0.024 in/0.60 mm	
								Bosch W230T30	0.024 in/0.60 mm	
								Bosch W250P21	0.024 in/0.60 mm	
911E, 911S (1970/71 models)	...	...	...	...	...	...	...	Bern 265/14/3P	0.024 in/0.60 mm	
								Bosch W265P21	0.024 in/0.60 mm	
911TV (1972/73 models)	...	...	...	...	...	...	...	Bosch W230T30	0.024 in/o.60 mm	
								Bern 225/14/3	0.024 in/0.60 mm	
911T USA (1972/73 models)	...	...	...	...	...	...	...	Bosch W235P21	0.020 to 0.024 in/0.50 to 0.60 mm	
911E, 911S (1972/73 models)	...	...	...	...	...	...	...	Bosch W265P21	0.020 to 0.024 in/0.50 to 0.60 mm	
								Bern 265/14/3P	0.020 to 0.024 in/0.50 to 0.60 mm	
Carrera 2.7 (1972 models onwards)	...	...	...	...	...	...		Bosch W265P21	0.022 in/0.55 mm	
								Bosch W260T2	0.028 in/0.70 mm	
								Bern 265/14/3P	0.022 in/0.55 mm	
								Bern 260/14/3	0.028 in/0.70 mm	
911 (1974/75 models)	...	...	...	...	...	...	...	Bosch W215T30	0.028 in/0.70 mm	
								Bern D215/14/3A	0.028 in/0.70 mm	
911S (1974/75 models)	...	...	...	...	...	...	...	Bosch W225T30	0.028 in/0.70 mm	
								Bern 255/14/3A	0.028 in/0.70 mm	

Note: *The spark plugs are generally as specified for European models; it is recommended that the advice of a Porsche dealer or spark plug manufacturer should be sought to ensure that the latest approved type is used for any particular vehicle.*

Torque wrench settings

									lbf ft	kgf m
Spark plugs	...	...	...	...	...	...	...	...	18 to 22	2.5 to 3

1 General description

1   The ignition system used on pre-1969 models is of conventional ignition coil and battery type. For 1969 models onwards, a capacitor discharge ignition system (CDS) was introduced for improved spark characteristics. All models use a distributor with a speed limiting rotor to prevent the engine speed exceeding a pre-determined limit.

Conventional ignition system

2   This system comprises the ignition switch, ignition coil, the distributor (which is driven at half engine speed) and spark plugs. The basic operation of the system can be summarised as follows:

For simplicity let us consider the system to be divided into two separate halves, the low tension (LT) and the high tension (HT). The LT side comprises the primary winding of the ignition coil, the ignition switch, the contact breaker, the condenser and the associated wiring to make the connections to and from the battery. The HT side is made up of the secondary winding of the ignition coil, the distributor cap and rotor, the spark plugs and their connecting leads.

As the distributor cam rotates, the contacts will be closed for a period of time. During this time, current will flow in the primary winding of the coil (which is only a transformer anyway) but due to its self inductance, which opposes current flow, a magnetic field is not set up immediately; hence there is no secondary induced voltage worth considering. As the cam rotates further, the contacts will open and at this instant of time a spark will try to jump the contact gap as the magnetic field in the coil rapidly collapses and current starts to flow again. This spark is absorbed by the condenser which then rapidly discharges back through the primary coil winding and speeds the collapse of the field.

At the time when the contacts opened, the distributor rotor had turned to a position which effectively connected the secondary winding of the coil to a particular spark plug, and since there is now a continuous secondary circuit, the decaying magnetic field induces a voltage in the secondary coil winding. This voltage is in the order of 15000 to 18000 volts and is sufficient to enable a spark to jump across the spark plug electrode gap. The distributor contacts will now close again as the cam rotates further and the cycle is repeated for the next spark plug.

Now that we have looked at some of the fundamental points of the ignition circuit we need to consider some of the refinements that are

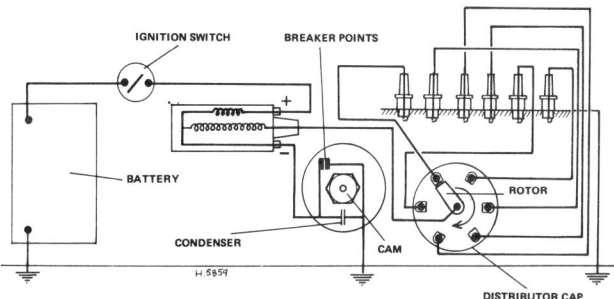

Fig. 3.1. Conventional ignition system - theoretical (Sec. 1)

required for correct timing under all conditions. For efficient combustion of the petrol/air mixture a spark is required just before the piston reached top-dead-centre (TDC), since there is a time lag between the spark occurring and development of the full force of the mixture burning. Unfortunately, this time lag varies with engine speed and load, so two devices are used to alter the timing of the spark. These are the centrifugal advance and retard mechanism which advances the point of ignition as engine speed increases, and the vacuum advance and retard which depends on the inlet manifold depression (or suction) for its operation. Where there is a relatively low depression, for example hill climbing with a wide throttle opening, the mechanism will rotate the contact assembly in the distributor in the direction of cam rotation, thus delaying or retarding the spark. Conversely, with a car cruising at a moderately fast speed on level surfaces there will be an increase in manifold depression and a tendency for a more advanced spark.
Note: The vacuum advance and retard is not applicable to all models.

A series resistor is added in the primary circuit of the ignition coil to limit the current flow and internal heat generated. This resistor is by-passed during the starting sequence in order to produce a bigger magnetic field and spark when it is most needed.

Capacitor discharge system (CDS)

3   Although adequate for most needs, the system described in Section 2 does have shortcomings, particularly where there are high engine crankshaft speeds; for this reason the CDS ignition circuit is used. This has the advantage of a higher HT voltage (20000 to 25000 volts) which

does not vary with engine speed, a larger permissible spark plug electrode gap which gives a more intensive spark, no sparking at the contact breaker points, a more precisely timed spark and due to its lower dynamic internal resistance, is less sensitive to any leakage resistance at the spark plug.

The princliple of operation is that a condenser within the CDS unit is charged to between 350 and 400 volts. When the distributor contacts open, the trigger unit fires a thyristor (a semi-conductor device which can loosely be described as a gate or switch), which in turn causes the capacitor to discharge via the primary winding of the ignition transformer (coil). A voltage is induced in the secondary winding and a spark is produced at the plug electrodes. The centrifugal advance and retard mechanism is retained, but there is no necessity for a condenser connected across the contact breaker points since this part of the circuit no longer switches the highly inductive coil primary voltage. The vacuum advance and retard mechanism is used on certain models. **Note:** In this ignition system there is a danger of severe electric shock from terminal 'A' of the CDS unit.

Care should therefore be taken, particularly when removing the ignition coil or CDS unit. The system should never be operated with the ignition coil disconnected or open-circuit, or where the storage capacitor is known to be defective.

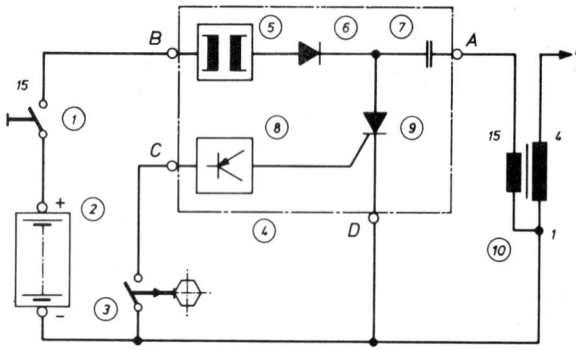

Fig. 3.2. CDS ignition circuit (Sec. 1)

1	Ignition switch	6	Rectifier
2	Battery	7	Capacitor
3	Contact breaker points	8	Trigger unit (electronic)
4	CDS unit	9	Thyristor
5	DC amplifier	10	Ignition voltage transformer (coil)

2 Contact breaker points - removal, cleaning and installation

Bosch distributor
1 Spring back the retaining clips and remove the distributor cap.
2 Remove the retaining screws and take off the rotor.
3 Loosen the nut of the screw which secures the leaf spring of the breaker arm.
4 Remove the lock ring from the breaker arm pivot stud, then pull the breaker arm out.
5 Remove the retaining screw from the fixed contact support then take the support out.
6 If the points are pitted they may be cleaned on a fine oilstone but if this has been done on a previous occasion it is preferable to obtain a new contact set. When refacing the points care should be taken so that when re-installed they will be flat and parallel, or very slightly domed.
7 Wipe the contact faces clean with a petrol moistened cloth, then install them by reversing the removal procedure. Adjustment of the points gap is given in the following Section.

Marelli distributor
8 Remove the distributor, as described in Section 4.
9 Remove the retaining screw(s) and take off the rotor.
10 Remove the securing screw(s) and take out the breaker point arm and stationary plate.
11 Refer to paragraphs 6 and 7.

3 Contact breaker points/dwell angle - adjustment

Bosch distributor - points gap
1 Remove the distributor cap and rotor as described in the previous Section.
2 Turn the crankshaft at the pulley until one lobe of the cam fully opens the contact breaker points.
3 Using a feeler gauge of the specified size, check the points gap. If correct, the gauge should be a firm sliding fit. If the points are pitted, they should either be cleaned or renewed (see previous Section) (photo).
4 If adjustment is required, loosen the screw in the fixed contact support and adjust the contacts as necessary. Tighten the screw and recheck the gap.
5 Fit the distributor rotor and cap, referring to the previous Section, if necessary. On completion, refer to paragraph 8, then check the ignition timing (Section 5).

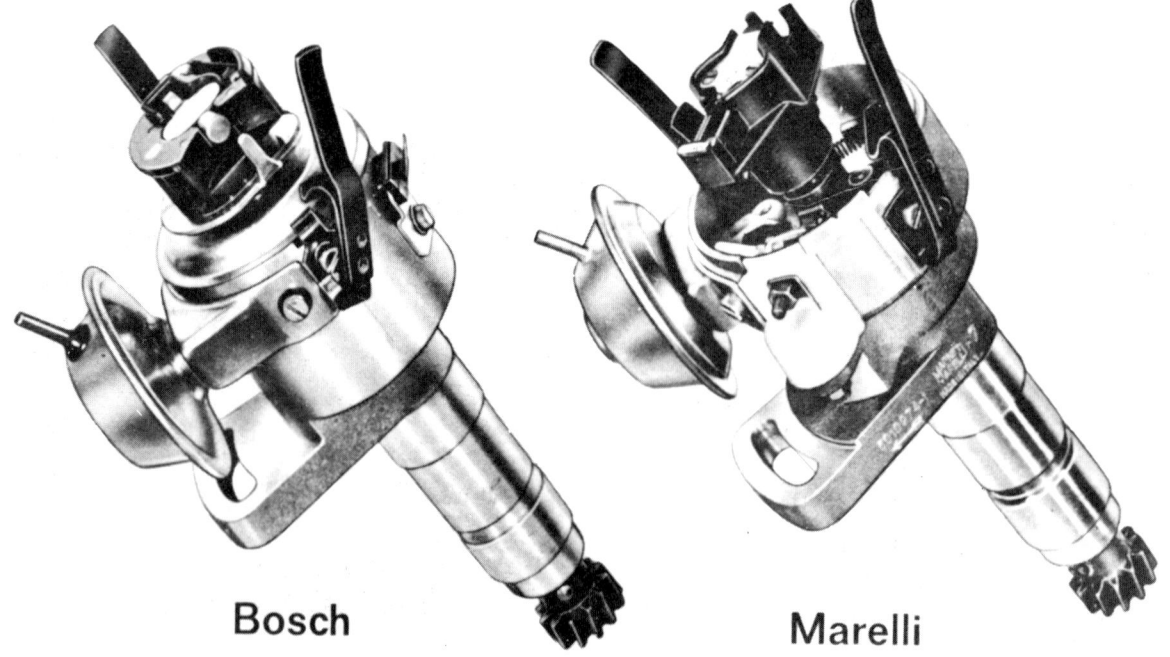

Bosch   Marelli

Fig. 3.3. Typical distributors (1972 model shown) (Sec. 2)

Marelli distributor - points gap

6　Remove the distributor cap and rotor, referring to the previous Section, if necessary.

7　Refer to paragraphs 3, 4 and 5. Note that on this distributor the front screw of the stationary contact plate is the one to be loosened.

Dwell angle

8　The dwell angle is directly related to the points gap and wherever possible should be checked after the points gap has been set. Although ideally a correctly set points gap will provide the correct dwell angle, there can be very slight differences due to small degrees of wear in the distributor.

9　Dwell angle can only be checking using a proprietary dwell angle meter which should be connected in accordance with the manufacturer's instructions (connect to distributor terminal 1 and earth for a CDS ignition circuit). (Fig. 3.7) If it is found that the dwell angle is too large, it indicates that the points gap is too small and vice-versa.

4　Distributor - removal and installation

1　In order to ensure that the ignition timing is not radically altered, it is essential that the exact relationship of the distributor body to the engine crankcase, and the distributor rotor/spindle to the crankshaft

Fig. 3.6. Contact assembly retaining screws (arrowed) — typical for later distributors (Sec. 2)

(top) Bosch　　　　　　　　*(bottom) Marelli*

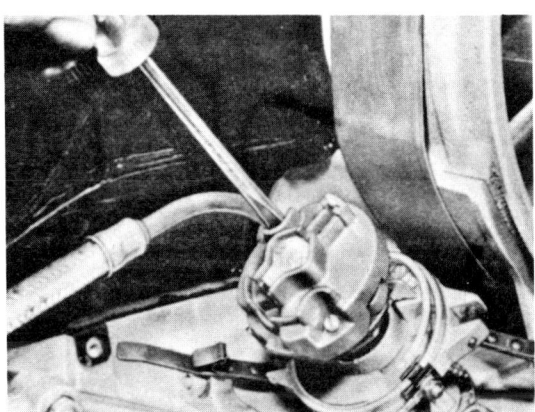

Fig. 3.4. Removing retaining screw for early Marelli distributor (Sec. 2)

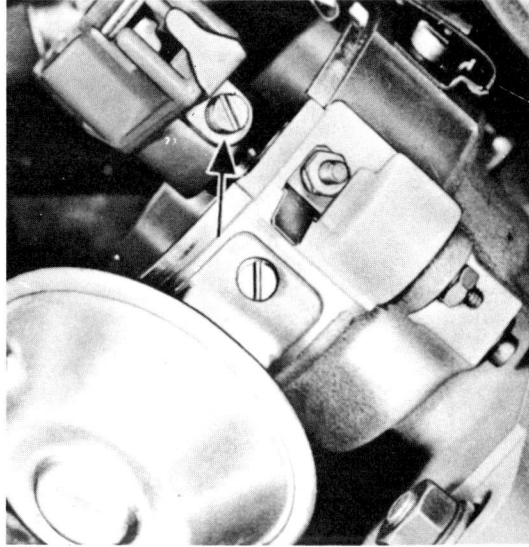

Fig. 3.5. Retaining screw (arrowed) for later Marelli distributor (Sec. 2)

3.3 Checking points gap

drive gear is not upset. Therefore, it is recommended that the crankshaft is rotated to align the timing marks for top-dead-centre (TDC) which will mean that either no. 1 or no. 4 piston is at the top of its stroke and the spark plug about to fire. Check whether the rotor is pointing towards no. 1 or no. 4 distributor cap segment and lead. If

Fig. 3.7. Connections for dwell angle meter (CDS) (Sec. 3)

1   Earth   2   Distributor terminal 1

4.4 Remove the clamping nut when removing the distributor (the engine is out of the car in this photograph)

Fig. 3.8. Typical ignition timing marks (Sec. 5)
The arrow shows 5° ATDC; 21 is TDC
Also shown are 30° and 35° ATDC
Note: 1° of advance is approximately 1 mm at the
pulley circumference

pointing to no. 4, rotate the crankshaft 360°; if pointing towards no. 1, all is well.

2   Now mark as accurately as possible, the relative position of the distributor body and crankcase, and the rotor and distributor body (on some distributors the no. 1 cylinder firing position is already marked).

3   Spring back the clips and remove the distributor cap.

4   Remove the nut securing the distributor clamp to the crankcase (not the clamping bolt) and lift out the distributor (photo).

5   Provided that the crankshaft is not rotated, installation is the reverse of the removal procedure with the markings being aligned. If the crankshaft has been rotated it will be necessary to rotate the crankshaft so that no. 1 piston is at its firing point (refer to paragraph 2 of the following Section).

5   Ignition timing

1   In order to obtain optimum performance, it is essential that the ignition timing is correctly set. If the ignition timing is known to be approximately correct, check that the distributor rotor is pointing towards no. 1 distributor cap segment; if it is pointing to no. 4 segment, rotate the crankshaft through 360°. If it is not pointing to either, refer to the following paragraph; otherwise proceed as described at paragraph 3.

2   Where the ignition timing setting has been lost completely (for example where the distributor was removed without making the alignment marks as described in Section 4), it will be necessary to set the crankshaft TDC marking (Z1) to align with the blower housing marking; this will bring nos. 1 and 4 pistons to TDC. To check whether no. 1 or no. 4 piston is on its firing stroke, remove both spark plugs and check which of the two cylinders has compression at TDC. Set the crankshaft so that no. 1 cylinder has compression at this point.

3   Having determined that no. 1 piston is on its firing stroke, rotate the engine at the crankshaft so that the distributor rotor moves back towards no. 5 segment, then rotate it the opposite way until the points *just* commence to open. This point may be difficult to judge accurately so remove the rotor and connect a 12V bulb of 6 watts maximum rating across the contact breaker points and switch on the ignition. The bulb will illuminate when the points are just opening.

4   If necessary, loosen the distributor clamp nut and reposition the distributor to obtain the static setting given in the Specifications. At this point the appropriate pulley mark should align with the marking on the blower housing. (Where the ignition timing was lost completely, and there is no specified static setting, set to TDC (Z1) to give an approximate setting then check dynamically as described in paragraphs 5 and 6). For all practical purposes it can be assumed that 1 degree of ignition advance is equal to 1 mm at the edge of the crankshaft pulley. Therefore, for those engines which require 5 degrees BTDC as an initial advance, the static timing point will be 5 mm to the right of the TDC (Z1) marking, and so on.

5   Having set the static advance, it is necessary to set the dynamic advance, which in most cases is done at 6000 rpm (with the vacuum line disconnected, where applicable). On certain models the dynamic advance is set at 900 ± 50 rpm; for these versions the vacuum line should remain connected. Refer to the Specifications for further information.

6   Dynamic ignition timing should be carried out using a proprietary stroboscopic light connected in accordance with the manufacturer's instructions (with a CDS ignition circuit, it is only permissible to connect to the fusebox for the stroboscopic light power supply). This is shone onto the appropriate timing mark on the crankshaft pulley which, when correctly set should align with the mark on the blower housing. Rotate the distributor as previously described to obtain the correct setting.

6   Condenser - checking

1   The condenser is only used in the conventional ignition system, where it is connected across the contact breaker points.

2   Condensers normally give many years of trouble-free life, but where there is evidence of excessive pitting of the contact breaker points together with engine starting problems, it is evidence of impending failure and the item should be renewed.

3   There is no simple and foolproof check for the condenser; if it is

Fig. 3.9. Connections for stroboscopic timing light (CDS) (Sec. 5)

1 *Power supply (from fuse)*   3 *No 1 cylinder HT lead*
2 *Earth connection*

suspected as being faulty, a replacement should be obtained. Considering its importance in the ignition system, it is a relatively cheap item to buy.

7 Ignition coil

Note: The ignition coil used in CDS ignition circuits is more properly described as an ignition voltage transformer. The word coil is used because of its obvious similarity to a conventional coil, particularly in appearance.

1 The ignition coil is normally trouble-free and requires no maintenance other than being kept clean, particularly at the end where the leads are.
2 The coils used on the two different ignition systems are very different internally and cannot be interchanged. If a coil is defective ensure that any replacement is the correct type for your particular vehicle.

8 Spark plugs and HT leads

1 The correct functioning of the spark plugs is vital for the proper running and efficient operation of the engine.
2 At the intervals specified, the plugs should be removed, examined, cleaned, and if worn excessively, renewed. The condition of the spark plug can also tell much about the general condition of the engine.
3 If the insulator nose of the spark plug is clean and white, with no deposits, this is indicative of a weak mixture, or too hot a plug (a hot plug transfers heat away from the electrode slowly - a cold plug transfers heat away quickly). (Fig. 3.11)
4 If the insulator nose is covered with hard black looking deposits, then this is indicative that the mixture is too rich. Should the plug be black and oily then it is likely that the engine is fairly worn, as well as the mixture being too rich.
5 If the insulator nose is covered with light tan to greyish brown deposits, then the mixture is correct, and it is likely that the engine is in good condition.
6 If there are any traces of long brown tapering stains on the outside of the white portion of the plug, then the plug will have to be renewed, as this shows that there is a faulty joint between the plug body and the insulator, and compression is being allowed to leak away.
7 Plugs should be cleaned by a sand blasting machine, which will free them from carbon more than by cleaning by hand. The machine will also test the condition of the plugs under compression. Any plug that fails to spark at the recommended pressure should be renewed.
8 The spark plug gap is of considerable importance, as, if it is too large or too small the size of the spark and its efficiency will be seriously impaired. The spark plug gap is given in the Specifications Section.
9 To set it, measure the gap with a feeler gauge, and then bend open, or closed, the outer plug electrode until the correct gap is achieved. The centre electrode should never be bent as this may crack the insulation

and cause plug failure, if nothing worse. (Fig. 3.10)
10 When installing the plugs, remember to connect the leads from the distributor cap in the correct firing order (see Specifications).
11 The HT leads require no maintenance other than being kept clean and wiped over regularly.

9 Ignition system - fault diagnosis

Conventional ignition system

1 Engine will not start.
a) The engine is so enclosed that the normal wet condition after leaving the car in the open over-night is not so prevalent. However, before running down the battery when the car will not start after being left in the open, have a look to see that everything is dry. If mist has penetrated then dry the moisture off, either with a cloth or with a proprietary type spray.
b) If the engine will not start when everything is dry, pull off a plug lead, turn back the plug cover and hold the metal end of the plug lead about 1/8 in (3mm) from the crankcase. With the ignition switched on, spin the engine with the starter. If there is a spark, a good fat one, then the ignition system is working. Check that the distributor body is held tight in the clamp ring, then check the timing setting. (see Section 5). If the spark is correct and the timing has not altered, then the fault is not in the ignition system.
c) If there is not a fat spark then the ignition system is at fault. Begin by checking the LT circuit in the following order:
  (i)   *Are the points opening correctly? Are they clean?*
  (ii) *Check the voltage at coil terminal 15. It should be at least 9 volts (ignition on). If no voltage then the wiring or the switch is at fault.*
  (iii) *Check the voltage at coil terminal 1, points closed - no volts, points open - reading on the meter. If no reading on the meter with points open, the coil has an open circuit.*
  (iv) *With the ignition switched on check the voltage across the contact breaker points; points closed - no volts, points open - meter reads. Points open - no reading, then the condenser is faulty.*
d) Check all the LT wiring and connections carefully, and if the LT circuit is functioning correctly then proceed to the HY circuit. Check the following in the order given (ignition switched on):
  (i)   *Pull the HT lead from the centre of the distributor and hold the end 1/8 in (3 mm) from the crankcase. Spin the engine. There should be a spark. No spark means a faulty HT winding in the coil.*
  (ii) *Turn off the ignition switch, put the lead back in the centre of the distributor cap and examine the carbon brush carefully. Is it making contact with the rotor arm spring? Examine the cap for cracks and tracking. Check that the segments are clean and that the rotor arm leading edge is not corroded. Clean these if they are.*
  (iii) *Check the rotor arm, check the drive by turning the rotor gently. There should be a slight movement. Anything more than a slight movement means that the drive is suspect or the automatic advance and retard has disintegrated. The latter is rare but it has happened.*
e) Finally remove a plug and check its condition. If it is oily, wet with petrol, or corroded, then clean it, and the other five. Check the gap. Oily or corroded plugs mean an engine overhaul or at least a checking of the exhaust gas composition by an expert. Wet plugs may be flooding during starting.
2 Engine runs sluggishly but does not misfire.
a) Check the contact breaker points, plug gaps and distributor rotor
b) Check the ignition timing
c) Check the octane rating of the fuel.
3 Engine misfires, runs unevenly and cuts out at low revolutions.
a) Check contact breaker and plug gaps. (CB gap too large?)
b) Check the distributor shaft for wear.
c) Check the fuel system.
d) Check the distributor rotor.
4 Engine misfires at high revolutions.
a) Check contact breaker and plug gaps (CB gap too small?)
b) Check the distributor shaft for wear.
d) Check the fuel system
5 Ignition faults are quite often exasperating. Work steadily through

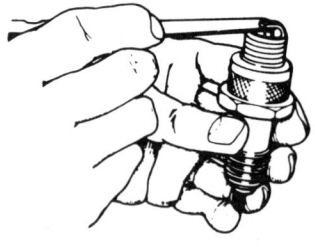

Checking plug gap with feeler gauges

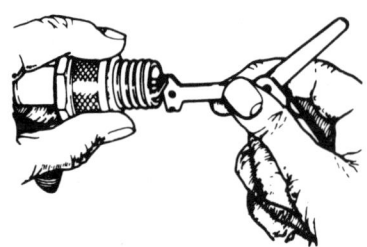

Altering the plug gap. Note use of correct tool

Fig. 3.10. Spark plug maintenance (Sec. 8)

White deposits and damaged porcelain insulation indicating overheating

Broken porcelain insulation due to bent central electrode

Electrodes burnt away due to wrong heat value or chronic pre-ignition (pinking)

Excessive black deposits caused by over-rich mixture or wrong heat value

Mild white deposits and electrode burnt indicating too weak a fuel mixture

Plug in sound condition with light greyish brown deposits

Fig. 3.11. Spark plug electrode conditions (Sec 8)

the system checking all leads and connections methodically. Test the components, check the battery, and if finally the fault cannot be located then go to the expert. He has instruments specially designed to locate faults. But if his respect is to be obtained do not go about testing in a haphazard manner; that will only result in more faults being installed and the original one may never be located.

Capacitive discharge system (CDS)
6   If the engine fails to start, first check for obvious faults such as disconnected leads, and condition of contact breaker points, spark plugs, etc.
7   If these are satisfactory, switch on the ignition and check for a whistling sound from the CDS unit. If there is no whistling sound, remove the connector from the CDS unit and connect a voltmeter between the connector centre terminal ('B') and earth. If there is 11 volts or more, ensure that the connector pins are clean and then refit it. If there is still no whistling sound, the CDS unit is defective and a replacement should be obtained.
8   If there is a whistling sound, it is possible to check for a voltage at terminal '4' of the ignition coil (the HT terminal). Remove the coil to distributor HT lead at the distributor, and support it 0.4 in (10 mm) away from a good earth point on the crankcase. Do not touch the lead, and do not move the lead further from the crankcase or cross-arcing may occur inside the coil causing damage. If there is no spark when the engine is cranked, or sparking is irregular, proceed to paragraphs 9 and 10 If there is regular sparking, the fault lies elsewhere (eg: ignition timing, fuel system, moisture in distributor, etc.)
9   Remove the ignition coil connections and connect an ohmmeter between the coil terminals 1 and 15 (primary); there should be a resistance of 0.4 to 0.6 ohms. Repeat the check between terminals 1 and 4; there should be a resistance of 650 to 790 ohms.

Fig. 3.12. Component layout for CDS ignition circuit (Sec. 9)

1   CDS unit
2   Ignition voltage transformer (coil)
3   RPM sensor

10 To check the current drawn by the CDS unit, connect an ammeter into the wire no. 15 from the ignition switch, then disconnect wire no. 1 at the distributor. With the ignition switched on, there should be a current of 1.0 to 1.9 amps. If outside this range, a replacement CDS unit should be obtained.
11 The rpm sensor can only be checked using an ohmmeter. Pull out the sensor and check for a resistance of 170 to 210 ohms between terminals 'A' and 'B', and 220 to 300 ohms between terminals 'A' and 'C'.

Chapter 4 Clutch

Contents

Specifications

Clutch type	Single dry plate with diaphragm spring and cable actuation
Pedal free-travel	1 in (25.4 mm)
Friction lining area	31.5 sq in (203 sq cm)
Release bearing type	Sealed ball

Torque wrench settings	**lb f ft**	**kg fm**
Pressure plate cover bolts	25	3.5
Release lever dowel pin	8	1.1
Release lever ball pin	16	2.2
Transmission to engine bolts	28	3.9

1 General description

1 The clutch fitted to all models which are equipped with a manually operated gearbox is of single dry plate, diaphragm spring type with cable actuation.

2 The design of the clutch release components and the cable mechanism differs between cars built up until 1970 and those built after that date.

3 The clutch fitted in conjunction with Sportomatic transmission is regarded as an intergral part of the transmission and is therefore included in Chapter 5.

4 When the clutch pedal is depressed, the connecting cable actuates the clutch release arm. The release arm pushes the release bearing forwards to bear against the release plate so moving the centre of the diaphragm spring inwards. The spring is sandwiched between two annular rings which act as fulcrum points. As the centre of the spring is pushed in, the outside of the spring is pushed out, so moving the pressure plate backwards and disengaging the pressure from the clutch disc.

When the clutch pedal is released the diaphragm spring forces the pressure plate into contact with the high friction linings on the clutch

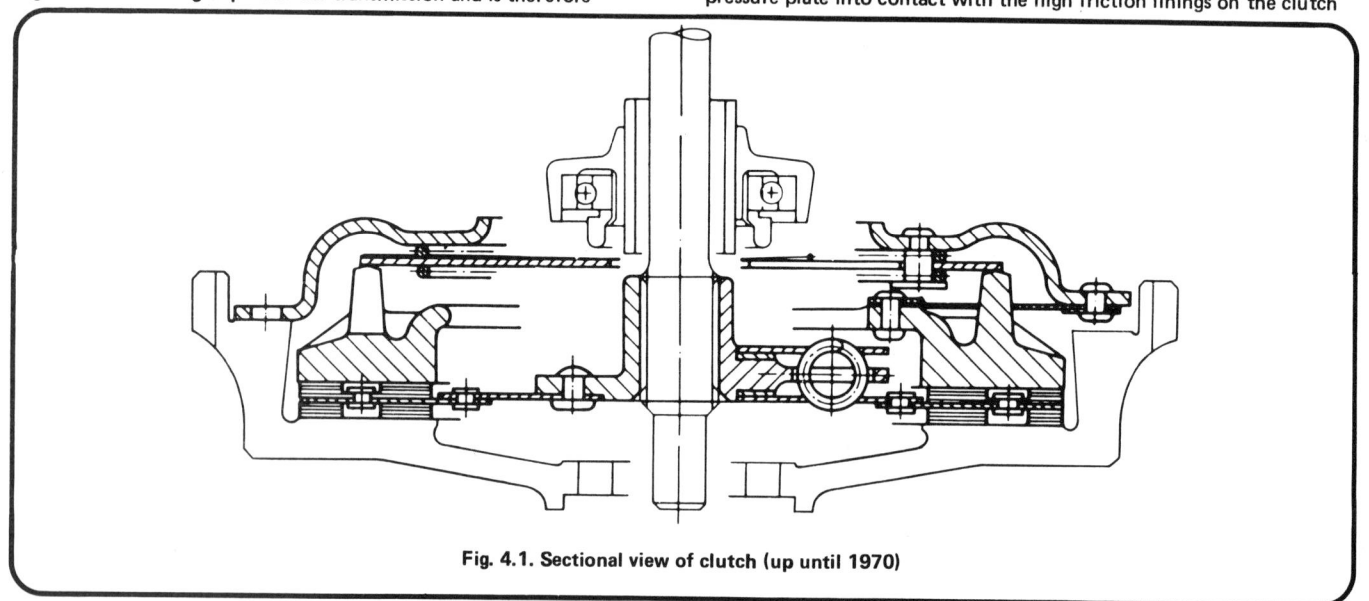

Fig. 4.1. Sectional view of clutch (up until 1970)

disc and at the same time pushes the clutch disc a fraction of an inch forwards on its splines so engaging the clutch disc with the flywheel.

The clutch disc is now firmly sandwiched between the pressure plate and the flywheel so the drive is taken up.

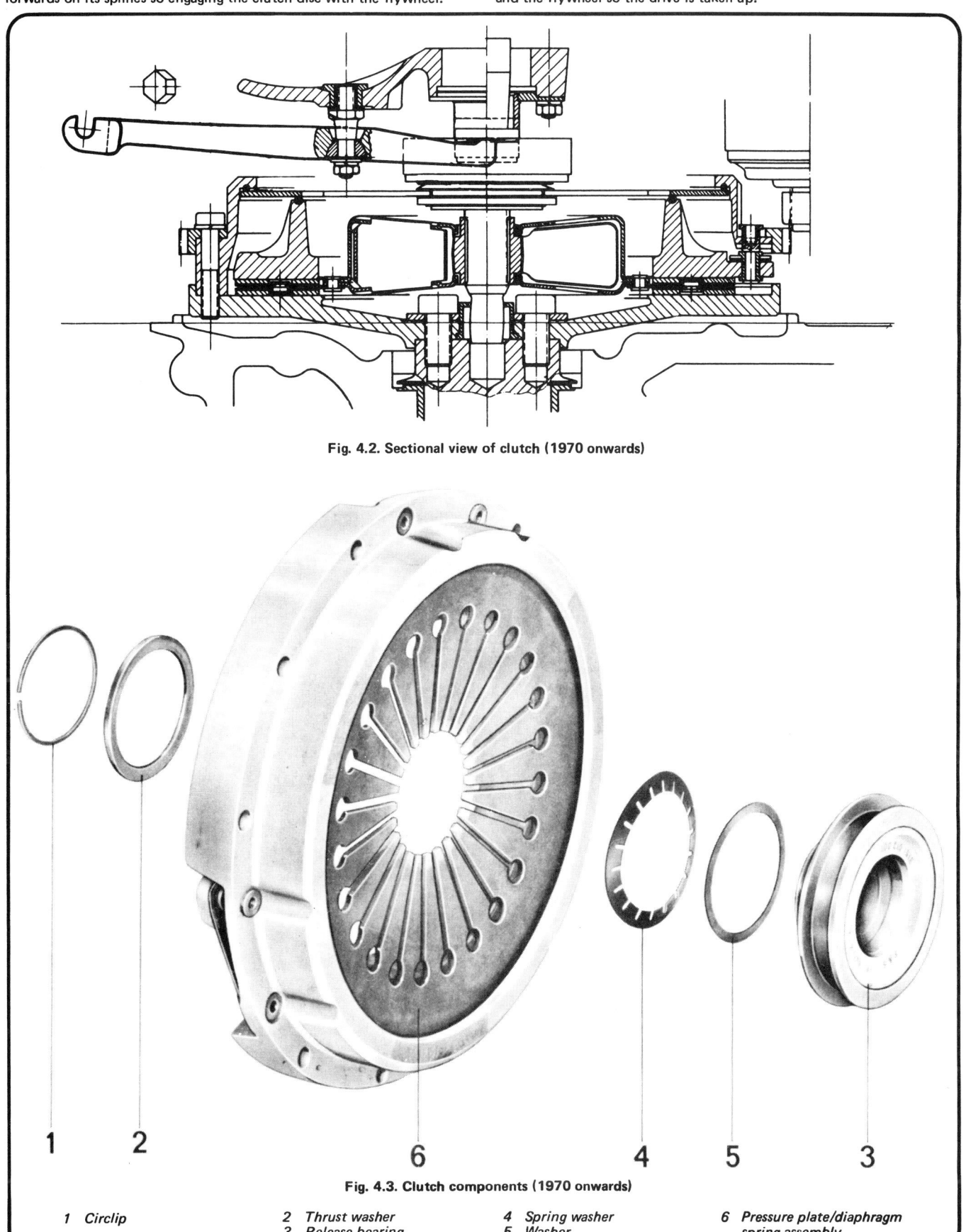

Fig. 4.2. Sectional view of clutch (1970 onwards)

Fig. 4.3. Clutch components (1970 onwards)

1 Circlip	2 Thrust washer	4 Spring washer	6 Pressure plate/diaphragm
	3 Release bearing	5 Washer	spring assembly

2 Clutch adjustment (up to 1970)

1 Two adjustment points are provided, one at the release lever and the second at the clutch pedal. Adjustment is normally carried out at the release lever unless new components have been fitted or all available adjustment at the release lever has been taken up.
2 Place the car on ramps or over a pit and release the locknut at the release lever end of the clutch cable.
3 Turn the adjusting nut until a free-movement is provided at the clutch pedal of 1 in (25.4 mm). When adjustment is correct, tighten the locknut.
4 Where adjustment must be made at the pedal end of the cable. remove the rubber mat from the passenger side and then peel back the rubber covering from the front end of the tunnel.
5 Release the clevis locknut and extract the clevis pin clip and clevis pin.
6 Turn the clevis fork as necessary to provide the necessary adjustment of the cable but do not screw the fork onto the cable so far that the

Fig. 4.4. Cable adjuster (up to 1970) at release lever (Sec. 2)

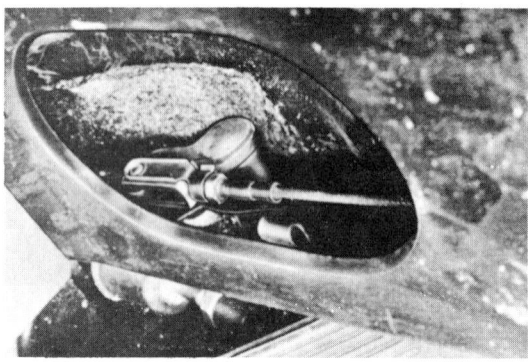

Fig. 4.5. Cable adjuster (up to 1970) at pedal (Sec. 2)

Fig 4.7. Direction of clutch pedal free-movement (1970 to 1972) (Sec. 3)

threaded part of the cable projects into the U shaped aperture of the fork.
7 Refit the clevis pin and spring and tighten the locknut.
8 If the correct adjustment of the clutch pedal cannot be obtained with these adjusters, then the clutch components are probably worn and must be renewed as described in Sections 6 to 10, of this Chapter.

3 Clutch adjustment (1970 to 1972)

1 Release the locknut on the clutch cable outer casing near the release lever.
2 Turn the adjuster nut until the clutch pedal free play is 1 in (25.4 mm) To check the free-play, pull the pedal back gently in the direction indicated in Fig. 4.7.
3 Tighten the locknut.
4 Start the engine and with it idling, select reverse gear. This should be obtainable without any grinding of gears.
5 If grinding does occur, check the inner cable adjustment in the following manner.
6 When the clutch pedal is fully depressed, the release fork should move approximately 0.6 in (15 mm) to completely disengage the clutch. Failure of the fork to move this distance is indicated if the clutch cable is tight against the bottom of its clamp when the pedal is fully depressed.
7 To rectify this situation, the inner cable must be adjusted at the clevis fork end.
8 Disconnect the clevis fork and measure from the outer face of the locknut to the end of the threaded part of the cable. This should be between 0.7 and 0.9 in (17 to 22 mm). Adjust as necessary, by turning the clevis and then tighten the locknut.
9 If the adjustment is not carried out correctly then the opposite condition may be obtained where the cable jumps out of the open end of its clamp when the pedal is fully depressed.

Fig. 4.6. Cable adjuster (1970 to 1972) (Sec. 3)

Fig. 4.8. Clutch cable at bottom of its guide clamp (1970 to 1972) (Sec. 3)

4 Clutch adjustment (1972 onwards)

1 The clutch actuating mechanism on these cars has been simplified and adjustment of the clutch pedal free-movemnet is carried out by holding the square on the end of the cable at the release lever and turning the self-locking nut. Check the pedal free-movement as shown in Fig. 4.7.

2 On 1975 and later models, the release arm and cable routing has been modified yet again. Measure the lever to transmission casing distance while prising the lever away with a screwdriver. After adjusting the cable, the movement of the lever (when the clutch pedal is fully depressed) should reduce the dimension previously taken by only 5/32 in (4 mm) which is in fact the total movement of the lever.

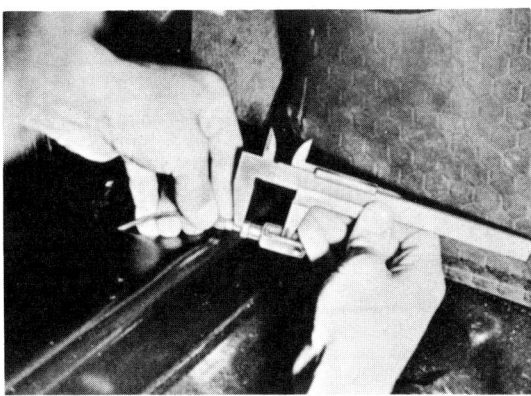

Fig. 4.9. Measuring cable projection (1970 to 1972) (Sec. 3)

Fig. 4.10. Clutch cable jumping from open end of guide clamp
(1970 to 1972) (Sec. 3)

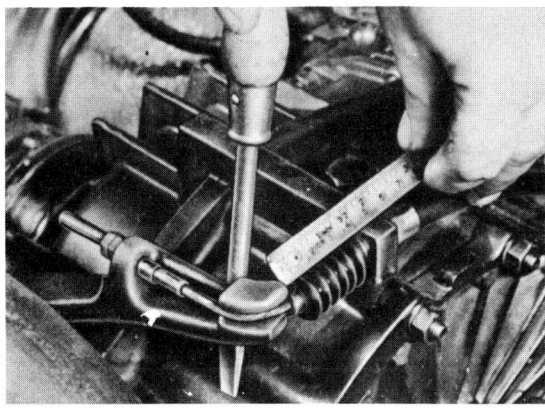

Fig. 4.12. Cable adjuster and routing of cable over release lever
(1975 onwards) (Sec. 4)

5 Clutch pedal travel (up to 1970) - adjustment

1 On early models, a movable stop is provided to limit the clutch pedal travel.

2 Provided the clutch cable has been correctly adjusted as described in Section 2, then the stop should be set so that the pedal has to be depressed the minimum distance to permit engagement of reverse gear without grinding of gears. Select reverse gear for this test when the gearbox has been warmed-up and pause for a few seconds in neutral with the clutch depressed before selecting the gear.

6 Clutch cable - renewal

1 Renewal of the clutch cable is simply a matter of disconnecting the cable at both ends from the pedal and the release lever.

2 Always renew any dust excluding bellows which have deteriorated and on completion of installation adjust the clutch pedal free movement.

3 Details of the clutch pedal are given in Chapter 2, Section 49.

7 Clutch - removal

1 Access to the clutch is obtained after removing the combined engine/transmission as described in Chapter 1, Section 4 and then separating the transmission from the engine as described in Section 5 according to car date production.

2 Unscrew and remove the bolts which secure the clutch pressure plate cover to the flywheel. Unscrew these bolts in diagonally opposite sequence, half a turn at a time until the pressure of the diaphragm spring is released.

3 Lift away the cover and extract the driven plate from the face of the flywheel.

4 Check and renew the clutch and clutch release components as described in the following Sections.

Fig. 4.11. Cable adjuster (1972 onwards) (Sec. 4)

Fig. 4.13. Clutch pedal movable stop (Sec. 5)

8 Clutch - inspection and renovation

1   Due to the slow-wearing qualities of the clutch, it is not easy to decide when to go to the trouble of removing the gearbox in order to check the wear on the friction lining. The only positive indication that something needs doing is when it starts to slip or when squealing noises on engagement indicate that the friction lining has worn down to the rivets. In such instances it can only be hoped that the friction surfaces on the flywheel and pressure plate have not been badly worn or scored.

A clutch will wear according to the way in which it is used. Much intentional slipping of the clutch while driving - rather than the correct selection of gears - will accelerate wear. It is best to assume, however, that the driven plate will need renewal every 35,000 miles (56,000 km) at least and that it will be *worth* replacing it after 25,000 miles (40,000 km). The maintenance history of the car is obviously very useful.

2   Examine the surfaces of the pressure plate and flywheel for signs of scoring. If this is only light it may be left, but if very deep the pressure plate unit will have to be renewed. If the flywheel is deeply scored it should be taken off and advice sought from an engineering firm. Refer to Chapter 1, Section 20.

3   The driven plate lining surfaces should be at least 1/32 in (0.8 mm) above the rivets, otherwise the disc is not worth putting back. If the lining material shows signs of breaking up or black areas where oil contamination has occured it should also be renewed. If facilities are readily available for obtaining and fitting new friction pads to the existing disc this may be done but the saving is relatively small compared with obtaining a complete new disc assembly which ensures that the shock absorbing springs and the splined hub are renewed also. The

same applies to the pressure plate assembly which cannot be readily dismantled and put back together without specialised riveting tools and balancing equipment. An allowance is usually given for exchange units.

9 Clutch release bearing and mechanism

1   The sealed, ball bearing type release bearing, although designed for long life, is worth renewing at the same time as the other clutch components are being renewed or serviced.

2   Deterioration of the release bearing should be suspected when there are signs of grease leakage or the unit is noisy when spun with the fingers.

Cars built up until 1970

3   Unscrew the dowel pin from the release arm, extract the spring, release arm/fork assembly and the thrust bearing (photo).

4   Withdraw the release arm/fork from the bearing, noting the positioning of the slides (photos).

5   If necessary, the ball pin can be unscrewed and renewed. On early models up to transmission no. 1020802 or 222706, the ball pin was driven into position and not screwed in.

Cars built after 1970

6   The release arm will already have been removed to permit separation of the transmission from the engine (see Chapter 1, Section 5).

7   The release bearing is captive on the diaphragm spring and will still be attached to the spring.

8   To remove the release bearing, press down on the thrust washer so that the circlip can be extracted.

9   Remove the release bearing and washers.

9.3 Removing release arm dowel pin with an Allen key   9.4a Removing release arm from bearing   9.4b Clutch release bearing and slides

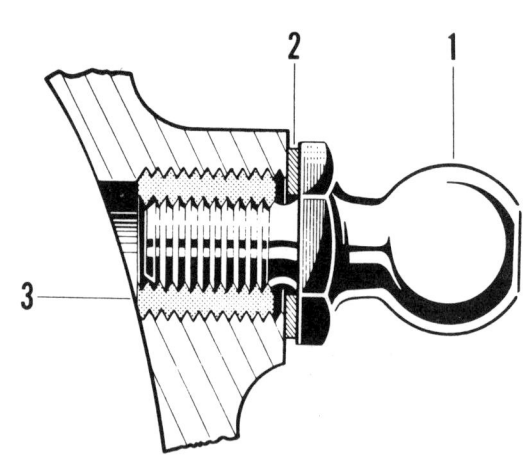
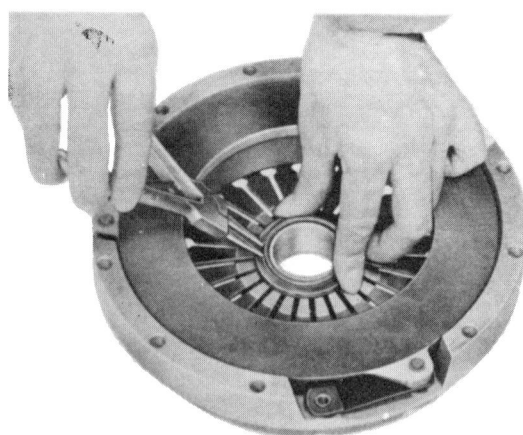

Fig. 4.14. Release lever ball pin (Sec. 9)

1   Ball pin   2   Sealing washer   3   Threaded insert

Fig. 4.15. Extracting release bearing circlip (1970 onwards) (Sec. 9)

Fig. 4.16. View of release bearing (1970 onwards) showing position of washers (Sec. 9)

10.2 Installing clutch driven plate

10 Refitting of the release components is a reversal of removal but apply a little grease to the ball pin on earlier models.

10 Clutch - installation

1 Make sure that the face of the flywheel is clean and free from oil.
2 Place the driven plate against the flywheel so that the larger projecting boss is towards the clutch release bearing (photo).
3 Offer the clutch pressure plate into position and insert the retaining bolts finger-tight. On cars built after 1970, the diaphragm spring tension must be relieved by the screws and spacers having been fitted to the three internally threaded rivets on the pressure plate assembly.
4 Now centralise the driven plate so that the transmission input

shaft spigot will enter it freely when the transmission is reconnected to the engine. The best way to do this is to insert an old input shaft through the splines of the driven plate and into engagement with the pilot bearing in the centre of the flywheel. Where such a shaft is not available, use a suitably stepped mandrel.
5 With the driven plate centralised, fully tighten the pressure plate cover bolts in diagonal sequence, half a turn at a time to the specified torque wrench setting.
6 Reconnect the transmission to the engine by reversing the disconnection operation and on cars built after 1970 remember to remove the temporary screws and spacers from the threaded rivets of the pressure plate after the release lever and fork have been reconnected to the release bearing.
7 Install the engine/transmission (Chapter 1) and then adjust the clutch pedal free-movement.

11 Fault diagnosis - clutch

Symptom	Reason/s
Judder when taking up drive	Loose engine or gearbox mountings Badly worn friction surfaces or contaminated with oil Worn splines on gearbox input shaft or driven plate hub Worn input shaft spigot bush in flywheel
Clutch spin (failure to disengage) so that gears cannot be meshed	Incorrect release bearing to diaphragm spring finger clearance caused by incorrect cable adjustment Driven plate sticking on input shaft splines due to rust. May occur after standing idle for long period. Damaged or misaligned pressure plate assembly
Clutch slip (increase in engine speed does not result in increase in vehicle road speed - particularly on gradients)	Incorrect release bearing to diaphragm spring finger clearance caused by incorrect cable adjustment. Friction surfaces worn out or oil contaminated
Noise evident on depressing clutch pedal	Dry, worn or damaged release bearing Insufficient pedal free travel Excessive play between driven hub splines and input shaft splines
Noise evident as clutch pedal released	Distorted driven plate Broken or weak driven plate cushion coil springs Insufficient pedal free travel Distorted or worn input shaft Release bearing loose on retainer hub

Chapter 5: Part 1 Manual transmission

Contents

Specifications

| Transmission type ... ... | Four or five-speed, synchromesh, incorporating final drive and differential gear |

Manual transmission (general)

Gear ratios ... ... See Section 1

Final drive ratio:
    All models except 1975 USA 7:31 (4.429:1)
    1975 USA models 8:31 (3.875:1)

Lubricant type ... ... SAE 90EP gear oil to Specification MIL-L-2105 or 2105B. For limited slip differential versions use oil to Specification M2C 28B (eg: Shell S 1747A) only

Lubricant capacity (approx):
    Pre-1972 models ... ... 4.3 Imp. pints (5.2 US pints/2.5 litres)
    1972 models onwards ... ... 5.3 Imp. pints (6.3 US pints/3 litres)

Fits, clearances and wear limits (5-speed transmission)

Backlash between gears:
    New ... ... 0.0023 to 0.0047 in (0.06 to 0.12 mm)
    Wear limit ... ... 0.0087 in (0.22 mm)

Gear play on shafts:
    New:
        1st ... ... 0.0118 to 0.0157 in (0.3 to 0.4 mm)
        2nd ... ... 0.0079 to 0.0118 in (0.2 to 0.3 mm)
        3rd (end play) ... ... 0.0079 to 0.0118 in (0.2 to 0.3 mm)
        4th ... ... 0.0079 to 0.0118 in (0.2 to 0.3 mm)
        5th ... ... 0.0079 to 0.0118 in (0.2 to 0.3 mm)
    Wear limit:
        1st ... ... 0.0197 in (0.5 mm)
        2nd ... ... 0.0157 in (0.4 mm)
        3rd (end play) ... ... 0.0157 in (0.4 mm)
        4th ... ... 0.0157 in (0.4 mm)
        5th ... ... 0.0157 in (0.4 mm)

Shift rods, radial play in guides (pre-1972 models):
    New ... ... 0.0037 to 0.0061 in (0.095 to 0.156 mm)
    Wear limit ... ... 0.0157 in (0.4 mm)

Shift rods, radial play in guides (1972 models onwards):
    New ... ... 0.0076 to 0.0093 in (0.195 to 0.236 mm)
    Wear limit ... ... 0.0157 in (0.4 mm)

Shift rods, out-of-true (max)	0.0039 in (0.1 mm)
Shift fork in shifting sleeve:	
New	0.0039 to 0.0118 in (0.1 to 0.3 mm)
Wear limit	0.0197 in (0.5 mm)
Synchro rings, installed, outside diameter (pre-1972 models):	
New	2.997 to 3.011 in (76.12 to 76.48 mm)
Wear limit	Molybdenum layer worn through
Synchro rings, installed outside diameter (1972 models onwards):	
New, 1st, 2nd	3.3937 to 3.4071 in (86.20 to 86.54 mm)
New, 3rd, 4th, 5th	2.997 to 3.011 in (76.12 to 76.48 mm)
Wear limit	Molybdenum layer worn through
Driveshaft (input shaft) nose out of true (max)	0.0039 in (0.1 mm)
Driveshaft (input shaft) radial play in crankshaft bush:	
New	0.0057 to 0.0091 in (0.145 to 0.231 mm)
Wear limit	0.0118 in (0.3 mm)
Shift rod short detent spring free-length (1st/reverse)	1.11 to 1.15 in (28.2 to 29.2 mm)
Shift rod long detent spring free-length (2nd, 3rd/4th, 5th)	1.47 to 1.5 in (37.3 to 38.5 mm)

Fits, clearances and wear limits (4-speed transmission)

Refer to the previous Section for 5-speed transmission, but note that for pre-1972 transmissions, references to gears 2, 3, 4 and 5 of the 5-speed transmission are equivalent to 1, 2, 3 and 4 of the 4-speed transmission. **Note:** *This similarity does not necessarily apply to assembly procedures - see Sections 15 and 27.*

Torque wrench settings

	lb f ft	kg fm
Drain plug	15 to 18	2 to 2.5
Filler plug	15 to 18	2 to 2.5
Transmission housing nuts	16 to 18	2.2 to 2.5
Reverse light switch	25 to 29	3.5 to 4
Input shaft flange nut (M30), 1972 onwards	116 to 130	16 to 18
Input shaft castellated nut (M18), 1972 onwards	87 to 101	12 to 14
Input shaft nut (M24), pre-1972	72 to 87	10 to 12
Input shaft crown nut (M12)	43 to 47	6 to 6.5
Input shaft reinforced crown nut (M14)	65 to 80	9 to 11
Driveshaft expansion bolt (M12), pre-1972	80 to 87	11 to 12
Retaining plate nut	15 to 17	2.1 to 2.3
Support attachment nut	15 to 17	2.1 to 2.3
Pinion shaft flange nut, 1972 onwards	174 to 188	24 to 26
Transmission housing breather	15 to 22	2 to 3
Shift fork nuts	17 to 19	2.4 to 2.6
Axle flange expansion bolt, 1972 onwards	19 to 22	2.6 to 3
Axle flange expansion bolt, pre 1972	33 to 36	4.5 to 5
Input shaft pressure line, Carrera	6 to 6.5	0.8 to 0.9
Pressure relief valve plug in front cover, Carrera	16 to 18	2.2 to 2.5
Oil pump cover, Carrera	6.6 to 7	0.9 to 1
Pick-up tube Allen bolt, Carrera	6 to 6.5	0.8 to 0.9
Gear housing pressure line bolt, Carrera	6 to 6.5	0.8 to 0.9

1 General description

The transmission unit (transaxle) is either 4- or 5-speed, and incorporates the transmission gears and final drive in a common housing. All forward gears have a synchronized meshing action (synchromesh), and are selected through a linkage from the floor-shift lever.

The gears and shafts are housed in a light alloy ribbed casing, which contains the clutch mechanism, and is bolted to the front of the engine. Although the gears and final drive unit are housed together, and use a common oil supply, they are entirely separate assemblies apart from the meshing of the pinion shaft with the differential ring gear.

Transmissions used up to 1972 are considerably different from those used from 1972 onwards. The two types can be easily distinguished; the early type had the reverse gear at the forward-left position of the gearshift lever while the later type had the reverse gear at the rear-right position. This basic ruling applies to both 4- and 5-speed transmissions which are very similar in design within their respective type grouping.

In the text, the transmissions are referred to as the early and later types. Because of the similarities, information of 4-speed transmission is limited to a single Section in each case. The same basic ruling applies for later transmissions with an oil pump lubrication system as used on Carrera models.

Dismantling and reassembly of the transmission gears is comparatively straightforward, but it is not recommended that any repair work is attempted on the final drive in view of the special tools, gauges and procedures involved. When the final drive is in need of repair, it is recommended that the gears and shafts are removed from the casing, then the casing and final drive entrusted to a Porsche dealer for the necessary repairs. **Note:** Porsche have provided different gear ratios for so many different vehicle applications on the 911 models that a list of ratios is meaningless. The quickest way of determining the actual ratio is to remove the spark plugs, engage a gear and note the number of wheel revolutions per crankshaft revolution when pushing the car. Divide this number by the final drive ratio and the gear ratio will be obtained.

2 Transmission - removal and installation

The transmission can only be removed complete with the engine. Refer to Chapter 1 for this procedure.

3 Five-speed transmission (early type) - dismantling into major assemblies, and reassembly

1 Initially remove the starter motor (refer to Chapter 9, if necessary) and clutch throwout (release) lever and bearing (refer to Chapter 4, if necessary).
2 Clean the exterior of the transmission with a water-soluble solvent, then transfer it to a suitable workbench. Have a supply of clean lint-free cloth available, together with several containers for putting the various parts in.

3   Commence the dismantling by removing the drain plug and draining the oil into a container of suitable size. The reverse light switch and pin can also conveniently be removed at this stage.
4   Remove the inner shift rod guide fork plate from the transmission housing. Now select 5th-gear by moving the selector linkage rod at the end cover, then use a screwdriver through the guide fork aperture to also engage 2nd or 3rd gear. In this way the gears can be locked in mesh.
5   If the differential is to be removed, proceed as described in paragraphs 6 and 7. **Note:** It is necessary to remove the differential if the outer race of the housing centre bearing is to be removed.
6   Using two screwdrivers, carefully prise out the caps from the driveshaft flange joints, where applicable. Remove the flange expansion bolts and withdraw the flanges.
7   Remove the transmission side cover and take out the differential assembly.
8   Remove the nuts and take off the front cover, taking great care that the reverse gear components do not fall off.
9   Remove the 1st/reverse gear selector fork retaining bolt, then take off the gear and selector fork together.
10 With the transmission still locked as at paragraph 4, remove the expansion bolt from the end of the mainshaft. If a suitable socket is not available, use a cranked drift to drive out the speedometer gear retaining pin, remove the speedometer gear, then drive the pin back in. A conventional socket can now be used on the expansion bolt.
11 Remove the locking pin and castellated nut from the forward end of the input shaft.
12 Disengage the 2nd or 3rd gear selector at paragraph 4, but leave the 5th gear engaged.
13 Pull out the inner shift rod through the rear access hole, then remove the intermediate plate complete with shafts and gears. At this stage it is very important to note the intermediate plate/housing gasket thickness. If this is not done, the pinion meshing depth will be upset, and have to be set up by a Porsche dealer or transmission specialist.
14 Support the intermediate plate in a vice using jaw clamps, and carefully draw or prise off the 1st/reverse guide sleeve.

15 Remove the 1st speed gear and the needle bearing cage.
16 Select neutral then remove the selector shaft detent plug; pull out the spring.
17 Withdraw the 1st/reverse selector shaft and take out the detent ball.
18 It is worthwhile at this stage to mark the exact position of the 2nd/3rd and 4th/5th shift forks on their respective shafts as this can be an aid to their adjustment when reassembling (see Section 4), particularly if these parts do not subsequently need renewing.
19 Now remove the 2nd/3rd selector fork retaining screw, then take

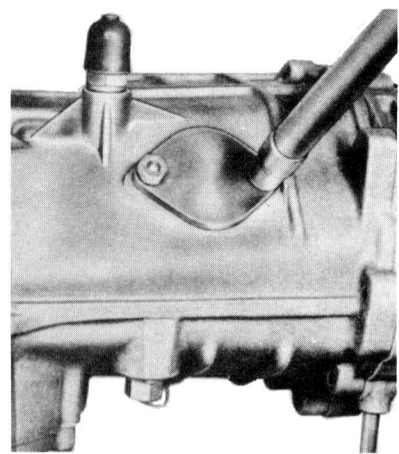

Fig. 5.1. Removing the guide fork (Sec. 3)

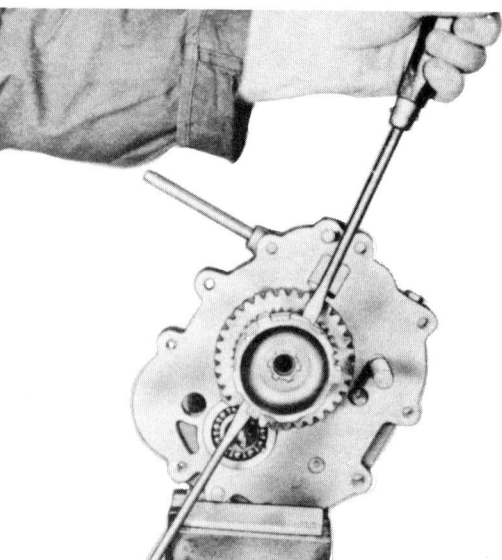

Fig. 5.3. Removing the 1st/reverse guide sleeve (Sec. 3)

Fig. 5.2. 1st/reverse selector fork retaining screw (arrowed) (Sec. 3)

Fig. 5.4. Removing the selector shaft detent plug (Sec. 3)

Fig. 5.5. 2nd/3rd selector fork retaining screw (arrowed) (Sec. 3)

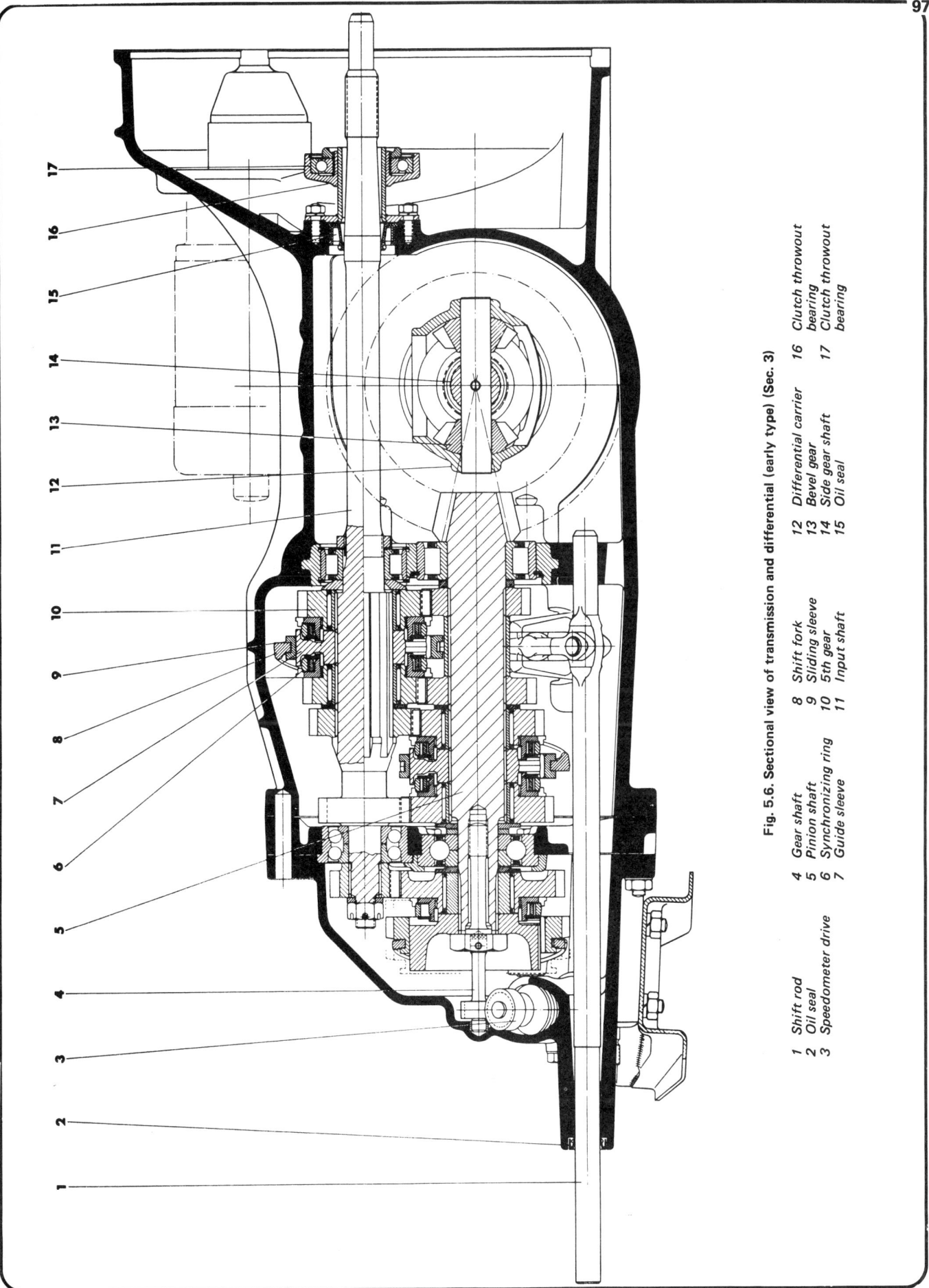

Fig. 5.6. Sectional view of transmission and differential (early type) (Sec. 3)

1 Shift rod
2 Oil seal
3 Speedometer drive
4 Gear shaft
5 Pinion shaft
6 Synchronizing ring
7 Guide sleeve
8 Shift fork
9 Sliding sleeve
10 5th gear
11 Input shaft
12 Differential carrier
13 Bevel gear
14 Side gear shaft
15 Oil seal
16 Clutch throwout bearing
17 Clutch throwout bearing

out the selector shaft, selector fork and detent pin. Mark the selector fork so that it is not confused with the 4th/5th fork when that is removed.

20 Remove the 4th/5th selector shaft, selector fork and detent ball in a similar way, marking the fork for identification purposes.

21 Remove the detent balls, pin and spring.

22 Apply blows from a soft-faced hammer to the shaft ends alternately, to drive them from the intermediate plate (while still meshed together). Ensure that the balls are not lost from the double-row ball bearing.

23 Remove the retainers from the centre web of the case if the input shaft bearing is to be removed (also remove the front retainer

for the pinion shaft). Heat the casing in a suitable oven to about 120ºC (250ºF) then drive out the bearings using a hammer and a suitable drift.

24 If necessary, remove the cover plate at the clutch housing end and take out the oil seal.

25 For further information on dismantling the shafts, transmission front cover, intermediate plate, transmission housing and synchro assemblies, together with inspection of these parts, refer to the appropriate following Sections.

26 In general, reassembly is the reverse of the removal procedure. Where removed, first install the retainer into the pinion shaft outer bearing race.

27 Insert the rear retainer into the bearing bore at an angle, and guide it into the groove using a small screwdriver.

28 Heat the housing to about 120ºC (250ºF), install the input shaft roller bearing outer race and secure it with the second retainer.

29 Install the pinion shaft roller bearing outer race (with the retainer already fitted), then install the front retainer (photo).

30 Install the input shaft oil seal, with the lips inwards, and install the cover plate. Lubricate the seal lips with a little general purpose grease (photos).

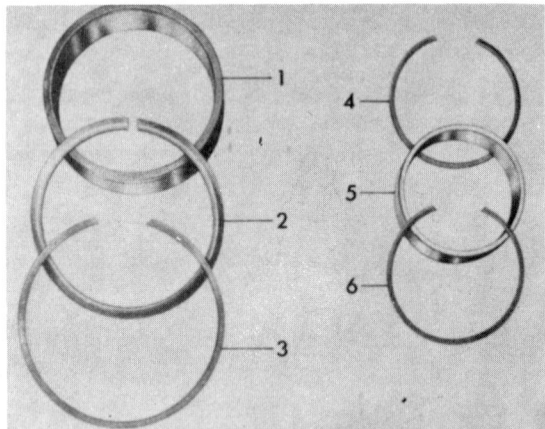

Fig. 5.7. Transmission casing races and retainers (Sec. 3)

1	Outer race - pinion shaft	4	Retainer
2	Retainer, mounted on outer race	5	Outer race - input shaft
3	Retainer	6	Retainer

Fig. 5.8. Inserting the input shaft bearing rear retainer (Sec. 3)

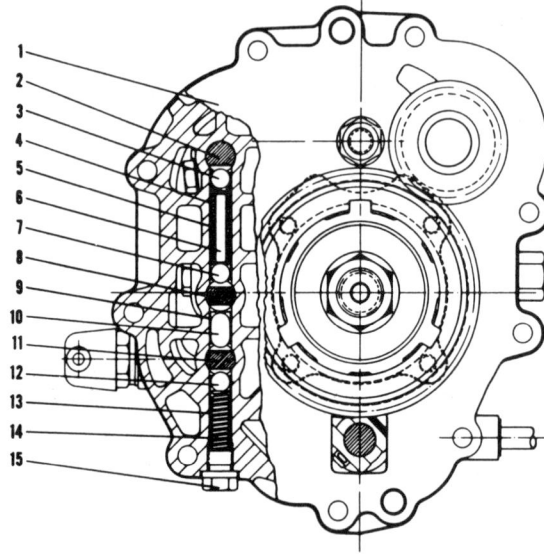

Fig. 5.9. Sectional view showing the detent components (Secs. 3 and 9)

1	Intermediate plate	9	Detent bushing
2	4th/5th selector shaft	10	Detent pin
3	Ball	11	1st/reverse selector shaft
4	Detent bushing	12	Ball
5	Long detent spring	13	Detent bushing
6	Detent pin	14	Reverse detent spring (short)
7	Ball	15	Plug
8	2nd/3rd selector shaft		

3.29 Pinion shaft outer bearing retainer

3.30a Input shaft oil seal ...

3.30b ... and retainer

31 Position the input and pinion shafts into engagement, and install them in the intermediate plate. Do not forget the bearing inner races; the X-marking on the pinion shaft inner race of early models must face outwards (photos).
32 Install the pinion shaft thrust washer with the small collar facing the bearing (photo).
33 Install the needle bearing race, pushing it on using a metal tube of suitable dimensions.
34 Install the needle bearing, followed by the 1st gear (photos).
35 Install the 1st gear on the input shaft (photo).
36 Install the thrust washer and castellated nut. Move the shift sleeves to lock the transmission gears in mesh, then tighten the nut to the lowest torque value specified (photo).
37 Install the reverse gear with the shift sleeve away from 1st gear. Lubricate the thrust face of the expansion bolt, then install it. If the speedometer drive pin was removed, press in the retaining pin before installing the expansion bolt. Tighten the bolt to the specified torque.
38 Where applicable, push the speedometer gear pin out as far as

necessary, then install the speedometer gear and push the pin back in (photo).
39 Further increase the tightening torque if necessary on the castellated nut (whilst not exceeding the specified maximum) and install a new locking pin (photo).
40 Select neutral then place the 4th/5th selector fork onto the appropriate sliding sleeve. Insert the selector shaft (the shift arm should have been already installed at this stage) until it enters the bore of the intermediate plate. Lightly tighten the fork retaining bolt and spring washer (photo).
41 Insert one detent ball, lubricate the long detent pin with grease, put it into the long spring, then put them both into the detent bore (photos).
42 Install the 2nd/3rd shaft fork and shaft in a similar manner, but ensure that the second ball is pressed in the detent bore before the selector shaft is pushed through the intermediate plate. Ensure that 4th/5th shift fork is in the neutral position while this is being done. Lightly tighten the shift fork bolt and spring washer (photo).

3.31a Pinion and input shafts meshed together ...

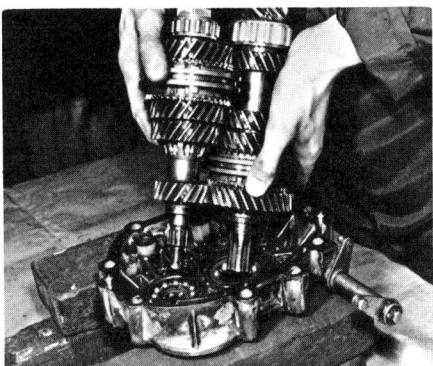
3.31b ... and installed into intermediate plate

3.32 Installing pinion shaft thrust washer

3.34a Install the needle bearing ...

3.34b ... followed by the 1st gear

3.35 Installing the 1st gear

3.36 Installing the thrust washer and castellated nut

3.38 Installing the speedometer gear

3.39 Installing the locking pin

3.40 Installing 4th/5th selector shaft

3.41a Inserting a detent ball ...

3.41b ... followed by the long detent pin and spring

3.42 Installing 2nd/3rd shift fork and shaft

3.43a Inserting the detent pin ...

3.43b ...and 1st/reverse selector shaft

3.44 Inserting the short spring

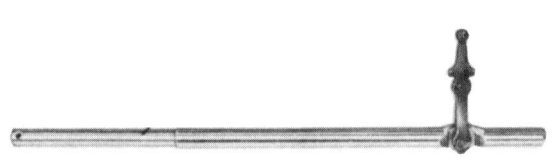

Fig. 5.10. The inner shaft rod assembled (Sec. 3)

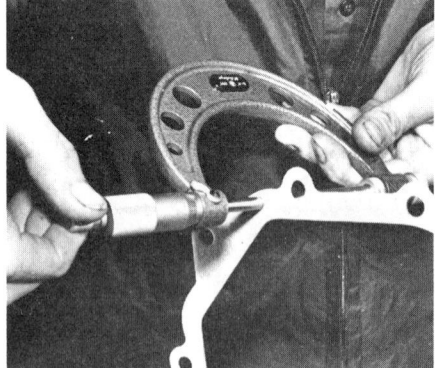

3.47a Measuring gasket thickness ...

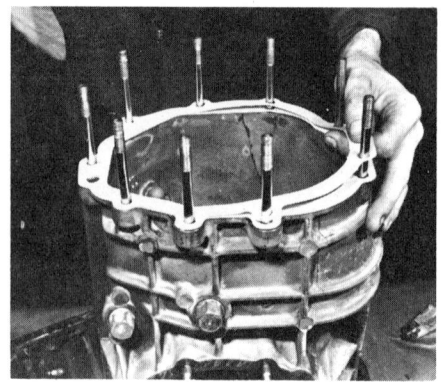

3.47b . . and installing them

3.48 Installing intermediate plate and inner shift rod

3.50 Installing the guide fork and gasket

3.51a Reverse gear parts on intermediate plate

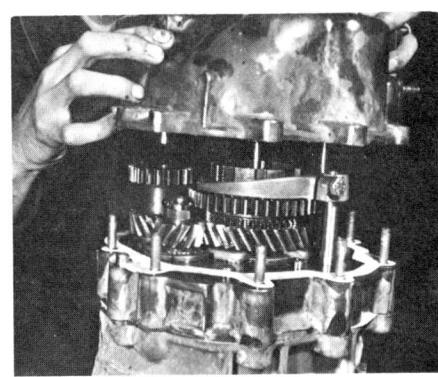

3.51b Installing the front cover

3.51c Speedometer drive in position

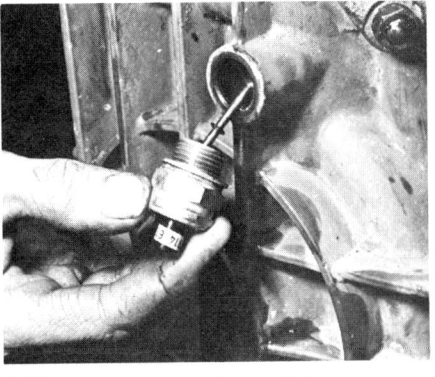

3.52 Installing reverse light switch

43 With the 2nd/3rd selector shaft in the neutral position, insert the detent pin, then install the 1st/reverse selector shaft, passing it through the fork positioned over the shift sleeve (photos).

44 Insert the detent ball and short spring, and tighten the detent plug to the specified torque (photo).

45 The next step is to adjust the shift forks. The procedure for this is given in Section 4, but also see paragraph 18.

46 If dismantled, assemble the inner shift rod, ensuring that the tapered bore in the rod points in the same direction as the inner shift rod. Install a new retaining pin and cotter key.

47 Place the correct thickness of gasket(s) on the housing (see paragraph 13) (photos).

48 Position the inner shift rod through the aperture in the intermediate plate, then select 5th gear and lower the assembly into the housing. The services of an assistant are very useful at this stage. Take great care that the input shaft oil seal is not damaged at this stage as the shaft splines pass through it (photo).

49 Select neutral, and guide the inner shift rod into position at the selector shaft tabs and into the rear bore.

50 Using a new gasket, install the guide fork (photo).

51 Using a new gasket install the assembled front cover (Section 11) and tighten the nuts progressively to the specified torque. **Note:** On the project car, it was found convenient to install the reverse gear parts on the intermediate plate rather than in the rear cover, due to the position of the transmission housing on the bench. If this is done, insert the bearing cages into the 1st/reverse gear, then put the thrust washer in position on the intermediate plate so that the cutout clears the mainshaft bearing. Install the axial thrust bearing, the gear and needle rollers (straight cut gear uppermost), then install the front cover. (Note that the bronze thrust washer is on the shaft in the front cover). The speedometer drive can then be installed (photos).

52 Install the reverse light switch and pin (photo).

53 Install the differential, side cover (using a new gasket or O-ring) and driveshaft flanges. Further information will be found in Section 14.

54 Install the clutch throwout lever and bearing, and add the transmission oil.

4 Shift forks (early type) - adjustment

1   Adjustment of the shift forks will not normally be necessary except where any dismantling has been done. However, it is possible that very slight wear of the selector parts can be compensated for by adjustment although this is an indication of general wear which may indicate that a more extensive general repair is really required. If this adjustment is to be attempted, it is carried out on the assembled intermediate plate which must have been removed from the main transmission housing, as described in paragraphs 1 to 13 of Section 3.

2   The official procedure for adjustment calls for the use of a template (tool no. P260) to hold the shafts in alignment. Using this, adjustment is simplified because the shafts can be adjusted in the horizontal plane and the shift sleeves on the synchro assemblies can easily be set to their mid-positions of travel. If the template is not available the shafts can be mounted horizontally in which case a certain amount of 'swash' can be expected, or mounted vertically which will mean that the synchro sleeves have to be held in their mid-positions of travel. Either of these two methods is liable to inaccuracies occuring if great care is not taken. The procedure below describes the template P260 in use (Fig. 5.11).

3   Select neutral. Position the assembled reverse idler twin gear axial bearing and thrust washer in position on the intermediate plate.

4   Check for a clearance of 0.04 in (1 mm) between the shift gear and reverse idler gear teeth when the shift fork and shift gear are in contact (Fig. 5.12). Adjust the shift fork on its shaft to obtain this clearance, then tighten the bolt to the specified torque. Check that the selector shaft actuating tabs on the 1st/reverse shaft have a side clearance of 0.08 to 0.12 in (2 to 3 mm) in relation to those of the 2nd/3rd shaft (Fig. 5.13.)

5   Ensure that the shift sleeves are in their mid-positions between the synchro rings, then adjust the 4th/5th and 2nd/3rd shift forks. Tighten the shift fork bolts to the specified torque. Check that a side-play of 0.08 to 0.12 in (2 to 3 mm) exists between the actuating tabs on the 4th/5th shaft in relation to those of the 2nd/3rd shaft.

Fig. 5.11. Template P260 in use (Sec. 4)

6   With neutral selected, check the operation of all gears, and adjust, if necessary.

5   Input shaft (early type) - dismantling and reassembly

1   Mount the input shaft between the jaws of a vice, gripping the section forward of the nut and tab washer which is not a bearing surface.
2   Fold back the washer tab and remove the nut from the threaded section.
3   Remove the input shaft from the vice, hold it vertically, loosened nut downwards, and support all the shaft components with the hand. By lightly tapping the shaft on the bench, the components will be loosened and can be taken off. Figs. 5.14 and 5.15 show the components in their correct order; do not interchange bearing parts or rapid wear will result.
4   Commence reassembly by sliding on 3rd gear, narrow flange towards the splined shoulder, followed by the thrust washer. Do not lubricate the faces of any of the gears, sleeves or spacers during the assembly procedure.
5   Install the needle bearing inner race and needle bearing, followed by the 4th gear (photo).
6   Install the shift sleeve and synchro hub (photo).
7   Install the remaining inner race and needle bearing, followed by the 5th gear (photo).
8   Install the thrust washer and roller bearing noting which way round it is fitted (photo).
9   Position a new tab washer on the shaft, lubricate the threads and

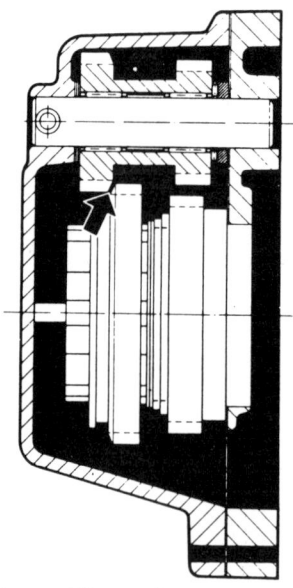

Fig. 5.12. Reverse idler gear clearance (arrowed) (Sec. 4)

Fig. 5.13. Side clearance (lower arrow) between 1st/reverse shaft and 2nd/3rd shaft. (The upper arrow shows the clearance between the 4th/5th and 2nd/3rd shaft) (Sec. 4)

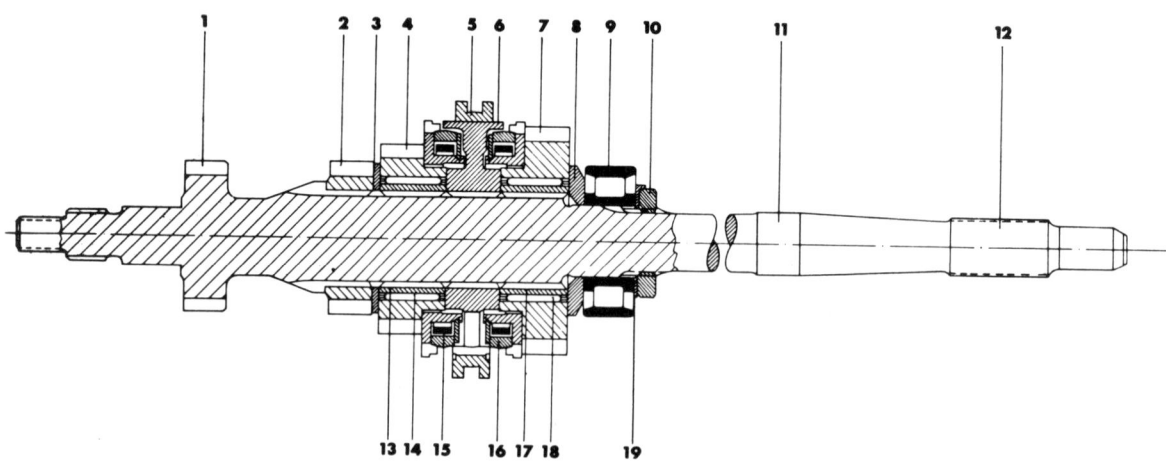

Fig. 5.14. Sectional view of input shaft (Sec. 5)

1 Input shaft	6 Spider (hub)	10 Nut	15 Brake band
2 3rd gear (fixed)	7 5th gear (free-wheeling)	11 Oil seal race	16 Synchronizing ring
3 Thrust washer	8 Thrust washer	12 Splined end	17 Needle bearing inner race
4 4th gear (free-wheeling)	(5.9 mm thickness)	13 Needle bearing inner race	18 Needle bearing cage
5 Sliding sleeve	9 Roller bearing	14 Needle bearing cage	19 Lock plate

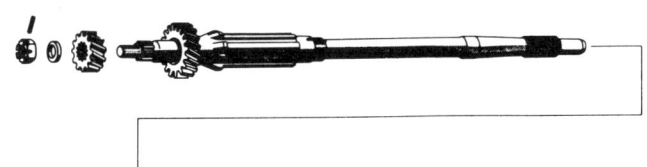

Fig. 5 15. Exploded view of input shaft (Sec. 5)

5.5 Installing the 4th gear

5.6 Installing shift sleeve and synchro hub

5.7 Installing 5th gear

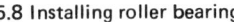

5.8 Installing roller bearing

5.9 Installing the input shaft nut

thrust face of the nut, and tighten to the specified torque while holding the shaft in a vice. Secure the nut with the washer tab (photo).
10 Install the bearing inner race on the opposite end of the shaft. If this is found to be tight, heat it in oil to approximately 100°C (210°F) and carefully press it on.

---

6 Pinion shaft (early type) - dismantling and reassembly

1 With the exception of the bearing, the components of the pinion shaft can easily be removed by holding the shaft vertically, pinion gear upwards, then tapping the lower end of the shaft on the bench whilst the components are supported with the hand. The components are shown in their correct order in Figs. 5.16 and 5.17; do not interchange bearing parts or rapid wear will result. Note the number and total thickness of spacers (items 7 and 17) (Fig. 5.16) which must not be altered, or the pinion meshing depth will need to be reset by a Porsche dealer
2 The bearing will only need to be removed if inspection shows that it is no longer serviceable, in which case the two parts of the inner race must also be renewed. To remove the bearing, either use a puller with

extended legs, or drive the pinion through the bearing with the latter supported across the open jaws of a vice. If a new bearing is required, it is essential that the total thickness of the bearing race (item 8) and spacers is not altered, or the pinion meshing depth will be upset. Therefore, if a new bearing is used, the spacer thickness may need altering to compensate for a different bearing thickness.
3 Where applicable, commence reassembly by pressing on the bearing, noting which way round it is fitted.
4 Install the spacers (17).
5 Install the spacer (7) and 5th gear. Do not lubricate the faces of any of the gears, sleeves or spacers during the assembly procedure.
6 Install the spacer bushing and 4th gear (photos).
7 Install the thrust washer followed by the needle bearing and race (photo).
8 Install the 3rd gear and the 2nd/3rd synchro assembly (photos).
9 Install the 2nd gear needle bearing and race, followed by the 2nd gear (photo).
10 Install the thrust washer (or thrust washer and spacer on transmissions prior to number 100407) with the plain face towards the needle bearing, then press the bearing inner race onto the shaft. If this is found to be tight, heat it in oil to approximately 100°C (210°F) and carefully press it on (photo).

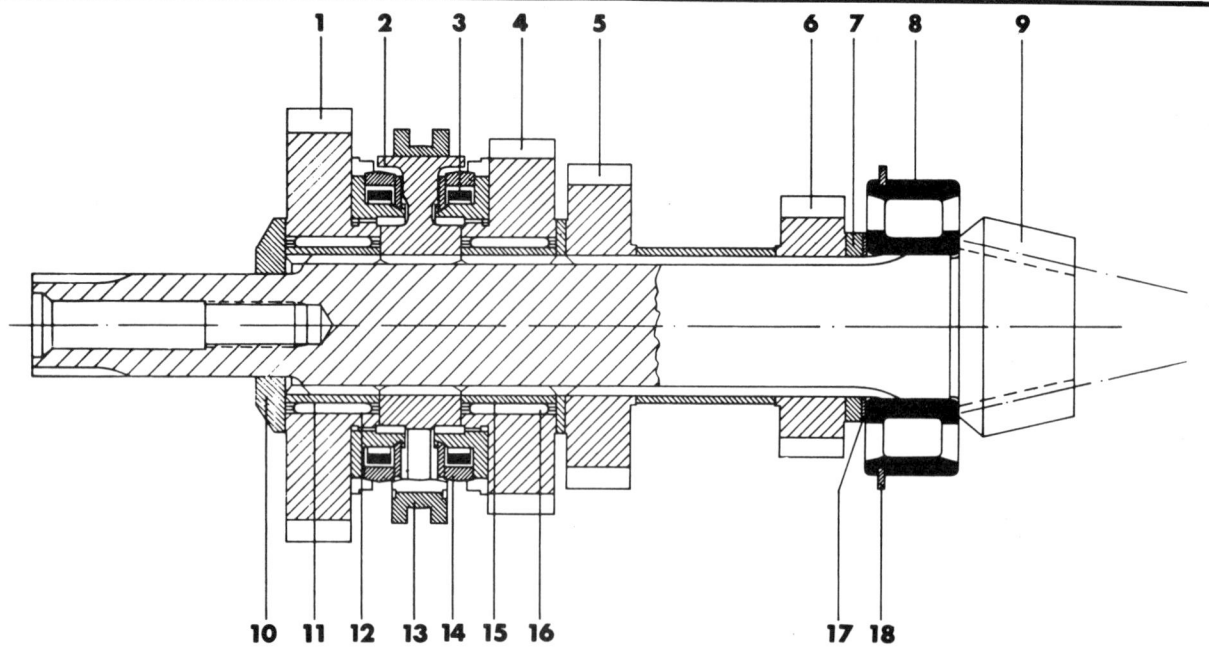

Fig. 5.16. Sectional view of pinion shaft (Sec. 6)

1   2nd gear (free-wheeling)
2   Spider (hub)
3   Brake band
4   3rd gear (free-wheeling)
5   4th gear (fixed)
6   5th gear (fixed)

7   Spacer
8   Roller bearing
9   Pinion shaft
10 Thrust washer (6.6 mm thickness)
11 Needle bearing inner race

12 Needle bearing cage
13 Sliding sleeve
14 Synchronizing ring
15 Needle bearing inner race
16 Needle bearing cage
17 Spacers
18 Retaining ring

Fig. 5.17. Exploded view of pinion shaft (Sec. 6)

6.6a Installing the spacer bushing (5th gear already installed)

6.6b Installing 4th gear

6.7 Thrust washer and bearing race installed

6.8a Installing 3rd gear ...

6.8b ... and the synchro assembly

6.9 Installing 2nd gear

6.10 Installing the thrust washer

7 Inspection of transmission components (early type) - general

1   Each component should be cleaned carefully and wiped dry. Spend a little time on this and get rid of all the old oil and grease; clean the place up and start the inspection with a clean bench, clean hands and clean wiping rag.

2   The inside as well as the outside of the castings should be clean and dry. Examine them for cracks or superficial damage. Studs should be checked for tightness and nuts tried on the stud threads.

3   Examine all the gears for tooth wear, chipped teeth and spalling (cracks and scoring). Damaged gears should be regarded with suspicion. If there is doubt about them consult the Porsche agent. However it is better to put a slightly worn gear back than to mate a new one with an old one. If new gears are installed consideration should be given to replacing the gear with which the new gear is to mesh.

4   Needle and roller bearings should be washed in isopropyl alcohol or clean petrol, lightly oiled and checked for axial and radial play. If they are alright then they should be greased lightly to retain the components in position. Not too much grease though or it may get in places it is not intended for, with disastrous results.

5   The synchronizer assemblies should be checked for wear. Further information on these items will be found in Section 8.

6   Check the shafts for signs of wear or scoring. Splines should not be in any way damaged. If they are, remove the burrs or damaged portions

carefully with a fine file.

7   Examine the shift rods and forks for wear and damage, particularly on the rubbing and sliding surfaces, renewing parts as necessary.

8   Check the detent springs for wear and fretting, and compare them with the length given in the Specifications. Renew them as necessary.

9   Finally if all the parts are laid out in good order, and new parts acquired have been cleaned and put ready in order with the old ones, have a good check round again. Lay out a set of gaskets in a safe place ready for installation. Note that the gasket set supplied may contain some gaskets which will not be used on certain transmissions.

8 Synchronizer assemblies (early type) - dismantling and reassembly

Note: Refer to Section 15 for information on the 1st speed synchronizer assembly used on early 4-speed transmissions. Also see Fig. 5.39 for the component parts of the synchronizers; the 1st gear components are as used in early type 4-speed transmissions and all later type transmissions.

1   Remove the retainer and take off the synchro ring, brake bands (one only on the 1st gear), anchor block and thrust block. Dismantle one assembly at a time and ensure that the parts from different assemblies are not mixed up.

2   Check the synchronizer parts for wear and damage, and obtain replacements, as necessary. If a major transmission overhaul is being

8.2 Typical synchronizer parts

8.5 Installing the retainer

Fig. 5.18. Assembled synchronizer - typical for all transmissions except early type 1st gear (Sec. 8)

Fig. 5.19. Early type 1st gear assembled synchronizer (Sec. 8)

undertaken, or where it has been possible to beat the synchromesh during past gearchanges, these parts should be renewed any way. Retainers may be re-used provided that they are a good spring-fit in the grooves (photo).
3   Examine the shift sleeve and synchro tab for wear and damage. Check each shift fork in its appropriate sleeve and, where excessive side-play exists (see Specifications), obtain replacement parts.
4   Ensure that the synchronizer parts are clean and lightly lubricated, then reassemble them, (see Figs. 5.18 and 5.19). Note that the rough surface of the synchro-ring faces the shift sleeve.
5   Position the tongue of the retainer into the anchor block cut-out. Push the retainer into the groove, whilst pressing the synchro-ring onto its seat, and spread it with circlip pliers (photo).
6   At this stage, check the overall diameter of the synchro-ring with a micrometer at its highest point. If outside the specified diameter limits, dismantle and reassemble with replacement parts.

9   Intermediate plate (early type) - dismantling and reassembly

1   The intermediate plate need only be dismantled where the ball bearing assemblies or detent drilling bushes require renewal.
2   To remove the ball bearing assemblies, remove the clamping plate and support plate. Heat the intermediate plate in an oven to approximately 120°C (250°F) then press out the bearings.
3   Where necessary, the detent drilling bushings can be extracted using a hook-ended tool.
4   Reassembly is the reverse of the dismantling procedure. Press in new bearings to full depth after heating the intermediate plate to 120°C (250°F). Ensure that the detent drilling bushes are installed in the correct order (see Fig. 5.9), and that they do not protrude into the shift rod bores. Use a suitably sized arbor to prevent damage while pressing them in. **Note:** If the intermediate plate is renewed it is essential that the pinion meshing depth is reset; this is a job for your Porsche dealer or a transmission specialist.

10 Transmission housing (early type) - breather

1   Early transmission of this type (prior to no. 100100) used a small breaker pipe and labyrinth in the front cover. Later transmissions use a breather which screws into the differential section of the housing.
2   The breather is removed by unscrewing it.
3   Before installing it, clean it in petrol and dry it with a lint-free cloth.
4   When installing, ensure that the breather vent hole is positioned as shown in Fig. 5.22.

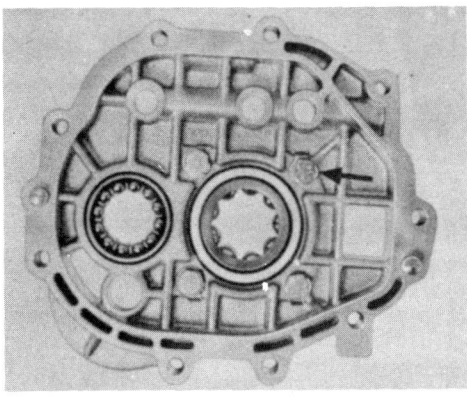

Fig. 5 20. Intermediate plate (early type, prior to 1968) (Sec. 9)
The arrow indicates a clamping plate bolt

Fig. 5.21. Intermediate plate (early type, 1968 onwards) (Sec. 9)
NOTE: On this type special washers are used between the keeper
plate and the support plate

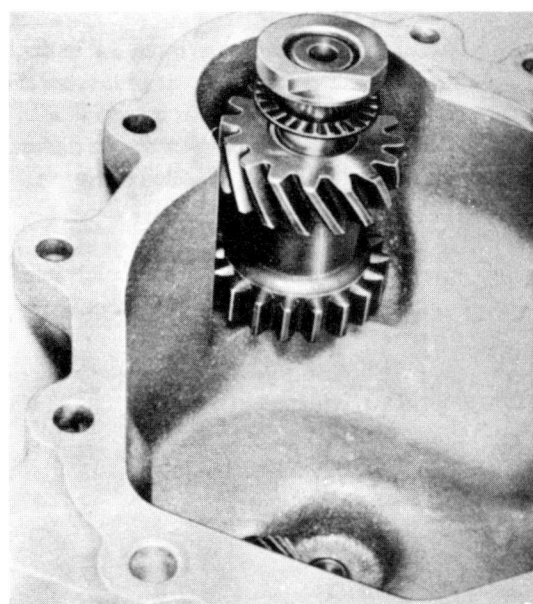

Fig. 5.23. 1st/reverse gear, axial thrust bearing and thrust washer
inside front cover (Sec. 11)

11 Transmission front cover (early type) - dismantling and reassembly

1   Having removed the front cover, take off the thrust washer, axial
thrust needle bearing and 1st/reverse gear.
2   Remove the bearing cages and spacer bushing.
3   Remove the locking screw and withdraw the speedometer elbow

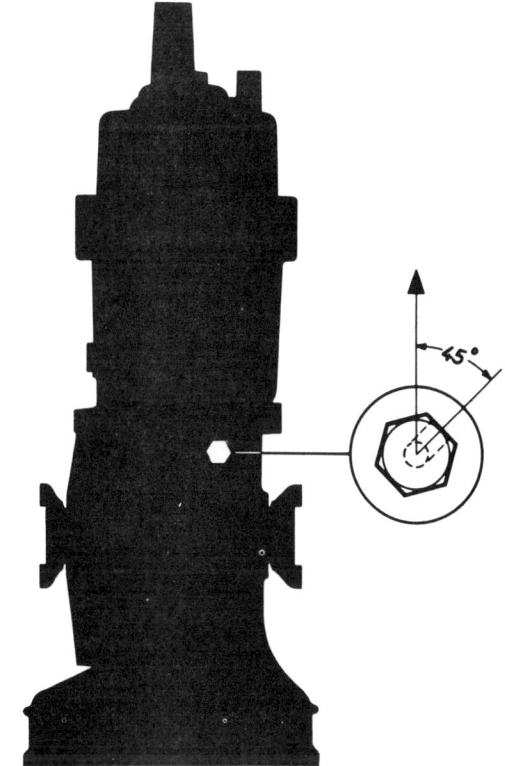

Fig. 5.22. Installed position of breather (Sec. 10)

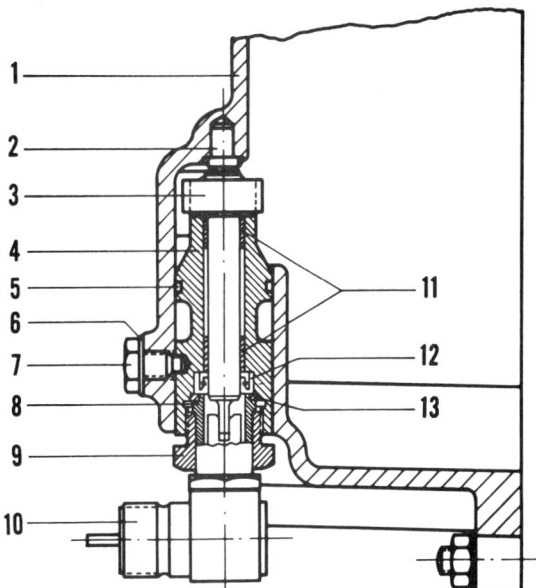

Fig. 5.24. Sectional view of speedometer drive. (Sec. 11)

1 Front cover of	7 Set screw
transmission	8 Elbow drive
2 Thrust stud	9 Coupling nut
3 Connecting shaft	10 Elbow drive
4 Bushing	11 Support bushings
5 O-ring	12 Oil seal
6 Spring washer	13 Central disc

drive.

4   If necessary, drive out the reverse gear shaft retaining pin, then heat the cover in an oven to approximately 120°C (250°F) and drive the shaft inwards to remove it.

5   Press the bronze thrust washer off the shaft.

6   Check the inner shift rod oil seal, and replace it if necessary (photo).

7   Clean all the parts in petrol and dry them with a lint-free cloth. Any parts showing wear or damage should be replaced.

8   Reassembly is basically the reverse of the dismantling procedure. As well as heating the cover to install the shaft, also heat the thrust washer to 120°C (250°F) and press it on so that it seats against the cover (photo).

9   Install a bearing cage, the spacer, then the second bearing cage on the shaft; then push on the gear, straight cut gear first (photo).

10   Install the axial thrust needle bearing and thrust washer, then install the speedometer drive gear (photo).

12 Gearshift linkage (early type) - removal, installation and adjustment

1   Remove both front seats, then remove the gearshift knob, heater knob, dust boot and tunnel cover.

2   Remove the retaining bolts and lift off the gearshift base.

3   Remove the retaining screws and lift off the tunnel rear cover.

4   Pull back the dust boot, then loosen the clamp bolt and push the shift rod off the coupling (photo).

5   Remove the shift rod clamp and boot.

6   At the shift lever end remove the lockwire, loosen the square headed screw and slide the shift rod joint off its base (Fig. 5.26).

7   Slide the shift rod joint off the shift rod.

8   Installation is the reverse of the removal procedure, but it will be necessary to adjust the linkage as described below before the rear tunnel cover is fitted.

11.6 Installing inner shift rod oil seal

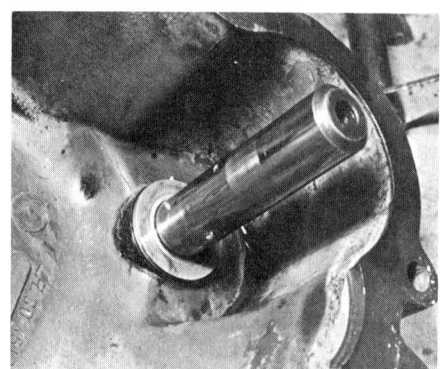
11.8 Thrust washer installed

11.9 Installing the idler gear

11.10 Installing the thrust washer

12.4 Shift rod coupling bolt removed

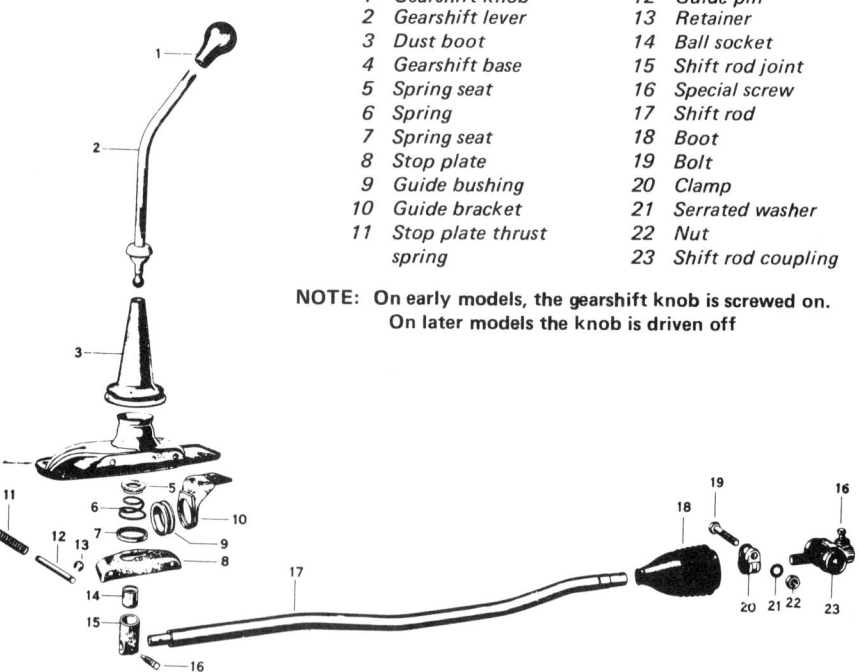

1 Gearshift knob	12 Guide pin
2 Gearshift lever	13 Retainer
3 Dust boot	14 Ball socket
4 Gearshift base	15 Shift rod joint
5 Spring seat	16 Special screw
6 Spring	17 Shift rod
7 Spring seat	18 Boot
8 Stop plate	19 Bolt
9 Guide bushing	20 Clamp
10 Guide bracket	21 Serrated washer
11 Stop plate thrust spring	22 Nut
	23 Shift rod coupling

NOTE: On early models, the gearshift knob is screwed on. On later models the knob is driven off

Fig. 5.25. Shift linkage components (Sec. 12)

Fig. 5.26. Removing the square-headed screw (Sec. 12)

14.12 Installing differential casing oil seal

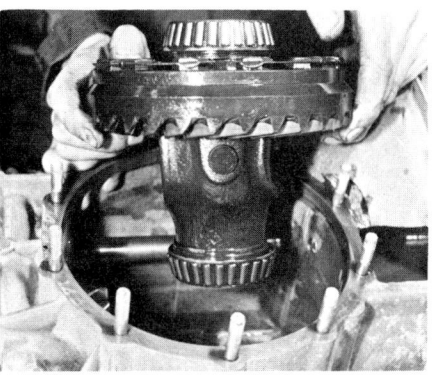

14.13 Installing differential

14.14 Installing differential cover

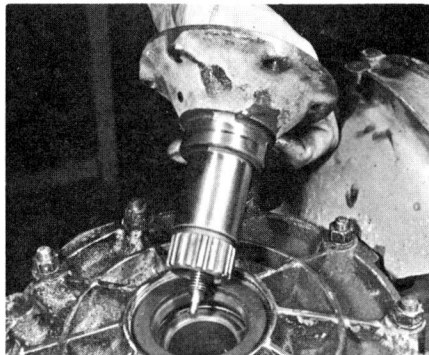

14.15 Installing the flange and stub shaft

Adjustment
9   With the shift rod clamp bolt loose, move the shift lever in the transmission pulley left to the stop while in the neutral position.
10 With the transmission in neutral, move the gearshift lever fully right to the stop.
11 Tighten the clamp bolt, check the shift lever operation, then install the rear tunnel cover.

13 Final drive differential (early type) - general description

The Porsche 911 models may be equipped with either a conventional differential or a limited-slip differential.

With a conventional differential the power is transferred to the wheel with the least traction, this can result in wheelspin during adverse accelerating or cornering conditions. With a limited-slip differential power is transferred to the wheel with the greatest traction, power being taken from the wheel with the least traction to prevent it from slipping. This is accomplished by transmitting the drive from the ring gear through a series of friction discs to the differential case and pinion gears, instead of transmitting it directly.

As stated in Section 1 of this Chapter, the only job which should be attempted is removal and installation of the differential.

14 Differential (early type) - removal and installation

1   It is possible to remove the differential with the transmission installed in the car. However, where any replacement parts or adjustment are required, it may be advantageous to remove the engine/transmission, as described in Chapter 1. If the differential is removed with the transmission installed, detach the driveshafts as described in Chapter 6. Also detach the clutch cable and rear throttle linkage.

2   Install two bolts in one of the driveshaft flanges and arrange a bar, so that as the expansion bolt is loosened, the turning effect of the flange will wedge the bar against the bolts and the transmission housing. Remove the bolt completely, and withdraw the flange and stub shaft.
3   Repeat this operation for the other flange.
4   Mark the installed position of the differential side cover, then remove it from the housing.
5   Lift out the differential assembly.
6   The only remaining job which can readily be done is renewal of the oil seals. If it is found that the bearing outer races (and the bearings on the differential) require renewal, these jobs can be done by reference to paragraphs 7 to 12, but it is possible that re-shimming of the bearings will be required. This will need to be checked by a Porsche dealer or transmission specialist.
7   Where necessary, drive out the bearing outer races from the transmission housing and cover.
8   Where necessary, pull off the differential bearings using a universal puller. Do not mix up the shims and spacer washers from side-to-side.
9   Inspect the parts for obvious damage whilst removed.
10 Press on new bearings using a suitable diameter tube, applying loads to the inner race only.
11 To install new outer races it will be necessary to heat the cover and housing to approximately 120ºC (250ºF) in an oven (do not use a naked flame). The bearing races can then be pressed in.
12 When the housing and cover have cooled, install new oil seals (photo).
13 Position the differential into the housing (photo).
14 Install the cover using a new O-ring lubricated with transmission oil. Install the washers and nuts, and tighten to the specified torque (photo).
15 Install the flange and stub shaft (photo).
16 Lock the universal flanges, as described in paragraph 2, and tighten the expansion bolts to the specified torque.

15 Four-speed transmission (early type) - general

1   Dismantling and reassembly procedures are similar to those given previously for the 5-speed transmission. However, the following important points should be noted:

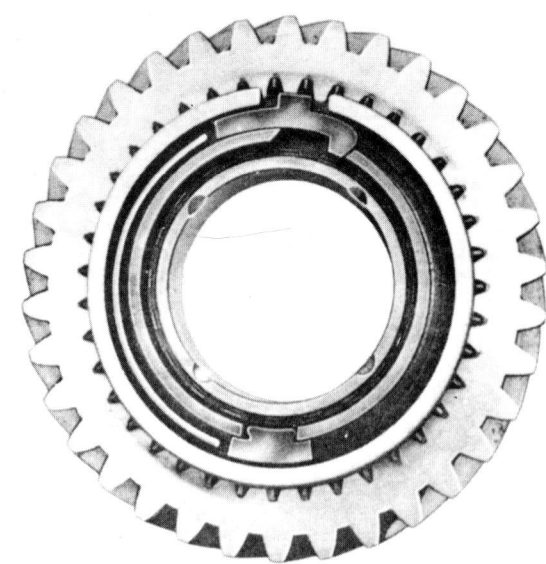

Fig. 5.27. Four-speed transmission (early type) 1st gear synchronizer assembly (Secs. 15, 21 and 40)

a) *The arrangement of the gears on the 4-speed pinion shaft is the same as gears 2 to 5 on the 5-speed pinion shaft.*

b) *The front cover houses the reverse gear only on the 4-speed transmission.*

c) *Due to the reversed action of the synchronizer assemblies of the 1st gear in the 4-speed transmission, the synchro components have to be assembled in the opposite way. When assembling the 4-speed transmission 1st gear synchronizer assembly, remember to use only one brake band - see Fig. 5.27. Note: Also refer to Section 21 and Fig. 5.39, which deal with the virtually identical synchronizer assembly used on later type transmissions.*

d) *The pinion shaft is shown in Figs. 5.28 and 5.29.*

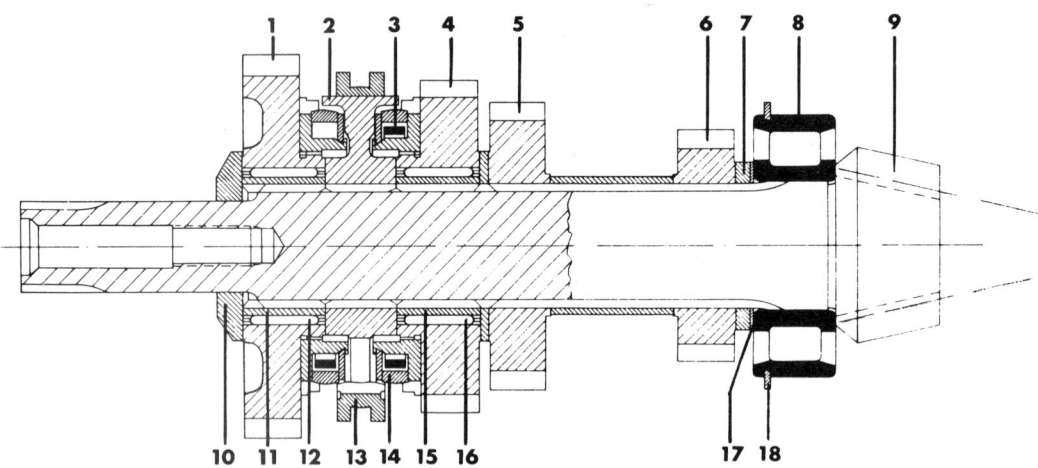

Fig. 5.28. Four-speed transmission (early type) — Sectional view of pinion shaft (Sec. 15)

1 Four-point ballbearing	7 Spacer	13 Sliding sleeve
2 1st gear (free-wheeling)	8 Roller bearing	14 Synchronizing ring
3 Brake band	9 Pinion shaft	15 Needle bearing inner race
4 2nd gear (Free-wheeling	10 Thrust washer (6.6 mm thickness)	16 Needle bearing cage
5 3rd gear (fixed)	11 Needle bearing inner race	17 Spacers
6 4th gear (fixed)	12 Needle bearing cage	18 Retaining ring

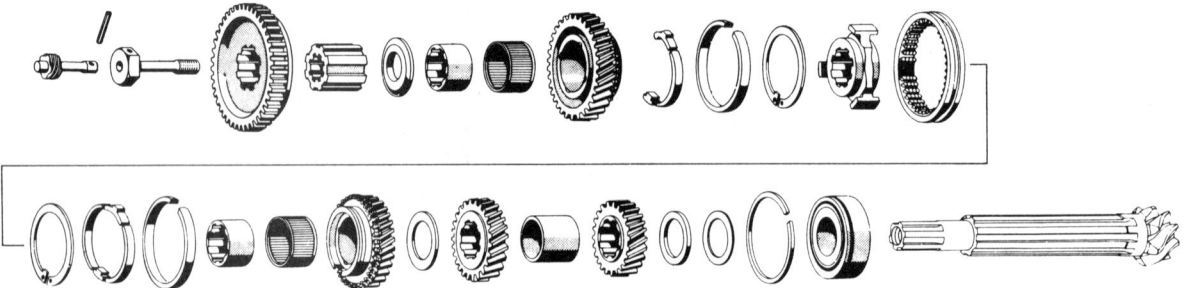

Fig. 5.29. Four-speed transmission (early type) — Exploded view of pinion shaft. (Sec. 15)

16 Five - speed transmission (later type) - dismantling into major assemblies, and reassembly

Note: It must be appreciated that adjustment of the shift forks on this type of transmission is not straightforward. It is recommended that paragraph 15 of this Section, and all of Section 17 is read before any dismantling is commenced.

1 Initially proceed as described in paragraph 1, 2 and 3 of Section 3.
Note: The transmission final drive housing is manufactured from magnesium alloy. Take care that any cleaning solvents are non-corrosive to this type of material.
2 Remove the transmission front cover.
3 Remove the cover and guide fork from the gear housing.
4 Select 5th gear using the shift rod, then move the selector fork to also select 1st, 2nd, 3rd or 4th gear to lock-up the transmission.
5 Remove the roll pin and castellated nut from the input shaft.
6 Remove the flange nut from the pinion shaft.
7 Remove the roll pin, then take out the bolt and take off the 5th/reverse shift fork.
8 Remove the 5th/reverse sliding gear.
9 Remove the O-ring, thrust washer, idler gear, bearing cages, intermediate ring and axial thrust bearing.
10 Remove the reverse gear from the input shaft, followed by the 5th speed fixed gear, and the 5th/reverse idle shaft.
11 Remove the guide sleeve, 5th gear, needle bearing cage, bushing and thrust washer from the pinion shaft. Ensure that the needle bearing does not get mixed up with others yet to be removed.
12 Select neutral.
13 Remove the nuts and washers, then separate the gear housing from the transmission housing. The 5th/reverse shift fork rod and the gear shift rod will remain with the gear housing; the shafts, gears and selector will remain with the transmission housing.
14 Remove the 3rd/4th shift detent plug, seal washer, spring and short detent.
15 To simplify the shift fork adjustment procedure during reassembly, carefully mark the installed position of the shift guide, and the 1st/2nd and 3rd/4th shift forks on their respective rods.
16 Remove the 1st/2nd shift fork bolt and washer, then carefully spread the gap of the clamping piece with a screwdriver to loosen it on the shift rod.
17 Remove the nuts and washers from the input and pinion shaft retaining plates.
18 Withdraw the input and pinion shafts (meshed together) complete with 3rd/4th shift rod and fork, and the 1st/2nd shift fork. The 1st/2nd shift rod remains in the transmission housing.
19 Remove the 1st/2nd shift fork before it accidentally falls off.
20 Remove the 3rd/4th shift rod, and the shift fork and guide.
21 Remove the plug and short detent from the top of the transmission housing.
22 Remove the plug, seal washer, spring and short detent, then pull out the 1st/2nd selector rod.
23 Take off the shim(s), noting the thickness and quantity. **Note:** This is very important since it will be necessary for the pinion meshing depth to be reset if the total shim thickness is altered. This will be a job for the Porsche dealer or a transmission specialist.
24 For further information on dismantling the shafts, transmission front cover, gear housing, transmission housing and synchro - assemblies, together with inspection of these parts, refer to the appropriate following Sections.
25 In general, reassembly is the reverse of the removal procedure, commencing with putting the correct number and quantity of shims (see paragraph 23) on the transmission housing studs.
26 Insert the 1st/2nd shift rod, followed by the shift detent, spring, seal washer and plug.
27 Position the 1st/2nd shift fork onto the shift sleeve, then offer the assembly up to the transmission housing and shift rod. Insert the pinion only far enough for the bearing to just rest in the race in the housing.
Note: If the shift fork binds in the rod, open up the gap in the damping piece with a screwdriver.
28 Insert the input shaft to mesh with the pinion shaft, and push them both fully home.
29 Install the washers and nuts on the clamping plate, and tighten to the specified torque.
30 Lightly tighten the 1st/2nd shift fork bolt.
31 Insert the short detent from the top of the transmission housing.

32 Position the 3rd/4th shiftfork and clamping piece loosely on the end of the shift rod, then position the fork in the shift sleeve groove. Push in the shift rod and lightly tighten the shift fork bolt.
33 Ensure that the short detent (paragraph 31) is between the two shift rods, and loose in its drilling, then install the plug in the top of the transmission housing.
34 Insert the 3rd/4th detent, spring, seal washer and plug.
35 The next step is to adjust the 1st/2nd and 3rd/4th shift forks. See Section 17 for further information, but also refer to paragraph 15.
36 Install the gear housing, complete with the 5th/reverse shift rod and the gearshift rod, using a new gasket. Tighten the nuts to the specified torque.
37 Push the 5th/reverse shift rod into the ball sleeve, and the gearshift rod into the shift pawl guides.
38 Install the idler gear shaft, turning it until it locates with the pin in the housing.
39 Install the 5th gear and reverse gear on the mainshaft, and turn the nut on a few turns to retain them. **Note:** Ensure that the small flange on the 5th gear faces the gear housing.

Fig. 5.30. Retaining bolts for cover and guide fork (arrowed) (Sec. 16)

Fig. 5.31. Removing the input and pinion shafts (Sec. 16)
The arrows indicate the 3rd/4th detent plug hole and the bolt removed from the 1st/2nd shift fork.

Fig. 5.32. Installing the pinion shaft (Sec. 16)

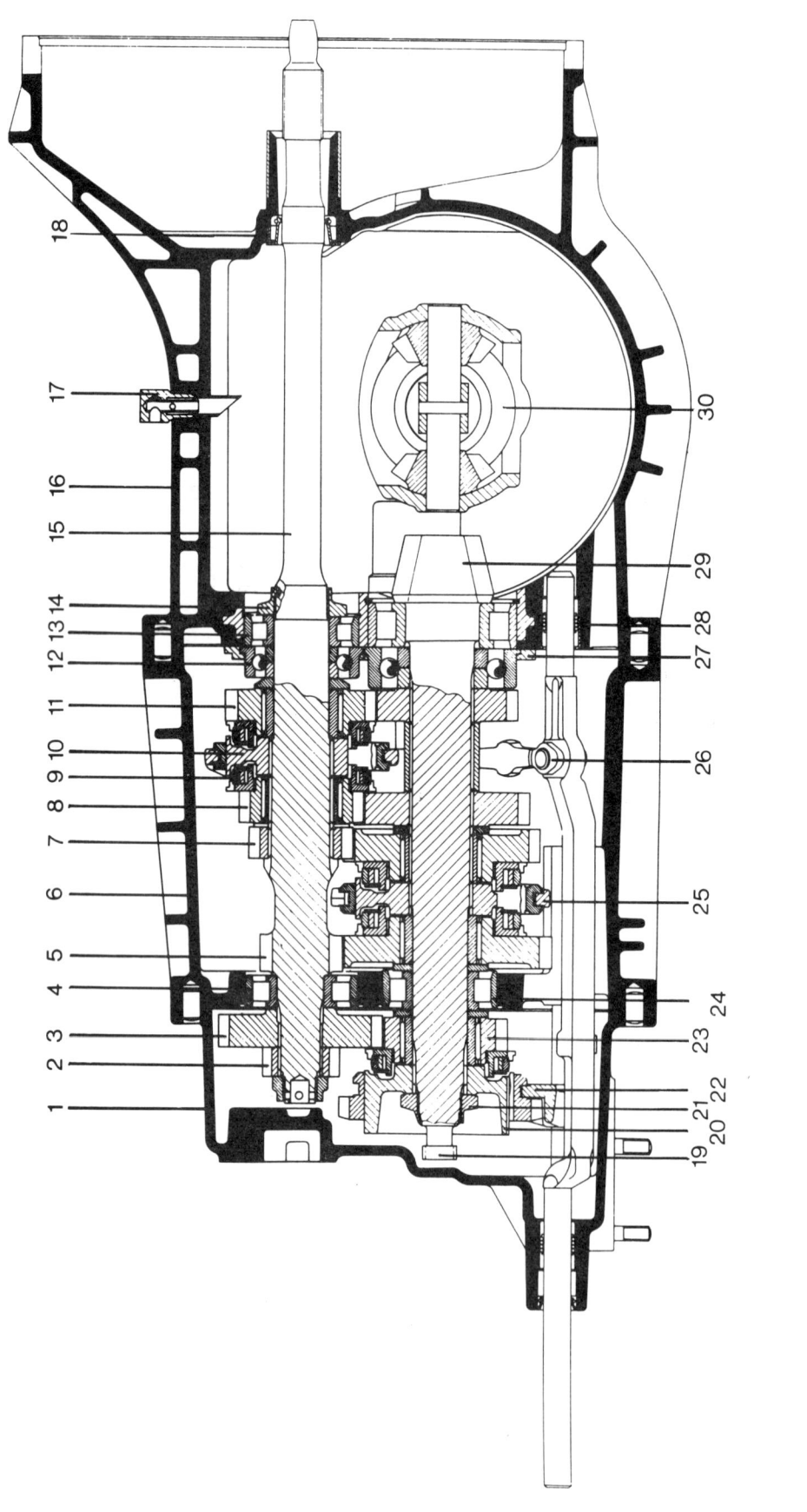

Fig. 5.33. Sectional view of transmission and differential (later type) (Sec. 16)

1 Transmission front cover
2 Reverse gear
3 5th gear (fixed)
4 Roller bearing
5 1st gear (fixed)
6 Gear housing
7 2nd gear (fixed)
8 3rd gear (free-wheeling)
9 Synchronizing ring
10 Spider (synchro hub)
11 4th gear (free-wheeling)
12 Ball bearing
13 Roller bearing
14 Flange nut
15 Input shaft
16 Transmission housing
17 Breather
18 Seal
19 Speedometer gear
20 Spider (5th/reverse)
21 Flange nut
22 Shift fork (5th/reverse)
23 5th gear (free-wheeling)
24 Roller bearing
25 Shift fork (1st/2nd)
26 Selector shaft
27 Bearing retaining plate
28 Ball sleeve
29 Pinion shaft
30 Differential

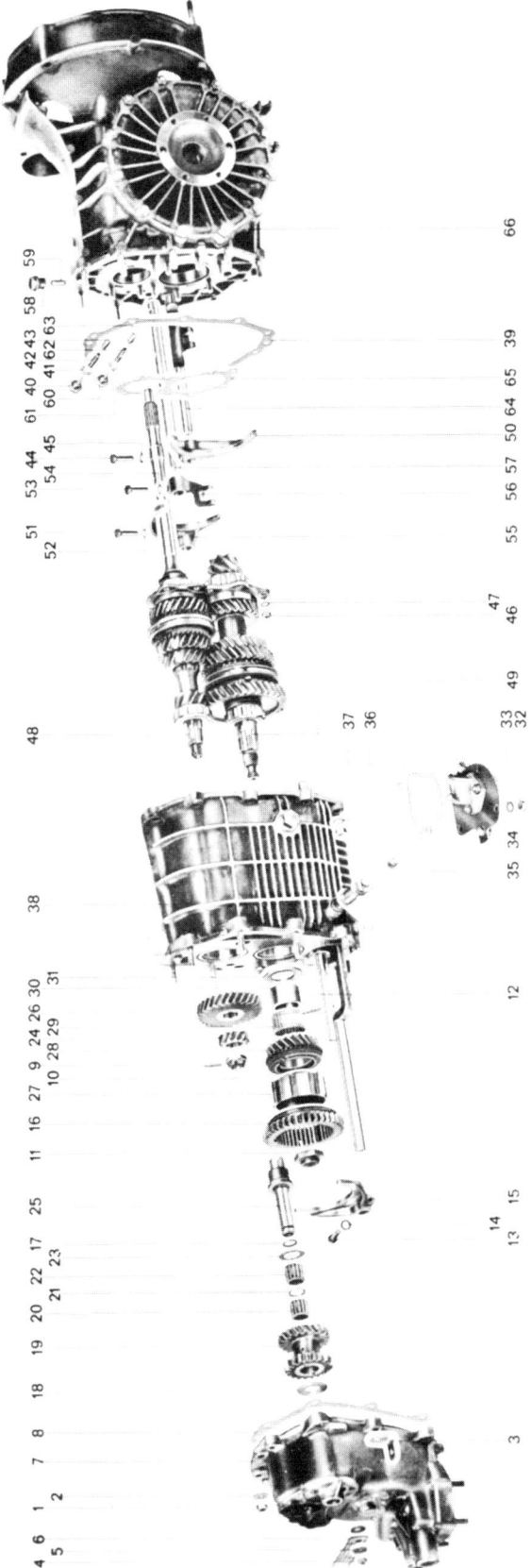

Fig. 5.34. Later type five-speed transmission — exploded view (Sec. 16)

1 Self-locking nut
2 Washer
3 Clutch cable bracket
4 Self-locking nut
5 Washer
6 Earth strap
7 Front cover
8 Gear housing gasket
9 Roll pin
10 Castellated nut
11 Flange nut
12 Roll pin
13 Bolt
14 Spring washer
15 Shift fork (5th/reverse

16 Sliding gear (5th/reverse)
17 O-ring
18 Thrust washer
19 5th/reverse idler gear
20 Needle bearing cage
21 Intermediate ring
22 Needle bearing cage
23 Thrust needle bearing cage
24 Reverse gear
25 Shaft for 5th/reverse idler gear

26 5th gear (fixed)
27 Guide sleeve
28 5th gear (free-wheeling)
29 Needle bearing cage
30 Bushing
31 Thrust washer
32 Self-locking nut
33 Washer
34 Cover and guide fork
35 Gasket
36 Self-locking nut
37 Washer
38 Gear housing
39 Gasket

40 Plug
41 Seal
42 Spring
43 Short detent
44 Nut
45 Spring washer
46 Nut
47 Lock washer
48 Input shaft
49 Pinion shaft
50 1st/2nd shift fork
51 Bolt
52 Spring washer
53 Bolt

54 Spring washer
55 3rd/4th shift fork
56 Shift guide
57 3rd/4th shift fork
58 Plug
59 Short detent
60 Plug
61 Seal
62 Spring
63 Short detent
64 1st/2nd selector fork rod
65 Shim
66 Transmission housing

40 Install the thrust washer on the pinion shaft, followed by the bushing, needle bearing and 5th gear.
41 Install the guide sleeve and turn the nut on a few turns to retain it.
42 Install the axial thrust needle bearing on the idler shaft, followed by a needle bearing cage, the intermediate ring, the second needle bearing cage, the 5th/reverse idler (straight cut teeth outwards) and the thrust washer.
43 Position the 5th/reverse shift fork on the 5th/reverse gear, slide the gear onto the guide sleeve while, at the same time, ensuring that the fork engages on the shift rod. If necessary open up the slot in the fork clamping piece with a screwdriver.
44 Install the shift fork bolt and washer, and lightly tighten it.
45 Lubricate a rear O-ring and install it on the idler shaft.
46 Lock-up the transmission as described in paragraph 4.
47 Tighten the input shaft nut to the minimum specified torque, then increase the torque until the pin hole aligns with one of the castellations. Install a new roll pin.
48 Tighten the mainshaft flanged nut to the specified torque, then lock it by centre punching.
49 Select neutral, then install the guide fork and cover, using a new gasket.
50 Adjust the 5th/reverse shift fork, as described in Section 17.
51 Install the reverse light switch and adjusting pin, recessed end of the pin towards the switch.
52 Install the front cover using a new gasket. Note that there is a flat washer on each side of the earth strap; tighten the nuts to the specified torque.
53 Coat the magnesium alloy transmission housing with an underbody paint to protect it from corrosion due to salt spray etc which may be encountered on roads.
54 Install the clutch throw out bearing, and add the transmission oil.

17 Shift forks (later type) - adjustment

1 Apart from adjustment of the 5th/reverse shift fork, it is not considered practicable to adjust the 1st/2nd and 3rd/4th shift forks. This is because the procedure requires the use of two special tools, one of which provides location for the shafts and shift rods, as well as acting as a distance piece of equivalent thickness to the front wall of the gear housing, while the other locks the shafts and gears against rotation

Fig. 5.35. 5th/reverse sliding gear clearance (arrowed) (Sec. 17)

while the input shaft and pinion shaft nuts are tightened. This operation must therefore be entrusted to the Porsche dealer, or a transmission specialist.
2 To adjust the 5th/reverse shift fork, install the idler gear and push it into contact with the 5th speed fixed gear on the input shaft.
3 Adjust the clearance between the idler gear and the 5th/reverse sliding gear on the pinion shaft to obtain 0.04 in (1 mm). This should be checked when applying light pressure to the sliding gear (away from the gear coming free) to ensure that the shift fork is against the sidewall of the groove.
4 Tighten the shift fork bolt to the specified torque when the correct adjustment is obtained.

18 Input shaft (later type) - dismantling and reassembly

1 The procedure is essentially as described in Section 5, although gears are installed in a different order owing to the different transmission layout.
2 Refer to Fig. 5.37 which shows the parts in their order of removal. Note that when installing the inner bearing races (items 3 and 6) they may be heated to approximately 120°C (250°F) if they cannot be pressed on readily when they are cold.
3 After installing and torque tightening the flanged nut, lock it by centre punching.

19 Pinion shaft (later type) - dismantling and reassembly

1 The procedure is essentially as described in Section 6. However, it may be necessary to press the gears off the pinion shaft if the roller bearing at the speedometer gear end is a tight fit. This operation is best achieved by supporting the shaft vertically, pinion gear downwards, so that the flanged side of the four point bearing is supported on a tube of suitable diameter. By applying blows from a soft-faced hammer the shaft can be driven downwards and out of the bearing.
2 The layout of the gears and associated parts are shown in Fig. 5.38. Do not remove the pinion end roller bearing unless its condition warrants renewal. If this bearing is renewed the pinion meshing depth will be upset. However, provided that the depth of the new and old bearing is known, this can be compensated for by altering the shim thickness (item 65 in Fig. 34). For example, if the new bearing is 0.001 in (0.025 mm) shorter than the old one, a shim of 0.001 (0.025 mm) increased thickness will be required, and vice-versa.
3 Note that when installing the inner bearing races (item 15), they may be heated to approximately 120°C (250°F) if they cannot be pressed on readily when they are cold.

20 Inspection of transmission components (later type) - general

1 Refer to Section 7, which gives all the necessary information on inspection of transmission components. The reference at paragraph 5 should read Section 21 for later type transmissions.

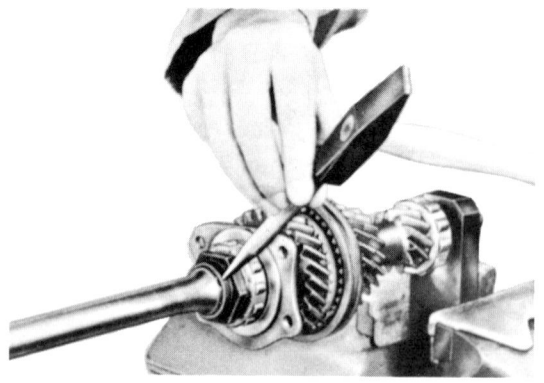

Fig. 5.36. Locking the input shaft flanged nut (Sec. 18)

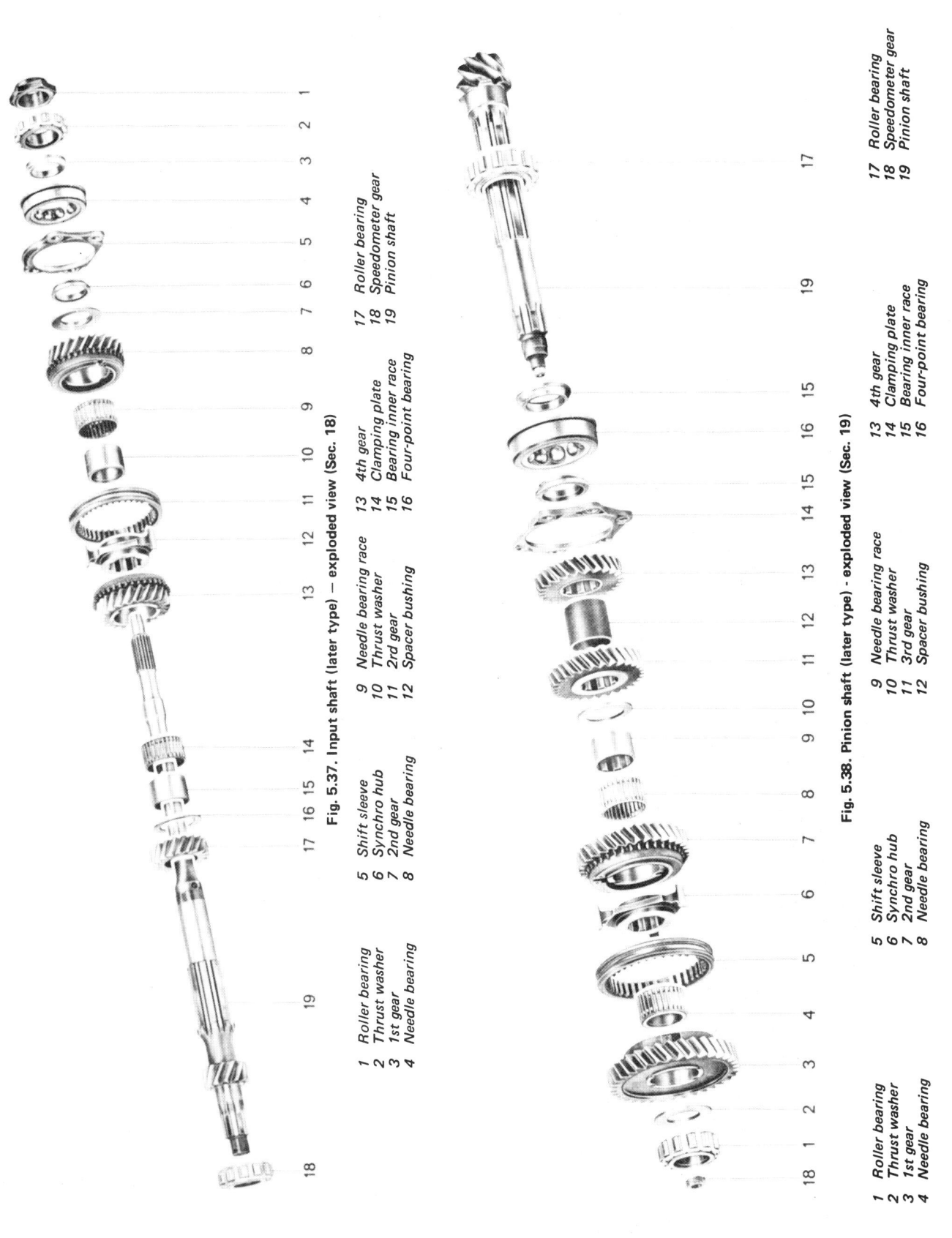

Fig. 5.37. Input shaft (later type) — exploded view (Sec. 18)

1	Roller bearing	5	Shift sleeve	9	Needle bearing race	13	4th gear	17	Roller bearing
2	Thrust washer	6	Synchro hub	10	Thrust washer	14	Clamping plate	18	Speedometer gear
3	1st gear	7	2nd gear	11	2nd gear	15	Bearing inner race	19	Pinion shaft
4	Needle bearing	8	Needle bearing	12	Spacer bushing	16	Four-point bearing		

Fig. 5.38. Pinion shaft (later type) - exploded view (Sec. 19)

1	Roller bearing	5	Shift sleeve	9	Needle bearing race	13	4th gear	17	Roller bearing
2	Thrust washer	6	Synchro hub	10	Thrust washer	14	Clamping plate	18	Speedometer gear
3	1st gear	7	2nd gear	11	3rd gear	15	Bearing inner race	19	Pinion shaft
4	Needle bearing	8	Needle bearing	12	Spacer bushing	16	Four-point bearing		

21 Synchronizer assemblies (later type) - dismantling and reassembly

1   Refer to Section 8 which gives all the necessary information on the synchronizer assemblies. Note that the first gear synchronizer is assembled in the opposite way to the early type - see Fig. 5.39. (In fact, the later type 1st speed synchronizer is similar to the early type 4-speed transmission 1st speed synchronizer - see Fig. 5.27).

22 Transmission front cover (later type)

Two types of front cover are used on the later type transmissions, the difference being that Carrera models have an oil pump driven from the input shaft. For further information see Section 28.

Dismantling and reassembly - general
1   The two types of front cover are shown in Figs. 5.40 and 5.41.

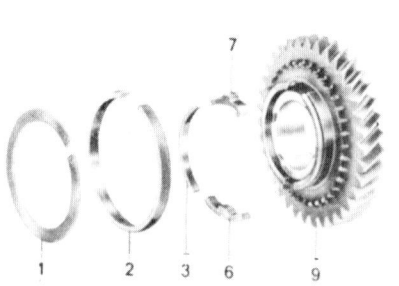
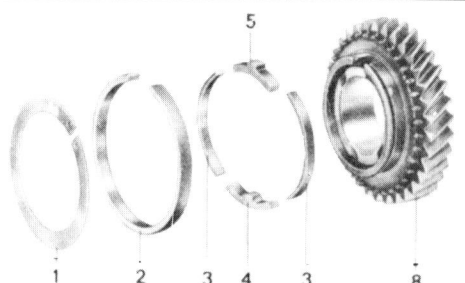

Fig. 5.39. Component parts of synchronize/assemblies used on later type transmissions (Secs. 8, 15 and 21)

1   Circlip
2   Synchronizing ring
3   Brake band, only 1 for 1st speed
4   Brake band anchor block, 2nd speed
5   Thrust block, 2nd speed
6   Brake band anchor block, 1st speed
7   Thrust block, 1st speed
8   Gear, 2nd speed
9   Gear, 1st speed

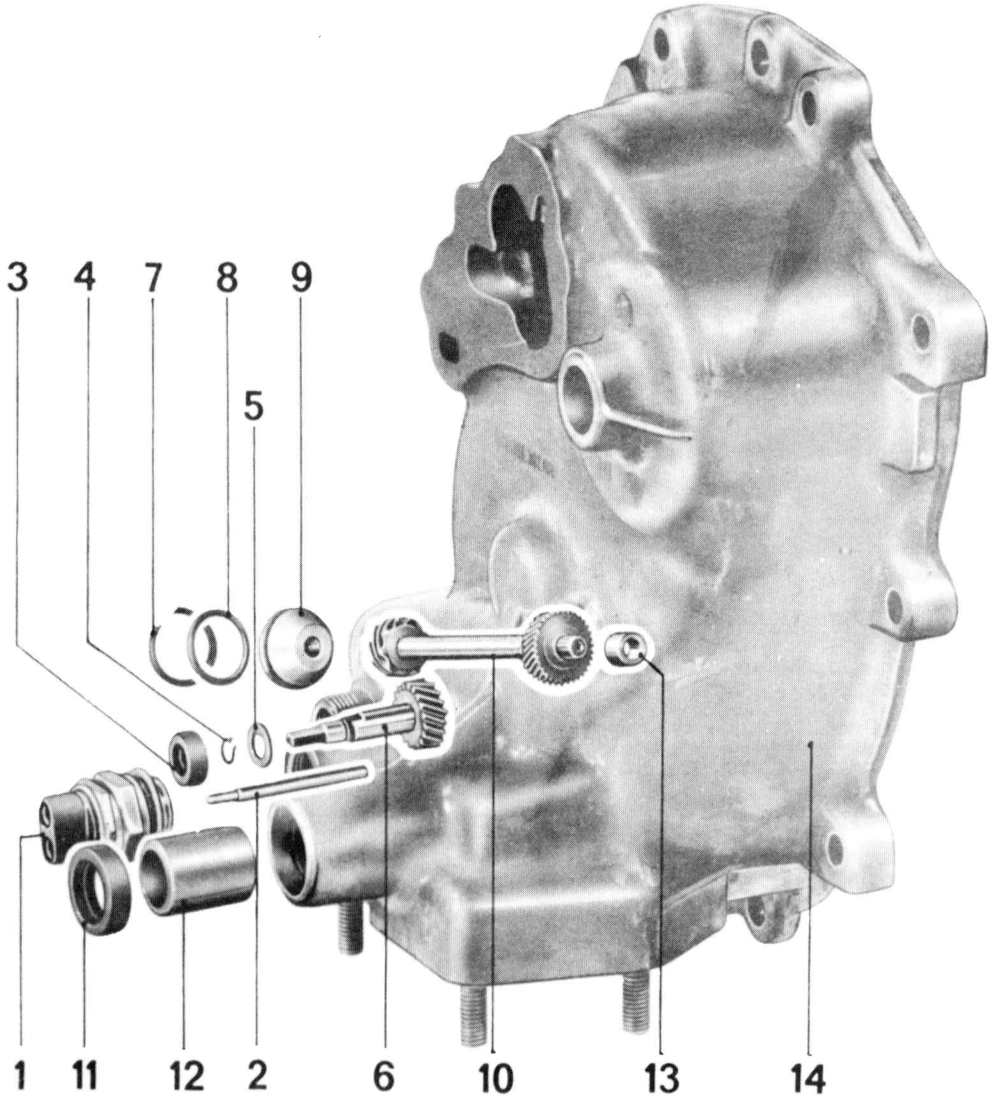

Fig. 5.40. Transmission front cover — later type (Sec. 22)

1   Reverse light switch
2   Actuating pin
3   Seal
4   Retainer
5   Thrust washer
6   Speedometer drive
7   Retainer
8   O-ring
9   Spacer
10 Worm shaft
11 Seal
12 Shift rod bushing
13 Bushing
14 Transmission front cover

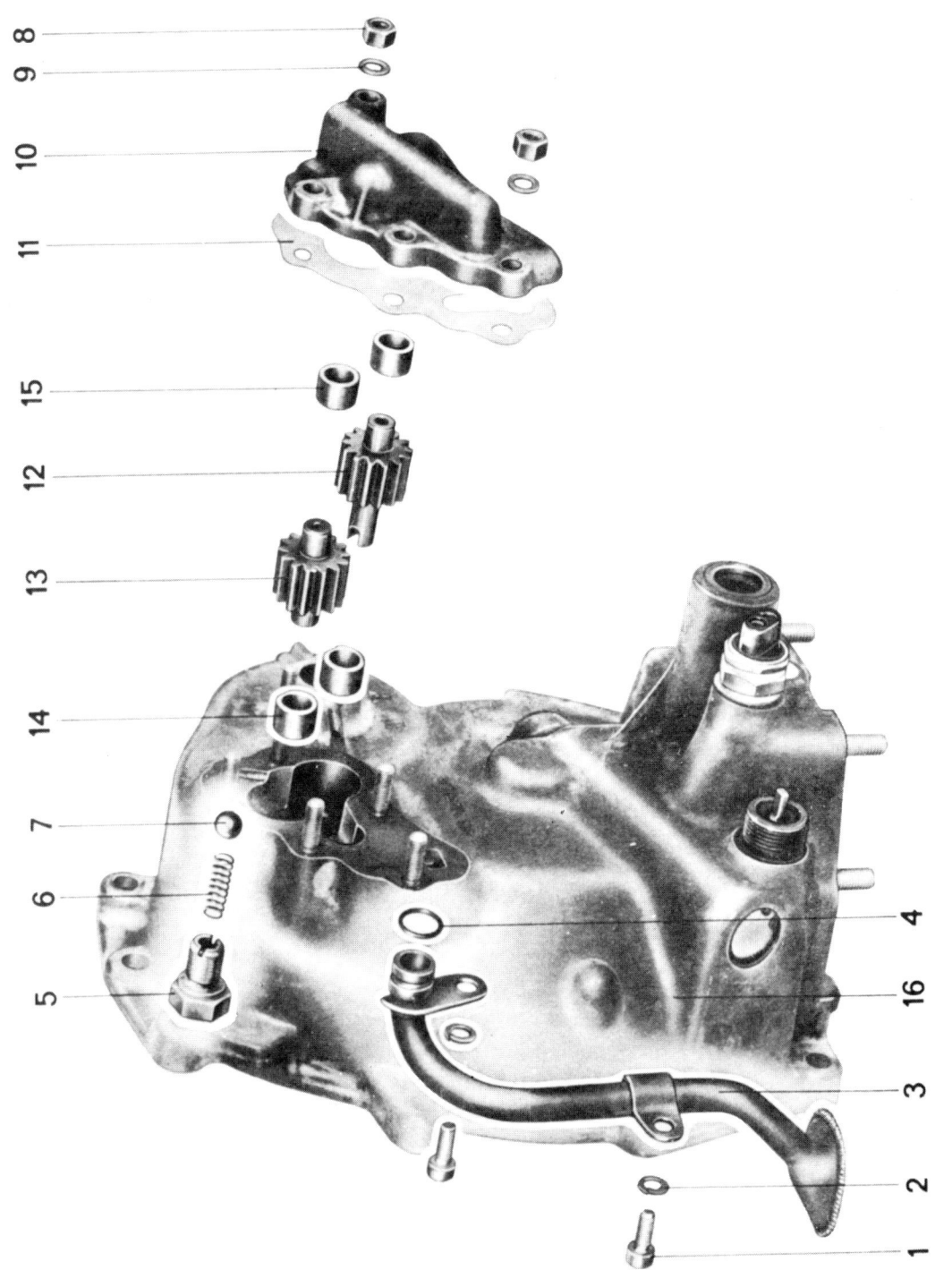

Fig. 5.41. Transmission front cover with oil pump — later type (Sec. 22)

1 Allen bolt
2 Lock washer
3 Pickup tube
4 O-ring

5 Plug
6 Spring
7 Ball
8 Self-locking nut

9 Washer
10 Pump cover
11 Gasket
12 Gear I

13 Gear II
14 Bushing
15 Bushing
16 Transmission front cover

Dismantling and reassembly procedure are straightforward. The only items which could possibly be troublesome to remove being the speedometer drive bushing and the oil pump cover bushings. **Note:** When removing an oil pump cover, note the thickness and number of gaskets used; the same total must be used when installing.

2   The speedometer drive bushing can be drilled out if worn, or removed using a suitable extractor after heating the cover to approximately 120°C (250°F). A new one can be driven in using a suitable arbor taking care that the end is not burred over.

3   Oil pump cover bushings can be removed and installed in a similar way if a proprietary inside puller is not available. Note that when installing, the orientation is very important; the milled ends of the oil pockets must face the pressure chamber or oil pump gears respectively. See Figs. 5.42 and 5.43.

4   Oil pump gears should be inspected for obvious wear and damage. Endfloat of approximately 0.002 in (0.05 mm) should be evident.

23 Gear housing (later type) - dismantling and reassembly

1   The component parts of the gear housing are shown in Fig. 5.44,

and are numbered in their order of dismantling.

2   The plug which retains the detent components can be removed by carefully prising out with a screwdriver blade or chisel. If damaged, a new plug should be used for reassembly.

3   Note that two roll pins are used to limit the travel of the two detents. These must obviously be removed before the detent components can be taken out. When installing, ensure that they are correctly located; it will be necessary to press down the sleeve in order to install the upper roll pin.

4   If the bearing outer races are to be removed, heat the casing to approximately 120°C (250°F), and drive them out with a suitable arbor. Installation is the reverse of this procedure.

24 Transmission housing (later type) - dismantling and reassembly

1   The component parts of the gear housing are shown in Fig. 5.46, main difference being the arrangement of the input shaft oil seal. From transmission numbers 733 7375, 783 0838 and 793 1031 onwards, the oil seal can be removed from the clutch bellhousing side without the need for dismantling the transmission. Take care that the garter spring

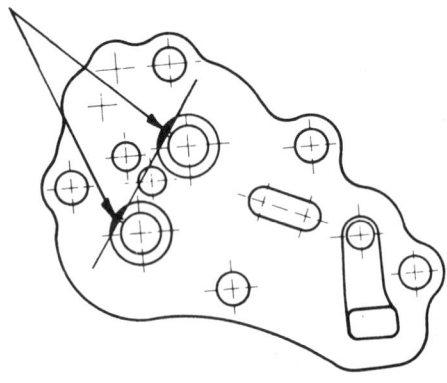

Fig. 5.42. Oil pump cover bushings — installed position (Sec. 22)

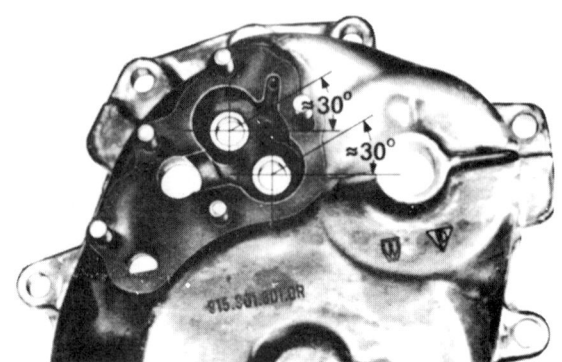

Fig. 5.43. Front cover bushings — installed position (Sec. 22)

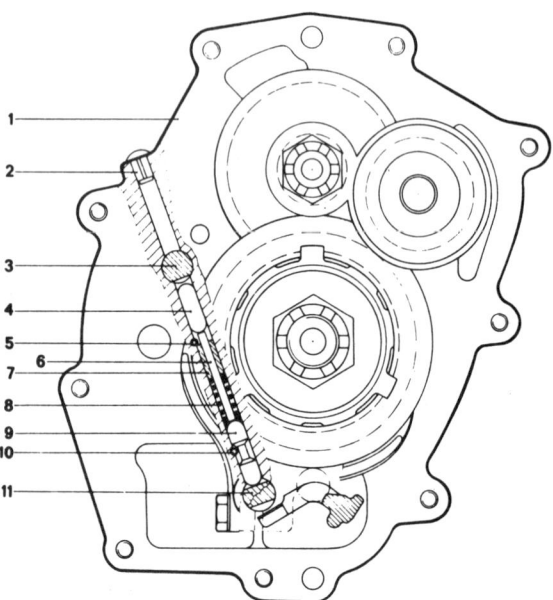

Fig. 5.44. Sectional view of gear housing showing detents (Sec. 23)

1	Gear housing	6	Pin
2	Plug	7	Sleeve
3	3rd/4th shift fork rod	8	Spring
4	Short detent	9	Long detent
5	Roll pin	10	Roll pin
		11	5th/reverse shift fork rod

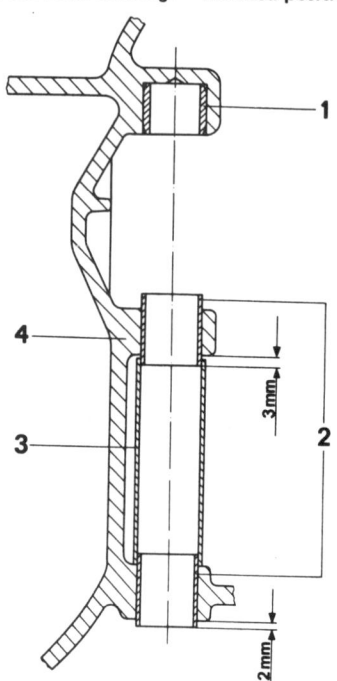

Fig. 5.45. Installation dimensions for clutch throwout lever bushings (Sec. 24)

1	Bushing	3	Shaft cover tube
2	Lever shaft bushing	4	Transmission housing

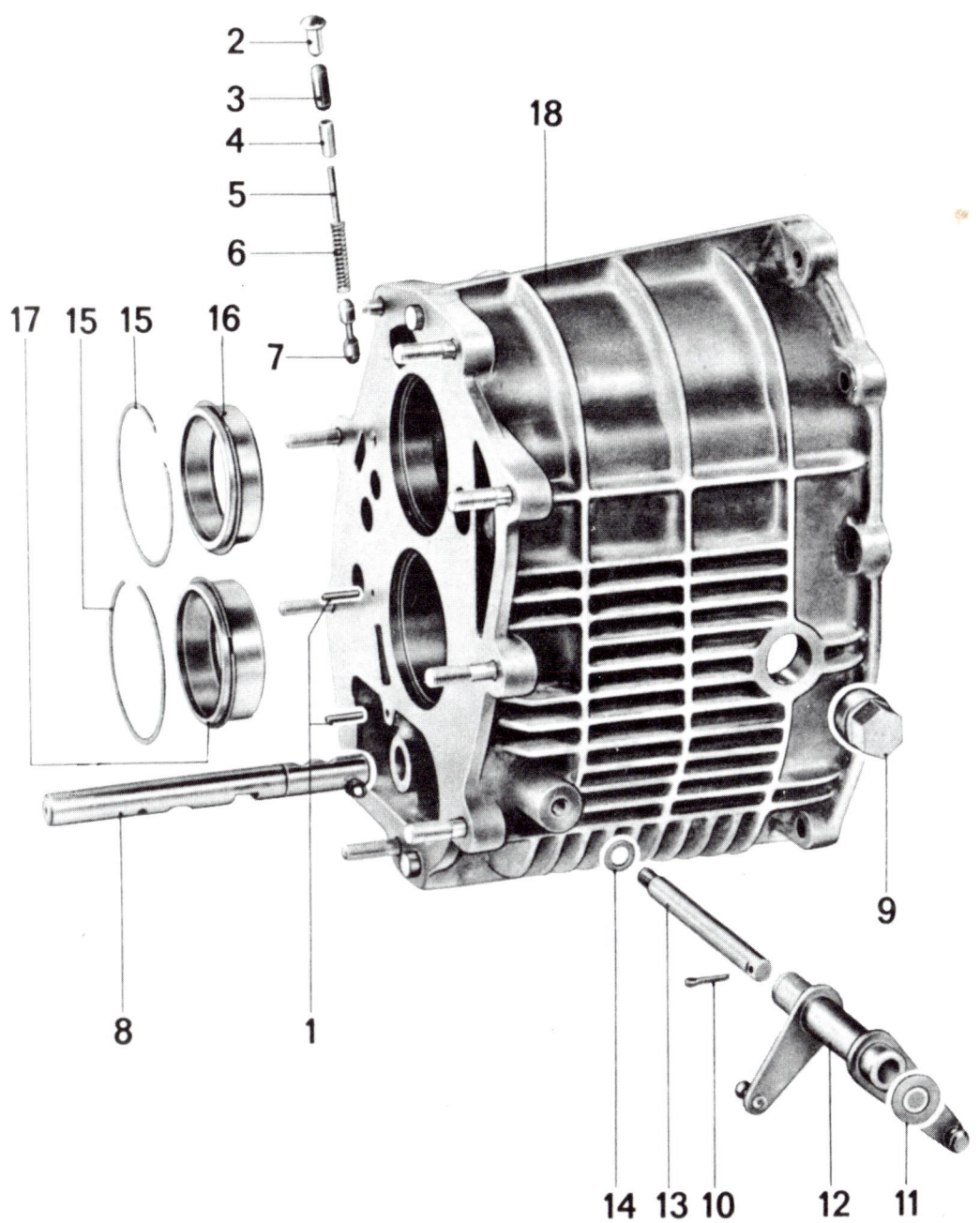

Fig. 5.46. Gear housing (later type) — exploded view (Sec. 23)

1	Roll pin	6	Spring
2	Plug	7	Long detent
3	Short detent	8	5th/reverse shift rod
4	Sleeve	9	Plug
5	Pin	10	Cotter pin
11	Washer	15	Retainer ring
12	Bellcrank (for	16	Bearing outer race
	accelerator linkage)	17	Bearing outer race
13	Shaft	18	Gear housing
14	Washer		

is not inadvertently left on the input shaft when installing the replacement.

2   Figs. 5.47 and 5.48 show the component parts for the two housings, the parts being numbered in the order of dismantling.

3   With the earlier type oil seal, this must be driven out towards the clutch bellhousing, and installed with the sealing ring in the same direction.

4   If the bearing outer races are to be removed, heat the casing to approximately 120°C (250°F), and drive them out with a suitable arbor. Installation is the reverse of this procedure.

5   If new bushings are required for the clutch throwout (release) lever,

ensure that replacements are installed to the dimensions shown in Fig. 5.48.

6   The release fork should be installed so that a dimension of 2.76 in (70 mm) exists between the tip of the fork and the bellhousing face, and 3.11 in (79 mm) exists between the bottom of the throwout lever and the bellhousing face.

7   Where the transmission has an oil pump, the pressure lines can be removed by removing the bolts shown in the illustrations. Note that the one at the pinion end has a nut on the pinion side also. Ensure that O-rings are lubricated with transmission oil when reassembling. (See Figs. 5.49 a and b).

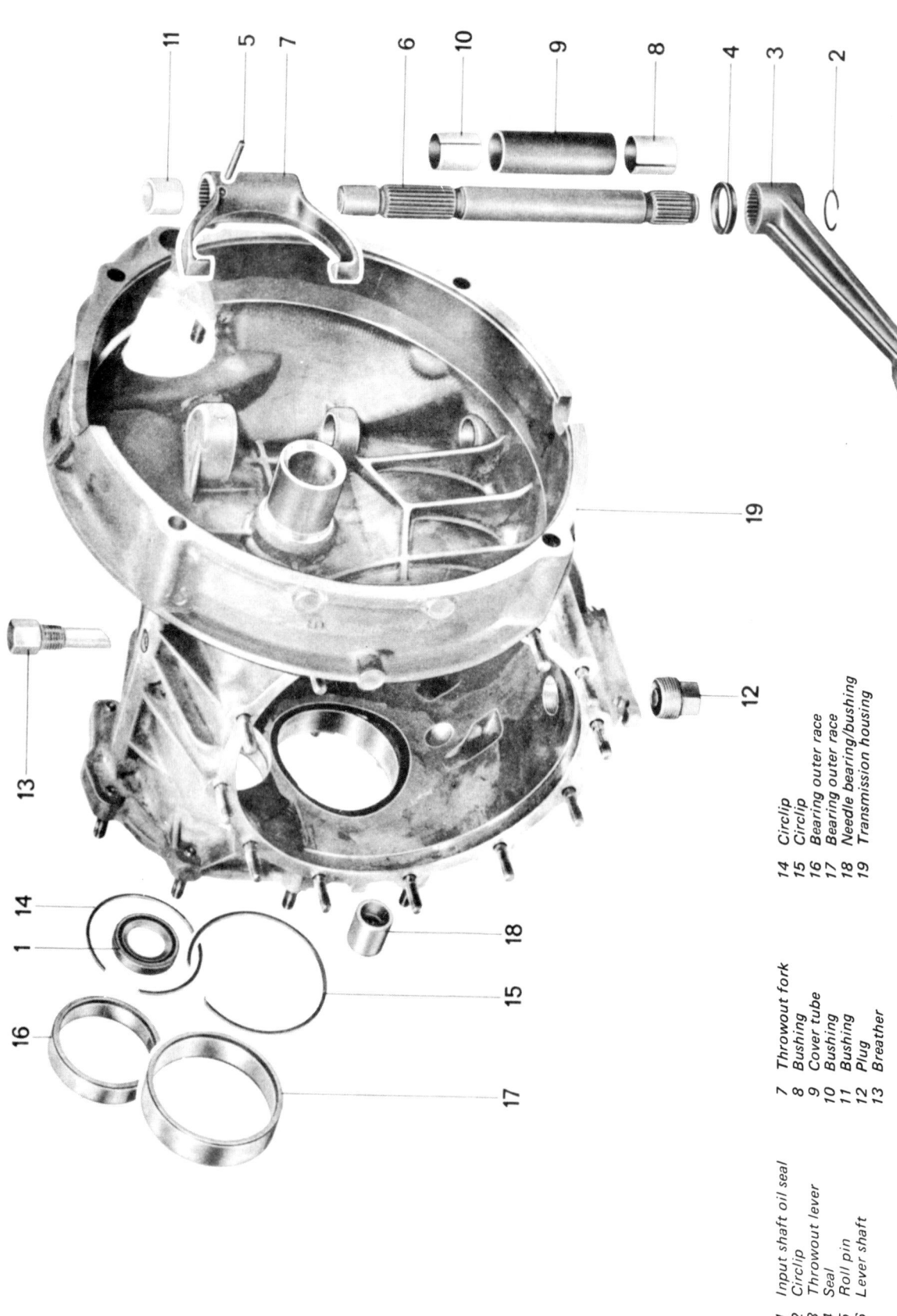

Fig. 5.47. Transmission housing (later type, prior to transmission Nos 733 7375, 783 0838 and 793 1031) (Sec. 24)

1 Input shaft oil seal
2 Circlip
3 Throwout lever
4 Seal
5 Roll pin
6 Lever shaft

7 Throwout fork
8 Bushing
9 Cover tube
10 Bushing
11 Bushing
12 Plug
13 Breather

14 Circlip
15 Circlip
16 Bearing outer race
17 Bearing outer race
18 Needle bearing/bushing
19 Transmission housing

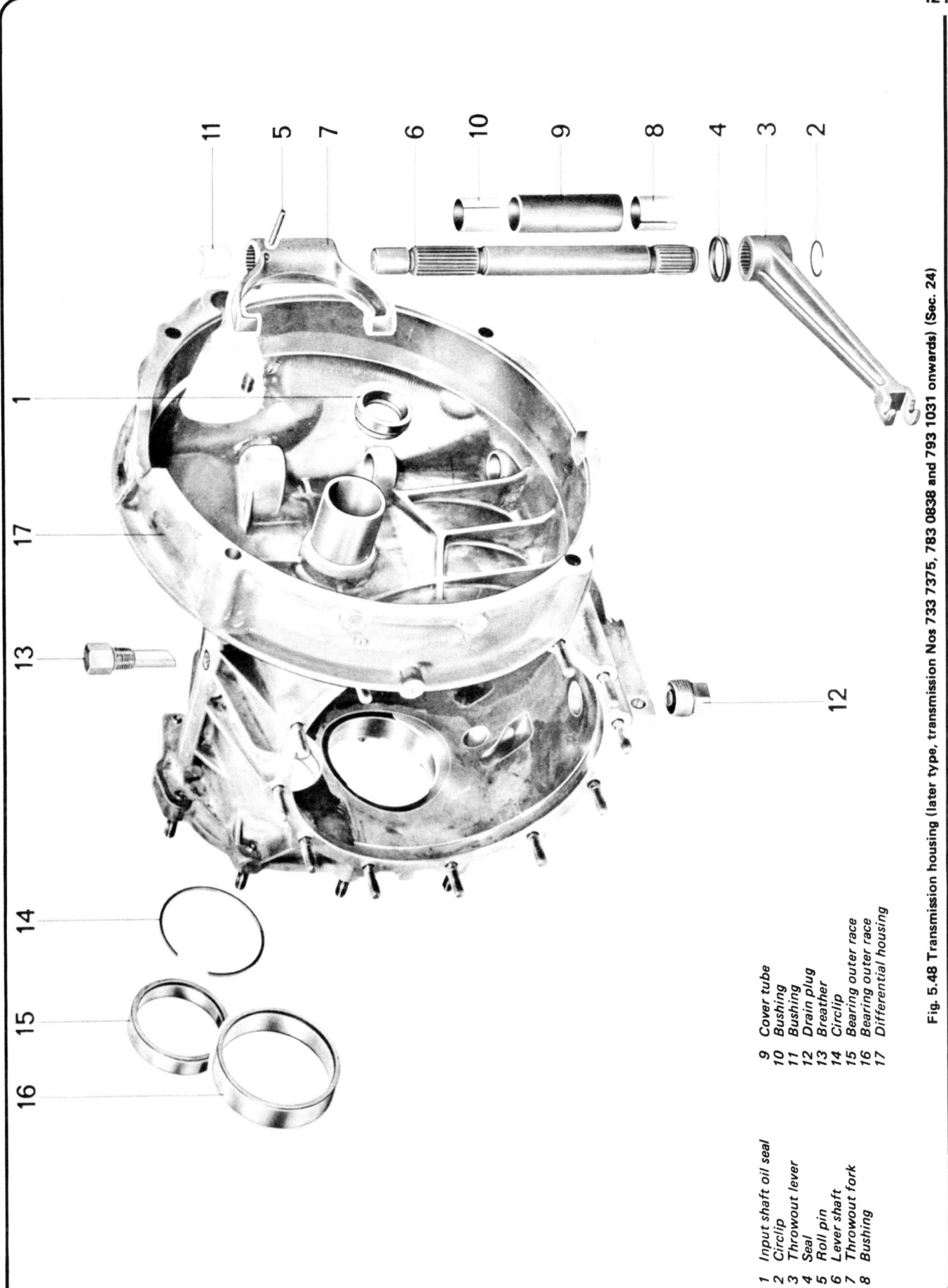

Fig. 5.48 Transmission housing (later type, transmission Nos 733 7375, 783 0838 and 793 1031 onwards) (Sec. 24)

1 Input shaft oil seal
2 Circlip
3 Throwout lever
4 Seal
5 Roll pin
6 Lever shaft
7 Throwout fork
8 Bushing

9   Cover tube
10 Bushing
11 Bushing
12 Drain plug
13 Breather
14 Circlip
15 Bearing outer race
16 Bearing outer race
17 Differential housing

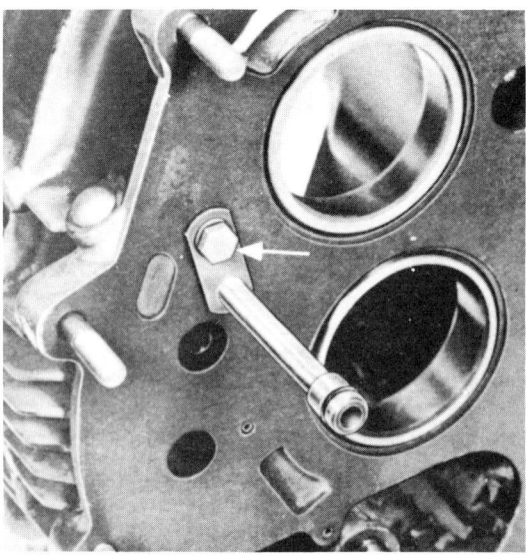

Fig. 5.49a. Pressure line retaining bolts (Sec. 24)

Fig. 5.49b. Pressure line retaining bolts (Sec. 24)

25 Gearshift linkage (later type) - removal, installation and adjustment

1   The component parts of the gearshift linkage are shown in Figs. 5.51 and 5.52. In general, the procedures given in Section 12 are applicable for the removal and installation.

Adjustment
2   Loosen the shift rod clamp, then turn the shift rod to the right.
3   Move the gearshift lever, starting from the neutral position, so that the lower part is vertical and touching the left stop.
4   Lightly tighten the shift rod clamp, then check that there is an equal amount of travel to select gears 1 to 4, and also that 5th and reverse gears can be selected easily
5   Correct the adjustment if necessary, then tighten the clamp bolt.
6   Select 5th gear then push back the dust boot and check that there is a definite amount of free-play in the selector shaft.

26 Differential (later type)

The information given in Sections 13 and 14 is equally applicable to the later type transmission.

27 Four-speed transmission (later type) - general

Apart from the lack of the 5th speed gear, the dismantling and reassembly procedures given in Section 16 onwards are applicable.
Unlike the early type 4-speed transmission there is no difference in the assembly procedure for the sychronizer assemblies.

28 Four-or five-speed transmission (later type) with oil pump - general

Transmissions used on Carrera models incorporate an oil pump in the transmission front cover, driven from the input shaft.
Oil is drawn from the transmission oil sump through a pick-up tube, and is forced through passages in the pump cover and into the pressure lines. The oil is distributed through discharge nozzles which direct the oil to the lubrication points for lubrication and cooling.
A pressure relief valve opens if one of the pressure lines becomes clogged, and the oil then spills back into the sump.
Dismantling and reassembly procedures of this type of transmission are similar to those for the normal 4- or 5-speed transmission. Refer to Sections 22 and 24 for information on the oil pump and pressure lines. The following additional points should be noted:

a)   When assembling the transmission, ensure that the pick-up tube and pressure line O-rings are lubricated with transmission oil.
b)   The gear housing is assembled with the pressure line in place. This passes through the hole in the 3rd/4th shift fork.
c)   When installing the transmission front cover, ensure that the input shaft coupling pin engages in the oil pump gear slot. Turn the input shaft slightly, if necessary, for this operation.

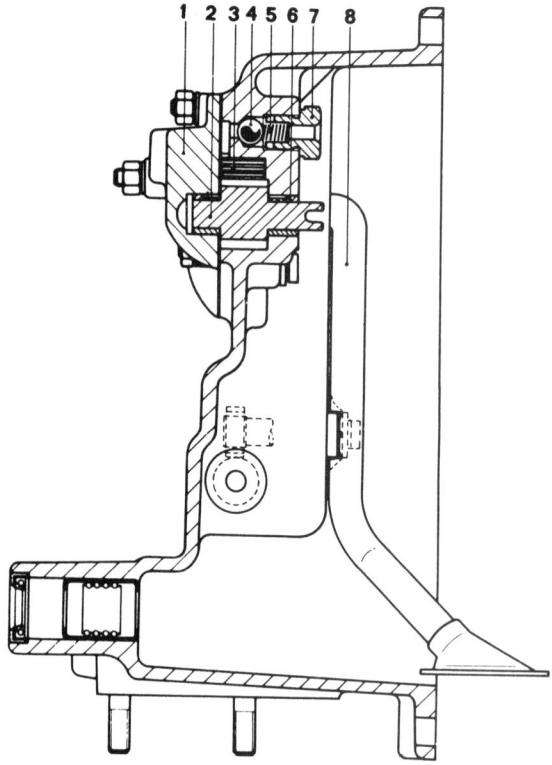

Fig 5.50. Sectional view of oil pump and front cover (Carrera models) (Sec. 28)

1   Oil pump cover
2   Pump gear I
3   Pump gear II
4   Pressure relief valve ball
5   Pressure relief valve spring
6   Bushing
7   Pressure relief valve plug
8   Pickup tube

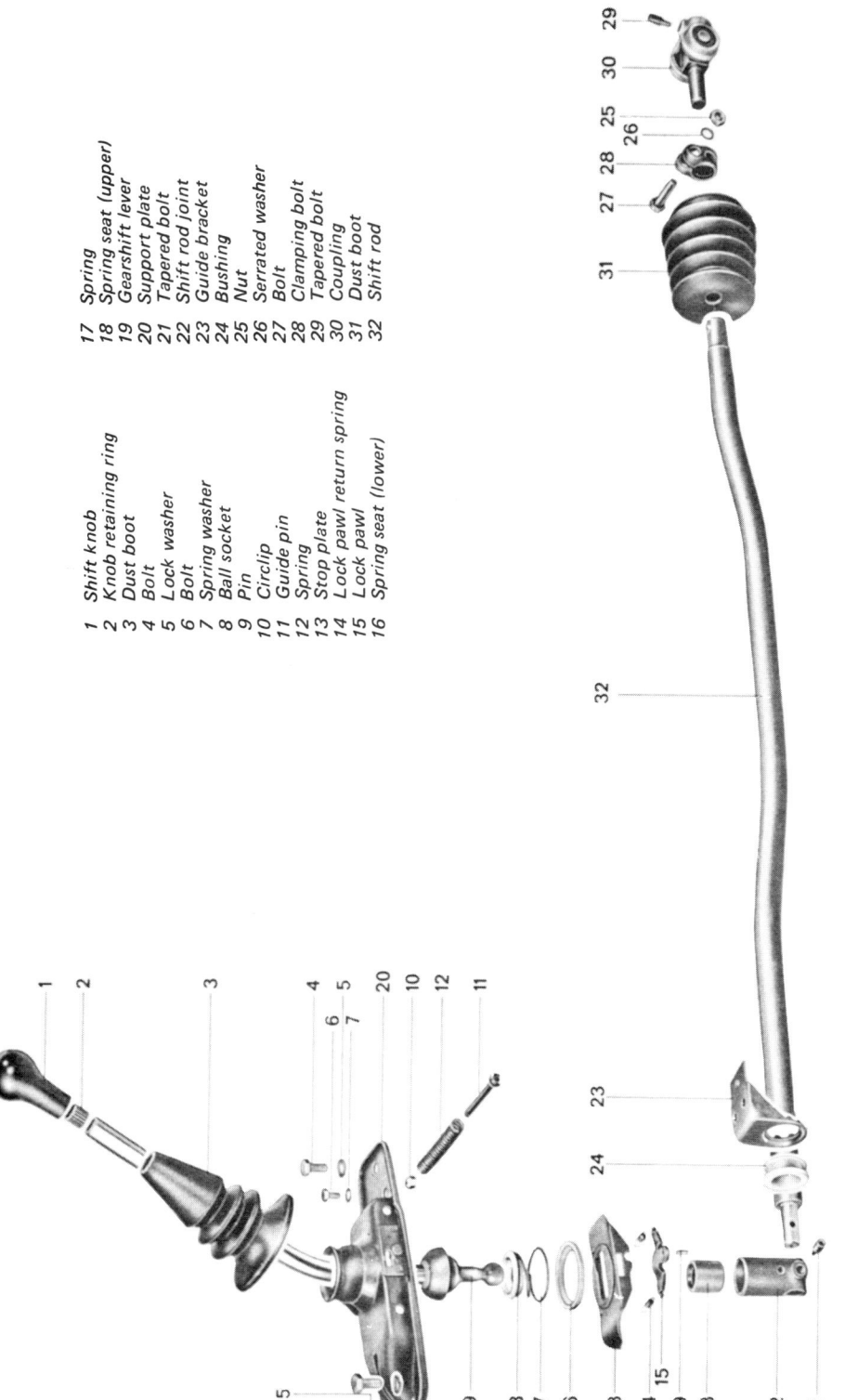

1 Shift knob
2 Knob retaining ring
3 Dust boot
4 Bolt
5 Lock washer
6 Bolt
7 Spring washer
8 Ball socket
9 Pin
10 Circlip
11 Guide pin
12 Spring
13 Stop plate
14 Lock pawl return spring
15 Lock pawl
16 Spring seat (lower)

17 Spring
18 Spring seat (upper)
19 Gearshift lever
20 Support plate
21 Tapered bolt
22 Shift rod joint
23 Guide bracket
24 Bushing
25 Nut
26 Serrated washer
27 Bolt
28 Clamping bolt
29 Tapered bolt
30 Coupling
31 Dust boot
32 Shift rod

Fig. 5.51. Grearshift linkage (later type) — except 1973 models onwards with five-speed transmission (Sec. 25)

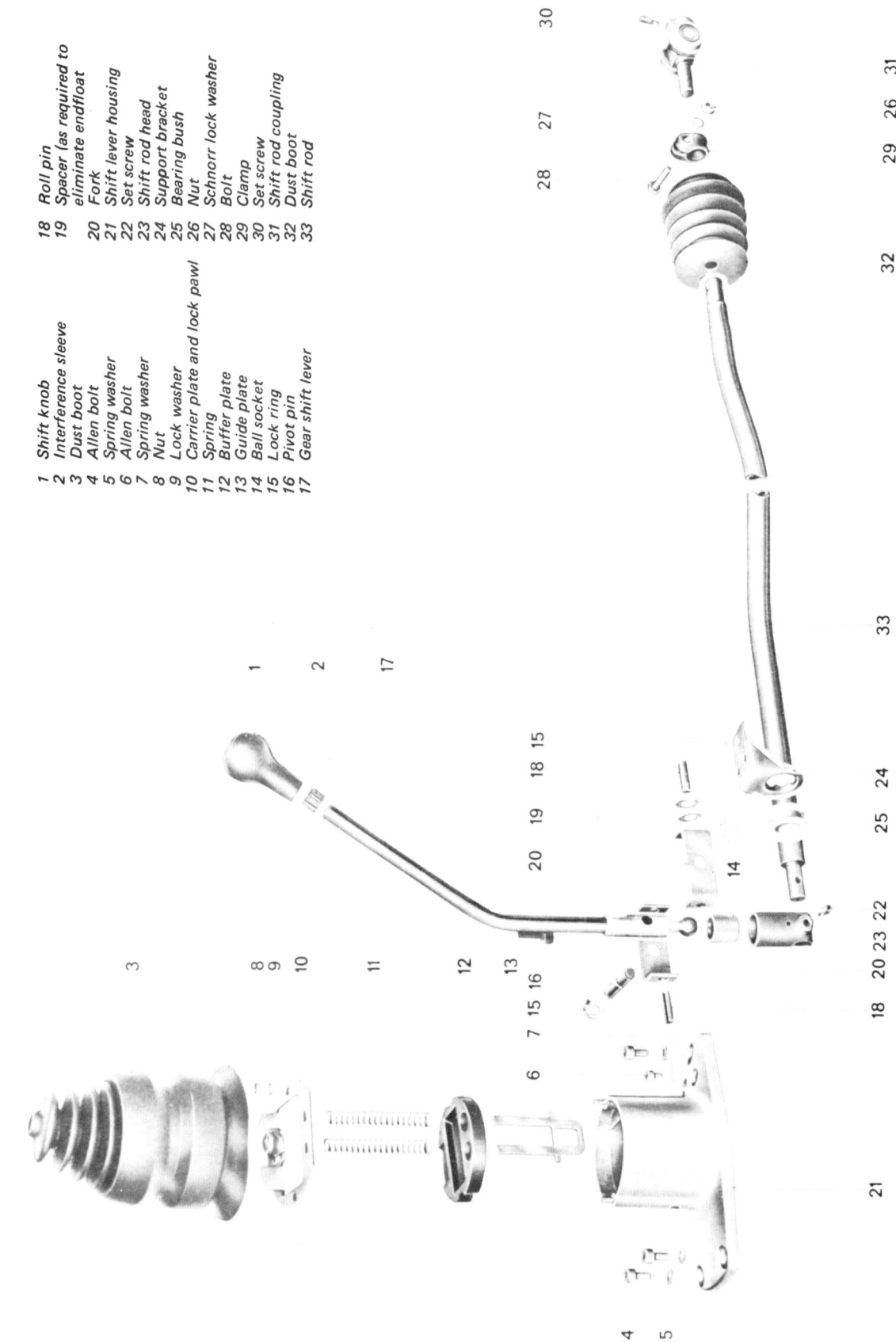

1 Shift knob
2 Interference sleeve
3 Dust boot
4 Allen bolt
5 Spring washer
6 Allen bolt
7 Spring washer
8 Nut
9 Lock washer
10 Carrier plate and lock pawl
11 Spring
12 Buffer plate
13 Guide plate
14 Ball socket
15 Lock ring
16 Pivot pin
17 Gear shift lever
18 Roll pin
19 Spacer (as required to eliminate endfloat
20 Fork
21 Shift lever housing
22 Set screw
23 Shift rod head
24 Support bracket
25 Bearing bush
26 Nut
27 Schnorr lock washer
28 Bolt
29 Clamp
30 Set screw
31 Shift rod coupling
32 Dust boot
33 Shift rod

Fig. 5.52. Gearshift (later type) — 1973 models onwards with five-speed transmission

29 Fault diagnosis - manual transmission

It is sometimes difficult to decide whether it is worthwhile removing and dismantling the transmission for a fault which may be nothing more than a minor irritant. Transmissions which howl, or where the synchromesh can be 'beaten' by a quick gear change, may continue to perform for a long time in this state. A worn transmission usually needs a complete rebuild to eliminate noise because the various gears, if re-aligned on new bearings, will continue to howl when different wearing surfaces are presented to each other.

The decision to overhaul therefore, must be considered with regard to time and money available, relative to the degree of noise or malfunction that the driver has to suffer.

Symptom	Reason/s	Remedy
Ineffective synchromesh	Worn synchro rings	Dismantle and renew.
Jumps out of one or more gears (on drive or over-run)	Weak detent springs, worn selector forks or worn gears (or all three)	Dismantle and renew.
Noisy, rough, whining and vibration	Worn bearings (initially), resulting in extended wear generally due to play and backlash	Dismantle and renew.
Noisy and difficult engagement of gear	Clutch fault Shift forks require adjustment	Examine clutch operation. Dismantle and adjust.

Chapter 5: Part 2 Sportomatic transmission

Contents

Specifications

Transmission type	Sportomatic four-speed synchromesh, incorporating torque converter, clutch, control mechanism, final drive and differential gear

Sportomatic transmission (general)

Gear ratios:

Transmission 905/00	...	...	...	...	...	...	...	1	15:36
(pre-1970 models)	...	...	...	...	...	...	...	2	19:31
								3	23:28
								4	26:25
								Reverse	15:38
Transmission 905/01	...	...	...	...	...	...	...	1	15:36
(pre-1970 models)	...	...	...	...	...	...	...	2	19:31
								3	23:28
								4	27:25
								Reverse	15:38
Transmission 905/20	...	...	...	...	...	...	...	1	15:36
(1970/71 models)	...	...	...	...	...	...	...	2	20:31
								3	24:27
								4	28:24
								Reverse	15:38
Transmission 925/00, 925/01	...	...	...	...	...	...	1	15:36
(1972/73 models except 911T models with carburettors)	...	...	2	20:31
								3	24:27
								4	28:24
								Reverse	15:38
Transmission 925/02	...	...	...	...	...	...	...	1	15:36
(1974 models, and 1975 models except USA and Canada)	...	...	2	20:31
								3	24:27
								4	28:23
								Reverse	15:38
Transmission 925/10	...	...	...	...	...	...	...	L	16:34
(1975 models, USA and Canada) ...	...	...	...	...	...	D	22:29
								D3	27:25
								Reverse	15:38

Final drive ratio:
1975 models	...	...	...	...	...	...	...	...	8:27 (3.375:1)
Other models	...	...	...	...	...	...	...	...	7:27 (3.857:1)

Torque converter:
Lubricant type ... ... Same Specification as engine oil - See Chapter 1
Lubricant capacity (additional to standard engine oil capacity):
Torque converter ... ... 4.4 Imp. pints (5.3 US pints/2.5 litres)
Oil cooler ... ... 4.4 Imp. pints (5.3 US pints/2.5 litres)

Transmission and final drive:
Lubricant type ... ... SAE 90EP gear oil to Specification MIL-L-2105 or 2105B
For limited slip differential versions use oil to Specification
M2C 28B (eg: Shell S 1747A)
Lubricant capacity (approx) ... ... 4.3 Imp. pints (5.2 US pints/2.5 litres)
Tow-start speed in 'L' ... ... 21 mph (35 km/hr)
Stall speed ... ... 2500/2700 rpm

Fits, clearances and wear limits (Sportomatic)
Refer to the Section dealing with the 4-speed transmission in the Specifications for manual transmissions, but note the following difference:

Shift rods, radial play in guides:
New ... ... 0.0077 to 0.0101 in (0.195 to 0.256 mm)
Wear limit ... ... 0.0157 in (0.4 mm)

Torque wrench settings

	lb f ft	kg f m
Transmission housing nuts ...	15 to 17	2.1 to 2.3
Elbow drive hexagon head screw ...	11	1.5
Elbow drive hollow screw in bush ...	16 to 17.5	2.2 to 2.4
Detent plug ...	18	2.5
Oil drain plug ...	14.5 to 18	2 to 2.5
Oil filler plug ...	14.5 to 18	2 to 2.5
Transmission housing breather ...	14.5 to 22	2 to 3
Brace plate bolts ...	18	2.5
Input shaft hexagon nut ...	72 to 87	10 to 12
Input shaft castellated nut (pre-1972) ...	65 to 80	9 to 11
Input shaft flanged nut (1972 onwards) ...	80 to 94	11 to 13
Pinion shaft expansion bolt ...	80 to 87	11 to 12
Selector fork bolts ...	18	2.5
Axle shaft flange expansion bolts (pre-1972) ...	33 to 36	4.5 to 5
Axle shaft flange expansion bolts (1972 onwards) ...	25 to 29	3.5 to 4
Torque converter and vacuum servo nuts (M8) ...	15 to 17	2.1 to 2.3
Parking lock plug ...	25 to 29	3.5 to 4
Clutch pressure plate cap screws ...	8.6 to 10	1.2 to 1.4
Torque converter freewheeling support cap screws ...	8.6 to 10	1.2 to 1.4
Torque converter-to-coupling plate cap screws ...	17 to 19	2.4 to 2.6
Reverse light switch ...	25 to 29	3.5 to 4
Bypass switch ...	25 to 29	3.5 to 4
Torque converter temperature sensor and switch ...	18 to 22	2.5 to 3
Hollow screw in guide bushing elbow drive ...	16 to 17	2.2 to 2.4

30 General description

The Sportomatic transmission comprises a 3-element hydraulic torque converter, a vacuum operated diaphragm clutch and a 4-speed transmission unit (transaxle). The transmission unit is very similar to the early type 4-speed manual transmission dealt with in Part 1, of this Chapter, but additionally has a parking lock arrangement on the reverse sliding gear.

The clutch is similar in principle to that described in Chapter 4, except that it is the opposite way round, with the release mechanism moving towards the engine. Its purpose is to isolate the engine from the transmission for gearchanging, which it does automatically by a vacuum servo arrangement.

When the gearshift lever is moved to select an alternative gear, switches at the base of the shift lever and on the shift linkage operate a solenoid valve which applies engine intake manifold vacuum to a diaphragm and linkage arrangement. This in turn operates the clutch through a typical release mechanism. A modulating valve adjusts the clutch engagement rate according to the relative position of the throttle butterfly.

The torque converter uses oil supplied from the car main oil tank, although this is in an independent circuit. Circulation is by means of a pump driven from the engine left-hand camshaft; there is no oil cooler on early transmissions, this function being taken care of by the engine oil cooler.

Modifications were made to the Sportomatic transmission for most 1972 models; these are associated with the increased torque output of the newly introduced 2.4 litre engine and have some effect on workshop procedures. Further modifications for 1974 models only affect the torque converter ratio.

1975 models supplied to the USA and Canada have a 3-speed transmission of the same basic type.

In the text, the transmissions are referred to as the early and later types, the early type being the 905 series and the later type being the 925 series (see Specifications).

Dismantling and reassembly of the Sportomatic transmission is comparatively straightforward, but it is not recommended that any repair work is attempted on the final drive in view of the special tools, gauges and procedures involved. Where the final drive is in need of repair, it is recommended that the torque converter, clutch, gears and shafts are removed from the casing, then the casing and final drive entrusted to a Porsche dealer for the necessary repairs.

During any dismantling of the torque converter, great care must be taken to prevent contamination by foreign matter which can have a disastrous effect on performance and component life.

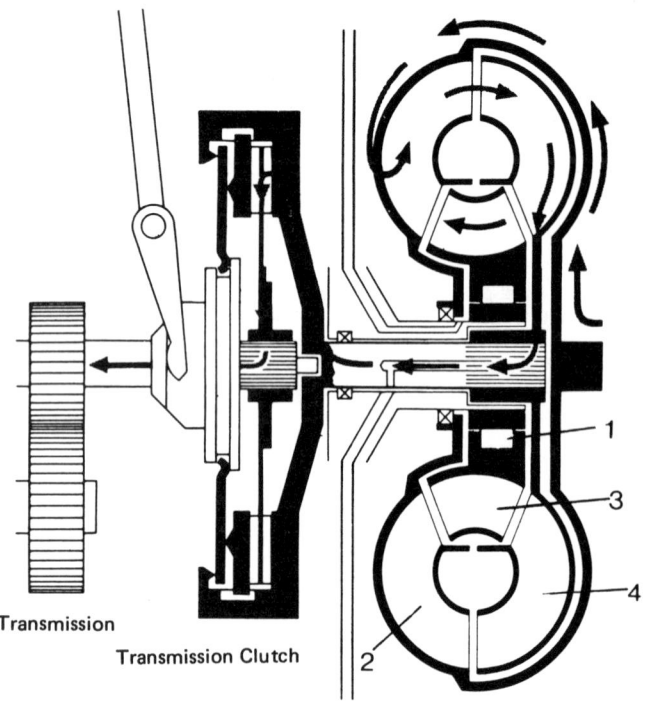

Transmission

Transmission Clutch

Torque converter

Fig. 5.53. Diagrammatic representation of power flow in the Sportomatic transmission (Sec. 30)

1 Freewheel unit   3 Stator
2 Pump   4 Turbine

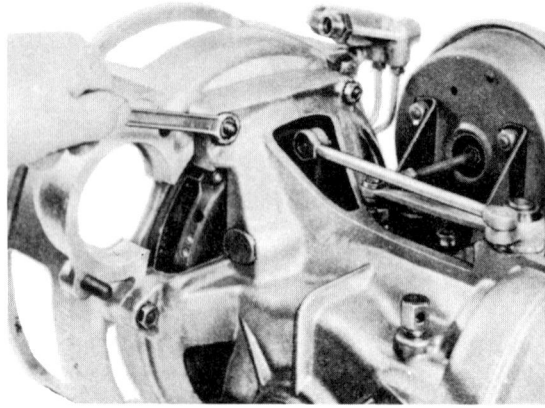

Fig. 5.54. Removing the torque converter housing nuts (Sec. 32)

31 Transmission - removal and installation

The Sportomatic transmission can only be removed complete with the engine. Refer to Chapter 1, for this procedure.

32 Torque converter and clutch - removal, dismantling, reassembly and installation

1   If not already removed, remove the starter motor (refer to Chapter 9, if necessary).
2   Withdraw the torque converter from the housing, wiping up any oil which is bound to spill out. Cover the torque converter with polythene or something similar and put it safely on one side.
3   Remove the nuts securing the transmission to the torque converter housing, not forgetting the two on the inside.
4   Remove the cotter key and detach the actuating rod from the intermediate lever.
5   Withdraw the torque converter housing, sliding the clutch release bearing out of the disengaging fork.
6   Remove the socket head bolts evenly and progressively, and take off the clutch pressure plate. Remove the release bearing before it falls off, by sliding it diagonally rearwards.
7   Take off the clutch plate, then remove the socket head screws from the freewheeling support. On early models removal may be made easier if the bolts are struck with a soft-faced hammer.
8   Screw in two 6 mm bolts in opposite positions, and carefully drive the freewheeling support and oil seal out of its seat.
9   Remove the circlip from the turbine shaft, then drive the turbine out of its seating with a soft-faced hammer. Ensure that the torque

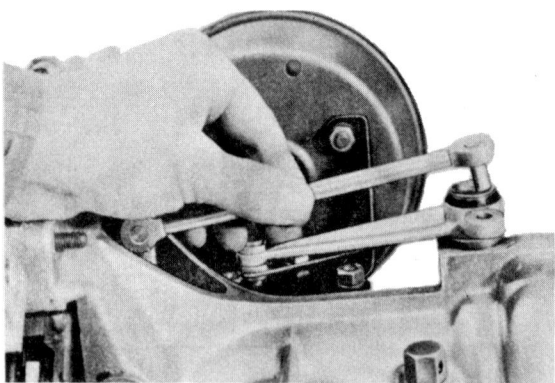

Fig. 5.55. Detaching the actuating rod (Sec. 32)

Fig. 5.56. Withdrawing the torque converter housing (Sec. 32)

Fig. 5.57. Removing clutch pressure plate (Sec. 32)

Fig. 5.58. Removing freewheeling support bolts (Sec. 32)

Fig. 5.59. Driving out the freewheeling support (Sec. 32)

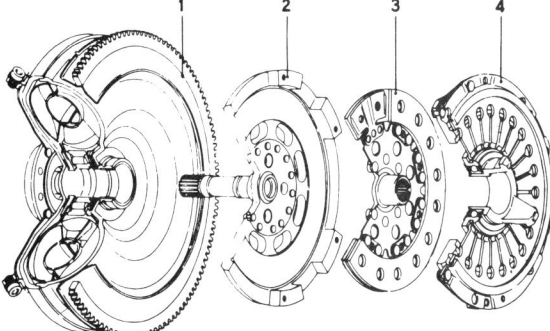

Fig. 5.60. Torque converter and clutch parts (Sec. 32)

1 Torque converter   3 Clutch friction plate
2 Turbine shaft   4 Clutch pressure plate

converter housing is adequately supported while doing this.
10 Carefully drive off the torque converter ball bearing, and push out the oil seal.
11 Check the torque converter for obvious wear and damage. A leakage test can be performed but will require a special rig and must therefore be entrusted to a Porsche dealer.
12 The turbine shaft and clutch pressure plate assembly must be checked for wear and scoring of the clutch contact surface. If severe wear is found, the assembly must be replaced. If the needle bearing is unserviceable it may be drawn out using a suitable puller, and a replacement installed; install a new oil seal and lightly smear the bearing with a molybdenum disulphide grease. Ensure that the turbine hub seating surface is undamaged, and the oil passage clear.
13 Check the clutch plate lining, and renew if damaged or where the lining thickness is less than 0.217 in. (5.5 mm). If possible, check the lateral runout of the clutch plate; the maximum permissible is 0.02 in. (0.5 mm). Also ensure that the clutch plate moves freely on its splines.
14 Check the clutch pressure plate for scoring and other damage, and particularly for wear on the diaphragm spring fingers. If necessary, obtain a replacement assembly. Wipe the release bearing clean and check that it rotates freely. Do not immerse it in any cleaning solvent or permanent damage will result.
15 Inspect the turbine shaft bearing for wear and damage, replacing as necessary. Check for wear in the bushes of the freewheeling support and turbine shaft, renewing parts as necessary. Ensure that the passages in the freewheeling support are clear.
16 Reassembly is essentially the reverse of the removal procedure, but ensure that everything is kept scrupulously clean. Commence by heating the torque converter housing to about 120°C (250°F), then drive in the ball bearing, pressing on the outer race only.
17 Lubricate the silicone ring oil seal and carefully drive it into the torque converter.
18 Attach the freewheeling support using three bolts at evenly spaced points, and carefully drive in the turbine shaft.
19 Now remove the three bolts, take out the support and install the shaft circlip.
20 Install the freewheeling support, then install the bolts using new O-rings and tighten in a cross-wise order to the specified torque.
21 Lubricate the silicone ring oil seal and carefully drive it in.
22 Install the clutch plate, using a suitable round wood or metal bar to centre it.
23 Lightly lubricate the clutch diaphragm spring fingers with a molybdenum disulphide grease, and slide in the release bearing, working diagonally from the inside to the outside.
24 Install the pressure plate, ensuring that it is aligned on the dowels. Tighten the bolts evenly and in a crosswise order to the specified torque.
25 Installation of the torque converter and clutch is now straightforward

Fig. 5.61. Turbine shaft circlip in position (Sec. 32)

provided that the following points are heeded:
   a) *Lightly lubricate the input shaft splines, and sliding surfaces of the clutch disengaging fork and release bearing with molybdenum disulphide grease before installation.*
   b) *Insert the mounting bolt and spring washer into the torque converter housing next to the temperature sensor housing, before offering the assembly up to the transmission, as the vacuum servo will prevent it being inserted later.*
   c) *Ensure that the release bearing aligns correctly with the disengaging fork.*
   d) *Before installing the torque converter, fill it with approximately 0.5 litres/½ pint of engine oil. If this is not done, serious damage may occur during initial running.*

33 Clutch operating linkage - removal and installation

Intermediate lever
1   Detach the intermediate rod from the intermediate lever, and the actuating rod at the clevis.
2   Remove the circlip, and take off the washer, grommet, spacer and intermediate lever.
3   Remove the O-ring, thrust ring and spring.
4   Check the pivoting and thrust surfaces for wear and damage, replacing parts as necessary.
5   Installation is the reverse of the removal procedure, parts being lubricated with a molybdenum disulphide grease.

Clutch disengaging fork
6   Detach the intermediate rod from the disengaging fork.
7   Carefully prise off the caps at the ends of the pivot.
8   Drive out the roll pin from the disengaging fork, then drive out the shaft. Remove the fork and washers.
9   If necessary, drive out the pivot bushings using a suitable drift.
10 Inspect the shaft and bushings for wear, obtaining replacements, as

necessary.
11 Installation is the reverse of the removal procedure. Apply a molybdenum disulphide grease to the shaft and bushings, and ensure that the roll pin aligns with the groove in the shaft.

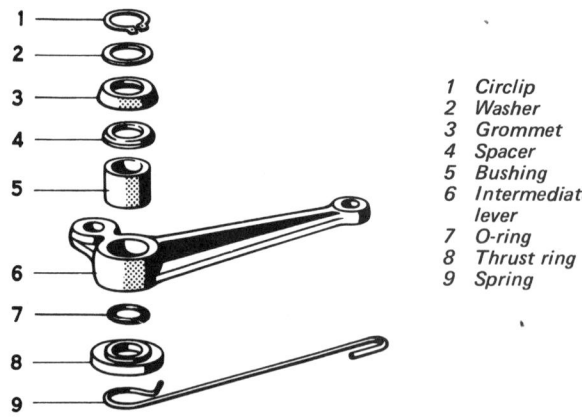

1	Circlip
2	Washer
3	Grommet
4	Spacer
5	Bushing
6	Intermediate lever
7	O-ring
8	Thrust ring
9	Spring

Fig. 5.62. Intermediate lever parts (Sec. 33)

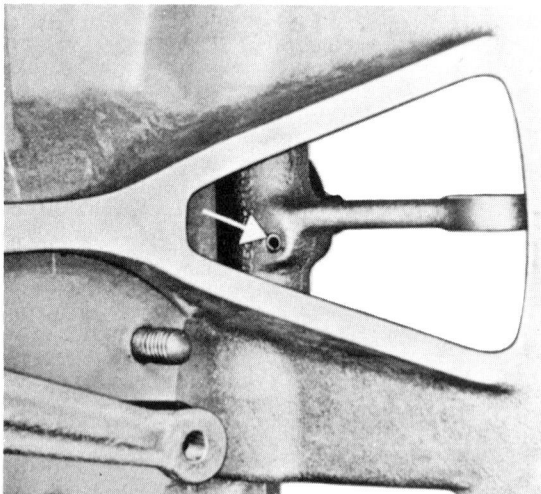

Fig. 5.64. Disengaging fork roll pin (arrowed) (Sec. 33)

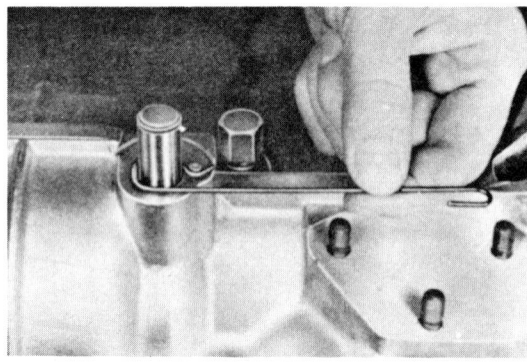

Fig. 5.63. Intermediate lever spring being installed (Sec. 33)

Fig. 5.65. Detaching engine mountings (Sec. 34)

Fig. 5.66. Temperature gauge sensor (1) and temperature switch (2) (Sec 34)

34 Temperature switch and temperature gauge sensor - removal and installation

1   Remove the air cleaner assembly, as described in Chapter 2. Where applicable, also detach the air pump hoses and remove the filter.
2   Detach cable no. 1 and the HT cable from the ignition coil.
3   Detach the hot air ducts from the heat exchangers (refer to Chapter 1, if necessary).
4   Position a jack with a suitable packer under the engine/transmission assembly. Take up the weight slightly and detach the engine mountings.
5   Carefully lower the jack until the switch and gauge sensor are accessible, then detach the cables and unscrew them.
6   Installation is the reverse of the removal procedure, but it is recommended that the copper washers are annealed by heating and quenching.

35 Transmission (early type) - dismantling into major assemblies and reassembly

1   Remove the torque converter and clutch, as described in Section 32.
2   Clean the exterior of the transmission with a water-soluble solvent, then transfer it to a suitable workbench. Have a supply of clean lint-free cloth available, together with several containers for putting the various parts in.
3   Detach the clutch intermediate rod (refer to Section 33, if necessary).
4   Remove the retaining nuts and take off the servo bracket (complete with the servo).
5   Remove the four nuts and take off the transmission mounting member.
6   Remove the parking lock plug and take out the spring and ball.
7   Unscrew the bypass switch, then remove the nuts and take off the

front cover.
8   Remove the parking lock pin and ball from the reverse selector fork.
9   Remove the circlip from the reverse selector fork rod, and withdraw the reverse gear and selector fork.
10 Detach the parking lock return springs and take off the parking lock lever and pawl.
11 With neutral selected, remove the nuts and take off the selector shaft guide fork.
12 Turn the selector rod clockwise and pull it out to select 4th gear.
13 Using a screwdriver through the guide fork aperture, also move the selector to engage another gear to lock-up the transmission.
14 Remove the expansion bolt from the end of the pinion shaft. If necessary, the pin can be driven out and the speedometer gear removed if found more convenient.
15 Remove the splined muff from the pinion shaft.
16 Drive out the roll pin, then remove the castellated nut and washer from the input shaft.
17 Remove the reverse light switch and take out the actuating pin.
18 Select neutral, then pull out the reverse/parking lock selector fork

Fig. 5.67. Removing servo bracket nuts (Sec. 35)

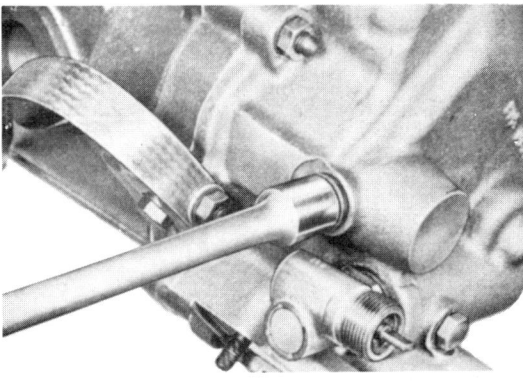
Fig. 5.68. Removing parking lock plug (Sec. 35)

Fig. 5.69. Removing the front cover (Sec. 35)

Fig. 5.70. The reverse selector fork rod circlip (arrowed) (Sec. 35)

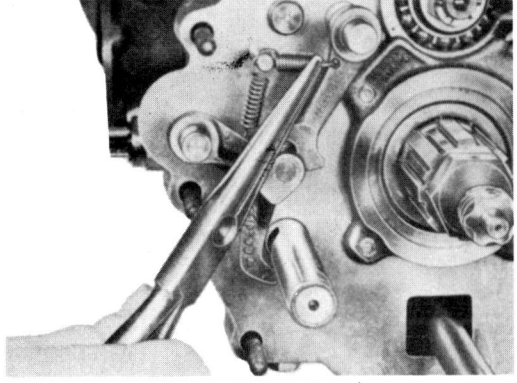
Fig. 5.71. Removing the parking lock return springs. (Sec. 35)

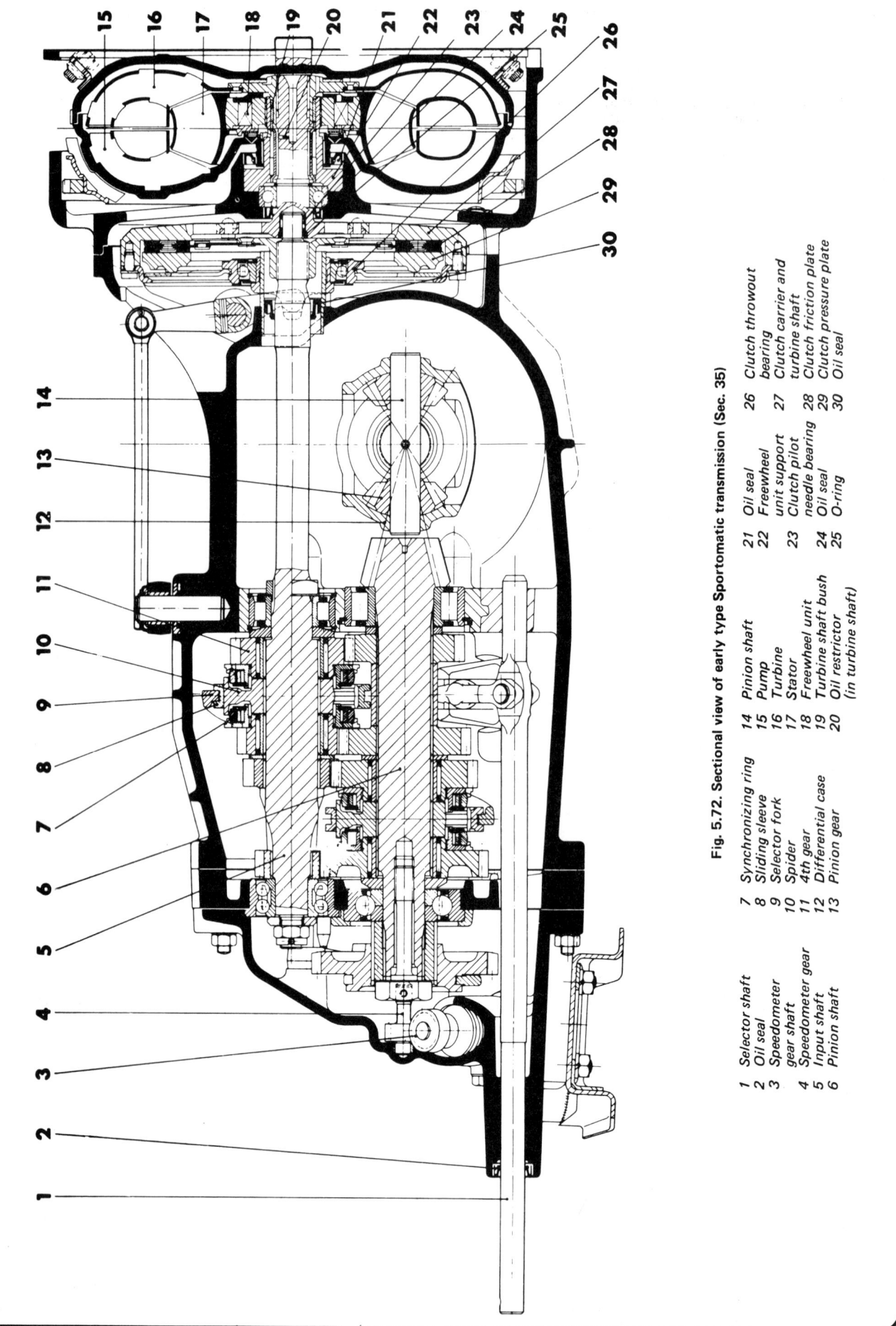

Fig. 5.72. Sectional view of early type Sportomatic transmission (Sec. 35)

1 Selector shaft
2 Oil seal
3 Speedometer gear shaft
4 Speedometer gear
5 Input shaft
6 Pinion shaft

7 Synchronizing ring
8 Sliding sleeve
9 Selector fork
10 Spider
11 4th gear
12 Differential case
13 Pinion gear

14 Pinion shaft
15 Pump
16 Turbine
17 Stator
18 Freewheel unit
19 Turbine shaft bush
20 Oil restrictor (in turbine shaft)

21 Oil seal
22 Freewheel unit support
23 Clutch pilot needle bearing
24 Oil seal
25 O-ring

26 Clutch throwout bearing
27 Clutch carrier and turbine shaft
28 Clutch friction plate
29 Clutch pressure plate
30 Oil seal

until it contacts the intermediate plate.

19 Withdraw the intermediate plate and turn it clockwise to remove it from the transmission housing. The gears and shafts will also come out, attached to the intermediate plate. At this stage note the number and total thickness of gaskets between the intermediate plate and the housing. If the same total thickness is not used for reassembly, the pinion meshing depth will be upset; this will then need resetting by a Porsche dealer or transmission specialist.

20 Mount the intermediate plate in a vice using protective jaw clamps to prevent damage.

21 Remove the detent plug and take out the spring and ball. Take the reverse/parking lock selector fork and the detent out of the intermediate plate.

22 Mark the installed position of the selector forks on the shafts to simplify the adjustment on reassembly. Also mark the orientation of the 3rd/4th fork to prevent mix-up.

23 Remove the 1st/2nd selector fork retaining bolt, then push out the rod leaving the fork in position. Take out the detent balls, pin and spring before they fall out.

24 Apply blows from a soft-faced hammer to the shaft ends alternately, to drive them from the intermediate plate whilst still meshed together. Ensure that the balls are not lost from the double-row ball bearing.

25 If the input shaft oil seal and casing bearing outer races are to be renewed, remove the differential. See Section 49.

26 Drive out the input shaft seal using a suitable drift.

27 Remove the retainers from the centre web of the case if the input shaft bearing is to be removed (also remove the front retainer for the pinion shaft). Heat the casing in a suitable oven to about 120°C (250°F) then drive out the bearings using a hammer and a suitable drift.

28 For further information on dismantling the shafts, transmission front cover, intermediate plate, transmission housing and synchro assemblies, together with inspection of these parts, refer to the appropriate following Sections.

29 In general, reassembly is the reverse of the removal procedure. Where removed, first install the retainer into the pinion shaft outer

bearing race (also see Fig. 5.7).

30 Insert the rear retainer into the bearing bore at an angle, and guide it into the groove using a small screwdriver.

31 Heat the housing to about 120°C (250°F), install the input shaft roller bearing outer race and secure it with the second retainer.

32 Install the pinion shaft roller bearing outer race (with the retainer already fitted), then install the front retainer.

33 Position the input and pinion shafts into engagement, and install them in the intermediate plate. Do not forget the bearing inner races; where applicable, the X-marking on the pinion shaft inner race must face outwards.

34 Install the input shaft washer, bevelled edge facing outwards, and turn the nut on a few turns.

35 Push the splined muff onto the pinion shaft with the inner splines facing outwards.

Fig. 5.73. Removing the detent plug (Sec. 35)

Fig. 5.74. 1st/2nd selector fork retaining bolt (arrowed) (Sec. 35)

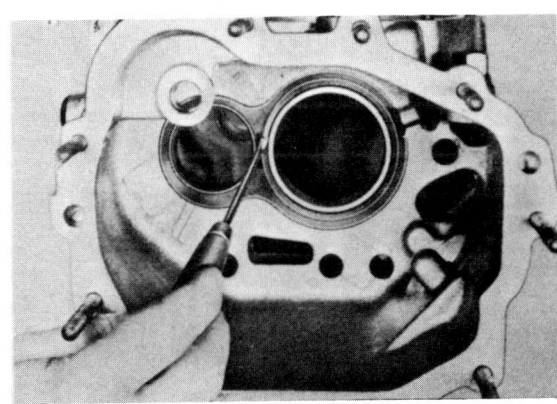

Fig. 5.75. Pinion shaft bearing retainer being removed (Sec. 35)

Fig. 5.76. Installing pinion shaft inner race (Sec. 35)

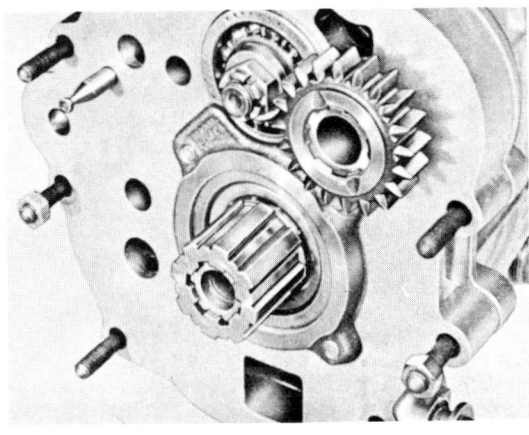

Fig. 5.77. Splined muff on input shaft (Sec. 35)

36 Lubricate the pressure face of the pinion shaft expansion bolt, and lightly tighten it.

37 Move the selector sleeves to lock the transmission gears in mesh, then tighten the castellated nut to the lowest specified torque. Increase this torque, as necessary, to allow a new roll pin to be installed, without exceeding the maximum permitted value.

38 Tighten the expansion bolt to the specified torque. If the speedometer drive gear was removed, it can now be refitted.

39 Select neutral, then place the 3rd/4th selector fork onto the appropriate sliding sleeve. Insert the selector shaft (the shift arm should have been installed at this stage) until it enters the bore of the intermediate plate. Lightly tighten the fork retaining bolt and spring washer.

40 Insert one detent ball lubricate the long detent pin with grease, put it into the long spring, then put them both into the detent bore.

41 Install the 1st/2nd selector fork and shaft in a similar manner, but ensure that the second ball is pressed in the detent bore before the

selector shaft is pushed through the intermediate plate. Ensure that the 3rd/4th selector fork is in the neutral position while this is being done. Lightly tighten the selector fork bolt and spring washer.

42 The next step is to adjust the selector forks. The procedure for this is given in Section 36, but also see paragraph 22.

43 With the 1st/2nd selector fork rod in the neutral position insert the fork rod detent pin.

44 Insert the reverse/parking lock selector fork rod. Take care that the fork rod detent pin does not fall out during this operation.

45 Stick the reverse gear thrust bearing in place using a general purpose grease, with the rollers towards the gear.

46 If dismantled, assemble the inner shift rod, ensuring that the tapered bore for the shift rod set screw aligns with the seat in the selector shaft. Fit the clevis pin and a new cotter key.

47 Place the correct thickness of gasket(s) on the housing (see paragraph 19).

48 Position the inner shift rod through the aperture in the intermediate plate, then install the assembled intermediate plate. Pull out the reverse/parking lock selector fork rod to rest against the intermediate plate.

49 Push the reverse/parking lock selector fork rod into its seat in the housing bore (in the neutral position), and insert the detent ball and spring. Check that the detent pin is in position by making a test shift.

50 Guide the selector shaft assembly into the fork rods and into the seat in the housing bore.

51 Using a new gasket, install the guide fork.

52 Slide the reverse gear selector fork and sliding gear onto the selector fork rod and pinion shaft. Install the selector fork circlip.

53 Grease the pin and parking lock ball and insert them (in that order)

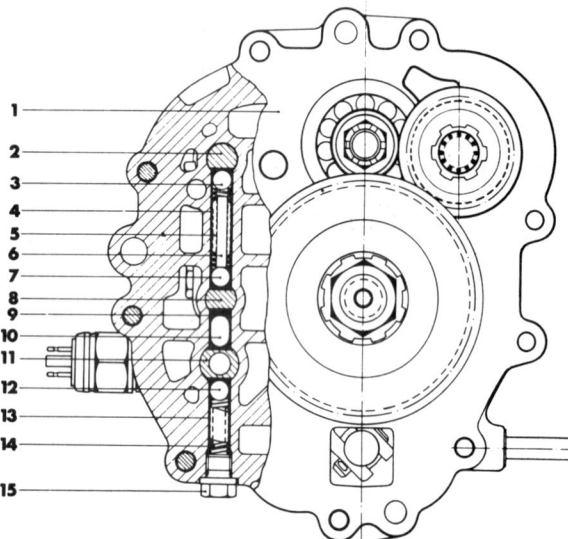

Fig. 5.79. Arrangement of the detent components (Sec. 35)

1 Intermediate plate	9 Detent bushing
2 Selector fork rod for gears 3/4	10 Detent pin
3 Ball	11 Selector fork rod for reverse gear and parking lock
4 Detent bushing	12 Ball
5 Detent spring for gears 1/4	13 Detent bushing
6 Detent pin	14 Detent spring for reverse gear/parking lock
7 Ball	15 Cap screw
8 Selector fork rod for gears 1/2	

Fig. 5.78. Shift arm installed on selector shaft (Sec. 35)

Fig. 5.80. Installing reverse gear thrust bearing (Sec. 35)

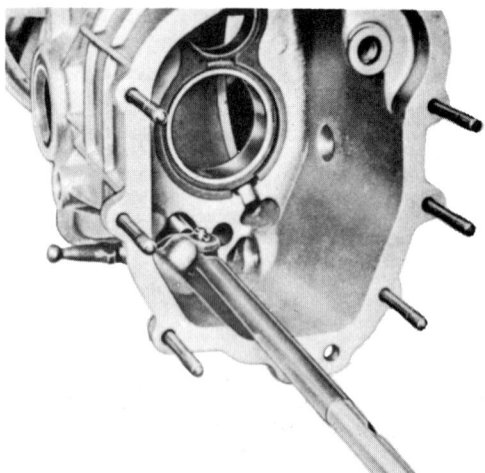

Fig. 5.81. Installing inner shift rod (Sec. 35)

Fig. 5.82 Parking lock lever and pawl installed (Sec. 35)

in the drilling in the selector fork and rod.

54 Install the parking lock lever and pawl and connect the return springs.

55 Install the front cover, tightening the nuts in a crosswise order to the specified torque.

56 Install the actuating pin and reverse light switch.

57 Install the input shaft oil seal. This can be tricky, but lubricate it with transmission oil and carefully press it in using a tube of suitable dimensions until the flat face is just in the smaller bore of the tube.

58 Install the differential, side cover (using a new gasket or O-ring) and drive shaft flanges. Further information will be found in Section 49.

59 Finally add the transmission oil.

36 Shift forks - adjustment

1　Refer to Section 47, paragraphs 1 and 2 of Part 1 of this Chapter.

2　With neutral selected, adjust the selector forks so that the sliding sleeve is positioned exactly in the centre between the synchronizing rings.

3　After adjusting, check the selection action then tighten the shift fork bolts to the specified torque.

4　Check that the 3rd/4th shift arm clears the 1st/2nd fork rod by approximately 0.08 in. (2 mm).

37 Input shaft (4-speed) - dismantling and reassembly

1　This input shaft is generally similar to the one used in the early type, 5-speed manual transmission, as described in Section 5, Part 1 of this Chapter.

2　The component parts are shown in Figs. 5.84 and 5.85.

38 Pinion shaft (4-speed) - dismantling and reassembly

1　The pinion shaft is generally similar to the one used in the early type, 5-speed manual transmission, as described in Section 6, Part 1 of this Chapter.

2　The component parts are shown in Figs. 5.86 and 5.87.

39 Inspection of transmission components - general

1　Refer to Section 7, Part 1 of this Chapter which gives all the necessary information on inspection of transmission components. The

Fig. 5.83. 1st/2nd to 3rd/4th shift arm clearance (arrowed) (Sec. 36)

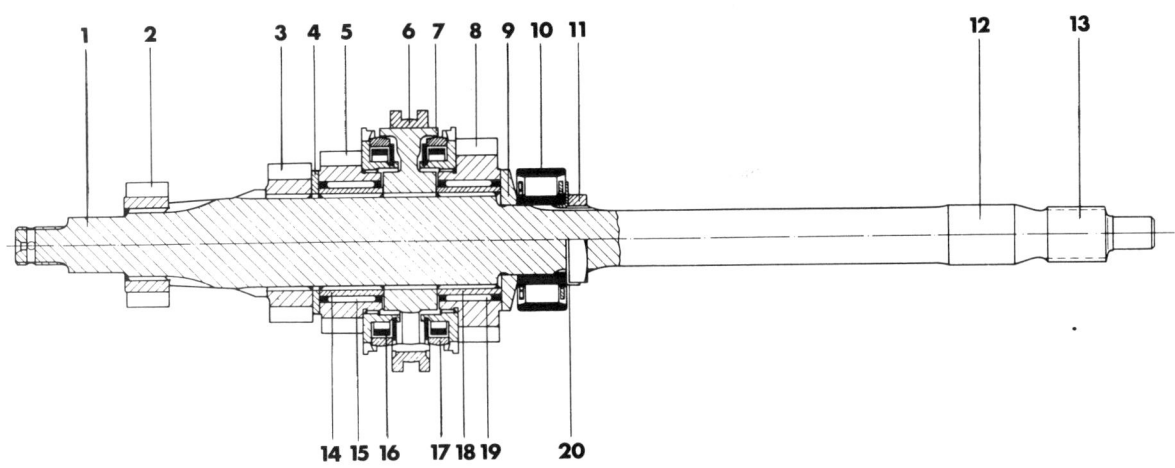

Fig. 5.84. Sectional view of input shaft (Sec. 37)

1　Input shaft	6　Sliding sleeve	11　Nut	16　Brake band
2　1st gear (fixed)	7　Spider	12　Oil seal race	17　Synchronizing ring
3　2nd gear (fixed)	8　4th gear (free-wheeling)	13　Spline for clutch plate	18　Needle bearing inner race
4　Thrust washer	9　Thrust washer (5.9 mm thick)	14　Needle bearing inner race	19　Needle bearing cage
5　3rd gear (free-wheeling)	10　Roller bearing	15　Needle bearing cage	20　Lock plate

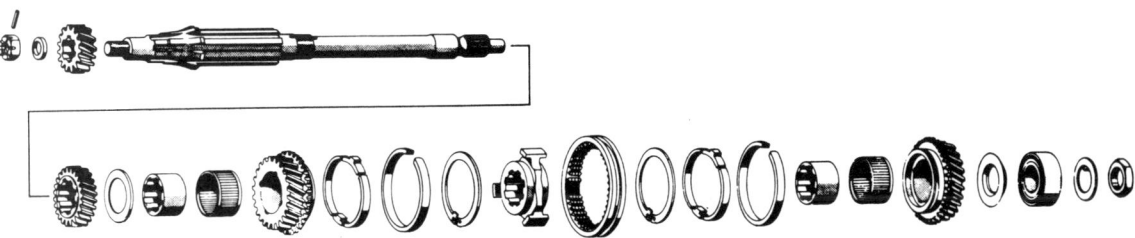

Fig. 5.85. Input shaft — exploded view (Sec. 37)

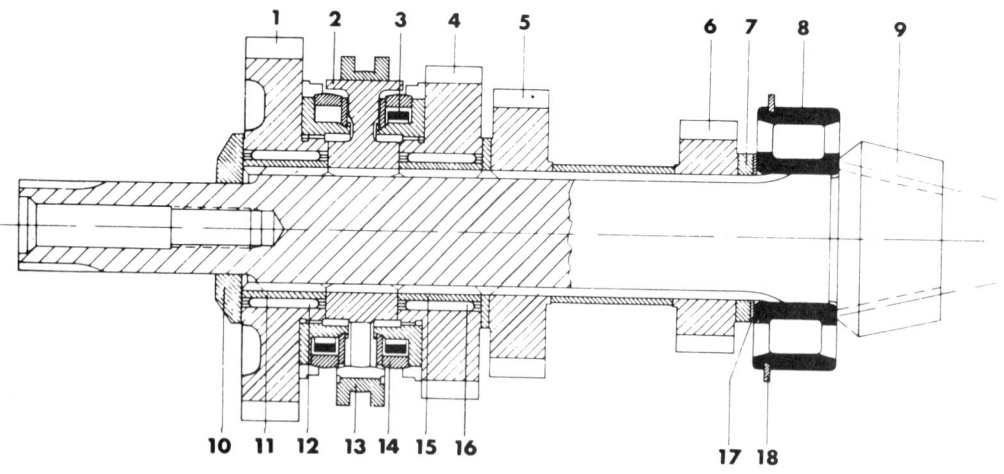

1   1st gear (free-wheeling)
2   Spider
3   Brake band
4   2nd gear (free-wheeling)
5   3rd gear (fixed)
6   4th gear (fixed)
7   Spacer
8   Roller bearing
9   Pinion shaft
10 Thrust washer (6.6 mm/
    0.260'' thick)
11 Needle bearing inner race
    (1st to 4th gear)
12 Needle bearing cage
    (1st to 4th gear)
13 Sliding sleeve
14 Synchronizing ring
15 Needle bearing inner race
16 Needle bearing cage
17 Spacers
18 Retaining ring

Fig. 5.86. Sectional view of pinion shaft (Sec. 38)

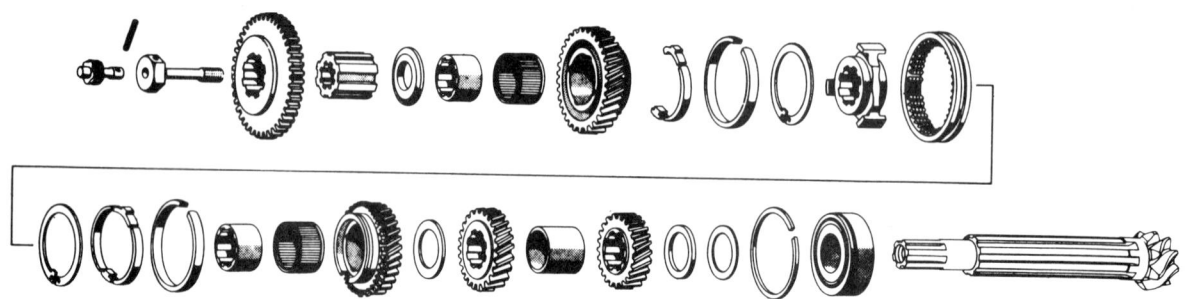

Fig. 5.87. Pinion shaft — exploded view (Sec. 38)

reference at paragraph 5 should read Section 40 for early type
Sportomatic transmissions.

40 Synchronizer assemblies - dismantling and reassembly

1   The synchronizer assemblies are similar to those used in the early
type, 4-speed manual transmission. For further Information refer to
Sections 8 and 15, Part 1 of this Chapter.
2   The 1st speed synchronizer assembly is shown in Fig. 5.27.

41 Intermediate plate (early type) - dismantling and reassembly

1   The intermediate plate is generally similar to the one used on the
early type, 5-speed manual transmission, referred to in Section 9, Part
1 of this Chapter. However, there is one important difference, which
is the reverse gear assembly.
2   Before any other dismantling is done, pull off the straight-cut reverse
gear using a universal puller. This will break the retaining ring, so ensure
that all fragments are removed.
3   When reassembling, first install the helical reverse gear so that the
splined sleeve projects through to the front cover side of the
intermediate plate.

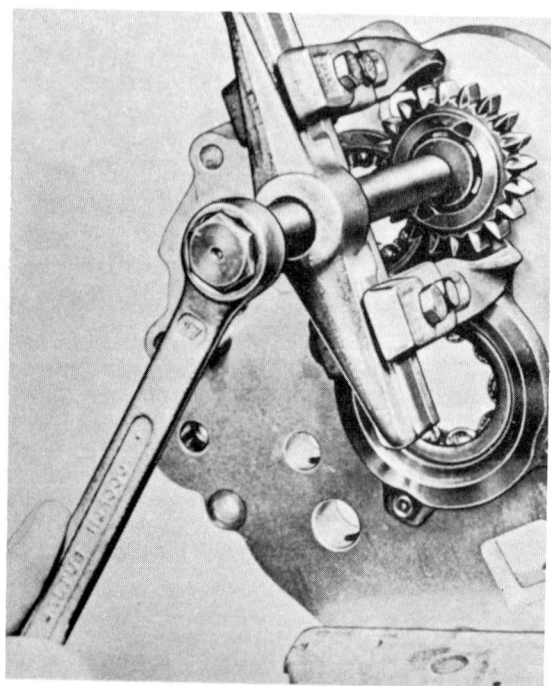

Fig. 5.88. Removing the intermediate plate reverse gear (Sec. 41)

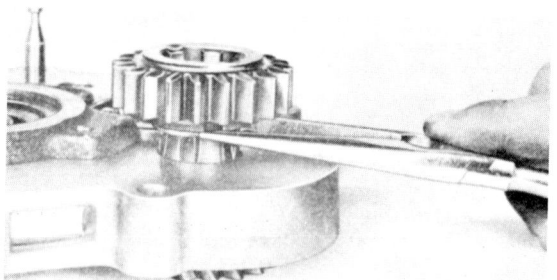

Fig. 5.89. Installing the reverse gear (Sec. 41)

4   Install the retaining circlip in the groove, then push on the straight-cut gear to contact it.
5   Compress the retaining circlip, then further press on the gear so that the circlip snaps into place in the gear.

42 Transmission housing - breather

1   Refer to the procedures given in Section 10, Part 1 of this Chapter.

43 Transmission front cover (early type) - dismantling and reassembly

1   The transmission front cover is generally similar to the one used in the early type, 5-speed manual transmission referred to in Section 11, Part 1 of this Chapter.

44 Gearshift linkage - removal, installation and adjustment

1   The gearshift linkage is generally similar to that used in the early type, 5-speed manual transmission referred to in Section 12, Part 1 of this Chapter.

45 Gearshift lever micro-switch - removal and installation

1   Push back the front seats and remove the floor covering from the centre tunnel.
2   Remove the retaining bolts and lift up the gearshift base so that the micro-switch leads can be detached.
3   Withdraw the entire base and mount the shift lever in a vice using jaw clamps.
4   Using a hammer and suitable tool (eg, an open-ended spanner) drive off the gearshift knob. Remove the locking sleeve from the knob using a suitable hook ended tool.
5   Pull off the dust boot and switch from the gearshift lever.
6   Installation is the reverse of the removal procedure. Ensure that the switch contacts are clean, and bend the outer contact tabs if necessary to obtain a gap of 0.012 to 0.016 in. (0.3 to 0.4 mm). Ensure that the slit in the switch is facing forwards when installed, and push down until it engages in the pin.

46 Clutch - adjustment

Engine/transmission installed
1   Raise the car to a suitable working height.

Fig. 5.90. Correct position of switch on gearshift lever (Sec. 45)

2   Push the throttle linkage cross-shaft to the fully open position to relieve the vacuum in the servo. With the left hand, push the clutch intermediate lever towards the right-hand rear wheel and check for a free-play of at least 0.2 in. (5 mm). If there is less than this, remove the engine/transmission and adjust the basic setting, as described below.

Engine/transmission removed
3   Remove the cotter key from the actuating rod/intermediate lever clevis pin; remove the clevis pin.
4   Pull the servo actuating rod fully out, whilst pushing the intermediate lever towards the servo as far as it will go.
5   In this position, adjust the actuating rod clevis so that the bore in the clevis extension extends 0.394 to 0.47 in. (10 to 12 mm) beyond the bore in the intermediate lever (dimension 'A' in Fig. 5.92).

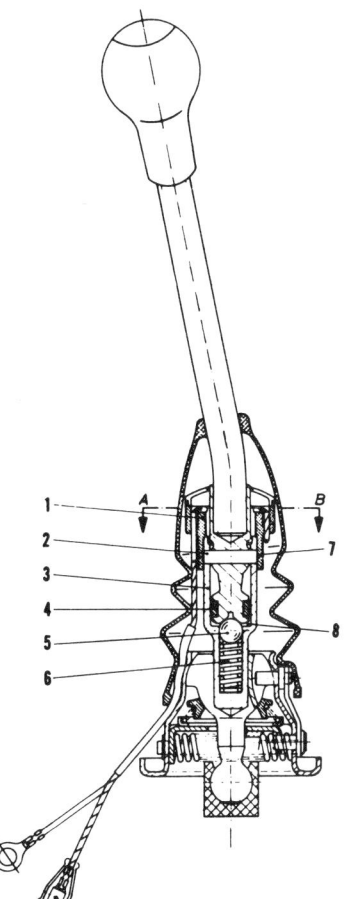

1   Switch
2   Retaining pin
3   Gearshift lever (lower)
4   Stop ring
5   Ball
6   Spring
7   Switch position when engaged with aligning pin
8   Internal parts lightly lubricate at time of reassembly

Fig. 5.91. Sectional view of gearshift lever assembly (Sec. 45)

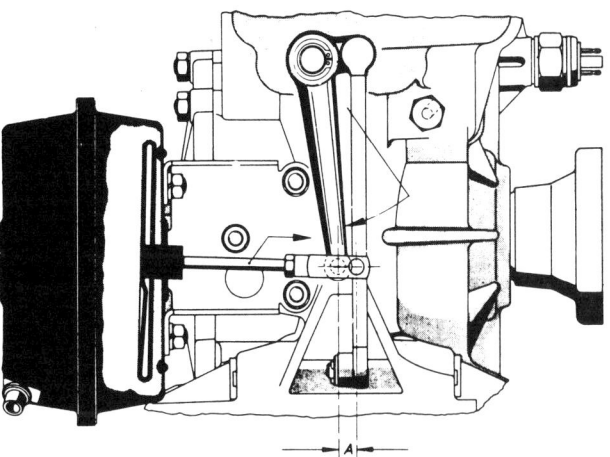

Fig. 5.92. Clutch adjustment (Sec. 46)
A = 0.394 to 0.47 in (10 to 12 mm)

6   Before installing the transmission, check the control valve plunger adjustment, as described in Section 47.
7   After installing, check that reverse gear can be selected without grating when the engine is running.

47 Control valve - adjustment

Note: Before any adjustments are made, ensure that the control linkage and engine idle speed have been correctly set.

Upshifting on acceleration - 1968 models
Note: The method described for 1969 models can also be used on 1968 models, but the layout of the operating linkage and throttle flaps must first be adjusted in relation to the injection pump or accelerator linkage.

1   With the cam in the fully returned position, adjust the control valve plunger so that a clearance of 0.06 in (1.5 mm) exists between it and the drag spring.
2   Place a 0.12 in (3 mm) gauge plate under the left idle speed stop screw, and adjust the cam by loosening the Allen screw so that the drag spring just contacts the control valve plunger. **Note:** If necessary, the 0.06 in (1.5 mm) clearance may be reduced to a minimum of 0.04 in (1 mm) to achieve this adjustment.

Upshifting on acceleration - 1969 911E models
3   Adjust the control valve plunger so that there is a reserve stroke of 0.02 in (0.5 mm) in the full throttle position.
4   Place a 0.12 in (3 mm) gauge plate beneath one throttle valve stop screw, and adjust the cam disc so that it just touches the plunger.
5   At the idling position, check that there is a small clearance between the control valve plunger and the cam disc.

Downshifting on deceleration - provisional setting
6   With the handbrake applied, allow the engine to idle then engage a gear. There should be a time lag of 0.3 to 0.5 seconds from the time

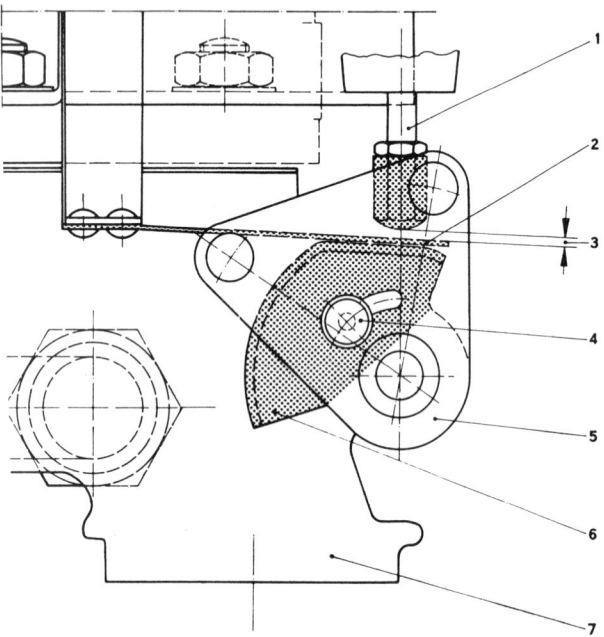

Fig. 5.93. Control valve plunger adjustment for 1968 models (Sec. 47)

1   Control valve plunger   4   Allen bolt
2   Drag spring   5   Throttle cross-shaft
3   Clearance   6   Cam disc
                               7   Intake manifold

Fig. 5.95. Control valve plunger adjustment — 1969 911E (Sec. 47)

Fig. 5.96. Gauge plate beneath throttle valve stop screw (Sec. 47)

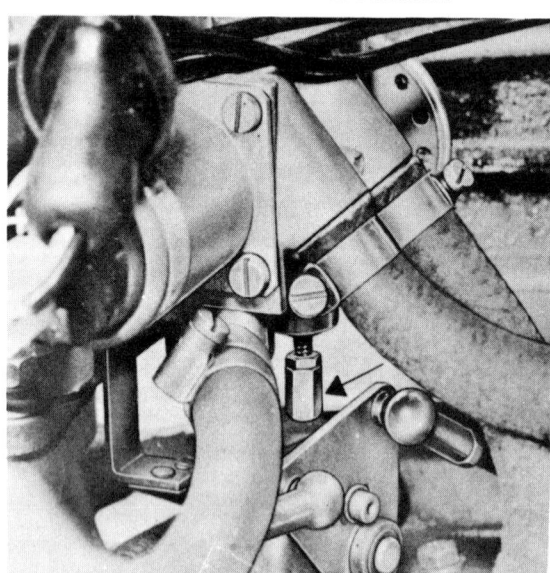

Fig. 5.94. Adjustment point (arrowed) for 1968 models (Sec. 47)

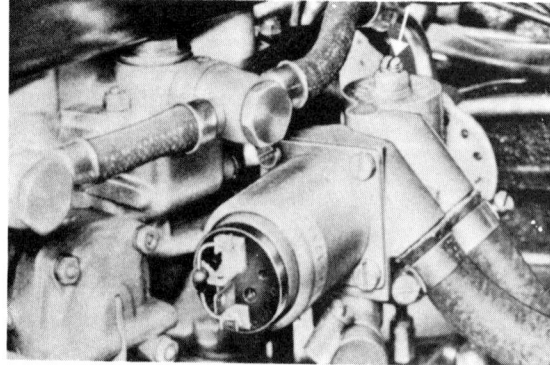

Fig. 5.97. Control valve adjustment screw (arrowed) — 1969 911E (Sec. 47)

the gearshift lever is released, to the time of gear engagement.

Downshifting on deceleration - road test

7   Drive the car with 'D' selected at an engine speed of 4500 rpm. Release the throttle and shift down to 'L'; there should be no time lag whilst the clutch engages, but at the same time there should be no momentary locking of the driving wheels. The clutch may be adjusted to suit individual tastes as described below.

Deceleration downshift phase - adjustment

8   Remove the air cleaners (except on 1969 911E models).
9   Remove the plastic cover from the adjustment screw, then either turn the screw inwards (for a softer, delayed clutch engagement) or outwards (for a firmer, faster clutch engagement). Adjustments should be made in increments of ¼ turn of the screw at a time.
10 Install the plastic cover and air cleaners (where applicable).

48 Control valve - removal and installation

1968 models

1   Detach the battery earth lead(s).
2   Remove the air cleaner (refer to Chapter 2, if necessary).
3   Take off the rubber cap from the control valve, then remove the cotter key and take off the wire connector.
4   Detach the vacuum hoses, then remove the control valve from its bracket.
5   Installation is the reverse of the removal procedure. Apply a little molybdenum disulphide grease to the top of the cam disc, and adjust the control valve after installation. Ensure that the cable connector is firmly fitted; if necessary the cotter key hole may be re-drilled.

1969 911E models

6   Detach the hoses, then remove the nuts and take off the control valve and holder together.
7   Remove the split pin and detach the plug-in connector.

Fig. 5.98. Control valve connector cotter key (arrowed) (Sec. 48)

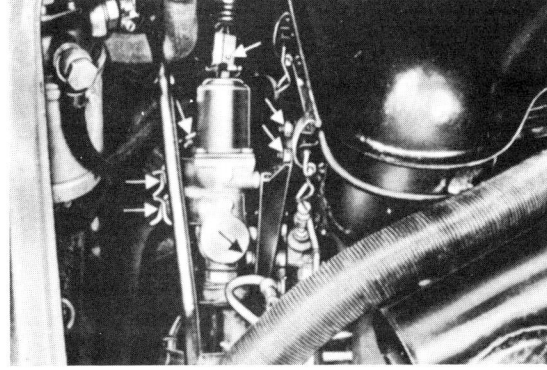

Fig. 5.99. Detachment points (arrowed) for control valve on 1969 911E models (Sec. 48)

8   Detach the control valve from the holder.
9   Installation is the reverse of the removal procedure, but it is preferable to adjust the reserve stroke (Section 47) before the control valve is installed. Coat the cam drive with a molybdenum disulphide grease where it contacts the plunger, then finally adjust the downshift (Section 47).

49 Differential

The information given in Part 1, Sections 13 and 14 is equally applicable to Sportomatic transmissions.

50 Transmission (later type) - dismantling into major assemblies, and reassembly

Note: This transmission is generally similar to the early type Sportomatic transmission, the differences being mainly associated with the gears assembled on the intermediate plate. Therefore, only those procedures which have been amended are given in this and subsequent Sections. Where information is not given, refer to the appropriate Section for the early type Sportomatic transmission.

1   With the torque converter, clutch and transmission front cover already removed, select neutral then remove the fork piece from the transmission housing.
2   Turn the shift rod clockwise and pull it out to select 4th gear.
3   Working through the fork piece aperture in the housing, select 1st or 2nd gear to lock-up the transmission.
4   Remove the pinion shaft expansion bolt and take off the speedometer gear.
5   Remove the circlip from the reverse shift rod and parking lock.
6   Push in the detent pin, and take off the shift fork and reverse sliding gear.
7   Take off the splined bushing, then remove the reverse idler gear assembly, needle cages and axial thrust needle bearing.
8   Remove the flanged nut from the input shaft.
9   Remove the bypass and reverse light switches, and their contact plungers.
10 Withdraw the gear assembly, noting the total number and thickness of gaskets used for the intermediate plate. If this is not done, the pinion meshing depth will need to be reset by a Porsche dealer on assembly.
11 Mark the installed position of the selector forks on the shafts, then remove the shafts from the intermediate plate as described in Section 35.

Fig. 5.100. Components on intermediate plate (Sec. 50)

1	Reverse gear	6	Parking lock springs
2	Flanged nut	7	Speedometer drive gear
3	Reverse idler gear assembly	8	Expansion bolt
4	Reverse selector gear	9	Parking lock lever
5	Parking lock springs	10	Reverse shift fork
		11	Circlip

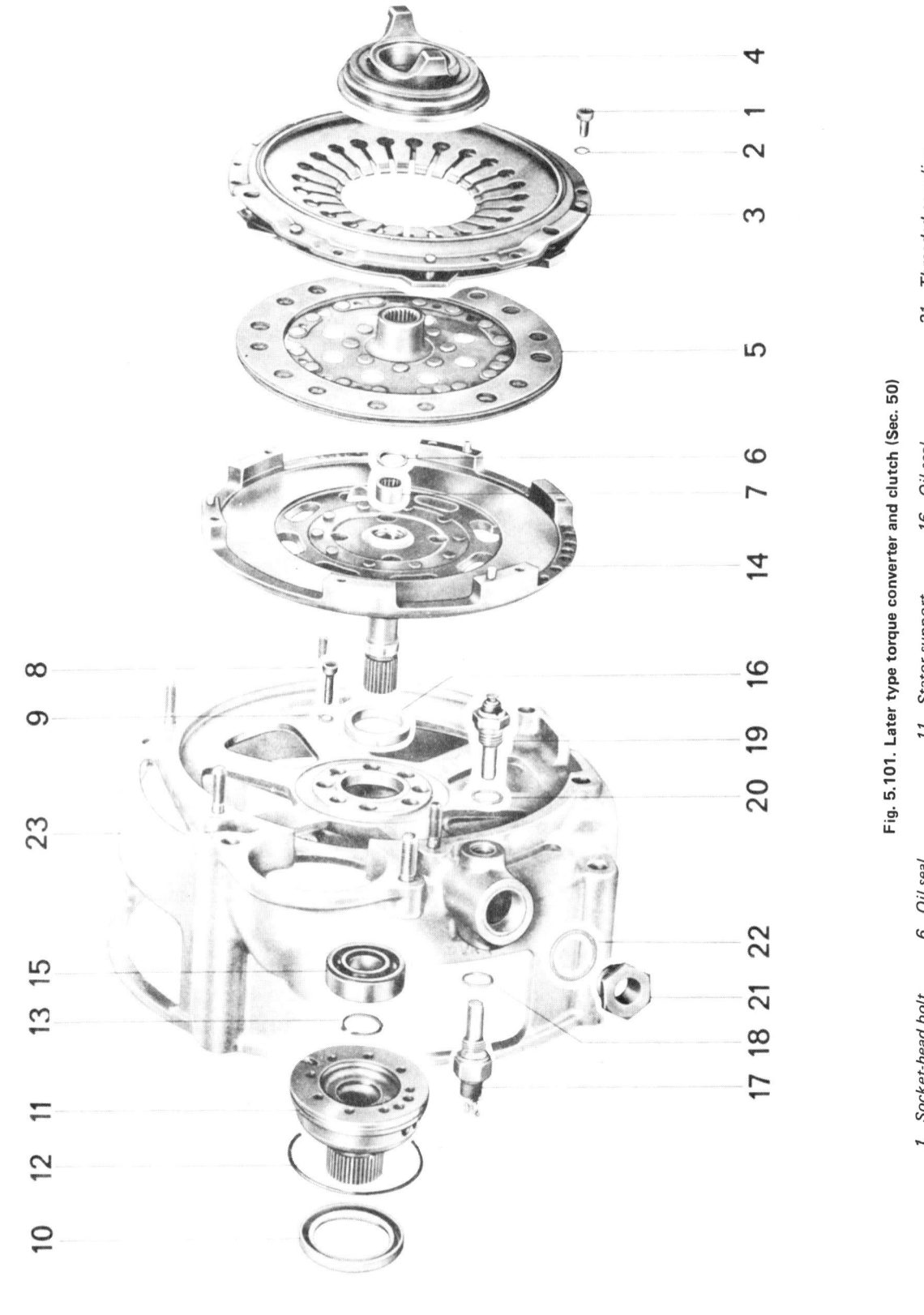

Fig. 5.101. Later type torque converter and clutch (Sec. 50)

1	Socket-head bolt	6	Oil seal	11	Stator support	16	Oil seal	21	Threaded coupling
2	Lock washer	7	Needle bearing	12	O-ring	17	Temperature switch	22	Oil seal
3	Pressure plate	8	Socket-head bolt	13	Circlip	18	Oil seal	23	Torque converter
4	Throwout bearing	9	Oil seal	14	Turbine shaft	19	Temperature		housing
5	Clutch disc	10	Oil seal	15	Ball bearing		coupling		
							20	Oil seal		

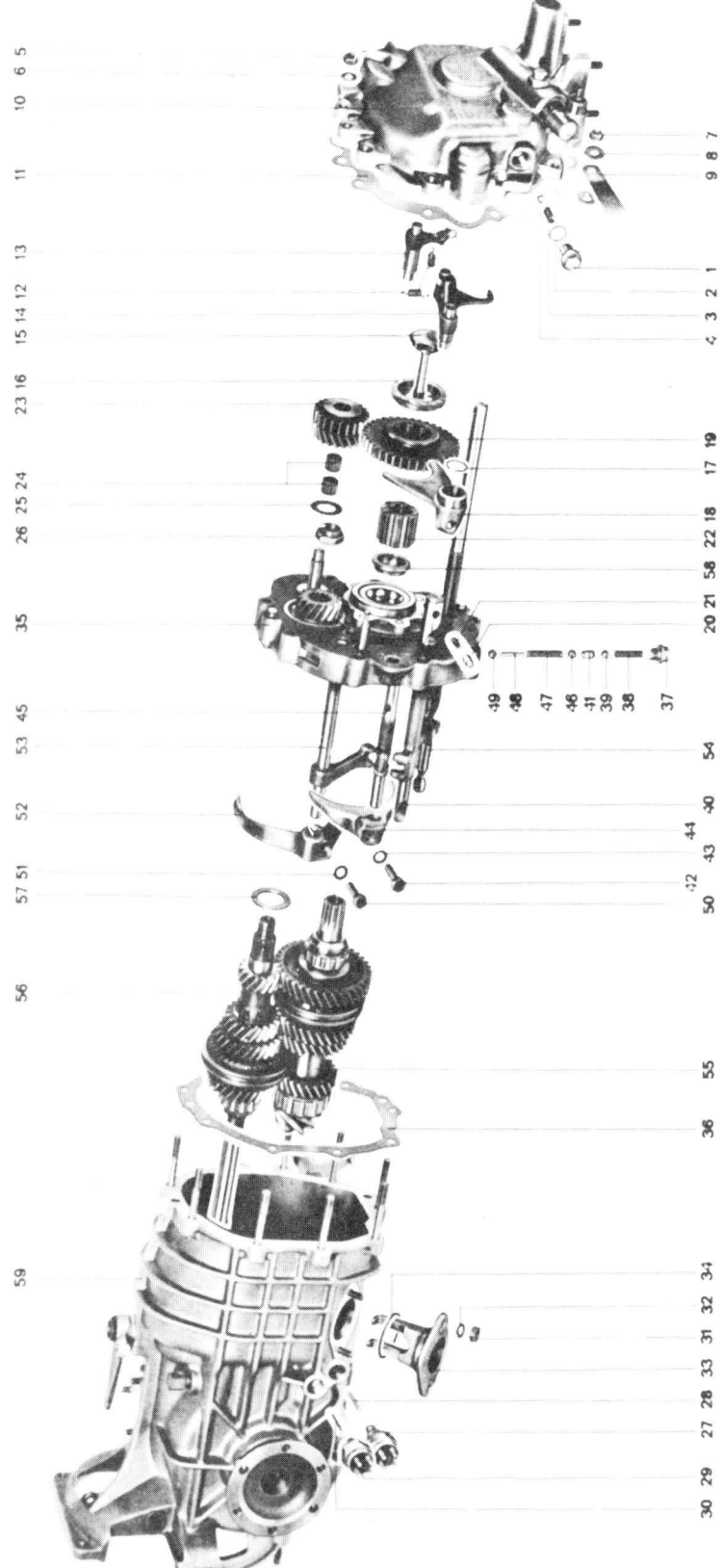

Fig. 5.102. Transmission (later type) — exploded view (Sec. 50)

1 Cap screw
2 Oil seal
3 Spring
4 Ball
5 Lock nut
6 Washer
7 Lock nut
8 Washer
9 Earth strap
10 Transmission
   front cover
11 Gasket
12 Spring
13 Parking lock lever

14 Parking lock pawl
15 Expansion bolt
16 Speedometer drive
   gear
17 Lock ring
18 Reverse shift
   fork
19 Reverse sliding gear
20 Detent pin
21 Spring
22 Splined bushing
23 Reverse idler
   gear assembly
24 Needle bearing cage

25 Thrust needle bearing
26 Flange nut
27 Bypass switch
28 Plunger
29 Reverse light switch
30 Plunger
31 Nut
32 Spring washer
33 Fork piece
34 O-ring
35 Immediate plate
36 Gasket
37 Plug
38 Spring

39 Ball
40 Reverse shift rod
41 Detent
42 Bolt
43 Spring washer
44 Shift fork,
   1st/2nd gear
45 Shift rod,
   1st/2nd gear
46 Ball
47 Spring
48 Detent (large)
49 Ball
50 Bolt

51 Spring washer
52 Shift fork,
   3rd/4th gear
53 Shift rod,
   3rd/4th gear
54 Shift fork rod and
   selector lever
55 Pinion shaft
56 Input shaft
57 Spacer
58 Bearing inner
   race half
59 Transmission housing

12 When reassembling the transmission, the following points should be noted:

a) *Install the spacer on the pinion shaft before installing the assembled shafts to the intermediate plate, then hand tighten the nut.*

b) *Lock-up the transmission, and tighten the pinion shaft expansion bolt and input shaft nut as described for the early type transmission (the speedometer gear need not be installed at this stage); then adjust the shift forks.*

c) *Assemble the selector lever, as described for the early type transmission.*

d) *Ensure that the correct quantity and thickness of gaskets is used when installing the assembled intermediate plate (see paragraph 10).*

e) *When installing the reverse sliding gear and shift fork, push in the detent pin in the shift rod.*

f) *To install the speedometer gear, remove the expansion bolt. Lubricate the expansion bolt contact surface before reinstalling.*

g) *Install the input shaft oil seal as described for the early type transmission.*

51 Intermediate plate (later type) - dismantling and reassembly

1 The intermediate plate is generally similar to the one used in the early type, 5-speed transmission. The differences are:

a) *The method of retention for the pinion shaft bearing; this now utilizes a circlip.*

b) *The combined grooved ball bearing and reverse driven gear.*

2 Refer to Section 41 of Part 1 of this Chapter for further information. The component parts are shown in Fig. 5.104.

52 Transmission front cover (later type) - dismantling and reassembly

1 The transmission front cover is generally similar to the one used in the early type, 5-speed manual transmission referred to in Section 43 of Part 1 of this Chapter.

2 The component parts are shown in Fig. 5.105.

Fig. 5.103. Detent pin (arrowed) in reverse shift fork (Sec. 50)

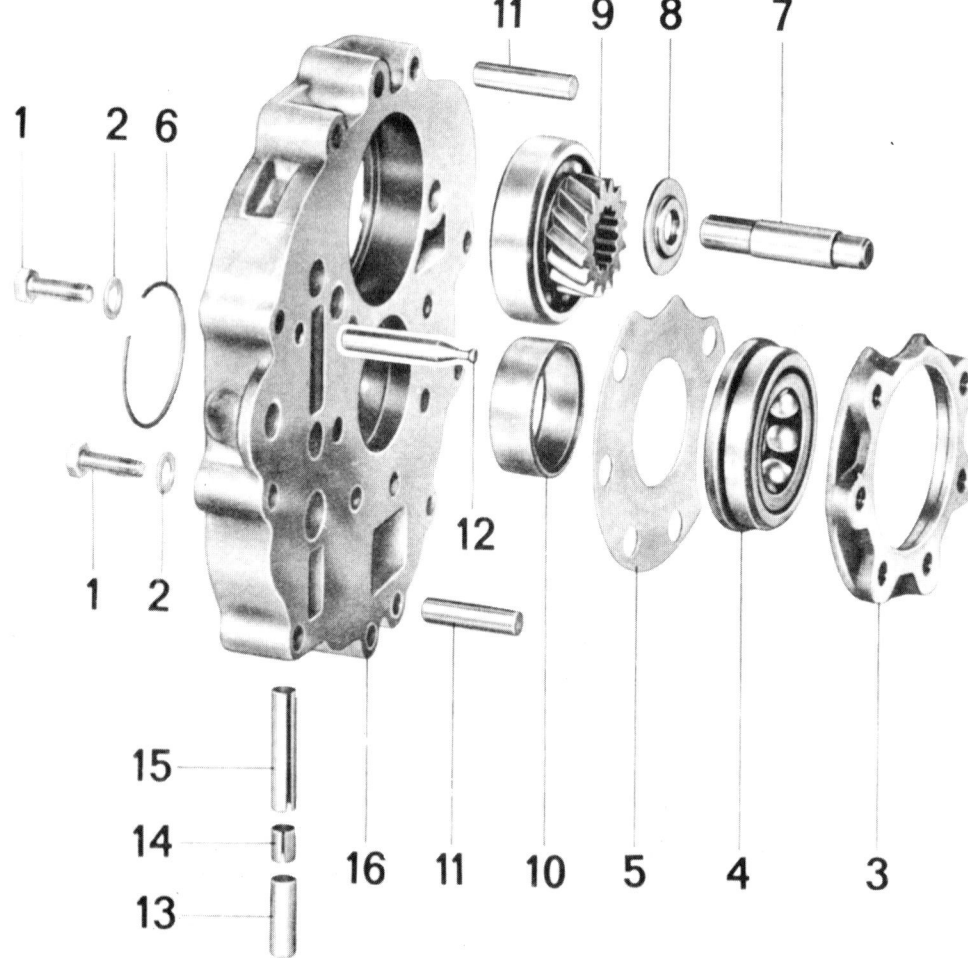

Fig. 5.104. Intermediate plate (later type) (Sec. 51)

1 Bolt
2 Washer
3 Clamping plate
4 Four-point ball bearing
5 Support plate
6 Snap ring
7 Reverse idler shaft
8 Thrust washer
9 Grooved ball bearing and reverse gear
10 Roller bearing outer race
11 Dowel
12 Spring anchor stud
13 Bushing
14 Bushing
15 Bushing
16 Intermediate plate

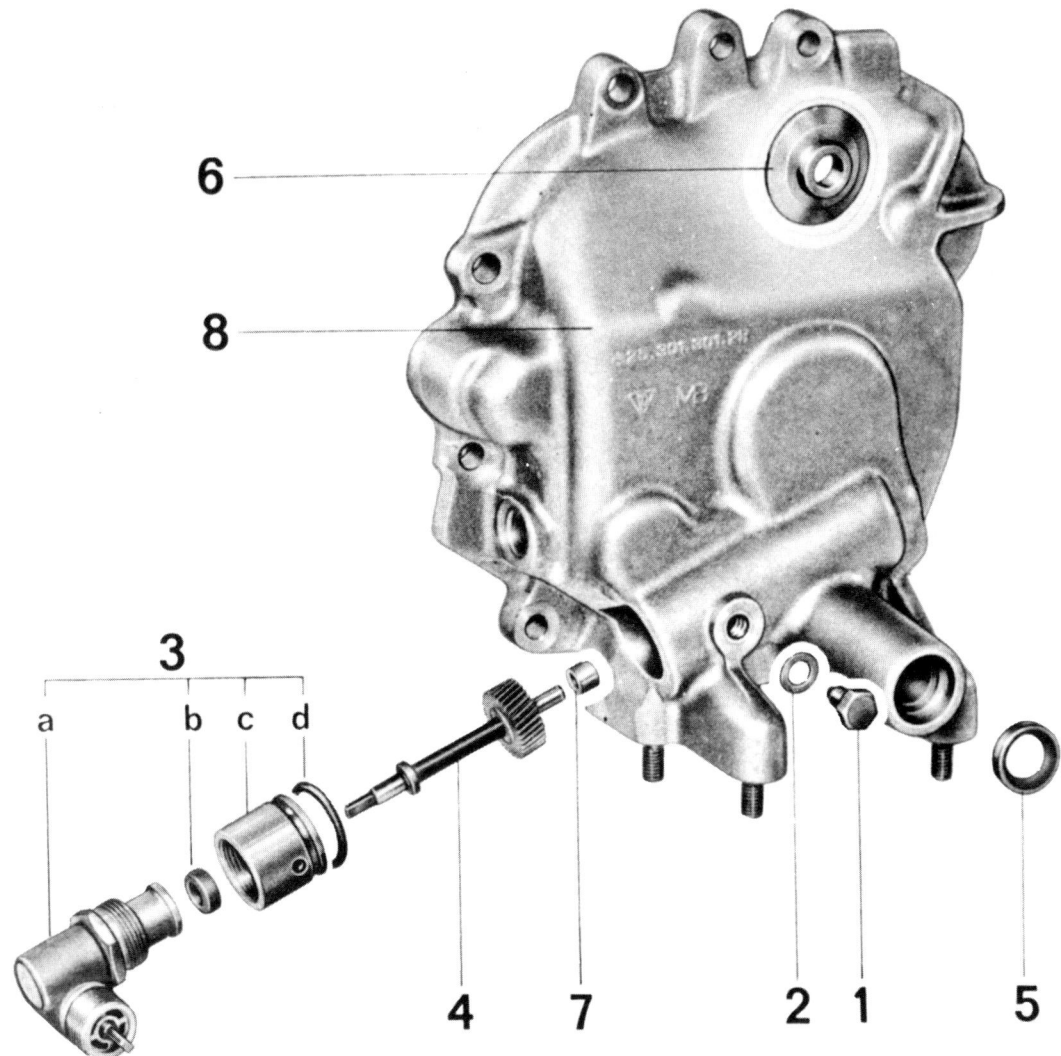

Fig. 5.105. Transmission front cover — later type (Sec. 52)

1 Retaining bolt	3d O-ring
2 Washer	4 Gear shaft
3 Speedometer drive (complete)	5 Seal
3a Elbow adaptor	6 Thrust washer
3b Seal	7 Bushing
3c Guide bushing	8 Transmission front cover

---

53 Three-speed transmission input shaft - dismantling and reassembly

1   This input shaft is generally similar to the one used in the early type, 5-speed manual transmission, as described in Section 5 of Part 1 of this Chapter.

2   The component parts are shown in Fig. 5.106.

54 Three-speed transmission pinion shaft - dismantling and reassembly

1   This pinion shaft is generally similar to the one used in the early type, 5-speed manual transmission, as described in Section 6 of Part 1 of this Chapter.

2   The component parts are shown in Fig. 5.107.

144

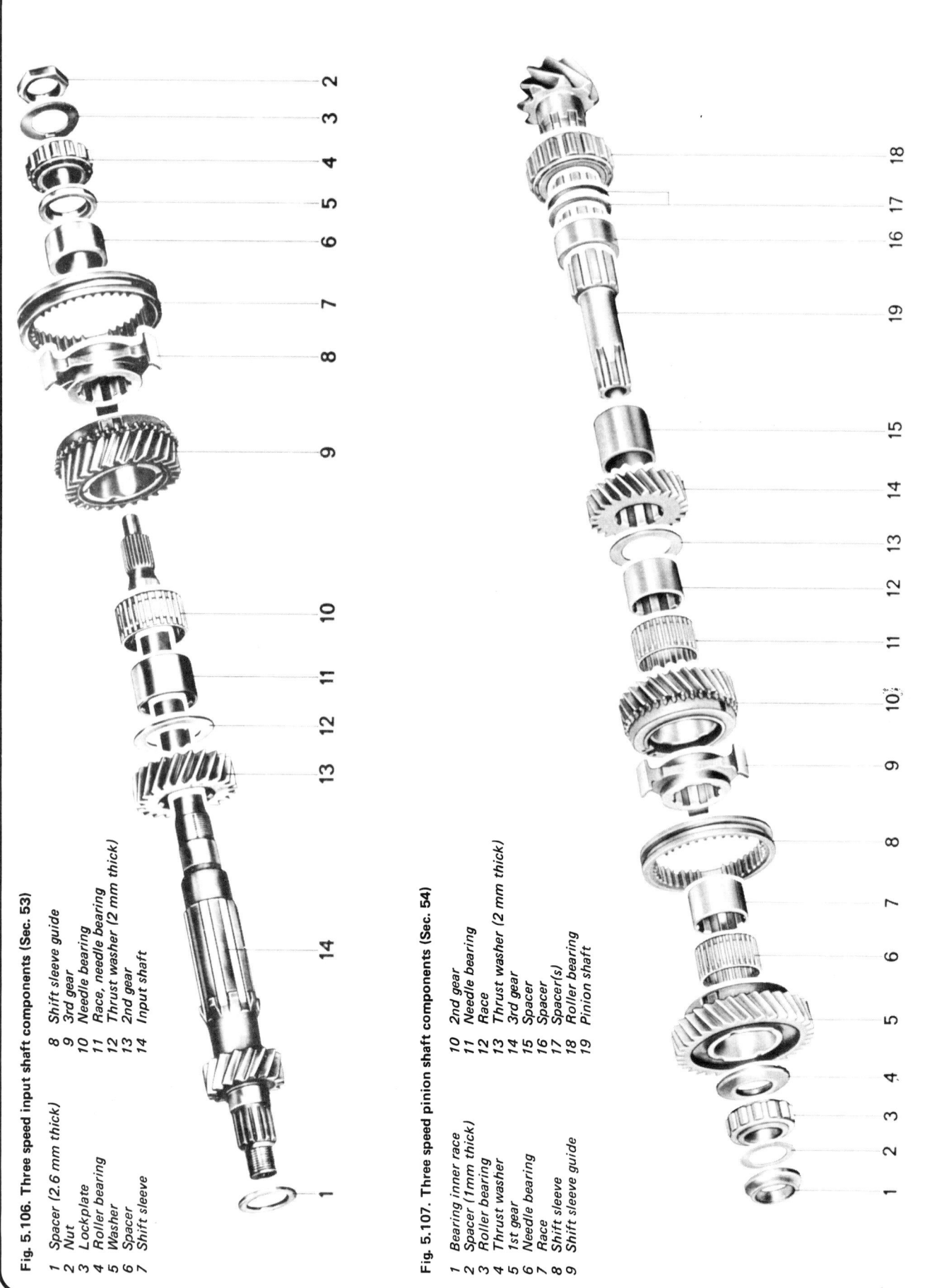

Fig. 5.106. Three speed input shaft components (Sec. 53)

1 Spacer (2.6 mm thick)
2 Nut
3 Lockplate
4 Roller bearing
5 Washer
6 Spacer
7 Shift sleeve

8 Shift sleeve guide
9 3rd gear
10 Needle bearing
11 Race, needle bearing
12 Thrust washer (2 mm thick)
13 2nd gear
14 Input shaft

Fig. 5.107. Three speed pinion shaft components (Sec. 54)

1 Bearing inner race
2 Spacer (1mm thick)
3 Roller bearing
4 Thrust washer
5 1st gear
6 Needle bearing
7 Race
8 Shift sleeve
9 Shift sleeve guide

10 2nd gear
11 Needle bearing
12 Race
13 Thrust washer (2 mm thick)
14 3rd gear
15 Spacer
16 Spacer
17 Spacer(s)
18 Roller bearing
19 Pinion shaft

55 Fault diagnosis - Sportomatic transmission

Symptom	Reason/s	Remedy
Clutch slipping under full throttle	Clutch linings contaminated	Replace clutch plate, eliminate source of contamination.
	Defective clutch	Replace clutch.
	Incorrectly adjusted clutch linkage	Adjust linkage. Check clutch free play; check clutch.
Excessive clutch slippage on completion of shift	Incorrectly adjusted control valve	Adjust control valve (for acceleration upshift).
Harsh or delayed clutch engagement on downshift	Incorrectly adjusted control valve	Adjust control valve (for deceleration downshift).
Clutch does not disengage	Incorrectly adjusted clutch linkage	Check adjustment.
	Leaks in connecting hoses or vacuum servo unit	Eliminate leaks.
	Defective diaphragm in vacuum servo unit	Replace servo unit.
	Defective input shaft needle bearing	Replace needle bearing and oil seal in turbine shaft.
	Solenoid or wiring open circuit	Repair damage (possibly by replacing the fuse).
	Dirty contact points in gearshift lever switch or poor earth to chassis	Clean contacts or install new switch; check earth connection.
	Defective solenoid in control valve	Replace control valve.
	Blocked or kinked hoses	Replace defective hoses.
Engine dies when a shift is made; idle speed cannot be adjusted	Leak in hose vacuum servo unit	Replace hose.
	Defective diaphragm in vacuum servo unit	Replace servo unit.
	Leaking check valves in inlet manifold	Replace check valves.
	Loose or defective hose between control valve and vacuum reservoir	Tighten/replace hose.
	Leak in vacuum reservoir	Rectify leak.
Clutch does not engage on completion of downshift, but engages harshly when throttle opened	Gearshift switch contacts sticking, or shorting	Clean or replace the switch.
	Short circuit in wire between switch and solenoid	Repair damage.
	Sticking control valve solenoid	Replace control valve.
Car jerks when gearshift lever is released while engine is idling and gear is engaged	Idle speed too high	Adjust.
	Incorrectly adjusted control valve	Adjust control valve (for deceleration downshift).
High-pitch whining from torque converter	Torque converter oil level low	Replenish oil in oil tank.
	Oil pressure too low	Check oil pump.
	Torque converter losing oil through pump hub seal	Replace seal in pump hub.
	Oil leaking through weld seam between pump and turbine	Replace torque converter.
Poor acceleration (not associated with an engine out-of-tune)	Defective torque converter. Check: Run engine with footbrake and handbrake applied, and D4 selected. Open throttle and check for an engine speed of 2400/2800 rpm. Ensure that temperature gauge pointer does not reach the red sector on the dial	Engine speed high, replace clutch. Engine speed low, replace torque converter.

Chapter 6 Rear suspension and driveshafts

Contents

Specifications

Rear suspension type	Independent with triangulated control arms, torsion bars and telescopic shock absorbers. Rear stabilizer bar used on some models
Driveshafts type	Nadella or Lobro with twin universal joints

Rear suspension geometry (degrees)

	Camber	Toe-in
1965 models	−1º 6'	0 to −2'
1966/67 models	−50' ± 20'	0 ± 10' each wheel
1968 models	−1º 15' ± 20'	0 ± 10' each wheel
1969/71 models	−50' ± 20'	0 ± 10' each wheel
1972/73 models	−1º ± 10'	0 to 20' each wheel
1974/75 on	−1º ± 10'	0 ± 20' each wheel

Radius arm adjustment

Pre-1968 models	36º
1968 models	39º
1969 onwards	36º 30' to 37º

Rear axle trim height setting	0.472 ± 0.197 in (12 ± 5 mm)
Maximum height difference (side-to-side)	0.315 in (± 8 mm)

Note: *All suspension geometry measurements must be made with correctly inflated tyres, a full fuel tank and the spare wheel in position.*

Torque wrench settings

	lb f ft	kg fm
Rear axle control arm nut	87	12
Radius arm (trailing arm) nut	65	9
Camber eccentric bolts	43	6
Tracking (toe-in) eccentric bolts	36	5
Shock absorber attachment - M12	54	7.5
Shock absorber attachment - M14	90	12.5
Halfshaft castellated nut	217/253	30/35
Halfshaft flange Allen bolts (Nadella)	34	4.7
Halfshaft flange Allen bolts (Lobro) - M8	31	4.3
Halfshaft flange Allen bolts (Lobro) - M10	60	8.3
Bearing cap bolts	34	4.7

1 General description

The rear suspension is of the triangulated control arm type with springing by an adjustable tranverse tension bow and hydraulic double-acting shock absorbers. The main axle load is taken by the axle control arms, the torsional loads being applied through trailing radius arms. The tension bars are adjustable through a vernier arrangement to provide alteration of the rear axle trim height. Eccentric adjuster bolts are provided for camber and tracking (toe-in).

Drive from the transmission is through twin shafts to the rear hubs. Early versions used either Nadella or Lobro driveshafts.

The Nadella shafts had Hookes-type universal joints; the inner joint having an arrangement which permits axial movement of the driveshaft through a special link. This is the only type of shaft used with early Sportomatic transmissions. The Lobro driveshaft had two constant velocity joints and, although modified at different times, subsequently replaced the Nadella shafts.

The rear suspension and driveshaft do not require routine maintenance and lubrication.

2 Suspension control arm - removal and installation

Pre - 1969 models

1 Remove the rear wheel caliper and the disc/drum assembly, as described in Chapter 8.
2 Remove the cotter pin from the castellated nut.
3 Using a bar between two of the wheel studs, wedged against the floor to stop the hub from rotating, unscrew the driveshaft castellated nut.
4 At the transmission end, remove the flange Allen bolts, then use a soft-faced hammer to tap off the driveshaft from the flange joint.
5 Using a tube or arbor of the appropriate size, drive out the rear hub.
6 Detach the handbrake cable, and remove the shield plate (where applicable) and the brake carrier plate, referring to Chapter 8, as necessary.
7 Using a suitable jack (one with a cradle-type head is preferable) raise the control arm and detach the shock absorber retaining bolt.
8 Mark the installed position of the camber and tracking eccentric

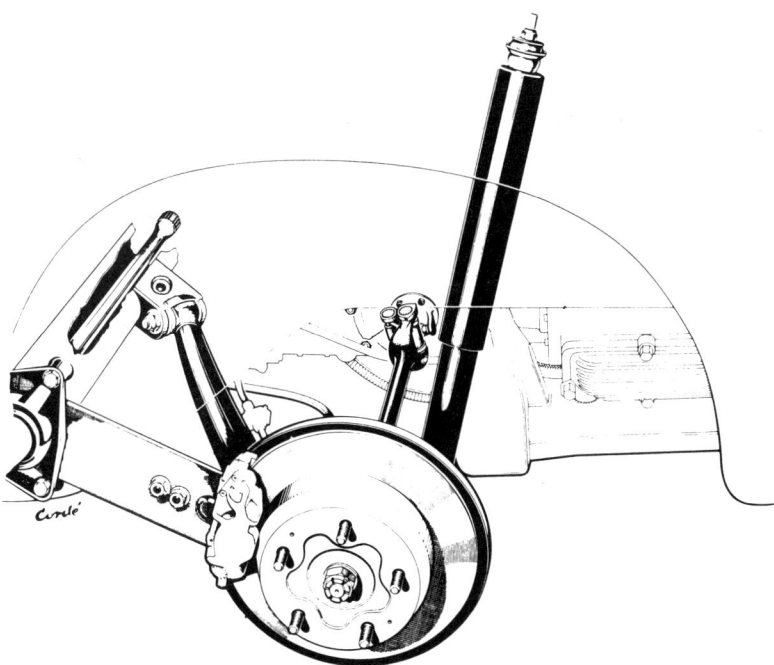

Fig. 6.1. Rear suspension layout — typical (Sec. 2)

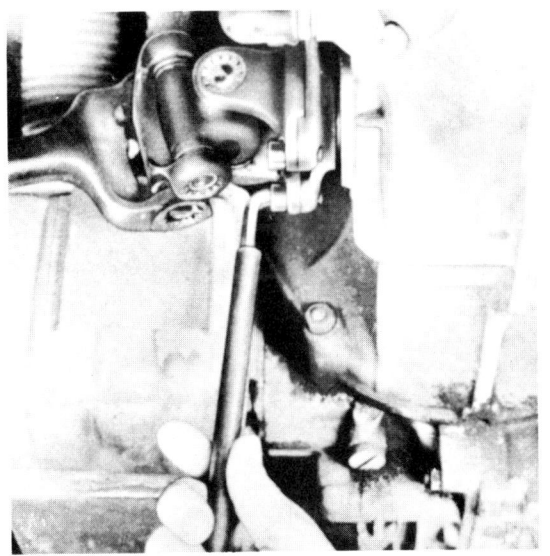

Fig. 6.2. Removing the flange Allen bolts (Nadella) (Sec. 2)

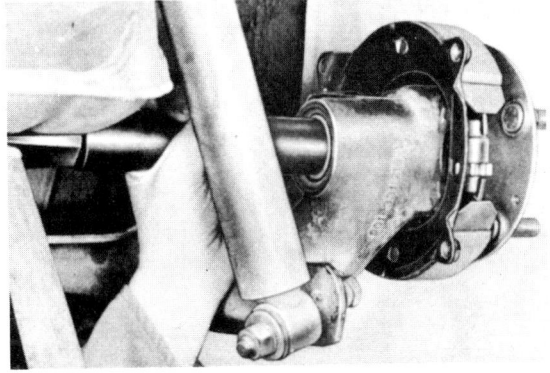

Fig. 6.3. Driving out the rear hub (Sec. 2)

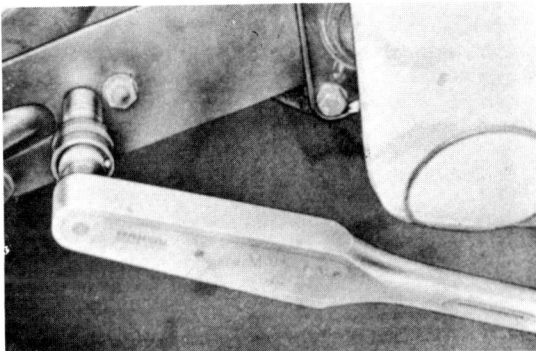

Fig. 6.4. Removing a camber eccentric bolt (Sec. 2)

bolts as a guide to installing, then remove the nuts from these and the arm retaining bolts.

9   Detach the brake hose from the control arm.

10 Remove the nut from the control arm mounting bolt, then drive the bolt out. It will be necessary to move the control arm slightly, and may also be necessary to loosen the transmission carrier retaining bolts, in order to release the control arm. (Fig. 6.5)

11 Mount the control arm in a vice and pull out the roller bearing inner ring. Move the spacer tube to one side and then use a suitable drift to drive out the ballbearing. Also remove the spacer tube.

12 Press or drive out the roller bearing, but ensure that the control arm is adequately supported during the process.

13 If the Flanbloc bushes are worn or damaged, they can only be removed by destroying them, then new ones pressed in to their full depth. This job is best entrusted to a Porsche agent who will have the necessary tools for the job. At the same time the control arm can be checked for alignment using a special fixture. Also check the radius arm rubber bushes for wear and damage, renewing as necessary. Note that from chassis no. 305 1015 (911S) and 307 325 (911), these are vulcanized to the radius arm, and the complete arm must be renewed.

14 Examine the ball and roller bearing for wear, corrosion, scoring and signs of overheating (bluish colour). It is recommended that the oil seals are renewed as a matter of course.

15 Assembly is basically the reverse of the removal procedure. After installing the roller bearing and oil seal, fit the spacer tube with the recess and wide thrust collar towards the roller bearing. Using approximately 1½ oz (40g) of general purpose grease, work it into the bearings, then put the remainder into the hub. At this stage check, and

Fig. 6.5. Control arm retaining bolt nut (arrowed) (Sec. 2)

Fig. 6.7. Install an O-ring in the groove around the ball bearing (Sec. 2)

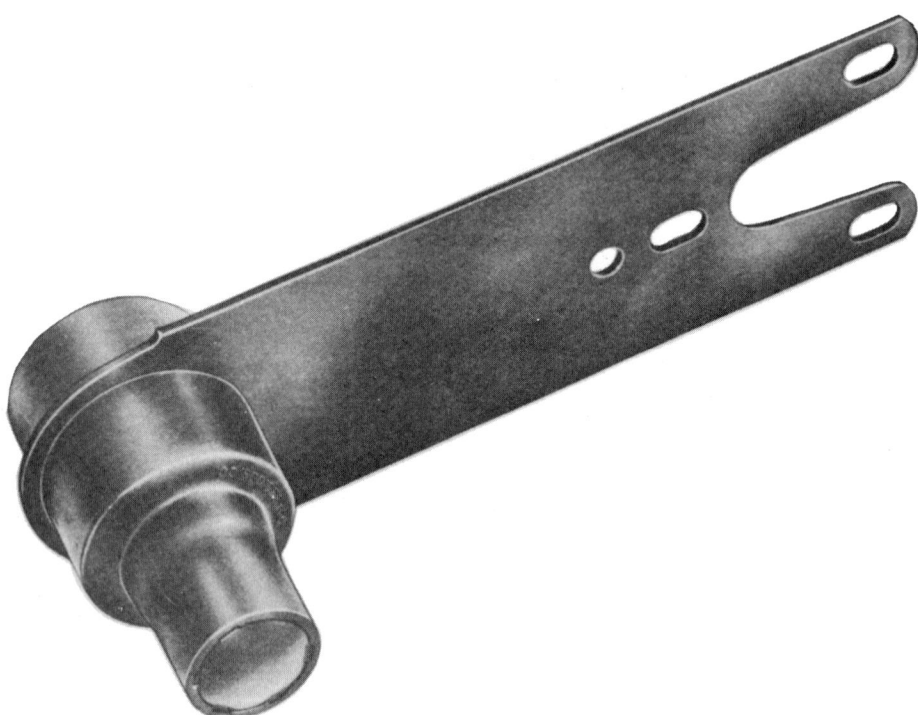

Fig. 6.6. Vulcanised radius arm bushes (Sec. 2)

renew if necessary, the oil seal in the brake carrier plate.

16 When installing, the procedure is basically the reverse of that used when removing. However, the following points should be noted:

a) Slide in the 14M bolt from inside whilst positioning the control arm to line it up. Do not forget the washer under the bolt head and under the nut. Do not tighten the nut until the car weight is taken on its wheels.

b) Tighten the eccentric bolts in their original positions. This must only be regarded as a provisional setting, and on completion the camber and tracking (toe-in) must be checked.

c) After installing the ball bearing, do not forget to place the oil seal in the groove. Use a little grease and make sure that it is correctly seated.

d) Refer to Chapter 8, if necessary, for information on installing the handbrake cables.

e) When installing the hub, place a new gasket on the driveshaft stub, then drive on the hub using a soft-faced hammer. Support the hub flange and drive the roller bearing inner ring into position.

f) Do not forget to tighten the flange nuts and castellated nut to the specified torque. Refer to Section 8, for further information if

Fig. 6.8. Removing the flange Allen bolts (Lobro) (Sec. 2)

required.

g) *Refer to Chapter 8 for torque wrench settings for the brake system, and for the handbrake adjustment and brake system bleeding procedure.*

h) *Tighten the control arm 14 mm bolt with the weight of the car on its suspension.*

j) *Refer to Section 7 for suspension geometry checks.*

1969/71 models

Note: If the control arm has been installed with the pivot bolt head towards the transmission, it will be necessary to remove the engine/transmission for the control arm to be released. Refer to Chapter 1, for this procedure.

17 Refer to the procedure given in paragraphs 1, 7, 2, 3, 4, 5 and 6 (in that order) of this Section. Note that paragraph 4 is only applicable if the control arm pivot bolts are installed with the heads outwards in which case it will not have been necessary to remove the engine/transmission.

18 Take off the handbrake cable guide.

19 Refer to the procedure given in paragraph 8, of this Section.

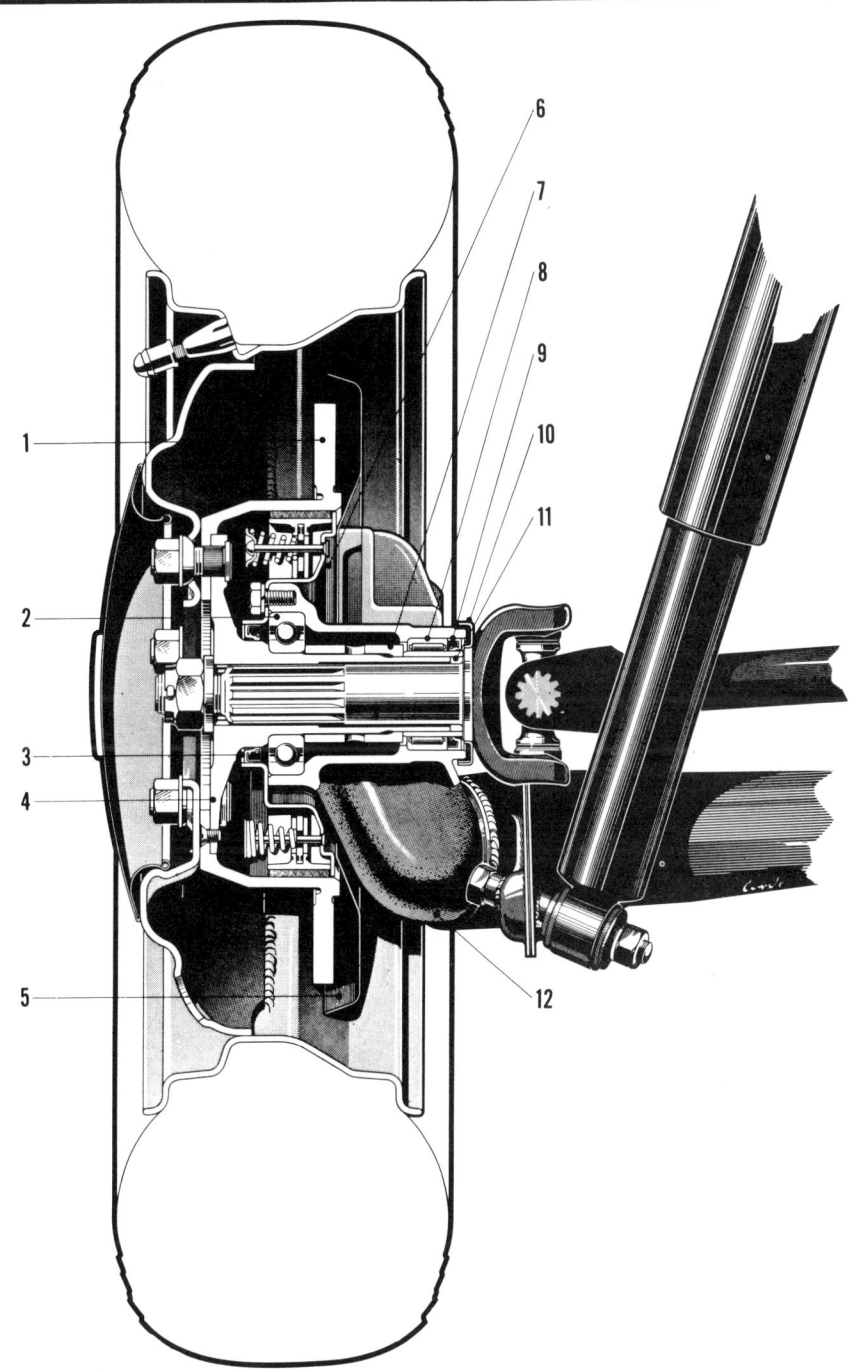

Fig. 6.9. Pre-1969 wheel bearing arrangement (left-hand side) (Secs. 2 and 3)

1 Brake disc	4 Hub	7 Spacer tube	10 Dust cap
2 Ball bearing	5 Disc shroud	8 Roller bearing	11 Gasket ring
3 Oil seal	6 Brake carrier plate	9 Oil seal	12 Control arm

20 With the control arm removed, press or drive out the radial thrust ball bearing if wear or damage is evident (see paragraph 22). A new one must be obtained for reassembly if it is removed, as it will almost certainly be damaged during the removal procedure.

21 If the Flanblocs are worn or damaged, they can only be removed by destroying them, then the new ones pressed in to full depth. This job is best entrusted to a Porsche agent who will have the necessary tools for the job. At the same time the control arm can be checked for alignment using a special fixture. Also check the radius arm rubber bushes for wear and damage, renewing as necessary.

22 Examine the ball bearing for signs of rough running and overheating

(a bluish colour); if evident it must be removed - see paragraph 20.

23 Installation is basically the reverse of the removal procedure, but the following points should be noted:

a) Heat the pivot bearing housing to approximately 120°C (250°F) when pressing in the thrust bearing. The bearing should be pressed in on the outer race only, and only needs light lubrication with grease as it is sealed.

b) Use a new self-locking nut for the M14 bolt on the control arm, and tighten it to the specified torque. At the same time, lift the

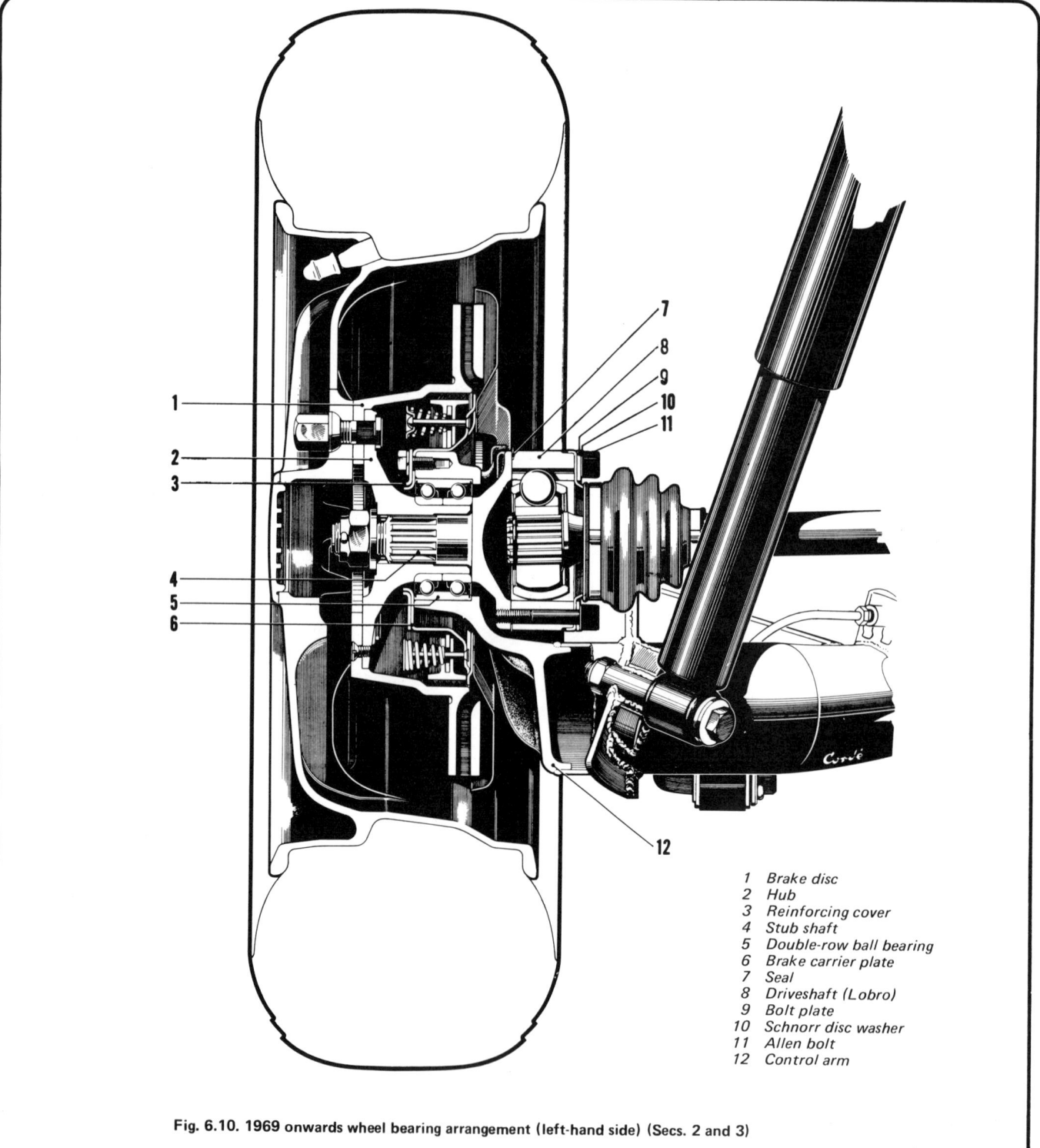

1 Brake disc
2 Hub
3 Reinforcing cover
4 Stub shaft
5 Double-row ball bearing
6 Brake carrier plate
7 Seal
8 Driveshaft (Lobro)
9 Bolt plate
10 Schnorr disc washer
11 Allen bolt
12 Control arm

Fig. 6.10. 1969 onwards wheel bearing arrangement (left-hand side) (Secs. 2 and 3)

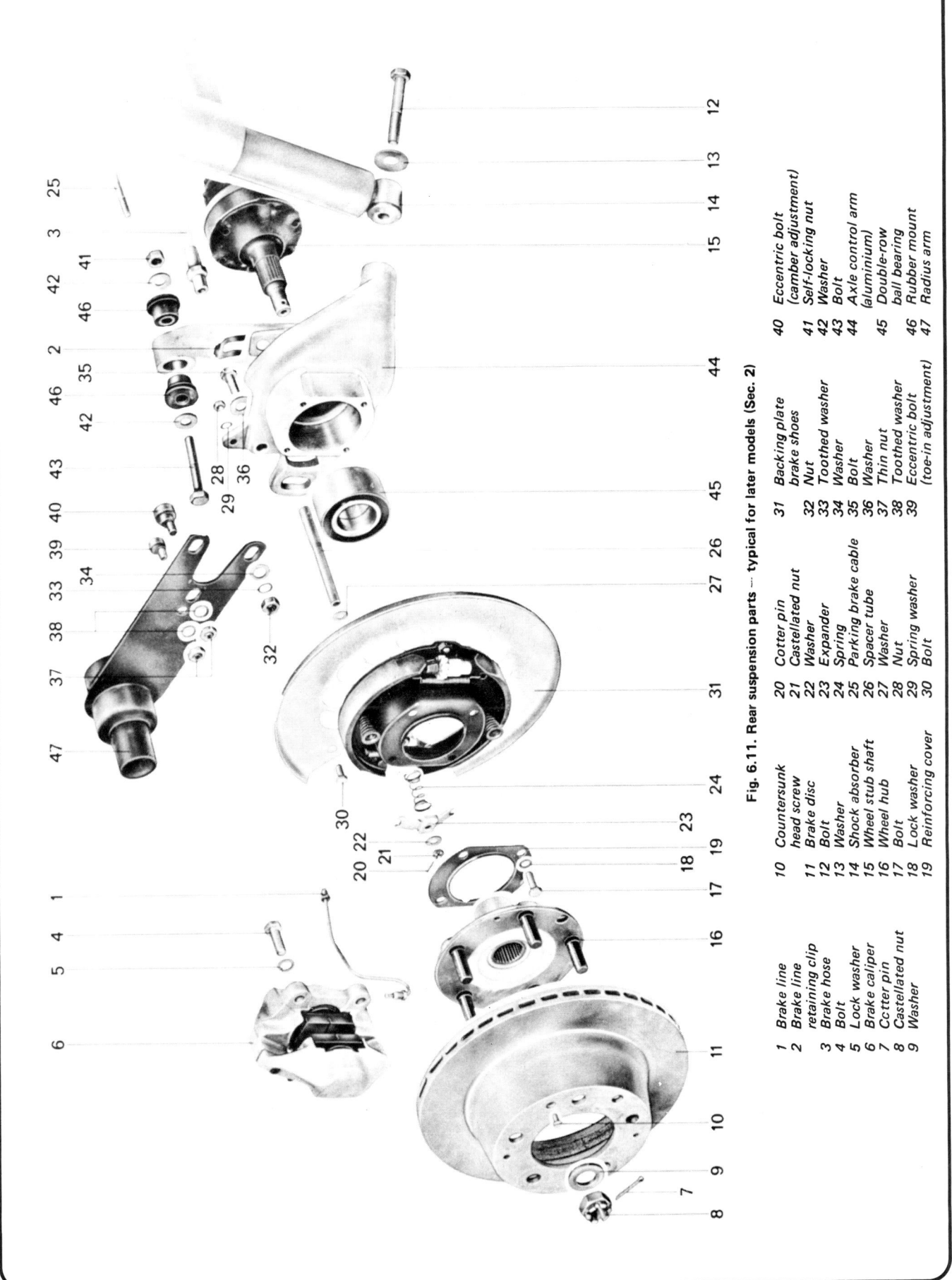

Fig. 6.11. Rear suspension parts — typical for later models (Sec. 2)

1 Brake line
2 Brake line retaining clip
3 Brake hose
4 Bolt
5 Lock washer
6 Brake caliper
7 Cotter pin
8 Castellated nut
9 Washer
10 Countersunk head screw
11 Brake disc
12 Bolt
13 Washer
14 Shock absorber
15 Wheel stub shaft
16 Wheel hub
17 Bolt
18 Lock washer
19 Reinforcing cover
20 Cotter pin
21 Castellated nut
22 Washer
23 Expander
24 Spring
25 Parking brake cable
26 Spacer tube
27 Washer
28 Nut
29 Spring washer
30 Bolt
31 Backing plate brake shoes
32 Nut
33 Toothed washer
34 Washer
35 Bolt
36 Washer
37 Thin nut
38 Toothed washer
39 Eccentric bolt (toe-in adjustment)
40 Eccentric bolt (camber adjustment)
41 Self-locking nut
42 Washer
43 Bolt
44 Axle control arm (aluminium)
45 Double-row ball bearing
46 Rubber mount
47 Radius arm

control arm until the lower surface is level with the upper surface of the rear wheel radius arm. Tighten the radius arm retaining bolts to the specified torque.

c) *Tighten the eccentric bolts in their original positions. This must only be regarded as a provisional setting, and on completion the camber and tracking (toe-in) must be checked.*

d) *Install the brake system parts by reference to Chapter 8, as necessary.*

e) *Lightly tap on the hub just far enough for the washer and castellated nut to be fitted, then tighten the nut to draw on the hub. Take care with this operation as the bearing is not designed to take excessive axial shock loads.*

f) *When installing the driveshaft at the transmission end, ensure that the flange surfaces are clean, and use a new gasket. Ensure that the locking washers for the cheesehead bolts are fitted with the hollow side against the spacing plate.*

g) *Don't forget to tighten the flange nuts and castellated nut to the specified torque. Refer to Section 8, for further information, if required.*

h) *Refer to Chapter 8, for torque wrench settings for the brake system bleeding procedures.*

j) *Refer to Section 7 for suspension geometry checks.*

1972 models onwards

24 The procedure for these models is similar to that for 1969/71 models, except that rubber mounts are used for the control arm pivots. These can be renewed if worn or damaged. The component parts are shown in Fig. 6.11 in their order of removal. Note that it is no longer necessary to remove the transmission before removing the control arms as the pivot bolts are installed with the heads outwards.

3 Rear wheel bearing - removal and installation

To remove the rear wheel bearings, it is necessary to remove the rear suspension control arm, then extract the bearing after the control arm has been removed. This procedure is given in the previous Section.

4 Shock absorbers - removal and installation

Note: When detaching the shock absorber it is important that the weight of the car is on its wheels. Therefore, it is necessary to place the car over an inspection pit or on ramps until the lower mounting is detached. Alternatively, provided that care is taken, the suspension control arm can be raised using a jack to partially compress the shock absorber.

1 Remove the rubber cap from the top of the shock absorber plunger rod. Whilst preventing the shock absorber plunger rod from turning, remove the self-locking nut.

2 Remove the low retaining bolt and detach the shock absorber.

3 If the exterior of the shock absorber is covered with oily deposits, it must be renewed as a matter of course. If apparently satisfactory, mount it vertically in a vice, plunger rod uppermost, and pump it over its full length of travel several times. If there is any free-travel a new shock absorber must be obtained. Check, and if necessary renew, the rubber buffer (see Fig. 6.13); any replacement must be of the same type. Where Koni adjustable shock absorbers are fitted, these may be

adjusted by reference to Chapter 7, Section 3.

4 Installation is the reverse of the removal procedure. If the rubber buffer was removed, ensure that the stop disc is fitted with the grooves towards the plunger to prevent loss of fluid. Do not use any lubricant on the buffer.

5 Torsion bar - removal, installation and adjustment

1 Raise the rear of the car and remove the roadwheels.

2 Support the weight of the rear control arms so that the shock absorber is slightly compressed from its point of maximum travel.

3 Remove the shock absorber lower mounting, and the retaining and eccentric bolts from the radius arm. Refer to Section 2 for further information, if necessary.

4 Remove the radius arm cover retaining bolts and withdraw the single spacer.

5 Using two large screwdrivers or similar tools, prise off the radius arm cover.

6 Allow the radius arm to be lowered, then remove the plug in the side of the body so that the radius arm can be removed. (On versions where the trim strap covers the plug, this will have to be removed first).

7 Withdraw the torsion bar, taking care that its protective paint is not damaged.

8 If the torsion bar has broken, in which case the inner part will remain in the car, remove the second torsion bar. then drive the broken piece out working from the second side, using a suitable steel rod.

9 Check the torsion bar for damaged splines and corrosion, and renew if either is evident. Touch-up any damaged paintwork using a suitable primer. If the rubber torsion bar support is damaged or has deteriorated, this too must be renewed.

10 Installation is the reverse of the removal procedure. Take care that the left (marked L) and right (marked R) torsion bars are not mixed up; they are marked on their end faces. Coat the torsion bar lightly with a general purpose grease and apply it generously to the splines. Adjust the torsion bar (see paragraphs 12 to 18), then coat the rubber support with glycerine or a similar rubber lubricant.

11 Install the radius arm and shock absorber bolt, referring to Section 2, as necessary. Do not forget to check the rear suspension geometry on completion (see Section 7).

Fig. 6.12. Removing a shock absorber top mounting nut (Sec. 4)

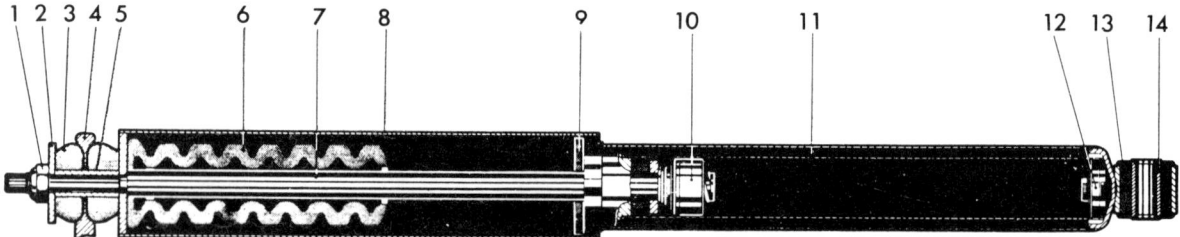

Fig. 6.13. Rear shock absorber — sectional view (Sec. 4)

1	Self-locking nut	5	Grommet bush	9	Stop disc	12	Check valve
2	Washer	6	Rubber buffer	10	Plunger	13	Grommet
3	Grommets	7	Plunger rod	11	Cylinder	14	Grommet bush
4	Seat (in vehicle)	8	Cover tube				

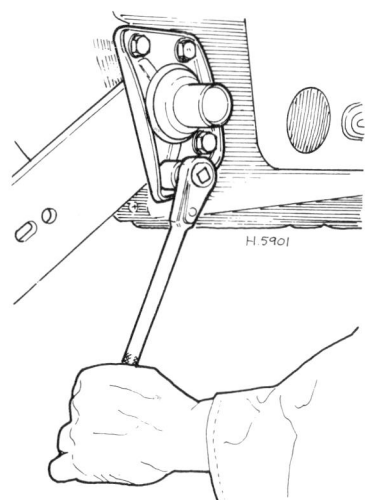

Fig. 6.14. Removing the radius arm cover bolts (Sec. 5)

Torsion bar - adjustment

12 If a torsion bar on one side of the car is adjusted, it is strongly recommended that the one on the opposite side is checked for adjustment also. The adjustment is checked by measuring the relative angle between the radius arm and the horizontal plane of the car, when the radius arm is hanging free.

13 Provided that care is taken, the following method will be found accurate, and does not require the use of expensive tooling.

14 Place the car on a flat level surface. If this cannot be done, place a spirit level on the lower edge of the door aperture and note the amount of deflection, on a protractor, by which the car is out-of-level (Fig. 6.15).

15 With the torsion bar installed in the car (the inner end has 40 splines), and the radius arm pushed onto the outer end (44 splines), measure the angle between the horizontal and the radius arm. Correct the angle, if necessary, for any amount by which the car was out-of-level (paragraph 14), then compare the angle with that given in the Specifications (Fig. 6.16).

16 If adjustment is required, either move the torsion bar on its spline, or the radius arm on its spline. Moving the torsion bar will provide an alteration of 9°; moving the radius arm will provide an alteration of $8^\circ 10'$. Therefore the minimum adjustment is equivalent to $50'$. Refer to the Specifications for the correct adjustment for your particular car.

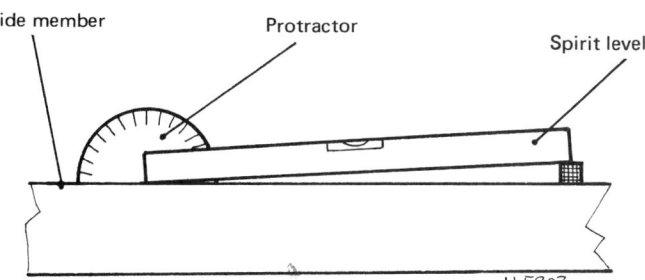

Fig. 6.15. Checking the level of the car (Sec. 5)

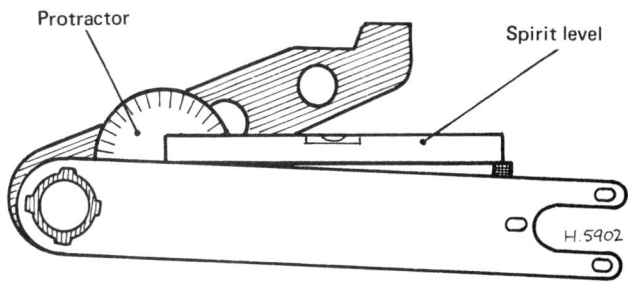

Fig. 6.16. Checking the radius arm angle (Sec. 5)

Fig. 6.17. Installed position of a typical rear stabilizer (Sec. 6)

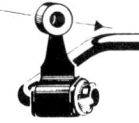

Fig. 6.18. Rear stabilizer showing the shackle grommets (Sec. 6)

17 Repeat the adjustment procedure for the other side of the car.
18 Refer to paragraphs 10 and 11 for the remainder of the assembly procedure.

6   Rear stabilizer - removal and installation

1 Using a large screwdriver, prise the upper end of the stabilizer shackle off the supporting ball on the control arm.
2 Remove the bolts and take off the mounting brackets to release the stabilizer.
3 Check the rubber bushings for wear and damage, replacing as necessary. Ensure that replacements are of the correct size for your particular stabilizer as they have been produced in several different sizes.
4 Installation is the reverse of the removal procedure. The shackle mounting grommets may be lubricated with glycerine or a similar product, but the rubber bushes should be installed dry. Use a little molybdenum disulphide general purpose grease on the upper shackle grommets before pressing them onto their supporting ballstuds.

7   Suspension geometry - checking

1 Whenever any repair work has been carried out where the rear torsion bar or radius arm has been disconnected, it is necessary to check the camber and tracking (toe-in). Unfortunately, this is not a job for the home mechanic, since special optical alignment equipment is required. It should therefore be entrusted to a Porsche dealer or other suitably equipped automobile repair shop. However, before this is done, the torsion bar adjustment can be set (Section 5), and the rear axle height adjustment checked.

Rear axle height adjustment
2 Depress the rear of the car several times by pushing down on the bumper horns and allowing the car to come to rest on the rebound.
3 Measure the vertical height from the wheel centre to the ground; call this dimension 'a'.
4 Measure the vertical height from the lower edge of the torsion bar bushing cover; call this dimension 'b1'.
5 To 'b1', add half the diameter of the bushing cover to find the centre line of the torsion bar; call this dimension 'b'.
6 When 'a' is subtracted from 'b', a dimension as given in the Specifications should be obtained. Having checked the first side, check the second side which again must be within the specified dimension, but must also meet the side-to-side height difference

dimension.
7 If these values cannot be obtained, it is likely that the front suspension geometry is incorrectly set (see Chapter 7) or that the rear torsion bar is incorrectly set (see Section 5).

8   Driveshaft (axle shaft) - removal, servicing and installation

Pre-1969 models
1 Jack-up the rear of the car and remove the roadwheel.
2 Remove the cotter pin from the castellated nut.
3 Using a bar between two of the wheel studs, wedged against the floor to stop the hub from rotating, unscrew the driveshaft castellated nut.
4 At the transmission end, remove the flange Allen bolts, then use a soft-faced hammer to tap off the driveshaft from the flange joint.
5 Check the universal joints for wear, and if evident obtain a replacement shaft. These are available on an exchange basis through Porsche dealers. Lobro driveshafts which have damaged dust boots can be fitted with replacements as described in paragraphs 7 to 13 below.
6 Installation of the driveshaft is the reverse of the removal procedure. Ensure that the correct tightening torques are used, according to which type of shaft is installed. The Lobro shafts must be installed with the hollow side of the Schnorr disc washer towards the base plate, and only the special Porsche bolts may be used (Part no. 900.067.073.01; these bear the markings 130-140 or 12K). Ensure that the gasket faces are clean, and that a new joint washer is used.

Lobro driveshaft dust boot- replacement
7 With the driveshaft removed from the car, remove the lock ring (circlip) and withdraw the universal joint and wire retainer from the shaft splines.
8 Remove the existing boot and clean the joint parts carefully.
9 Install the new dust boot on the shaft, then slide the wire retainer and universal joint on; secure them with the lock ring.
10 Fill the joint with approximately 2½ oz (70 g) of molybdenum disulphide general purpose grease. Any surplus of this quantity should be placed inside the flange area.
11 Clean the contact surface of the large end of the dust boot and its mating flange, and apply a non-setting jointing compound.
12 Install the clip, tighten it and bend over the tab. Tap it down with a hammer.
Note: Installation of the clip is made easier if two small holes are

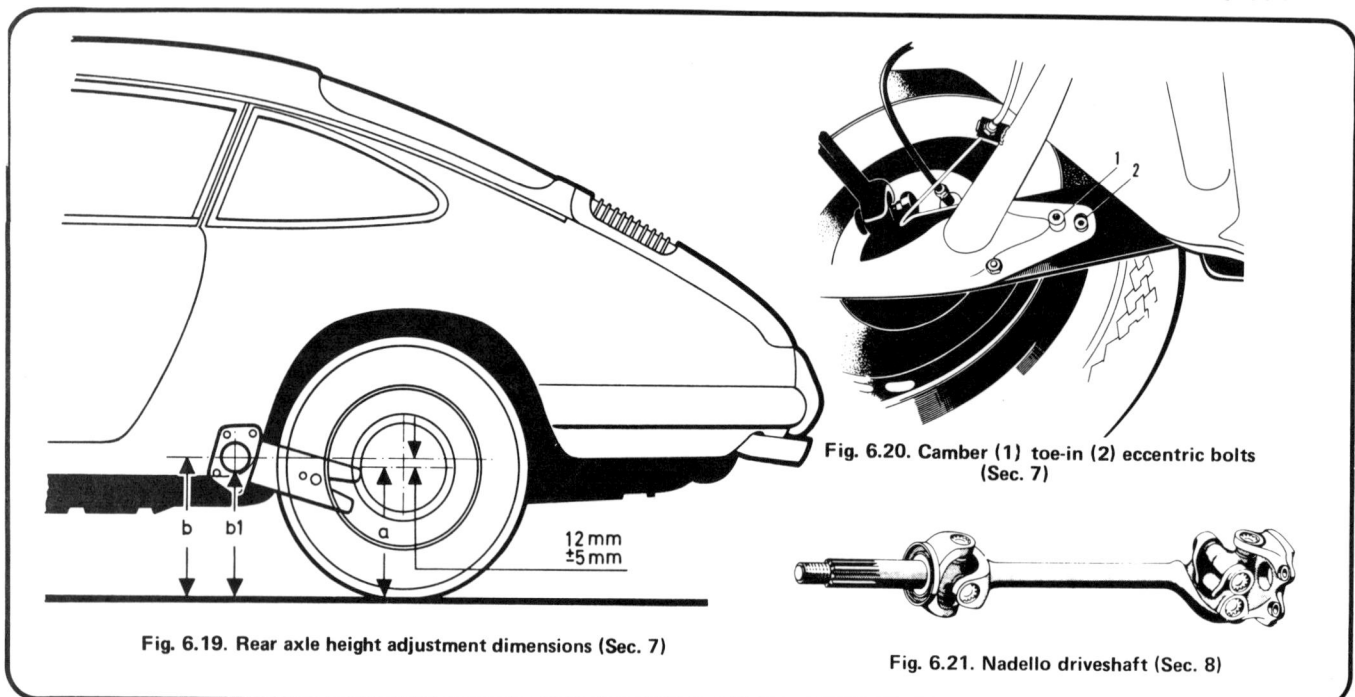

Fig. 6.19. Rear axle height adjustment dimensions (Sec. 7)

Fig. 6.20. Camber (1) toe-in (2) eccentric bolts (Sec. 7)

Fig. 6.21. Nadello driveshaft (Sec. 8)

Fig. 6.22. Lobro driveshaft (typical) (Sec. 8)

A = 1.26 in (32 mm) – pre-October 1971
A = 1.575 in (40 mm) – October 1971 onwards

Fig. 6.23. Removing a universal joint lock ring (circlip) (Sec 8)

Fig. 6.24. Drill 2 holes in the clip for early types (Sec. 8)

Fig. 6.25. Later type securing clip (ears arrowed) (Sec. 8)

8.14 Removing a driveshaft flange bolt on a 1969 model

drilled (5/64 in/2 mm/no. 47 drill) so that round nose or circlip pliers can be used to draw the ends together.

13 On completion, install the driveshaft as described earlier in this Section.

1969/71 models

14 This procedure is similar to that described for the pre-1969 models, except that the shock absorber lower mounting bolt must be removed. For further information refer to the note at the beginning of Section 4. When reassembling, note that there is an increase in the specified torque for the joint flange bolts, which have been increased in size to M10 (photo).

Lobro driveshaft dust boot - replacement

15 The procedure is similar to that described for pre-1969 dust boots, but the following points should be noted:

a) If only the outer dust boot requires renewal, it is only necessary to detach the driveshaft at the transmission flange end.

b) A modified type of clip is used. This can be cut off with pliers, and the ears pressed together with blunt nosed pliers when installing.

c) Ensure that the sheet metal protective cap has not become detached from the driveshaft joint section. This may be refitted using Loctite or a similar locking varnish.

October 1971 models onwards

16 A lighter driveshaft is used for these models. The constant velocity joints are 1.26 in (32 mm) long, compared with 1.575 in (40 mm) for the earlier type. These shafts can be used for all models from 1969 onwards on an individual basis, provided that the longer M10 Allen bolts are used, together with the new supporting plates. Workshop procedures are similar to those for the 1969 models.

9   Fault diagnosis - rear suspension and driveshafts

Symptom	Reason/s	Remedy
'Clunks' from driveshafts	CV joint worn or disintegrated	Dismantle and repair.
	Worn splines at wheel or differential end	Remove driveshaft and examine.
Wheel wobble and vibration	Worn wheel bearings or loose wheels	See Chapter 8.
Noise from control arm pivot	Pivot loose or worn	Examine and repair as necessary.
Poor handling and/or roadholding	Dampers defective	Fit replacements.
	Control arm pivot loose or worn	Examine and repair as necessary.
	Incorrect axle alignment	Arrange for your Porsche dealer to check.
	Incorrect tyre pressures	Inflate as necessary, see Chapter 8.

Chapter 7 Front suspension and steering

Contents

Specifications

Front suspension

Type	MacPherson strut and torsion bar with single wishbone and transverse stabilizer. Self-levelling suspension struts used on certain variants from 1969 onwards, with optional transverse stabilizer
Shock absorber type	Koni self-adjusting, Boge or Bilstein
Self-levelling suspension strut type:	
Pre-1972	Porsche or Boge
1972 onwards	Koni or Boge

Steering

Type	ZF rack and pinion
Steering ratio:	
Prior to 1969 model	16.5:1
1969 models onwards	17.78:1
Steering wheel turns, lock-to-lock:	
Prior to 1969 model	2.8 approx.
1969 models onwards	3.1 approx.

Steering/suspension geometry (degrees)

	Camber	Toe-in	Caster
1965 and 66 models	+ 4'	15/20'	7° 45'
1967 models	0° ± 20'	0°	6° 45' ± 45'
1968 models	0° ± 20'	+ 40/− 20'	6° 45' ± 45'
1969/71 models (2.2 litre)	0° ± 20'	0°	6° 05' ± 15'
1972 models onwards (except as given below)	0° ± 10'	0°	6° 05' ± 15'
1975 onwards 911S USA and Carrera USA	+ 30' ± 10'	0°	6° 05' ± 15'
Maximum camber difference, side-to-side	10'		
Front axle trim height setting (except as given below)	4.25 ± 0.2 (108 ± 5 mm)		
1975 Carrera	4.45 ± 0.2 in (113 ± 5 mm)		
1975 911S USA and Carrera USA	3.66 ± 0.2 in (93 ± 5 mm)		
Self-levelling suspension units	4.88 ± 0.4 in (124 ± 10 mm)		
Maximum height difference, side-to-side	0.20 in (5 mm)		

Note: *All suspension geometry measurements must be made with correctly inflated tyres, a full fuel tank and the spare wheel in position.*

Torque wrench settings

	lb f ft	kg fm
Shock absorber strut upper mounting	58	8
Clamping sleeve on tie-rod	11	1.5
Strut upper mounting plate	34	4.7
Auxiliary support to body	65	9
Undershield bolt (M10)	34	4.7
Undershield bolt (M8)	18	2.5
Flanbloc attachment bolt	34	4.7
Auxiliary support attachment bolt	34	4.7
Steering unit attachment bolt	34	4.7

Torque wrench settings

								lb f ft	kg fm
Steering unit tie rod bolt	...	...	...	...	...	...	...	34	4.7
Stabilizer mount to body	...	...	...	...	...	...	...	18	2.5
Stabilizer lever to stabilizer	...	...	...	...	...	...	...	18	2.5
Wheelbearing clamping nut to axle (Allen bolt)	...	...	...	...	...	...	...	10	1.5
Balljoint to shock absorber strut (nut)	...	...	...	...	...	...	...	16	2.2
Balljoint to shock absorber strut (bolt)	...	...	...	...	...	...	...	33	4.5
Balljoint to wishbone	...	...	...	...	...	...	...	109	15
Plug for Boge shock absorber strut	...	...	...	...	...	...	...	87 + 14	12 + 2
Plug for Koni shock absorber strut	...	...	...	...	...	...	...	145	20
Steering coupling to steering shaft	...	...	...	...	...	...	...	18	2.5
Steering shaft to steering unit	...	...	...	...	...	...	...	18	2.5
Steering support attachment	...	...	...	...	...	...	...	18	2.5
U-joint to steering shaft	...	...	...	...	...	...	...	18	2.5
Steering wheel attachment	...	...	...	...	...	...	...	54	7.5
Dust boot support to steering rack	...	...	...	...	...	...	...	51	7
Balljoint to steering knuckle	...	...	...	...	...	...	...	33	4.5
Coupling flange to steering pinion (self-locking nut)	...	...	...	...	...	...	...	34	4.7
Housing cover to steering housing	...	...	...	...	...	...	...	11	1.5

1 General description

The front suspension is of the MacPherson strut type with a single lower wishbone on each side.

All models prior to 1969 use torsion bars and shock absorber struts to provide the springing medium with a transverse stabilizer bar connecting the wishbones. The torsion bars are adjustable so that the car trim height can be altered.

For 1969, the 911E models, and certain other models to special order, were equipped with Porsche or Boge self-levelling suspension bar and torsion bars.

For 1972 onwards, Koni or Boge self-levelling suspension struts were available for all models as an option, but the stabilizer bar was reintroduced as standard equipment for most models and optional on the 911T and 911E.

Rack and pinion steering has been used throughout the production run, but the original 'pot'-type rack was superseded in mid-1970 by a type already in use in the Porsche 914 models. A safety (collapsible) steering column is used for 1974 models onwards.

This manual cannot go into great detail regarding the suspension options due to lack of space, but it should be noted that items such as the stabilizer bar can be added where necessary, or an existing type can be replaced by one of a larger or smaller cross-sectional area. Your Porsche dealer will be able to advise you on the most suitable item(s) for your car. The same goes for suspension units, but here it is of the utmost importance to ensure that where replacement parts are installed, they do not differ from side-to-side on the car. Provided that the steering shaft, shaft tube and switch assembly are changed, the safety (collapsible) steering column can be installed in 1968 and later models.

The steering and front suspension do not require routine maintenance and lubrication.

2 Front wheel bearings - removal, installation and adjustment

1 Remove the brake disc/hub, as described in Chapter 8.

2 If necessary, index mark the brake disc and wheel hub, then remove the disc retaining bolts and remove the hub.

3 Heat the hub evenly in an oven to 120/150°C (250/300°F) then press out the inner bearing and seal using a suitable press and steel tubing or anchor.

4 Repeat this procedure for the outer bearing race, but make up a spacer as shown (Fig. 7.2) to prevent press loads from being taken by the wheel studs.

5 Clean all the parts in paraffin or petrol, and dry with a lint-free cloth. Examine carefully for wear, damage, scoring and overheating (a bluish colour). Replace a complete bearing if any part is suspect; take care not to mix up parts from two different hubs.

6 Reassembly is basically the reverse of the removal procedure. Again heat the hub to 120/150°C (250/300°F) and press in the outer race of the inner roller bearing.

7 Smear general purpose grease on the inner race, insert it into the outer race, then carefully press in a new oil seal.

8 Press in the outer race of the outer bearing, then align the hub and brake disc marking, and install the bolts from the inside. Use new spring

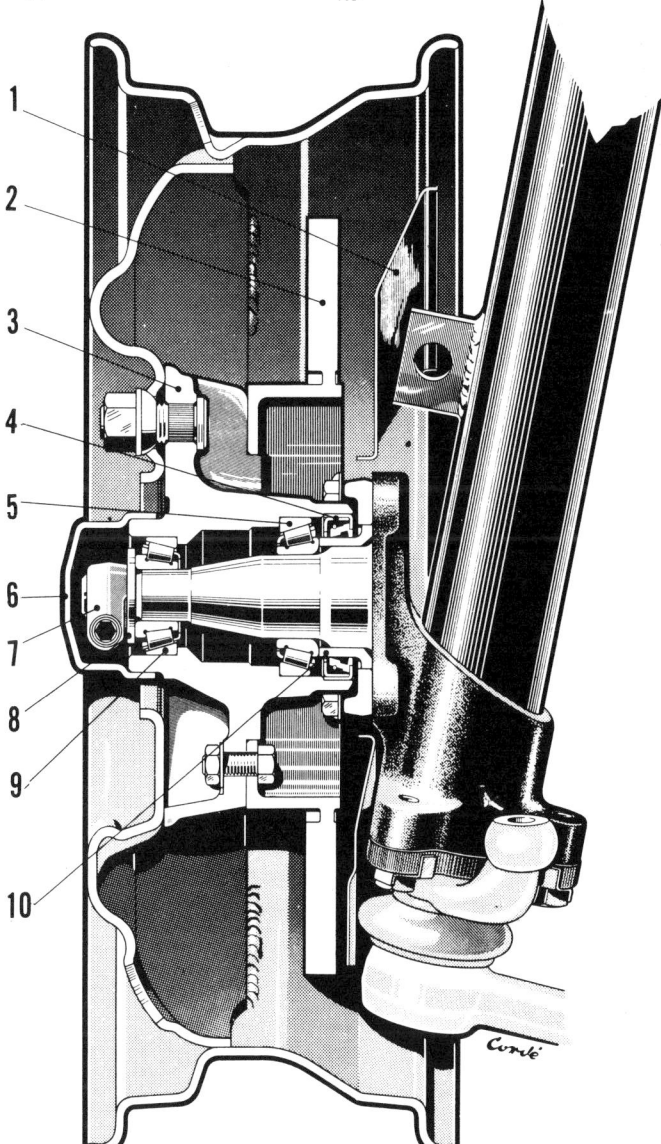

Fig. 7.1. Wheel bearing (typical) - sectional view (Sec. 2)

1 Cover shroud	6 Grease cap
2 Brake disc	7 Clamping nut
3 Hub	8 Washer
4 Seal	9 Tapered roller bearing
5 Tapered roller bearing	10 Distance ring

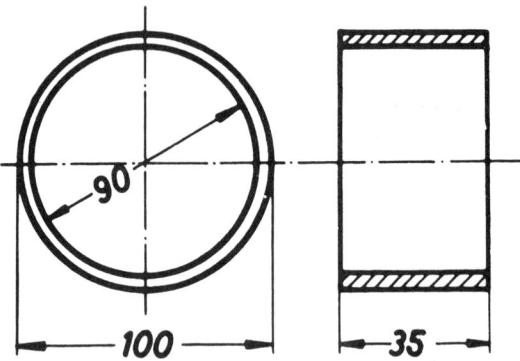

Fig. 7.2. Spacer dimensions (mm) for removing outer bearing race (Sec. 2)

3.543 in = 90 mm   3.937 in = 100 mm   1.380 in = 35 mm

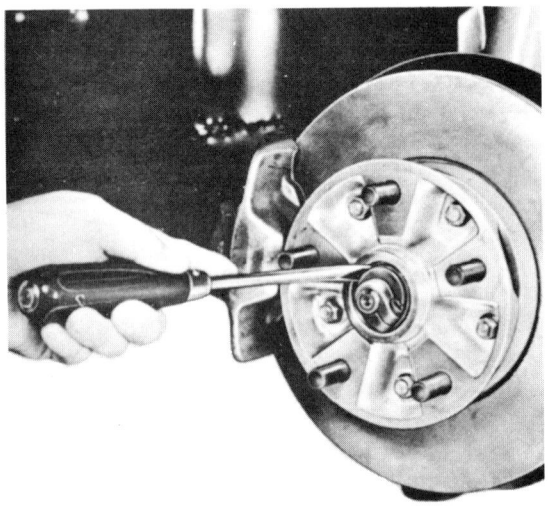

Fig. 7.3. Check that the thrust washer can just be removed (Sec. 2)

Fig. 7.4. Tightening the clamping nut Allen screw (Sec. 2)

washers under the nuts and tighten to the specified torque.

9   Pack the hub with approximately 50 cc (1.6 oz/45 g) of general purpose grease for pre-1969 models or 65 cc (2.1 oz/60 g) for 1969 models onwards. Ensure that the grease is thoroughly worked into the bearings, and fill the space between the sealing lip of the sealing ring also, so that the outer sealing ring does not run without lubrication.

10 Install the brake disc and hub, placing the thrust washer beneath the clamping nut.

11 Whilst rotating the hub, tighten the clamping nut to approximately 10 lbf ft (1.5 kgf m) to seat the bearings.

12 Loosen the clamping nut until the thrust washer can *just* be moved sideways under light pressure. At this time there should be no detectable axial play in the bearing. (Fig. 7.3).

13 Without altering the position of the clamping nut, tighten the Allen screw to the specified torque. Recheck that the thrust washer is still just free to move sideways under light pressure.

14 Lightly grease the clamping nut and thrust washer, then tap on the grease cap (without filling it with grease) with a soft-faced hammer.

15 Install the brake caliper (refer to Chapter 8, if necessary). Do not forget to bleed the brakes on completion.

3   Shock absorber strut (pre-1969 models) - removal, servicing and installation

Note: Before removing a shock absorber strut it is important to realise that the suspension geometry may need resetting on completion. It is recommended that Section 11 is read before any work is started.

1   Remove the brake disc/hub, as described in Chapter 8.

2   Fold back the tabs on the brake carrier lockplates, remove the bolts and take off the carrier.

3   Remove the steering balljoint cotter pin and castellated nut.

4   Using a proprietary balljoint separator or by driving in split wedges, separate the balljoint from the steering knuckle. **Note:** Provided that care is taken, it is possible to drive in the taper of a cold chisel between the eye of the steering knuckle and the balljoint end of the steering tie-rod (trackrod).

5   Remove the cotter pins and castellated nuts from the suspension strut attachment of the wishbone (transverse control arm).

6   Fold back the lock tab at the top of the suspension strut, then use a C-spanner to prevent the notched washer from turning and remove the nut. The strut is now free to be removed.

7   To dismantle the shock absorber strut, mount it in a vice using

Fig. 7.5. Detaching the strut from the wishbone (Sec. 3)

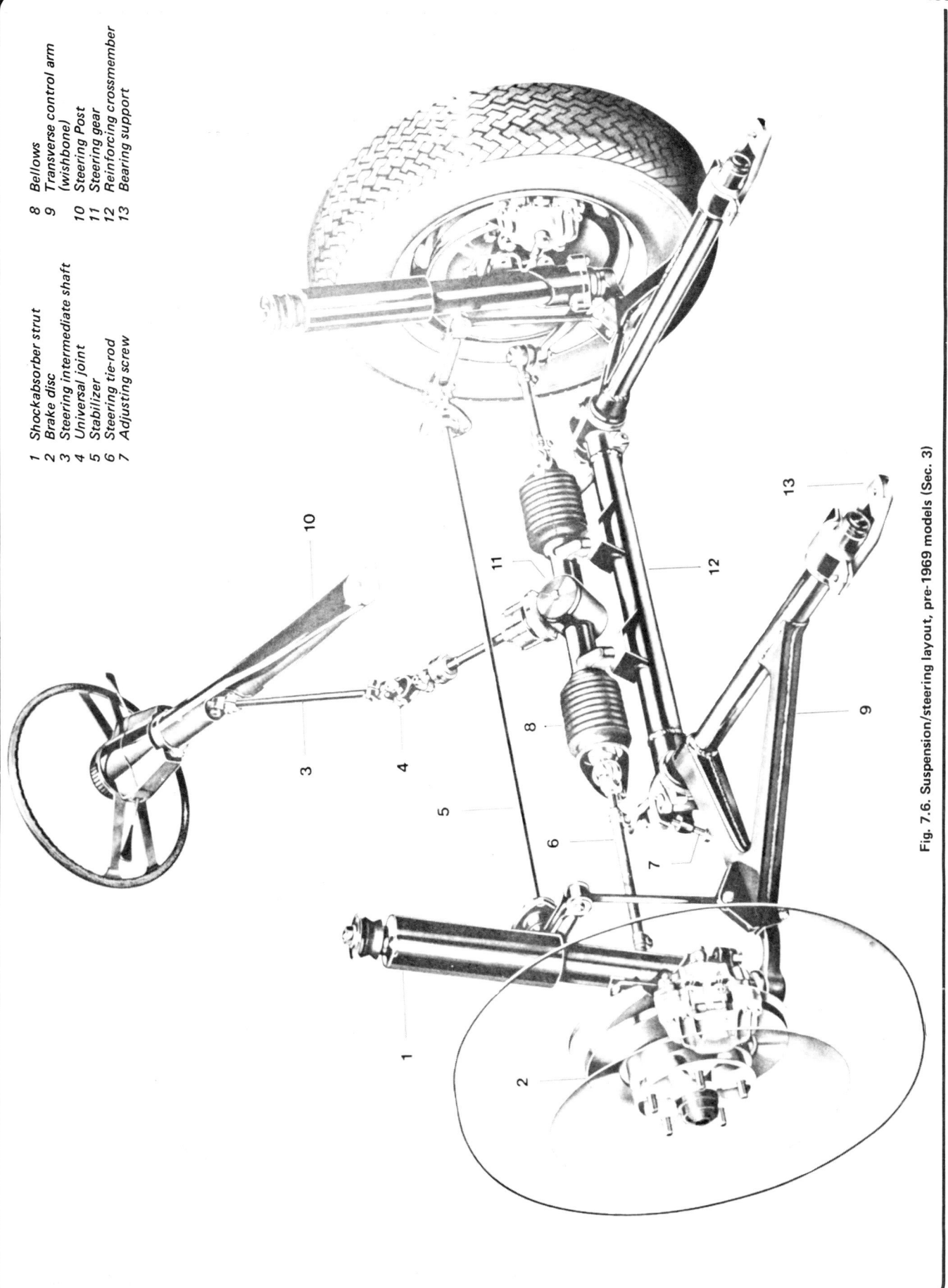

1 Shockabsorber strut
2 Brake disc
3 Steering intermediate shaft
4 Universal joint
5 Stabilizer
6 Steering tie-rod
7 Adjusting screw
8 Bellows
9 Transverse control arm (wishbone)
10 Steering Post
11 Steering gear
12 Reinforcing crossmember
13 Bearing support

Fig. 7.6. Suspension/steering layout, pre-1969 models (Sec. 3)

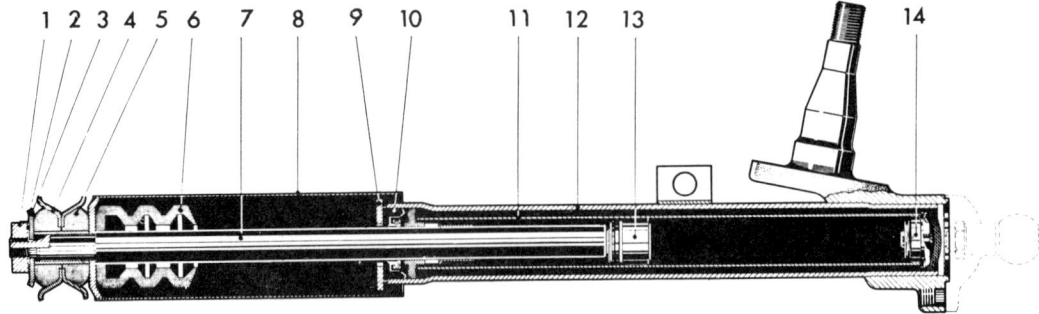

Fig. 7.7. Front shock absorber strut (pre-1969) (Sec. 3)

1 Nut	4 Bracket (on car)	8 Shielding tube	12 Strut tube
2 Safety plate	5 Rubber bushing	9 Stop disc	13 Piston
3 Notched washer	6 Rubber buffer	10 Oil seal	14 Valve
	7 Piston rod	11 Cylinder	

Fig. 7.8. Detaching the strut top mounting (Secs. 3 and 5)

Fig. 7.9. Removing the balljoint castellated nut (Secs. 3 and 5)

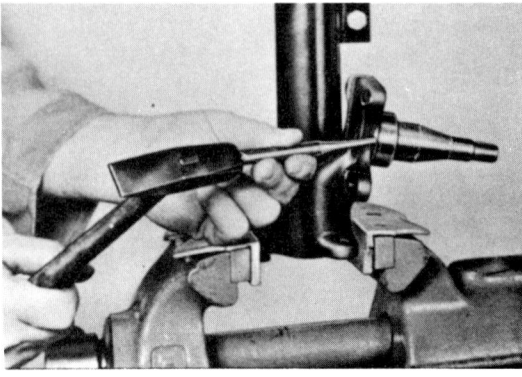

Fig. 7.10. Removing the distance ring (Secs. 3 and 5)

jaw clamps, then fold back the lockplate tabs and remove the steering knuckle taking care that the bushing is not lost.

8 Remove the shielding tube and withdraw the rubber buffer.

9 Secure the steering knuckle in a vice, then unlock and remove the castellated nut. Remove the balljoint using a press or puller, or by carefully driving it out without causing damage to the screw threads if it is to be re-used.

10 Carefully drive or pull off the distance ring from the knuckle wheel spindle.

11 The struts can be checked for damage by a Porsche dealer using a special alignment jig but unless the car has been involved in an accident this is unlikely to be necessary. If there are signs of oil leakage the strut should be considered as unserviceable; also, if when the strut is mounted vertically and then pumped three or four times, it should be found that there is free-travel, the strut is unserviceable. A strut replacement kit is available for models from Chassis no. 301800 onwards, details of this being given in Section 5. Note that Koni shock absorber struts are adjustable; details of the adjustment procedure are given in paragraphs 17 to 24, towards the end of this Section. Check the balljoint and, if there is axial play, obtain and install a replacement. Replace the rubber dust boot if damaged.

12 Reassembly and installation is basically the reverse of the removal procedure. Ensure that an O-ring (R32-2.5) is installed between the distance piece and knuckle spindle to prevent rust formation, and heat the distance ring to approximately 150°C (300°F) before driving it on.

13 If new balljoints are installed the boot should be filled with 0.2 oz (6.5 g) of molybdenum disulphide general purpose grease, but do not apply grease to the ball stud taper.

14 If the cotter pin drilling stands proud of the nut castellation, it is permissible to use a spacer washer.

15 When installing the shock absorber buffer, do not use any lubricant.

16 The remainder of the installation procedure is straightforward but use a new lock tab for the top mounting. Do not forget to bleed the braking system (Chapter 8), check the wheel bearing play (Section 2) and the suspension geometry (Section 11) on completion.

Koni shock absorber struts - adjustment

17 If the shock absorbers are to be adjusted while still on the car, raise the front end and remove the roadwheels. Support the wishbones on jacks or blocks, then detach the top mounting, as described in paragraph 6.

18 If the strut has been removed from the car, mount it vertically in a vice at the knuckled end using jaw clamps.

19 To adjust, press down the plunger rod and shielding tube then, without using undue force, turn the plunger rod clockwise so that it engages in the mating recess in the bottom valve.

20 Mark the engagement point on the shock absorber body and shielding tube.

21 To determine whether an adjustment has previously been made, rotate the shielding tube further clockwise (harder adjustment) and note how much it can be turned.

22 Starting from the original position, turn the tube ½ turn anticlockwise until the required damping action has been obtained (maximum adjustment is 2¼ turns). Pull up the plunger rod to disengage the adjusting mechanism.

23 Adjust the second shock absorber to obtain an equal amount of damping action.

24 Install the shock absorber by following the reverse of the removal procedure, using a new lock tab for the top mounting.

---

4 Self-levelling suspension struts

1 Self-levelling hydro-pneumatic suspension struts have been available as a standard fitment or to special order (according to the model) since late 1968. The original types were of Boge or Porsche manufacture but later models had Koni or Boge types.

2 A typical Boge self-levelling suspension strut is shown in Fig. 7.13 in its various operating modes. Figs. 7.14 and 7.15 show Porsche and Koni self-levelling struts.

Checking

3 Ideally, special gauging plugs should be obtained (Porsche tool P301b) for inserting in the transverse support arms (see paragraph 5, and Fig. 7.16), but locally made-up plugs can be used.

4 Load the front luggage compartment with a weight of 220 lb (100 kg) evenly distributed over the front axle.

5 Insert the gauging plugs from within the reinforcing support member compartment to the stop in the left and right-hand transverse support arms. Use a little grease to hold them in place.

6 Measure the vertical distance from the ground to the centre of the front wheel (a) (Fig. 7.17), then measure from the gauging plug tip to the ground (b). Measurement 'b' should 5 in (124 mm) less than measurement 'a'.

7 Now raise the car at the front, in the centre, until the correct distance 'b' is obtained, and note the distance from the bottom of the wing across the centre of the front wheel on each side.

8 Before lowering the jack, measure from the wheel flange to the ground, then lower the jack and repeat this measurement. This gives the static deflection of the tyres, and this must be deducted from measurements obtained between the ground and the bottom of the wing.

9 Drive the car for approximately 1¼ miles (2 km) over relatively straight but rough ground without severe braking, then stop on a level surface.

10 Without the car occupant(s) getting out, have a second person recheck the measurements from the front wings to the ground. These values should be within ± 13/32 in (10 mm) of the ones previously obtained.

11 If these values are not obtained it is possible that a new strut will be required, and the advice of a Porsche dealer should be sought.

---

5 Self-levelling suspension strut or shock absorber strut (1969 models onwards) - removal, servicing and installation

Note: The procedure given is for struts installed from 1969 to 1971 which had a clamp-type attachment at the wishbone. For 1972, a double-wedge cotter bolt arrangement was used; further information on this will be found in paragraph 23. If a shock absorber strut is to be serviced using a replacement kit, there is no need to detach the brake disc/hub and caliper. This procedure is given in paragraphs 9 to 17.

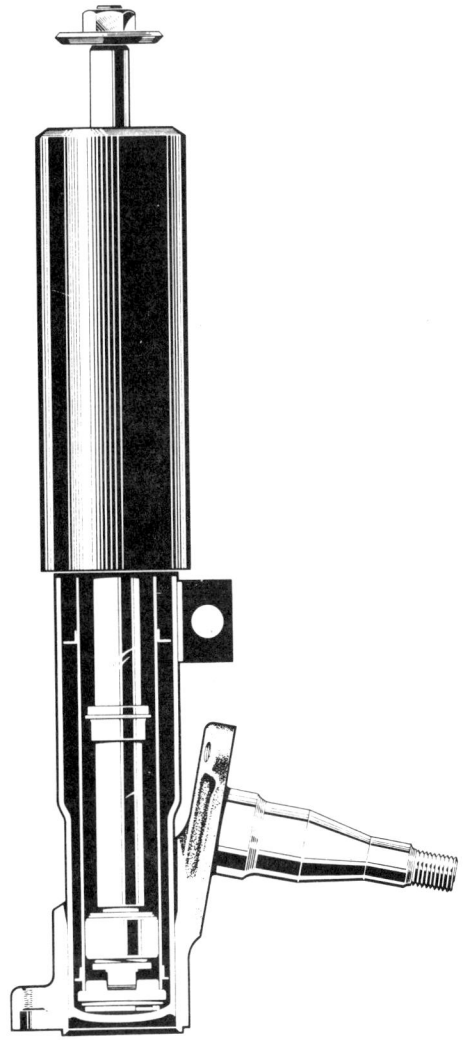

Fig. 7.11. Plunger rod engaged in mating recess (Koni) (Sec. 3)

Removal

1 Remove the brake disc/hub, as described in Chapter 8.

2 Remove the retaining bolts and take off the shield plate.

3 Remove the steering balljoint cotter pin and castellated nut.

4 Using a proprietary balljoint separator or by driving in split wedges, separate the balljoint from the steering knuckle. **Note:** Provided that care is taken, it is possible to drive in the taper of a cold chisel between the eye of the steering knuckle and the balljoint end of the steering tie-rod (trackrod).

5 Remove the clamp bolt at the balljoint end of the suspension strut or shock absorber strut, then press down on the wishbone to remove it. **Note:** Where shock absorber struts are fitted, the torsion bar adjusting screw must first be loosened and the adjusting arm removed.

6 Fold back the lock tab at the top of the suspension strut, then use a C-spanner to prevent the notched washer from turning and remove the nut. The strut is now free to be removed.

7 If considered necessary, drive or pull off the distance ring from the knuckle wheel spindle.

8 The shock absorber strut can now be checked, as described in paragraph 11 of Section 3. Where applicable, a new suspension or shock absorber strut should be obtained, and installed, as described in paragraphs 18 to 22. If an existing shock absorber strut is to be serviced, proceed as described in paragraph 9 to 17 below.

Servicing using a shock absorber strut replacement kit.

9 If the shock absorber strut has not been removed from the car, raise the car and remove the front roadwheels.

10 Either place a polythene film over the brake fluid reservoir filler orifice and install the cap, or wedge the brake pedal in a partially depressed position, to prevent fluid from draining out.

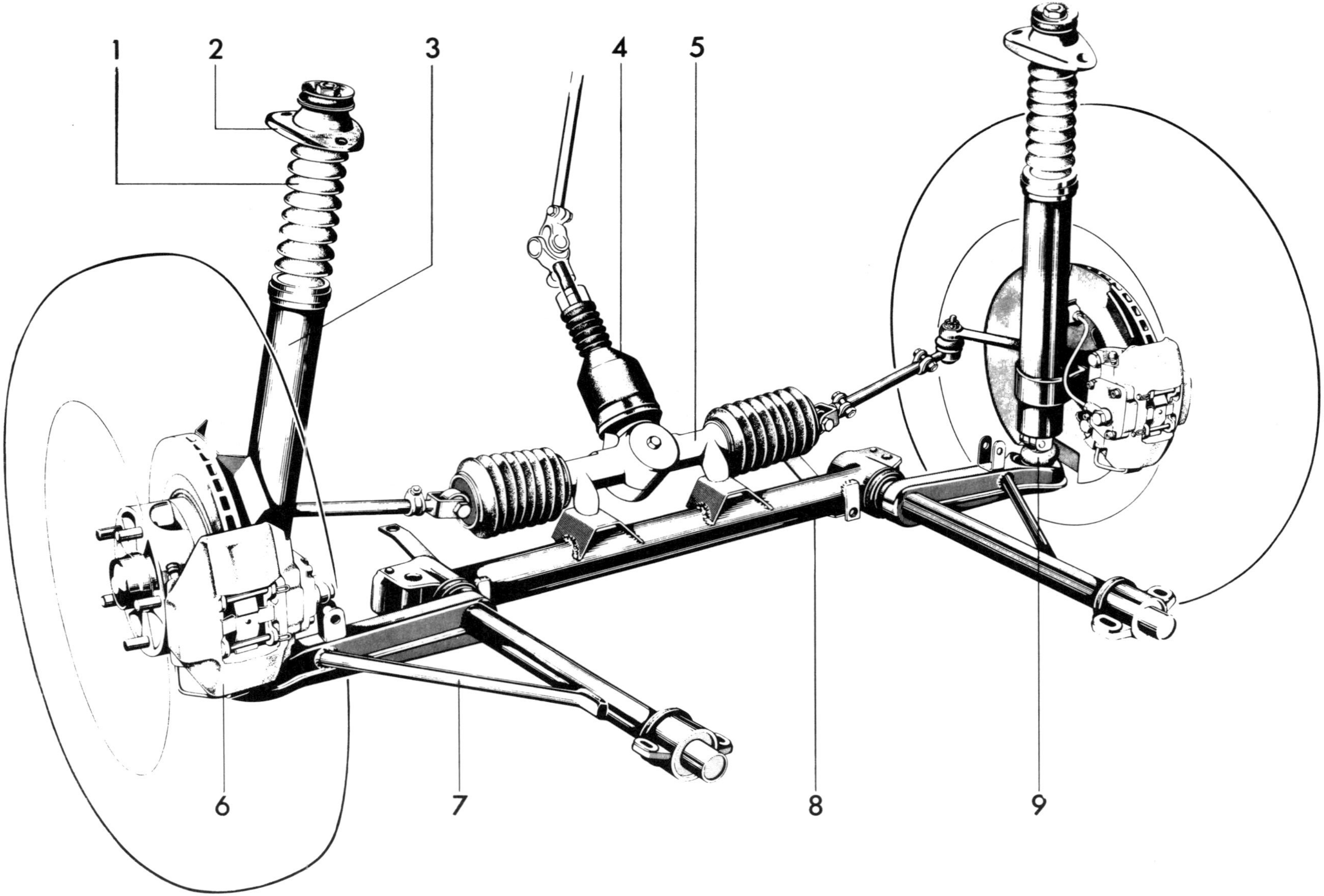

Fig. 7.12. Suspension/steering layout showing early type self/levelling suspension struts original 'pot-type' steering gear (Sec. 4)

1 Vukollan-spring
2 Step bearing and rubber bearing
3 Self-levelling hydro-pneumatic suspension strut
4 Rubber sleeve
5 Steering gear
6 Brake caliper
7 Wishbone
8 Auxiliary support (reinforcing crossmember)
9 Ball joint

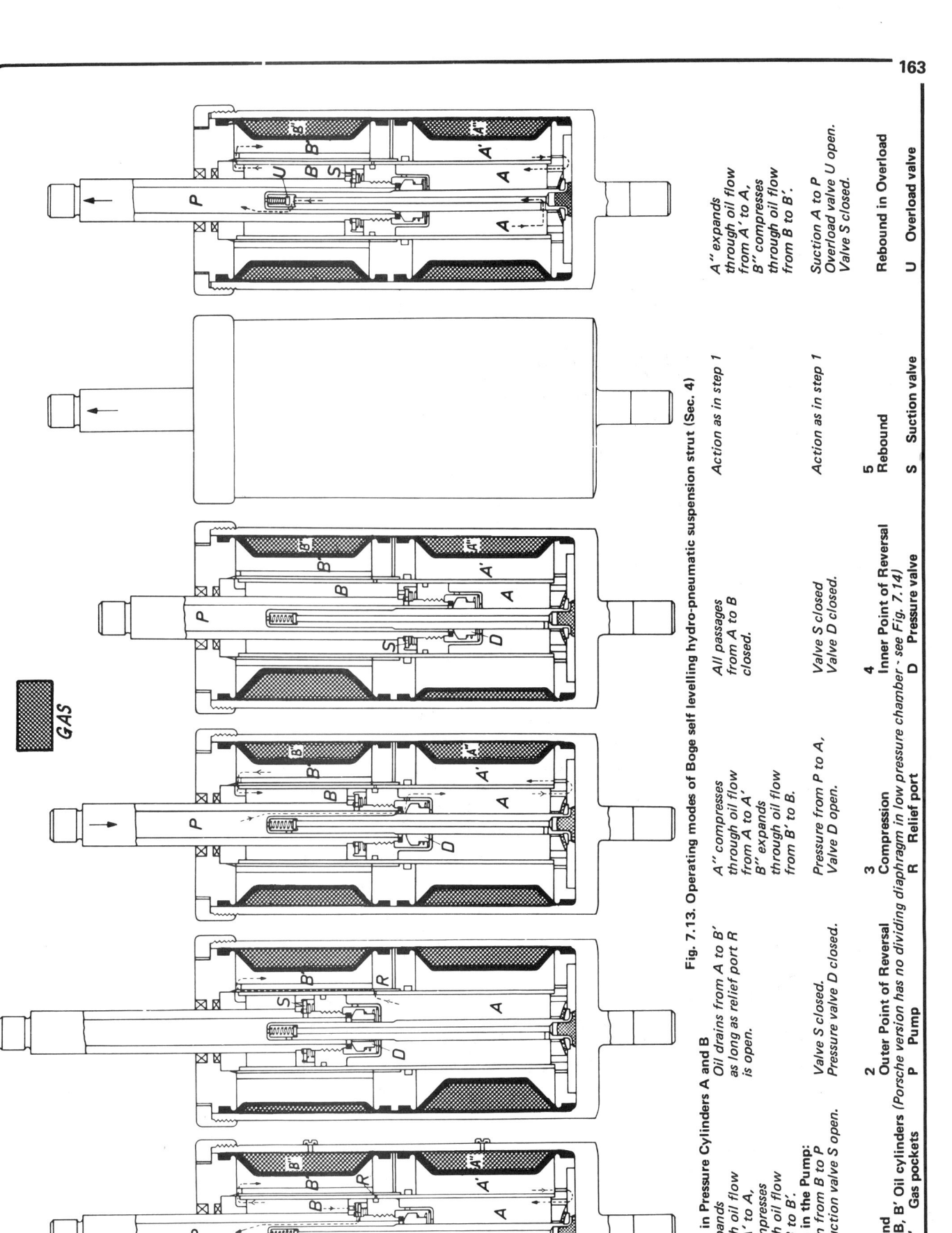

GAS

Fig. 7.13. Operating modes of Boge self levelling hydro-pneumatic suspension strut (Sec. 4)

Action in Pressure Cylinders A and B

A'' expands
through oil flow
from A' to A,
B'' compresses
through oil flow
from B to B'.

Action in the Pump:
Suction from B to P
with suction valve S open.

Oil drains from A to B
as long as relief port R
is open.

A'' compresses
through oil flow
from A to A'
B'' expands
through oil flow
from B' to B.

All passages
from A to B
closed.

Action as in step 1

A'' expands
through oil flow
from A' to A,
B'' compresses
through oil flow
from B to B'.

Suction A to P
Overload valve U open.
Valve S closed.

Valve S closed.
Pressure valve D closed.

Pressure from P to A,
Valve D open.

Valve S closed
Valve D closed.

Action as in step 1

1	2	3	4	5	
Rebound	Outer Point of Reversal	Compression	Inner Point of Reversal	Rebound	Rebound in Overload

A, A', B, B' Oil cylinders (Porsche version has no dividing diaphragm in low pressure chamber - see Fig. 7.14)

A'', B'' Gas pockets

P Pump

R Relief port

D Pressure valve

S Suction valve

U Overload valve

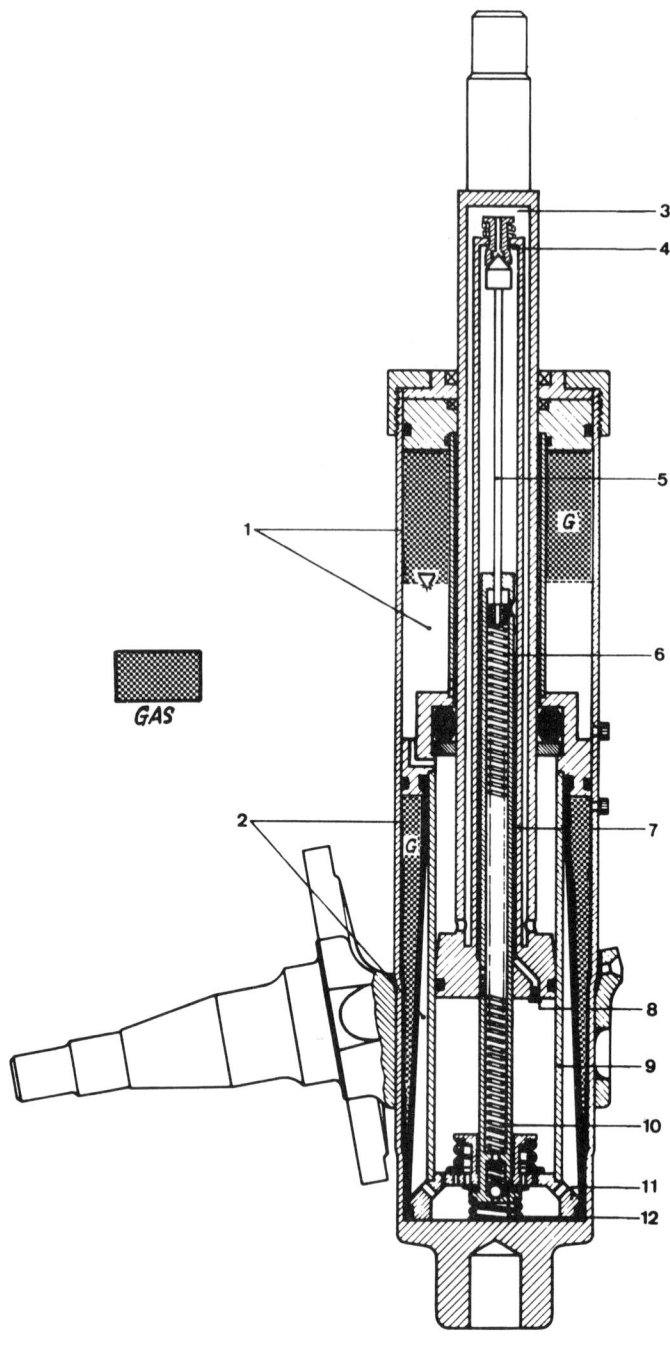

Fig. 7.14. Sectional view of Porsche
self-levelling suspension strut (Sec. 4)

Fig. 7.15. Sectional view of Koni self-levelling suspension strut (Sec. 4)

1	Low pressure chamber	7	Pump cylinder
2	High pressure chamber	8	Pressure valve
3	Return orifice	9	Main cylinder
4	Suction valve	10	Pump rod
5	Needle valve	11	Damper housing
6	Spring	12	Overload valve

G - Gas cushions

Fig. 7.16. Gauging plug in position (arrowed) (Sec. 4)

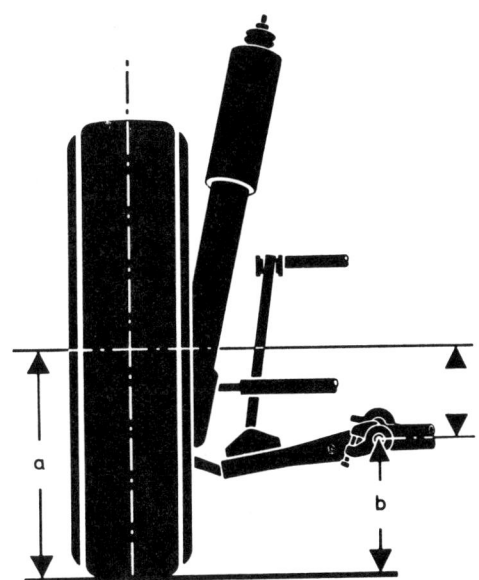

Fig. 7.17. Checking the self-levelling suspension struts (Sec. 4)

Fig. 7.18. Removing the shield plate (Sec. 5)

11 Detach the hydraulic line at the banjo connection on the caliper.

12 Proceed as described in paragraphs 3, 4, 5 and 6, of this Section.

13 Mount the strut in a vice using jaw clamps. Remove the cover tube and take out the rubber buffer.

14 Using a locally manufactured tool as shown in Figs. 7.19 and 7.20, remove the retaining nut and take out the old insert components.

15 Drain the hydraulic fluid from the strut casing, and wipe it clean using a lint-free cloth.

16 Install the new insert and tighten the retaining nut to the specified torque according to the strut type.

17 Installation of the strut complete with disc/hub and caliper is now straightforward, the braking system being bled on completion, as described in Chapter 8. If the strut was removed as described in paragraphs 1 to 7, it should now be installed as described below.

Fig. 7.21. Removing the strut insert (Sec. 5)

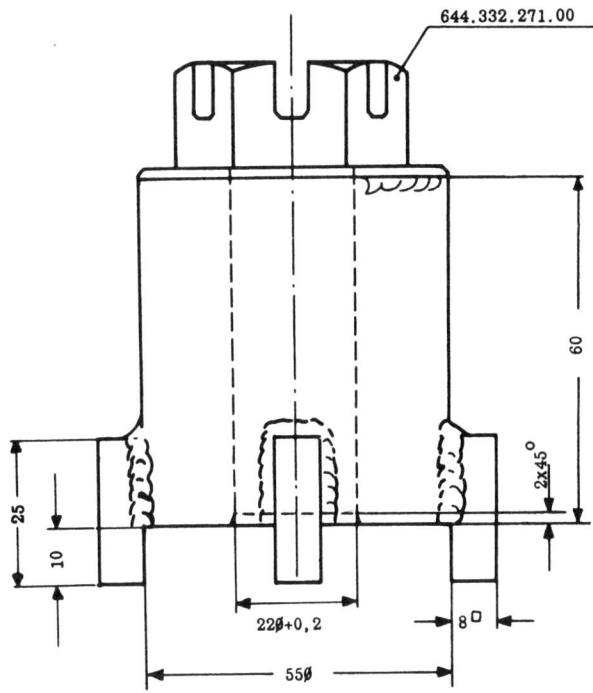

Fig. 7.19. Insert retaining nut tool dimensions (BOGE) (Sec. 5)

Dimensions in mm
0.984 in = 25 mm
0.394 in = 10 mm
2.165 in = 55 mm
0.008 in = 0.2 mm

0.315 in = 8 mm
2.362 in = 60 mm
0.866 in = 22 mm

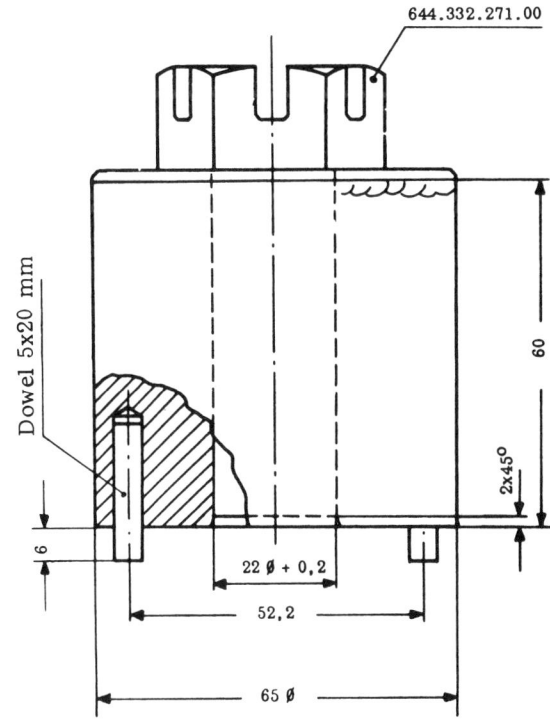

Fig. 7.20. Insert retaining nut tool dimensions (KONI) (Sec. 5)

Dimensions in mm
0.236 in = 6 mm
0.866 in = 22 mm

2.055 in = 52.2 mm
2.559 in = 65 mm
2.362 in = 60 mm

0.197 in = 5 mm
0.787 in = 20 mm

Installation
18 Installation is basically the reverse of the removal procedure. If the distance ring was removed from the steering knuckle it should be heated to approximately 150°C (300°F) before being pressed on. Always fit a cord ring seal (OR 25.3 X 2.4) between the spacer ring and the steering knuckle to prevent corrosion occurring.
19 When installing the hollow rubber spring, do not use any lubricant.

Fig. 7.22. The Schnorr disc washer in place (Sec. 5)

20 When installing the lower balljoint, use a new bolt and Schnorr disc washer. Do not lubricate the balljoint, and do not forget the steel washer between the suspension or shock absorber strut.
21 When installing a shock absorber strut torsion bar adjusting lever, lever downwards on the wishbone until the strut is fully extended and contacting its lower stop. Push the adjusting lever onto the torsion bar as close as possible to the adjusting screw stop on the subframe. Ensure that the adjusting lever is fitted with a dust cap. Apply a molybdenum disulphide general purpose grease to the adjusting screw thread and screw it in a few turns. Also check that a dust cap is fitted in the wishbone; this prevents the torsion bar from creeping out of engagement from the splines.
22 The remainder of the installation procedure is straightforward. Do not forget to bleed the braking system (Chapter 8), check the wheel bearing play (Section 2) and the suspension geometry (Section 11).

Suspension strut balljoint (1972 models onwards)
23 The modified suspension strut balljoint is shown in Fig. 7.23, the parts being numbered in the order of removal. The following points should be noted on reassembly:

a) *The double-wedge bolt should be lubricated with general purpose grease*
b) *Ensure that the bolt is installed with the notch towards the disc/hub, and the nut on the forward side (Fig. 7.24)*
c) *Before torque tightening the nut, tap the double-wedge bolt to seat it properly.*

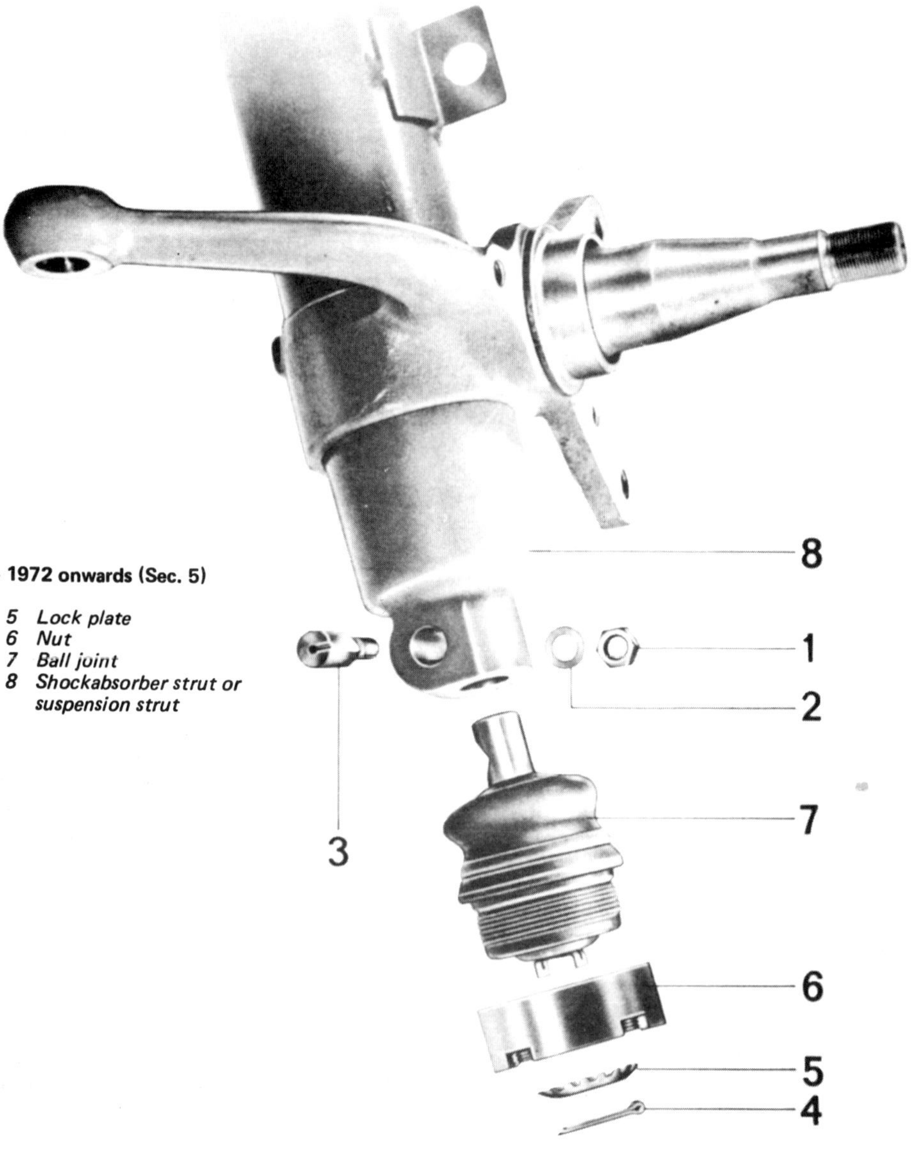

Fig. 7.23. Suspension strut balljoint - 1972 onwards (Sec. 5)

1 *Nut*	5 *Lock plate*
2 *Washer*	6 *Nut*
3 *Double-wedge bolt*	7 *Ball joint*
4 *Cotter pin*	8 *Shockabsorber strut or suspension strut*

Fig. 7.24. Installed attitude of double wedge bolt (Sec. 5)

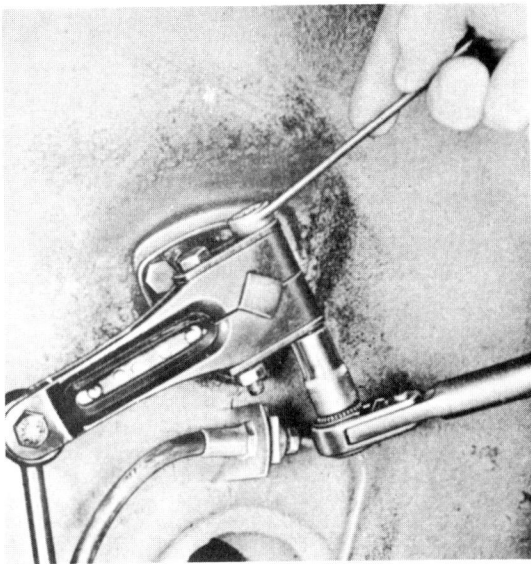

Fig. 7.25. Stabilizer lever clamping bolts being removed (Sec. 6)

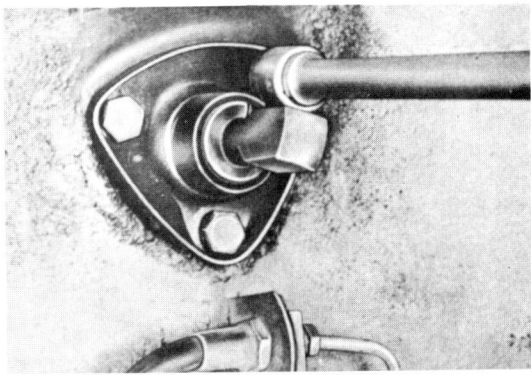

Fig. 7.26. Removing the bush support retaining bolts (Sec. 6)

6 Stabilizer bar (anti-roll bar) - removal and installation

1   The stabilizer used up to 1974 comprised a tranverse rod with twin levers and link rods, the latter being connected to the wishbones (transverse control arms). For 1974 a single cranked stabilizer was introduced as shown in Fig. 7.27. The two types are not interchangeable, but each type can be obtained in different standard sizes according to the vehicle and application. It is recommended that the advice of a Porsche dealer is sought if a stabilizer bar is to be fitted or where one of different size is thought to be necessary.

Pre-1974 models

2   Loosen the clamping bolts and withdraw the stabilizer lever.
3   Remove the bush support retaining bolts. Apply a little penetrating oil to the bush support and rubber bush, then prise off the support and bush using two screwdrivers or similar tools.
4   Remove the retaining bolts on the other side, and pull out the stabilizer complete with the bush and its support.
5   Apply penetrating oil, then press off the support and bush.
6   Remove the shackle bolt, then remove the shackle and stabilizer lever.
7   Inspect the rubber parts for wear and damage, and obtain replacements as necessary.
8   Installation is the reverse of the removal procedure, the bushes being treated with glycerine or a similar rubber lubricant. Lightly tighten the bush supports, then centre the stabilizer and tighten the bolts to the specified torque. Allow approximately 0.04 in (1 mm) protrusion of the stabilizer through the lever before tightening the clamping bolts.

1974 models onwards

9   From beneath the car remove the stone guard.
10 Remove both support clamps from the auxiliary support (reinforcing crossmember).
11 Draw the stabilizer rearwards out of the wishbone bushings, first one side, then the other.
12 Inspect the rubber parts for wear and damage, and obtain replacements, as necessary.
13 Installation is the reverse of the removal procedure, using glycerine or a similar rubber lubricant for the bushings.

7 Wishbone (transverse control arm) removal and installation

Pre-1968 models

1   Jack-up the front of the car and remove the roadwheel.
2   Remove the undershield and turn back the torsion bar adjustment screw. (Fig. 7.28)
3   Unlock and remove the wishbone castellated nuts, pull out the bolts and slide the strut/balljoint out of the control arm.
4   Remove the bolts, then take off the control arm bushing bracket and bracket cap. (Fig. 7.29)
5   Remove both torsion bar dust caps, then remove the circlip in the front part of the wishbone.
6   Drive the torsion bar out forwards using a suitable drift.
7   Remove the Flanbloc retaining bolt in the reinforcing crossmember, then withdraw the wishbone and Flanblok by pushing the wishbone forwards and turning it about its axis. (Fig. 7.30)
8   Drive out the torsion bar lever, using a drift through the hole in the reinforcing crossmember. Take care that the splines are not damaged.
9   Examine the rubber bushes and Flanbloc for wear. If the Flanbloc is damaged it can only be removed by destroying it. This job is best entrusted to a Porsche agent who will have the necessary tools for the job. At the same time the wishbone can be checked for alignment using a special fixture. Torsion bars with damaged splines or severe rusting must be renewed; if only the paint finish is damaged, this should be touched up using a suitable primer.
10 Installation is the reverse of the removal procedure but the following points must be observed:

   a) *The wishbone end which carries the ball support must be at an angle of 10° to the reinforcing crossmember before the Flanbloc clamping bolt is torque tightened. (Fig. 7.31)*
   b) *Lightly coat the torsion bar with general purpose grease, paying particular attention to the splines. When installing, do not mix-up the left (marked 'L' on the end/and right (marked 'R' on the end) versions; install the lockring and dust cap when in*
   d) *When fitting the torsion bar adjusting lever into the reinforcing crossmember, attach the strut to the wishbone, then lever downwards on the wishbone and, with the adjusting screw turned back, insert the torsion bar adjusting lever into the reinforcing crossmember and onto the torsion bar splines. Leave as little clearance at the adjusting point as possible, and*

168

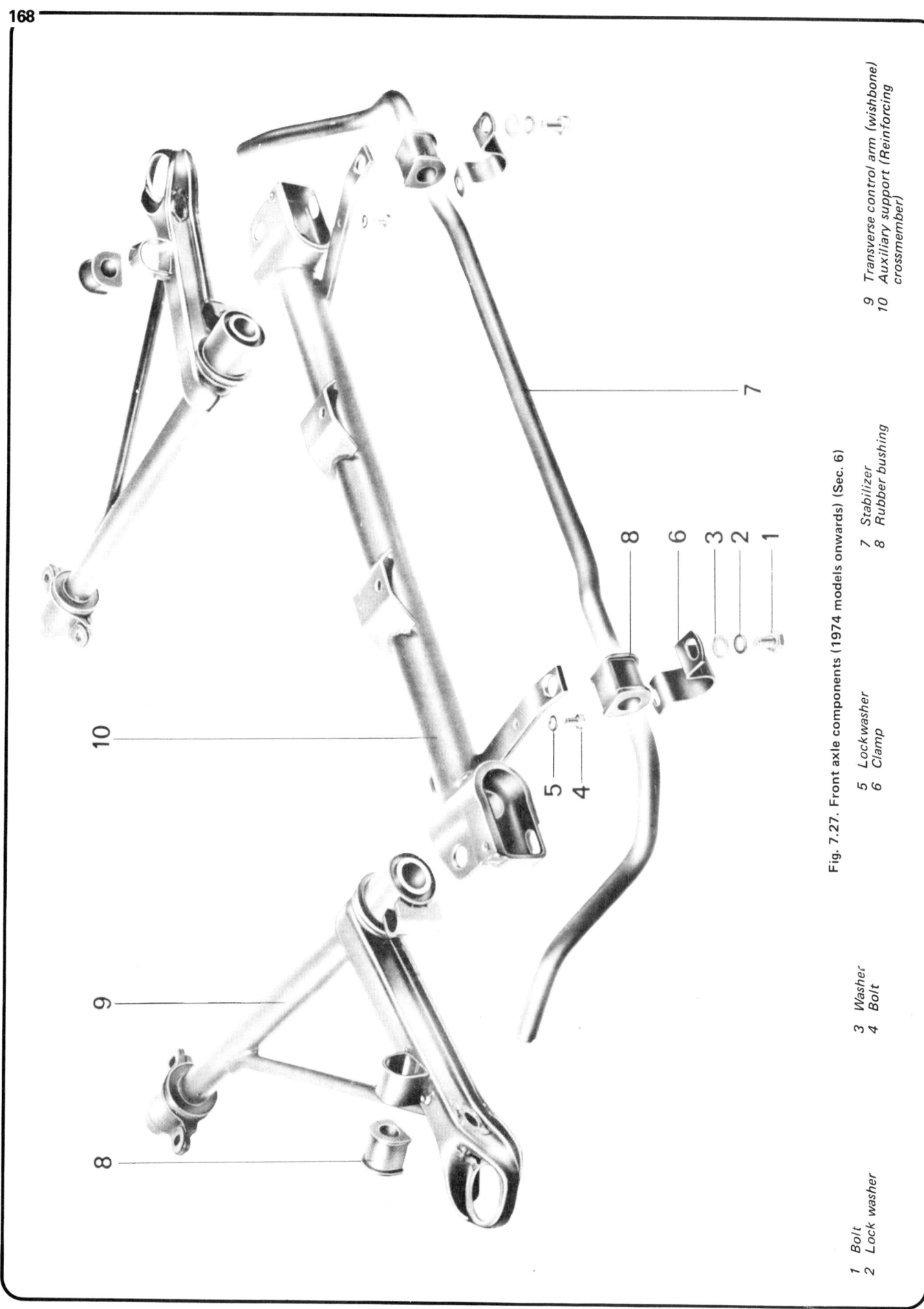

Fig. 7.27. Front axle components (1974 models onwards) (Sec. 6)

1 Bolt
2 Lock washer
3 Washer
4 Bolt
5 Lockwasher
6 Clamp
7 Stabilizer
8 Rubber bushing
9 Transverse control arm (wishbone)
10 Auxiliary support (Reinforcing crossmember)

Fig. 7.28. Turning back the torsion bar adjustment screw (Sec. 7)

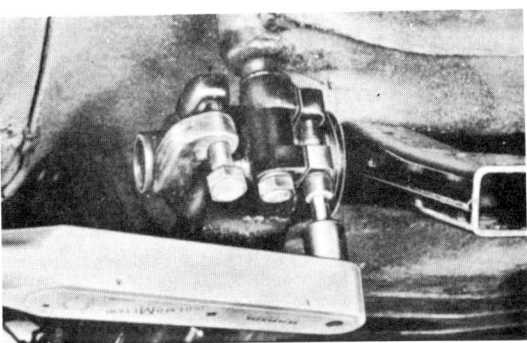

Fig. 7.30. Removing the Flanbloc retaining bolt (Sec. 7)

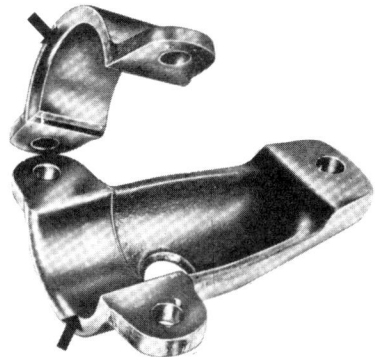

Fig. 7.32. Correct alignment of the bracket and cap (Sec. 7)

coat the lever with a molybdenum disulphide general purpose grease prior to installing into the support arm. Lightly tighten the adjusting screw, then install the lockring and dust cover.
e) Check the suspension geometry, as described in Section 11.

1968 models

11 The procedure for removing and installing the wishbone is similar to that previously described except that, because of the different reinforcing crossmember used, the attachment at this end is different. It is therefore important to note that where both wishbones are to be removed, the support member must be secured in position, after the first wishbone has been removed, using the retaining bolt. Also note the seal which is installed at the rear end of the torsion bar where it passes through the reinforcing crossmember.

Fig. 7.29. Removing the bracket and bracket cap (Sec. 7)

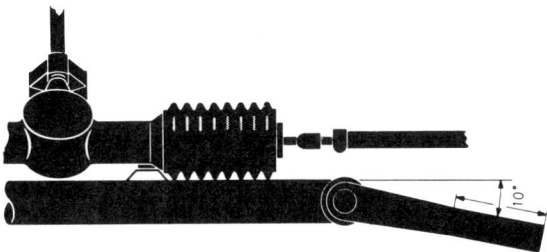

Fig. 7.31. Angle for setting the wishbone end (Sec. 7)

1969 models onwards

12 The procedure for removing and installing the wishbone is similar to that for 1968 models with regard to the reinforcing crossmember attachment point. However, a different method of attachment is provided at the base of the strut for the balljoint. These are dealt with in Section 5 for both pre-1972 versions (clamp mounting type) and 1972 models onwards (double-wedge bolt type). Where self-levelling suspension struts are used, reference to the torsion bar and its adjustment should be ignored.

8 Suspension upper thrust bearing and rubber pad - removal and installation

Note: Before removing an upper thrust bearing, it is important to realize that the suspension geometry will require checking on completion. For further information see Section 11.
1　Raise the front of the car and remove the roadwheel(s).
2　Fold back the lock tab at the top of the suspension strut, then use a C-spanner to prevent the notched washer from turning, and remove the nut.
3　Press down on the suspension strut and extract the piston rod from the rubber pad.
4　Remove all sealing compound from around the pressure plates, then mark around the pressure plates as a guide to installation.
5　Using a suitable Allen key, remove the bolts, then remove the thrust bearing and pad. (Fig. 7.34)
6　Installation is the reverse of the removal procedure, using a new lock tab for the top strut mounting. On completion, even though the pressure plates are installed in the same position, the suspension geometry should be checked. After this is done, seal around the Allen screws with sealing compound such as underbody paint (photo).

9 Torsion bar - removal and installation

The torsion bar has to be removed whenever a wishbone is removed. Therefore, refer to the procedure given in paragraphs 1, 2, 4, 5 and 6, of Section 7. For 1968 models onwards, note the seal which is installed at the rear end of the torsion bar where it passes through the reinforcing crossmember (see Fig. 7.33). Do not forget to carry out the suspension geometry checks, as described in Section 11, on completion.

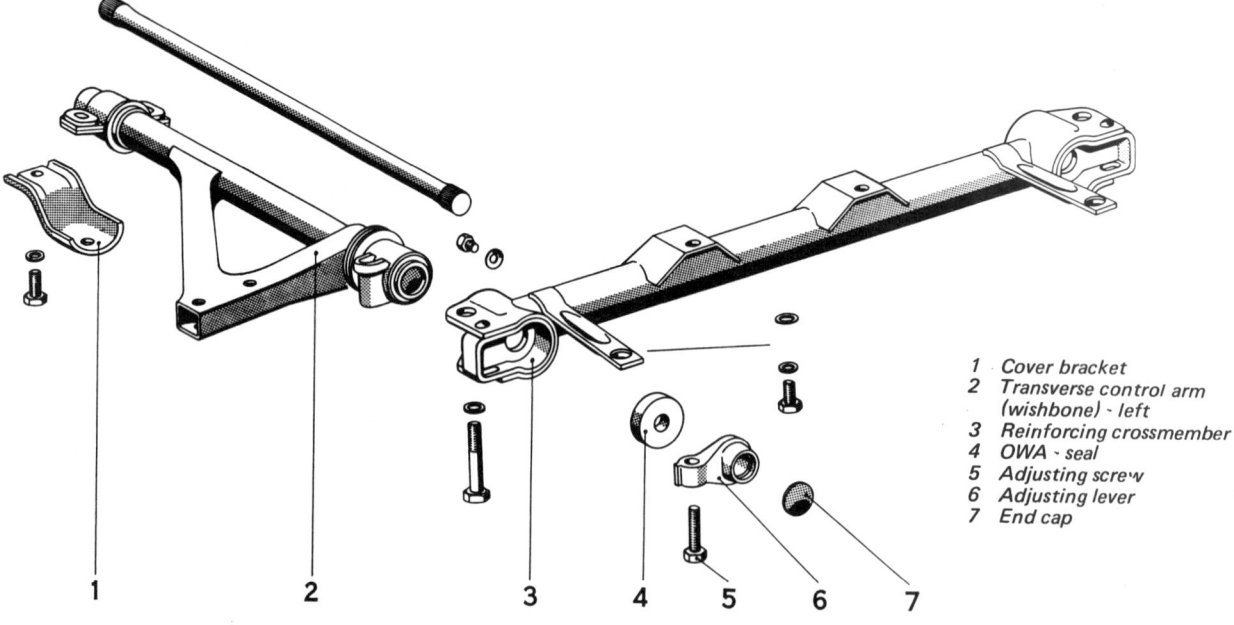

1 · Cover bracket
2 · Transverse control arm
(wishbone) - left
3 · Reinforcing crossmember
4 · OWA - seal
5 · Adjusting screw
6 · Adjusting lever
7 · End cap

Fig. 7.33. Suspension components on 1968 models (Secs. 7 and 9)

Fig. 7.34. Removing an upper thrust bearing (Sec. 8)

8.6 Upper thrust bearing correctly installed

10 Reinforcing crossmember - removal and installation

1   Remove the wishbones, as described in Section 7.
2   Detach the steering gear from the crossmember, referring to Section 12, if necessary.
3   Detach the crossmember reinforcing braces.
4   Loosen the crossmember retaining bolts, then knock or lever it off the locating studs. Now remove the screws fully and take away the crossmember. It is recommended that the steering gear is supported while the crossmember is off the car.
5   Installation is the reverse of the removal procedure, but before tightening the crossmember bolts, ensure that it is correctly aligned on the locating studs.

11 Suspension geometry - checking

Cornering and roadholding qualities are influenced by vehicle height adjustment and wheel alignment. Whenever any major work has been carried out on the front suspension, the vehicle trim height, tracking (toe-in), camber and caster should be checked. Refer to Chapter 6 for suspension geometry checks for the rear of the car.

Trim height: This is the difference between the hub centre line and the wishbone or suspension arm. Where self-levelling suspension struts are fitted, refer to Section 4 for the checking procedure. The adjustment procedure for conventional suspensions is given below.

Toe-in: This is the amount by which the front wheels must point inwards at their leading edges. This is expressed as an angle and can therefore only be checked using optical alignment gauges; it is therefore not a task which can be readily attempted by the home mechanic. Adjustment is made by lengthening or shortening the steering tie-rods, by rotating them.

Camber: This is the angular difference between the plane of the wheel and a vertical line passing through the point of contact of the tyre with the ground. Adjustment is made at the suspension strut top mounting but because optical alignment gauges are required for checking, this

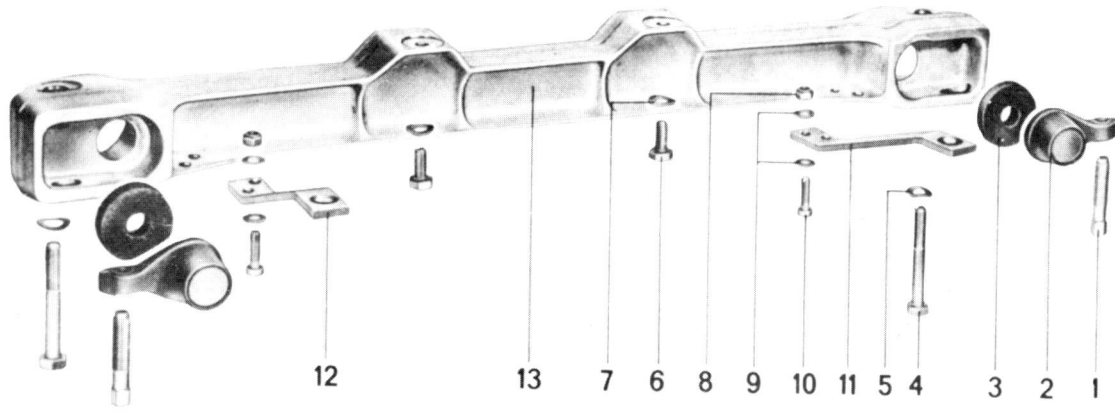

Fig. 7.35. Reinforcing crossmember used on Carrera 2.7 models (Sec. 10)

1 Adjusting screw	4 Bolt	7 Spring washer	10 Allen bolt
2 Adjusting lever	5 Spring washer	8 Self-locking nut	11 Right brace
3 OWA-gasket	6 Bolt	9 Washer	12 Left brace
			13 Reinforcing crossmember

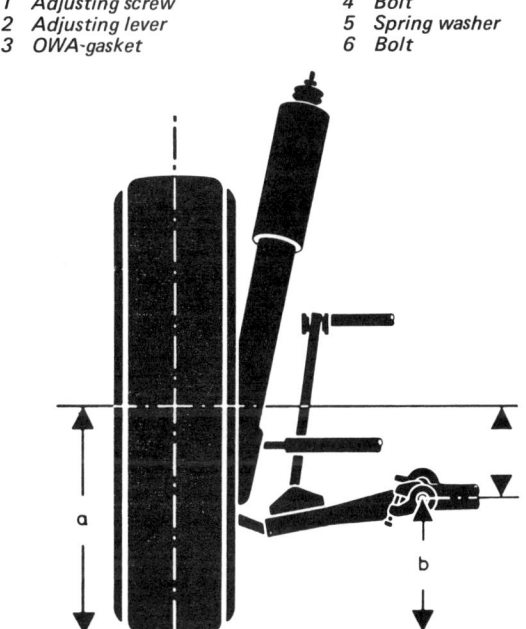

Fig. 7.36. Front axle height checking (Sec. 11)

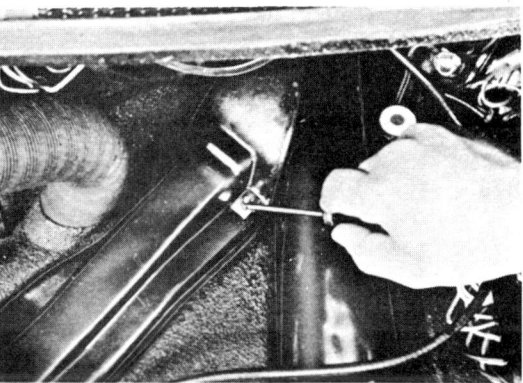

Fig. 7.37. Access to the intermediate shaft (Sec. 12)

should not be attempted by the home mechanic.

Caster: This is the angular difference between a line drawn through the suspension strut and a vertical line passing through the point of contact of the tyre with the ground. Adjustment for this is also made at the suspension strut top mounting and should not be attempted by the home mechanic.

Trim height - adjustment

Note: This check must be made with correctly inflated tyres, a full fuel tank and the spare wheel in position.

1   Press the car down several times at the bumper and allow it to come to rest naturally.

2   Note the distance from the ground to the centre of the hub cap or wheel (dimension 'a' in Fig. 7.36).

3   Measure the height from the centre of the torsion bar to the ground (dimension 'b'), and subtract this from dimension 'a'. The difference, the front axle trim height, should be as given in the Specifications for the particular model.

4   If adjustment is required, remove the torsion bar dust cover at the adjusting lever to gain access to the torsion bar centering mark which is used as a reference point. Adjust the torsion bar (at the adjusting screw) until the correct dimension 'b' is obtained, again bouncing the car several times before any measurement is made.

12 Rack and pinion steering gear - removal and installation

1   Remove the carpeting in the luggage compartment and detach the auxiliary heater heating duct from the steering post. Lay the duct on one side.

2   Open the access door and remove the intermediate shaft cover. It is advantageous to prise up one of the two prongs of the spring clip using a small screwdriver.

3   Remove the three heater fuel pump retaining bolts and lay the pump on one side.

4   Remove the cotter pin from the lower bolt of the universal joint, loosen the nut and pull the joint off the steering shaft.

5   Remove the Allen bolts from the cap of the steering shaft bushing; remove the cap, then pull out the bushing and dust boot. (Fig. 7.38)

6   Unlock and remove the retaining bolts from the steering coupling. (Fig. 7.39)

7   Remove the retaining nuts and bolts, and remove the undershield.

8   Detach the tie-rod balljoint (see paragraph 4, in Section 3, for the procedure).

9   Unscrew the steering gear housing retaining bolts. (Fig. 7.40)

10 Remove the right reinforcing crossmember brace, then withdraw the steering gear assembly towards the right of the car.

11 Mark the installed position, then unlock and remove the tie-rod yoke bolt so that the tie-rod can be detached.

12 Installation is basically the reverse of the removal procedure. If any play is detectable in the tie-rod balljoints, these should be renewed. Apply a molybdenum disulphide general purpose grease to yoke bolts when fitting them. Note that the steering coupling should be installed with the larger hole contacting the flanges. On completion it is essential that the car toe-in is checked (see Section 11).

Fig. 7.38. Removing the bushing cap Allen bolts (Sec. 12)

Fig. 7.40. Steering gear housing retaining bolts (arrowed) (Sec. 12)

13 Steering gear eyebolts

Different types of steering gear eyebolts have been used according to the type of steering and the steering geometry for the particular vehicle. If replacements are required, it is essential that they are correctly aligned and for this reason the job should be entrusted to a Porsche dealer who will have the appropriate setting-up jig.

14 Steering gear - dismantling, reassembly and adjustment

This operation is considered beyond the scope of the home mechanic due to the need for special tools and setting-up jigs. If the need for major repair occurs, the job should be entrusted to a Porsche dealer, or an exchange unit obtained.

15 Steering wheel - removal and installation

1   Disconnect the battery earth lead.
2   On pre-1974 models, rotate the horn pad anticlockwise and withdraw it. Pull out the contact pin. On 1974 models onwards (collapsible steering wheel), pull off the horn pad and detach the wire.
3   Remove the steering wheel nut and washer.
4   Mark the relative position of the steering wheel and steering upper shaft, then pull off the steering sheel. Do not try to use a hammer if the wheel is stubborn, but use the ball of the hand as near to the hub as possible.
5   On pre-1974 models, note the bearing support ring and spring beneath the steering wheel.
6   Installation is the reverse of the removal procedure. Lightly lubricate the horn contact using a little petroleum jelly.

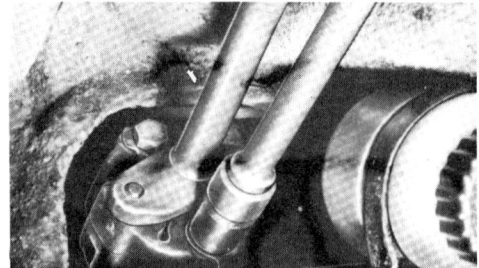

Fig. 7.39. Detaching the steering coupling (Sec. 12)

Fig. 7.41. Removing the horn pad (early type) (Sec. 15)

Fig. 7.42. Bearing support ring and spring (early type) (Sec. 15)

16 Steering column shafts - removal and installation

Pre-1969 models
1   Remove the steering wheel, as described in the previous Section.
2   Proceed as described in paragraphs 1 to 4, of Section 12.
3   Remove the Allen bolts retaining the bushing cap in the lower shaft; remove the cap.
4   Pull the universal joint off the steering lower shaft, then drive the intermediate shaft out of the upper universal joint. Remove the intermediate shaft and lower universal joint.
5   Where applicable, remove the light switch and steering lock, as described in Chapter 9, Section 26.
6   Remove the Allen bolt in the switch assembly retaining clamp, then turn the clamp so that the retaining pin can be pulled out.
7   Detach the electrical leads from the switch assembly, marking each one for ease of identification on assembly.
8   Withdraw the switch assembly complete with upper shaft and universal joint; draw the cables through the opening in the instrument panel.
9   Unlock and remove the steering post attaching bolts.

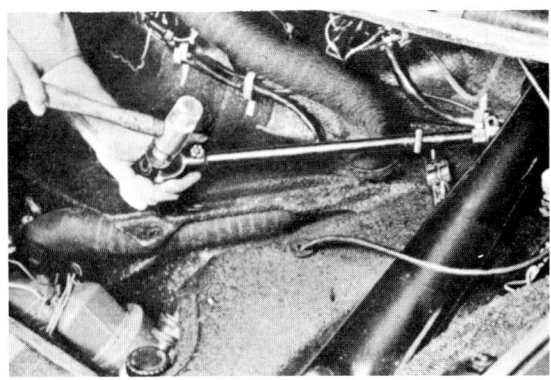
Fig. 7.43. Driving the intermediate shaft out of the upper universal joint (Sec. 16)

Fig. 7.44. Removing the switch assembly retaining clamp Allen bolt (Sec. 1 (Sec. 16)

Fig. 7.45. Withdrawing the switch assembly (Sec. 16)

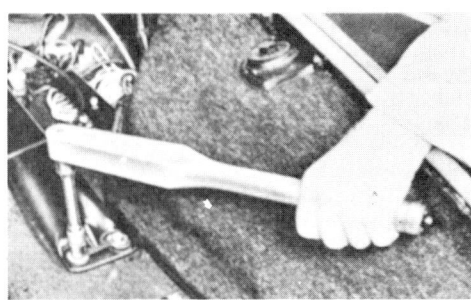
Fig. 7.46. Removing the steering post attaching bolts (Sec. 16)

10 Apply a little glycerine around the steering post grommet, then rotate the shaft and remove it.

11 Check the universal joints for wear and damage, obtaining replacements as necessary. Note that from Chassis No. 305101 onwards the universal joints have internal splines which mate with those on the upper shaft, intermediate shaft and lower shaft. These joints are not interchangeable with non-splined types, and if required, the appropriate shaft(s) must also be obtained.

12 Installation of the shafts and switches is basically the reverse of the removal procedure. However, the following points should be noted:

> a) Apply glycerine or a similar rubber lubricant to the steering post grommet and steering post extension sealing ring for ease of assembly.
> b) When installing the retaining clamp for the switch assembly, place it on the steering post so that the threaded part is on the right, in order that the Allen bolt can be inserted from below.
> c) Adjust the position of the steering post so that there is about 0.8 in (2 mm) clearance between the switch assembly and the instrument panel.
> d) Refer to Chapter 9 for information on installing the steering lock.

1969/73 models

13 Remove the steering wheel, as described in the previous Section.

14 Remove the luggage compartment mat, then remove the panelling in front of the fresh air plenum box.

15 Remove the four screws and take off the air grille and frame.

16 Detach the fresh air plenum chamber (2 screws).

17 Detach the connecting hoses on the control boxes.

18 Detach the electrical wires. Detach the control cable from the flap lever then push off the outer cable retaining clip. (Fig. 7.49)

19 Bend up one of the prongs of the retaining clip, then take off the intermediate steering shaft cover plate.

20 Remove the retaining bolt nuts on the universal joint and take out the bolts (photo).

21 Remove the Allen bolts on the steering shaft bearing cap; take off the cap.

22 Pull the lower joint out of the steering shaft and remove the

Fig. 7.47. Fresh air plenum box panelling (Sec. 16)

Fig. 7.48. Detaching the fresh air plenum chamber (Sec. 16)

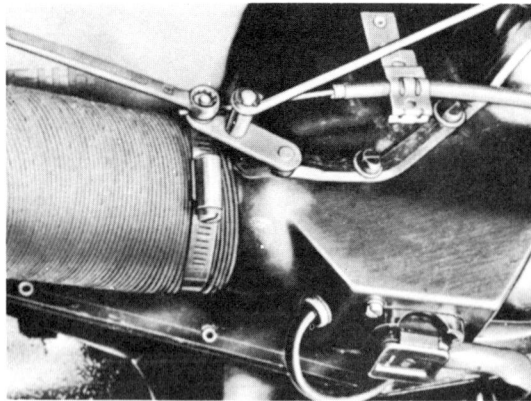

Fig. 7.49. Detaching the control cable (Sec. 16)

16.20 Column shaft universal joint

Fig. 7.50. Pulling off the steering column bearing (Sec. 16)

intermediate shaft with its universal joints.
23 Using an extractor, pull off the steering column bearing.
24 Remove the circlip from the steering shaft and drive the shaft out upwards.
25 Remove the circlip from the ball bearing in the outer column tube, then drive the bearing out downwards.
26 Check the shaft splines, universal joints and ball bearing for wear and damage, renewing parts as necessary.
27 Installation is basically the reverse of the removal procedure, but

Fig. 7.51. Removing the seal ring retainer (Sec. 17)

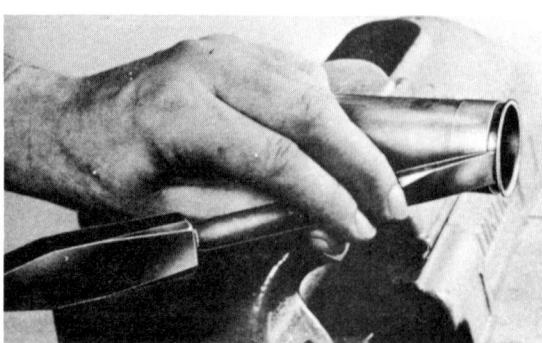

Fig. 7.52. Removing the drive spindle bearing (Sec. 17)

the following points should be noted:

a) *The ball bearing should be packed with general purpose grease before it is installed. Ensure that the bearing cover faces outwards.*
b) *Tighten the steering shaft bearing cap before the universal joint bolts are tightened.*
c) *When installing the fresh air plenum box and blower, first insert the air inlet aperture, followed by the water drain hoses which connect to the drain tube in the luggage compartment floor. Before finally tightening the securing bolts and clips, ensure that everything is correctly aligned and that the air flaps open and shut satisfactorily.*

1974 models onwards
28 This procedure is essentially the same as that for 1969/73 models. Note that it will also be necessary to remove the knee strip, light switch, tachometer, ignition switch/ steering lock and column switch assembly. The components are shown in Fig. 7.53.

17 Upper shaft and steering post extension (pre-1969 models) - dismantling and reassembly

1 Remove the upper shaft and switch assembly, as described in the first part of the previous Section.
2 Remove the bolt and take off the universal joint.
3 Prise off the seal ring retainer, then remove the seal washer, seal and second seal retainer.
4 Remove the post extension Allen bolts, then carefully drive the extension out of the switch assembly.
5 Remove the circlip from the upper shaft and drive the shaft out of the bearing.
6 Remove the second circlip and drive the bearing out of the post extension.
7 Using a blunt chisel carefully drive out the drive spindle bearing.
8 Check the bearings, universal joint and shaft for wear and damage, obtaining new parts where necessary.
9 Installation is the reverse of the removal procedure, but the following points should be noted:

a) *Pack the ball bearing with general purpose grease and install it so that the shield is outwards.*

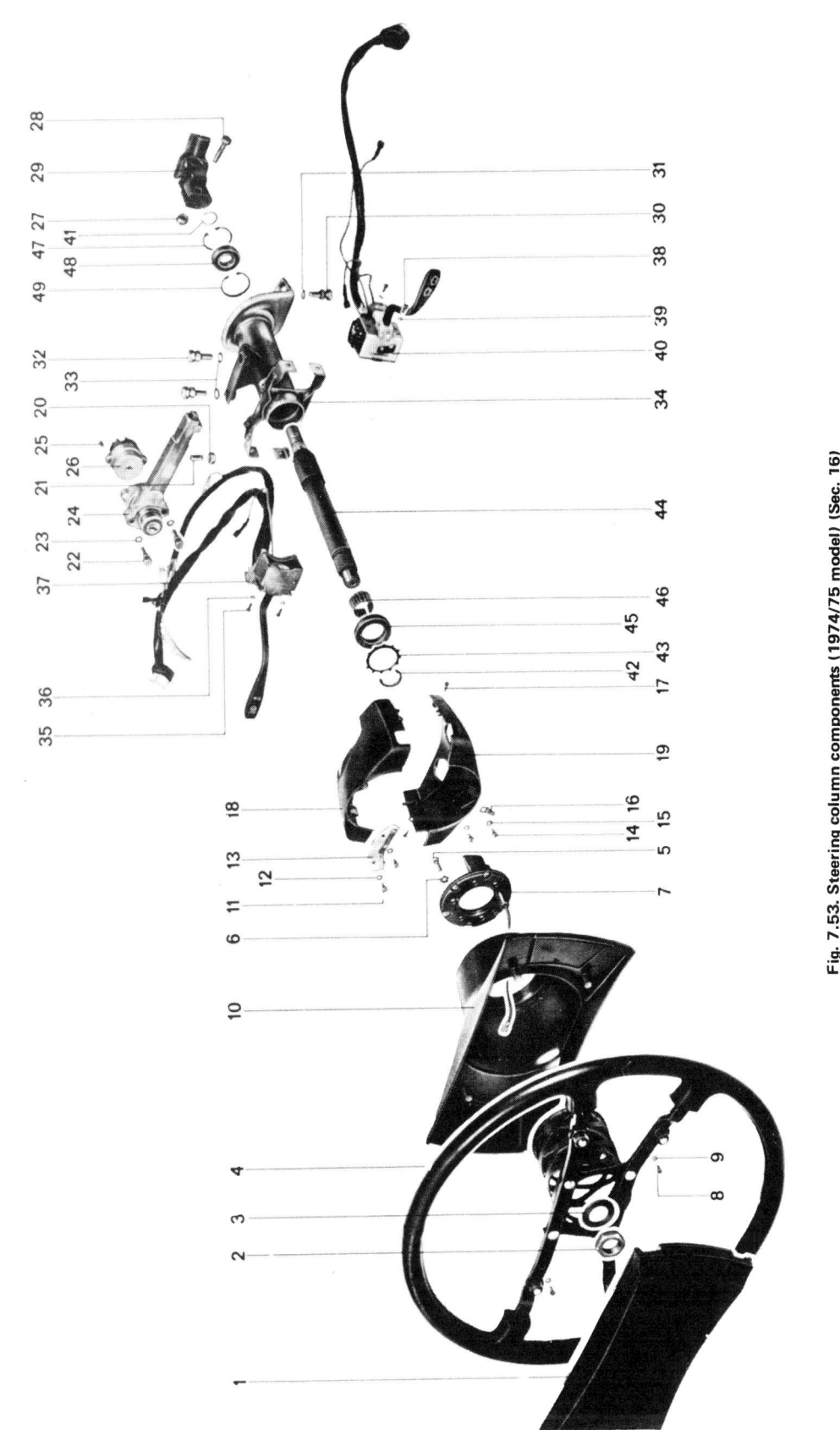

Fig. 7.53. Steering column components (1974/75 model) (Sec. 16)

1 Pad
2 Nut
3 Spring washer
4 Safety steering wheel hub and energy absorbing support
5 Oval head screw
6 Special lock washer
7 Contact ring
8 Allen screw
9 Lock washer

10 Hub cover
11 Allen screw
12 Lock washer
13 Contact plate
14 Allen screw
15 Lock washer
16 Contact tab
17 Allen screw
18 Switch housing top
19 Switch housing bottom

20 Nut
21 Stud
22 Shear head bolt
23 Lock washer
24 Ignition steering lock
25 Allen screw
26 Ignition/starter switch
27 Self-locking nut
28 Bolt
29 Universal joint

30 Shear head bolt
31 Lock washer
32 Shear head bolt
33 Lock washer
34 Steering shaft tube
35 Allen screw
36 Lock washer
37 Directional signal and dip switch
38 Allen screw
39 Lock washer

40 Wiper/washer switch
41 Lock washer
42 Lock washer
43 Retaining ring
44 Steering shaft
45 Ball bearing
46 Contact ring
47 Circlip
48 Ball bearing
49 Circlip

b) Ensure that the rectangular lock opening in the post extension is central in the opening in the switch assembly.

c) Align the post extension to obtain a dimension 'A' (Fig. 7.55)

of 9/32 in (7 mm).

d) Use a new Schnorr disc washer under the universal joint castellated nut; also use a new bolt.

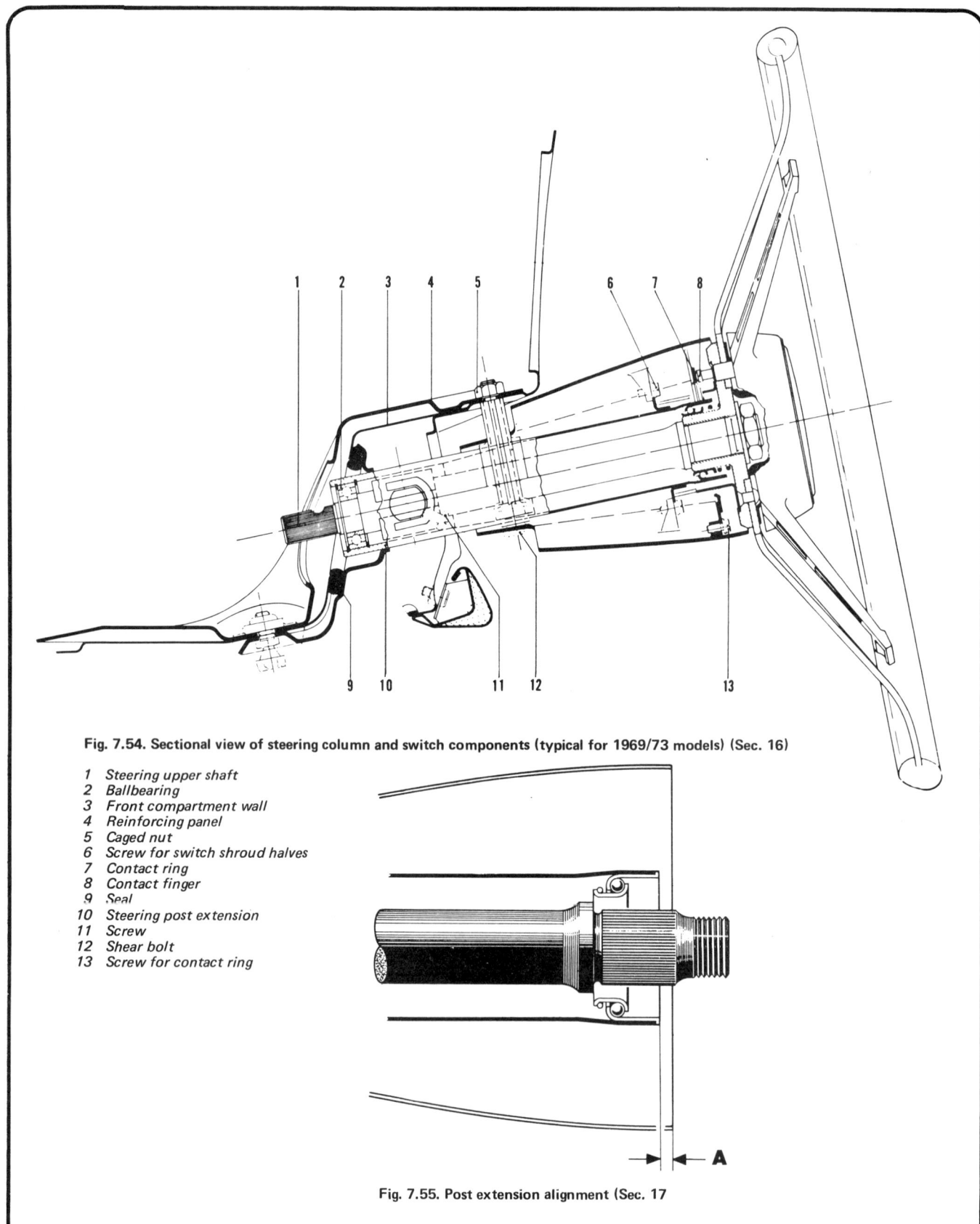

Fig. 7.54. Sectional view of steering column and switch components (typical for 1969/73 models) (Sec. 16)

1   Steering upper shaft
2   Ballbearing
3   Front compartment wall
4   Reinforcing panel
5   Caged nut
6   Screw for switch shroud halves
7   Contact ring
8   Contact finger
9   Seal
10 Steering post extension
11 Screw
12 Shear bolt
13 Screw for contact ring

Fig. 7.55. Post extension alignment (Sec. 17

18 Fault diagnosis - front suspension and steering

Before diagnosing faults in the mechanics of the suspension and steering itself, check that any irregularities are not caused by:

1   *Binding brakes*
2   *Incorrect 'mix' of radial and crossply tyres*
3   *Incorrect tyre pressures*
4   *Misalignment of the bodyframe and suspension due to accident damage*

Symptom	Reason/s	Remedy
Steering wheel can be moved considerably before any sign of movement of the wheels is apparent	Wear in the steering linkage, gear and column coupling	Check movement in all joints and steering gear. Repair/renew as required.
Vehicle difficult to steer in a consistent straight line (wandering)	As above	As above.
	Wheel alignment incorrect (indicated by excessive or uneven tyre wear)	Check wheel alignment.
	Front wheel hub bearings loose or worn	Adjust or renew as necessary.
	Worn suspension balljoints	Renew as necessary.
Steering stiff and heavy	Incorrect wheel alignment (indicated by excessive or uneven wear)	Check wheel alignment.
	Excessive wear or seizure in one or more of the joints in the steering linkage or suspension	Repair as necessary.
	Excessive wear in the steering gear unit	Adjust if possible, or renew.
Wheel wobble and vibration	Roadwheels out of balance (see Chapter 8)	Balance wheels.
	Roadwheels buckled (see Chapter 8)	Check for damage.
	Wheel alignment incorrect	Check wheel alignment.
	Wear in the steering linkage or suspension	Check and renew as necessary.
Excessive pitching and rolling on corners and during braking	Defective shock absorbers and/or broken torsion bar springs	Check and renew as necessary.
	Defective self-levelling suspension struts	Check and renew as necessary.

Chapter 8 Braking system, wheels and tyres

Contents

Specifications

Brakes

System type	Hydraulic, discs front and rear, with cable operated rear drum-type handbrake. Dual circuit system from 1968 onwards

Pre-1968 models except 911S:

Disc type	Solid
Disc diameter:	
Front	11.1 in (282 mm)
Rear	11.2 in (285 mm)
Disc thickness:	
Front	0.500/0.492 in (12.7/12.5 mm)
Rear	0.386/0.394 in (9.8/10 mm) or 0.406/0.413 in (10.3/10.5 mm)
Minimum disc thickness:	
Front	0.43 in (11 mm)
Rear	0.33 in (8.5 mm)
Maximum lateral run out (installed)	0.008 in (0.02 mm)
Minimum pad lining thickness	0.08 in (2 mm)
Caliper cylinder diameter:	
Front	1.89 in (48 mm)
Rear	1.378 in (35 mm)
Master cylinder bore diameter	0.75 in (19.05 mm)
Handbrake drum diameter	7.087 in (180 mm)
Handbrake lining width	1.26 in (32 mm)
Minimum handbrake lining thickness	0.08 in (2 mm)

Pre-1968 911S (differences):

Disc type	Ventilated
Disc diameter:	
Front	11.12 in (282.5 mm)
Rear	11.26 in (286 mm)
Disc thickness (front and rear)	0.780/0.787 in (19.8/20 mm)
Caliper spacer thickness:	
Front	0.287 in (7.3 mm)
Rear	0.417 in (10.8 mm)
Caliper cylinder diameter, rear	1.496 in (38 mm)

1968 models (differences):

Disc type:	
911T except Sportomatic	Solid
911L, 911S, 911T Sportomatic	Ventilated
Caliper cylinder diameter:	
911T (except Sportomatic), rear	1.378 in (35 mm)
911L, 911S, 911T Sportomatic, rear	1.496 in (38 mm)

1969 model (differences):

Disc type:	
911T (except Sportomatic)	Solid
911E, 911S, 911T Sportomatic	Ventilated

Disc diameter:

Front	...	...	...	...	...	...	...	...	11.12 in (282.5 mm)
Rear	...	...	...	...	...	...	...	...	11.42 in (290 mm)
Caliper cylinder diameter, rear			...	...	...	...	...	...	1.496 in (38 mm)
Handbrake lining width	...	...	...	...	...	...	...	...	0.984 in (25 mm)
Master cylinder bore diameter, 911E, 911S, 911T Sportomatic								...	0.813 in (20.64 mm)

1970 model onwards (differences):

Disc type (all models)	...	...	...	...	...	...	...	...	Ventilated
Brake master cylinder diameter		...	...	...	...	...	...	...	0.75 in (19.05 mm)

Brake fluid type	...	...	...	...	...	...	...	...	Ate Blau S or SAE J1703

Wheels and tyres

Pre-1968 models:

Wheels	...	...	...	...	...	...	...	...	Perforated disc, 4½J x 15
Tyres:									
911S	...	...	...	...	...	...	...	...	165 VR 15
Other models	...	...	...	...	...	...	...	...	165 HR 15

1968 models:

Wheels	...	...	...	...	...	...	...	...	Perforated disc, 5½J x 15
Tyres:									
911S	...	...	...	...	...	...	...	...	165 VR 15
Other models	...	...	...	...	...	...	...	...	165 HR 15

1969/71 models:

Wheels (911T):									
Standard fitment	...	...	...	...	...	...	...	...	5½J x 15
Optional fitment	...	...	...	...	...	...	...	...	5½J x 14 or 6J x 15
Tyres (911T):									
Standard fitment	...	...	...	...	...	...	...	...	165 HR 15
Optional fitment	...	...	...	...	...	...	...	...	185 HR 14 or 185/70 VR 15
Wheels (911E):									
Standard fitment	...	...	...	...	...	...	...	...	6J x 15
USA and Sportomatic	...	...	...	...	...	...	...	...	5½J x 14
Tyres (911E):									
Standard fitment	...	...	...	...	...	...	...	...	185/70 VR 15
USA and Sportomatic	...	...	...	...	...	...	...	...	185 HR 14
Wheels (911S)	...	...	...	...	...	...	...	...	6J x 15
Tyres (911S)	...	...	...	...	...	...	...	...	185/70 VR 15

1972/73 models:

Wheels (911T):									
Standard fitment	...	...	...	...	...	...	...	...	5½J x 15
Optional fitment	...	...	...	...	...	...	...	...	5½J x 14 or 6J x 15
Tyres (911T):									
Standard fitment	...	...	...	...	...	...	...	...	165 HR 15
Optional fitment	...	...	...	...	...	...	...	...	185 HR 14 or 185/70 VR 15
Wheels (911E, 911S)	...	...	...	...	...	...	...	...	6J x 15
Tyres (911E, 911S)	...	...	...	...	...	...	...	...	185/70 VR 15

1975 models onwards:

Wheels:									
All models (except Carrera USA)		...	...	...	...	...	...	...	6J x 15
Carrera USA	...	...	...	...	...	...	...	...	7J x 15
Tyres:									
911	...	...	...	...	...	...	...	...	185/70 HR 15
Other models (except Carrera USA)		...	...	...	...	...	...	185/70 VR 15
Carrera USA	...	...	...	...	...	...	...	...	215/60 VR 15

Note: *Wheels are made from steel pressings, cast magnesium alloy or forged magnesium alloy. Consult your Porsche dealer when replacements are required.*

Tyre pressures (nominal, cold tyre), pre-1973 models:

Front	...	...	...	...	...	...	...	...	26 lb f/sq. in (1.8 kg f/sq. cm)
Rear	...	...	...	...	...	...	...	...	29 lb f/sq. in (2.0 kg f/sq. cm)

Tyre pressures (nominal, cold tyre), 1973 models onwards:

Front	...	...	...	...	...	...	...	...	29 lb f/sq. in (2.0 kg f/sq. cm)
Rear	...	...	...	...	...	...	...	...	34 lb f/sq. in (2.4 kg f/sq. cm)

Note: *Where applicable, the collapsible spare tyre should be inflated to 29 lb f/sq. in (2 kg f/sq. cm).*

Torque wrench settings

	lb f ft	kg fm
Master cylinder attachment nuts	18	2.5
Bottom shield:		
Nuts	47	6.5
Bolts	34	4.7
Brake disc/hub nuts (front)	17	2.3
Caliper carrier plate (front)	34	4.7
Disc shroud	18	2.5
Brake caliper attachment (front)	51	7
Brake caliper attachment (rear)	43	6
Handbrake carrier plate	18	2.5
Handbrake lever support housing	18	2.5
Hydraulic connections	14.5	2
Bleed nipples	2.2	0.3
Wheel nuts	94	13

1 General description

All Porsche 911 cars utilize a four-wheel hydraulic disc brake system, with a mechanically operated handbrake (parking brake) operating through cables to shoes inside the rear disc/drums.

During the production run of this model there have been numerous changes to components such as calipers, brake pads and shoes, but the most obvious differences are the introduction of ventilated discs to replace the original solid discs, and the dual-circuit braking system introduced for 1968 models. For USA models, the dual master cylinder incorporates a brake failure warning switch, although the cylinder is similar to that in general use in other respects.

Whenever spare parts are required for the braking system, it is essential that the chassis and engine number are quoted in order to obtain the correct parts for any particular model.

Wheels of different types have been used, manufactured from steel or magnesium alloy; it is essential that where replacements are required individually they are obtained from a Porsche dealer to ensure that the correct types are obtained.

A collapsible spare tyre is used on certain models where the provision of a large fuel tank has precluded the use of a standard tyre. This tyre is stored in the deflated condition and thus requires less room for its accommodation.

Note: If the car is to be used for competition work or continued hard driving, the disc shrouds should be removed. Deflector shields should be installed in their place on the front brakes; these are obtainable from Porsche dealers under the part no. 901 351 801/802 15.

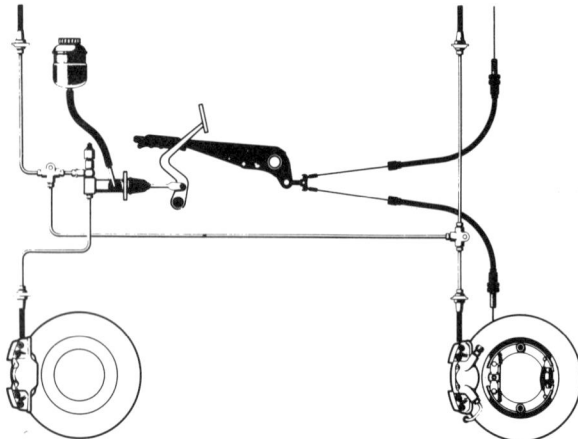

Fig. 8.1a. Brake system layout - single master cylinder (Sec. 1)

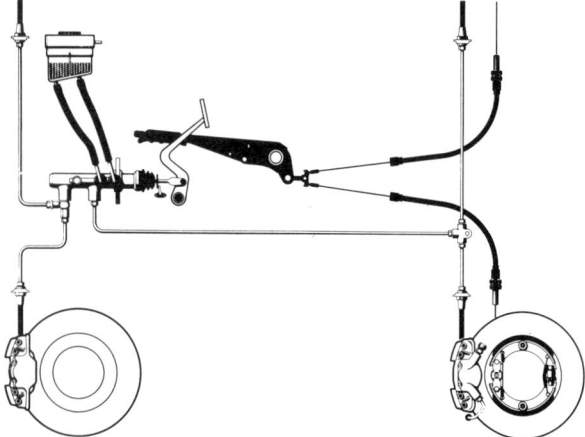

Fig. 8.1b. Brake system layout - dual master cylinder (Sec. 1)

2 Brake pads - renewal

1   The installed thickness of a new brake pad and backing plate is approximately 0.6 in (15 mm), and when the pad lining material has worn down to 0.08 in (2 mm), or when the pad segment touches the cross spring, it is time for renewal. Your Porsche dealer will be able to supply different pads according to the car model, and the type of use to which it is put.
2   Raise the car to a suitable working height and remove the roadwheel.
3   Withdraw the pin retainers, depress the cross spring and push out the retaining pins (photos).
4   Make-up a suitable wire hook and pull out the brake pads. If they are to be reused, mark them so that they can be installed in their original positions.
5   Using a hardwood or aluminium bar, press the pistons back into the caliper as far as they will go. Do this carefully as the reservoir

Fig. 8.2. Brake pad checks (Arrows indicate wear limit) (Sec. 2)

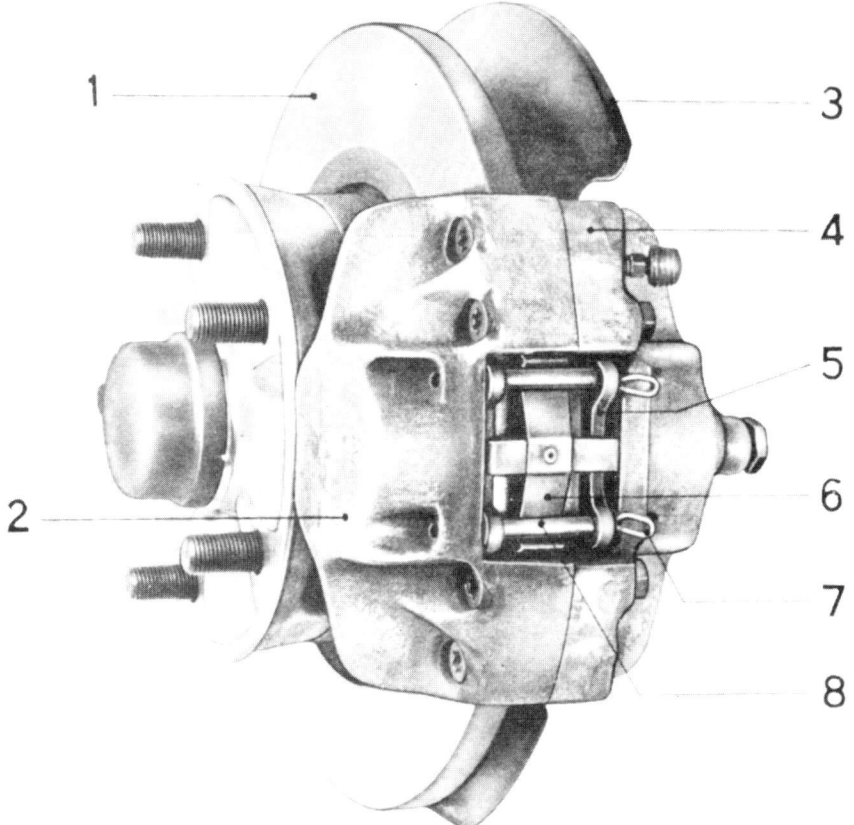

Fig. 8.3. Early solid disc and brake caliper

(Secs. 2, 3 and 4)

1   Disc
2   Caliper cover
3   Disc shroud
4   Caliper base housing
5   Brake pad
6   Cross spring
7   Pin retainer
8   Retaining pin

2.3a Withdraw the pin retainers ...

2.3b ... and the retaining pins.

2.7 Installing brake pads.

fluid level will rise and it may be necessary to syphon some fluid off.
6   Blow out any dirt from the caliper using an airline, and if necessary clean it with methylated spirit or isopropyl-alcohol. Check the dust boots and clamping rings for damage, and replace, if necessary. If necessary the discs may be cleaned using a fine grade of emery cloth.
7   Installation is now the reverse of the removal procedure. Ensure that the pads move freely in the calipers and finally pump the brake pedal repeatedly to force the caliper piston into the operating position. Check and top-up the reservoir fluid level, as necessary. For the first 125 miles (200 km) avoid heavy braking if possible, to allow the pads to bed in. During this period there may be noticed a 'once only' tendency for the pads to fade; this is a normal occurrence and is not to be confused with brake malfunction (photo).

---

3   Brake disc/hub - removal and installation

1   Remove the brake pads, as described in the previous Section.
2   Either place a polythene film over the brake fluid reservoir filler

orifice and install the cap, or wedge the brake pedal in a partially depressed position, to prevent fluid from draining out.

Front brakes
3   Detach the hydraulic line at the banjo-connection on the caliper.
4   Remove the retaining bolts and withdraw the caliper and shield. (Fig. 8.4)
5   Carefully prise off the hub bearing cap, then loosen the Allen screw so that the clamping nut and thrust washer can be removed. (Fig. 8.5)
6   Grip the disc firmly at opposite sides and pull it off. If it cannot be removed readily, do not use a hammer but obtain a suitable puller.
7   Remove the retaining bolts and pull off the disc shroud.
8   Remove the retaining bolts and pull off the brake carrier.
9   If necessary, mark the relative position of the disc and hub, then remove the retaining nuts and separate the two halves.
10 If the disc is considered unserviceable, it is strongly recommended that a replacement item is obtained. The alternative is to have the existing one reconditioned by a suitably equipped engineering workshop, but remember that this is a very specialised job.

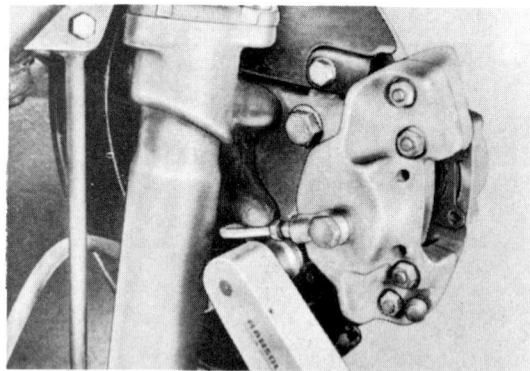

Fig. 8.4. Removing the caliper retaining bolts (Sec. 3)

Fig. 8.5. Loosening the clamping nut Allen screw (Sec. 3)

Fig. 8.6. Removing the caliper retaining bolts (Sec. 3)

Fig. 8.7. Handbrake cable attachment (Sec. 3)

Fig. 8.8. Removing the brake adjuster (Sec. 3)

11 Installation is basically the reverse of the removal procedure. Ensure that all parts are clean and free from grease, and tighten the disc-to-hub nuts to the specified torque. Apply approximately 50 cubic cm (45 gm/1.6 oz) of general purpose grease to each bearing. Tighten the brake carrier, shroud and caliper bolts to the specified torques, using new locking plates and spring washers. Adjust the wheel bearing, as described in Chapter 7, then check that the lateral runout of the disc does not exceed that specified. Install the brake pads and finally bleed the braking system, as described in Section 7.

Rear brakes
12 Remove the retaining bolts and withdraw the disc shrouds.
13 Detach the hydraulic line at the brake caliper.
14 Remove the retaining bolts and withdraw the caliper.
15 Remove the countersunk screws, and take off the brake disc and spacer ring, where applicable (ensure that the handbrake is released) (photo).
16 Remove the cotter pin, castellated nut and washer, so that the handbrake cable can be detached. Take off the mechanical expander and spring.
17 Remove the retainer disc from the holddown pin on the upper brake shoe, pulling the shoe outwards if necessary. Rotate the spring to remove it and pull out the pin from behind the backplate.
18 Using a screwdriver, raise the upper brake shoe, then remove the adjuster and unhook the spring.
19 Withdraw the spring and pin from the lower brake shoe, then remove both shoes, drawing them towards the front of the car so that the special return spring can be unhooked.
20 Installation is basically the reverse of the removal procedure, but the following points should be noted:

a) *When installing the handbrake cable, do not forget the washer which is between the spacer tube and expander.*

b) *Install the special return spring (the one at the handbrake cable side) with the spring coils orientated towards the axle centre.*

c) *Having positioned the brake shoes, insert the inner expander into the seats in the brake shoes.*

d) *Ensure that the handbrake adjuster assembly sprocket wheel is downwards on the right brake and upwards on the left brake.*

e) *After installing the brake shoes turn the cable adjuster, then install the spring, second expander half, washer and castellated nut.*

f) *Check that the disc lateral runout does not exceed that specified after installation.*

g) *When installing the caliper, use new spring washers and tighten the bolts to the specified torque.*

h) *Bleed the braking system (Section 7) and adjust the handbrake (Section 9) on completion.*

4 Brake caliper - overhaul

1 Remove the caliper, as described in the previous Section.
2 Remove the bleed nipples and blow out the fluid using compressed air from an air line or tyre pump (approximately 15 lb f/sq. in/1 kg/sq. cm).
3 Hold the caliper in a vice using jaw protectors, then prise the clamping ring out carefully using a screwdriver. Also remove the dust boot.
4 Place a wooden block between the two pistons, then apply air pressure to the fluid supply part to force out the piston. The pressure required may be anything from 30 lb f/sq. in (2 kg/sq. cm upwards), so it is likely that an airline will be required.
5 Prise out the piston seal using a non-metallic tool such as a plastic knitting needle.
6 On early models, in the unlikely event of fluid leaking from the seal between the caliper halves, the front calipers may be dismantled as described below. If leakage occurs from the rear calipers, replacements must be obtained.

Fig. 8.9. Correct installation of the brake return springs (Sec. 3)

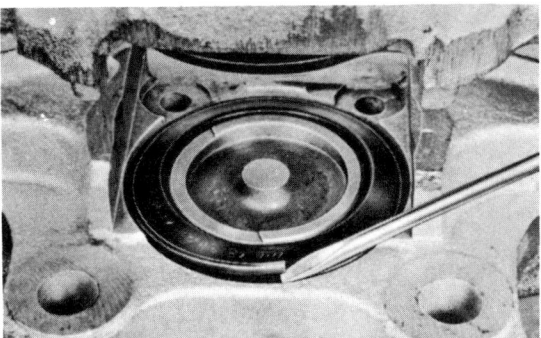
Fig. 8.10. Prising out the caliper clamping ring (Sec. 4)

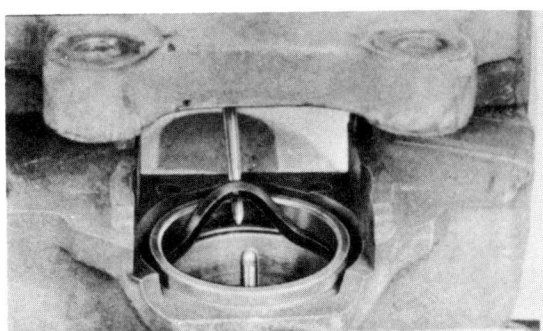
Fig. 8.11. Removing the piston seal (Sec. 4)

7 Remove the caliper clamping bolts, separate the caliper halves and remove the O-rings.
8 Discard all the rubber parts and carefully clean the metal parts in methylated spirit, isopropyl alcohol or clean brake fluid. Renew the appropriate parts if there is any evidence of wear, scoring or corrosion. Ensure that the fluid inlet port is clean and unobstructed. If any part of the automatic pad adjustment device in the piston is defective, a new piston assembly must be obtained.
9 Assembly is now basically the reverse of the removal procedure, all moving parts being lubricated with clean brake fluid. If the front brake caliper halves were separated, ensure that new O-rings, bolts, spring washers and nuts of the approved type are used. Ensure that the caliper halves are aligned before tightening the bolts to 12 lb f ft (1.7 kg f m) in the order shown in Fig. 8.12. Retighten them in the same order to 25 lb f ft (3.4 kg f m).
10 When installing the piston, ensure that the stepped part is as shown in Fig. 8.13. A suitable gauge can be made up from stiff cardboard for this purpose. Take care that the pistons do not jam as they are being pressed in; if difficulty is experienced in turning them after installation, it is better to remove them rather than trying to turn them with a

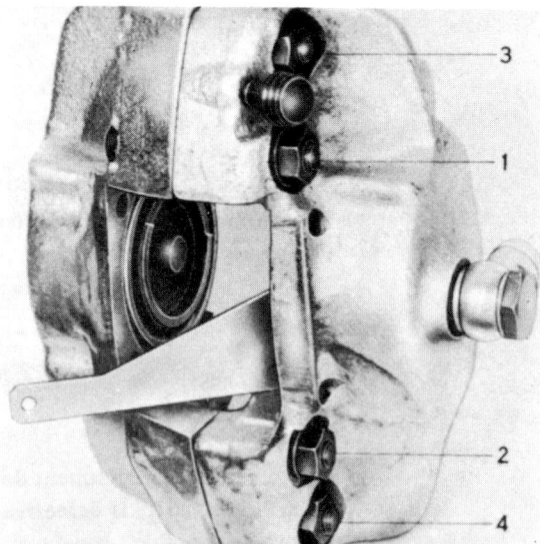

Fig. 8.12. Bolt tightening sequence for caliper halves (Sec. 4)

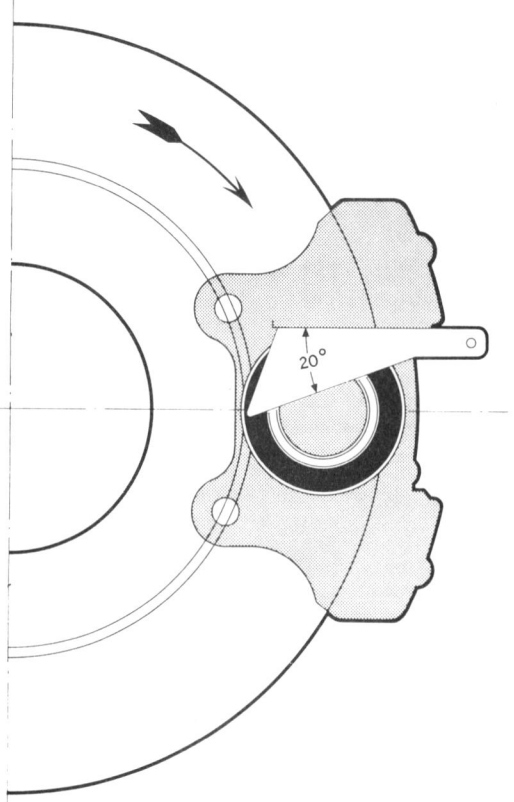

Fig. 8.13. Aligning the caliper piston using a gauge plate (Sec. 4)

Fig. 8.14. Floorboard retaining nut (arrowed) (Sec. 5)

Fig. 8.15. Bottom shield retainer nuts and bolts (Sec. 5)

remove the floor mat on the driver's side.
3   Remove the retaining nut and plate, then manoeuvre the floorboard out and away from the pedals.
4   Remove the dust boot from the master cylinder.
5   Drain or syphon the fluid from the master cylinder. Alternatively place a polythene film over the brake fluid reservoir filler orifice and install the cap to prevent excessive fluid loss.
6   Remove the front axle undershield.

Single master cylinder
7   Detach the hydraulic lines and stoplight switch wires (where applicable) at the brake master cylinder.
8   Loosen the hose clamp which connects the fluid reservoir to the master cylinder; withdraw the hose.
9   Remove the retaining nuts at the mounting flange and withdraw the master cylinder.

Dual master cylinder
10 Detach the brake lines from the master cylinder. On USA models also detach the wires from the brake failure warning switch.
11 Remove the retaining nuts at the mounting flange.
12 Detach the fluid connecting lines at the master cylinder then

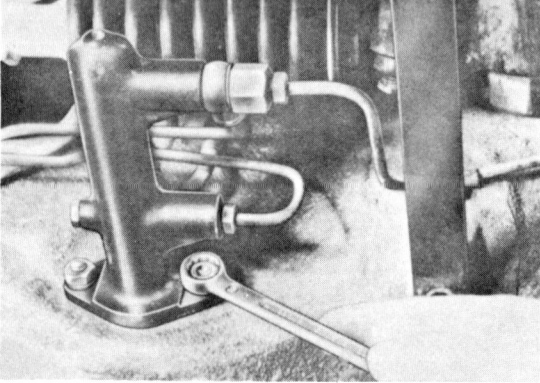

Fig. 8.16. Removing the master cylinder (Sec. 5)

screwdriver or similar tool. Finally, install the caliper, referring to the previous Section if necessary, then bleed the system as described in Section 7.

---

5   Brake master cylinder - removal and installation

1   Raise the car or place it over an inspection pit to provide access to the master cylinder (adjacent to the steering rack).
2   Pull back the throttle pedal to detach it from the pushrod, then

withdraw it from the mounting.

13 Installation is basically the reverse of the removal procedure, but the following points should be noted:

Single master cylinder:

a) *When installing, use a sealing compound to prevent water and dirt entering the car at the flange joint. Ensure that the piston rod is correctly positioned, then adjust it to provide 0.04 in (1 mm) clearance (endfloat) between it and the master cylinder piston.*

b) *After refilling or topping-up the system, bleed it as described in Section 7, then check the stoplight operation.*

c) *Tighten the bottom shield retaining bolts to the specified torque.*

Dual master cylinder:

d) *Follow the procedure notes given for the single master cylinder. On USA cars it is necessary to check the brake failure warning switch. To do this, switch on the ignition and arrange for a second person to open one brake bleed nipple while you depress the brake pedal; the warning light should now illuminate. The nipple should now be tightened and the pedal released. Repeat this procedure on another bleed nipple on the other half of the braking circuit (ie: a rear nipple if the first one was a front nipple, and vice versa).*

6 Brake master cylinder - overhaul

1 Secure the master cylinder in a vice using jaw clamps, then carefully remove the lock ring using a screwdriver.

Single master cylinder

2 Withdraw the piston stop plate and piston.

3 Applying air from an air line or tyre pump at the pressure port (approximately 15 lb f/sq. in/1 kg/sq. cm), blow out the piston cup, spring and check valve.

4 Remove the piston cup from the piston.

5 Discard all the rubber parts, and carefully clean the metal parts in methylated spirit, isopropyl alcohol or clean brake fluid. Renew the appropriate parts if there is any evidence of wear, scoring or corrosion. Ensure that the inlet and pressure ports are clean and free from obstruction; similarly check the purging passage in the check valve. (Fig. 8.20)

6 Assembly is now the reverse of the dismantling procedure, all parts being lubricated with clean brake fluid. Do not forget the washer between the piston and the primary piston cup, and finally ensure that the lock ring is correctly seated.

Dual master cylinder

7 Remove the stop plate together with the primary piston assembly.

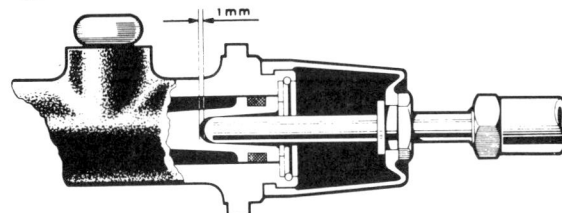

Fig. 8.17. Adjusting the master cylinder piston rod (Sec. 5)

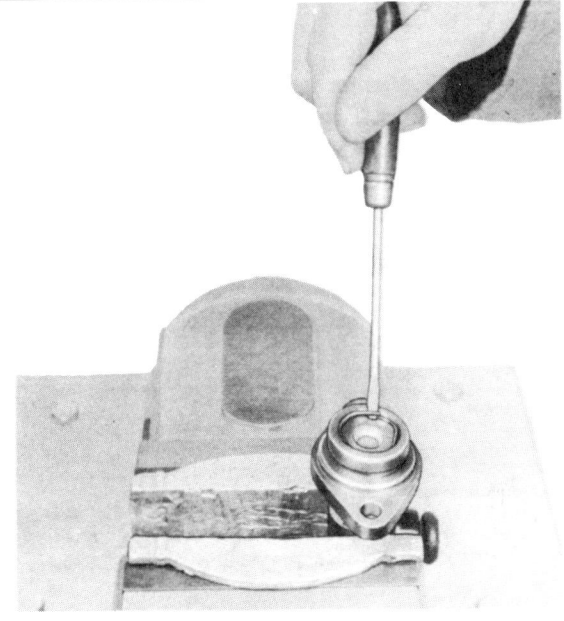

Fig. 8.18. Removing the lock ring (Sec. 6)

Fig. 8.19. Single master cylinder-exploded view (Sec. 6)

1 Housing	7 Piston stop plate
2 Special check valve	8 Lock ring
3 Spring	9 Washer
4 Primary piston cup	10 Grommet
5 Piston and washer	11 Boot
6 Secondary piston cup	

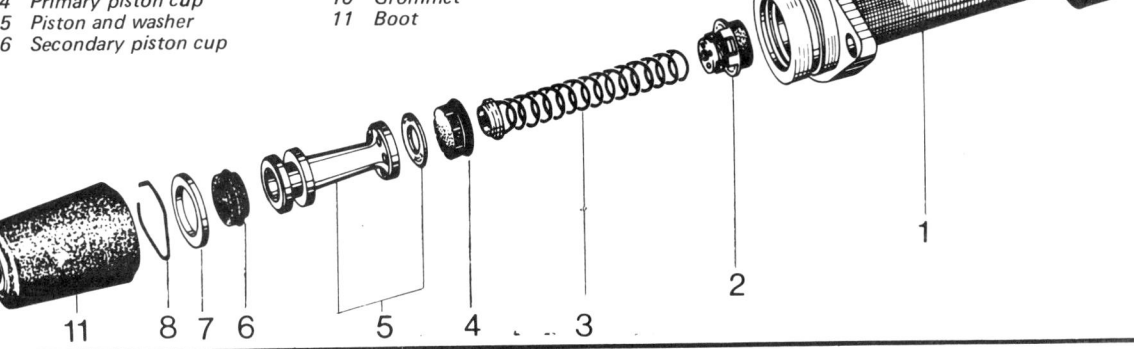

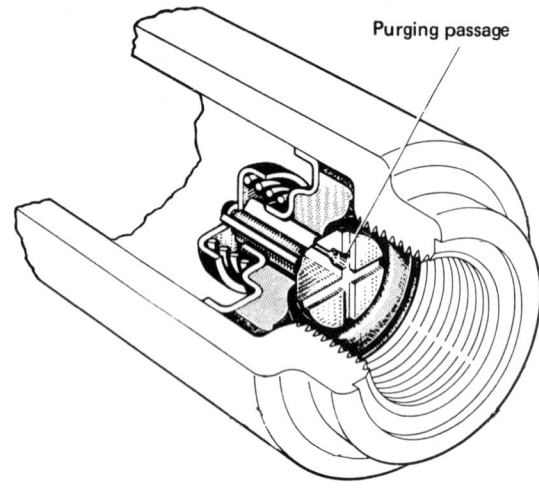

Fig. 8.20. Check valve purging passage (Sec. 6)

8   Remove the secondary piston stop bolt and gasket, then apply air from an air line or tyre pump at the secondary pressure port (approximately 15 lb f/sq. in/1 kg/sq. cm) to blow out the secondary piston. Cover the holes from which air is escaping as necessary.

9   Remove the spring, spring seat and supporting washer.

10 Secure the stem of the primary piston in a vice, using jaw clamps and, whilst depressing the spring to avoid damaging the screw threads, remove the stroke limiting bolt.

11 Remove the stop sleeve, stroke limiting bolt, spring, spring seat and supporting washer from the primary piston.

12 On USA models remove the brake failure warning light switch and cap screw. Blow out the plungers and springs using compressed air from an airline or tyre pump.

13 Discard all the rubber parts, and carefully clean the metal parts in methylated spirit, isopropyl-alcohol or clean brake fluid. Renew the appropriate parts if there is any evidence of wear, scoring or corrosion. Ensure that all drillings and passageways are clean and free from obstruction.

14 Assembly is now the reverse of the removal procedure, all parts being lubricated with clean brake fluid. Assemble the parts to the secondary piston, as shown in Fig. 8.21 and install with the large

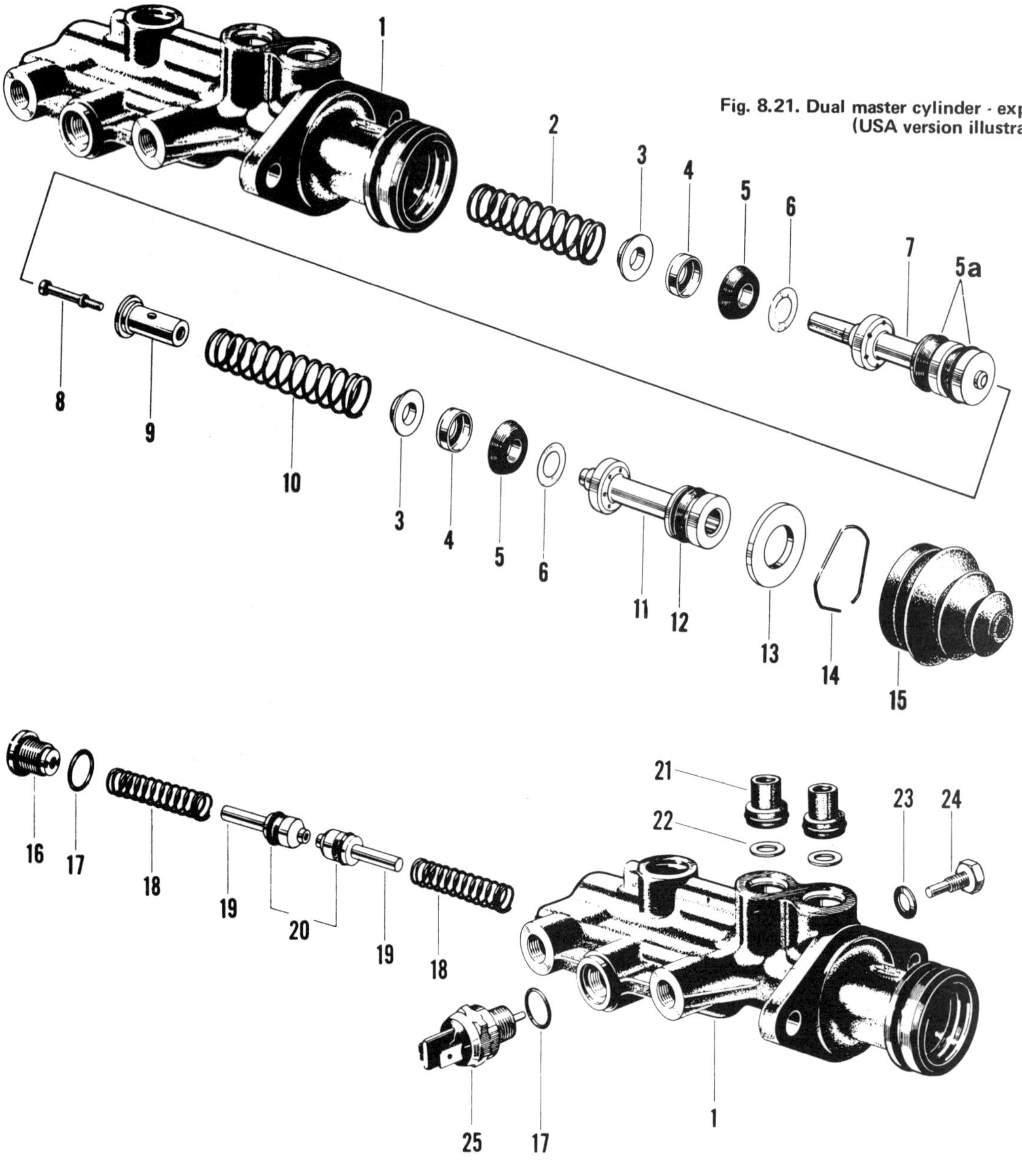

Fig. 8.21. Dual master cylinder - exploded view (Sec. 6)
(USA version illustrated)

1   Housing
2   Secondary piston return spring
3   Spring seat
4   Supporting washer
5   Primary cup
5a Primary collar
6   Filler disc
7   Secondary piston
8   Stroke limiting bolt
9   Travel stop sleeve
10 Primary piston return spring
11 Primary piston
12 Secondary cup
13 Stop plate
14 Lock ring
15 Boot
16 Bolt
17 O-ring
18 Spring
19 Piston
20 Piston cup
21 Grommet
22 Washer
23 Gasket
24 Stop bolt
25 Circuit failure warning switch

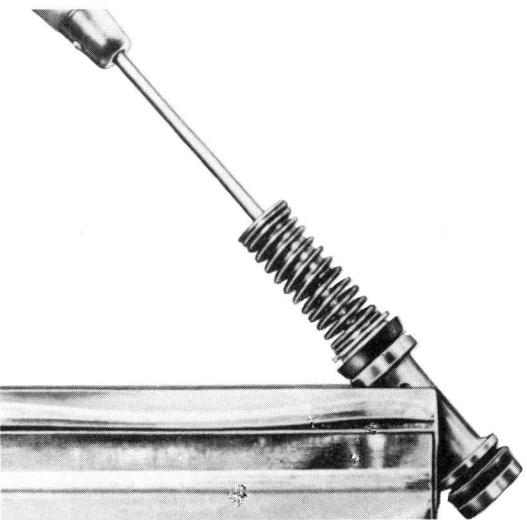

Fig. 8.22. Removing the stroke limiting bolt (Sec. 6)

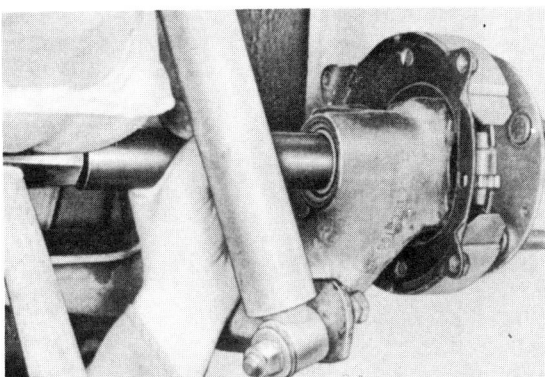

Fig. 8.23. Removing the rear hub (Sec. 8)

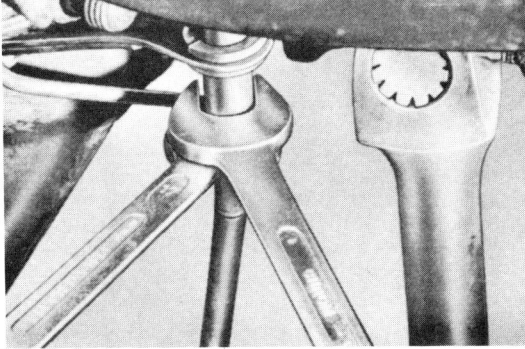

Fig. 8.24. Slackening the outer cable adjusting nuts (Sec. 9)

coil of the spring towards the bottom of the housing.

15 Push in the secondary piston with a non-metallic tool to clear the stop bolt hole, then install the stop bolt using a new gasket.

16 Assemble the primary piston as shown in Fig. 8.21, securing the assembly with the stroke limiting bolt. Install the piston and retain it with the stop plate and lock ring; ensure that the lock ring is correctly seated.

17 On USA models, install the parts associated with the brake failure warning light switch.

7 Hydraulic brake system - bleeding

Bleeding the hydraulic system is not part of any routine maintenance programme but will be needed where air has entered the system after items have been disconnected. If excessive pedal travel or 'sponginess' is experienced, a temporary cure may be effected by bleeding the system, but this must be taken as a warning that a leak in the system has occurred. This may be due to a leaking seal or pipe, and must be attended to without delay.

1   To bleed the system, first obtain help from an assistant then gather together a clean glass or plastic jar, a 12 in (300 mm) length of rubber or plastic tubing which will fit firmly over the bleed nipple, and a tin of brake fluid to the correct specification.

2   Place the end of the tube in the jar, together with about ½ in (13 mm) of brake fluid. Wipe the first bleed nipple clean and push the other end of the tube over it, working in the following order:

Right-hand drive cars
    a) *Right rear wheel, outer bleed nipple*
    b) *Right rear wheel, inner bleed nipple*
    c) *Left rear wheel, outer bleed nipple*
    d) *Left rear wheel, inner bleed nipple*
    e) *Left front wheel*
    f) *Right front wheel*

Left-hand drive cars
Follow the procedure for right-hand drive cars but for left read right, and vice versa.

3   Pump the pedal two or three times, then arrange for the assistant to open the bleed nipple by about ½ turn. The pedal will move to the floor, and air and fluid will be forced out. Before releasing the pedal the bleed valve should be closed.

4   Repeat the procedure until no more air is forced out, but all the time keep an eye on the reservoir fluid level.

5   Repeat the procedure on the remaining bleed nipples.

6   On completion, top-up the reservoir to approximately ¾ in (2 cm) from the top ridge. Do not re-use any of the fluid which has been bled from the system as it may contain moisture and other impurities. Finally check the brake action during a brief road test; on USA models also check the brake failure warning switch, as described in Section 5.

8 Handbrake carrier plate - removal and installation

1   Remove the rear brake caliper, as described in Section 3.

2   Remove the driveshaft, as described in Chapter 6.

3   Remove the rear hub by driving it out using a metal tube of suitable diameter.

4   Remove the retaining bolts and withdraw the brake carrier plate.

5   Installation is basically the reverse of the removal procedure. Ensure that all parts are clean, and if necessary renew the oil seal in the carrier plate. Pack the bearing races with a general purpose grease, and after installation use a new O-ring before the carrier plate is installed. Refer to Chapter 6 for the axle shaft nut tightening torque.

9 Handbrake cables - removal, installation and adjustment

1   Remove the handbrake support housing, as described in Section 10, then raise the car and remove both rear roadwheels.

2   Detach the cables from the equalizer.

3   Remove the caliper and brake disc, as described in Section 3.

4   Remove the cotter pin, castellated nut and disc, then pull out the cable from behind the brake assembly.

5   Pull the other end of the cable out of the tube in the centre tunnel.

6   When installing, coat the cable with a general purpose grease, then feed it into the centre tunnel tube.

7   At the brake/hub end, place one washer between the spacer sleeve and brake expander, and the other under the castellated nut. Turn the nut to align a slot with the cotter pin hole, then install a new cotter pin. Take care to ensure that the expander is seating correctly.

8   Install the caliper (Section 3), install the handbrake support housing (Section 10), bleed the brake system (Section 7) and adjust the handbrake, as described below.

Handbrake adjustment

9   With the rear wheels raised from the ground and the car supported on axle stands, release the handbrake and push back the brake pad so that the disc rotates freely.

10 Slacken the outer cable adjusting nuts on the brake backplate to

remove any pre-tensioning of the cable.

11 Insert a screwdriver through the hole in the drum and fully tighten the adjusting sprocket so that the drum cannot be turned by hand.

12 Repeat this procedure for the other brake, then tighten the adjusting nuts to just remove any cable slackness.

13 Pull up the tunnel cover and handbrake lever boot sufficiently to check the position of the equalizer by looking through the two inspection holes. Adjust the equaliser if necessary, so that it is at right-angles to the major axis of the car, by repositioning the adjuster nuts. Ensure that the locknuts are tightened afterwards .

14 Back-off the adjusting sprocket by 4 to 5 teeth on each wheel so that the disc can turn freely.

15 Check that the handbrake lever is operating correctly. When pulled up four notches of the ratchet, the handbrake should be on.

16 Before driving the car, depress the brake pedal repeatedly to force the pistons into the operating position, then check the reservoir fluid level.

Handbrake warning light switch adjustment

17 Pull up the tunnel cover and handbrake lever boot, then raise the handbrake lever by one notch of the ratchet.

18 Loosen the single screw and reposition the switch contact block, if necessary, so that the warning light just comes on.

19 Tighten the screw and recheck the operation

10 Handbrake support housing - removal, dismantling, reassembly and installation

1   Remove the tunnel cover and handbrake lever duct boot, then tap off the heater control lever knob(s).

2   Remove the bolts retaining the handbrake support housing.

3   On pre-1975 models, remove the nut securing the heater control lever, then withdraw the cup spring, pressure disc, friction disc and heater control lever.

4   On 1975 models remove the nut securing the hand throttle lever, then remove the friction disc.

5   Raise the handbrake support housing, then unsnap and pull out the cable equalizer retainer stud.

6   Detach the electrical wires and control cables from the support housing.

7   If necessary, the handbrake support housing can be dismantled. Figs. 8.31 and 8.32 show the two types in sectioned views; when assembling, ensure that all components are installed in the order shown and adjust the self-locking nuts to obtain the correct operating load.

8   Installation of the handbrake support housing is the reverse of the removal procedure. Adjust the heater controls, as described in Chapter 1, adjust the hand throttle, as described in Chapter 2, and the handbrake as described in Section 9.

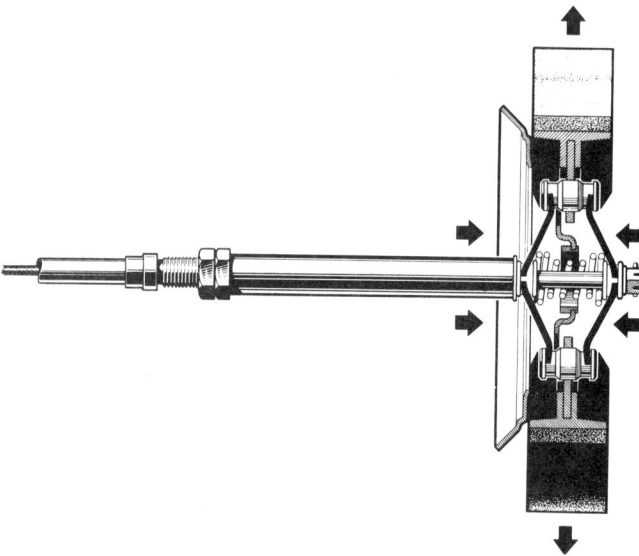

Fig. 8.25. Handbrake assemblied - sectional view (Sec. 9) Arrows show direction of relative movement

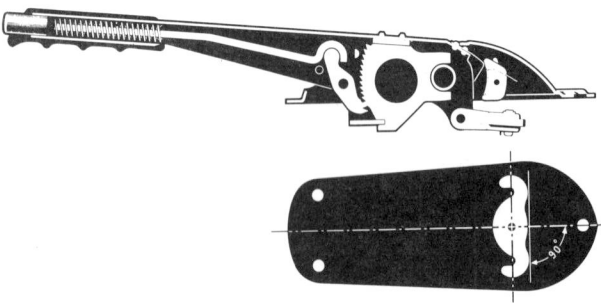

Fig. 8.26. Handbrake lever - sectional view, showing position of equalizer (Sec. 9)

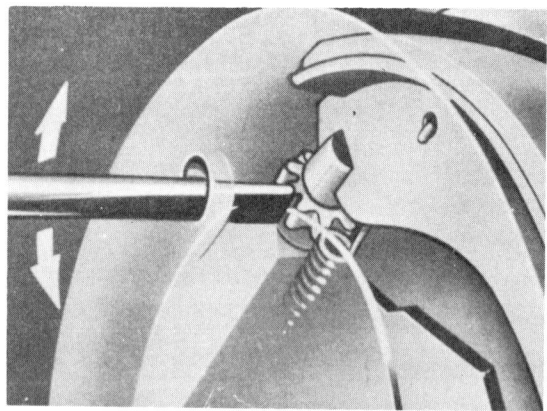

Fig. 8.27. Rotating the adjusting sprocket with a screwdriver (Sec. 9)

Fig. 8.28. Handbrake switch contact block screw (arrowed) (Sec. 9)

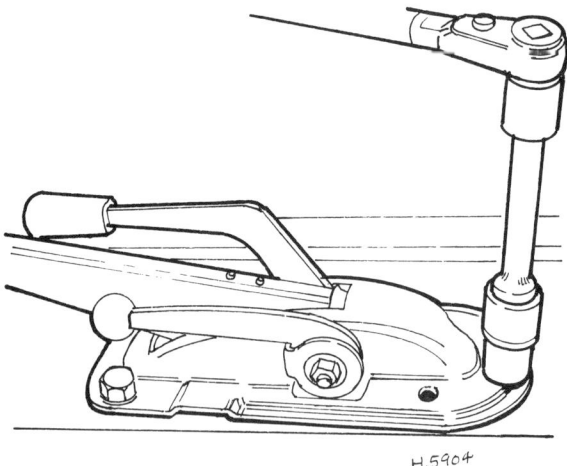

H.5904

Fig. 8.29. Removing the handbrake support housing (Sec. 10)

Fig. 8.30. Cable equalizer retainer (arrowed) (Sec. 10)

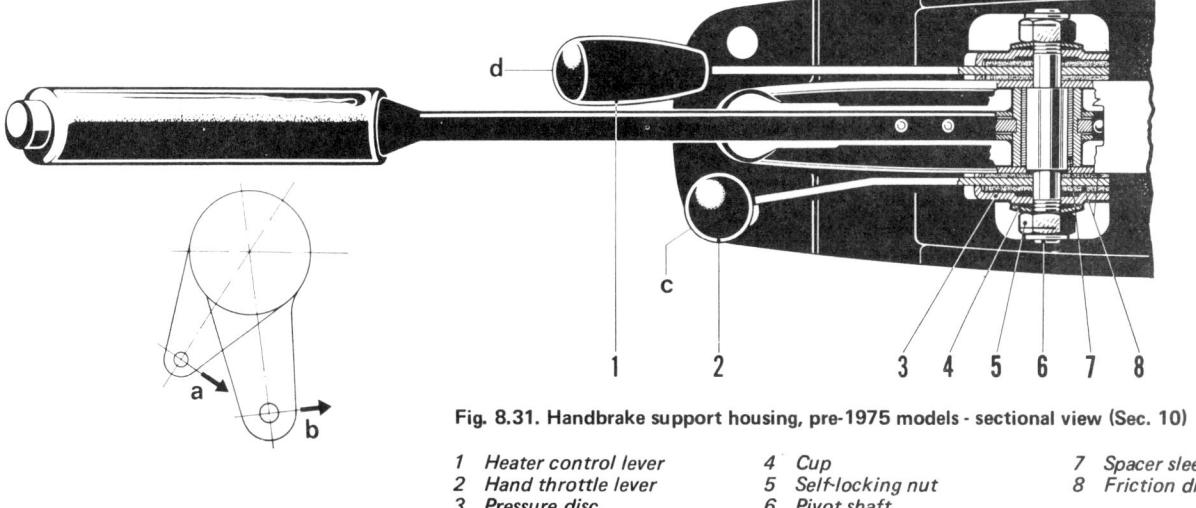

Fig. 8.31. Handbrake support housing, pre-1975 models - sectional view (Sec. 10)

1 Heater control lever   4 Cup   7 Spacer sleeve
2 Hand throttle lever   5 Self-locking nut   8 Friction disc
3 Pressure disc   6 Pivot shaft

a Limiting friction of heater lever clutch is 10 kg (22 lb)
b Limiting friction of hand throttle clutch is 6 kg (13 lb)
c Hand throttle lever knob is pressed on (avoid damaging the knob)
d Heater lever knob is screwed on

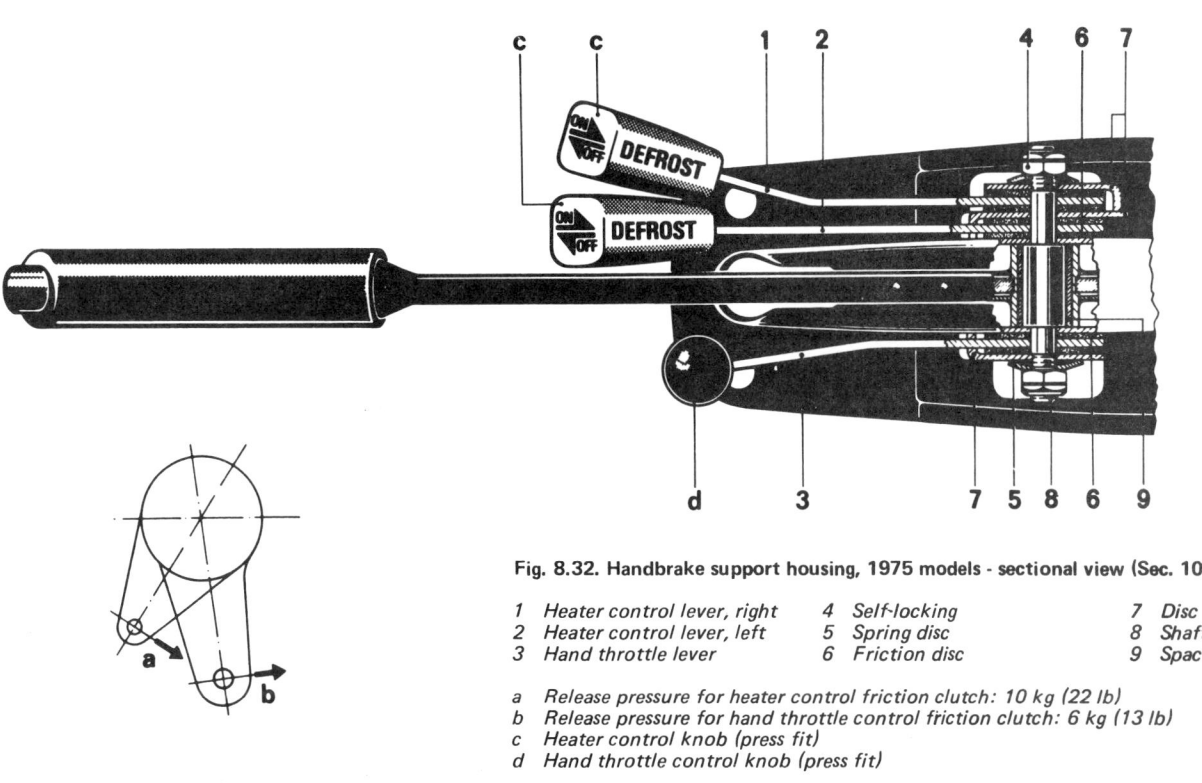

Fig. 8.32. Handbrake support housing, 1975 models - sectional view (Sec. 10)

1 Heater control lever, right   4 Self-locking   7 Disc
2 Heater control lever, left   5 Spring disc   8 Shaft
3 Hand throttle lever   6 Friction disc   9 Spacer

a Release pressure for heater control friction clutch: 10 kg (22 lb)
b Release pressure for hand throttle control friction clutch: 6 kg (13 lb)
c Heater control knob (press fit)
d Hand throttle control knob (press fit)

11 Stoplight switch - removal, installation and adjustment

Note: Some early models may have a hydraulic stoplight switch on the master cylinder. Removal is described in paragraphs 5, 6 and 7 of Section 5, but it is not necessary to remove the hydraulic lines. No adjustment is required, but it will be necessary to bleed the hydraulic system, as described in Section 7, on completion. The procedure given below is for the switch mounted on the fork pedal assembly.

1   Pull back the throttle pedal and detach it from the pushrod.
2   Remove the carpeting, then remove the single retaining nut and take out the floorboard, manœuvring it around the pedals.
3   Remove the two screws to release the switch, then detach the leads and withdraw the switch.
4   Installation is the reverse of the removal procedure, but to obtain the correct adjustment, place a packing piece 5/32 in (4 mm) thick between the brake pedal and its travel return stop. This is equivalent to a pedal travel of 0.827 in (21 mm) at the pedal pad. Now loosen the switch adjusting screw locknut, and adjust the screw so that the stop lights just illuminate. Lock the nut on completion.

12 Brake pedal - removal and installation

This forms part of the clutch and brake pedal assembly and is dealt with in Chapter 4.

13 Wheels and tyres

1   Many different types of wheels have been used on the Porsche 911 models and it is important that replacements are of the type originally fitted.
2   Wheels do not need any special maintenance but it is important that they are not damaged by careless driving such as hitting a kerb. If damage does occur to a wheel, it should be examined by a Porsche dealer and if found to be cracked or out-of-true, a replacement obtained.
3   Tyre fitting must be left to a specialist for fear of damaging the rims. Prior to March 24th 1971 where light alloy wheels were fitted, the tyres must be removed and installed from the inner side of the rim. After this date tyres should be removed and installed from the outer side of the rim.
4   The recommended tyres should be fitted with inner tubes, and new tubes used each time new tyres are fitted. After new tyres have been fitted, and at any time where undue tyre wear or wheel vibration is experienced, wheel balancing must be carried out. Where steel disc wheels are installed, conventional balance weights with spring clips are used; these should be used on the inside rim, if necessary, with 5½ J x 14 light-alloy wheels. For all other applications Porsche self-adhesive balance weights must be used.
5   When removing a wheel it is recommended that the installed position is noted to retain the optimum balance. When installing, a

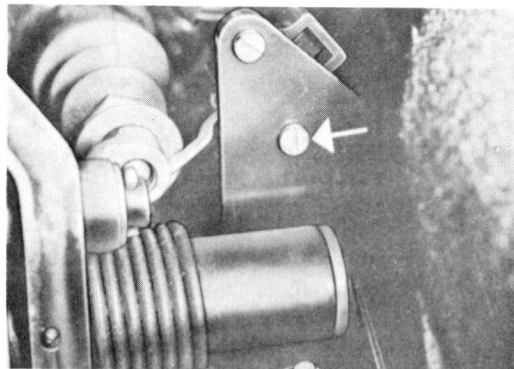

Fig. 8.33. Stoplight switch retaining screws (one arrowed) (Sec. 11)

Fig. 8.34. Stoplight switch showing adjusting screw (Sec. 11)

little molybdenum disulphide general purpose grease should be used to prevent the nuts from scuffing on the wheels.
6   Tyre pressures should be checked regularly when the tyres are cold. The recommended pressures are given in the Specifications, but individual drivers may find that slight adjustment is advantageous according to driving habits.
7   Cars with an 80 or 85 litre (17.5 or 18.6 Imp. gal/21.1 or 22.4 US gal) fuel tank have a collapsible tyre for use in emergencies. This should never be used for road speeds above 100 mph (160 km/hr). If this tyre is to be removed from the rim, it must be cut off. Fitting follows normal practice for conventional tyres.
8   For certain markets, studded (snow) tyres are available. Where these are considered necessary further information should be sought from a tyre specialist of a Porsche dealer.
9   In the event of a car being 'laid-up' for any length of time, it is recommended that the tyres are inflated to 60 lbf/sq.in. (4 kg/sq.in) to prevent flat spots from forming

14 Fault diagnosis - braking system

Before diagnosing faults in the braking system check that irregularities are not caused by any of the following faults:

1. *Incorrect mix of Radial and Crossply tyres*
2. *Incorrect tyre pressures*
3. *Wear in the steering mechanism, suspension or shock absorbers*
4. *Misalignment of the bodyframe*

Symptom	Reason/s	Remedy
Pedal travels a long way before the brakes operate	Disc pads worn past limit	Inspect and renew as necessary.
Stopping ability poor, pedal pressure firm	Pads or discs worn, contaminated, or wrong type	Renew pads and discs as necessary.
	One or more caliper piston seized	Inspect and repair as necessary.
Car veers to one side when brakes are applied	Brake pads on one side contaminated with oil or hydraulic fluid	Remove and renew. Repair source of oil leakage.
	Hydraulic pistons in calipers seized or sticking	Overhaul caliper.
	Wrong pads fitted	Install correct pads.
Pedal feels spongy when brakes are applied	Master cylinder or brake caliper loose	Tighten bolts.
	Air in the hydraulic system	Bleed brakes and check for signs of leakage. Top up reservoir.
	Spring weak in master cylinder	Repair master cylinder.
	Brake disc distorted	Renew brake disc.
Pedal travels right down with no resistance and brakes do not operate	Fluid reservoir empty	Check refill and bleed all brakes.
	Hydraulic lines fractured	Trace through and replace as necessary.
	Seals in master cylinder have failed	Dismantle cylinder and rebuild with new seals.
Brakes overheat or bind when car is in motion	Compensating port in master cylinder blocked	Rebuild cylinder.
	Reservoir air vent blocked	Clean vent.
	Connecting rod required adjustment	Adjust.
	Caliper piston seals swollen	Replace.
	Unsuitable brake fluid	Drain and refill system.
Brakes judder or chatter and tend to grab	Pads worn	Replace.
	Dirt in calipers	Clean.
	Discs runout excessive	Replace.
Disc pads squeak	Wrong type of pad fitted	Fit new pads.
	Pad guide surfaces dirty	Clean.
	Spreader spring deficient or broken	Fit new spring.
	Pads glazed	Fit new pads.
	Lining on pad not secure	Fit new pads.
Handbrake ineffective	Cable requires adjustment	Adjust as necessary.
	Linings worn or contaminated	Inspect and renew or repair.
	Brake drums worn or contaminated	Inspect and renew or repair.

15 Fault diagnosis - tyres

Wear description	Probable cause
Rapid wear of the centre of the tread all round the circumference	Tyre overinflated.
Rapid wear at both edges of the tread, wear even all round the circumference	Tyre underinflated.
Wear on one edge of the tyre:	
Front wheels only	Steering geometry needs checking.
Rear wheels only	Check rear suspension for damage.
Scalloped edges, wear at the edge at regular spacing around the tyre	Maybe wheel out of balance, or more likely wear on the steering knuckle.
Flat or rough patches on the tread	Caused by harsh braking. Check the brake adjustment.
Cuts and abrasions on the wall of the tyre	Usually done by running into the kerbstone.

Chapter 9 Electrical system

Contents

Specifications

System type	12 Volt, negative earth (ground)

Battery

Up to 1969	45 Amp hr.
1969/1973	Twin 36 Amp hr.
1974 onwards	66 Amp hr.

Alternator

Up to 1969	Bosch 500 W or Motorola 490 W
1969/1974	770 W
1975 (early)	840 W
1975 (Late, onwards)	980 W

Alternator regulator	Electromagnetic type (must be same make as alternator)

Starter motor

Up to 1972	0.8 HP Bosch pre-engaged
1972	1.5 HP Bosch pre-engaged (except 911 TV/Sportomatic models)
1973 onwards	1.5 HP Bosch pre-engaged (northern hemisphere and Canada)
	0.8 HP Bosch pre-engaged (other markets except 2.7 litre Carrera)

Lighting system bulb chart

Up to 1969

	Wattage or candle power (C.P.)
Headlamps	45/40 W
Sealed beam inserts (US)	50/40 W
Parking number plate	4 W
Parking lamps (Italy)	3 W
Direction indicators	18 W
Direction indicators (Italy)	15 W
Direction indicators/back-up lamps (USA)	32 CP
Stop/tail (USA)	32/4 CP
Stop/tail	18/5 W
Reverse lamps	25 W
Interior lights	10 W
Luggage compartment light	5 W
Instrument and control lights	2 W
Parking lamps (USA)	2 CP

Specifications

1969 model onwards:	Wattage or candle power (CP)
Quartz-iodine headlamps (H1-up to 1973)	55 W
Quartz-iodine headlamps (H4 - 1973 onwards)	60/55 W
Sealed beams (USA)	50/40 W
Double filament headlamps	45/40 W
Foglights (quartz-iodine)	55W
Foglights (spherical bulbs)	35 W
Direction indicators (Europe)	21 W
Front turn signals, stop lights, rear lights (USA)	32/4 CP
Rear turn signals (USA)	32 CP
Sidelight, number plate light (except USA)	4 W
Sidelight, number plate light (USA)	2 CP
Stop/tail (Europe)	5W
Reverse lights (Europe)	18 W
Back-up lights (USA)	15 CP
Interior light	10 W
Luggage compartment light	5 W
Instrument and control lights	2 W

Fuses and protected circuits

1965/68 models

Fuse No.	Protected circuits	Fuse rating (amps)
1	Stop, reverse, indicator lights	8/15
2	Interior light, clock, cigarette lighter	8/15
3	Auxiliary heater	25/40
4	Windscreen wipers, washers	25/40
5	Foglamps	8/15
6	Number plate light, luggage compartment light	8/15
7	Sidelight, RH	8/15
8	Sidelight, LH	8/15
9	Dipped beam, RH	8/15
10	Dipped beam, LH	8/15
11	Main beam, RH and warning light	8/15
12	Main beam, LH	8/15

Late 1968/69 models:

	Fuse rating (amps)
Electric windows, windscreen wipers, emergency flashers	25/40
Cigarette lighter, stop lights, sunroof	16/25
Headlight high and low beams	8/15
Direction indicators, parking (side) lights, number plate lights ...	5/9

1970/73 models:

Fuse box no. 1 (top)		Fuse box no. 2 (lower)		Fuse box no. 3 (in engine compartment)	
Fuse No.	Rating (amps)	Fuse No.	Rating (amps)	Fuse No.	Rating (amps)
1	5	1	8	1	5
2	16	2	8	2	8
3	25	3	8	3	25
4	16	4	8		
5	16	5	5		
6	25	6	5		
7	25	7	5		
8	16	8	16		
9	5				
10	5				

1974/75 models:

Fuse No.	Protected circuits	Fuse rating (amps)/Luggage compartment fuse box
1	Fog lights	16
2	Number plate light	5
3	Side lights, right	5
4	Side lights, left	5
5	Dipped beam, right	8
6	Dipped beam, left	8
7	Main beam, right	8
8	Main beam, left and warning light	8
9	Front indicator, right	5
10	Front indicator, left	5
11	Stoplights, reverse lights, flasher relay	16

1974/75 models:
Fuse No.
Fuse rating (amps)/Luggage compartment fuse box

12	Rear window defroster relay, fresh air blower, rear window defroster warning light	25
13	Windscreen wiper, washer pump	25
14	Electric sunroof, rear window wiper	16
15	Auxiliary heater, cigarette lighter, blower switch control light	16
16	Power windows	25
17	Emergency flasher	16
18	Interior lights, clock, glove compartment light, luggage compartment lighting	5

Note: *An additional 3-fuse block may be installed on some models, the middle fuse (25 amp) being for the headlamp washer system.*

Engine compartment fusebox

Fuse No.	Protected circuits	Fuse rating (amps)
1	Heater fan relay, Sportomatic	5
2	Starting valve (Carrera only) heater fan	25
3	Rear window defroster	25

Torque wrench settings

	lbf ft	kgf m
Alternator pulley nut	29	4

1 General description

1   The electrical system is a 12 volt, negative earth type, comprising an alternator and its associated regulator, one or two batteries (according to the particular model), the starter motor, the ancillaries such as lighting equipment, windscreen wipers, etc., and the associated wiring and protective circuits.
2   The battery provides starting power and a reserve of energy should the loading of the system exceed the alternator output. Where any reference is made to the battery in this Chapter, it is equally applicable to the second battery (if so equipped), unless otherwise stated.
3   When installing electrical accessories to your vehicle it is important to ensure that they are suitable for negative earth vehicles (most vehicles are negative earth, but accessories are still available for positive earth systems). Equipment which incorporates semi-conductor devices may well be permanently damaged if they are not suited to your particular system.
4   If the battery is to be boost-charged from an external charging source, it is important to disconnect the battery positive cable in order to protect the semi-conductor devices in the alternator and possibly any electrical accessories which may have been installed. Similarly, when any electric (arc) welding or power tools are used the same precaution should be taken.

2 Battery - removal and installation

The battery is housed in the luggage compartment at the left-hand side, and is usually beneath the floor covering. 1969/73 models have a second battery at the opposite side, connected in parallel to the first one.
1   To remove a battery, first disconnect the earth lead, followed by the positive lead, then remove the retaining bracket bolt(s). The battery can then be lifted out. NOTE: Where two batteries are installed, and only one is being removed, do not allow the two disconnected leads to touch together, or the positive lead to become earthed (photo).
2   Installation is the reverse of the removal procedure. Ensure that the terminals and leads are clean, and lightly smear them with a little petroleum jelly before tightening them.

3 Battery - maintenance

1   Normal weekly battery maintenance consists of checking the electrolyte level of each cell to ensure that the separators are covered by ¼ inch of electrolyte. If the level has fallen, top-up the battery using distilled or de-ionized water. Do not overfill. If the battery is

2.1 Removing the right-hand battery on a 1969 model

overfilled, or any electrolyte spilled, immediately wipe away the excess, as electrolyte attacks and corrodes any metal it comes into contact with very rapidly. In an emergency, where the electrolyte level is too low, it is permissible to use boiled drinking water which has been allowed to cool but this is not recommended as a regular practice.
2   If the battery terminals are showing signs of corrosion, brush or scrape off the worst, taking care not to get the deposits on the vehicle paintwork or your hands. Prepare a solution of household ammonia, washing soda or bicarbonate of soda and water. Brush this onto all the corroded parts, taking care that none enters the battery. This will neutralize the corrosion and when all the fizzing and bubbling has stopped the parts can be wiped clean with a dry, lint-free cloth. Do not forget to smear the terminals and clamps with petroleum jelly afterwards to prevent further corrosion.
3   Inspect the battery clamp and mounting tray and treat these in the same way. Where the paintwork has been damaged, after neutralizing, the area can be painted with a zinc based primer and the appropriate finishing colour, or an underbody paint can be used.
4   At the same time inspect the battery case for cracks. If a crack is found, clean and plug it with one of the proprietary compounds marketed for this purpose. If leakage through the crack has been excessive then it will be necessary to refill the appropriate cell with fresh electrolyte as described later. Cracks are frequently caused at the top of the battery case by pouring in distilled water in the middle

of winter *after* instead of *before* a run. This gives the water no chance to mix with the electrolyte and so the former freezes and splits the battery case.

5   If topping-up becomes excessive and the case has been inspected for cracks that could cause leakage, but none are found, the battery is being overcharged and the voltage regulator will have to be checked and reset.

6   With the battery on the bench, measure the specific gravity with a hydrometer to determine the state of charge and condition of the electrolyte. There should be very little variation between the different cells and, if a variation in excess of 0.025 is present, it will be due to either:

    a) *Loss of electrolyte from the battery at some time caused by spillage or a leak, resulting in a drop in the specific gravity of the electrolyte when the deficiency was replaced with distilled water instead of fresh electrolyte.*

    b) *An internal short circuit caused by buckling of the plates or similar malady pointing to the likelihood of total battery failure in the near future.*

7   The specific gravity of the electrolyte for fully charged conditions at the electrolyte temperature indicated, is listed in Table A. The specific gravity of a fully discharged battery at different temperatures of the electrolyte is given in Table B.

Table A

Specific gravity - battery fully charged.

1.268 at 100°F or 38°C electrolyte temperature
1.272 at 90°F or 32°C electrolyte temperature
1.276 at 80°F or 27°C electrolyte temperature
1.280 at 70°F or 21°C electrolyte temperature
1.284 at 60°F or 16°C electrolyte temperature
1.288 at 50°F or 10°C electrolyte temperature
1.292 at 40°F or 4°C electrolyte temperature
1.296 at 30°F or -1.5°C electrolyte temperature

Table B

Specific gravity - battery fully discharged.

1.098 at 100°F or 38°C electrolyte temperature
1.102 at 90°F or 32°C electrolyte temperature
1.106 at 80°F or 27°C electrolyte temperature
1.110 at 70°F or 21°C electrolyte temperature
1.114 at 60°F or 16°C electrolyte temperature
1.118 at 50°F or 10°C electrolyte temperature
1.122 at 40°F or 4°C electrolyte temperature
1.126 at 30°F or -1.5°C electrolyte temperature

4   Battery - electrolyte replenishment

1   If the battery is in a fully charged state and one of the cells maintains a specific gravity reading which is 0.025 or lower than the others, and a check of each cell has been made with a voltage meter to check for short circuits (a four to seven second test should give a steady reading of between 1.2 and 1.8 volts), then it is likely that electrolyte has been lost from the cell with the low reading at some time.

2   Topup the cell with a solution of 1 part sulphuric acid to 2.5 parts of distilled or de-ionized water. If the cell is already fully topped up draw some electrolyte out of it with a pipette.

3   **When mixing the sulphuric acid and water never add water to sulphuric acid** — always pour the acid slowly onto the water in a glass container. **If water is added to sulphuric acid it will explode.**

4   Continue to top up the cell with the freshly made electrolyte and to recharge the battery and check the hydrometer readings.

5   Battery - charging

Note: If a battery is to remain in the vehicle when being charged always disconnect the battery positive lead.

1   In winter when a heavy demand is placed on the battery, such as when starting from cold, and much electrical equipment is continually in use, it is a good idea to occasionally have the battery fully charged from an external source at a rate of approximately 4 amps.

2   Continue to charge the battery at this rate until no further rise in specific gravity is noted over a four hour period.

3   Alternatively, a trickle charger, charging at the rate of 1.5 amps

can be safely used overnight.

4   Special rapid 'boost' charges which are claimed to restore the power of the battery in 1 to 2 hours are most dangerous unless they are thermostatically controlled as they can cause serious damage to the battery plates through overheating.

5   While charging the battery note that the temperature of the electrolyte should never exceed 100°F (37.8°C).

6   Alternator - general information and precautions

1   The alternator charging system comprises the alternator, the regulator, the battery and the associated wiring.

2   The alternator is driven by a 'V' belt from the engine. Current is supplied from the alternator/regulator system to slip rings, via two brushes.

3   Power is generated in the form of alternating current which is then rectified by six diodes for battery charging. The alternator regulator automatically adjusts the field current to maintain the prescribed output voltage.

4   When the ignition is switched on, current passes to the alternator field and as the engine is started the alternator field rotates causing the alternator to generate a voltage.

5   It must be appreciated that the semi-conductors in the alternator can easily be permanently damaged by inadvertently reversing the battery terminals or disconnecting one battery lead while the engine is running.

6   The manufacturers recommend that Bosch alternators are dismantled annually or at major engine overhauls for inspection of the brushes and relubrication of the bearings. No servicing is recommended for the Motorola alternator.

7   Alternator - testing in the car

Under normal circumstances there is no need to check the alternator operation. However, if the ignition (alternator) warning light does not illuminate when the ignition is switched on, or it does not extinguish when the engine is running above idle speed, or where its operation is erratic, or where the battery fails to hold a charge and has been established as being serviceable, the following check-out procedure may be performed.

Bosch alternators

1   Obtain a voltmeter (0.20V dc), an ammeter (0.60 amp dc) and a variable resistor of 500 watt rating (0.5 ohm, approx), and connect as shown in Fig. 9.1. Ensure that the drive belt tension is correct - see Chapter 1.

2   Run the engine and keep the speed steady at 3000 rpm. Check that at a load current of 28 to 30 amp, the voltage is 13.5 to 14.5 volts. If these values cannot be obtained, further testing of the alternator and/or regulator should be carried out by your Porsche dealer or auto electrical specialist.

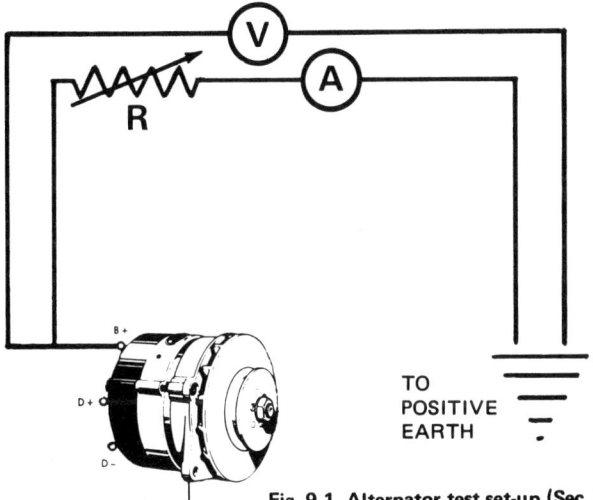

TO POSITIVE EARTH

Fig. 9.1. Alternator test set-up (Sec. 7)

Fig. 9.2. Shroud attaching bolts (arrowed) (Sec. 8)

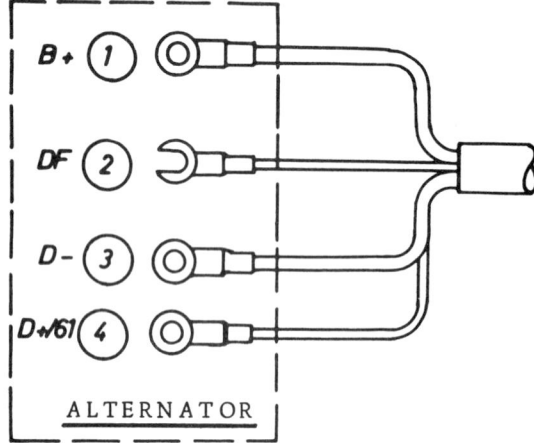

Fig. 9.3. Alternator lead connections (Sec. 8)

1 *Red/white*   2 *Black*   3 *Brown*   4 *Red*

Fig. 9.4. Removing the brush plate (Bosch) (Sec. 9)

Fig. 9.5. Separating the two halves of the alternator (Bosch) (Sec. 9)

Motorola alternators

3 The procedure is as described for the Bosch alternator except that a voltage of 13.4 to 14.6 volts should be obtained at an engine speed of 2500 ± 150 rpm.

8 Alternator - removal and installation

1 Remove the battery earth lead.
2 Remove the air intake silencer (refer to Chapter 2, if necessary), and the upper blower shroud attaching bolts.
3 Using a suitable peg spanner to prevent the impeller from turning (tool P 208 is available for this purpose), remove the pulley nut and take off the drivebelt.
4 Remove the bolts from the blower housing strap, ease the blower housing and alternator rearwards, and detach the alternator wires.
5 Installation is the reverse of the removal procedure. Ensure that the blower housing seals in the dowel in the crankcase, then tighten the nut to the specified torque. If necessary, check and adjust the drivebelt tension, as described in Chapter 1.

9 Alternator - dismantling, testing, servicing and reassembly

Note: Before attempting to dismantle and repair the alternator, it must be appreciated that more harm than good can be done by anyone not familiar with repair techniques on semi-conductor devices. Also, before dismantling, ensure that there are spare parts available since it is unlikely that any individual components will be capable of being repaired. If parts are not available, or you feel that you do not have the knowledge and experience to do the job yourself, either purchase an exchange unit or entrust the job to a specialist in this type of work.

Bosch alternator

1 Remove the pulley nut, pulley, hub and key.
2 Mark the installed position of the alternator in the blower housing.
3 Unscrew and remove the brush plate complete with brushes.
4 Remove the retaining bolts and separate the two halves of the alternator.
5 Using a suitable press, press the rotor assembly out of the end frame. If necessary, remove the rotor bearing using a puller, or support the assembly on suitable plates and press off the rotor. Take care to apply loads to the inner race only; if this is not possible damage may occur and a new bearing will be required.
6 Carefully open the lead retaining clamps and remove the insulating sleeves. Cut the wires as close to the soldered joint as possible.
7 The exciter diodes can now be tested using a continuity tester with a supply voltage not exceeding 24V dc. Ensure that there is continuity in one direction only. If only the exciter diodes are defective they may be renewed at this stage and no further dismantling need be carried out. Even if only one exciter diode is defective all three (positive or negative) must be renewed; make careful note of the connections before diodes are removed to ensure that replacements are correctly installed.
8 If rectifier diodes require renewal, the frame on the slip ring side will require further dismantling. Note the insulating bushes beneath the positive diode carrier; to remove the negative diode carrier use a

Fig. 9.6. Opening the lead retaining clamps (Bosch) (Sec. 9)

Fig. 9.7 . Removing exciter diodes (arrow shows diode) (Bosch) (Sec. 9)

Fig. 9.8. Removing rectifier diodes (Bosch) (Sec. 9)

Fig. 9.9. The longer fastening clip (arrowed) (Bosch) (Sec. 9)

Fig. 9.10. Cable ends ready for soldering (Bosch) (Sec. 9)

socket or box spanner to remove the threaded studs.

9   Parts may be cleaned by wiping with a petrol or solvent moistened cloth; do not soak any parts.

10 Stator windings can be checked for earthing using a 40V ac supply. Rotor windings can be checked in a similar manner.

11 Using a resistance tester (ohmmeter) check for a resistance of 0.26 ohm ± 10% between the phase output terminals. Check for a resistance of 4.0 ohms ± between the rotor slip rings.

12 If necessary, the slip rings may be dressed on a lathe. The maximum permissible run-out is 0.001 in (0.03 mm); the minimum diameter is 1.24 in (31.5 mm); the maximum permissible run-out of the complete rotor is 0.002 in (0.05 mm).

13 To remove the brushes, unsolder them at their terminals; renew them if they are less than 0.55 in (14 mm) long. Ensure that replacements are not binding in the brush holder, and that solder does not run excessively into the lead braiding.

14 Reassembly is now basically the reverse of the removal procedure, but the following points must be observed:

 a Lubricate the bearings with high melting point grease.

 b Install the negative diode plate and fastening clips, with the shorter threads of the studs facing outwards. Note that the left clip is the longer one.

 c Install the positive diode plate, insulating washers and spring washers, and install the insulating caps.

 d Put the stator in position, then connect together the strands of the positive and negative diode leads. Retain the leads with a sleeve, solder the ends together, then insulate them with a further sleeve or insulating tape.

Motorola alternator

15 A number of checks can be carried out on this alternator without the need for dismantling, and it is recommended that these are done before any repairs are considered. First remove the brush assembly retaining screws, then withdraw the cover plate and brush holder.

16 *Brush assembly test:* Using a suitable ohmmeter, there should be negligible resistance between one brush and the 'DF' terminal, and the other brush and the brush holder. There should be no continuity between the two brushes.

17 *Rotor test:* Using an ohmmeter there should be no continuity between the 'D-' terminal and the slip rings, but there should be a resistance of 4.5 to 6.5 ohms between the slip rings. If these readings are not obtained a new rotor must be installed. (Fig. 9.13)

18 *Isolation diode test:* To check for earthing of the isolation diode heat sink, connect an ohmmeter between terminal 'D+/61' and 'D-'. Change the lead polarity and check for an infinitely high resistance in one direction and less than 50 ohms in the other direction. If these values are not obtained it is likely that the diode heat sink insulator at the rear housing is faulty. To check the diodes, connect the ohmmeter between terminal 'D+/61' and 'B+'. Change the lead polarity and check for an infinitely high resistance in one direction and less than 50 ohms in the other. If these values are not obtained, renew the complete diode assembly. (Fig. 9.14)

19 *Rectifier diode test:* To check the neagative diodes, connect an ohmmeter between the diode terminal and 'D-'. Change the lead

Fig. 9.11. Removing the brush holder (Motorola) (Sec. 9)

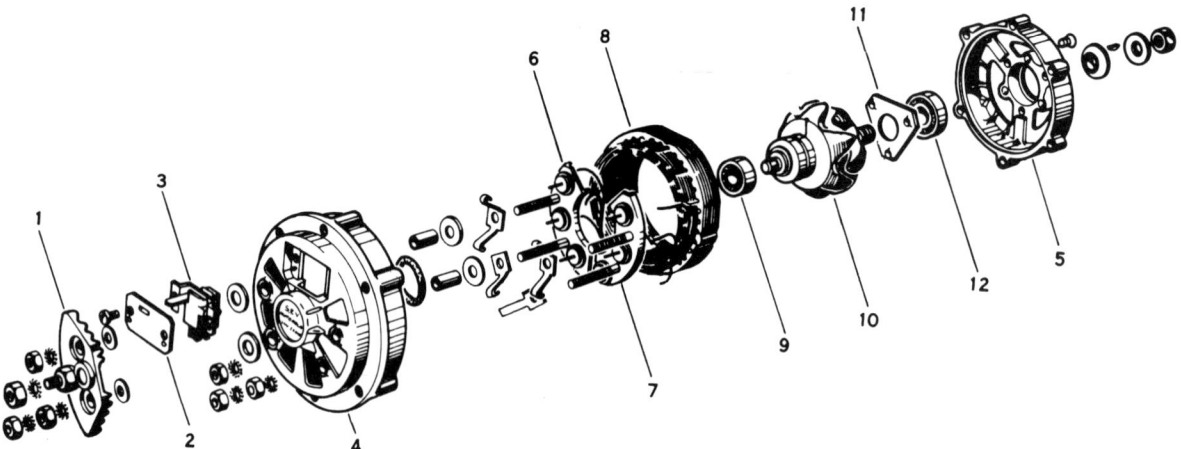

Fig. 9.12. Motorola alternator - exploded view (Sec. 9)

1 Isolation diode heat sink
2 Brush cover plate
3 Brush holder
4 Rear housing, (supporting bearing and rotor)
5 Front housing, (supporting bearing and rotor)
6 Positive diode heat sink
7 Negative diode heat sink
8 Stator
9 Ball bearing
10 Rotor
11 Bearing cover plate
12 Ball bearing

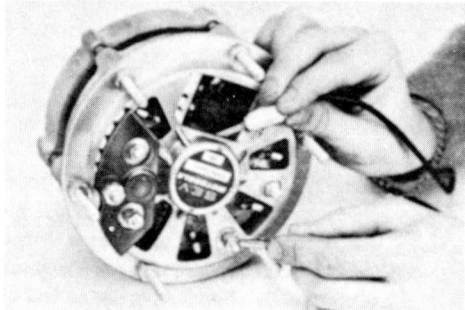

Fig. 9.13. Checking D-terminal to slip ring (Motorola) (Sec. 9)

Fig. 9.14. Checking for earthing of isolation diode heat sink (Motorola) (Sec. 9)

Fig. 9.15. Rectifier diode test (Motorola) (Sec. 9)

Fig. 9.16. Heat sink retaining nuts (Motorola) (Sec. 9)

polarity and check for an infinitely high resistance in one direction and less than 50 ohms in the other. If these values are not obtained, renew the complete diode assembly. Repeat this check for the positive diodes, but connect between the diode terminal and 'D+/61'.

20 To dismantle the alternator further, remove the retaining nuts from both ends of the heat sink and remove the isolation diode assembly.

21 Remove the nuts from the six through-bolts and separate the two halves of the alternator.

22 Press out the rotor from the front housing, then draw off the ball bearing from the rear of the rotor shaft using a suitable puller.

23 Remove the bearing cover and press out the bearing from the front cover.

24 Remove the diode assembly retaining nuts from the rear housing, then withdraw the stator and diode assemblies.

25 Mark the diode leads for identification, then unsolder them from the diodes.

26 Examine the stator coil for evidence of burning and/or local hot-spots. Using an ohmmeter, check that there is no short circuit between any of the stator leads and earth.

27 Parts may be cleaned by wiping with a petrol or solvent moistened cloth; do not soak any parts.

28 Reassembly is now basically the reverse of the removal procedure, but the following points must be observed:

a   *Ensure that the positive (red) diodes and negative (black) diodes are not mixed up.*

b   *When installing the stator and diode assemblies into the rear housing, place an insulating washer and sleeve on each of the retaining bolts of the positive diode assembly. Place two insulating washers onto the retaining bolts of the positive diode assembly after it is installed.*

c   *Ensure that the compensating bore in the rear housing is clean and unobstructed, and that the O-ring is in good condition.*

10 Voltage regulator

1   The alternator regulator is mounted on the left-hand sidewall of the engine compartment. It cannot be adjusted without the use of special equipment; if it is not operating correctly, it must be renewed or adjusted by a Porsche dealer or auto-electrical specialist.

2   If the regulator is to be removed, disconnect the battery earth lead, remove the regulator leads, noting their colours, and detach the regulator from its mounting.

3   Installation is the reverse of the removal procedure.

11 Starter motor - general description

1   The starter motor is a four-brush, four-pole, four-field wound type.

2   The main frame encloses a wound armature running in two bushings; this rotates between four pole shoes around which are four field coils.

3   The field coils are series-parallel connected, and are retained by the pole shoes which are attached to the starter frame.

4   A rubber grommet which prevents foreign matter entering the starter also isolates the field coil strap from the starter frame.

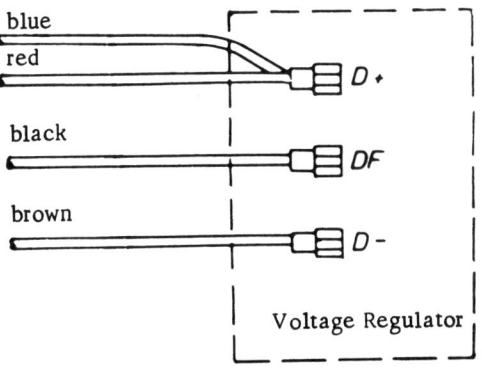

Fig. 9.17. Voltage regulator and connections (Sec. 10)

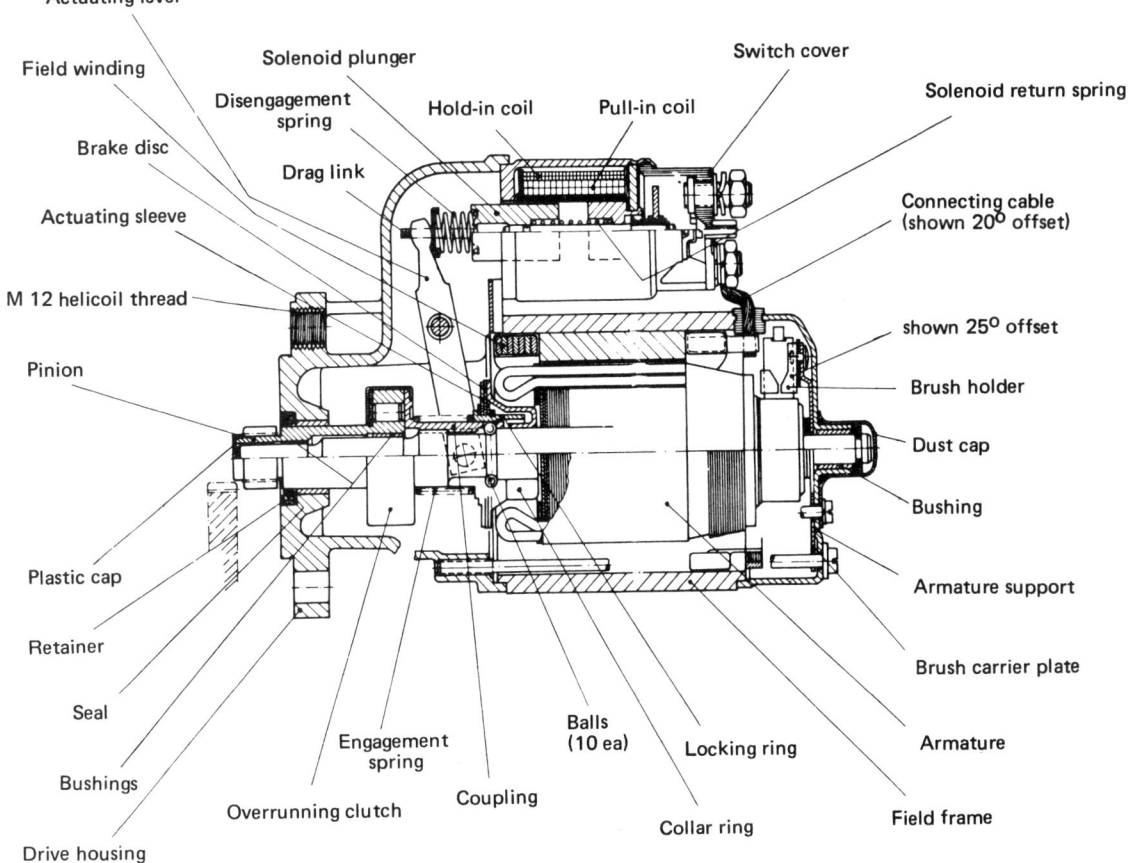

Fig. 9.18. Sectional view of typical starter motor (Sec. 11)

5   The solenoid assembly is mounted on the starter drive end housing and lies parallel to the motor body. The plunger and shift fork are enclosed in the drive end housing where they are protected from mud, dirt, grease, etc.

6   In the engine starting sequence the solenoid is energized from the ignition switch which moves the starter drive gear into mesh with the flywheel ring gear. At the same moment, the solenoid main contacts close and the motor is energized and starts to rotate.

7   As soon as the engine fires and the ignition key returns to the normal running position, the solenoid is de-energized. This cuts the supply to the motor and the solenoid return spring causes the shift fork to disengage the drive from the flywheel ring gear.

8   To prevent excessive motor speed as the engine fires, an overrunning clutch is incorporated in the drive gear assembly. The drive gear can therefore run at a faster speed than the armature during this brief period of time and disengages itself from the flywheel ring gear.

12 Starter motor - removal and installation

1   Disconnect the battery earth strap, then detach the battery and alternator cables from the starter motor (terminal 30).
2   Detach the solenoid feed wire (terminal 50) from the starter motor.
3   Remove the flange attachment bolts and lift out the starter.
4   Installation is the reverse of the removal procedure.

13 Starter motor - dismantling, testing, servicing and reassembly

Solenoid
1   Detach the braided wire from the lower terminal, then remove the retaining bolts to detach the solenoid.
2   Pull out the starter pinion a little so that the solenoid switch can be withdrawn.
3   Installation is the reverse of the removal procedures, but take care not to overtighten the cable retaining nuts or the switch contacts may be damaged. When installing a new solenoid switch, adjust the connecting end of the solenoid plunger so that a distance of 1.276 $\pm$ 0.004 in (32.4 $\pm$ 0.1 mm) exists between the hole centre in the plunger clevis to the switch mounting flange, when the plunger is in position. This provides a solenoid plunger travel of 0.394 $\pm$ 0.008 in (10 $\pm$ 0.2 mm).

Brush and commutator checks
4   Remove the end cover and examine the amount of brush material remaining. Brushes which do not protrude out of the brush holders must be renewed; ensure that replacements move freely in the brush holders.
5   Check the brush spring tension, which should be 1150 to 1350 gm (40.6 to 47.6 oz). If unsatisfactory, obtain replacements and install them.
6   Wipe the commutator clean with a petrol moistened cloth. If necessary, the surface can be skimmed on a lathe after further dismantling.
7   Installation of the brush gear is the reverse of the removal procedure.

Starter motor - 0.8 HP
8   Remove the dust cover, locking ring and spacers, taking care not to lose the O-rings.
9   Remove the solenoid as previously described, unhooking the solenoid plunger from the actuating lever.
10 Remove the through bolts and the commutator support.
11 Withdraw the brushes from the holders. The positive brushes are soldered to the field winding, and the negative ones to the brush holders.
12 Remove the brush carrier plate, noting the insulating washer and metal disc.
13 Take the field frame off the drive housing, noting the sealing rubber and metal plate. Take out the stud bolt from the housing.
14 Remove the armature and actuating lever from the drive housing.
15 Whilst holding the motor in a vice, press the actuating sleeve against the overrunning clutch. Remove it from the shaft, noting the locking balls.

Fig. 9.19. Removing the brushes (Sec. 13)

Fig. 9.20. After removing the brush carrier plate, remove the washer and metal disc (Sec. 13)

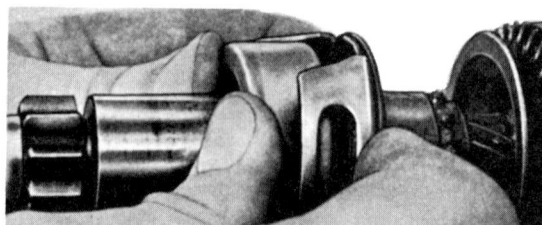

Fig. 9.21. Dismantling the overrunning clutch (Sec. 13)

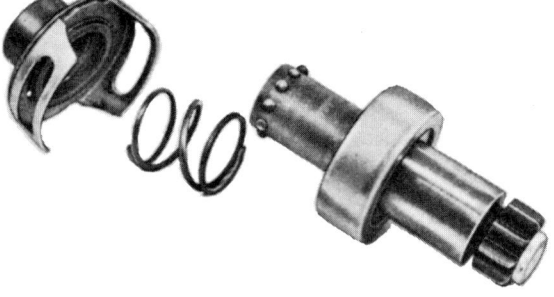

Fig. 9.22. The overrunning clutch parts (Sec. 13)

16 Clean the parts with compressed air, and a petrol or solvent moistened cloth. Do not immerse the armature or overrunning clutch in any solvent.
17 Examine all parts for wear and damage, obtaining replacements where necessary. Check the field coil for continuity using an ohmmeter. Test for earthing between the brush carrier plate and ground, between the field coils and ground, and between the armature segments and core, using a test voltage of 40 V AC.

18 Where necessary, the commutator can be skimmed provided that a minimum diameter of 1.319 in (33.5 mm) is maintained. The maximum permissible run-out is 0.002 in (0.05 mm). The segment insulation should be approximately 0.031 in (0.8 mm) below the commutator surface.

19 Bearing bushings can be replaced in the drive housing, but take care that replacements are not damaged as they are pressed in. When replacing the sintured metal bushing and sealing ring, use screws, nuts and spring washers and peen over the screw ends. Lubricate the bushing with engine oil, and other running parts with a general purpose grease.

20 When reassembling, first place the balls into the locking ring and retain them with grease.

21 Hold the armature in a vice, then push the overrunning clutch and actuating sleeve/brake disc onto the armature shaft until the balls engage the groove in the shaft.

22 Ensure that the pinion and overrunning clutch are properly seated on the armature shaft, then push the armature and actuating lever into the drive housing.

23 Screw the pivot stud of the actuating lever into the drive housing. The tab of the rubber grommet must seat in the cutout within the field frame.

24 Push the field frame over the armature, not forgetting the steel shims and insulating washer on the commutator side.

25 Place the brush carrier plate onto the commutator shaft and ensure that the spring tension is correct (see paragraph 5).

26 Install the dust cover. Ensure that the earth connections between the brush carrier plate and cover, and between the cover and housing, are bare and clean.

27 Install the spacer discs and lock ring so that an axial play of 0.004 to 0.006 in (0.1 to 0.15 mm) is obtained.

28 Install the commutator bearing cap followed by the solenoid plunger. Install the solenoid as previously described.

Starter motor - 1.5 HP

29 This starter is basically similar to the 0.8 HP starter, and is dismantled in a generally similar way. The component parts are shown in the order of dismantling in Fig. 9.23.

---

14 Headlamps

Headlamp bulb (early type) - renewal

1 Remove the crosshead screw in the lower centre of the lamp bezel and withdraw the lamp assembly.

2 Remove the cable connector, press in the retaining ring and rotate in an anticlockwise direction. Remove the retainer and take out the bulb.

3 Installation of the new bulb is straightforward but ensure that the aligning tab in the base of the bulb engages properly in the reflector cut-out. It is recommended that the beam alignment is checked on completion.

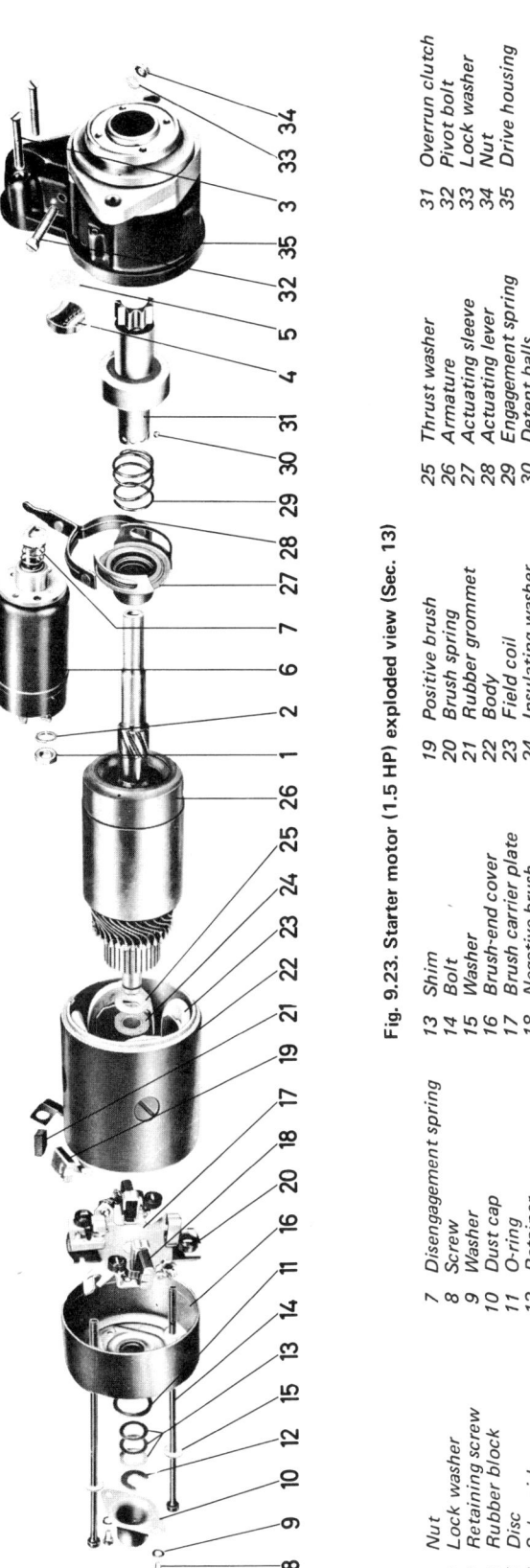

Fig. 9.23. Starter motor (1.5 HP) exploded view (Sec. 13)

1   Nut
2   Lock washer
3   Retaining screw
4   Rubber block
5   Disc
6   Solenoid
7   Disengagement spring
8   Screw
9   Washer
10 Dust cap
11 O-ring
12 Retainer
13 Shim
14 Bolt
15 Washer
16 Brush-end cover
17 Brush carrier plate
18 Negative brush
19 Positive brush
20 Brush spring
21 Rubber grommet
22 Body
23 Field coil
24 Insulating washer
25 Thrust washer
26 Armature
27 Actuating sleeve
28 Actuating lever
29 Engagement spring
30 Detent balls
31 Overrun clutch
32 Pivot bolt
33 Lock washer
34 Nut
35 Drive housing

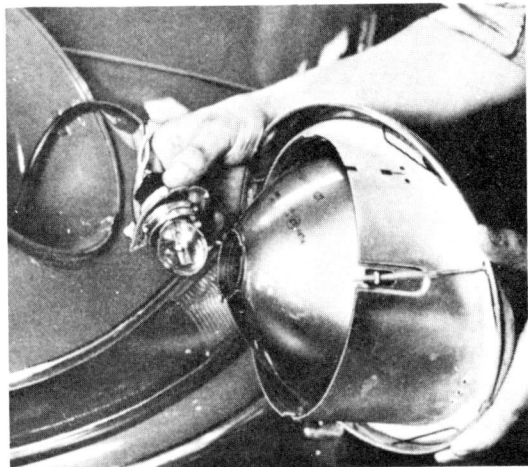

Fig. 9.24. Removing an early type headlamp bulb (Sec. 14)

Headlamp sealed beam unit - renewal

4   Remove the lamp bezel, as described in paragraph 1 (photo).
5   Remove the three lens unit retaining screws (do not touch the beam alignment screws) and remove the retaining ring (photo).
6   Withdraw the lens unit and detach the electrical connector (photo).
7   Installation is the reverse of the removal procedure. It is recommended that the beam alignment is checked on completion.

Quartz-iodine (H1) headlamp bulbs - renewal

8   Remove the lamp assembly, as described in paragraph 1.
9   Pull off the cable from the plug of the appropriate bulb. Press down the retaining clip and move it aside.
10   Remove the bulb and install the replacement following the reverse of the removal procedure. Do not touch the bulb glass; handle it with a clean cloth or tissue. It is recommended that the beam alignment is checked on completion.

Quartz-iodine (H4) headlamp bulbs - renewal

11   Remove the lamp assembly, as described in paragraph 1. For 1974 models onwards a very long screwdriver will be required to clear the front of the car.
12   Remove the connector, depress and unhook both retaining springs, then take out the bulb.
13   Install the replacement following the reverse of the removal procedure. Do not touch the bulb glass; handle it with a clean cloth or tissue. It is recommended that the beam alignment is checked on completion.

Headlamp lens (early type) - renewal

14   Remove the headlamp unit and bulb as previously described.
15   Remove the retaining screws and take out the reflector.
16   Remove the lens retainers from the rim using a screwdriver, then withdraw the reflector support and take out the glass.
17   Place a new sealing ring onto the lens, then install the lens with the word Bosch upright. The remainder of the installation procedure is the reverse of that used when removing. It is recommended that the beam alignment is checked on completion.

Quartz-iodine (H1) headlamp lens - renewal

18   Take out the headlight as previously described.
19   Remove the springs from the bezel, then remove both adjusting screws for the low beam.
20   Remove the horizontal adjusting screw for the high beam.
21   Ease the screws to one side and lift off the housing.
22   Install a sealing ring on the new lens, then align the lens to the centre line of the screw hole (small mark).
23   Install the housing, moving the screws to one side as necessary, then partly screw in the horizontal adjustment screw for the low beam.
24   Install the lens retaining springs, the longer ones on the wider side of the headlight ring and the shorter ones on the narrow side. At the top, the bezel must not contact the springs.
25   Install the low beam adjustment screws, then further tighten the high beam horizontal adjustment screw.
26   Install the headlamp and check the beam alignment.

Quartz-iodine (H4) headlamp lens - renewal

27   The procedure is similar to that given for the H1 headlamp lens.

Quartz-iodine headlamp bezels - removal and installation

28   Remove the headlamp and dismantle as described for lens renewal.
29   Remove the flexible-shaft main beam vertical adjusting screw from its retaining rubber and the reflector hoop.
30   Replace the bezel following the reverse of the removal procedure.

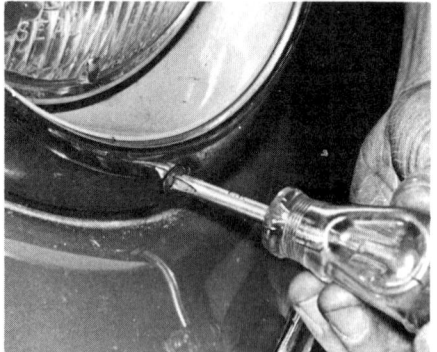      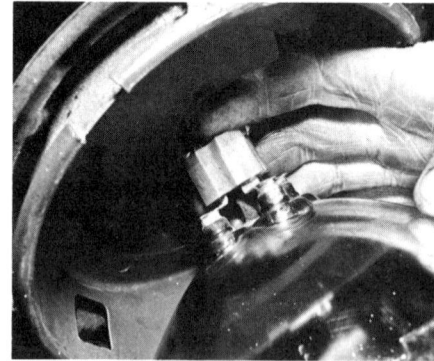

14.4 Headlamp bezel retaining screw   14.5 Removing a lens retaining screw   14.6 Electrical connector on lens unit

   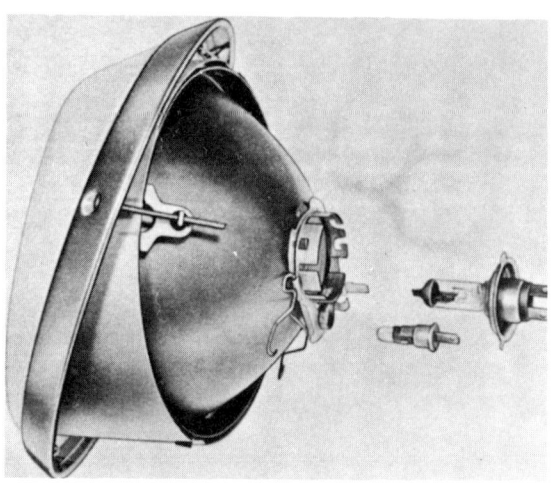

Fig. 9.25. Removing a quartz-iodine (H1) headlamp bulb (Sec. 14)

Fig. 9.26. Quartz-iodine (H4) headlamp bulb and lens assembly
The parking light bulb is for 1974/75 models (Sec. 14)

Fig. 9.27. Position the bezel springs as shown (Sec. 14)
Dimension is 30 mm (1.18 in) each side of centre

Headlamp beam alignment

31 Headlamp beam alignment screws are provided on each headlamp, but it is not recommended that these are used haphazardly in an attempt to obtain a satisfactory illumination pattern. Beam alignment requirements vary according to which country the car is being used in, so the only satisfactory method is to entrust this job to a suitably equipped service station. Figs. 9.28, 9.29 and 9.30 show the beam alignment screws; these may be used after component parts of the headlamps have been renewed to obtain the best possible settings, but these settings must be re-checked without delay using the proper equipment.

---

15 Side, tail, reverse and direction indicators - bulb renewal

---

Note: On 1974 models onwards, cars with H4 quartz-iodine headlights incorporate a side (parking) lamp bulb in the headlight unit. This is accessible after the lamp unit has been removed - see paragraphs 11 to 13, of the previous Section.

Early models

1 Take out the screws and remove the lamp unit.
2 Using a screwdriver lift off the holder at the cut-away corner to reveal the bulb.
3 Press in the bulb and turn it anticlockwise to remove it.
4 Installation is the reverse of the removal procedure.

Later models

5 Remove the retaining screws and take off the lens unit (photos).
6 Press in the bulb and turn it anticlockwise to remove it.
7 Installation is the reverse of the removal procedure.

---

16 Fog lamps - bulb renewal

---

1 Remove the screws from the lens retaining ring and withdraw the lamp unit.
2 Pull the snap-fit socket from the lamp unit, then press in the bulb and rotate it clockwise.
3 Install the new bulb, taking care not to touch the glass, then reverse the removal procedure for the remainder of the installation procedure.

---

17 Miscellaneous bulbs - renewal

Interior lamp

1 Carefully press out the lamp from the rear end using a screwdriver, remove the defective bulb and install the replacement. (Fig. 9.31)
2 Press in the lamp base to retain it.

Luggage compartment lamp

3 Remove the lens glass from the lower part of the lid for access to the bulb (photo).
4 Remove the bulb, install the replacement, then install the lens galss.

Fig. 9.28. Headlamp beam alignment screws - Early and H4 types
(Sec. 14)

Upper screw - vertical adjustment   Lower screw - horizontal adjustment

Fig. 9.29. Headlamp beam alignment screws - Sealed beam types
(Sec. 14)

a - horizontal adjustment   b - vertical adjustment

Fig. 9.30. Headlamp beam alignment screws - H1 types (Sec. 14)

A (top) - vertical adjustment, dipped beam
B (bottom) - horizontal adjustment, dipped beam
A (top) - vertical adjustment, main beam
B (bottom) - horizontal adjustment, dipped beam

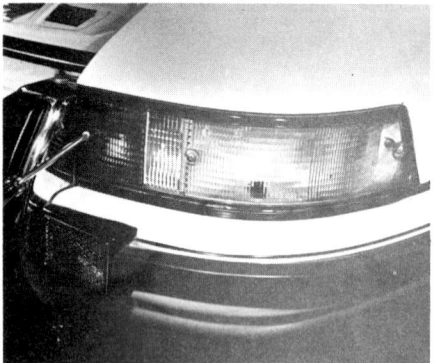

15.5a Remove the screws ...

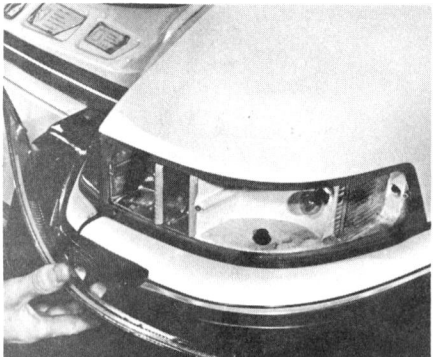

15.5b ... and take off the lens unit

17.3 Luggage compartment light lens (and switch)

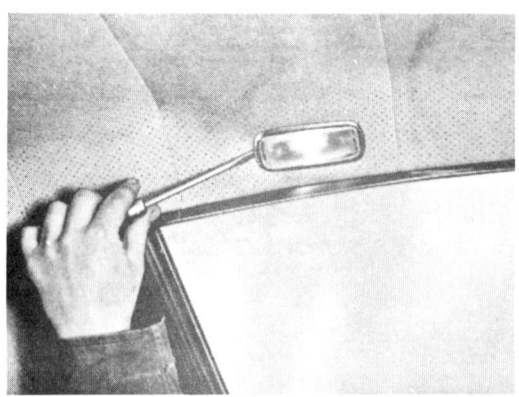

Fig. 9.31. Interior lamp removal (Sec. 17)

17.6 Number plate (license plate) lamp

Number plate (licence plate) lamp

5   Remove the two screws securing the lamp assembly to the engine compartment lid.

6   Withdraw the lamp, replace the bulb, then install it by following the reverse of the removal procedure (photo).

---

18 Steering column mounted switches - removal and installation

---

1   Disconnect the battery earth lead.

2   Remove the steering wheel, as described in Chapter 7.

3   Remove the retaining screws and detach the horn contact ring.

4   Remove the upper and lower column tube housings.

5   Disconnect all the cable connectors.

6   Remove the appropriate switch from the column tube.

7   Installation is the reverse of the removal procedure. Where twin switches are installed, the connections should be as follows:

Terminal		Wire colour
30		Red/white
57a	Ignition switch	Grey
56		Yellow and white/black
58L	Light switch	Grey/black
58R		Grey/red
L		Black/white
R	Warning light switch	Black/green
49a		Black/white/green

---

19 Reverse light (back-up light) switch - removal and installation

---

1   Jack-up the car to provide access to the right-hand side of the

Fig. 9.32. Switch housing retaining screws (arrowed) - later type (Sec. 18)

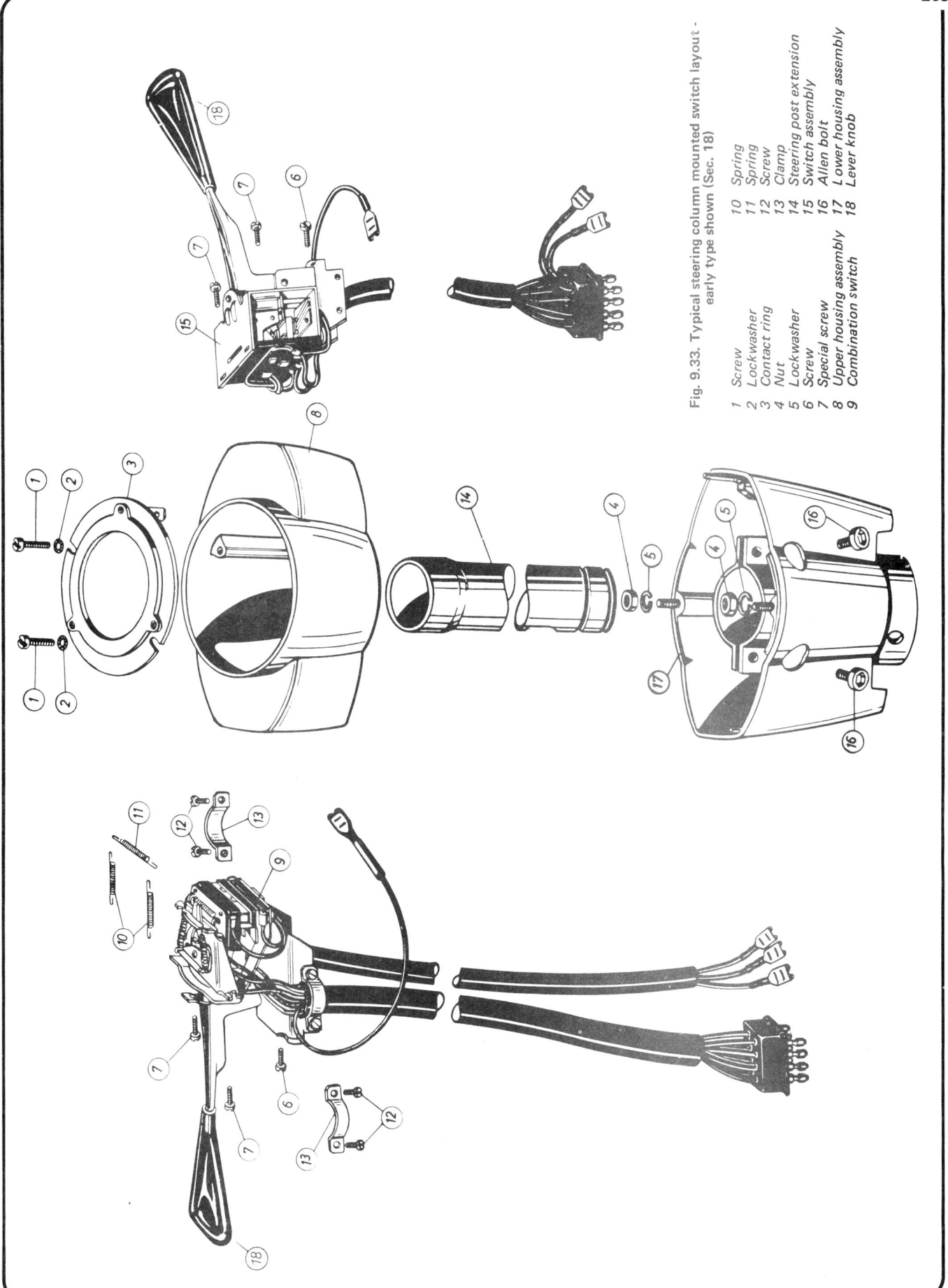

Fig. 9.33. Typical steering column mounted switch layout - early type shown (Sec. 18)

1	Screw	10	Spring
2	Lockwasher	11	Spring
3	Contact ring	12	Screw
4	Nut	13	Clamp
5	Lockwasher	14	Steering post extension
6	Screw	15	Switch assembly
7	Special screw	16	Allen bolt
8	Upper housing assembly	17	Lower housing assembly
9	Combination switch	18	Lever knob

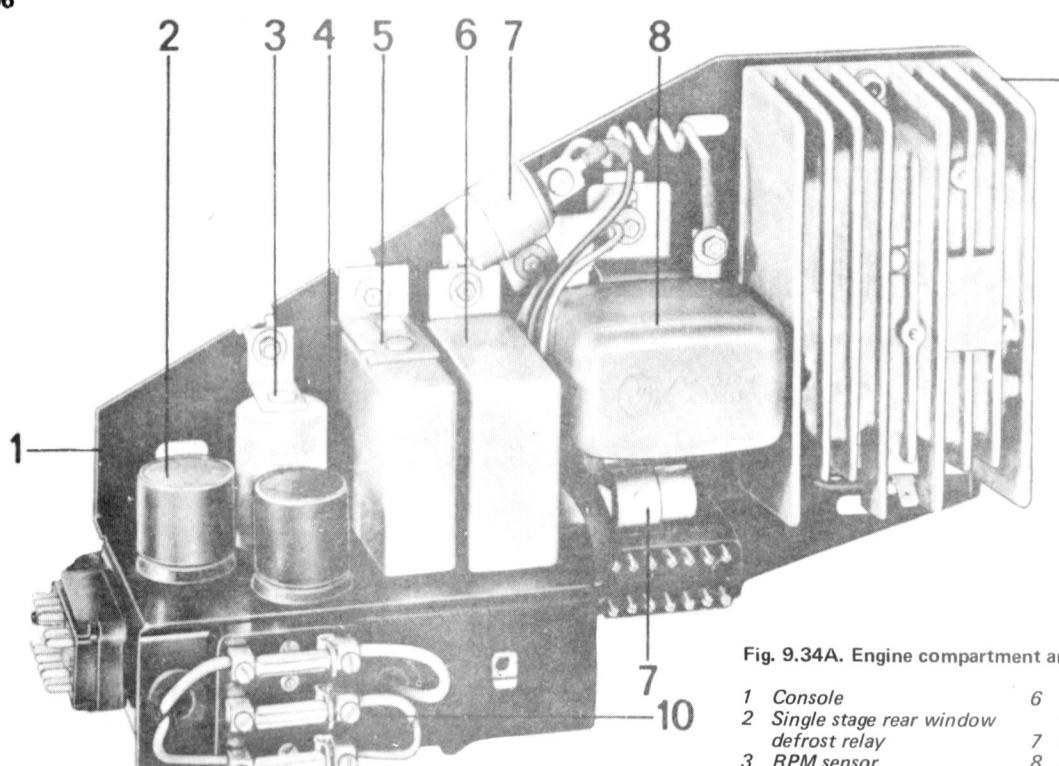

Fig. 9.34A. Engine compartment and fuses (typical) (Sec. 22)

1 Console
2 Single stage rear window
   defrost relay
3 RPM sensor
4 Start enrichment relay
5 RPM transducer

6 Two-stage rear window
   defrost relay
7 Radio noise suppressor
8 Regulator
9 Ignition trigger unit (CDS)
10 Fuse box III

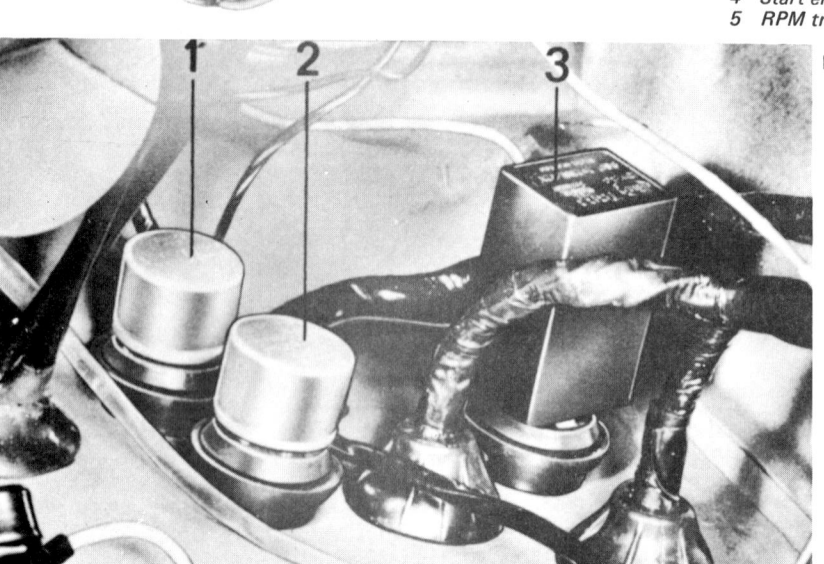

Fig. 9.34B. Luggage compartment relay panel (rear)
(Sec. 22)

1 Headlight dipper relay
2 Windscreen demist relay
3 Turn signal relay

22.1 Typical fuse panel installation

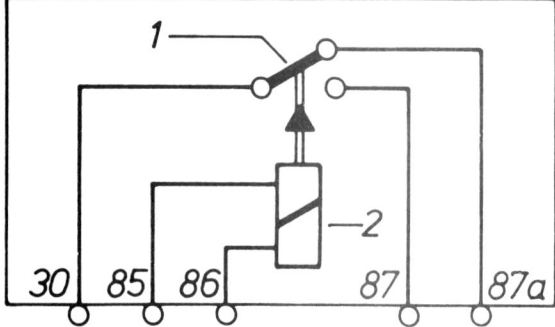

Fig. 9.34C. General arrangement of relay contacts (Sec. 22)

1 Relay contacts
2 Coil winding (shown de-energized)

The relay is an electrically controlled switch. When the coil windings are energized (terminal 85 and 86) the electromagnetic force actuates the switch contacts. This interrupts the circuit from terminal 30 to terminal 87a. The circuit from terminal 30 to 87 is then completed. In this way it is possible to use low current (control current) for switching a main power circuit.

transmission.

2 Remove the protective cap from the switch and pull off the connections.

3 Unscrew the switch from the transmission housing, taking care that the switch plunger does not fall out.

4 Installation is the reverse of the removal procedure.

20 Door contact switch - removal and installation

1 Remove the rubber cap from around the switch, then unscrew the switch from the door pillar.

2 Detach the wire and connect it to the new switch.

3 Installation of the switch is the reverse of the removal procedure.

21 Horns - removal and installation

The horns are installed on flexible mountings beneath the front wings (fenders).

1 To remove a horn, detach the snap-on connectors, remove the retaining nut and take the horn out.

2 Installation is straightforward but ensure that no part of the horn touches the car body or the operation will be impaired.

22 Relays and fuses

Note: For relays associated with the fuel system, refer to Chapter 2. Refer to Section 25 for the headlamp washer relay (where applicable).

1 Relay and fuse panels are installed in the luggage compartment at the front left-hand side, and in the engine compartment on the left sidewall (photo).

2 Early models incorporate one relay only, this being the headlight flasher relay. Later models may also incorporate foglamp and air-conditioning relays as standard items, but there is provision for four further relays should any additions be made to the electrical system.

3 The protected circuits are marked inside the fusebox lid, the fuses being numbered from top to bottom, or front to rear, as appropriate.

4 Later models incorporate a separate fusebox mounted on the left sidewall of the engine compartment beneath the relay panel cover. It contains fuses for the rear window heater, fuel system and Sportomatic transmission.

5 In the event of a fuse blowing it is important that the fault is isolated before a replacement is installed. Under no circumstances should a fuse of a higher rating be used in an attempt to stop a fuse blowing or serious component damage may result.

6 A list of the fuse ratings is given in the Specifications.

23 Windscreen wiper motor and linkage - removal and installation

The windscreen wiper motor and linkage are serviced as an assembly, and in the event of failure it should be repaired by a suitably equipped Porsche dealer or auto-electrical specialist, or a replacement unit obtained.

1 Working from the rear of the luggage compartment, remove the retaining clip and air duct, then remove the ventilating case.

2 Detach the five wire terminals from the wiper motor, noting the terminals to which they are connected.

3 Remove the nut from the wiper spindle and remove the wiper arms (photos).

4 Remove the rubber protectors from the spindles and unscrew the retaining nuts.

5 Withdraw the wiper motor and linkage downwards.

6 Installation is the reverse of the removal procedure. Adjust the wiper arms to obtain a satisfactory sweep; ensure that the outer arm does not contact the decorative strip, and maintain a gap of 25/32 in (20 mm) between the arms at rest. Fig. 9.36 shows the difference between the pre-February 1972 wiper arms and the later type.

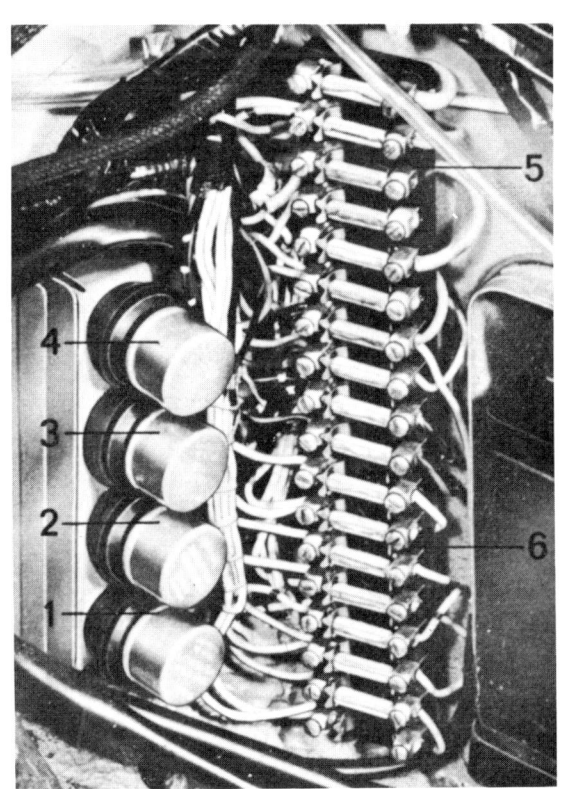

1 Horn

2 Fog lights/auxiliary driving lights/air conditioning
1 Horn

3 Auxiliary driving lights/air conditioning
2 Fog lights/auxiliary driving lights
1 Horn

4 Air conditioning
3 Auxiliary driving lights
2 Fog lights
1 Horn

Fig. 9.34D. Luggage compartment relay panel (front)(Sec. 22)

1 - 4 Standard relay   5, 6 Fuse panel
Relays depend on equipment options.

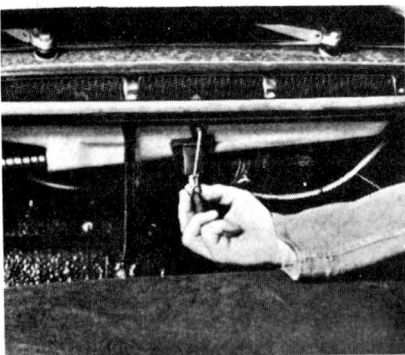

Fig. 9.35. Removing the retaining clip prior to removing the windscreen wiper motor and linkage (Sec. 23)

23.3a Removing the wiper arm ...

23.3b ... and blade

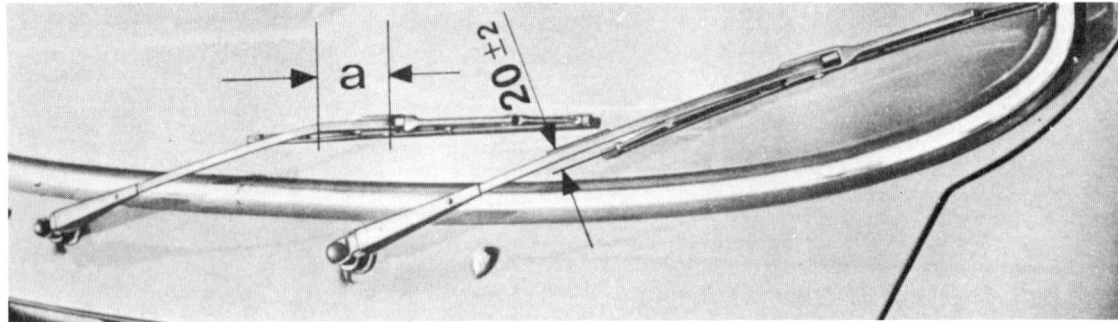

Fig. 9.36. Windscreen wiper arm setting (Sec. 23)

a = 35 mm/1 3/8 in. (early type)   *a = 60 mm/ 2 3/8 in. (later type)*

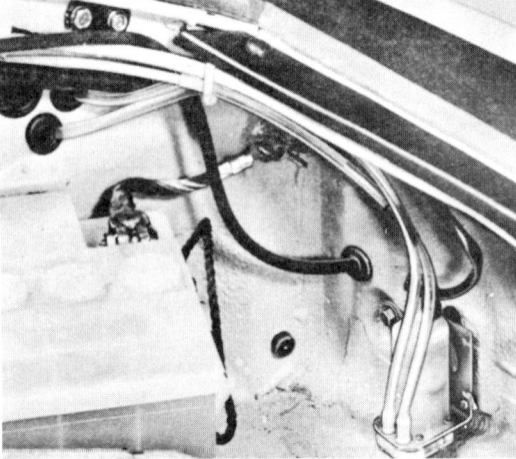

Fig. 9.37. Windscreen washer pump, 1974/75 models (Sec. 24)

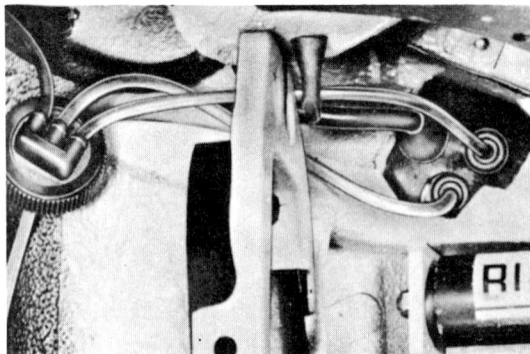

Fig. 9.38. Windscreen washer hoses, 1974/75 models (Sec. 24)

---

24 Windscreen washer system

Up to Chassis no. 302695 the washer reservoir was installed in a recess along the side of the luggage compartment floor. The washer pump was installed in the right-hand rear part of the luggage compartment under the mat. For later models, up to 1974, the washer pump is installed in the front luggage compartment next to the washer reservoir; for 1974 models onwards the washer pump is located in the lock transverse panel near the battery, and the reservoir is under the left-hand front wing (fender).

Reservoir (up to Chassis no. 302695) - removal and installation
1   Pump the reservoir completely dry, then remove the cap and hose. Remove the reservoir by turning it.
2   Installation is the reverse of the removal procedure.

Pump (up to Chassis no. 302695) - removal and installation
3   Detach the pump cables, followed by the pressure and suction hoses.
4   Loosen the pump retaining straps and pull the pump out.
5   Installation is the reverse of the removal procedure.

Washer pump and reservoir (Chassis no. 302695 onwards, except 1974/75 models) - removal and installation
6   Remove the reservoir (two screws) and detach the pump wires.
7   Loosen the pump retaining straps and lift out the pump.
8   Installation is the reverse of the removal procedure.

Windscreen washer pump (1974/75 models)
9   Prior to removal of the pump, the electrical wires and water hoses must be detached. When reconnecting, ensure that the brown wire is on the negative (-) terminal. The nipple marked 'D' is connected to the nozzle supply hose through the T-joint. A hose leads from each nozzle (connection 'B' and a connection in the T-joint) to the threaded cap in the reservoir which is located under the left front wing (fender). An additional vent connection in the reservoir cap leads to the water filler neck within the tank filler compartment.

Windscreen washer reservoir (1974/75 models) - removal and installation
10 Jack-up the car and remove the left front wheel.
11 Unfasten the retaining clip, remove the filler hose and threaded cap, then remove the reservoir rearwards.
12 Installation is the reverse of the removal procedure.

25 Headlamp washer system

An optional fitment on later models is a headlamp washer system. A facia-mounted switch supplies current to a relay and an electric pump which delivers water through spray jets to the headlamp glasses.

Spray jets - removal and installation
1 Remove the direction indicator housing from the bumper. On the left side of the car remove the water reservoir as described in the previous Section. (The reservoir supplies the windscreen washers and headlamp washers).
2 Push the spring rearwards to release the spray jet.

3 Installation is the reverse of the removal procedure. Note that the left and right jets are different.

Water pump - removal and installation
4 Disconnect the wiring and hoses at the pump.
5 Remove the retaining strap and remove the pump.
6 Installation is the reverse of the removal procedure. Ensure that the hoses and wires are connected correctly.

Headlamp washer switch - removal and installation
7 Disconnect the battery earth lead, then pull out the switch and disconnect the wires.
8 Installation is the reverse of the removal procedure.

Spray jets - adjustment
9 To adjust the spray jets it will be necessary to make up a tool to the dimensions shown in Fig. 9.42.
10 Insert the inner rod into the tubular piece, insert the chamfered end of the tubular piece into the jet, then extend the inner rod. Adjust the jet so that the inner rod touches the centre of the headlamp lens.

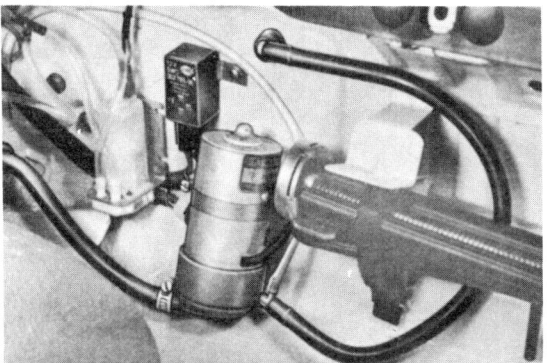

Fig. 9.40. Headlamp washer pump location (Sec. 25)

Fig. 9.39. Windscreen washer reservoir location, 1974/75 models (Sec. 24)

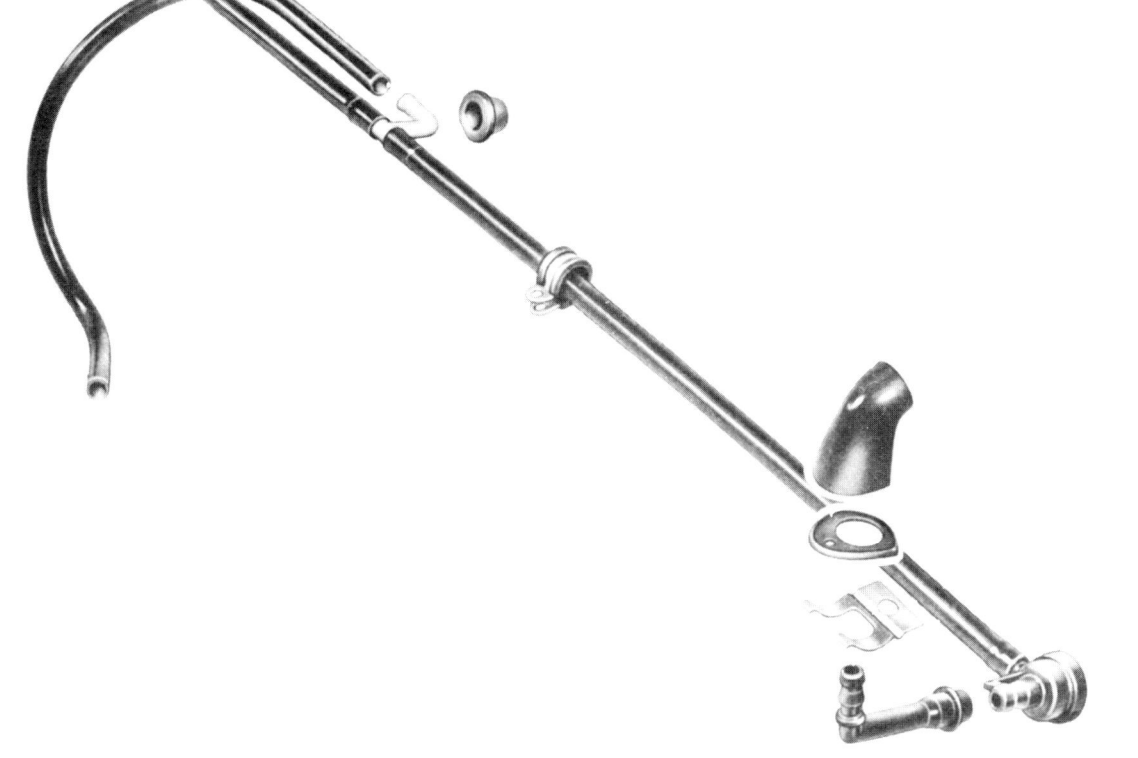

Fig. 9.41. Headlamp washer components (Sec. 25)

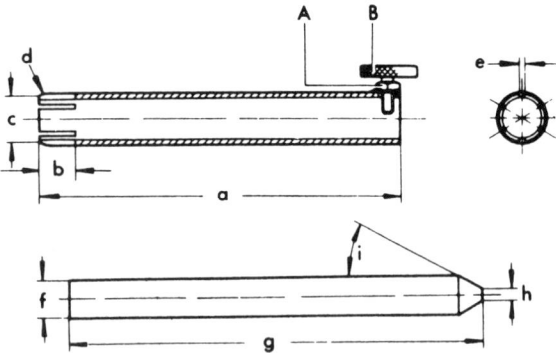

Fig. 9.42. Spray jet adjustment tool dimensions (Sec. 25)

a	100 mm	(3.94 in.)	f	10.5 mm	(0.413 in.) dia.
b	10 mm	(0.394 in.)	g	115 mm	(4.527 in.)
c	12.5 mm	(0.492 in.)	h	3 mm	(0.118 in.) dia.
d	5 mm	(0.197 in.)	1	30°	
e	1 + 0.2 mm	(0.039 + 0.008 in.)			

A   M 4 nut, soldered   or equivilent
B   M 4 knurled head screw   sizes

Fig. 9.44. Later type instrument rubber retaining ring (Sec. 26)

---

26 Instrument panel

Instruments (pre-1970 models) - removal and installation
1   Pull back the carpet in the front luggage compartment and detach the cables from the rear of the instrument(s) to be removed. Make a note of where the cables are connected to prevent mix-up when installing.
2   If the speedometer is to be removed, unscrew the knurled nut and pull out the cable end.
3   Remove the clamping nuts and clamp, then withdraw the instrument(s) from inside the car.
4   Installation is the reverse of the removal procedure.

Instruments (1970 models onwards)
5   Taking care not to damage the instrument panel, carefully prise an instrument out of the panel and detach the cables. Make a note of where the cables are connected to prevent mix-up when installing. If the speedometer is being removed, unscrew the knurled nut and pull

Fig. 9.43. Spray jet adjustment (Sec. 25)

out the cable end.
6   Remove other instruments as necessary by pushing them out, working through the aperture from where the first instrument was removed.
7   When installing, position the rubber ring up to the protruding part of the instrument housing, then connect the wires and position the gauge in the opening. Ensure that the instrument is correctly aligned, then press it firmly in.

Installing later instruments in earlier type instrument panels
8   Where replacement instruments have been obtained of a later type (ie, where the instrument seat has been widened to 0.71 in /18 mm), the rubber mounting rings should be used (see paragraph 7) and the earlier mounting rings and clamps discarded.

Instrument bulbs - renewal
9   The instrument bulbs can be removed from their sockets after the instruments have been removed, as previously described.

Headlight switch - removal and installation
10 Disconnect the battery earth lead, then unscrew the switch knob.
11 Make-up a suitable peg spanner to remove the retaining ring, but take care that it is not damaged (Porsche tool P281 is available for this purpose).
12 Push out the switch and detach the wires, making a note of the connections.
13 Installation is the reverse of the removal procedure.

Ignition switch - removal and installation
14 Disconnect the battery earth lead, then remove the switch cover.
15 *On models without a steering lock,* remove the screws and take out the switch.
16 *On models with a steering lock,* drill out the shear-head bolts and remove the switch from the panel.
17 Note the lead connections to the switch, then detach them.
18 Installation of the switch is straightforward, but where a steering lock is fitted ensure that the switch is properly installed and aligned before the bolt heads are sheared when tightening.

Speedometer cable - renewal
Note: The procedure given is for cars intended for the California market which have an EGR elapsed mileage odometer switch. For other cars, ignore the reference to the odometer switch and blower housing.
19 Remove the blower housing, taking care that the operating cables are not kinked.
20 Detach the speedometer cable at the EGR elapsed mileage odometer switch, or at the speedometer as previously described.
21 Tie a strong drawcord to the speedometer cable at the forward end.
22 Remove the tunnel cover and gearshift lever housing, then remove

the plastic strap.
23 Remove the cover at the rear of the tunnel, then remove the second plastic strap (photo).
24 Disconnect the speedometer cable at the transmission, then draw it out towards the rear.
25 Installation is the reverse of the removal procedure, the new cable being drawn in from the front using the drawcord.

Exhaust gas recirculation elapsed mileage odometer switch - removal, resetting and installation

26 The EGR elapsed mileage odometer switch operates a warning lamp after 30000 miles to warn that inspection of the system is required. During normal operating conditions the warning lamp illuminates when the ignition is switched on and extinguishes when the engine is started. To reset the switch proceed as follows.
27 Disconnect the battery earth strap and remove the tachometer as described previously.
28 Using a small screwdriver or similar tool press in the reset pin on the odometer switch housing.

27 Control illumination

1   On later models an illuminated heater control lever and fan control is used. To gain access to the heater control lever bulb, lift off the square lens on the centre tunnel.
2   The bulbs for the fan control switch (two for 1972/73 models, three for 1974/75 models) are installed in sockets behind the fan control panel. These are accessible from behind the instrument panel without removing the knee-guard.
3   The control lamp in the hazard warning switch is connected to the light switch through a 150 ohm resistor. The lamp glows at a much reduced intensity when the hazard flashers are not in operation.

28 Seatbelt warning system

General description

1   From January 1972, USA models incorporate a seatbelt warning system for the front passenger's seat. In the event of the seat being occupied without a seatbelt being used, the 'Fasten Seatbelt' lamp will illuminate and a buzzer will operate. This buzzer also operates when the ignition is switched on and the parking brake is fully released.
2   For 1974 models, a modified system was introduced which additionally prevents the engine from being started if either front seat is occupied without a seatbelt being used. The car can be started without the seats being occupied, or can be restarted without fastening the seatbelt, if the restarting occurs within 1 to 3 minutes of being switched off.

Seatbelt buckle (standard seat) - removal and installation

3   Remove the two countersunk screws to release the front plastic cover of the buckle.
4   Remove the buckle retaining screws, then carefully disconnect the wires whilst preventing the tabs from being strained.
5   Installation is the reverse of the removal procedure.

'Fasten seatbelt' lamp - removal and installation

6   Carefully prise off the loudspeaker cover and remove the loudspeaker (or detach the bonded plastic foil).
7   Detach the connector, then press the lamp forwards out of the instrument panel.
8   Open the lamp for access to the bulb.
9   Installation is the reverse of the removal procedure.

Seat contact (standard seat) - removal and installation

10 Remove the seat, as described in Chapter 10.
11 Remove the seat recliner retaining screws and detach the backrest.
12 Pull back the seat cover to gain access to the seat contact, then remove it, if necessary, noting its installed position.
13 Installation is the reverse of the removal procedure; the polarity of the wires is not important.

26.23 Remove the cover at the rear of the tunnel

Fig. 9.45. EGR elapsed mileage odometer switch (arrowed) (Sec. 26)

Seatbelt lock (Sport seat) - removal and installation

14 Remove both countersunk screws and take off the plastic cover.
15 Push the rear cover aside and remove the lock assembly by taking out the retaining bolt.
16 Carefully prise the clips open to free the wire, then detach it at the plug connector.
17 Installation is the reverse of the removal procedure.

Seat contact (Sport seat) - removal and installation

18 Remove the seat, as described in Chapter 10.
19 From beneath the seat, disconnect the wires, then detach the contact switch.
20 Installation is the reverse of the removal procedure. Bond the contact switch in position using a contact adhesive 5.1 in (130 mm) from the base of the seat back (see Fig. 9.46).

Logic relay switch (1974/75 models) - removal and installation

21 Remove the small combination instrument, as described in Section 26.
22 Withdraw the relay switch from its socket.
23 Installation is the reverse of the removal procedure.

Warning system (1974/75 models) - fault finding

24 If the starter does not operate after the seatbelts have been fastened, first replace the logic switch. If this does not cure the fault the problem may be in the starter motor, ignition/starter switch circuit, or in the seatbelt/seat contact/logic relay switch wiring.

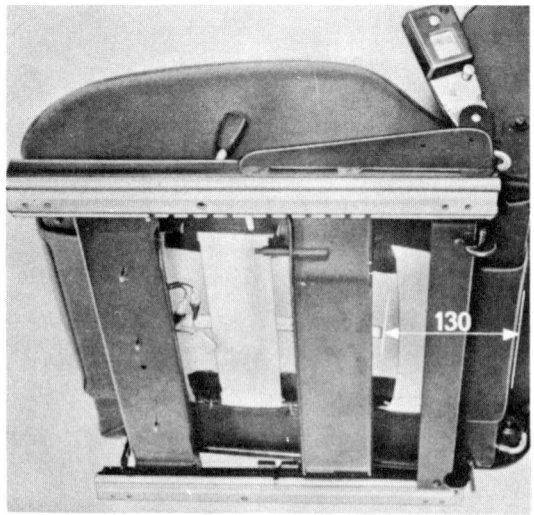

Fig. 9.46. Installed position of sport seat contact (Sec. 28)

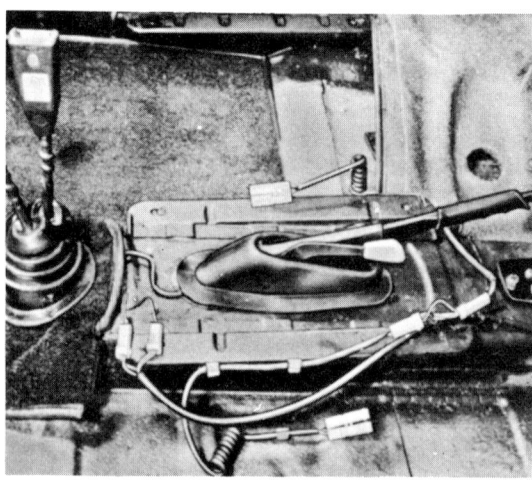

Fig. 9.47. Wiring layout for 1974/75 seat belt system (Sec. 28)

25 Remove the logic relay (paragraphs 21 and 22), and jumper terminals 'C' and 'SO' in the relay socket ensuring that a good contact is made. If the engine will now start, a fault in the seatbelt/seat contact/ logic relay switch wiring is indicated.

26 If the engine still fails to start, check the starter motor, ignition/ starter switch and appropriate wiring.
27 If the audible or visual warning devices fail to operate, but the engine starts, check these items and their associated wiring.

29 Fault diagnosis - electrical system

Starting system

Symptom	Possible fault	Remedy
Starter does not operate when key is turned to "start" position	Turn on the lights for this test	
	Lights go out - loose connections, corroded terminals, flat battery	Check circuit and replace battery.
	Lights go dim - battery run down	Recharge or replace battery.
	Connect a cable between terminals 30 and 50. If starter now turns either cables or ignition switch is faulty	Replace cables, starter to ignition switch and/or ignition switch.
	Lights stay bright, Connect cable from terminal 30 to connector strip terminal - starter now turns	Solenoid needs servicing or replacement.
Drive pinion sticks in mesh with starter ring	Coarse thread damaged	Overhaul starter.
	Solenoid not working	Replace solenoid.
Starter turns slowly and will not start engine	Battery run down	Charge or replace.
	Loose connections	Check circuit.
	Brushes not making proper contact	Overhaul or replace starter,
	Commutator dirty, burnt or damaged	Overhaul or replace starter.
	Windings damaged	Overhaul or replace starter.
Erratic starting i.e. sometimes it will and sometimes it will not, particularly from cold	Battery has internal fault.	Replace battery if necessary.
	Load test battery with tongs	

Charging system

Symptom	Possible fault	Remedy
Ignition switch on but not warning light	Battery flat or defective	Replace.
	Bulb requires replacement	Replace
	Battery terminals loose or dirty	Clean and tighten.
	Broken or damaged wiring	Repair or replace.
	Ignition switch not working	Replace.
	Alternator brushes open circuit	Overhaul alternator.
	Regulator faulty	Replace.
Light glows when engine is running	Fan belt broken or slipping	Adjust.
	Regulator faulty	Replace.
	Alternator not delivering charge	Test and repair.
Light remains on when engine switched off	Regulator points closed, probably burnt and stuck	Replace.

Windshield wipers and washers

Symptom	Possible fault	Remedy
Motor does not start, runs slowly, cuts out or stops	Brushes worn, stuck in holders or weak brush spring	Clean and if necessary replace brush gear
	Cummutator dirty, worn or grooved	Clean and if necessary skim commutator. If too worn replace armature.
	Armature open circuit or short circuit	Replace armature.
	Linkage or spindle bearing seized	Free, lubricate and if necessary replace.
	Loose connections in motor or switch	Locate and reconnect.
	Battery run down	Charge battery.
Motor runs when switched off, or will not park blades in the correct position	Contacts in cover faulty	Clean and adjust. Replace cover if necessary.
	Earth wire from terminal 31b to switch and earth faulty	Reconnect. Replace if necessary
Wiper works slowly with squeaky noise *	Spindle bearings faulty	Remove and service.
	End clearances in gear shaft and armature shafts incorrect	Adjust.
	Drive housing not correctly assembled to motor body	Dismantle and assembly correctly.

* *Note:* *If the symptom is allowed to continue the motor will overheat and the commutator will be damaged*

Fuel gauge

Symptom	Possible fault	Remedy
Fuel gauge gives no reading	Fuel tank empty! Electric cable between tank sender unit and gauge earthed or loose Fuel gauge supply cable interrupted Fuel gauge unit broken	Fill fuel tank. Check cable to earthing and joints for tightness. Check and replace cable if necessary. Replace fuel gauge.
Fuel gauge registers full all the time	Electric cable between tank unit and gauge broken or disconnected	Check over the cable and repair as necessary.

Horn

Symptom	Possible fault	Remedy
Horn operates all the time	Horn push either earthed, or stuck down Horn cable to horn push earthed	Disconnect battery earth, Check and rectify source of trouble. Disconnect battery earth. Check and rectify source of trouble.
Horn fails to operate	Blown fuse Cable or cable connection loose, broken or disconnected Horn has an internal fault	Check and renew if broken. Ascertain cause. Check all connections for tightness and cables for breaks. Replace horn.
Horn emits intermittent or unsatisfactory noise	Cable connections loose Horn incorrectly adjusted	Check and tighten all connections. Adjust horn until best note obtained.

Lights

Symptom	Possible fault	Remedy
Lights do not come on	If engine not running, battery discharged Light bulb filament burnt out or bulbs broken. Wire connections loose, disconnected or broken Light switch shorting or otherwise faulty	Push-start car, charge battery. Test bulbs in live bulb holders. Check all connections for tightness and wire cable for breaks. By-pass light switch to ascertain if fault is in switch and fit new switch as appropriate.
Lights come on but fade out	If engine not running battery discharged Light bulb filament burnt out or bulbs or sealed beam units broken Wire connections loose, disconnected or broken Light switch shorting or otherwise faulty	Push-start car, and charge battery. Test bulbs in live bulb holder; renew sealed beam units. Check all connections for tightness and wire cable for breaks. By-pass light switch to ascertain if fault is in switch and fit new switch as appropriate.
Lights give very poor illumination	Lamp glasses dirty Reflector tarnished or dirty Lamps badly out of adjustment Incorrect bulb with too low wattage fitted Existing bulbs old and badly discoloured	Clean glasses. Fit new reflectors. Adjust lamps correctly. Remove bulb and replace with correct grade. Renew bulb units.
Lights work erratically - flashing on	Battery terminals or earth connection loose Lights not earthing properly Contacts in light switch faulty	Tighten battery terminals and earth connection. Examine and rectify By-pass light switch to ascertain if fault is in switch and fit new switch as appropriate

Wiring diagrams

Special note
   Porsche have produced more than thirty wiring diagrams for the 911 models covered by this manual. For obvious reasons it is not practical to include all of these diagrams here, therefore, the wiring diagrams in this section are a representitive selection only.
   Wiring diagrams for models built prior to 1969 are not included as these will be found in the Porsche handbook supplied with the car. For the period 1969 to 1974 diagrams are included for alternate years. Should your car have been manufactured in one of the years not included, you should find that the diagram for the preceding or following year will be accurate enough for all practical purposes.
   A wiring diagram for 1975 models onwards is included.

Using 'Current Flow' type wiring diagrams
   The current flow diagrams used for the later models have been introduced by Porsche to simplify computer diagnostic checks, and at first glance may not be followed very easily. However, the numbering along the bottom line gives the current track number which, by reference to the diagram key, enables any component to be readily located. The interconnecting leads between components, terminals, connectors, earth points, etc., are shown in heavy lines with a wiring colour code reference. Where thin lines are shown, either internal connections are used or the component is directly connected to earth (ground).

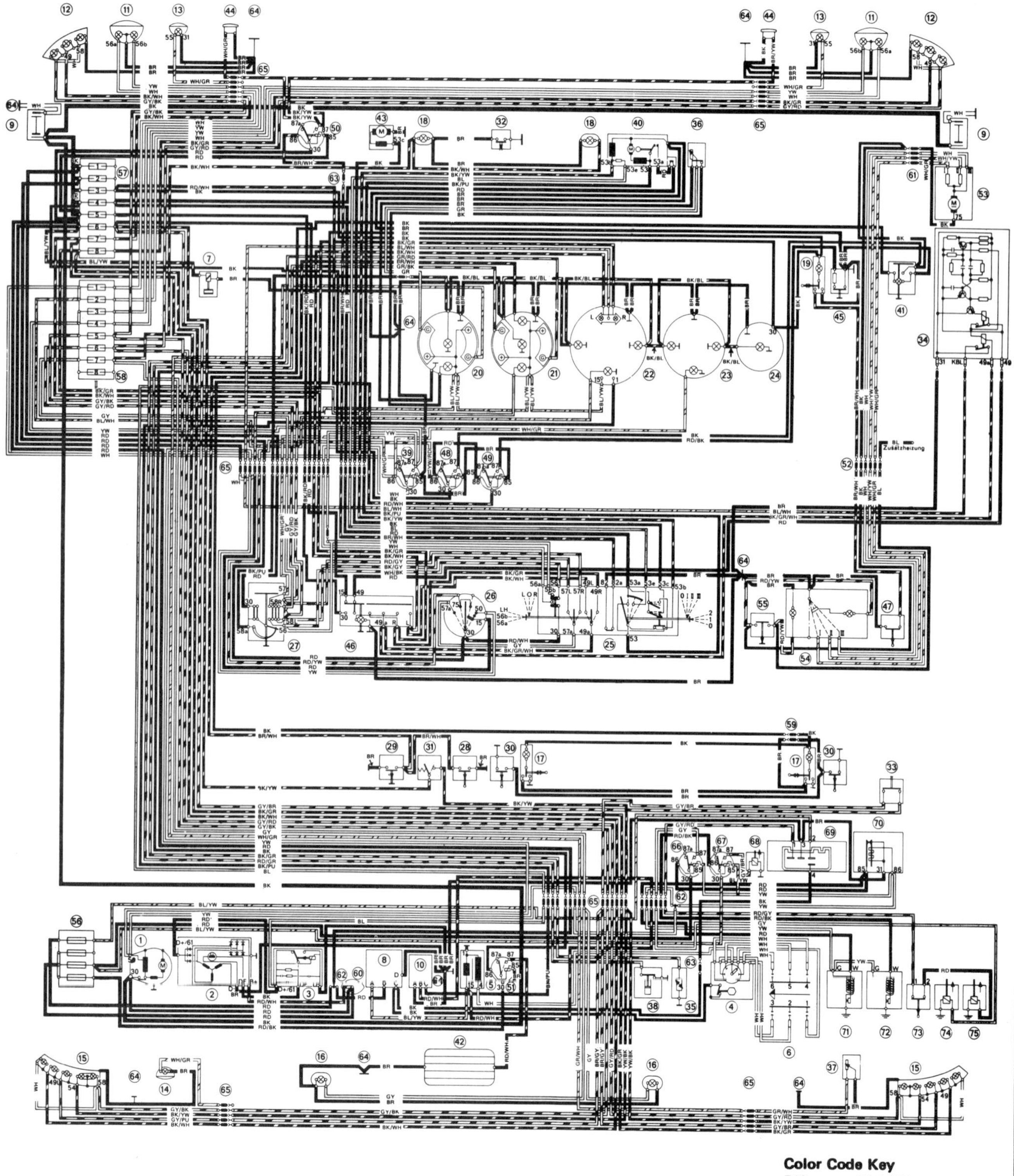

Fig. 9.48. Wiring diagram, 911E, 911S - 1969 models

Color Code Key

BK	–	BLACK
BL	–	BLUE
BR	–	BROWN
GR	–	GREEN
GY	–	GREY
PU	–	PURPLE
RD	–	RED
WH	–	WHITE
YW	–	YELLOW

Key to wiring diagram, 911E, 911S - 1969 onwards

1 Starter
2 Generator
3 Regulator
4 Distributor
5 Ignition coil
6 Spark plugs
7 Fuel pump
8 CDS oscillator
9 Battery
10 Swtiching SCR
11 Headlamps
12 Blinker, parking and side marker lights (side marker USA only)
13 Fog lamps (special order)
14 Fog tail lamp (special order)
15 Tail, stop, blinker, backup and side marker lights (side marker USA only)
16 License plate lights
17 Interior light
18 Luggage compartment light
19 Glove compartment light
20 Small instrument cluster
21 Large instrument cluster
22 Transistorized tachometer
23 Speedometer
24 Electric clock
25 Blinker, dim, headlamp flasher wiper, washer switch with horn button in steering wheel
26 Ignition/starter switch in steering column lock
27 Light switch
28 Brake failure warning switch (USA only)
29 Handbrake control lamp
30 Door contact switch
31 Stoplight switch
32 Luggage compartment light switch
33 Backup light switch
34 Blinker flasher
35 Oil temperature sender

36 Fuel gauge sender
37 Oil level sender
38 Diaphragm oil pressure sender
39 Headlamp flasher relay switch
40 Wiper motor
41 Rear window heating switch
42 Rear window heating circuit
43 Washer pump
44 Signal horn
45 Cigarette lighter
46 Emergency blinkers
47 Glove compartment light switch
48 Blower/heater relay switch
49 Cigarette lighter relay
50 Signal horn relay
51 Rear window heating relay switch
52 Multiple-pole connector
53 Blower motor
54 Blower and heater switch
55 Gasoline heater switch (special order)
56 Rear fuse box
57 Fuse box I
58 Fuse box II
59 Two-pole connector
60 Terminal bar
61 Multiple-pole connector
62 WECO-connector
63 Single-pole connector
64 Earth taps
65 Terminal connectors
66 Starting relay switch
67 Auxiliary starting relay switch (standard)
68 Starting solenoid
69 RPM transducer
70 Time limit switch
71 Temperature switch (start)
72 Temperature switch (start assist)
73 Microswitch (throttle linkage)
74 Shut-off solenoid (start)
75 Shut-off solenoid (stop)

Key to wiring diagram (Part 1), 911T, 911E, 911S, - 1971 models

1 Battery
17 Headlamps
18 Blinker, clearance and side marker lamps (side marker lamps USA only)
19 Tail, brake, blinker, side marker and back-up lamps (side marker lamps USA only)
20 Fog lamps (optional)
21 License plate lamp
22 Trunk lamp
23 Interior lamp
24 Glovebox lamp
25 Ashtray lamp
30 Blinker, dimming, headlamp flasher, wiper washer switch with signal button in steering wheel
31 Steering ignition starter switch
32 Light switch
33 Warning light switch (not applicable in Italy)

36 Door contact switch
37 Switch for trunk room light
39 Brake light switch
41 Backup light switch
42 Switch for glovebox light
48 Direction warning blinker indicator
50 Headlight flasher changeover relay
67 Transistor revolution counter
68 Speedometer
69 Electric time clock
78 Fuse box I 10-pole
79 Fuse box II 8-pole
84 Plug connection 14-pole
85 Plug connection 6-pole
87 Plug connection 1-pole
89 Earth connection - body
91 Switch for fog lamps (optional)
93 Fog tail light (optional)

Fuses:

Fusebox I;
1 Interior light, time clock, trunk light
2 Warning light
7 Fresh air fan
8 Brake, blinker, backup lights
9 Blinker light front left
10 Blinker light front right

Fusebox II:
1 High beam left
2 High beam right
3 Dimmer left
4 Dimmer right
5 Clearance light left
6 Clearance light right
7 License plate light
8 (Fog lights)

Fuses:

Fuse box I
1 (Electric window regulator)
2 (Electric window regulator)
3 Cigarette lighter, electric clock
4 Windshield wipers and washer
5 Hazard warning light
6 Stop light, blinkers back up lights
7 Blinker, LH
8 Blinker, RH

Fuse box II
1 High beam, LH
2 High beam, RH
3 Low beam, LH
4 Low beam, RH
5 Parking light, LH
6 Parking light, RH
7 License plate light, trunk light
8 (Sunroof)

Rear fuse box
Shut-off solenoid (start)
(Rear window wipers)
Shut-off solenoid (stop)
Rear window heating circuit

Earth leads or cables:
Battery-body
Transmission-chassis
Supporting plate-body
Fuel spout-body
Steering column control switch-body
Instruments body

218

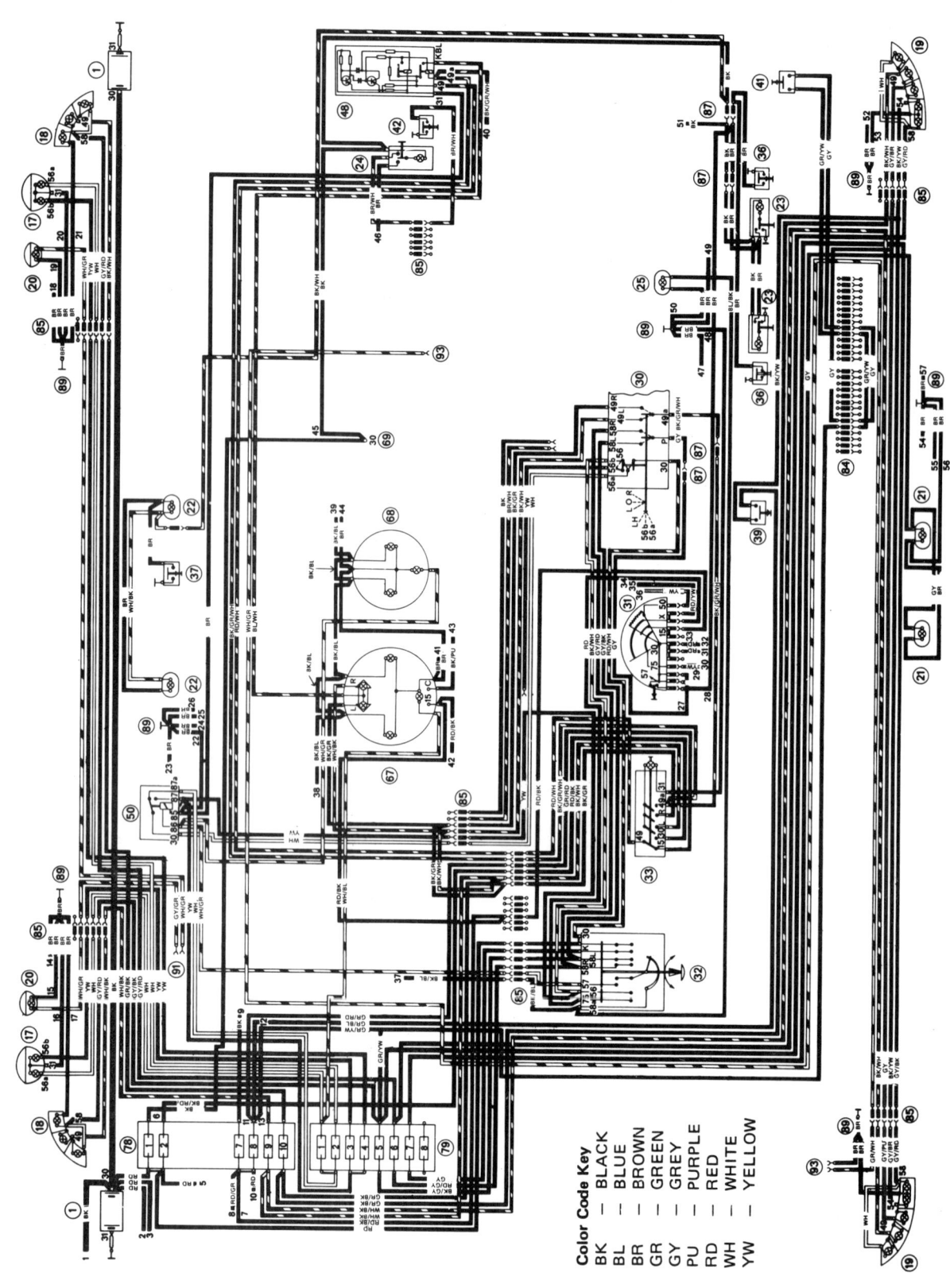

Fig. 9.49. Wiring diagram (Part 1), 911T, 911E, 911S - 1971 models (See page 217 for key)

Color Code Key
BK – BLACK
BL – BLUE
BR – BROWN
GR – GREEN
GY – GREY
PU – PURPLE
RD – RED
WH – WHITE
YW – YELLOW

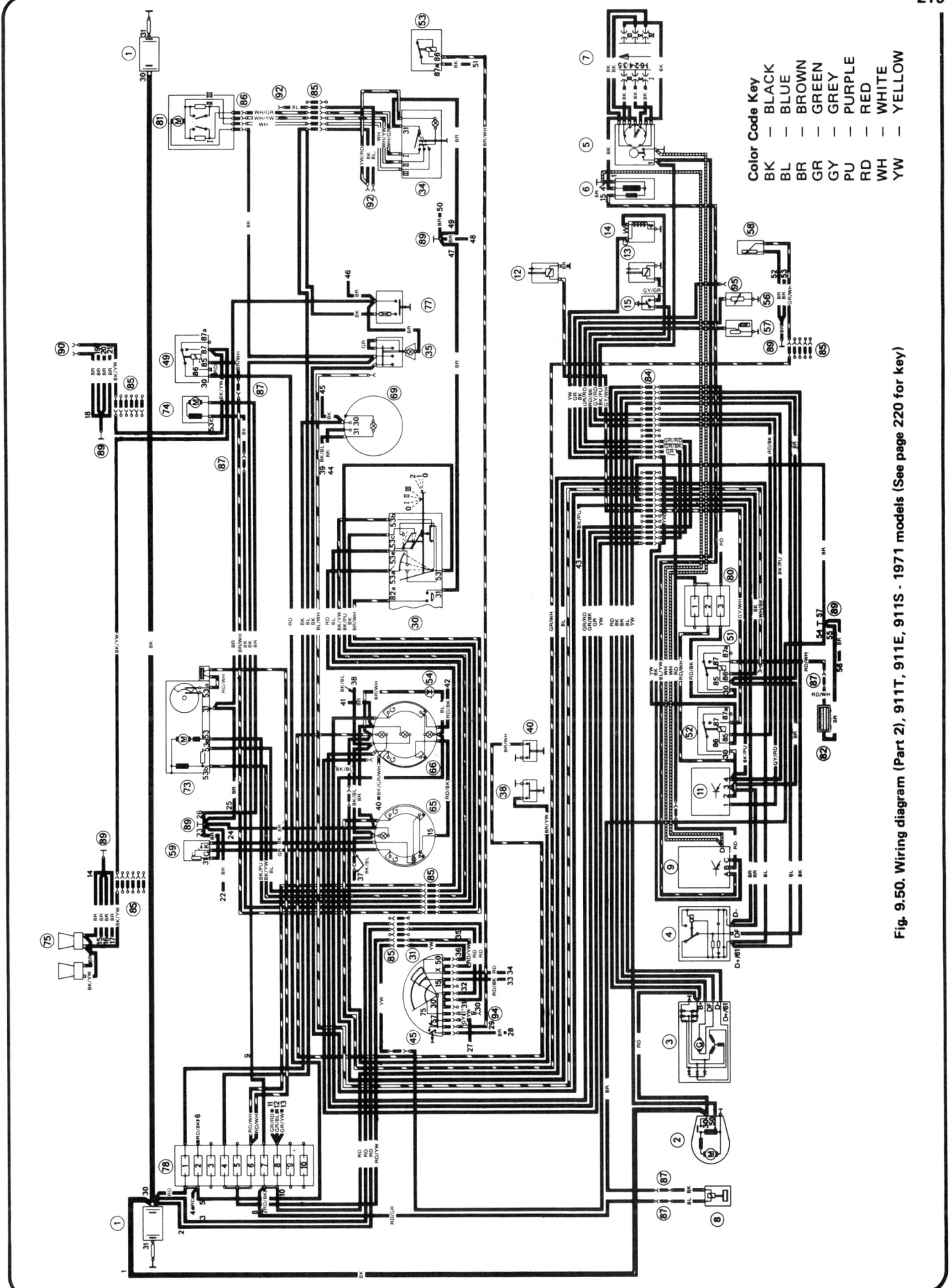

(See page 220 for key)

Fig. 9.50. Wiring diagram (Part 2), 911T, 911E, 911S - 1971 models

Color Code Key

BK — BLACK
BL — BLUE
BR — BROWN
GR — GREEN
GY — GREY
PU — PURPLE
RD — RED
WH — WHITE
YW — YELLOW

Key to wiring diagram (Part 2) 911T, 911E, 911S - 1971 models

1	Battery	34	Fan and separate heater switch	73 Wiper motor
2	Starter	35	Rear window heater switch	74 Washer pump
3	Alternator	38	Hand brake contact	75 Fanfare horn
4	Governor	40	Brake warning switch (USA only)	77 Cigarette lighter

1 Battery
2 Starter
3 Alternator
4 Governor
5 Ignition distributor
6 Ignition transformer
7 Spark plugs
8 Gasoline pump
9 BHKZ unit
11 Speed switch (E,S and 911T USA only)
12 Electromagnetic control valve (E and S only)
13 Lifting magnet (stop) (E and S only; on 911T USA solenoid valve)
14 Temperature time switch
15 Microswitch (E, S and 911T USA only)
30 Blinker, dimming, headlamp flasher, wiper-washer switch with signal button in steering wheel
31 Steering ignition starter switch

34 Fan and separate heater switch
35 Rear window heater switch
38 Hand brake contact
40 Brake warning switch (USA only)
45 Buzzer contact (USA only)
49 Horn relay
51 Rear window heater relay
52 Auxiliary starting relay (E and S only)
53 Buzzer (USA only)
54 Diode (USA only or optional)
56 Oil temperature indicator
57 Oil pressure indicator
58 Oil level indicator
59 Indicator for fuel gauge
65 Small combination instrument
66 Large combination instrument
69 Electric time clock

73 Wiper motor
74 Washer pump
75 Fanfare horn
77 Cigarette lighter
78 Fuse box I 10-pole
80 Fuxe box III 3-pole
81 Fan motor
82 Heated pane
84 Plug connection 14-pole
85 Plug connection 6-pole
86 Plug connection 4-pole
87 Plug connection 1-pole
89 Earth connection - body
90 Extra fanfare horn (optional)
92 Separate heater (optional)
94 Radio (Optional)
95 Oil temperature switch for SPM (optional)

FUSES:

Fusebox I:
1 Interior light, time clock, trunk light
2 Warning light
3 (Window lifter)
4 Cigarette lighter
5 (Slide roof)
6 Windshield wiper, washer pump
7 Fresh air fan
8 Brake, blinker, backup lights
9 Blinker light front left
10 Blinker light front right

Fusebox II:
1 (Sportomatic)
2 Stop magnet, solenoid valve starting valve
3 Rear window heater

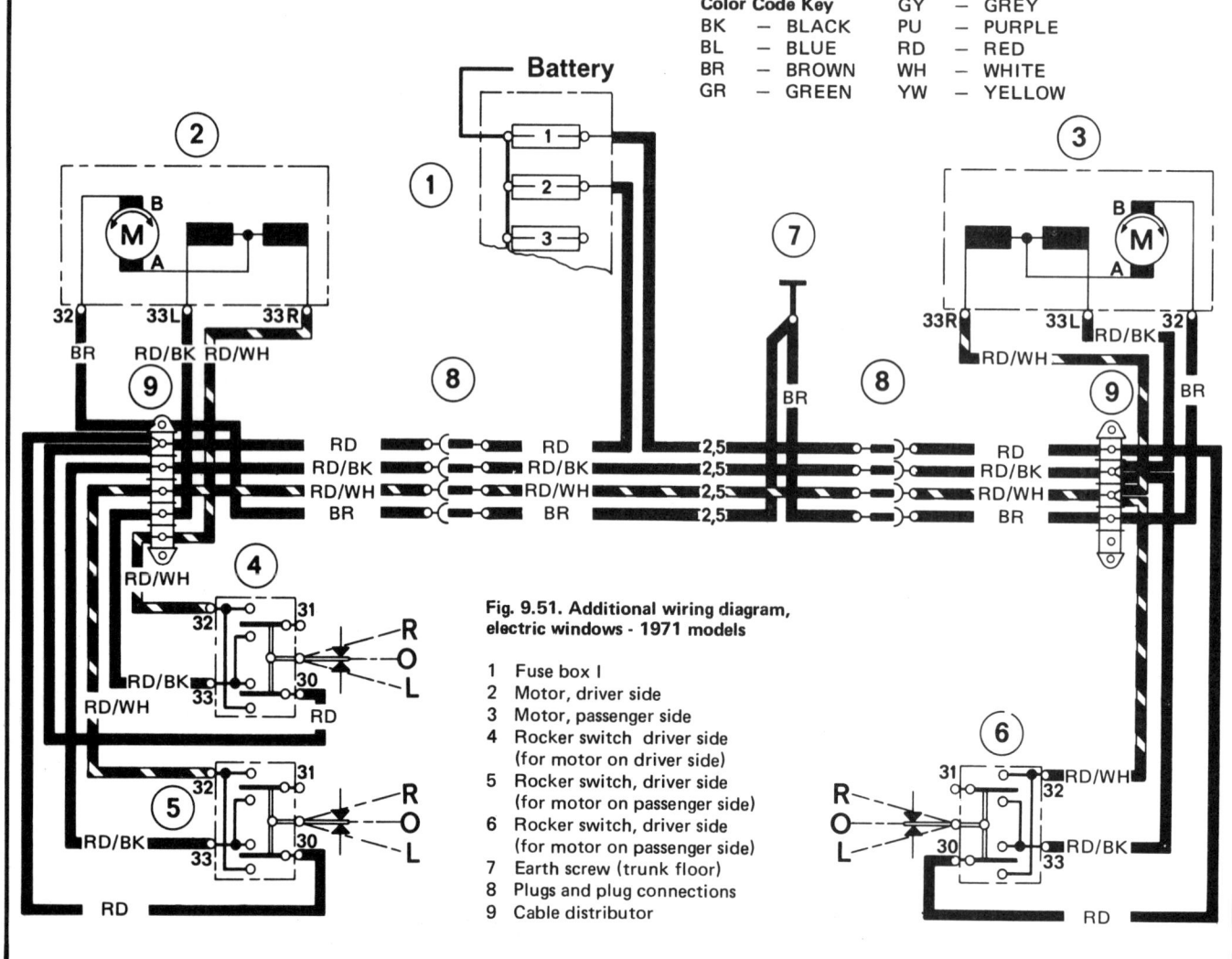

Color Code Key
BK — BLACK
BL — BLUE
BR — BROWN
GR — GREEN
GY — GREY
PU — PURPLE
RD — RED
WH — WHITE
YW — YELLOW

Fig. 9.51. Additional wiring diagram, electric windows - 1971 models

1 Fuse box I
2 Motor, driver side
3 Motor, passenger side
4 Rocker switch driver side (for motor on driver side)
5 Rocker switch, driver side (for motor on passenger side)
6 Rocker switch, driver side (for motor on passenger side)
7 Earth screw (trunk floor)
8 Plugs and plug connections
9 Cable distributor

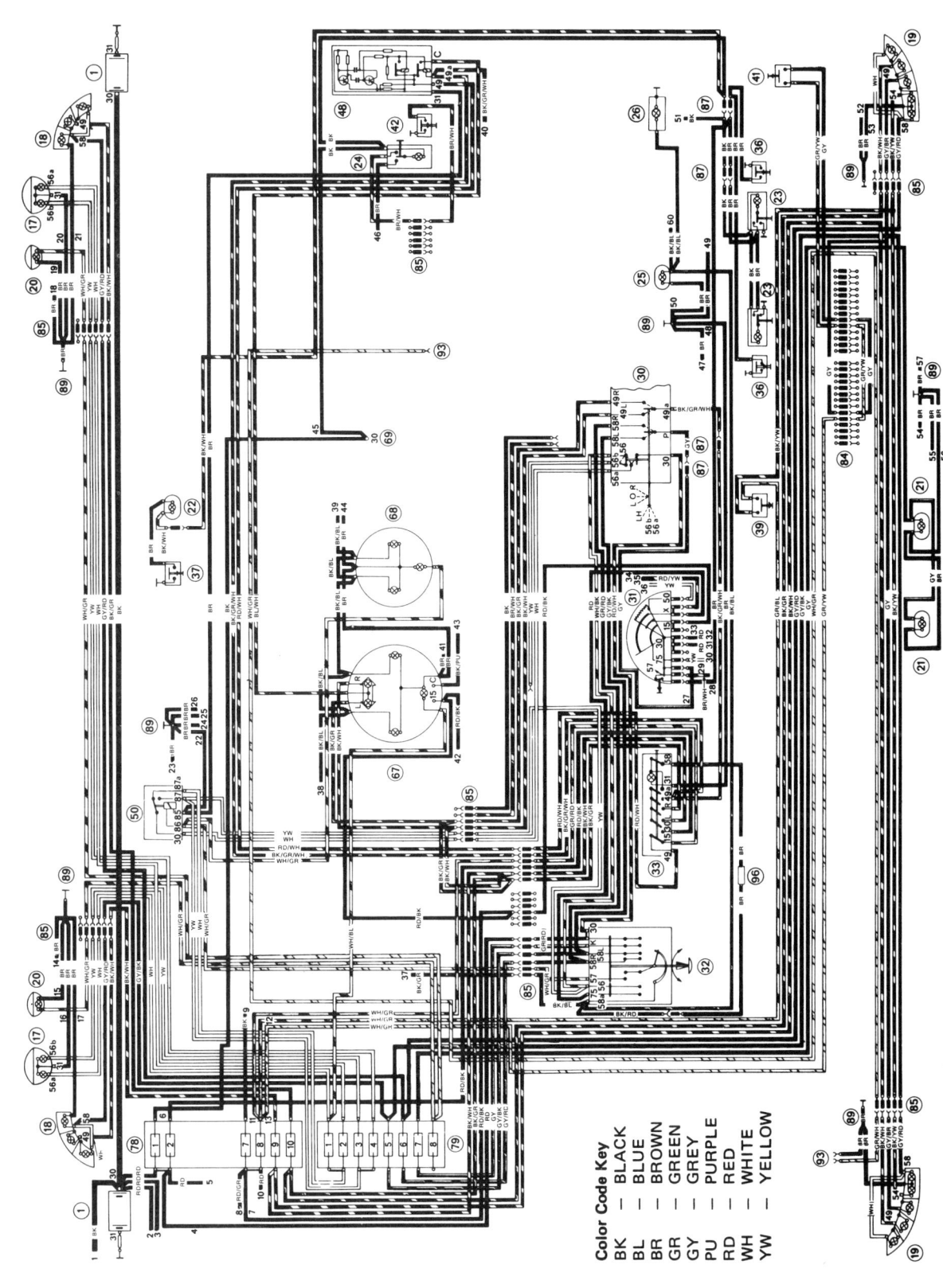

Color Code Key

BK – BLACK
BL – BLUE
BR – BROWN
GR – GREEN
GY – GREY
PU – PURPLE
RD – RED
WH – WHITE
YW – YELLOW

Fig. 9.52. Wiring diagram (Part 1), 911T, 911E, 911S, Carrera 2.7 - 1973 models (See page 222 for key)

Key to Wiring Diagram (Part 1), 911T, 911E, 911S, Carrera 2.7 - 1973 models

1 Battery
17 Headlights
18 Turn signal, parking and side marker lights (side marker lights USA only)
19 Tail, stop, turn, backup and side marker lights (side marker lights USA only)
20 Fog lights (optional)
21 License plate light
22 Luggage compartment light
23 Interior light
24 Glove compartment light
25 Ashtray light
26 Illumination for heating lever (USA only)
30 Flasher, dimmer, wiper-washer switch with horn ring on steering column
31 Ignition starter switch and steering lock
32 Light switch
33 Emergency flasher switch (not applicable in Italy and France)
36 Door contact switch
37 Switch for luggage compartment light
42 Switch for glove compartment light
48 Turn signal/emergency flasher unit
50 Headlight relay
67 Tachometer
68 Speedometer
69 Electric clock
78 Fuse box I (10 terminal)
79 Fuse box II (8 terminal)
84 Multi-connector (14 terminal)
85 Multi-connector (6 terminal)
87 Connector (single contact)
89 Earth connection-body
93 Rear fog light (optional)
96 Resistor (USA only)

FUSES:

Fuse box I:
1 Interior light, clock, luggage compartment light
2 Emergency flasher
7 Fresh air fan
8 Stop, turn and backup lights
9 Left front turn signal light
10 Right front turn signal light

Fuse box II:
1 High beam, left
2 High beam, right
3 Low beam, left
4 Low beam, right
5 Side marker, left
6 Side marker, right
7 License plate light
8 (Fog lights)

Key to Wiring Diagram (Part 2) 911T, 911E, 911S, Carrera 2.7 - 1973 models

1 Battery
2 Starter
3 Alternator
4 Governor
5 Distributor
6 Ignition transformer
7 Spark plugs
8 Fuel pump
9 High tesnion ignition un
11 Speed switch
12 Cold start solenoid (except 911 TV)
13 Shut-off solenoid (911 TV: solenoid valve)
14 Thermo-time switch (except 911 TV)
15 Micro switch
30 Flasher, dimmer, wiper-washer switch with horn ring on steering column
31 Ignition starter switch and steering lock
34 Switch for fan and auxiliary heater
35 Rear window defogger switch
38 Parking brake control
40 Brake warning light switch (USA only)
43 Safety belt contact, driver side (USA only)
44 Safety belt contact, passenger side (USA only)
45 Buzzer contact (USA only)
46 Seat contact, passenger side (USA only)
49 Horn relay
51 Rear window defogger relay
52 Auxiliary starting relay (except 911 TV)
53 Buzzer (USA only)
56 Oil temperature indiactor
57 Oil pressure indicator
58 Oil lever indicator
59 Indicator for fuel gauge
60 Safety belt warning light (USA only)
65 Fuel gauge dial
66 Oil temperature gauge dial
69 Electric clock
73 Wiper motor
74 Washer pump
75 Horns
77 Cigarette lighter
78 Fuse box I (10 terminal)
80 Fuse box III (3 terminal)
81 Fan motor
82 Rear window defogger element
83 Sportomatic (optional)
84 Multi-connector (14 terminal)
85 Multi-connector (6 terminals)
86 Multi-connector (4 terminal)
87 Connector (single contact)
88 Gear lever contact SPM (optional)
89 Earth connection-body
90 Optional horn
92 Auxiliary combustion heater (optional)
94 Radio (optional)

FUSES:

Fuse box I:
1 Interior light, clock luggage compartment light
2 Emergency flasher
3 (Electric windows)
4 Cigarette lighter
5 (Sliding roof)
6 Windshield wiper, washer pump
7 Fresh air fan
8 Stop, turn and backup lights
9 Left front turn signal light
10 Right

Fuse box II:
1 (Sportomatic)
2 Shut-off solenoid, solenoid valve, Solenoid for cold starting unit
3 Rear window defogger

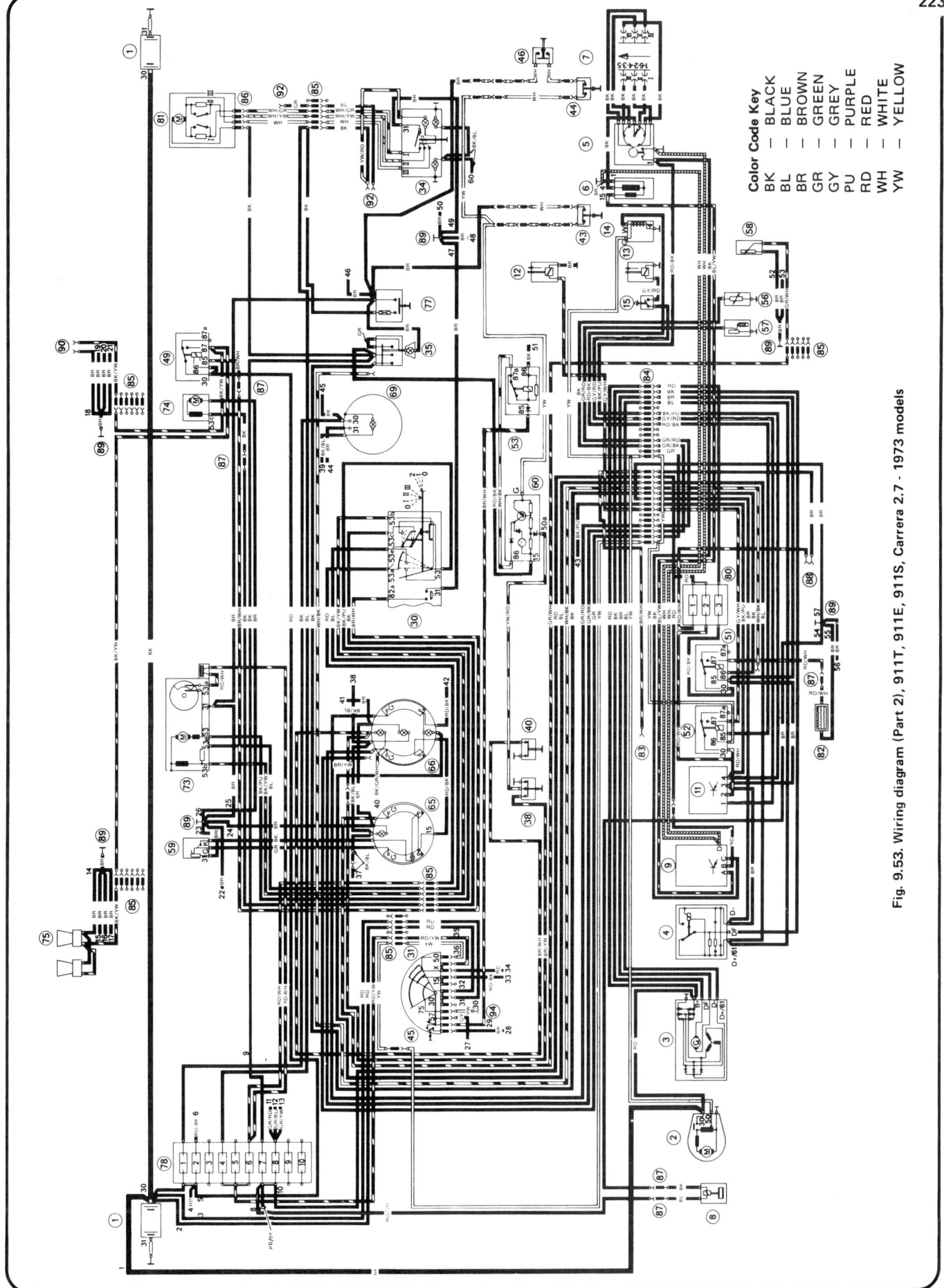

Color Code Key

BK — BLACK
BL — BLUE
BR — BROWN
GR — GREEN
GY — GREY
PU — PURPLE
RD — RED
WH — WHITE
YW — YELLOW

Fig. 9.53. Wiring diagram (Part 2), 911T, 911E, 911S, Carrera 2.7 - 1973 models

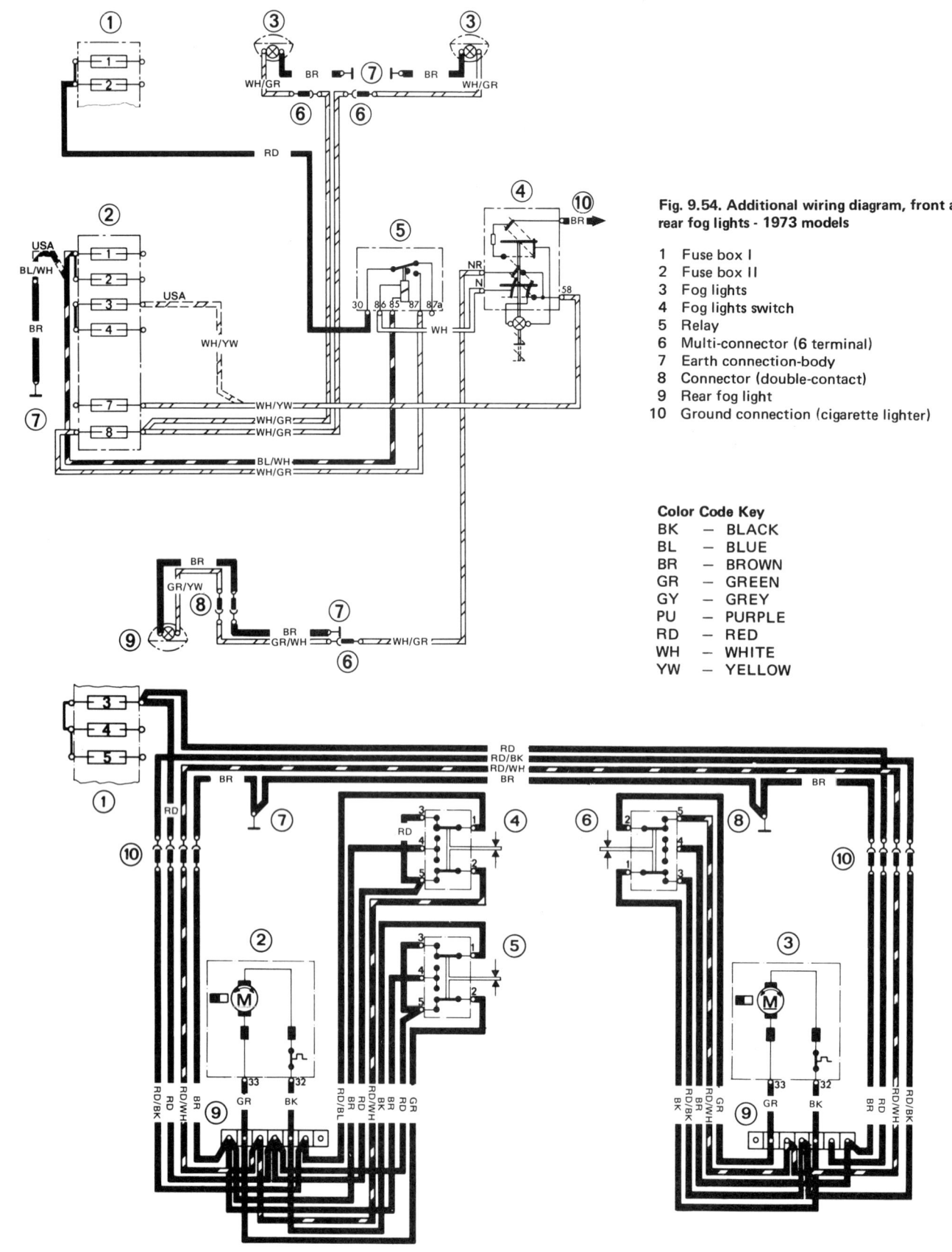

Fig. 9.54. Additional wiring diagram, front and rear fog lights - 1973 models

1 Fuse box I
2 Fuse box II
3 Fog lights
4 Fog lights switch
5 Relay
6 Multi-connector (6 terminal)
7 Earth connection-body
8 Connector (double-contact)
9 Rear fog light
10 Ground connection (cigarette lighter)

Color Code Key

BK	–	BLACK
BL	–	BLUE
BR	–	BROWN
GR	–	GREEN
GY	–	GREY
PU	–	PURPLE
RD	–	RED
WH	–	WHITE
YW	–	YELLOW

Fig. 9.55. Additional wiring diagram, electric windows - 1973 models

1 Fuse box I	4 Switch for passenger side, left	6 Switch for passenger side, right	8 Earth connection, right
2 Motor, driver side	5 Switch for driver side	7 Earth connection, left	9 Terminal strip
3 Motor, passenger side			10 Connector

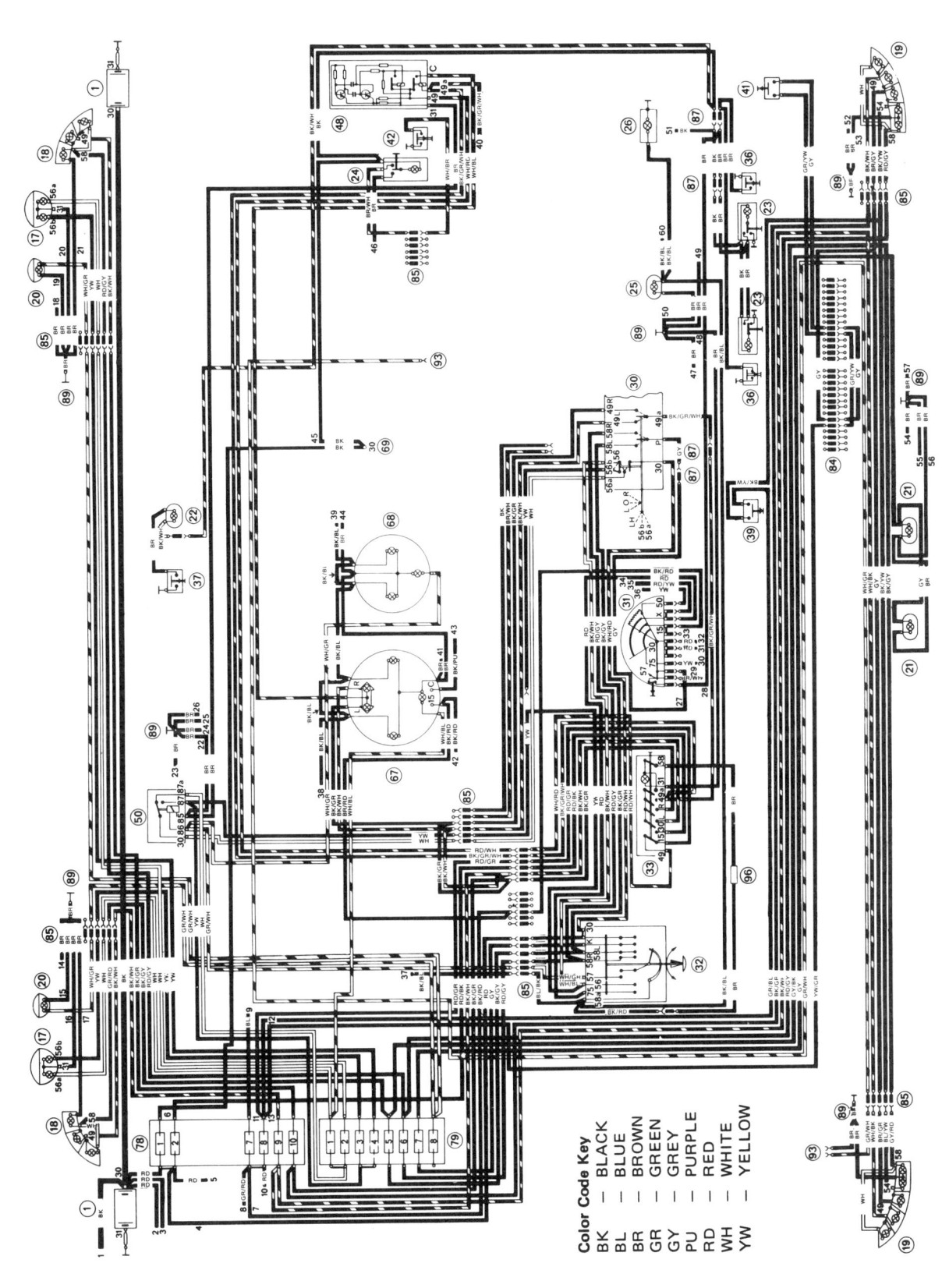

Color Code Key
BK — BLACK
BL — BLUE
BR — BROWN
GR — GREEN
GY — GREY
PU — PURPLE
RD — RED
WH — WHITE
YW — YELLOW

Fig. 9.56. Wiring diagram (Part 1), 911T with CIS - 1973 models (See page 226 for key)

Key to Wiring Diagram (Part I). 911T with C1S - 1973 models

1 Battery
17 Headlights
18 Turn signal, parking and side marker lights
   (side marker lights USA only)
19 Tail, stop, turn, backup and side marker lights
   (side marker lights USA only)
20 Fog lights (optional)
21 License plate light
22 Luggage compartment light
23 Interior light
24 Glove compartment light
25 Ashtray light
26 Illumination for heating lever (USA only)
30 Flasher, dimmer, wiper-washer switch with horn ring on steering column
31 Ignition starter switch and steering lock
32 Light switch
33 Emergency flasher switch (not applicable in Italy and France)
36 Door contact switch
37 Switch for luggage compartment light
39 Stop light switch
41 Back up light switch
42 Switch for glove compartment light
48 Turn signal/emergency flasher unit
50 Headlight relay
67 Tachometer
68 Speedometer
69 Electric clock
78 Fuse box I (10 terminal)
79 Fuse box II (8 terminal)
84 Multi-connector (14 terminal)
85 Multi-connector (6 terminal)
87 Connector (single contact)
89 Earth connection-body
93 Rear fog light (optional)
96 Resistor (USA only)

FUSES:

Fuse box I:
1 Interior light, lock, luggage compartment light
2 Emergency flasher
7 Fresh air fan
8 Stop, turn and backup lights
9 Left front turn signal light
10 Right front turn signal light

Fuse box II:
1 High beam, left
2 High beam, right
3 Low beam, left
4 Low beam, right
5 Side marker, left
6 Side marker, right
7 License plate light
8 (Fog lights)

Key to Wiring Diagram (Part 2) 911T with C1S - 1973 models

1 Battery
2 Starter
3 Alternator
4 Governor
5 Distributor
6 Ignition transformer
7 Spark plugs
8 Fuel pump
9 High tension ignition unit
12 Cold start solenoid
13 Control pressure regulating valve with warm-up compensation
14 Micro-switch
30 Flasher, dimmer, wiper-washer switch with horn ring on steering column
31 Ignition starter switch and steering lock
34 Switch for fan and auxiliary heater
35 Rear window defogger switch
38 Parking brake contact
40 Brake warning light switch (USA only)
43 Safety belt contact, driver side (USA only)
44 Safety belt contact, passenger side (USA only)
45 Buzzer contact (USA only)
46 Seat contact, passenger side (USA only)
49 Horn relay
51 Rear window defogger relay
53 Buzzer (USA only)
56 Oil temperature indicator
57 Oil pressure indicator (optional)
58 Oil level indicator (optional)
59 Indicator for fuel gauge
60 Safety belt warning light (USA only)
65 Fuel gauge dial
66 Oil temperature gauge dial
69 Electric clock
73 Wiper motor
74 Washer pump
75 Horns
77 Cigarette lighter
78 Fuse box I (10 terminals)
80 Fuse box III (3 terminal)
81 Fan motor
82 Rear window defogger element
83 Sportomatic (optional)
84 Multi-connector (14 terminal)
85 Multi-connector (6 terminal)
86 Multi-connector (4 terminal)
87 Connector (single contact)
88 Gear lever contact SPM (optional)
89 Earth connection-body
90 Optional horn
92 Auxiliary combustion heater (optional)
94 Radio (optional)

FUSES:

Fuse box I:
1 Interior light, lock, luggage compartment light
2 Emergency flasher
3 (Electric windows)
4 Cigarette lighter
5 (Sliding roof)
6 Windshield wiper, washer pump
7 Fresh air fan
8 Fresh air fan
9 Left front turn signal light
10 Right front turn signal light

Fuse box III:
1 (Sportomatic)
3 Rear window defogger

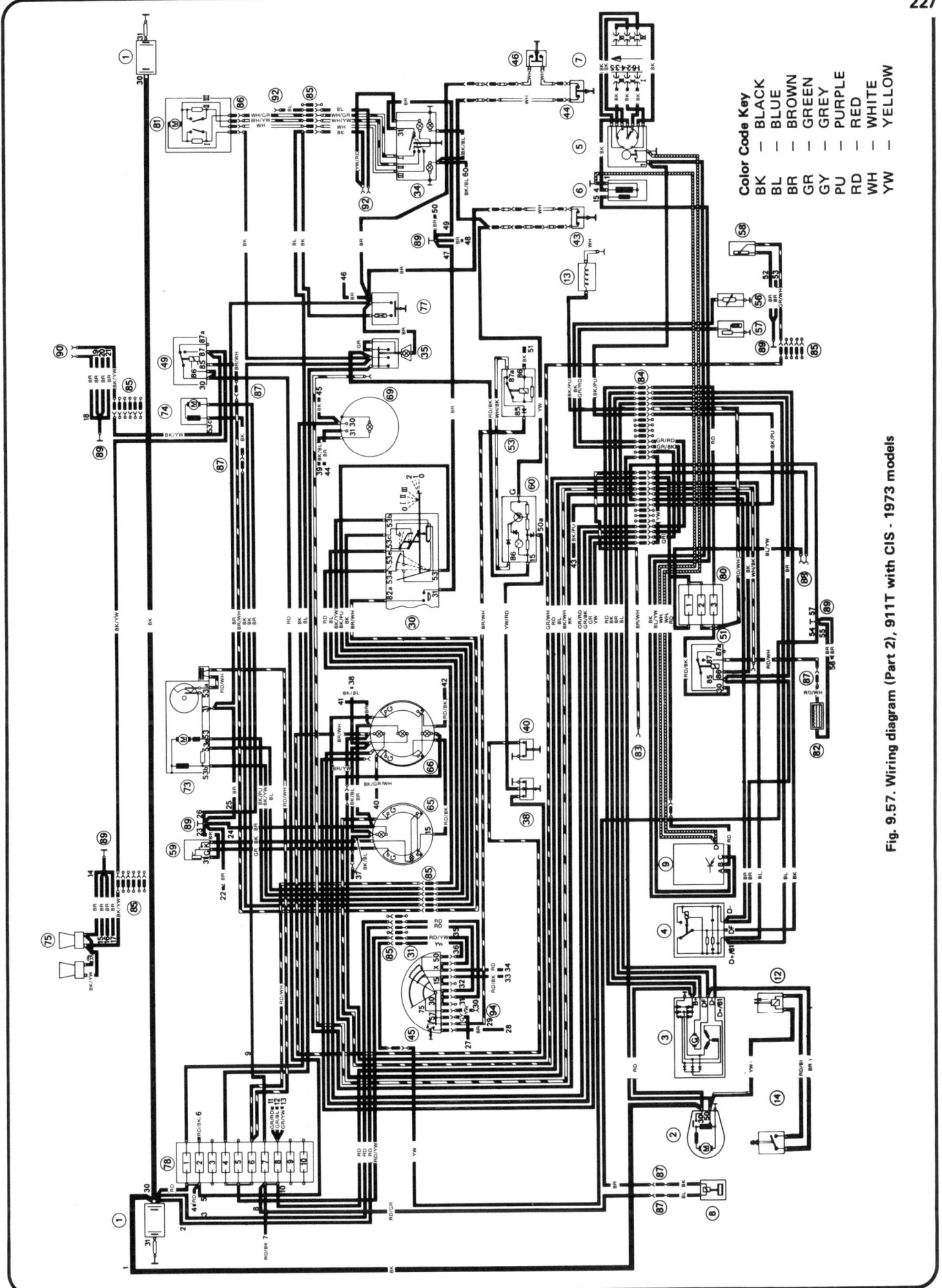

Color Code Key

BK	– BLACK
BL	– BLUE
BR	– BROWN
GR	– GREEN
GY	– GREY
PU	– PURPLE
RD	– RED
WH	– WHITE
YW	– YELLOW

Fig. 9.57. Wiring diagram (Part 2), 911T with CIS - 1973 models

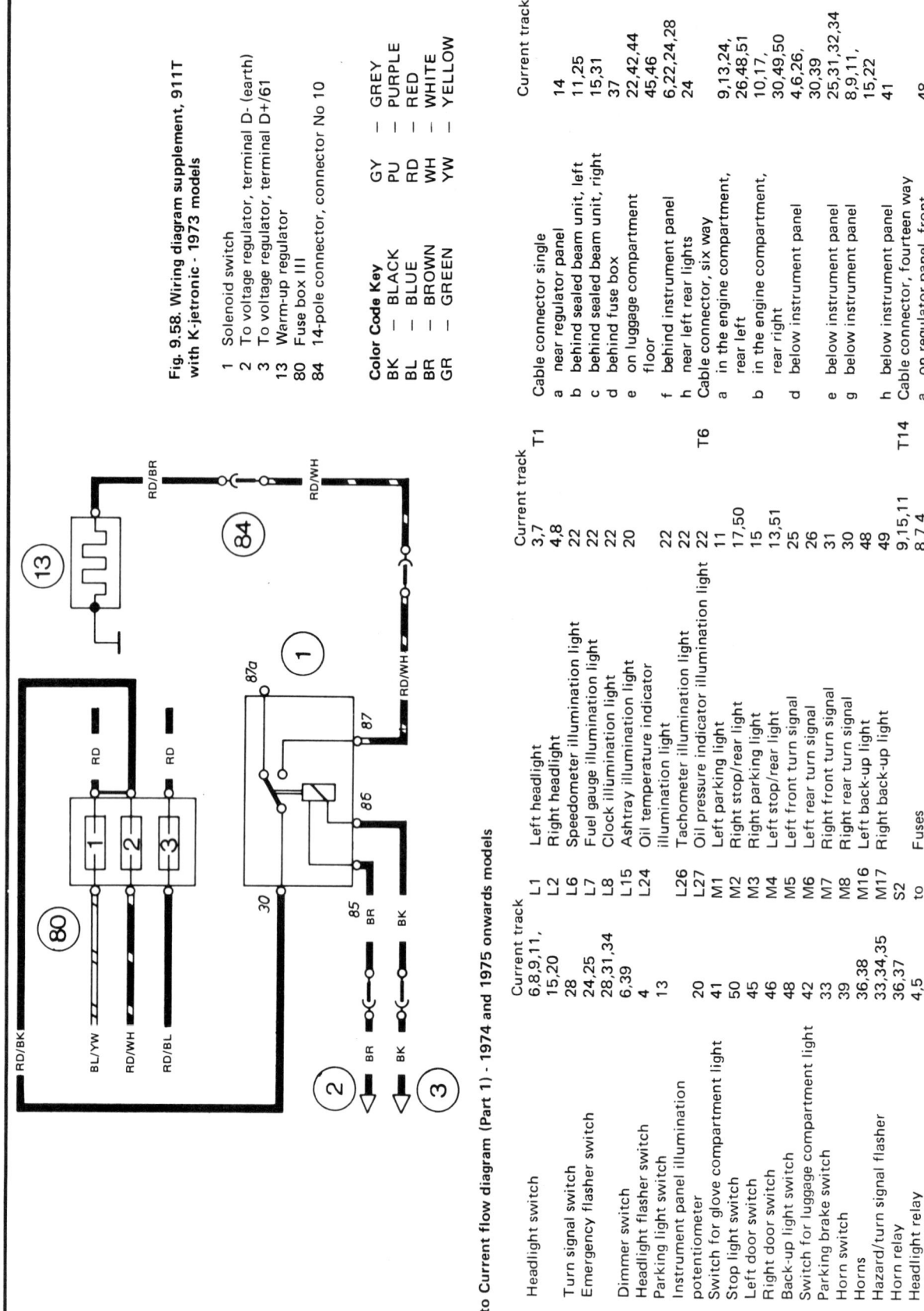

228

Fig. 9.58. Wiring diagram supplement, 911T with K-jetronic - 1973 models

1 Solenoid switch
2 To voltage regulator, terminal D- (earth)
3 To voltage regulator, terminal D+/61
13 Warm-up regulator
80 Fuse box III
84 14-pole connector, connector No 10

Color Code Key

BK	— BLACK	GY	— GREY
BL	— BLUE	PU	— PURPLE
BR	— BROWN	RD	— RED
GR	— GREEN	WH	— WHITE
		YW	— YELLOW

		Current track
T1	Cable connector single	
	a near regulator panel	14
	b behind sealed beam unit, left	11,25
	c behind sealed beam unit, right	15,31
	d behind fuse box	37
	e on luggage compartment floor	22,42,44 45,46
	f behind instrument panel	6,22,24,28
	h near left rear lights	24
T6	Cable connector, six way	
	a in the engine compartment, rear left	9,13,24, 26,48,51
	b in the engine compartment, rear right	10,17, 30,49,50
	d below instrument panel	4,6,26, 30,39
	e below instrument panel	25,31,32,34
	g below instrument panel	8,9,11, 15,22
	h below instrument panel	41
T14	Cable connector, fourteen way	
	a on regulator panel, front	48
	b on regulator panel, rear	48
W	Interior light	45,46
W3	Luggage compartment light	42
W6	Glove compartment light	41
X	License plate light	9,10
Y	Clock	40

Key to Current flow diagram (Part 1) - 1974 and 1975 onwards models

Code	Description	Current track
E1	Headlight switch	6,8,9,11, 15,20
E2	Turn signal switch	28
E3	Emergency flasher switch	24,25 28,31,34
E4	Dimmer switch	6,39
E5	Headlight flasher switch	4
E19	Parking light switch	13
E20	Instrument panel illumination potentiometer	20
E26	Switch for glove compartment light	41
F	Stop light switch	50
F2	Left door switch	45
F3	Right door switch	46
F4	Back-up light switch	48
F5	Switch for luggage compartment light	42
F9	Parking brake switch	33
H	Horn switch	39
H2	Horns	36,38
J1	Hazard/turn signal flasher	33,34,35
J4	Horn relay	36,37
J25	Headlight relay	4,5
K1	High beam indicator light	2
K4	Parking lights indicator light	1
K5	Turn signal indicator light	27,29
K6	Hazard flasher indicator light	24
K14	Parking brake indicator light	34

Code	Description	Current track
L1	Left headlight	3,7
L2	Right headlight	4,8
L6	Speedometer illumination light	22
L7	Fuel gauge illumination light	22
L8	Clock illumination light	22
L15	Ashtray illumination light	20
L24	Oil temperature indicator illumination light	22
L26	Tachometer illumination light	22
L27	Oil pressure indicator illumination light	22
M1	Left parking light	11
M2	Right stop/rear light	17,50
M3	Right parking light	15
M4	Left stop/rear light	13,51
M5	Left front turn signal	25
M6	Left rear turn signal	26
M7	Right front turn signal	31
M8	Right rear turn signal	30
M16	Left back-up light	48
M17	Right back-up light	49
S2	Fuses	9,15,11
to	on the	8,7,4
S11	fuse box	3,31,25,48
S17		34
S18		40

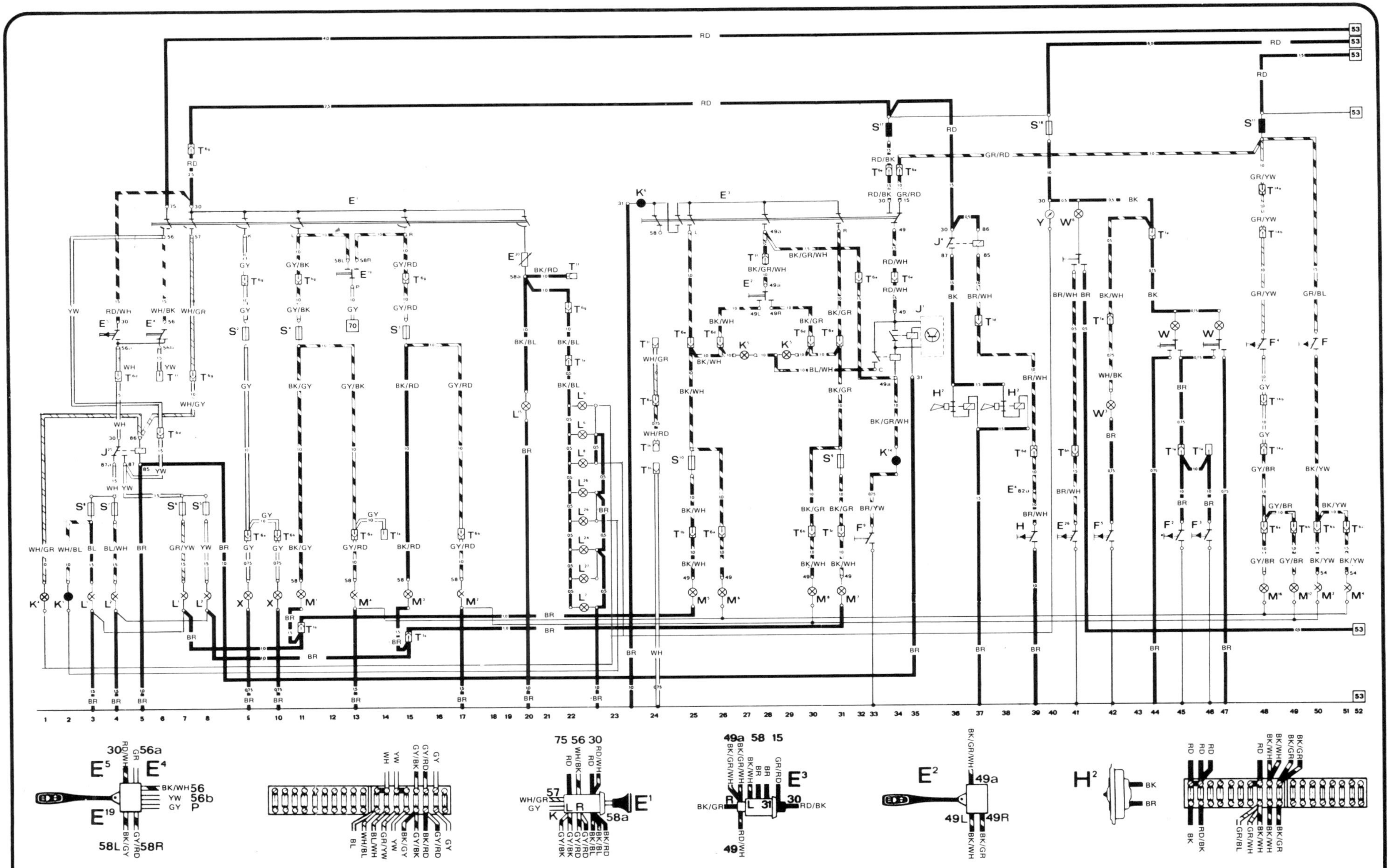

Color Code Key

BK	— BLACK	GY	— GREY
BL	— BLUE	PU	— PURPLE
BR	— BROWN	RD	— RED
GR	— GREEN	WH	— WHITE
		YW	— YELLOW

Fig. 9.59. Current flow diagram (Part 1), - 1974 and 1975 onwards models

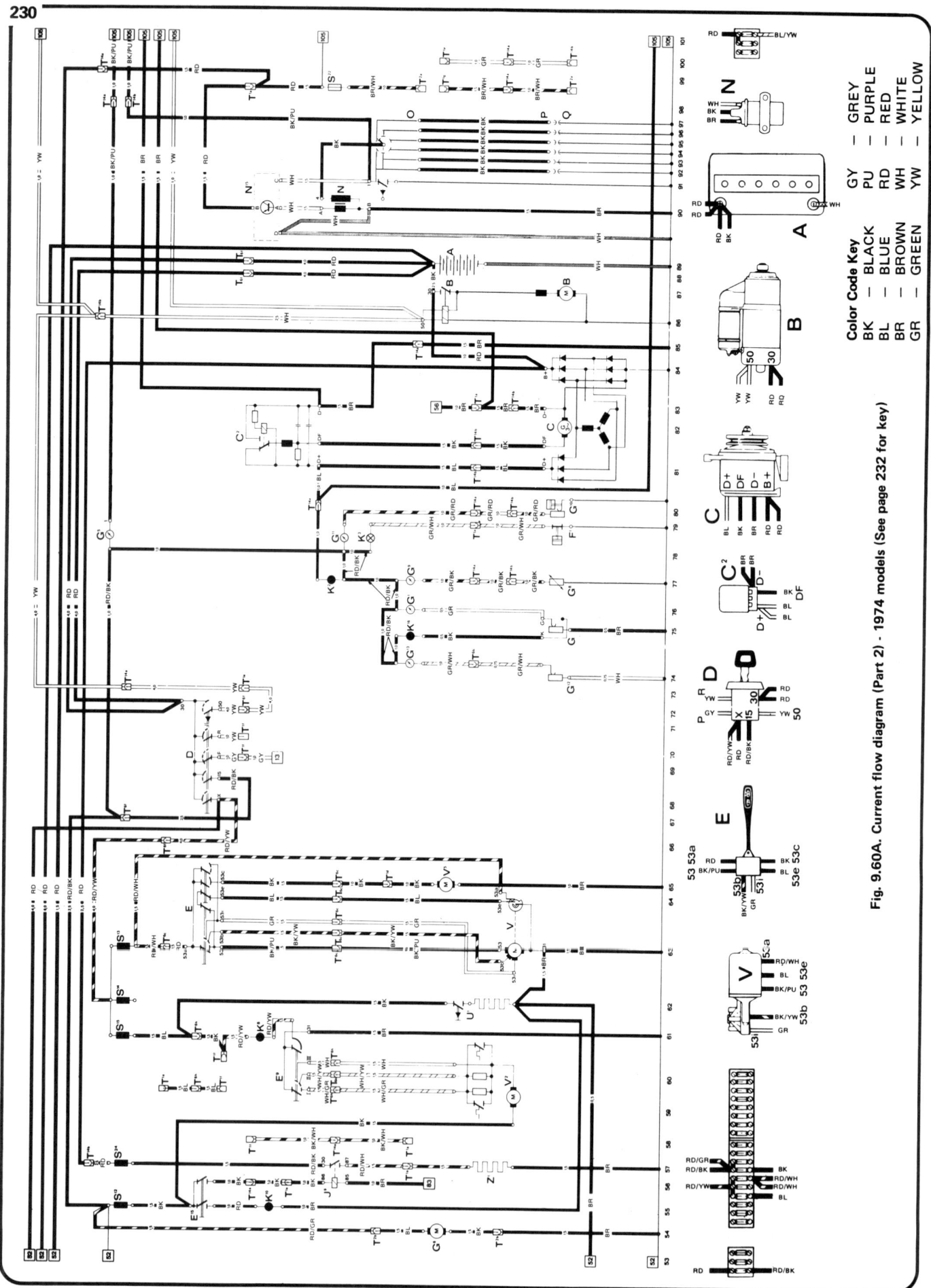

Fig. 9.60A. Current flow diagram (Part 2) - 1974 models (See page 232 for key)

Color Code Key

BK	— BLACK	GY	— GREY
BL	— BLUE	PU	— PURPLE
BR	— BROWN	RD	— RED
GR	— GREEN	WH	— WHITE
		YW	— YELLOW

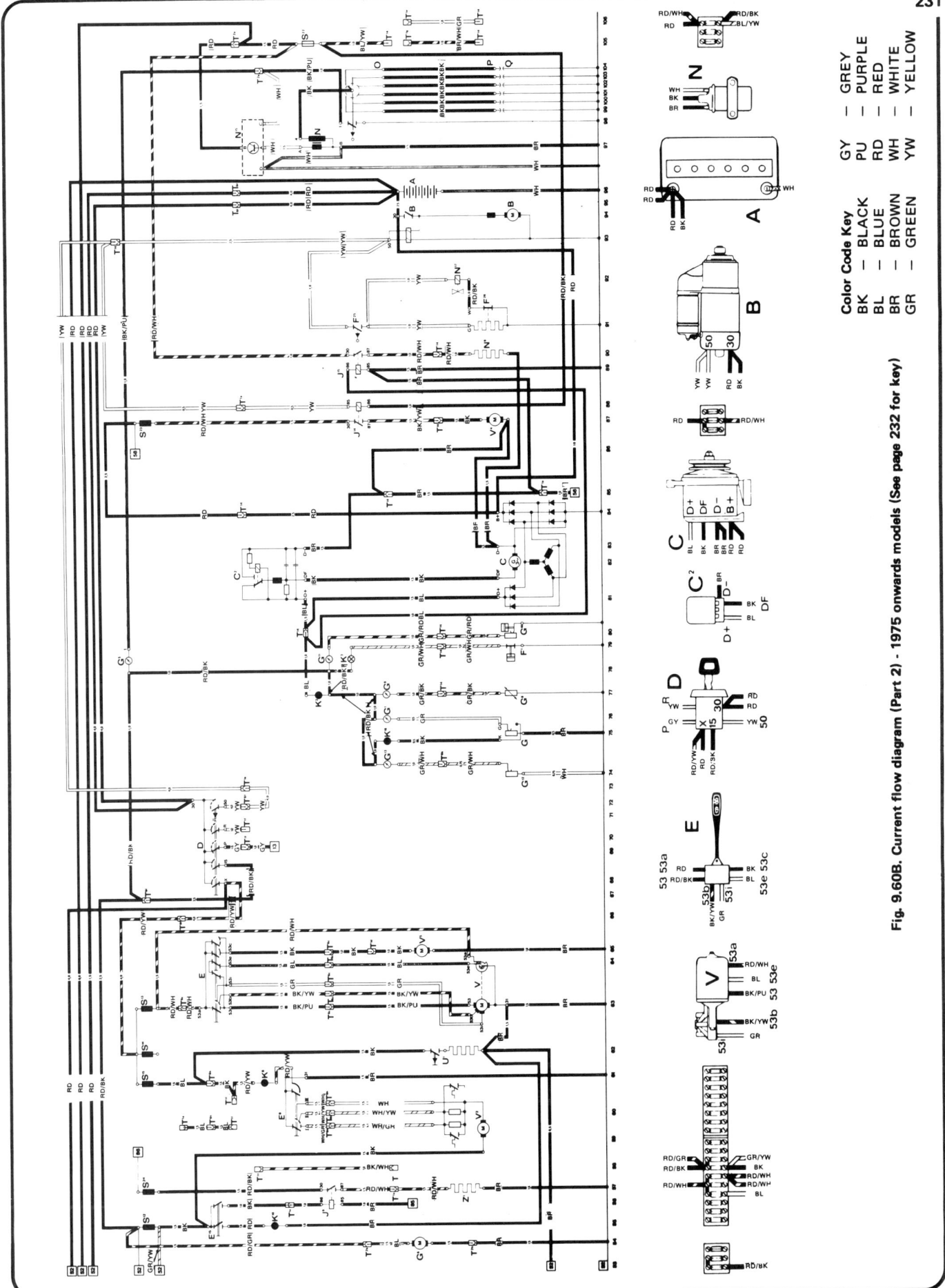

Fig. 9.60B. Current flow diagram (Part 2) - 1975 onwards models (See page 232 for key)

Color Code Key

BK — BLACK
BL — BLUE
BR — BROWN
GR — GREEN
GY — GREY
PU — PURPLE
RD — RED
WH — WHITE
YW — YELLOW

Key to Current flow diagrams A and B (Part 2) - 1975 onwards models

		Current track
A	Battery	89
B	Starter	86,87
C	Generator	81,82,83,84
C2	Voltage regulator	81,82,83
D	Ignition/starter switch	68,69,70,71,72
E	Windshield wiper switch	63,64,65
E9	Fresh air blower switch	60
E15	Rear window defogger switch	55,56
F1	Oil pressure switch	79
G	Fuel sender unit	75
G1	Fuel gauge	76
G5	Tachometer	78
G6	Fuel pump	54
G8	Oil temperature sender unit	77
G9	Oil temperature indicator	77
G10	Oil pressure sender unit	80
G11	Oil pressure indicator	78
G12	Oil level sender unit	74
G13	Oil level gauge	74
J9	Rear window defogger relay	56,57
K2	Generator charge indicator light	77
K3	Oil pressure indicator	78
K8	Blower indicator light	61
K10	Rear window defogger indicator light	55
K16	Low fuel warning light	75
N	Ignition transformer	90
N15	High tension ignition unit	90
O	Distributor	91,92,93,94 95,96,97
P	Spark plug connector	92,93,94 95,96,97
Q	Spark plug	92,93 94 95,96,97
S12	Fuses	55,63
to	on the	62
S15	fuse box	61
S22	Fuses on the	99
S24	rear fuse box (regulator panel)	57
T1	Cable connector, single	
	a near regulator panel	56,57,58 79,83,99
	d behind fuse box	65
	e on luggage compartment floor	60,73,100
	f behind instrument panel	58,60,61 69,70
	g below shift lever housing	99
T2	Cable connector, double	
	a below regulator panel	99
	b in engine compartment, left	54
T6	Cable connector, six way	
	b in engine compartment, right	74
	c below instrument panel	63,64,65
	f below instrument panel	66,67,72, 88,89
	h below instrument panel	60,61
T14	Cable connector, fourteen way	
	a on regulator panel, front	56,58,73,77 80,85,98,99 100
	b on regulator panel, rear	57,77,80,81 83,86,98,100
U1	Cigar lighter	62
V	Windshield wiper motor	63,64
V2	Blower motor	60
V5	Washer pump	65
Z1	Rear window defogger	57

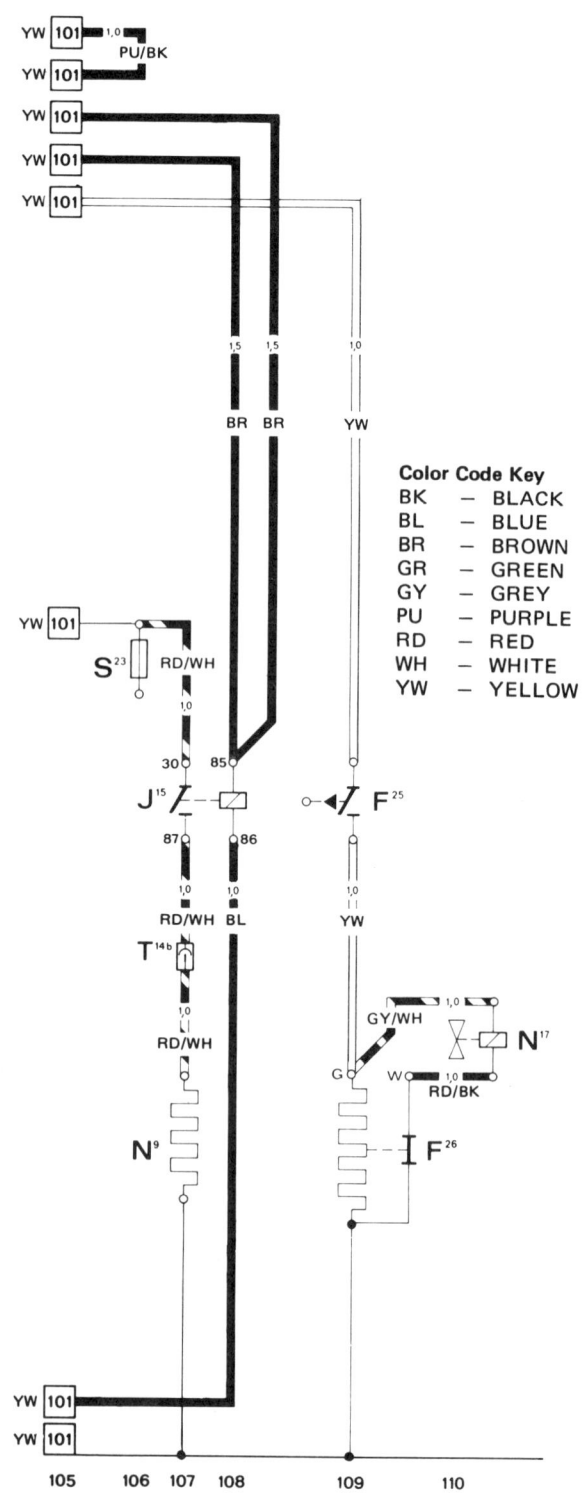

Color Code Key

BK	–	BLACK
BL	–	BLUE
BR	–	BROWN
GR	–	GREEN
GY	–	GREY
PU	–	PURPLE
RD	–	RED
WH	–	WHITE
YW	–	YELLOW

Fig. 9.61. Additional current flow diagram, 911 with K-jetronic - 1974 models

		Current track
F25	Throttle valve switch	109
F26	Thermo-switch for cold start valve	109
J15	Relay for warm-up regulator	107, 108
N9	Warm-up regulator	107
N17	Cold start valve	110
S23	Fuse on the rear fuse box	106
T14b	Cable connector, fourteenway on regulator panel, rear	107

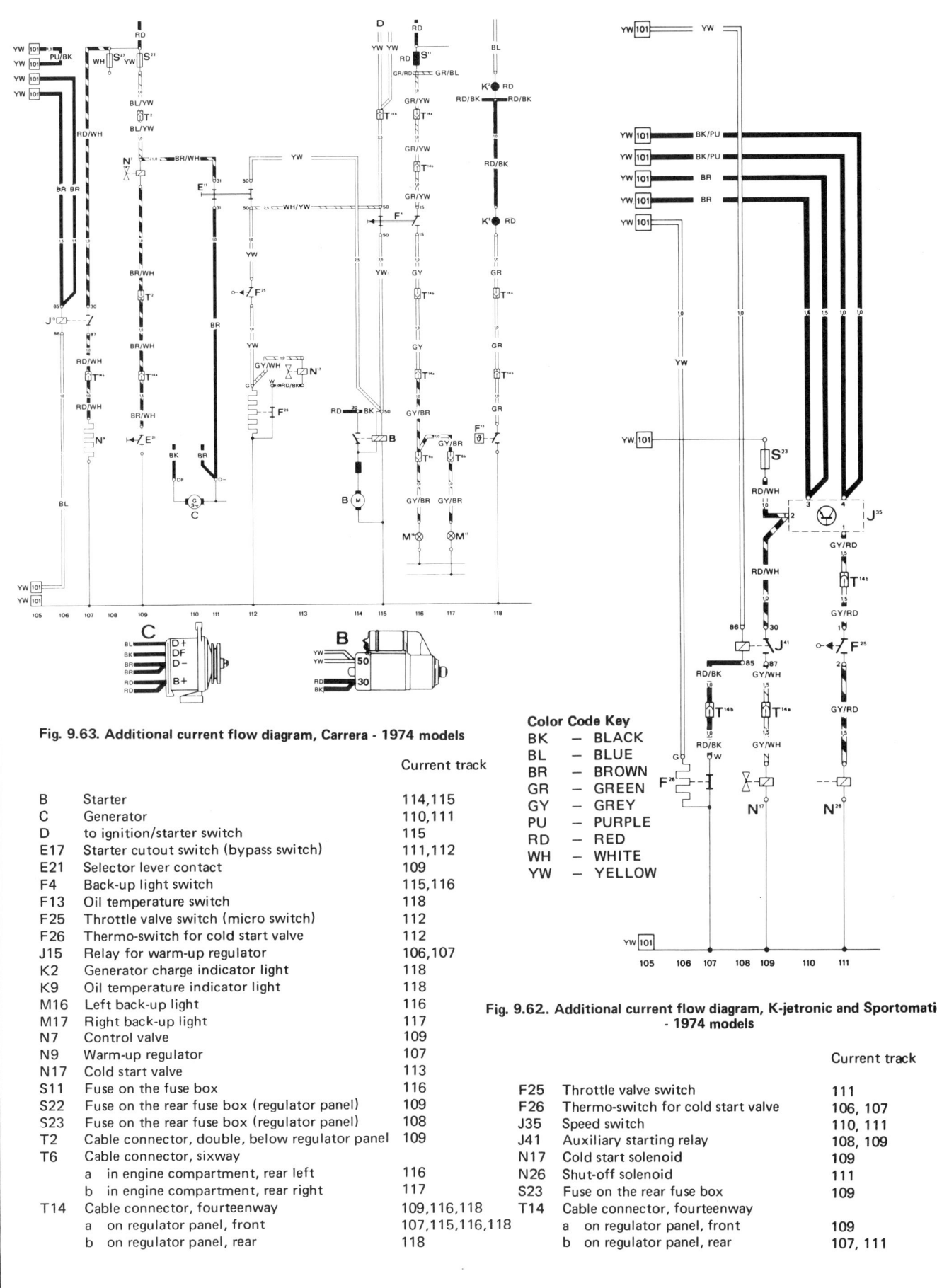

Fig. 9.63. Additional current flow diagram, Carrera - 1974 models

		Current track
B	Starter	114,115
C	Generator	110,111
D	to ignition/starter switch	115
E17	Starter cutout switch (bypass switch)	111,112
E21	Selector lever contact	109
F4	Back-up light switch	115,116
F13	Oil temperature switch	118
F25	Throttle valve switch (micro switch)	112
F26	Thermo-switch for cold start valve	112
J15	Relay for warm-up regulator	106,107
K2	Generator charge indicator light	118
K9	Oil temperature indicator light	118
M16	Left back-up light	116
M17	Right back-up light	117
N7	Control valve	109
N9	Warm-up regulator	107
N17	Cold start valve	113
S11	Fuse on the fuse box	116
S22	Fuse on the rear fuse box (regulator panel)	109
S23	Fuse on the rear fuse box (regulator panel)	108
T2	Cable connector, double, below regulator panel	109
T6	Cable connector, sixway	
	a in engine compartment, rear left	116
	b in engine compartment, rear right	117
T14	Cable connector, fourteenway	109,116,118
	a on regulator panel, front	107,115,116,118
	b on regulator panel, rear	118

Color Code Key

BK	–	BLACK
BL	–	BLUE
BR	–	BROWN
GR	–	GREEN
GY	–	GREY
PU	–	PURPLE
RD	–	RED
WH	–	WHITE
YW	–	YELLOW

Fig. 9.62. Additional current flow diagram, K-jetronic and Sportomatic - 1974 models

		Current track
F25	Throttle valve switch	111
F26	Thermo-switch for cold start valve	106, 107
J35	Speed switch	110, 111
J41	Auxiliary starting relay	108, 109
N17	Cold start solenoid	109
N26	Shut-off solenoid	111
S23	Fuse on the rear fuse box	109
T14	Cable connector, fourteenway	
	a on regulator panel, front	109
	b on regulator panel, rear	107, 111

Chapter 10 Bodywork and fittings

Contents

1 General description

The body is an aerodynamically efficient, all-steel construction, integral with the underframe. The pillars and frame members are fabricated from deep-drawn thin wall steel sheet; the main outer skin is welded to the floor group, wheel arches and pillars to form the integral unit. The front luggage compartment and rear engine compartment have hinged lids, opened by cable pulls from inside the car. The front wings (fenders), are bolted onto the main body structure.

The doors are attached to the front body pillars by internally fitted hinges, and are adjustable both at the hinges and striker plates for alignment with the body contours. The curved door windows are of safety glass, as is the rear window; the windscreen is of laminated safety glass.

For sound-proofing and insulation, all hollow sections and non-painted areas are treated with rust inhibitors and/or anti-drum compound.

For heating, an engine-driven fan blows hot air through ducts into the car interior, the amount being controlled by a lever on the tunnel and by slides in the footwell areas. A ram-air ventilation system is incorporated, and cold air can be boosted, or mixed with hot air, by the fan and control system. An auxiliary combustion heater is available on left-hand drive models. Details of this system are not included in this manual; if adjustment or repair is required, your Porsche dealer should carry out the necessary work.

2 Maintenance - bodywork and underframe

1 The condition of your car's bodywork is of considerable importance as it is on this that the second-hand value of the car will mainly depend. It is much more difficult to repair neglected bodywork than to renew mechanical assemblies. The hidden portions of the body, such as the wheel arches, fender skirts, the underframe and the engine compartment are equally important, although obviously not requiring such frequent attention as the immediately visible paintwork.

2 Once a year or every 12000 miles it is a sound scheme to visit your local dealer and have the underside of the body steam cleaned. All traces of dirt and oil will be removed and the underside can then be inspected carefully for rust, damaged hydraulic pipes, frayed electrical wiring and similar maladies.

3 At the same time, clean the engine and the engine compartment either using a steam cleaner or a water-soluble cleaner.

4 The wheel arches and fender skirts should be given particular attention as under-sealing can easily come away here, and stones and dirt thrown up from the roadwheels can soon cause the paint to chip and flake, and so allow rust to set in. If rust is found, clean down to the bare metal and apply an anti-rust paint.

5 The bodywork should be washed once a week or when dirty.

Thoroughly wet the car to soften the dirt and then wash the car down with a soft sponge and plenty of clean water. If the surplus dirt is not washed off very gently, in time it will wear paint down.

6 Spots of tar or bitumen coating thrown up from the road surface are best removed with a cloth soaked in gasoline.

7 Once every six months, give the bodywork and chromium trim a thoroughly good wax polish. If a chromium cleaner is used to remove rust on any of the vehicle's plated parts remember that the cleaner also removes part of the chromium so use sparingly.

3 Maintenance - upholstery and carpets

1 Remove the carpets or mats, and thoroughly vacuum clean the interior of the vehicle every three months or more frequently if necessary.

2 Beat out the carpets and vacuum clean them if they are very dirty. If the upholstery is soiled apply an upholstery cleaner with a damp sponge, and wipe off with a clean dry cloth.

4 Maintenance - PVC external roof covering

Under no circumstances try to clean any external PVC roof covering with detergents, caustic soaps or spirit cleaners. Plain soap and water is all that is required, with a soft brush to clean dirt that may be ingrained. Wash the covering as frequently as the rest of the vehicle.

5 Bodywork repairs - minor damage

The photo sequence on pages 235, 236 and 237 illustrates the operations detailed in the following sub. Sections.

Repair of minor scratches in the vehicle's bodywork

If the scratch is very superficial, and does not penetrate to the metal of the bodywork - repair is very simple. Lightly rub the area of the scratch with a paintwork renovator or a very fine cutting paste, to remove loose paint from the scratch and to clear the surrounding bodywork of wax polish. Rinse the area with clean water.

Apply touch-up paint to the scratch using a thin paint brush; continue to apply thin layers of paint until the surface of the paint in the scratch is level with the surrounding paintwork. Allow the new paint at least two weeks to harden, then, blend it into the surrounding paintwork by rubbing the paintwork, in the scratch area with a paintwork renovator, or a very fine cutting paste. Finally apply wax polish.

An alternative to painting over the scratch is to use a paint transfer. Use the same preparation for the affected area; then simply, pick a patch of a suitable size to cover the scratch completely. Hold the patch against the scratch and burnish its backing paper; the paper will adhere to the paintwork, freeing itself from the backing paper at the same

Typical example of rust damage to a body panel. Before starting ensure that you have all of the materials required to hand. The first task is to ...

... remove body fittings from effected area, except those which can act as a guide to the original shape of the damaged bodywork - the headlamp shell in this case.

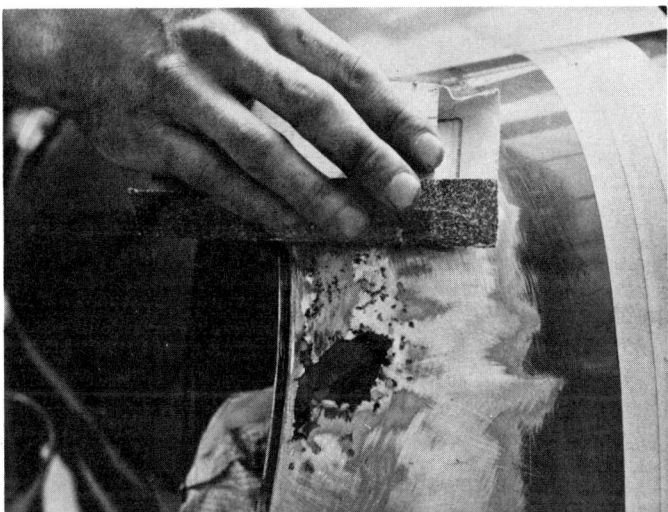

Remove all paint from the rusted area and from an inch or so of the adjoining 'sound' bodywork - use coarse abrasive paper or a power drill fitted with a wire brush or abrasive pad. Gently hammer in the edges of the hole to provide a hollow for the filler.

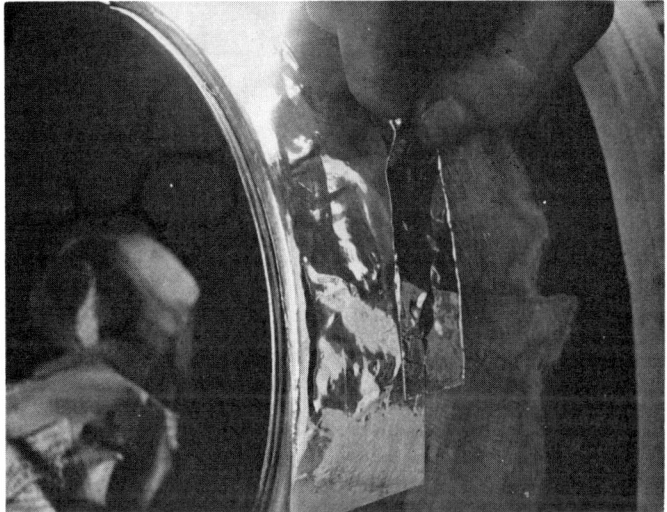

Before filling, the larger holes must be blocked off. Adhesive aluminium tape is one method; cut the tape to the required shape and size, peel off the backing strip (where used), position the tape over the hole and burnish to ensure adhesion.

Alternatively, zinc gauze can be used. Cut a piece of the gauze to the required shape and size; position it in the hole below the level of the surrounding bodywork; then ...

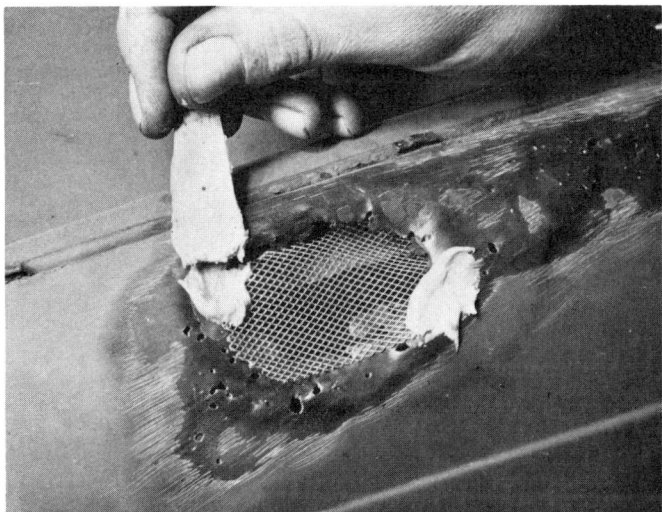

... secure in position by placing a few blobs of filler paste around its periphery. Alternatively, pop rivets or self-tapping screws can be used. Preparation for filling is now complete.

Mix filler and hardener according to manufacturer's instructions - avoid using too much hardener otherwise the filler will harden before you have a chance to work it.

Apply the filler to the affected area with a flexible applicator - this will ensure a smooth finish. Apply thin layers of filler at 20 minute intervals, until the surface of the filler is just 'proud' of the surrounding bodywork. Then ...

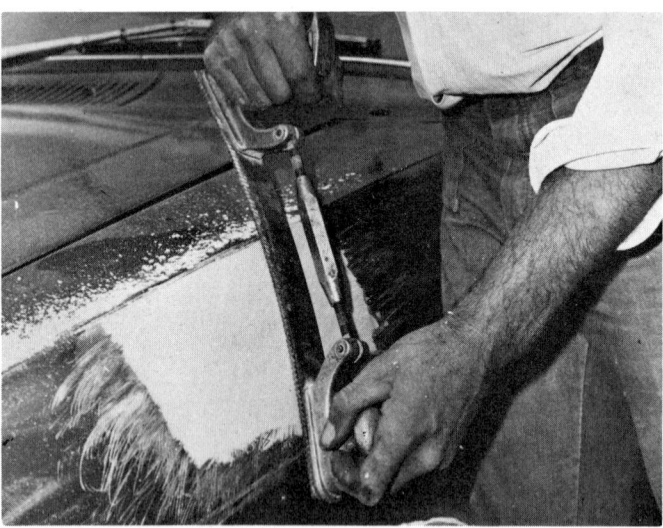

... remove excess filler and start shaping with a Surform plane or a dreadnought file. Once an approximate contour has been obtained and the surface is relatively smooth, start using ...

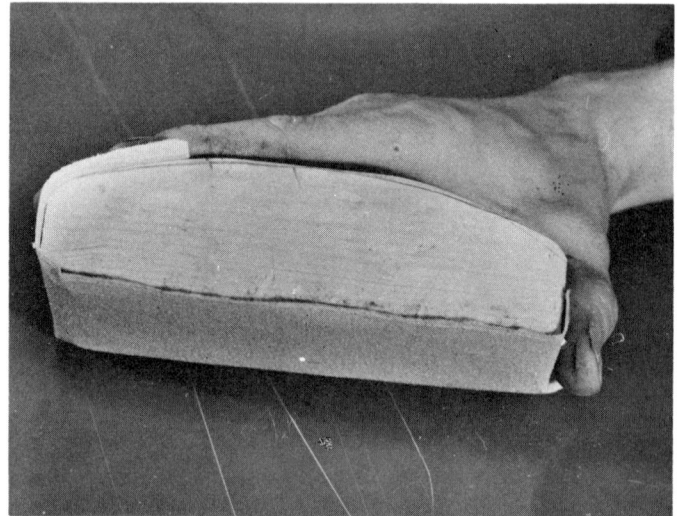

... abrasive paper. The paper should be wrapped around a flat wood, cork or rubber block - this will ensure that it imparts a smooth surface to the filler.

40 grit production paper is best to start with, then use progressively finer abrasive paper, finishing with 400 grade 'wet-and-dry'. When using 'wet-and-dry' paper, periodically rinse it in water ensuring also, that the work area is kept wet continuously.

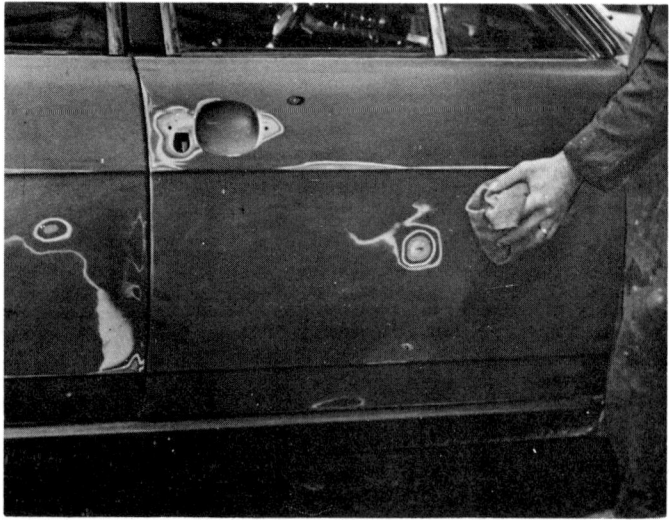

Rubbing-down is complete when the surface of the filler is really smooth and flat, and the edges of the surrounding paintwork are finely 'feathered'. Wash the area thoroughly with clean water and allow to dry before commencing re-spray.

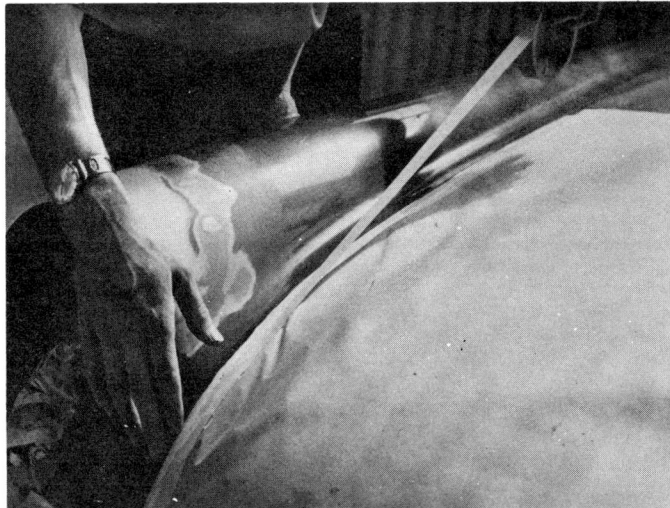

Firstly, mask off all adjoining panels and the fittings in the spray area. Ensure that the area to be sprayed is completely free of dust. Practice using an aerosol on a piece of waste metal sheet until the technique is mastered.

Spray the affected area with primer - apply several thin coats rather than one thick one. Start spraying in the centre of the repair area and then work outwards using a circular motion - in this way the paint will be evenly distributed.

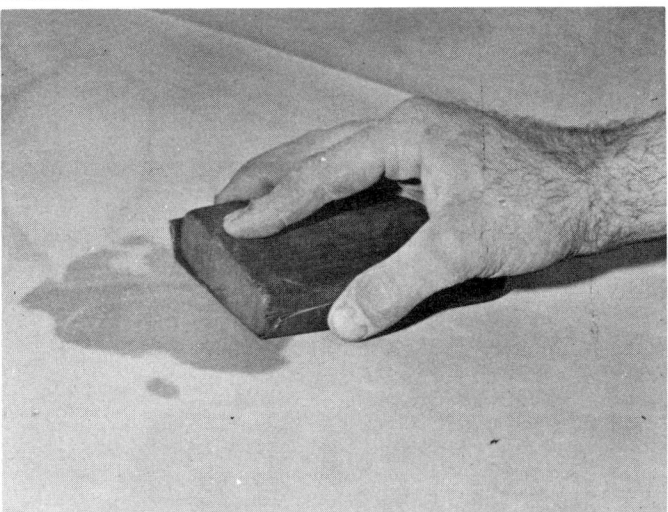

When the primer has dried inspect its surface for imperfections. Holes can be filled with filler paste or body-stopper, and lumps can be sanded smooth. Apply a further coat of primer, then 'flat' its surface with 400 grade 'wet-and-dry' paper.

Spray on the top coat, again building up the thickness with several thin coats of paint. Overspray onto the surrounding original paintwork to a depth of about five inches, applying a very thin coat at the outer edges.

Allow the paint two weeks, at least, to harden fully, then blend it into the surrounding original paintwork with a paint restorative compound or very fine cutting paste. Use wax polish to finish off.

The finished job should look like this. Remember, the quality of the completed work is directly proportional to the amount of time and effort expended at each stage of the preparation.

time. Polish the affected area to blend the patch into the surrounding paintwork.

Where a scratch has penetrated right through to the metal of the bodywork, causing the metal to rust, a different repair technique is required. Remove any loose rust from the bottom of the scratch with a penknife; then apply rust inhibiting paint to prevent the formation of rust in the future. Using a rubber or nylon applicator, fill the scratch with bodystopper paste. If required, this paste can be mixed with cellulose thinners to provide a very thin paste which is ideal for filling narrow scratches. Before the stopper paste on the scratch hardens, wrap a piece of smooth cotton rag around the tip of a finger. Dip the finger in cellulose thinners and then quickly sweep it across the surface of the stopper-paste in the scratch; this will ensure that the surface of the stopper-paste is slightly hollowed. The scratch can now be painted over as described earlier in this Section.

Repair of dents in the vehicle's bodywork

When deep denting of the vehicle's bodywork has taken place, the irst task is to pull the dent out, until the affected bodywork almost attains its original shape. There is little point in trying to restore the original shape completely; as the metal in the damaged area will have stretched on impact and cannot be reshaped fully to its original contour. It is better to bring the level of the dent up to a point which is about 1/8 inch (3 mm) below the level of the surrounding bodywork. In cases where the dent is very shallow anyway, it is not worth trying to pull it out at all.

If the underside of the dent is accessible, it can be hammered out gently from behind, using a mallet with a wooden or plastic head. Whilst doing this, hold a suitable block of wood firmly against the outside of the dent. This block will absorb the impact from the hammer blows and thus prevent a large area of bodywork from being 'belled-out'.

Should the dent be in a section of the bodywork which has a double skin or some other factor making it inaccessible from behind, a different technique is called for. Drill several small holes through the metal inside the dent area - particularly in the deeper sections. Then screw long self-tapping screws into the holes just sufficiently for them to gain a good purchase in the metal. Now the dent can be pulled out by pulling on the protruding heads of the screws with a pair of pliers.

The next stage of the repair is the removal of the paint from the damaged area , and from an inch or so of the surrounding 'sound' bodywork. This is accomplished most easily by using a wire brush or abrasive pad on a power drill, although it can be done just as effectively by hand using sheets of abrasive paper. To complete the preparations for filling, score the surface of the bare metal with a screwdriver or the tang of a file, or alternatively, drill small holes in the affected area. This will provide a really good 'key' for the filler paste.

To complete the repair see the Section on filling and re-spraying.

Repair of rust holes or gashes in the vehicle's bodywork

Remove all paint from the affected area and from an inch or so of the surrounding 'sound' bodywork, using an abrasive pad or a wire brush on a power drill. If these are not available a few sheets of abrasive paper will do the job just as effectively. With the paint removed you will be able to gauge the severity of the corrosion and therefore decide whether to replace the whole panel (if this is possible) or to repair the affected area. Replacement body panels are not as expensive as most people think and it is often quicker and more satisfactory to fit a new panel than to attempt to repair large areas of corrosion.

Remove all fittings from the affected area except those which will act as a guide to the original shape of the damaged bodywork (eg, headlamp shells etc). Then, using tin snips or a hacksaw blade, remove all loose metal and any other metal badly affected by corrosion. Hammer the edges of the hole inwards in order to create a slight depression for the filler paste.

Wire brush the affected area to remove the powdery rust from the surface of the remaining metal. Paint the affected area with rust inhibiting paint; if the back of the rusted area is accessible treat this also.

Before filling can take place it will be necessary to block the hole in some way. This can be achieved by the use of one of the following materials: Zinc gauze, Aluminium tape or Polyurethane foam.

Zinc gauze is probably the best material to use for a large hole. Cut a piece to the approximate size and shape of the hole to be filled, then position it in the hole so that its edges are below the level of the surrounding bodywork. It can be retained in position by several blobs

of filler paste around its periphery.

Aluminium tape should be used for small or very narrow holes. Pull a piece off the roll and trim it to the approximate size and shape required, then pull off the backing paper (if used) and stick the tape over the hole; it can be overlapped if the thickness of one piece is insufficient. Burnish down the edges of the tape with the handle of a screwdriver or similar, to ensure that the tape is securely attached to the metal underneath.

Polyurethane foam is best used where the hole is situated in a section of bodywork of complex shape, backed by a small box section (eg, where the rocker panel meets the rear wheel arch - most vehicles). The usual mixing procedure for this foam is as follows: Put equal amounts of fluid from each of the two cans provided in the kit, into one container. Stir until the mixture begins to thicken, then quickly pour this mixture into the hole, and hold a piece of cardboard over the larger apertures. Almost immediately the polyurethane will begin to expand, gushing frantically out of any small holes left unblocked. When the foam hardens it can be cut back to just below the level of the surrounding bodywork with a hacksaw blade.

Having blocked off the hole, the affected area must now be filled and sprayed - see Section on bodywork filling and re-spraying.

Bodywork repairs - filling and re-spraying

Before using this Section, see the Sections on dent, deep scratch, rust hole, and gash repairs.

Many types of bodyfiller are available, but generally speaking those proprietary kits which contain a tin of filler paste and a tube of resin hardener are best for this type of repair. A wide, flexible plastic or nylon applicator will be found invaluable for imparting a smooth and well contoured finish to the surface of the filler.

Mix up a little filler on a clean piece of card or board - use the hardener sparingly (follow the maker's instructions on the pack), otherwise the filler will set very rapidly.

Using the applicator, apply the filler paste to the prepared area, draw the applicator across the surface of the filler to achieve the correct contour and to level the filler surface. As soon as a contour that approximates the correct one is achieved, stop working the paste - if you carry on too long the paste will become sticky and begin to 'pick-up' on the applicator.

Continue to add the layers of filler paste at twenty-minute intervals until the level of the filler is just 'proud' of the surrounding bodywork.

Once the filler has hardened, excess can be removed using a Surform plane or Dreadnought file. From then on, progressively finer grades of abrasive paper should be used, starting from a 40 grade 'wet-and-dry' paper. Always wrap the abrasive paper around a flat rubber, cork or wooden block - otherwise the surface of the filler will not be completely flat. During the smoothing of the filler surface the 'wet-and-dry' paper should be periodically rinsed in water - this will ensure that a very smooth finish is imparted to the filler at the final stage.

At this stage the 'dent' should be surrounded by a ring of bare metal, which in turn should be encircled by the finely 'feathered' edge of the good paintwork. Rinse the repair area with clean water, until all of the dust produced by the rubbing-down operation is gone.

Spray the whole repair area with a light coat of grey primer; this will show up any imperfections in the surface of the filler. Repair these imperfections with fresh filler paste or bodystopper, and once more smooth the surface with abrasive paper. If bodystopper is used, it can be mixed with cellulose thinners to form a really thin paste which is ideal for filling small holes. Repeat this spray and repair procedure until you are satisfied that the surface of the filler, and the feathered edge of the paintwork are perfect. Clean the repair area with clean water and allow to dry fully.

The repair area is now ready for spraying. Paint spraying must be carried out in a warm, dry, windless and dust free atmosphere. This condition can be created artificially if you have access to a large indoor working area, but if you are forced to work in the open, you will have to pick your day very carefully. If you are working indoors, dousing the floor in the work area with water will 'lay' the dust which would otherwise be in the atmosphere. If the repair area is confined to one body panel, mask off the surrounding panels; this will help to minimise the effects of a slight mis-match in paint colours. Bodywork fittings (eg, chrome strips, door handles etc) will also need to be masked off. Use genuine masking tape and several thicknesses of newspaper for the masking operation.

Before commencing to spray, agitate the aerosol can thoroughly, then spray a test area (an old tin, or similar) until the technique is mastered. Cover the repair area with a thick coat of primer; the thickness should be built up using several thin layers of paint rather than one thick one. Using 400 grade 'wet-and-dry' paper, rub down the surface of the primer until it is really smooth. While doing this, the work area should be thoroughly doused with water. Allow to dry before spraying on more paint.

Spray on the top coat, again building up the thickness by using several thin layers of paint. Start spraying in the centre of the repair area and then using a circular motion, work outwards until the whole repair area and about 2 inches of the surrounding original paintwork is covered. Remove all masking material 10 to 15 minutes after spraying on the final coat of paint. Allow the new paint at least 2 weeks to harden fully; then, using a paintwork renovator or a very fine cutting paste, blend the edges of the new paint into the existing paintwork. Finally, apply wax polish.

6 Bodywork repairs - major damage

1 Because the body is built on the unitized principle and is integral with the underframe, major damage must be repaired by competent mechanics with the necessary welding and hydraulic straightening equipment.
2 If the damage has been serious it is vital that the body is checked for correct alignment as otherwise the handling of the car will suffer and many other faults such as excessive tyre wear, and wear in the transmission and steering may occur.
3 There is a special body jig which most large body repair shops have and to ensure that all is correct it is important that this jig be used for all major repair work.

7 Front bumpers - removal and installation

Several different types of front bumpers have been used. In all cases they are comparatively easy to remove and install, and only an outline procedure is given. When installing, ensure that the bumper is correctly aligned before finally tightening the attachment nuts and bolts.
1 *Pre-1969 models:* These bumpers are retained by brackets on the wings and spring brackets on the wheel arches. If a new sealing strip is required, it should be installed on the cross panel first, then the projections bonded to the wing bottom edges using a contact adhesive.
2 *1969/71 models:* These are retained by angle brackets at the outer edges, and by brackets (accessible from the front compartment) on the wheel boxes. The brackets can be detached after the bumper is removed. If a new sealing rubber is required, bond it to the lower edge of the wing with a contact adhesive, and pull the centre section into the shaped rails at the front compartment block bulkhead.
3 *1972 models:* These bumpers incorporate a front spoiler, but are otherwise similar to the 1969/71 bumpers. Early ones are of fibreglass but later ones are of steel; they can be installed on all 911's from 1969 onwards.
4 *1973 USA models:* These bumpers have energy absorbing rubber bumper horns and reinforced brackets. When removing the bumpers, detach them from the wing sides (disconnect any electrical wires if additional lights are installed) then detach the bumper brackets from the body. If air-conditioning is installed, detach the impact protection boss from the suspension arm attachment points. New seals can be bonded into position where necessary; new trim strips are simply pressed into position after prising out the old ones. (Fig. 10.4)
5 *1974/75 models:* These bumpers are made up from several parts and may include hydraulic dampers and/or side marker lamps. Fig. 10.3 shows the bumper parts which are numbered in the removal sequence. The insert (44) is bonded to the deformation tube (38).
6 A nose spoiler is used on later models. This is attached with nuts and bolts.

8 Rear bumpers - removal and installation

Several different types of rear bumpers have been used. In all cases they are comparatively easy to remove and install, and only an outline procedure is given. When installing, ensure that the bumper is correctly aligned, before finally tightening the attachment nuts and bolts.
1 *Pre-1969 models:* The bumpers are retained by nuts and bolts at

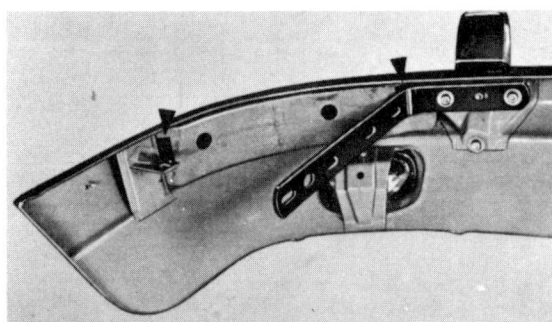

Fig. 10.1. The bumper brackets - pre-1969 models (Sec. 7)

The arrows show rubber packing pieces at the ends of the reinforcements

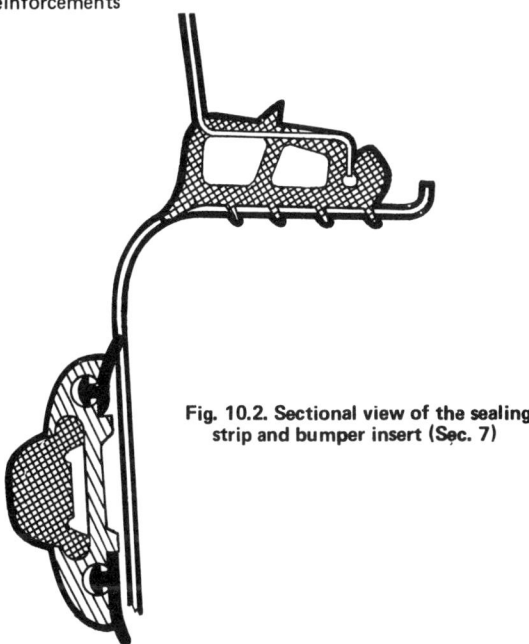

Fig. 10.2. Sectional view of the sealing strip and bumper insert (Sec. 7)

the wing bracket, side member and centre section. Where overriders are installed, these must be removed first, by removing the plastic plugs and undoing the bolts.
2 *1969/73 models:* Although the bumper pattern is changed, the basic instructions for the pre-1969 models are applicable.
3 *1973 USA models:* The bumpers are attached to support pipes and side brackets. The bumper brackets should be detached at the longitudinal members and removed complete with the bumper. If necessary they can then be dismantled, starting with removal of the cover plugs from the bumper horn, then removeing the horns from the bumper.
4 *1974/75 models:* The bumper components are shown in Fig. 10.5 and are numbered in the removal sequence.

9 Front lid

Removal and installation
1 With the lid raised, mark around the hinge positions with a soft pencil.
2 With help from an assistant to support the lid, remove the hinge bolts and lift the lid off.
3 Installation is the reverse of the removal procedure, adjusting the hinge positions, if necessary, for satisfactory alignment. On the early type lock with the dovetail bolt the lid lock spring should be tensioned with the cable so that the catch opens automatically if the cable breaks.

Lid locks
4 Different patterns of lid lock have been used, but removal and

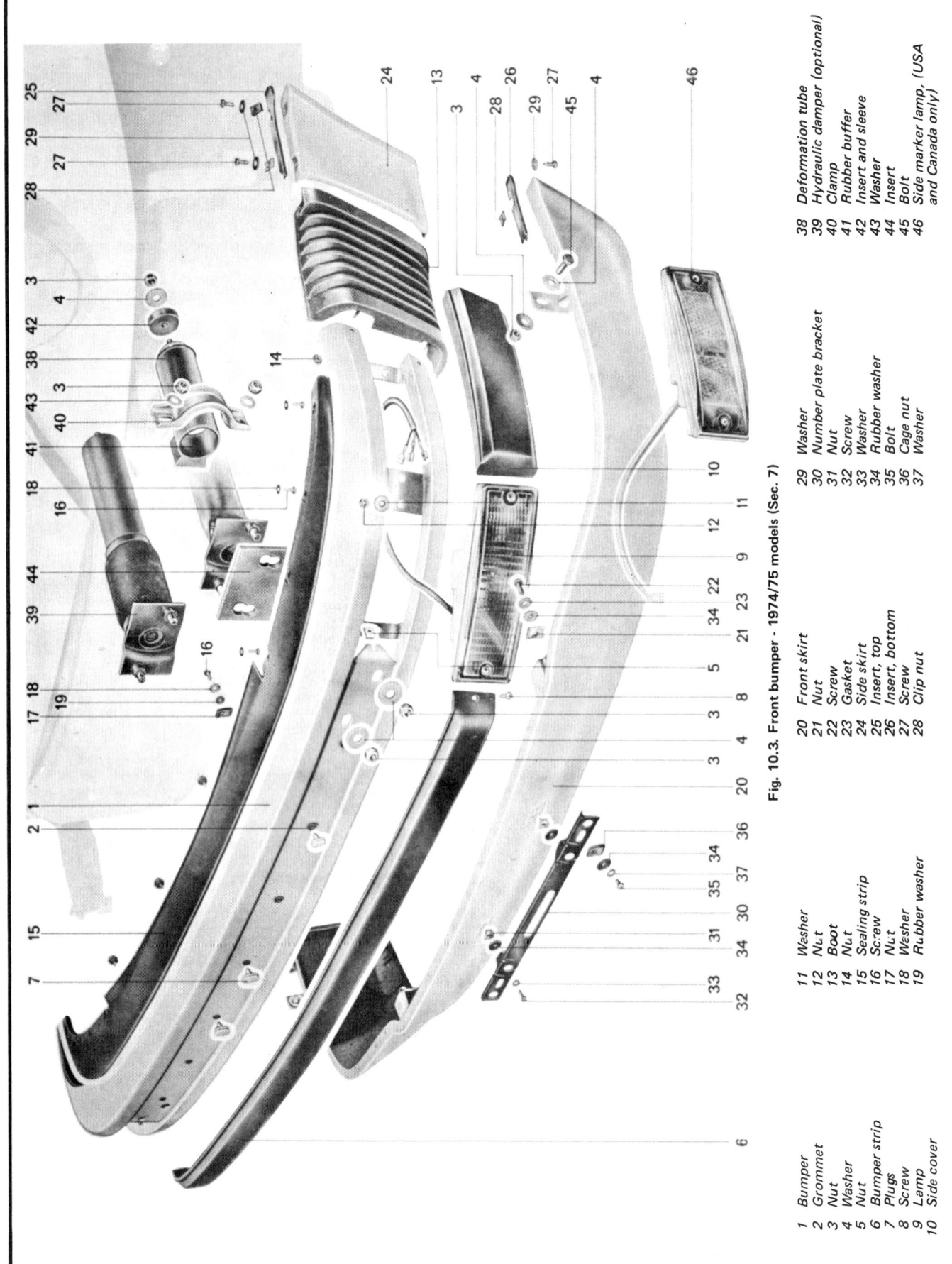

Fig. 10.3. Front bumper - 1974/75 models (Sec. 7)

1 Bumper
2 Grommet
3 Nut
4 Washer
5 Nut
6 Bumper strip
7 Plugs
8 Screw
9 Lamp
10 Side cover

11 Washer
12 Nut
13 Boot
14 Nut
15 Sealing strip
16 Screw
17 Nut
18 Washer
19 Rubber washer

20 Front skirt
21 Nut
22 Screw
23 Gasket
24 Side skirt
25 Insert, top
26 Insert, bottom
27 Screw
28 Clip nut

29 Washer
30 Number plate bracket
31 Nut
32 Screw
33 Washer
34 Rubber washer
35 Bolt
36 Cage nut
37 Washer

38 Deformation tube
39 Hydraulic damper (optional)
40 Clamp
41 Rubber buffer
42 Insert and sleeve
43 Washer
44 Insert
45 Bolt
46 Side marker lamp, (USA and Canada only)

Fig. 10.4. Front bumper attachments - 1973 USA models

installation is straightforward after removing the plastic cover (later type), bolts (and cable, where applicable). On the early type, the dovetail bolt should be adjusted for satisfactory lock operation; on the later type the position of the lower lock is adjusted for satisfactory operation.

Opening the lid when the operating cable breaks

5   On the early type lid locks, the catch opens automatically if the cable breaks (see paragraph 3). On the later types, remove the front bumper and drill a hole 5/16 in. (8 mm) diameter in the transverse panel (Fig. 10.6).
6   Make up a wire hook from a 15 in. (400 mm) length of steel rod approximately 3/16 in. (5 mm) diameter, insert the rod through the hole and press the wire clamping piece to the right.
7   After installing a new cable, plug the hole (plug '999 703 044 50' is available from Porsche dealers for this purpose). Finally, install the bumper.

10 Rear lid

Removal and installation - lid without spoiler

1   With the lid raised, mark around the hinge positions with a soft pencil.
2   Where applicable, remove the number plate lights and pull out the cable from the lid frame.
3   Remove the air intake grille.
4   With help from an assistant to support the lid, remove the hinge bolts and lift the lid off.
5   Installation is the reverse of the removal procedure, adjusting the hinge positions, if necessary, for satisfactory alignment. Tension the lid lock spring with the cable, if necessary, so that the catch opens automatically if the cable breaks.

Removal and installation - lid with spoiler

6   Refer to the procedure given in the previous paragraphs. If the spoiler is to be removed, remove the lower air inlet grille screws and the guard screws. Bend the guard (or if preferred, remove the upper section of the lid lock) to remove it, then remove the spoiler retaining nuts and screws.
7   Installation is the reverse of the removal procedure.

Lid locks

8   Removal and installation is straightforward after removing the retaining bolts (and cable, where applicable). The dovetail bolt should be adjusted as necessary for satisfactory operation.

11 Door - dismantling, removal, installation and reassembly

Pre-1969 models

1   Unscrew the trim strip and button on the door catch.
2   Prise off the cover from the window winder, remove the screw and pull off the handle.
3   Unscrew the armrest covering then disengage the door interior catch. To remove the armrest remove the three bolts at the bottom.
4   Remove the door panel screws, then pull the panel away from the door.
5   Remove the cover strip from the window glass well.
6   Pull out the pin from the door check strap.
7   Remove the window frame screws, then detach the frame, leaving the glass in the door.
8   Disengage the window glass and remove it, loosening the crank gear, if necessary. Remove the crank gear.
9   Remove the exterior door handle and the door lock/remote control mechanism. (Fig. 10.7)
10 A special tool (slide hammer no. P290) will now almost certainly be required to drive out the door hinge pins. Ensure that the door is adequately supported as it is removed.
11 Installation of the door is basically the reverse of the removal procedure, but the following points should be noted:

a) *Align the door if necessary, by loosening the hinge bolts and repositioning the hinges to obtain a gap of 0.12 to 0.16 in. (3 to 4 mm) at the bottom, front and rear. At the top there should be a maximum gap of 0.16 in. (4 mm) from the windscreen pillar. Slight bending of the hinges is permissible for fore-and-aft adjustment.*
b) *If necessary, a packing piece may be used for the striker plate.*
c) *Various types of door lock have been used. Your Porsche dealer will be able to advise which type is suitable for your particular model, since if incorrectly mated parts are used as replacements it is possible for the catch to disengage and the door to spring open.*
d) *When installing the crank gear it is recommended that replacement types with plastic slides are used in place of the types with metal rollers, as the latter are prone to rattling.*
e) *When fitting the window glass, set the crank gear in the halfway position, and push the glass and raiser bar backwards onto the slide pieces of the crank gear. Tighten the crank gear after the window frame is installed. (Fig. 10.9)*

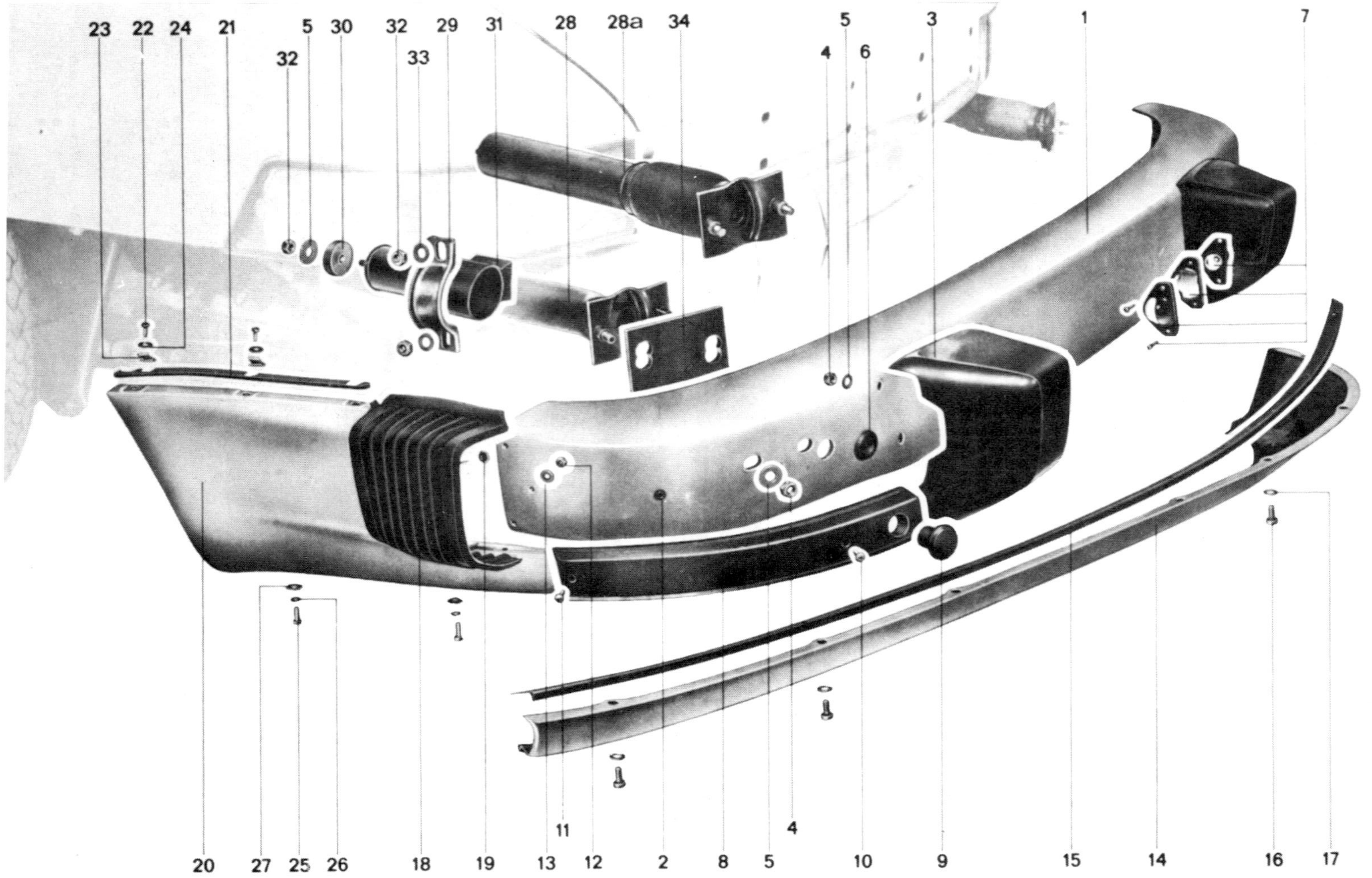

Fig. 10.5. Rear bumper - 1974/75 models (Sec. 8)

1 Bumper
2 Grommet
3 Bumper guard
4 Nut
5 Washer
6 Grommet (for wire)
7 Number plate lamp

8 Bumper strip
9 Cap for towing attachment
10 Bolt
11 Bolt
12 Nut
13 Washer
14 Rear skirt

15 Insert
16 Screw
17 Washer
18 Boot
19 Self-tapping nut
20 Fender lower section
21 Insert

22 Screw
23 Nut
24 Washer
25 Bolt
26 Lock washer
27 Washer
28 Deformation tube

28a Hydraulic damper
29 Clamp
30 Rubber Insert
31 Rubber buffer
32 Nut
33 Washer
34 Insert for mounting plate

Fig. 10.6. Drilling point for emergency opening of the front lid (Sec. 9)

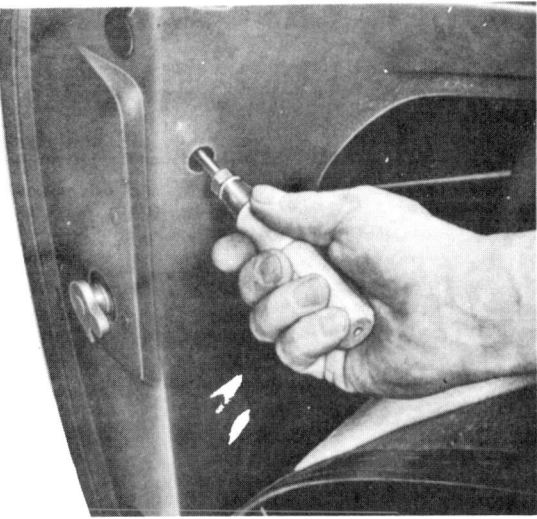

Fig. 10.7. Access to the door exterior handle screws (Sec. 11)

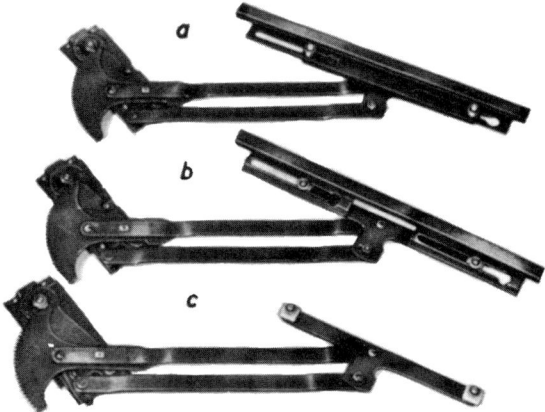

Fig. 10.8. Replacement crank gears (Sec. 11)

a metal rollers, short fixing plate
b plastic slide, short fixing plate
c plastic slide, long fixing plate

Fig. 10.9. Window glass installed in raiser bar (Sec. 11)

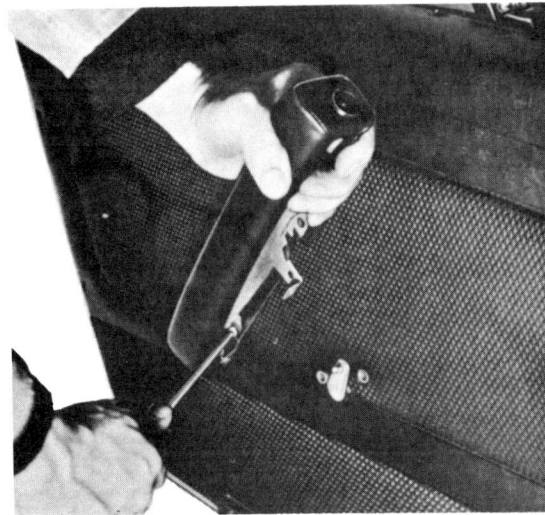

Fig. 10.11. Installing the armrest (Sec. 11)

f) Install the window frame with the window halfway up, and tighten the window frame screws in the order shown (Fig. 10.10).

g) If the type 'a' crank gear (Fig. 10.8) is used glue a plastic foam strip on the raiser bar to prevent it from rattling against the crank gear.

h) Install the weatherstrip, and cover over the inner panel apertures as applicable.

j) When installing the armrest, position it vertically as shown in Fig. 10.11, to install the first screw, then pivot it forwards to install the remaining screws. Secure the handle on the passenger's

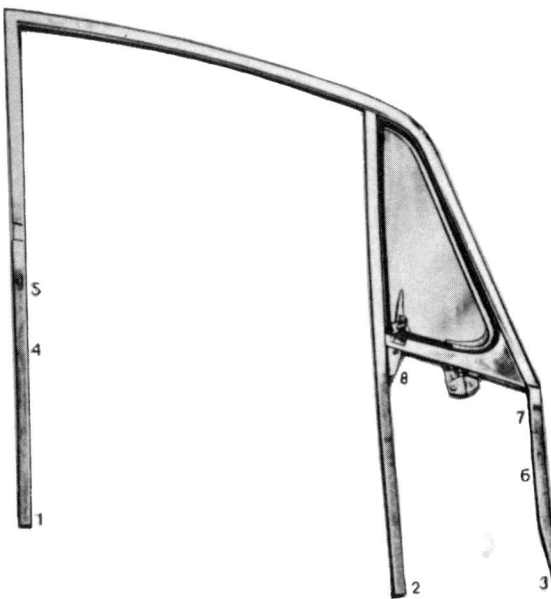

Fig. 10.10. Window frame screw tightening sequence (Sec. 11)

No. 3 screw is not used on some frames

side, then insert the lock remote control pushbutton backwards
into the armrest and push on the nipple. Bend the control rod,
if necessary, to obtain a satisfactory button operation.

   *k) Install the winder handle so that with the window closed, the
handle points diagonally downwards parallel to the window
frame.*

1969 models onwards

Note: Some modifications were made to the door locks and door stops
for 1970/73 models; these are covered in paragraphs 25 to 33. The door
panel used for 1974 models is of a new type although the basic 1970/
73 mechanism have not been altered; for information on this door
panel see paragraphs 34 to 41. A modified door stop was also introduced
at this date - see paragraph 42.

12 Remove the decorative strip and internal door lock knob.
13 Take off the winder handle cover, and remove the screw and winder
handle.
14 Take off the rubber surround from the folding storage box. Detach
the box from its retaining spring and unscrew the box.
15 Remove the armrest, detaching the lock operating lever from its
connecting linkage.
16 Loosen the plastic sheet. Working from the inside, remove the rear
attachment screw of the door closing bar. Remove the front attachment
screw and unscrew the pocket at the bottom.
17 Separate the trim panel from the inner frame, unscrew the
spring plate, pull off the window aperture seal and the plastic sheet.
Lift off the chrome strip from the upper edge of the door.
18 Unscrew all the threaded connections for the window frame (or
window guide rail on Targa models), and pull the frame up and out.
19 *Coupe version:* Push the glass forwards until the regulator sliding
block can be freed from the lift rail, and take out the window. Now
remove the lift regulator assembly (photo).
20 *Targa version:* Detach the window lift retaining screws, then remove
the window.
21 Remove the outside door handle, then unscrew the door lock
complete with inside locking mechanism and remote control, and
remove it from the door.

22 If necessary, unscrew the door outside mirror.
23 A special tool (slide hammer no. P290) will now almost certainly
be required to drive out the door hinge pins. Ensure that the door is
adequately supported as it is removed.
24 Installation of the door is basically the reverse of the removal
procedure. However, there are differences between the Coupe and
Targa versions and the following points should be noted:

   Coupe version:
   *a) After assembling the lock, remote control and inner catch on a
new door, attach the small felt pads beneath the connecting rods
using a contact adhesive.*
   *b) When installing the window regulator, tighten the bolts to 8.7
lb f ft (1.2 kg fm) torque.*
   *c) After installing the window glass, attach the rubber pad to the
base using a contact adhesive.*
   *d) If the window glass or window frames are being replaced, note
that the glass used with chrome frames is 0.12 in. (3 mm)
thicker than that used with light alloy frames.*
   *e) Fill between the window frame and the inside door panel near
the ventilator with a sealing compound, checking that the
winding action is satisfactory.*
   *f) When attaching the retaining spring plate to the inner door panel,
ensure that the door pocket and armrest holes align with the
inner panel holes.*
   *g) Connect the pull-up door handle in the armrest to the joint and
remote control mechanism, then install the armrest (photo).*
   *h) After attaching the folding storage box hinges, pull the rubber
strip through the retaining plates, the folding pocket and the
retaining eyes on the inner panel; insert the ends through the
inner panel on both sides. Attach the retaining spring, check the
operation and if necessary alter the run of the rubber strip.*

11.19 The left regulator assembly attaching screws

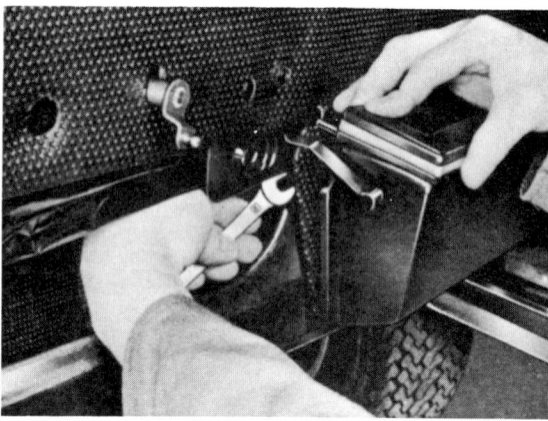

Fig. 10.12. Removing the door pocket (Sec. 11)

Fig. 10.13. Installing the lock, remote control and inner catch (Sec. 11)

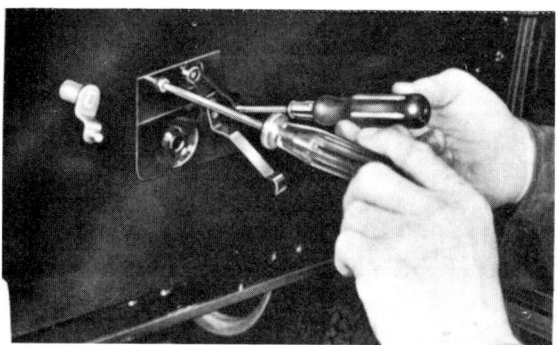

Fig. 10.14. Attaching the retaining spring plate (Sec. 11)

Fig. 10.15. Connecting the pull-up handle (Coupe) (Sec. 11)

11.24g Remote control mechanism joint

Targa version:
j) Refer to paragraph a).
k) Insert the door window and window regulator separately, then connect the two parts together and screw on the lift mechanism. Tighten the 8 mm screws to 16 lb f ft (2.2 kg fm) torque and the 6 mm screws to 8.7 lb f ft (1.2 kg fm) torque.
l) After installing the regulator mechanism, attach the rubber pad in the door well, to support the lift mechanism, with contact adhesive.
m) When installing the window frames, use rubber corner pieces where these were not originally fitted to improve the joint with the folding roof.
n) Apply sealing compound to the joint between the window frame and the inner door panel near the ventilator window.
o) Refer to paragraphs f), g) and h).

Outside door handle and door lock (1970/73 models) - removal and installation

25 Detach the door window frame and pull it upwards as necessary. (Refer to paragraphs 12 to 18).
26 Remove the self-locking nuts and washers, then remove the handle and plastic trim.
27 If the handle has been binding, remove the trigger and drive out the pivot pin from the pivot joint. Enlarge the hole in the inner pivot to 3.5 mm (no. 28 or 29 drill) and reassemble using a low temperature grease on the moving parts.
28 If the lock cylinder is binding, remove and clean it, using a mixture of glycerine and alcohol, then reassemble.
29 Installation of the handle is the reverse of the removal procedure.

Door lock (1970/73 models) - removal and installation
30 Remove the three countersunk screws and move the lock pawl to the closed position.
31 Remove the door ledge, pushbutton and interior door release lock, then remove the rubber bushing from the door inner panel.
32 Push the door lock out together with the actuating rods.

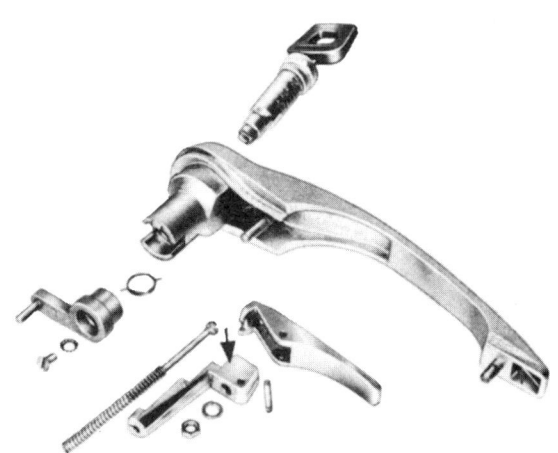

Fig. 10.16. Outside door handle (1970/73 models) - exploded view (Sec. 11)

Fig. 10.17. Door lock-assembly and extension rod attachments (1970/73 models) (Sec. 11)

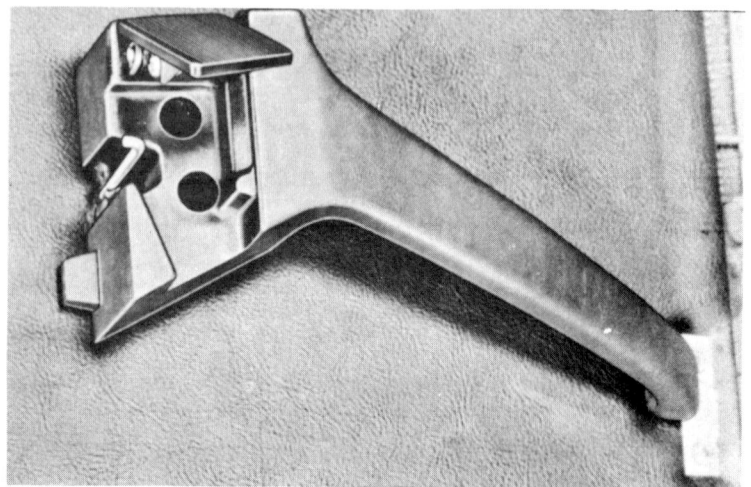

Fig. 10.18. Installing the hand grip (1974 models onwards) (Sec. 11)

Revised door stop (1970/73 models)

33 A revised door stop is used on these models. It is not interchangeable with the earlier types, although the later type (see paragraph 42) can be used in place of the 1970/73 type. Removal and installation details are similar for all types up to this date.

Door panel - removal and installation (1974 models onwards)

34 Remove the self-tapping screws and take off the storage compartment.

35 Unscrew the door lock button, remove the self-tapping screws and remove the door ledge cover.

36 Remove the rear of the storage compartment cover.

37 Detach the connecting rod at the handle, and unscrew the fasteners from the top and bottom of the handgrip.

38 Remove the regulator handle and supporting brackets, then unhook the door panel.

39 Remove the control lever from the door inner panel and disconnect the spring.

40 If the door is to be dismantled further, refer to paragraphs 12 to 24.

41 Installation is the reverse of the removal procedure.

Revised door stop (1974 models onwards)

42 A roll pin is used with the modified door stop. If this is removed it must be installed with the slit towards the outside of the car.

---

12 Electric window regulators - removal and installation

1   Remove the lock button and window ledge rail.

2   If possible, position the window about 4 in (100 mm) from the bottom, then remove the toggle switches after making a note of the connections.

3   Remove the door panel and sealing foil, then carefully prise off the chrome strip at the base of the window.

4   Remove the window frame, then push the window glass forwards and detach the regulator.

5   Remove the upper door well weather seal and take out the glass.

6   Disconnect the wiring, making a note of the connections.(If the loom is to be renewed, the door must be removed).

7   Remove the regulator and stop wedge from the door base.

8   Installation is the reverse of the removal procedure. As soon as the regulator and stop wedge are installed, operate the regulator from a battery or battery charger (positive to green motor wire, negative to black motor wire) to bring it 4 in (10 mm) from the bottom. Reverse the connections, if necessary, to achieve this.

---

13 Vent windows - removal and installation

Front

1   Remove the trim strip, pushbutton and window crash handle.

2   Disengage the front of the door panel to obtain access to the hole for the vent window fixing.

3   Loosen the vent window fixing friction catch.

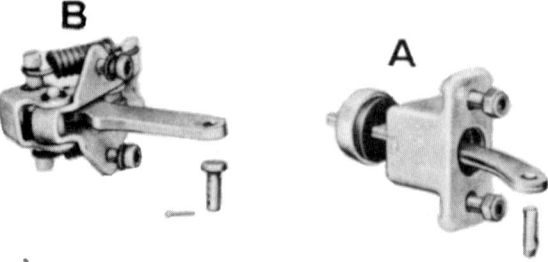

Fig. 10.19. Modified door stop (Sec. 11)

a   1974 models onwards   *b   1969/73 models*

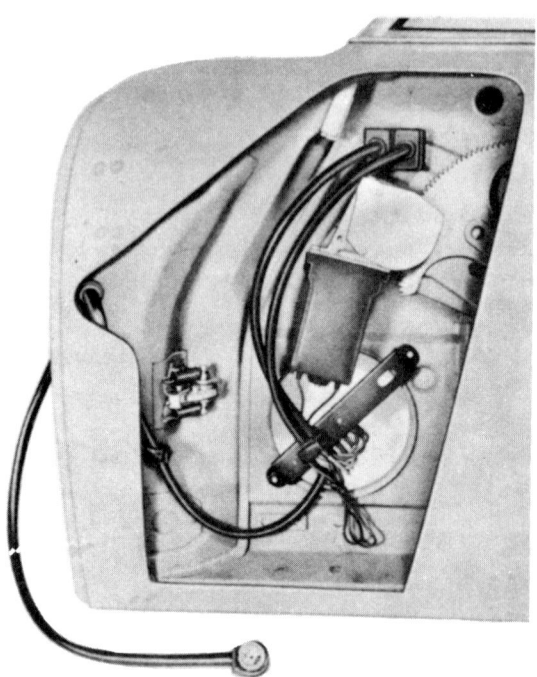

Fig. 10.20. Electric window regulator - 1972 model (Sec. 12)

Earlier models are slightly different in certain details

Extract the sealing strip frame by the top pivot, then unscrew the pivot using a 7 mm AF spanner.

5   Extract the window upwards. Note that on early models there are spacing washers on the friction catch; take care that these do not fall into the door.

6   Installation is the reverse of the removal procedure.

Rear

7   Unscrew the bolts on the lock pillar and the window catch self-tapping screws on the roof frame.
8   With the palm of the hand push the vent window forwards and outwards.
9   Remove the chrome trim strip *either* from above (self-tapping screws) *or* under the wing (self-tapping nuts)
10 When installing, cut the rubber strips to the size shown (Fig. 10.21). and attach them with adhesive. Fit sealing strips to the rim of the lock pillar and roof frame.
11 Place an underlay of Terostat strip beneath the chrome trim strip before it is fitted.
12 Insert the vent window, pushing the perforated metal tabs on the vent window in behind the retaining lips in the lock pillar.
13 The remainder of the installation procedure is the reverse of that used for removal. Ensure that the seal in the chrome bezel is a satisfactory fit.

14 Windscreen and rear window glass - removal and installation

Windscreen

1   Fold the windscreen wiper arms forwards, then cut away the rubber seal from outside the bezel.
2   Carefully prize away the bezel then cut through the rubber seal parallel to the windscreen.
3   Assuming that the windscreen glass has not shattered, press it out from the inside with an assistant outside to support it.
4   Carefully scrape away any sealing compound from the sealing edge, and touch up any bare paintwork or rusted areas with a rust inhibiting paint.
5   Obtain a new rubber moulding, and smear a little soap and water solution into the bezel groove. Install the bezel so that there is approximately 0.4 in (1 mm) gap at the top and bottom in the middle.
6   Place the moulding on the windscreen, and draw a piece of strong cord into the moulding at the top so that the cord overlaps by about 12 in (30 cm) in the top moulding.
7   Smear the sealing lip with glycerine then insert the windscreen glass at the bottom.
8   Slowly pull out the cord from each end so that the sealing lip is drawn over the sealing edge of the body aperture.
9   Ensure that the windscreen is firmly and evenly installed, then slide in the central pieces over both bezels.
10 Carefully prise the seal away from the metal, then from the glass, then inject a mastic-type sealing compound. Ensure that the bezel is kept an even distance from the windscreen aperture.
11 Remove any excess sealing compound with petrol.

Coupe rear window

12 Refer to the procedure given for the windscreen.

Targa rear window

13 With the folding top removed, remove the trunk clips and rear panelling.
14 Remove the left- and right-compartment trim strips, and the rear panel top section.
15 Remove the interior light, then detach the safety bar inside covering and remove it rearwards.
16 Undo the front seal frame along the safety bar and remove the chrome cover plate (self-tapping screws and screws beneath the wing). Pull off the rear seal.
17 Disconnect the heated rear window cables (where applicable) and remove the glass.
18 Fit the sealing strip and bezel to the glass, and install as described for the windscreen earlier in this Section.
19 The remainder of the installation procedure is the reverse of the removal procedure.

Glued-in weatherstrip and windscreen - USA models

20 From December 1969 USA models have a glued-in windshield. Apart from the use of the glue, rather than of the mastic sealing compound, installation is the same as for the type already described. Fig. 10.23 shows the position of the draw-cord and sealing lip, and the points to which the glue should be applied. Your Porsche dealer will be able to supply the glue for this application.

Fig. 10.21. Vent window rubber strips (Sec. 13)

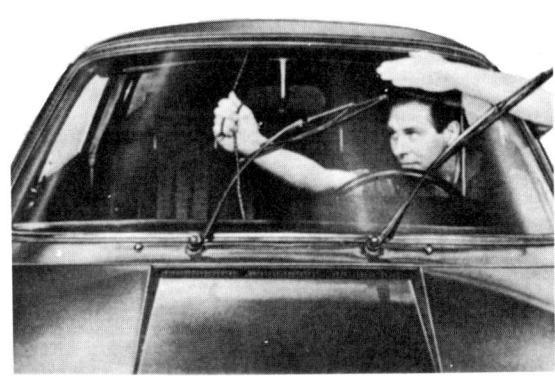

Fig. 10.22. Installing the windscreen (Sec. 14)

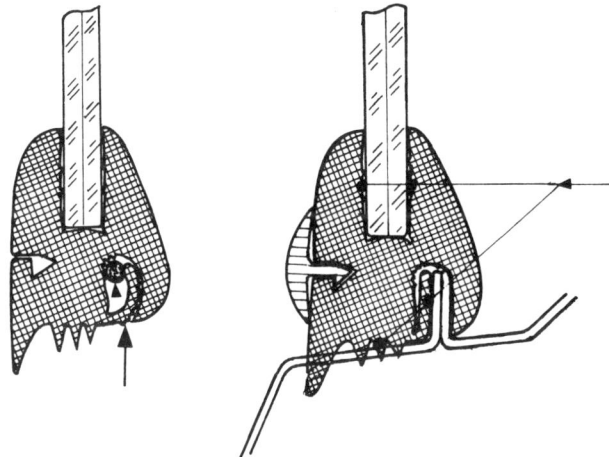

Fig. 10.23. Sectional views of glued-in windscreen weather strip (Sec. 14)

(left)   *showing the cord position*
(right)   *showing areas to which glue is applied*

Heated rear windows

21 Instructions for removal and installation of heated rear windows are basically as for the types already described. Take extreme care that the heater elements are not damaged by scratching; note that it will probably be necessary to make holes in the sealing rubber for the cables to pass through. (Fig. 10.24)

15 Sliding roof, guides and guide rails - removal and installation

1   Open the sliding roof approximately 4 in (100mm) and undo the clips at the front edge.
2   Push the roof cover back, then close the sliding roof.
3   Remove the screws and take off the left- and right-hand guides. Lift off the spring catch for the rear guide and turn it sideways.
4   Remove the screws and detach the cover reinforcements for the rear guides.
5   Lift the sliding roof and remove it in a forward direction.

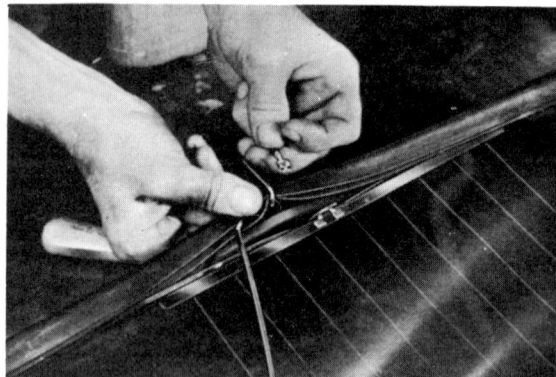

Fig. 10.24. Cable attachments for heated rear window (Sec. 14)

Fig. 10.25. Removing a guide rail (Sec. 15)

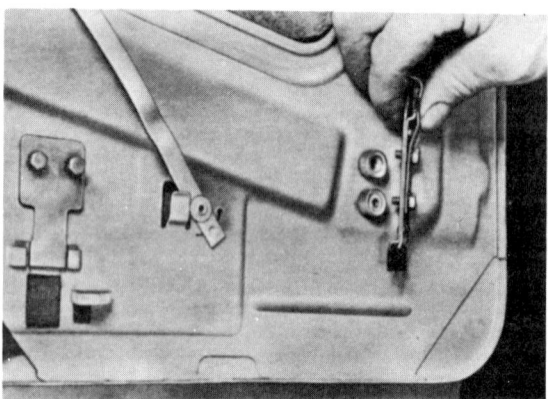

Fig. 10.26. Rear height adjustment for the sunroof (Sec. 15)

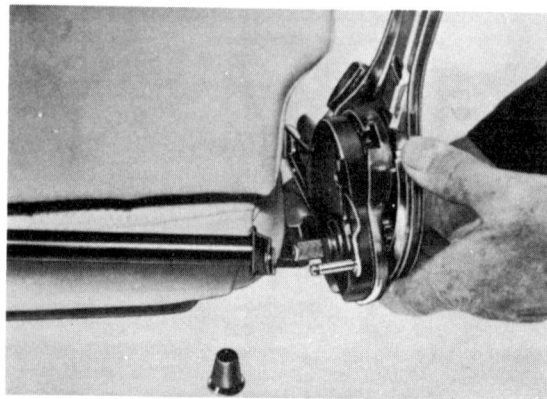

Fig. 10.27. Detaching the seat bracket (Sec. 16)

6   Remove one of the left- or right-hand guide rails forwards, having removed the spacer.
7   If the guides and guide rails are to be removed, open the zipper and remove the bolts to detach the driving gear.
8   Remove the spacer of the second guide rail and pull out the guide rail forwards.
9   Pull out and check the condition of the cables, renewing as a pair if possible to ensure satisfactory roof operation.
10   Grease the cables and push them into the tubular supports until the threaded plate is in the rear part of the roof aperture.
11   Push the guide rails into the cables, and push rearwards until the end of the tube and the plastic pin in the rear part of the top frame slide completely into the rail section and thus secure the rear of the guide rail.
12   Insert the top frame and push it rearwards, then secure the second rail.
13   Adjust the cables at the attachment plates on each side to approximately 2 in (50 mm) before the end of the rear roof aperture.
14   Install the drive gear.
15   To install the sliding roof, introduce the guide rails into the pegs and tube ends at the rear of the roof base.
16   Introduce the rear guides, with the operating cable in front, into the guide rails and grease them lightly.
17   Assemble the cable covers and wind deflector.
18   Introduce the top frame into the guide rails, push it to the rear, and secure the guide rails and spacers.
19   Insert the roof cover panel and secure the guides at the front so that the cover has a maximum of 0.04 in (1 mm) side-play. Do not forget to fit the safety plates.
20   Adjust the guides at the rear so that the reinforcements can be pushed in, with the guides bolted on the cover. Swivel the leaf springs under the guide pins.
21   To adjust the roof height slacken the front guides and turn the knurled nuts; if additional front height adjustment is required, the front guides can be turned round. The roof can be adjusted at the rear by means of the adjusting screws. If lateral adjustment is required the front guides can be repositioned.

22   The remainder of the installation procedure is the reverse of the removal procedure.

16 Seats - removal, repair and installation

Removal
1   *Pre-1969 models:* Raise the adjuster lever, then slide the seat fully forward and lift it out.
2   *1969 models onwards:* Slide the seat forwards and remove the rear guide rail screws; slide the seat rearwards and remove the front guide rail screws. The seat can now be lifted out, but on 1972 USA models onwards, detach the seat contact cable at the connector.

Repair
3   Remove the bracket half from the seat back rest, then from the seat frame.
4   Push the bracket half out of the square on the seat frame, then pull the bracket out of the connecting tube.
5   Reassemble the bracket halves in the reverse order to dismantling, then check the seat action.

Installation
6   Installation of the seats is the reverse of the removal procedure, general purpose grease being used on the sliding rails. On pre-1969 models special brackets are available to raise the seat by approximately 0.8 in (20 mm) if required.

17 Ventilation system - removal and installation

1   Detach the fresh air grille from the windscreen centre section.
2   Undo the wing nut of the water drain trough clamp bar, disengage the clamp bar, then remove the plate.
3   Pull the trough downwards and detach the water drain hose. If necessary renew the water trough sealing ring.

4   Detach the control lever cable in the front luggage compartment.
5   Remove the bolts from the left- and right-hand support brackets on the control box. Remove the support bracket outwards to extract the fresh air control flap.
6   Installation of the seats is the reverse of the removal procedure.
7   If the cable and guide tube for the fresh air control flap are to be removed, remove the windscreen wiper (refer to Chapter 9, if necessary). Pull the tension spring out of the sleeve at the rear of the control box, unscrew the clip at the back of the guide tube, and disengage the cable.
8   Installation is the reverse of the removal procedure.

18 Accessories - general

A wide range of accessories is available for the Porsche 911 models but it is regretted that space limitations prevent their inclusion in this Manual.

Typical of the range of accessories is the Webasto heating and ventilating unit, a kit for converting the Wesbasto unit from glow-plug to transistorized ignition, an air-conditioning unit and a ventilating air blower.

Metric conversion tables

Inches	Decimals	Millimetres
1/64	0.015625	0.3969
1/32	0.03125	0.7937
3/64	0.046875	1.1906
1/16	0.0625	1.5875
5/64	0.078125	1.9844
3/32	0.09375	2.3812
7/64	0.109375	2.7781
1/8	0.125	3.1750
9/64	0.140625	3.5719
5/32	0.15625	3.9687
11/64	0.171875	4.3656
3/16	0.1875	4.7625
13/64	0.203125	5.1594
7/32	0.21875	5.5562
15/64	0.234275	5.9531
1/4	0.25	6.3500
17/64	0.265625	6.7469
9/32	0.28125	7.1437
19/64	0.296875	7.5406
5/16	0.3125	7.9375
21/64	0.328125	8.3344
11/32	0.34375	8.7312
23/64	0.359375	9.1281
3/8	0.375	9.5250
25/64	0.390625	9.9219
13/32	0.40625	10.3187
27/64	0.421875	10.7156
7/16	0.4375	11.1125
29/64	0.453125	11.5094
15/32	0.46875	11.9062
31/64	0.484375	12.3031
1/2	0.5	12.7000
33/64	0.515625	13.0969
17/32	0.53125	13.4937
35/64	0.546875	13.8906
9/16	0.5625	14.2875
37/64	0.578125	14.6844
19/32	0.59375	15.0812
39/64	0.609375	15.4781
5/8	0.625	15.8750
41/64	0.640625	16.2719
21/32	0.65625	16.6687
43/64	0.671875	17.0656
11/16	0.6875	17.4625
45/64	0.703125	17.8594
23/32	0.71875	18.2562
47/64	0.734375	18.6531
3/4	0.75	19.0500
49/64	0.765625	19.4469
25/32	0.78125	19.8437
51/64	0.796875	20.2406
13/16	0.8125	20.6375
53/64	0.828125	21.0344
27/32	0.84375	21.4312
55/64	0.859375	21.8281
7/8	0.875	22.2250
57/64	0.890625	22.6219
29/32	0.90625	23.0187
59/64	0.921875	23.4156
15/16	0.9375	23.8125
61/64	0.953125	24.2094
31/32	0.96875	24.6062
63/64	0.984375	25.0031

Millimetres to Inches	
mm	Inches
0.01	0.00039
0.02	0.00079
0.03	0.00118
0.04	0.00157
0.05	0.00197
0.06	0.00236
0.07	0.00276
0.08	0.00315
0.09	0.00354
0.1	0.00394
0.2	0.00787
0.3	0.1181
0.4	0.01575
0.5	0.01969
0.6	0.02362
0.7	0.02756
0.8	0.3150
0.9	0.03543
1	0.03937
2	0.07874
3	0.11811
4	0.15748
5	0.19685
6	0.23622
7	0.27559
8	0.31496
9	0.35433
10	0.39270
11	0.43307
12	0.47244
13	0.51181
14	0.55118
15	0.59055
16	0.62992
17	0.66929
18	0.70866
19	0.74803
20	0.78740
21	0.82677
22	0.86614
23	0.90551
24	0.94488
25	0.98425
26	1.02362
27	1.06299
28	1.10236
29	1.14173
30	1.18110
31	1.22047
32	1.25984
33	1.29921
34	1.33858
35	1.37795
36	1.41732
37	1.4567
38	1.4961
39	1.5354
40	1.5748
41	1.6142
42	1.6535
43	1.6929
44	1.7323
45	1.7717

Inches to Millimetres	
Inches	mm
0.001	0.0254
0.002	0.0508
0.003	0.0762
0.004	0.1016
0.005	0.1270
0.006	0.1524
0.007	0.1778
0.008	0.2032
0.009	0.2286
0.01	0.254
0.02	0.508
0.03	0.762
0.04	1.016
0.05	1.270
0.06	1.524
0.07	1.778
0.08	2.032
0.09	2.286
0.1	2.54
0.2	5.08
0.3	7.62
0.4	10.16
0.5	12.70
0.6	15.24
0.7	17.78
0.8	20.32
0.9	22.86
1	25.4
2	50.8
3	76.2
4	101.6
5	127.0
6	152.4
7	177.8
8	203.2
9	228.6
10	254.0
11	279.4
12	304.8
13	330.2
14	355.6
15	381.0
16	406.4
17	431.8
18	457.2
19	482.6
20	508.0
21	533.4
22	558.8
23	584.2
24	609.6
25	635.0
26	660.4
27	685.8
28	711.2
29	736.6
30	762.0
31	787.4
32	812.8
33	838.2
34	863.6
35	889.0
46	914.4

1   Imperial gallon = 8 Imp pints = 1.16 US gallons = 277.42 cu in = 4.5459 litres

1   US gallon = 4 US quarts = 0.862 Imp gallon = 231 cu in = 3.785 litres

1   Litre = 0.2199 Imp gallon = 0.2642 US gallon = 61.0253 cu in = 1000 cc

Miles to Kilometres		Kilometres to Miles	
1	1.61	1	0.62
2	3.22	2	1.24
3	4.83	3	1.86
4	6.44	4	2.49
5	8.05	5	3.11
6	9.66	6	3.73
7	11.27	7	4.35
8	12.88	8	4.97
9	14.48	9	5.59
10	16.09	10	6.21
20	32.19	20	12.43
30	48.28	30	18.64
40	64.37	40	24.85
50	80.47	50	31.07
60	96.56	60	37.28
70	112.65	70	43.50
80	128.75	80	49.71
90	144.84	90	55.92
100	160.93	100	62.14

lb f ft to Kg f m		Kg f m to lb f ft		lb f/in^2 : Kg f/cm^2		Kg f/cm^2 : lb f/in^2	
1	0.138	1	7.233	1	0.07	1	14.22
2	0.276	2	14.466	2	0.14	2	28.50
3	0.414	3	21.699	3	0.21	3	42.67
4	0.553	4	28.932	4	0.28	4	56.89
5	0.691	5	36.165	5	0.35	5	71.12
6	0.829	6	43.398	6	0.42	6	85.34
7	0.967	7	50.631	7	0.49	7	99.56
8	1.106	8	57.864	8	0.56	8	113.79
9	1.244	9	65.097	9	0.63	9	128.00
10	1.382	10	62.330	10	0.70	10	142.23
20	2.765	20	144.660	20	1.41	20	284.47
30	4.147	30	216.990	30	2.11	30	426.70

Index

Printed by
J. H. HAYNES & Co. Ltd
Sparkford Yeovil Somerset
ENGLAND